Second Edition

Human Communication

Motivation, Knowledge, and Skills

Sherwyn P. Morreale
University of Colorado

Brian H. Spitzberg
San Diego State University

J. Kevin Barge
University of Georgia

THOMSON
─────────────
WADSWORTH

Australia • Brazil • Canada • Mexico • Singapore • Spain
United Kingdom • United States

THOMSON

WADSWORTH

Human Communication: Motivation, Knowledge, and Skills, **Second Edition**
Sherwyn P. Morreale, Brian H. Spitzberg, J. Kevin Barge

Publisher: Holly J. Allen
Acquisitions Editor: Jaime Perkins
Senior Development Editor: Renee Deljon
Assistant Editor: John Gahbauer
Editorial Assistant: Laura Localio
Senior Technology Project Manager: Jeanette Wiseman
Senior Marketing Manager: Kimberly Russell
Marketing Assistant: Alexandra Tran
Senior Marketing Communications Manager: Shemika Britt
Project Manager, Editorial Production: Catherine Morris
Creative Director: Rob Hugel
Executive Art Director: Maria Epes
Print Buyer: Karen Hunt

Permissions Editor: Bob Kauser
Production Service: Gretchen Otto, G & S Book Services
Compositor: G & S Book Services
Text Designer: Cheryl Carrington
Photo Researcher: Stephen Forsling
Copy Editor: Mary Ann Short
Illustrator: G & S Book Services
Cover Designer: Hiroko Chastain
Cover Images: Front cover, clockwise from the top: Walter Bibikow/
    Getty Images, Emely/zefa/Corbis, Dan Hallman/Getty Images,
    Randy Faris/Corbis, Jose Luis Pelaez, Inc./Corbis, Kerstin
    Hamburg/zefa/Corbis. Back cover, left to right: Corbis, Corbis
Text and Cover Printer: CTPS

Library of Congress Control Number: 2005930579

ISBN-13: 978-0-534-57024-8
ISBN-10: 0-534-57024-0

Thomson Higher Education
10 Davis Drive
Belmont, CA 94002-3098
USA

For more information about our products, contact us at:
Thomson Learning Academic Resource Center
1-800-423-0563

For permission to use material from this text or product, submit a request
online at **http://www.thomsonrights.com.**
Any additional questions about permissions can be submitted by e-mail
to **thomsonrights@thomson.com.**

About the Authors

Sherwyn P. Morreale served as Associate Director of the National Communication Association for eight years, from 1997 to 2005, and recently returned to a career of teaching and research at the University of Colorado, Colorado Springs. She earned an undergraduate degree in communication at the University of Colorado and her Ph.D. at the University of Denver. In her position as NCA Associate Director, she provided consulting services to communication departments and college campuses in her areas, which include public speaking, interpersonal and gender communication, diversity issues, and the assessment of communication competence. She served as the National Director of the undergraduate communication honor society Lambda Pi Eta and represented the communication field as the disciplinary liaison to interdisciplinary organizations such as the American Association for Higher Education, the American Association of Colleges and Universities, the Carnegie Foundation, and the Council of Graduate Schools. Sherry lives in Colorado Springs. In her spare time, she can be found on a hiking trail, in an aerobics class, or taking advantage of the rich natural environment of Colorado.

Brian H. Spitzberg is Professor and Director of Graduate Studies in the School of Communication at San Diego State University. A native of Dallas, Texas, Brian engaged actively in forensics in high school and college, majoring in communication. He received his B.A. at the University of Texas at Arlington and his M.A. and Ph.D. at the University of Southern California. He taught for a year as a visiting professor at the University of Wisconsin, Madison, and at the University of California at Santa Barbara and for six years at the University of North Texas and has been at San Diego State University since 1989. His main research interests are in communication competence, assessment, and areas deemed the "dark side" of interpersonal communication and relationships, including conflict, coercion, violence, and stalking. He has authored, coauthored, and/or co-edited over 80 scholarly works, including two books on communication competence, a book on stalking, and two edited books on the dark side, and presented over 100 papers at professional conferences. Brian lives in San Diego and enjoys dining out, wine, collecting art, jogging, biking, and trying to write while his two Siamese cats, Copo Cielo and Kundo, sit on his lap (or laptop).

J. Kevin Barge is an Associate Professor of Speech Communication at the University of Georgia. He has published over 40 articles and book chapters as well as two books: *Leadership: Communication Skills for Groups and Organizations* and *Managing Group Life: Communicating in Decision-Making Groups.* He is an active organizational consultant and facilitator, who works with team members in the United States and Europe to enhance their ability to collaborate, learn, and innovate. He is a member of the Public Dialogue Consortium, a group of academics and communication practitioners who are interested in developing innovative communication forums that allow community members to talk about polarized and polarizing issues in constructive ways. Kevin received his B.A. at Millikin University, in Decatur, Illinois, and his M.A. and Ph.D. at the University of Kansas. Kevin lives in Athens, Georgia, with his wife Courtney and son Jackson, and enjoys traveling, cooking, theater, and golf.

Brief Contents

Contents

Preface

Few textbooks have a single model around which all of the materials of the course can be organized and understood. This one does. By providing a model of communication competence, *Human Communication: Motivation, Knowledge, and Skills*, Second Edition, gives students and instructors the benefit of a framework that aids learning. The model also reinforces the fact that the study of communication has an underlying conceptual foundation. What is our model for communication competence? It is straightforward: A communicator, to be viewed as competent by self and others, needs to be motivated, knowledgeable, and skilled in a given context.

Throughout this text, we use the communication competence model to introduce the sources of motivation and the knowledge and skills that are essential in each of four communication contexts: interpersonal, small group, public speaking, as well as mediated and mass communication. The first edition of this book grew out of our research and writing in the area of communication assessment, as we believe strongly in the pedagogical value of articulated skills and methods of measuring them. Together, articulated skills and measurements help to demystify communication processes. They also help to give students control of their learning and development as communicators—a key motivating factor.

Proven Features

While this edition is significantly different from the first edition, we have retained not just our basic approach but also those features and topics from the first edition that we considered most essential to our vision of the introductory course. Gratifyingly, both instructors and students have praised these features and confirmed that they work:

- *An integrated model of communication competence.* Again, our model for communication competence is based on the premise that a communicator, to be viewed as competent by her- or himself and others, needs to be motivated, knowledgeable, and skilled in a given context. Specifically, the model helps students evaluate the appropriateness and effectiveness of their communication in various contexts.

- *An emphasis on assessment and practice.* The major topics in this book have parallels with assessable communication behaviors in the classroom. To facilitate self-assessment and evaluation by others, the text includes numerous easy-to-use assessment instruments. For example, Building Motivation self-assessments are provided throughout in chapter-ending activities, and competence skills grids are provided for each communication context. Additionally, multiple sets of skill-building discussion questions and exercises for both individuals and small groups conclude each chapter. In an era of increasing expectations of instructional accountability, and students' preference for efficient learning, this textbook offers practical tools that satisfy such demands.

- *Chapter-opening vignettes.* The real-world experiences of students highlighted in chapter-opening vignettes help to engage readers with the chapter content and reinforce the application of concepts. The vignettes are referred to throughout the chapters and serve as the basis for examples that model ways to approach the competence skills grids.

- *Integrated active reading and critical thinking tools.* Chapter-opening learning objectives are supported with intermittent learning links in the margins of each chapter to encourage active reading and students' critical thinking about the "what" and "how" of competent communication. The links present questions that help students track and connect concepts for greater information retention within and across chapters.

- *High-interest side bars.* Close-Up boxes throughout the text highlight current topics such as diversity, culture, gender, ethics, and conflict as they apply to the different communication contexts.

- *Straightforward organization.* A quick look at the book's table of contents shows that the "building knowledge" chapter for each communication context precedes its counterpart "developing skills" chapter. Our two-part pedagogical structure ensures that students know what they need to do before they are asked to do it.

- *Attention to real-world communication challenges.* Challenges to communication competence are addressed throughout the text for each context and accompanied by practical recommendations for overcoming those challenges. For example, the human tendency toward self-centeredness is addressed in the interpersonal context, with empathy and perspective taking presented as practical ways to overcome this common challenge.

- *Emphasis on ethics.* The text integrates and emphasizes ethics across all topic areas, such as ethics in interpersonal and group communication and when presenting informative or persuasive speeches.

- *Responsibility to the research.* The basic communication course traditionally takes responsibility for covering certain "tried and true" topics. As researchers ourselves, we struggled to be as responsible to the classic and current research on those topics as possible. We strove to strike a balance between student accessibility and scientific accountability, and we think we largely succeeded. We hope you will agree.

New to the Second Edition

Our discipline has advanced since this book's first edition was published, and the world has changed in myriad ways. In addition to being updated for currency in every respect, this new edition represents changes that students and instructors requested, including the coverage of new topics. The result is a more succinct, focused, and relevant text that provides streamlined instruction and better examples within a simplified organization—in short, a leaner book that is easier to read, covers the traditional topics and some critical new ones, and does so with greater focus and clarity. Highlights include

- *A new Part 5, Communication Competence in a Mediated World.* Separate chapters on computer-mediated communication (Chapter 15) and mass communication (Chapter 16) complete our examination of human communication in the 21st century. While Chapter 15, Computer-Mediated Communication, has been thoroughly updated, Chapter 16, Mass Communication, is entirely new.

- *A new synthesis of perception and culture.* Everyone acknowledges that culture influences perception and perceptions of reality, so it seemed obvious that we should integrate these two topics more effectively in the new edition. As a result, Chapter 3, Perception and Culture, now fully explores the interconnections and influences of culture on communication processes.

- *New sample student speeches.* Two new award-winning student speeches on topics of current interest—AIDS research and story-telling in society—are used to illustrate competent public speaking in Part 4. The first- and second-place speeches at the 132nd Annual Interstate Oratorical Association National Competition are integrated into the chapters on informative and persuasive speaking (Chapters 13 and 14, respectively), annotated at the end of the chapters, and are available on video on the book's website.

- *A new approach to communication and motivation.* Of the three factors included in the book's model of communication competence, motivation is the factor that is most similar across communication contexts. The benefits or rewards for communicating competently, and the nature of communication apprehension and anxiety, are often the same in various contexts. Therefore, three separate chapters that covered motivation in the first edition have been consolidated into one comprehensive chapter (Chapter 2) in this edition. Individual chapters for each of the three contexts (interpersonal, group, public speaking) still focus on knowledge and skills, which do vary considerably from context to context.

- *Interactive assessment instruments.* The book's website offers new interactive versions of the book's various self-assessments and competency grids. With automatic scoring capabilities, the interactive assessment tools make completing diagnostics easier and more fun for students, who can also e-mail results directly to you at your request. For more information about the second edition's extensive new online resources for students, please see the descriptions that follow.

We aimed to write a new edition that is as theoretically sound and substantive as its predecessor but that is also more accessible and efficient. As always, you and your students will be the judge.

Accompanying Resources: An Exclusive Teaching and Learning Package

Human Communication: Motivation, Knowledge, and Skills, Second Edition, offers a comprehensive array of supplements to assist in making the introduction to human communication course as meaningful and enjoyable as possible for both students and instructors, and to help students succeed. Thomson Wadsworth has prepared the following descriptions of the print and electronic resources available for your consideration.

Resources for Students

Strictly optional, these resources are bundled with student copies of the text only at your request for free or at a small additional cost.

Guide to Technology Resources for Human Communication. Packaged with an access code for Thomson's 1pass portal, the *Guide to Technology Resources for Human Communication* provides a comprehensive overview of and introduction to the many valuable resources for students available online, including the book's premium companion website, InfoTrac College Edition, Speech Builder Express, and vMentor. This handy guide, which can be packaged with the text at no additional charge, offers helpful information about and strategies for using each of these valuable online resources. **Please note:** If you want your students to have access to the book's premium online resources, please be sure to order **ISBN 0-495-20787-X,** which will ensure that this guide and a 1pass access code are bundled with every new copy of the text at no additional charge to your students. Students with used books may purchase the guide and access code by visiting **http://communication .wadsworth.com/morreale2.**

Descriptions of each of the component online resources follow:

- **Human Communication Premium Book Companion Website.** The premium companion website (accessed through Thomson's 1pass portal) features a wealth of interactive and multimedia learning resources, including online versions of the book's self-assessments and competency grids, and videos of complete student speeches from the book, professional speeches, and additional speech clips. The videos help students prepare for their own presentations and give effective feedback to their peers by providing practice in critiquing different types of speeches. After responding to the questions for analysis, students can e-mail their responses to you and see how their answers compare to the authors' own evaluations.

  The premium companion website also includes numerous chapter-by-chapter interactive resources to help students understand and apply the text's instruction such as live and updated Web links for every URL mentioned in the book, self-quizzes, key term crossword puzzles and flashcards, InfoTrac College Edition readings with critical questions, and an online glossary.

- **Speech Builder Express™ Speech Organization and Outlining Program.** This award-winning Web-based tool coaches students through the speech organization and outlining process. By completing interactive sessions that help them write a thesis statement, develop main and subordinate points, integrate support material, craft transitions, plan visual aids, compose an introduction and conclusion, and prepare a bibliography, students can create full-sentence and keyword outlines, formatted according to the principles presented in the text. The program's prompts are customized depending on the type of speech a student is preparing and the many other variables of speech preparation such as organizational pattern. Within the program, students also have access to embedded resources such as text and video models, a timeline, a dictionary, and a thesaurus. For more information about Speech Builder Express, visit **http://thomson.sbe.com.**

- **InfoTrac College Edition with InfoMarks™.** With their four-month subscription to this online library's more than 18 million reliable, full-length articles, students are able to use keyword searches to retrieve almost instant results from over 5,000 academic and popular periodicals in the InfoTrac College Edition database. Students also have access to InfoMarks—stable URLs that can be linked to articles, journals, and searches to save valuable time when doing research—*and* to the InfoWrite online resource center, where students can access grammar help, critical thinking guidelines, guides to writing research papers, and much more. For more information about InfoTrac College Edition and the InfoMarks linking tool, visit **http://www .infotrac-college.com** and click on "User Demo."

- VMentor gives your students access to virtual office hours—one-on-one, online tutoring help from a subject-area expert, at no additional cost. In vMentor's virtual classroom, students interact with the tutor and other students using two-way audio, an interactive whiteboard for illustrating the problem, and instant messaging. To ask a question, students simply click to raise a "hand."

Again, please note: If you want your students to have access to these premium online resources, please be sure to order **ISBN 0-495-20787-X,** which will ensure that the technology guide with a 1pass access code is bundled with every new copy of the text at no additional charge to your students. If you do not order this option, your students will not automatically have free access to this online content. Also again, students with used books may purchase the guide and access code by visiting **http://communication.wadsworth .com/morreale2** and clicking on "Purchase 1pass Now!" *Contact your local Thomson sales representative for more details.*

The following print and multimedia resources are also available for students and can be packaged with the text in a combination of your choice:

- ***Speech Builder Express Student Guide.*** This user-friendly guidebook offers students assistance with using the Speech Builder Express speech outlining and organizing software. Students will receive help every step of the way—from choosing their speech topic, to selecting an appropriate organizational pattern, to incorporating visual aids, and beyond.
- ***InfoTrac College Edition Student Activities Workbook for Public Speaking.*** The workbook features guidelines and an extensive selection of individual and group activities designed to help instructors and students get the most from InfoTrac College Edition. Referenced throughout the Annotated Instructor's Edition.
- ***Election 2004: Speeches from the Campaign.*** Featuring selected full speeches and excerpts from the 2004 Democratic and Republican conventions, this dynamic CD-ROM is a great way to help students understand the power and the impact of public speaking—both when it's effective and when it fails. Students may view some of the 2004 conventions' more noted speeches, including those by Barack Obama, Arnold Schwarzenegger, Bill Clinton, Laura Bush, and many more.
- ***A Guide to the Basic Course for ESL Students.*** Designed to assist nonnative speakers of English, the guide features FAQs, helpful URLs, and strategies for accent management and speech apprehension.

■ ***The Art and Strategy of Service Learning Presentations,*** **Second Edition.**
Written by Rick Isaacson and Jeff Saperstein of San Francisco State University, this brief book is an invaluable resource for students in basic courses that integrate a service-learning component. The handbook provides guidelines for connecting service learning work with classroom concepts and advice for working effectively with agencies and organizations. It also provides model forms and reports and a directory of online resources.

Resources for Instructors

Human Communication: Motivation, Knowledge, and Skills, Second Edition, also features a full suite of resources for instructors The following class preparation, classroom presentation, assessment, and course management resources are available:

■ **Annotated Instructor's Edition (AIE).** The *Human Communication* AIE is a student text enhanced with marginal class-tested and reviewer-validated teaching tips and suggestions for integrating the extensive ancillary program. Fully cross-referenced with the Instructor's Resource Manual, the Instructor Resources with Multimedia Manager CD-ROM, and the book's premium companion website, this tool is a must-have for the first-time instructor or graduate teaching assistant and a great refresher for the veteran professor.

■ **Instructor's Resource Manual.** Cross-referenced with the Annotated Instructor's Edition, the Instructor's Resource Manual, by Billy Fallon at San Diego State University, provides a comprehensive teaching guide featuring course outlines and sample syllabi, as well as the following for every text chapter: chapter goals and an outline, suggestions for integrating print supplements and online resources, supplementary research notes, suggested discussion questions and activities, additional InfoTrac College Edition exercises, an ABC news clip correlation guide for classroom use, and a comprehensive test bank with answer key that includes multiple-choice, true-false, short-answer, essay, and fill-in-the-blank test questions.

This manual is also available on the instructor's website and the Multimedia Manager with Instructor Resources CD-ROM, which includes ExamView Computerized Testing. You'll find more information about these electronic tools below.

■ **Instructor's Website.** The password-protected instructor's website includes electronic access to the Instructor's Resource Manual, downloadable versions of the book's PowerPoint slides, and a link to the Opposing Viewpoints Resource Center. To gain access to the website, simply request a course key by opening the site's home page.

■ **Instructor Resources CD-ROM with Multimedia Manager.** This disc contains an electronic version of the Instructor's Resource Manual, the ExamView® Computerized Testing program, JoinIn on Turning Point question slides, and ready-to-use Microsoft® PowerPoint® presentations, prepared by Mark Zeigler and Kelly Alvarez of Florida State University, based on material in the text. The PowerPoint slides contain text, images, and cued videos of speeches from the premium companion website and can be used as is or customized to suit your course needs. This all-in-one lecture tool makes it easy for you to assemble, edit, publish, and present custom lectures for your course. More information about ExamView and JoinIn follow:

ExamView®

- **ExamView® Computerized Testing** enables you to create, deliver, and customize tests and study guides (both print and online) in minutes using the test bank questions from the Instructor's Resource Manual. Exam-View offers both a *Quick Test Wizard* and an *Online Test Wizard* that guide you step by step through the process of creating tests, while its "what you see is what you get" interface allows you to see the test you are creating on screen exactly as it will print or display online. You can build tests of up to 250 questions, using up to 12 question types. Using the complete word processing capabilities of ExamView, you can even enter an unlimited number of new questions or edit existing ones.

- **JoinIn™ on TurningPoint®** Thomson Wadsworth is now pleased to offer you JoinIn™ content for Response Systems tailored to *Human Communication,* Second Edition, allowing you to transform your classroom and assess your students' progress with instant in-class quizzes and polls. Our exclusive agreement to offer TurningPoint® software lets you pose book-specific questions and display students' answers seamlessly within the Microsoft® PowerPoint® slides of your own lecture, in conjunction with the "clicker" hardware of your choice. Enhance how your students interact with you, your lecture, and each other.

- **Turn-It-In.** This proven online plagiarism-prevention software promotes fairness in the classroom by helping students learn to correctly cite sources and allowing instructors to check for originality before reading and grading papers and speeches. Turn-It-In quickly checks student papers and speeches against billions of pages of Internet content, millions of published works, and millions of student papers and within seconds generates a comprehensive originality report.

- **Student Speeches for Critique and Analysis on Video and DVD.** These eight volumes offer a variety of sample student speeches that your students can watch, critique, and analyze on their own or in class. All of the speech types are included, as well as speeches featuring nonnative English speakers and the use of visual aids.

- *The Teaching Assistant's Guide to the Basic Course.* This guidebook is designed for today's communication teacher. Based on leading communication teacher training programs, the guide covers general teaching and course management topics, as well as specific strategies for communication instruction, such as providing effective feedback on performance, managing sensitive class discussions, and conducting mock interviews.

These resources are available to qualified adopters, and ordering options for student supplements are flexible. Please consult your local Thomson sales representative for more information, to evaluate examination copies of any of these instructor or student resources, or product demonstrations. You may also contact the Wadsworth Academic Resource Center at 800-423-0563, or visit us at **http://communication.wadsworth.com.**

Acknowledgments

Special thanks go to our wonderful colleagues and friends with Thomson Learning who helped envision and create this new second edition: Elisa Adams, Holly Allen, Barbara Armentrout, Lucinda Bingham, Renee Deljon, Maria Epes, Stephen Forsling, John Gahbauer, Stephanie Lee, Annie Mitchell, Jaime Perkins, Catherine Morris, Gretchen Otto, Kimberly Russell, Alexandra Tran, Jeanette Wiseman, and Joy Westberg. We also acknowledge the most important source of guidance and inspiration, our students. We may do the research and writing, but it is students who help to test the *truth* of our ideas. They are our touchstones and, ultimately, our mission and our charge. As this textbook finds acceptance in coming years, we will look more and more to our own and our colleagues' experiences with students, and to the students themselves, to tell us where the value is in this book and where the value yet needs to be.

Finally, we exist in a community of scholars where individuals are committed to improving their teaching and research. We would like to thank the following colleagues for their feedback, suggestions, and comments that helped make the pedagogy and scholarship in *Human Communication* cutting edge, accessible, and meaningful.

Jabar Al-Obaidi, Bridgewater State University
Peter J. Bicak, Rockhurst University
Victoria Clements, University of Southern Maryland–Prince Frederick
Mary Ann Danielson, Creighton University
Randy Duncan, Henderson State University
Eric Fife, James Madison University
Michael Harsh, Hagerstown Community College
Paul T. M. Hemenway, Miami-Dade College–Wolfson
Mark Henderson, Jackson State University
Jesse Jackson, Austin Community College–Eastview Campus
Lori Norin, University of Arkansas–Fort Smith
Penny O'Connor, University of Northern Illinois
Cheryl Robinson, University of Tennessee–Chattanooga
Thomas E. Ruddick, Edison Community College

We would also like to thank the following colleagues for completing our survey: Your feedback, suggestions, and comments helped make the book a stronger teaching and learning tool.

Johnny Mac Allen, Oral Roberts University
Sandra Alspach, Ferris State University
Jacqueline Barker, St. Louis Community College–Meramec
Catherine Becker, University of Hawaii–Hilo
Kathy Berggren, Cornell University
Mark Buckholz, New Mexico State University
John Chetro-Szivos, Fitchburg State College
Kathleen D. Clark, University of Akron
Mary Ann Danielson, Creighton University
Thomas Downard, Northeastern University
Karen Foss, University of New Mexico
Jay Frasier, Lane Community College

Carla Harrell, Old Dominion University
Mike Hazen, Wake Forest University
Mark G. Henderson, Jackson State University
Marcia Hudson, Mississippi Delta Community College
Sunday A. Isang, Manchester College
Linda Kalfayan, Westchester Community College
Beverly Merrill Kelley, California Lutheran University
Larry J. King, Stephen F. Austin State University
Charles J. Korn, Northern Virginia Community College
Mark Kosinski, Manchester Community College
Lori Kuhn-Hancock, Bainbridge College
Mary P. Lahman, Manchester College
Sandra Lakey, Pennsylvania College of Technology
Robert P. Lauman, Webster University
Drew Lobenstein, Moorpark College
Linda Long, North Lake College
Mary Mater, Houston Baptist University
Thomas J. Mickey, Bridgewater State College
Kenneth Bruce Montgomery, Milligan College
Donna R. Munde, Mercer County Community College
Kay E. Neal, University of Wisconsin–Oshkosh
John Nicholson, Angelo State University
Vincent T. Niehaus, East Central College
John E. O'Connor, Fairmont State University
Mark Paustian, Martin Luther College
Rita Rahoi-Gilchrest, Winona State University
Melanie J. Reese, Boise State University
Cheryl M. Robinson, University of Tennessee–Chattanooga
Ken Robol, Halifax Community College
Chris Roberts Sawyer, Texas Christian University
Glynis Holm Strause, Coastal Bend College
Sarah J. Tracy, Arizona State University
Dudley Turner, University of Akron
Kyle James Tusing, University of Arizona
Curtis Vangeison, St. Charles Community College
David W. Worley, Indiana State University
Julie Ann Zink, University of Southern Maine

Finally, to our friends, family members, and peers, who have faithfully tended to our questions, complaints, and ongoing progress reports regarding this book, many thanks for your patience and support. That you have remained loyal throughout is evidence of the wisdom of our choices and luck of our birthrights.

Human Communication

© Tim Pannell /Corbis

1. Define communication and explain how messages, management, and meaning relate to communication.

2. Compare and contrast communication as information transfer, as sharing meaning, as persuasion, and as community.

3. Distinguish between the interactive and transactional models of communication.

4. Outline the seven assumptions underlying communication.

5. Explain why communication is crucial to constructing healthy relationships, groups, and communities.

6. Distinguish between communication and communication competence.

Introducing Communication

Monday, 8 p.m.—Kathryn returned to her apartment after attending a team-building workshop hosted by her university's Student Life Department. Even though she had extensive experience as a committee chair, Kathryn had been looking forward to this workshop because her new position as chair for her service club's fund-raising committee held many challenges.

As she walked into her apartment, she noticed she had received 6 phone messages; two were from a good friend confirming their lunch date on Tuesday. When she turned on her computer, she downloaded 7 e-mail messages from her classmates. Kathryn immediately called her friend Kwan and made a mental note to respond to the other phone calls, e-mails, and a couple of unreturned instant messages when she had some spare time on Tuesday. Tonight, her task was to finish her presentation for her 9 a.m. marketing class. She had done all her research; it was now time to outline her presentation of the marketing plan. She knew speaking to large groups wasn't her strength—Kathryn always felt nervous in front of an audience, and as a result, she typically fumbled for the right words and phrases. She began typing an outline for her presentation.

Tuesday, 10:30 a.m.—The speech had gone poorly. Even though she had prepared thoroughly and knew the information, Kathryn still had not overcome her nervousness. She lost her place on more than one occasion and introduced awkward silences into the presentation. Her nervousness did not escape her classmates; their evaluations showed that they felt it distracted from her speech.

Tuesday, 1 p.m.—Kathryn's lunch with her friend Kwan went much more smoothly than her presentation. Kwan was conflicted about whether to transfer to another college. Kathryn didn't have a hard time listening to him but felt awkward giving advice. She knew in her heart that she wanted her friend to stay but felt that saying so would put more pressure on him. Kathryn wanted to tell Kwan how she really felt but couldn't find a way of putting her feelings into words.

3

Tuesday, 5 p.m.—The fund-raising committee meeting had gone very well. Kathryn received several compliments from committee members about how well she had organized the meeting and how effective she was in keeping the discussion on track.

Tuesday, 8 p.m.—Kathryn returned to her apartment, exhausted after a long day. She looked at her answering machine and saw 7 new messages. She also found 13 new e-mails. She glanced at her date book and made note of her two other meetings in addition to her two classes on Wednesday. What would tomorrow be like? ■

Most of our waking hours are spent communicating with other people. Whether we are talking to someone over the phone, making a presentation to a group, responding to e-mail, working in a committee, or chatting with a friend, we are communicating and relating to people. Sometimes the vast number of people we talk to and the wide range of topics we must discuss leave us overwhelmed and unsure of our ability to communicate. Although we may want to cut off communication with others and withdraw as a means of coping with communication overload, a reality of contemporary life is that we must continually engage with others to do work and maintain relationships to sustain healthy lives.

What Is Communication?

The key to managing all this lies in the quality of our communication with others. High-quality communication is **competent**—both appropriate and effective for a particular situation. **Appropriate** communication means that you act in ways suitable to the norms and expectations of contexts and situations you encounter. **Effective** communication means you are able to achieve the most desirable objectives or outcomes in contexts. Your communication competence can vary from situation to situation. For example, Kathryn was perceived as very competent by her fellow committee members but as less competent by her professor and classmates during her marketing presentation.

What factors influence our ability to communicate appropriately and effectively? Kathryn's story highlights some of them. One possible explanation for Kathryn's poor performance in her marketing class is that she suffered from stage fright. She had written a solid outline of the most important points but was held back by her fear of public speaking. In her conversation with her friend Kwan, however, she was not at all nervous or anxious. Rather, she was highly motivated and knew what she wanted to say—but couldn't find a way to say it without pressuring him to stay. We could probably attribute Kathryn's ability to communicate successfully in the committee meeting to her motivation to lead the group and her extensive experience and training in leading committees.

To understand these and other factors that contribute to our competence, let us first define what we mean by communication. A wide variety of terms have been used to define communication such as symbols, speech, understanding, process, transmission, channel, intention, meaning, and situation (Littlejohn & Foss, 2005). A broad definition that applies to different situations and to a diversity of people is most useful. **Communication** is the process of managing messages and media for the purpose of creating meaning (Frey, Botan, & Kreps, 2000). The following four key terms make up this definition: messages, meaning, media, and managing.

Messages

Messages are the words, sounds, actions, and gestures that people express to one another when they interact. Messages may be expressed verbally in words or nonverbally in sounds, actions, and gestures. Messages may be symbolic. A **symbol** is a word, sound, action, or gesture that refers to something else. The relationship between symbols and the things or concepts to which they refer is arbitrary.

The arbitrary relation between symbols and their **referent,** or the thing to which they refer, deserves further consideration. Think of the word *nuts*. To begin with, it has several potential conventional meanings, as in "That guy is nuts!" "Let's get down to nuts and bolts." "The mixed nuts they served at that party were great." A commander at the Battle of the Bulge in World War II, when the encompassing German forces demanded he surrender, simply replied, "Nuts!" But to what reality do these words refer? There are edible seeds that we call nuts, but would the word *nut* typically conjure up images of a peanut, hazelnut, almond, pistachio, or some other member of that plant group? If a mechanic says, "Hand me that nut," is it a reference to a bolt's fastener or a snack? Furthermore, different cultures will have different words for what in English is referred to as nuts. So what we call something is merely a product of history, culture, and our ability to communicate using these arbitrary labels we place on things.

The arbitrary nature of the relationship between symbols and referents is often central to understanding communication problems in the world. And many of our most important referents are themselves quite abstract. We live in a republic, but it is commonly referred to as a democracy. The latter word seems to carry greater patriotic weight in political rhetoric, yet the American Pledge of Allegiance clearly labels the country a republic. Would people be as easily motivated to fight today to spread republicanism to the world as to spread democracy? When a politician says that we need to spread democracy around the world, what exactly does that mean in terms of actual political changes: does it mean changes in the constitution, voting processes, marketplace, authority of the military, family and gender relations, or all of the above? And if you interpret democracy differently than someone else does, how could you determine who has the more "true" conception of its meaning?

The most common set of verbal symbols we use is language, which we need to talk about our physical, social, and psychological worlds. **Language** is a verbal symbol system that allows us to take messages and utterances, in the form of words, and translate them into meaning. For example, in the English language, we use words such as *house* and *car* to refer to physical objects in our world and words such as *love* and *anger* to refer to our inner feelings. Verbal symbols may take either spoken or written form.

Symbolic behavior is not limited to verbal messages; it can be nonverbal as well. **Nonverbal symbols** are those sounds, actions, or gestures that people agree have a common meaning. Nonverbal symbols may be communicated by behaviors such as the use of eyes, posture, gestures, and the way we use space and time. An example of a nonverbal

learning link

What is the difference between a verbal and a nonverbal symbol?

● ● ●

symbol in North America is the joining of the forefinger and thumb to signal to others that we are OK. However, in some cultures, the same symbol sends an obscene message! Nonverbal symbols can also be used to communicate emotion. When people use e-mail they may include the nonverbal symbol called an emoticon, :-) or ☺, to show they feel good or happy. What distinguishes these symbolic nonverbal gestures from other nonverbal behaviors is that people have agreed on the meaning of the arbitrary gesture.

Media

Media are any means through which symbols are transmitted and meanings are represented. Humankind's earliest efforts at communication probably used their natural abilities as a medium—such as through grunts, growls, howls, and other vocalizations. Later, they probably employed various instruments of nature as a medium, by making sounds on tree trunks, signals with smoke, and tattoos on skin with sharpened bones. Now our everyday speaking and listening occur through the use of our own voice, gestures, and body to communicate through *natural media*.

Added to natural media today are *technological media*. Pens and papers were early media for writing, and now electronic personal digital assistants permit screens to display writing as digital text. Telephones transfer voice, text (in the form of faxes), and images (through videophones and cellphone cameras). The Internet, e-mail, instant messaging, and even biometric identification permit the transfer of written, visual, physical, and audio information. The options for communicating through technological media have vastly expanded in the past century.

Nonverbal symbols represent one way for people to communicate with one another.

Whether through natural or technological media, we have to have some way of assigning meaning to our behavior and communicating that meaning to other people.

Meaning

Meaning refers to the interpretation people assign to a message—how it is recognized or understood. Meaning for words and events may be personal and unique or it may be shared with others. As people are socialized into a group or culture, they develop meanings for certain words and events shared with others. Take, for example, the words *spam, virus,* and *firewall*. If you are a cook, *spam* refers to spiced ham in a can. If you are a doctor, the term *virus* refers to an infectious agent that invades and takes over human cells. If you are a forest firefighter, the word *firewall* refers to a line of defense where you will attempt to stop a fire. But if you are a computer programmer, these words take on different meanings. The word *spam* refers to junk mail that you receive on e-mail; *virus* refers to a rogue computer program that corrupts your files or does other damage; and a *firewall* restricts access to data on a computer network.

People may agree at some level on the meaning of particular words or events, but meaning can also be personal and unique and can depend on your own personal history, your culture, your political and religious beliefs, the volunteer organizations you belong to, and so on. It is not enough to ask, "What does that mean?" Instead, the question needs to be rephrased as "What does that mean *to you*?"

CALVIN & HOBBES *by BILL WATTERSON*

The meaning of words is both shared among people as well as unique to individuals.

Managing

Managing typically refers to the handling or supervising of people or some process or material. In communication, we manage the process of creating, receiving, and responding to verbal and nonverbal messages and media. Consider the various choices you make when performing a simple ritual such as greeting a friend in a hallway. You choose among several possible verbal or nonverbal behaviors. Do you wave your hand as you pass by your friend, extend a handshake, or give your friend a hug? Do you say, "Hello!" "Hey, it's good to see you!" or "What's happening?"

One way to sort out messages, media, meanings, and their management is to examine the models that people have created to describe the communication process. Models play an important role in changing our awareness of a process and, therefore, changing the process itself. Consider two consultants working with different models of forecasting election outcomes for their candidates. One consultant's model predicts that people will vote "on their pocketbooks," meaning that if the economy is thriving, people will vote for the incumbent. Another consultant's model predicts that people will vote based on their pocketbooks and, more specifically, whether their wages are keeping up with inflation, whether they have experienced growth in their career, and whether they subjectively feel better off today than they did a year ago. The latter model has more potential information and probably a better chance at predicting an election outcome. Our models of processes, therefore, play an important role in guiding our actions.

Models of Communication

Four different models that depict the communication process have evolved over the last century: (1) communication as information transfer, (2) communication as shared meaning, (3) communication as persuasion, and (4) communication as community.

Communication as Information Transfer

An early model of communication still used today is the **information transfer model.** Sometimes called an action or linear model of communication, this perspective adopts a one-way view of communication in which a message is sent by a **source** through a **channel**

learning link

What kinds of noise may interfere with a source clearly conveying a message to a receiver?

• • •

to a **receiver.** A source, or sender, is the original producer of the message and in human communication is a person. The channel is the medium through which a message is sent. Channels may be written, as in letters and memos; oral, as in face-to-face verbal communication and telephone conversations; nonverbal, as in shared looks or raised eyebrows; or mediated, as in e-mail or videoconferencing. The receiver of the message is the person or group of people who is the ultimate audience for the message.

The most direct version of this model, and the one for which it was originally developed, is a television program developed by the producers and station, or the source, sent through television signals and transmitters to television sets where people receive the programming. It is very unidirectional, and tends to treat the receiver as a passive receptacle of information and the source as the one in control of the communication event. It also tends to treat the medium, or channel, as something that, for the most part, simply has the potential to get in the way of more complete communication by limiting how the message gets transmitted.

As Figure 1.1 illustrates, the source encodes a message, or puts a thought into words, and transmits it through a channel, or a medium through which the message travels to a receiver. The receiver then decodes, or assigns meaning to, the message. These messages may be interrupted, intercepted, or altered by **noise,** which is any type of interference that distracts us from the communication. Noise can be competing sounds that make it difficult for the receiver to hear or other distractions in the environment such as heat or a seat in the back of a crowded room. Noise can also come from within the communication in the form of daydreaming, illness, or nervous tics. This model of communication suggests that we can understand a communication situation by answering five simple questions (Lasswell, 1948/1964): Who? Says what? To whom? Through what channel? With what effect?

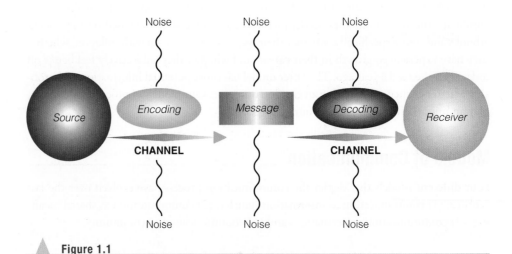

Figure 1.1

The Information Transfer Model of Communication

One of the earliest models of communication was the action or linear model of communication developed by Shannon and Weaver (1949). This model views communication as a one-way process in which a source encodes a message through a channel to a receiver who decodes the message. Noise can influence whether the message sent by the source is accurately received by the receiver.

Viewing communication as information transfer emphasizes the role of the message source in making intentional choices about the kinds of verbal and nonverbal messages needed to make the point. Message sources must find ways to express clearly what they are thinking and wanting. The key question in the information transfer model is "Did the source successfully convey his or her meaning to the receiver of the message? Did the receiver understand precisely what the speaker intended?" (Eisenberg & Goodall, 2004).

Imagine you are a vice president for Student Life at a college and you are trying to evaluate whether students understand the new policies and procedures your office has developed for student organization events, dances, and parties. If you were to use the communication as information transfer model, you would probably ask yourself the following kinds of questions:

- What does the Student Life office want students to understand about the new policies and procedures?
- What is the content of the message that the Student Life office is distributing to students?
- What channels does the Student Life office use to distribute the message? Presentations at club meetings? Posters? E-mail? Posting on a website?
- What might interfere with students' clear reception of the message?
- What message might students perceive that they received?
- Does the message sent by the Student Life office match the message received by students?

As a vice president for Student Life, you would be concerned with clearly identifying your organization's intent and anticipating and observing what obstacles, if any, might have interfered with the reception of the message.

Communication as Sharing Meaning

One difficulty with the information transfer model is that it assumes communication travels in only one direction, that it is unidirectional. Receivers are viewed as passive absorbers of information sent by sources with no way of responding to the message and communicating their viewpoint.

An alternative to the information transfer model views communication as sharing meaning and assumes that communication flows both ways—from source to receiver and from receiver to source. This model is illustrated less by the transmission of televised messages and more by a simple telephone conversation or a family discussion in which a decision has to be made about some future event. The most important outcome of communication is that each person understands the other and together they agree on the meaning of the message. Two distinct models have been developed that view communication as sharing meaning: (1) the interactive model, and (2) the transactional model.

The **interactive model** views communication as sharing meaning and adds a feedback loop that links the receiver to the source. This model shifts the perspective away from communication as a simple linear process and instead views it as a circular process in which both communicators alternate as senders and receivers of messages. As Figure 1.2

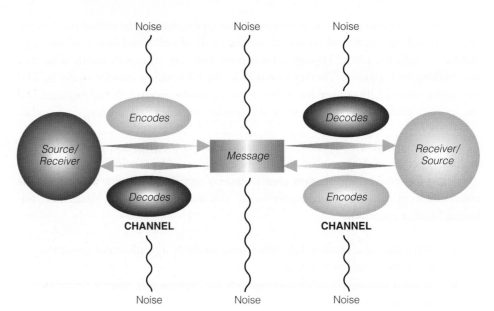

Figure 1.2

The Interactive Model of Communication

An interactive model of communication emphasizes two-way communication between communicators. Notice that, although both parties perform all the functions of the sender and receiver in the information transfer model (encoding and decoding), they take turns acting as sender and receiver.

illustrates, a distinguishing aspect of this model is that people can perform the role of only sender or receiver during interaction; they cannot perform both functions simultaneously.

Unlike the interactive model in which people alternate between acting as message sources and receivers, the **transactional model** maintains that people are simultaneously senders and receivers of messages. According to this model, even when you are listening carefully to another person and receiving his or her message, you are sending nonverbal messages through your level of eye contact, vocal "uh-huh's," hand gestures, and head nods. As Figure 1.3 illustrates, the transactional model also differs from the interactive model because it accounts for fields of meaning—the values, attitudes, beliefs, and ideas that a person has developed over a lifetime. The overlap between the receiver's and the sender's personal fields of meaning represents their shared field of meaning.

The transactional model of communication as sharing meaning focuses on identifying areas where shared meaning exists, areas where people disagree about meaning, and the communication processes people can use to create shared meaning. This model recognizes that individuals come to situations with different fields of personal meaning that may or may not overlap. For example, imagine a friend tells you he has just had a misunderstanding with his boss. The misunderstanding occurred because his boss told him to complete a project "as soon as possible." But when he completed the project, his boss was annoyed with him for being "late" with his work. If you were to apply the model of communication as shared meaning to this situation, you might ask your friend the following kinds of questions to help him understand his boss's personal field of meaning and look for commonalities with his own personal field of meaning:

- What does "as soon as possible" mean to you? What in your personal experience has led you to believe this?
- What do you think "as soon as possible" means to your boss? What in your boss's experience has led her to believe this?

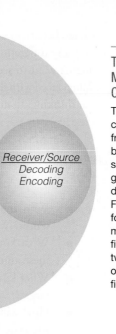

Figure 1.3

The Transactional Model of Communication

The transactional model of communication differs from the interactive model because it views the source and receiver as engaging in encoding and decoding simultaneously. Furthermore, it accounts for personal fields of meaning. The personal fields of meaning of the two communicators can overlap, creating a shared field of meaning.

- Where do the two of you agree on what "as soon as possible means?" Where do you disagree?
- For those areas where you disagree, what could you say or do to carve out an agreement on what "as soon as possible" means? What could your boss say or do?

These questions apply the transactional model by identifying areas of agreement and disagreement over meaning and highlighting possible ways of communicating to establish shared meaning where none exists.

How can we use communication to create shared meaning? One way is to simply see where shared meaning might already exist by asking questions about the other person's field of meaning and about what can be done to create shared meaning where it doesn't already exist. In other situations, people create shared meaning more actively by using persuasion.

Communication as Persuasion

Since Aristotle offered his first course in rhetoric in the 4th century BCE, communication scholars have studied the way speakers use the tools of persuasion to convince audiences. **Persuasion** is the use of communication to reinforce, change, or modify an audience's attitudes, values, beliefs, or actions. Persuasion is commonly viewed as a form of influence and occurs in many different contexts, for example, when we talk a friend into seeing a movie she doesn't want to see, or when a salesperson persuades us to purchase a product or service. When faced with decision making in small groups, group members make arguments to sway our thinking. In many arenas of life, politicians and advertisers bombard us with persuasive messages.

Communication as persuasion relies on influencing others to achieve your own goals. When trying to persuade others, you might typically ask yourself questions such as these:

- Who am I attempting to persuade? Who is the target of my persuasive attempt? What are the target person's key attitudes, values, and beliefs?
- What kinds of arguments can I use to persuade the target person? How do these arguments fit the target person's key attitudes, values, and beliefs?
- What kinds of appeals or arguments would most successfully persuade my target?
- How will the target of my persuasion need to act for me to know I have succeeded?

From this viewpoint, communication is successful to the degree to which you are able to get other people to do what you want. Successful communication is measured by your ability to persuade others and move them in the direction you choose.

Organizations such as Coca-Cola, Microsoft, Dell, Ford Motor Company, and Nike use a variety of persuasive techniques such as incentive systems, employee orientation programs, performance appraisals, and in-house newsletters to create shared meaning between their employees and the organization. If employees share an organization's values and views, they will pursue goals beneficial to the organization as well as to themselves. These organizations highlight a contemporary view of communication as a way of building community within interpersonal, group, and public situations.

Communication as Community

Many people have come to view communication as so powerful that it creates our social worlds (Pearce, 1994). A **community** is a group of people who come together in the same physical, mental, or virtual space to interact or pursue a common goal. Public institutions such as governments and schools; organizations such as Microsoft, Saturn, or Paine Webber; groups such as families, work teams, e-mail distribution lists, and sports teams; and romantic or friendship relationships represent the vast variety of communities to which we belong. How do these various kinds of communities get created? As Figure 1.4 illustrates, communication permeates our environment and creates the various communities we belong to. Moreover, different forms of communication create different forms of community. For example, when people in a group show little interest in completing an assigned task, the kind of community these members create is significantly different from the community created by a group whose members feel passionate about the task and are willing to devote the time and energy necessary to complete it.

The transactional model we previously looked at suggests that what needs to get done as we communicate is sharing meaning. However, when we view communication as

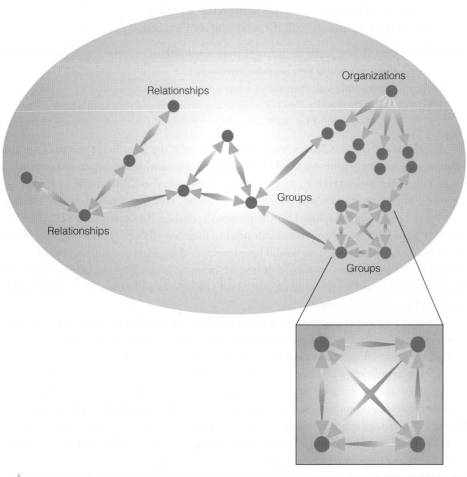

SOCIETY

Relationships

Organizations

Relationships

Groups

Groups

▲ **Figure 1.4**

The Community and Communication Model

Community permeates our existence as members of society, organizations, groups, and relationships. Understanding the idea of community is challenging because people may belong to multiple communities simultaneously, and the way we communicate can create different types of community. To understand how community is created, examine the form of communication occurring between people as indicated by the lines connecting individuals in their relationships, groups, organizations, and society.

community, creating shared meaning is only one possible outcome among many. Take for example, the following snippet of conversation:

Sally: I think you really need to get your act together.
Chris: [Silence.]
Sally: Chris, don't you care about what I'm saying?
Chris: [Silence.]

What is getting accomplished in this conversation? Sally appears to be the dominant partner in a relationship, seeking to move Chris to do things the way Sally wants them done. But Chris' communication appears to function as withdrawal from this very relationship.

What is the key difference between viewing communication as community and the transactional model of communication?

• • •

Other possibilities include an oppressive relationship where Sally is the oppressor or even a passive-aggressive relationship in which Chris is the aggressor.

Contrast the first episode with the following conversation:

Sally: I think you really need to get your act together.
Chris: Since when did you become my mother?
Sally: Chris, don't you care about what I'm saying?
Chris: No, Sally, I really don't. I wish in the future you'd just keep your mouth shut and let me live my life.

In this conversation, Chris is responding differently; she is no longer silent. This dialogue represents a very different kind of community, one in which an argument occurs because Sally and Chris actively disagree over an issue—whether Chris needs to get her act together. The community they create and the way they create it—together—is different from all the possibilities explored for the previous exchange. To understand a community, whether relational, group, or public, you need to focus on what people do together. If we viewed only Sally's messages, we would have interpreted the kind of community being created in both conversations similarly. When we examine how Chris responds to Sally, we begin to understand that the kind of community being created in their relationship is different in the two conversations.

Communication as community is about coordinating our actions with others to bring about desirable goals. For example, in the context of a job interview, the interviewer's goal is to discover information about a job applicant that will facilitate making a good hiring decision. The job applicant wants to present information that will promote a positive evaluation on the part of the interviewer. Sometimes these two interests come into conflict: interviewers may request information less than flattering to an applicant and job applicants do their best to avoid divulging that information. In interviews where the communication is coordinated, skillful interviewers and job applicants coordinate their questions and answers seamlessly to achieve their own personal goals.

All four models of communication—information transfer, sharing meaning, persuasion, and community—are useful when deciding how to communicate in different situations. The information transfer model is useful in mass communication or when giving instructions to a large group of people. Viewing communication as shared meaning may help a work team adopt the organization's vision. If a salesperson needs to fulfill a quota to keep his or her job, communication as persuasion may best accomplish the task. However, each model provides only partial insight into the communication process because it allows us to focus on only what it highlights as important. If we believe in communication as information transfer, we neglect the way shared meaning is created and the persuasive elements of communication. If we believe in communication as shared meaning, we do not focus on how information is transferred or how people persuade one another. If we believe in communication as persuasion, we do not focus on how people create shared meaning.

Consider an example of this dilemma. Many public health campaigns aimed at reducing teen pregnancy adopt an information transfer model of communication. They provide

© Rhoda Sidney/Monkmeyer Press

Viewing communication as shared meaning is sometimes useful.

detailed information about pregnancy and contraception. Why do so many of these campaigns fail? One explanation may be that by focusing on disseminating detailed information clearly, the proponents of such campaigns may have overlooked the importance of shared meaning. They may not be providing words and images in a way that taps into a teenager's field of experience.

Assumptions about Communication

If we view communication as community and as the process of managing messages to create meaning, what assumptions do we make about communication? Test your own beliefs about communication in the Test Your Assumptions box and then read the following detailed descriptions of these common assumptions.

Communication Is a Process

One of the turning points in any relationship with romantic potential occurs when two people look each other in the eye and say, "I love you." With these three simple words the relationship moves from a friendship to romantic involvement and love. Look 6 months into the future of this relationship. After an argument, both people look at each other and utter those same three words, "I love you." Does this phrase mean what it did 6 months earlier? Although the words may be the same, the meaning is probably quite different. The first time the couple said "I love you," it meant their relationship was moving to a new level of intimacy. The second "I love you" came after the couple had shared many more experiences—both positive and negative. The meaning of "I love you" changes from being a significant milestone to words intended to smooth over a conflict. Although you may be able to say the same words twice, the words never mean the same thing. Statement 1 in the Test Your Assumptions box then is false.

The fact that communication is a process does not mean that it must follow a specific series of steps to be effective. Rather, it suggests that the meaning of an utterance depends on where it falls in the process—what has happened before the words are spoken and what happens afterward. To understand the process of communication, we must ask questions such as what was said, to whom, in what context, and how did they respond? The statement "That's just nuts" could be an insult or a statement of how enjoyable something was, depending on what it is responding to. Thus Statement 2 is false.

Test ✓ Your Assumptions

Assumptions about Communication

INSTRUCTIONS: Please read the following statements and decide whether you think each is true or false.

TRUE	FALSE	
☐	☐	1. Saying something twice communicates exactly the same thing both times.
☐	☐	2. The meaning of a symbol is the same regardless of the situation in which it occurs.
☐	☐	3. Communication reflects reality rather than creates it.
☐	☐	4. The most important function communication serves is to achieve something.
☐	☐	5. High-quality communication must conform to the norms of the relationship or culture.
☐	☐	6. It is important to be consistent in the way you communicate.
☐	☐	7. The audience for a message determines the effectiveness of the message.
☐	☐	8. Knowing the intent of the sender's message is important to understanding the communication process.
☐	☐	9. Understanding one another and sharing meaning is the sole foundation for good communication.
☐	☐	10. To be effective, communication must be clear and unambiguous.

Answers: 1: F; 2: F; 3: F; 4: T; 5: F; 6: F; 7: T; 8: T; 9: F; 10: F

Communication Creates Our Social Worlds

Return to the Test Your Assumptions box. Statement 3 claims that communication reflects reality rather than creating it. In popular culture, we see this question debated in discussions about the effect of media messages on society. Some argue that violence on television, in the movies, and in video games creates a society desensitized to violence and causes people to act out their violent impulses. Others argue that the violent content of television, movies, and video games simply reflects the violence going on in society. The debate centers on whether life imitates art, art imitates life, or art and life are totally separate.

Communication does much more than simply transmit our internal states, such as thoughts and feelings, to others and allow us to refer to external events and people. Rather, it creates and re-forms our understanding of those states, events, and people. It is communication that provides us with meaning and expectations about people and situations. Because the way we communicate is responsible to a large extent for creating our social worlds, Statement 3 is false.

learning link

How does communication create our social worlds?

• • •

Communication performs a variety of functions. It can help us accomplish work as well as build relationships.

© Steven Rubin / The Image Works

Communication Is Functional

Statement 4 in the Test Your Assumptions box suggests the central reason for communicating is to accomplish something. If you are a member of a work team and need to make a decision, communication with other team members helps make that decision. When you are negotiating the purchase of a car, your ability to persuade can help you accomplish your goal of getting a good deal. Communication functions by helping us explain, brainstorm, negotiate, direct, and make decisions in many situations. It allows us to complete the task at hand. In short, communication is functional—that is, communication serves a particular purpose in any interaction. In addition to getting things done, communication also helps us build relationships and maintain a healthy supportive climate around us.

To understand the functional nature of communication, ask yourself the following questions:

- What has led the speaker to utter this message?
- What is the effect of this message on listeners?

By understanding the purpose of the message and the effect it has on others, you can begin to determine what functions the message is serving. So Statement 4 is true.

Communication Is Limiting and Liberating

When you think about communicating in a situation that is new to you, such as a first date, it is natural to think about how people typically communicate in that situation. However, there are times when acting in new or atypical ways opens up more possibilities. For instance, the auctioneer of a national art auction house often mentions that art auctions make great first dates because they are so different from what is expected, can be fun to people watch, are educational, and suggest that one either has, or is interested in, learning about culture.

In fact, people sometimes communicate in ways that intentionally or unintentionally violate pre-existing expectations and boundaries. When people communicate in ways that are creative and liberating, they reshape norms, values, and beliefs. Moreover, they may do it in such a way that others view it as appropriate. When Bono took up the cause of relieving the debt of poorer countries, traditional politicians and bankers found it odd for a rock star to seriously engage in the cause. But it was in part because of his celebrity as well as his ability to learn the technical aspects of the issue and his commitment to the cause that he began to be taken very seriously.

Said a different way, human beings both create and conform to contexts. When we conform to context, that context limits or imposes constraints on our communication. For example, in the context of a college classroom, students know they should take notes during class; they also know playing loud music and dancing is prohibited. When we create context, we open up new and innovative ways of acting and liberate people from their constraints. So Statement 5, "High-quality communication must conform to the norms of the relationship or culture," is false.

Communication Is Adaptive

Rather than being consistent in our communication and always saying the same thing in the same way, as competent communicators we need to adapt our messages to the time and place in which we are communicating and to the audience we are trying to reach. This is not to say you should change what you say or do to match what other people want you to say or do. This type of behavior would compromise your ethical code and make you seem inconsistent or unpredictable to others. However, people who are sensitive to the complexities of communication recognize the unique characteristics of their context and create messages that allow them to be heard by others while retaining their own viewpoints. In essence, communication competence requires the careful balancing of being consistent (being yourself) and adapting to others and the contexts in which you encounter them. Statement 6, that you should always be consistent, is thus false.

Communication Is Holistic

Understanding communication holistically means the speaker, the audience, and what they do together need to be viewed as complex sets of processes operating simultaneously. To understand communication holistically, focus on:

- what the communicators do together
- what they do at a specific time
- what they do in a specific place
- what has led up to this interaction
- what their hopes are for the future

Taking a holistic approach to examining communication is important because focusing only on the speaker's intent or on the audience's perceptions of a message limits our understanding of the entire communication process. Can we understand the complete communication process if we focus on only the speaker's intention apart from the audience

People sometimes adapt their communication to fit into situations. Adapting your communication to the situation may help you achieve your goals.

to whom he or she is speaking? Can we say a message is effective if the audience for that message views it as such, but the sender of the message does not? The simple answer is no. Understanding communication holistically requires examining the past, looking to the future, and focusing on the situation itself. Statements 7 and 8, then, are both true.

Communication Is Ambiguous

In the late 1970s, Douglas Adams wrote his science fiction novel, subsequently a movie, *The Hitchhiker's Guide to the Galaxy*. In it, he identifies one problem facing space travelers: the inability to communicate clearly with one another because of the wide variety of languages spoken. Yet a little creature that came to be called Babel Fish evolved that, when placed in the ear, would automatically and clearly translate what a person was saying into the listener's own language. Surprisingly, rather than helping relationships among different races by promoting clear understanding, the end results of using Babel Fish were some of the bloodiest wars known to the universe. Once people clearly understood one another and assigned similar meanings to words, this clarity sharply defined their differences and led to war.

Most of us assume that for people to communicate well they must share precise meanings for events and words (Statement 9 in the Test Your Assumptions box) and that people always need to be clear and unambiguous to achieve good communication (Statement 10). Of course, people often need to share meaning and clarity in communication. During crisis situations, medical personnel need to agree on what certain procedures mean and doctors must give clear instructions on the procedures that must be performed. Yet there are times when we may need or want to be less than clear in our communication. Being ambiguous can have two main benefits (Eisenberg & Goodall, 2004). First, ambiguity can help people with diverse sets of opinions collaborate with each other. If there is ambiguity about what beliefs or values are important, people may assume they share the same beliefs and values and be willing to work together. When communication is clear, the differences between people become more distinct and may lead to excessive conflict. Second, ambiguous communication can promote creativity. For example, sometimes teachers may be ambiguous in their instructions about how to complete a particular assignment to encourage students to be creative in the way they accomplish the task. So Statements 9 and 10 are both false.

Communication Is Crucial to a Quality Life

Given how much time we devote to speaking, listening, writing, informing, persuading, and talking, human beings communicate almost constantly. There is an assumption many scholars articulated decades ago: "One cannot *not* communicate" (Watzlawick, Beavin, and Jackson, 1967). You are even communicating when just being silent. Like Kathryn in the opening chapter vignette, we communicate with a large number of people daily through a wide variety of channels. We literally live in a communication world. And the way we communicate has direct consequences on the kinds of lives we lead, the kinds of relationships we create, and the kinds of communities we build. The ability to build strong interpersonal relationships depends on our changing the form of communication when necessary. When couples allow their conversations to be influenced by criticism, contempt, defensiveness, and withdrawal, they create relationships that are unstable and prone to divorce (Gottman & Silver, 1999). Rather than choosing to be negative, couples can choose more positive forms of communication that encourage them to describe their conflict, maintain fondness and admiration for each other, craft solutions that allow both people to meet their needs, and offer mutual support. Relationships are constantly being made and remade by communication—changing the form of communication can result in more positive, fulfilling, and long lasting interpersonal relationships.

The ability to create strong groups and teams also depends on communication. The last decade has seen an explosion in the use of groups in social and work settings. More than 40 million people in the United States currently participate in support groups such as Alcoholics Anonymous, cancer survivor groups, and consciousness-raising groups (Wuthnow, 1994). Moreover, in an era of increased domestic and international competition and corporate downsizing, organizations increasingly rely on work teams to maintain a competitive edge. In both our social and work lives, groups are becoming a more powerful presence. When group members choose forms of communicating that allow the creation of collective goals, the blending of individual members' knowledge, and the promotion of learning, they are more likely to be successful (Katzenbach & Smith, 2001; Kayes, 2002).

Finally, the way we communicate influences our ability to build strong and healthy communities. Traditional ways of building communities have emphasized debate and argument. For example, the United States has a strong tradition of using town hall meetings to deliberate important issues within communities (Barge, in press). In these settings, advocates for each side of the issue present arguments for their positions. Public issues such as health care, abortion, economic development, and environmental protection have been discussed in such public forums. Yet for debate and argument to work well, people need to come to such forums with similar assumptions and values. The shared assumptions and values serve as a backdrop for the discussion. However, as society becomes more diverse, the likelihood that people share assumptions and values diminishes. As a result, forms of communication such as argument and debate become polarized because people do not share the same foundation for understanding. In this situation, debate and argument may drive communities apart as opposed to bringing them together.

Many people interested in community building contend that we need to shift our forms of communication to include more dialogue (Pearce & Pearce, 2004; Spano, 2001). **Dialogue** is a way of communicating that allows people to stand their own ground while being open to and respectful of other perspectives. As people begin to participate in more community dialogues about significant issues, the community has more opportunity to pull together and unify.

Close Up *on Community*

Integrating Community Concerns with Your Experience

OUR COMMUNITIES ARE BECOMING INCREASINGLY diverse. How can you begin to understand those who are different from you? How can you begin to grasp how communication can make a difference in building strong, healthy communities? During your college experience, one way to connect with people who may be different from you is to make a commitment to work for social justice, to be willing to engage with and advocate for people in a community who are "economically, socially, politically, and/or culturally underresourced" (Frey, Pearce, Pollock, Artz, & Murphy, 1996, p. 110). The goal of working for social justice is not only to learn about people who may be different from you, but to take action to help those who are disadvantaged in your community because of a lack of resources (Hatch, 1996).

One way to integrate a commitment to social justice with your education is to engage in service learning, a collaboration between students and communities in which students apply their classroom learning to help communities manage significant issues or problems, and in turn, the community experience broadens the students' classroom learning (O'Hara, 2001). Service learning may take several different forms:

- Courses with service-learning components are not designed to be service-learning intensive, but they allow or require you to use a service experience, often something you may be doing already, such as tutoring high-risk children, visiting the elderly, working in domestic-abuse shelters, or supporting the chronically ill, as the basis for one assignment.
- Courses with service-learning motifs may or may not have been designed with service learning in mind, but they allow or require you to use service as the basis for all or a major part of your course assignments. An example would be a class developing and producing radio programs that respond to local community needs and interests.
- An internship or fieldwork provides an opportunity to spend several hours each week working with a community organization in a position that builds professional skills. Habitat for Humanity,

for example, has developed a public relations internship position that offers valuable public relations experience while participating in an effort to provide affordable housing to people who might otherwise live in deplorable conditions. The intern produces press packets, coordinates interviews, writes press releases and public service announcements, and assists in the editing and publishing of a newsletter.

- A capstone course is a department- or program-based, senior-level course that involves significant community service, as well as guided discussion and written analysis of previous service experience based on intellectual frameworks designed by the instructor or team of instructors. (Adapted from Frey et al., 1996, pp. 120–121)

Service learning is one way to learn about people who may be different from you. However, your school may not offer opportunities in service learning. In that case, how could you learn about others who may be different from you and still maintain a social justice commitment? Consider the following ideas:

- Mentor someone who is underresourced.
- Volunteer at a soup kitchen or a homeless shelter.
- Encourage campus groups to make a commitment to service.
- Facilitate the planning and execution of service projects on campus.
- Present a speech about people who are underresourced or about an issue that relates to social justice as an assignment for one of your classes.
- Research the underresourced in your community and submit an article based on this research to your school newspaper.

Even if formal classes that emphasize service and social justice are not offered, you can undertake any number of interpersonal, small group, or public speaking opportunities to facilitate your learning about people who may be different from you and to help those who have fewer resources.

SOURCE: Frey et al. (1996).

Communication and Competence

As you can see by now, communication is much more complex than it first appears. Like Kathryn at the beginning of this chapter, you probably communicate with a large and diverse number of people, over a number of topics and issues, and in a wide variety of settings. Given this diversity, it is impossible to construct rules for communication that specifically detail what messages are obligated, permitted, or prohibited given a specific situation. Thus building a comprehensive model of communication that can prescribe what people must do or say in all situations is impossible. There are times when it is effective to be ambiguous in your communication, when shared meaning is not important, and when the goal of the communication is not persuasion. However, if we can't make general rules for communicating, what kind of model of communication can we create? It is possible to construct a model of communication for making informed choices about messages that will help you act in competent ways—ways in which your communication is perceived as appropriate and effective by others. See the Close-Up on Community box for ways to acquire communication competence and work for social justice.

As Chapter 2 shows, communication competence requires acting in ways that are perceived as appropriate and effective by you and by others. Competent communication can be clear or ambiguous, it can create shared meaning or not, and it can function to persuade others or not. All forms of communication have the potential to be viewed as competent depending on the situation. This idea requires that you develop a framework for choosing among communication messages that will allow you to act competently within a situation.

Three requirements to constructing messages are perceived as competent by others. First, you must be motivated to communicate competently. Second, you must be knowledgeable about the situation you are communicating in and the kinds of messages that are obligated, permitted, or prohibited. Third, you must be skilled at actually transmitting the kinds of messages you know you should perform in the situation. Motivation, knowledge, and skills are the foundations to managing communication competently, whether in interpersonal, group, public speaking, or mass communication contexts. The remainder of this book will provide you with the motivation, knowledge, and skills critical to improving how you communicate in all of these contexts.

 ## Chapter Summary

Communication is a pervasive force in our everyday life as we relate and connect to a wide variety of people through face-to-face and mediated channels in a large number of social and work contexts. Communication is a process of managing messages for the purpose of creating meaning. There are various models by which this process can be understood, such as information transfer, sharing meaning, as persuasion, and as community. The model of communication as community is the most inclusive model and draws attention to the role that elements of the other models play in the creation of a sense of connection and engagement with others.

Communication is a process that unfolds over time and creates our social worlds. Communication is functional in that it helps us perform important tasks and build strong relationships. Our ability to create new ways of thinking and being requires being sensitive to the holistic nature of communication and taking actions that allow us to coordinate our collective behavior. To develop your communication competence you need to develop your abilities in three areas: (1) motivation, (2) knowledge, and (3) skills.

Study and Review

The premium companion website for *Human Communication* offers a broad range of resources that will help you better understand the material in this chapter, complete assignments, and succeed on tests. The website resources include

- Interactive self-assessments, competency grids, and other tools
- Web links, practice activities, self-quizzes, and a sample final exam

For more information about this text's electronic learning resources, consult the *Guide to Online Resources for Human Communication* or visit **http://communication .wadsworth.com/morreale2.**

 ## Key Terms

The key terms below are defined in the chapter on the pages indicated. They are also presented alphabetically with definitions in the Glossary, which begins on page 467. The book's website includes flashcards and crossword puzzles to help you learn these terms and the concepts they represent.

competent 4
appropriate 4
effective 4
communication 4
message 5
symbol 5
referent 5
language 5
nonverbal symbol 5
media 6
meaning 6

managing 7
information transfer model 7
source 7
channel 7
receiver 8
noise 8
interactive model 9
transactional model 10
persuasion 11
community 12
dialogue 19

 ## Building Knowledge

The questions below are among the practice activities on the book's website.

1. How are relatively new communication technologies such as e-mail, chat rooms, instant messaging, and video conferencing influencing the communication process?
2. Identify at least three situations where it would make sense to use communication as information transfer, communication as sharing meaning, and communication as persuasion.

3. How else can you define communication besides as information transfer, shared meaning, persuasion, and community?

4. Think of a time when you felt a person was flexible in his or her communication, yet was not perceived as being wishy-washy or adapting just to meet someone else's needs. How did that person make his or her communication flexible?

5. Why is understanding communication important to our daily lives? Are there ever situations where communication doesn't make a difference? Explain.

 ## Building Skills _____

The exercises below are among the practice activities on the book's website.

Individual Exercises

1. Think of a recent conversation you would characterize as poor communication. On a piece of paper, draw a vertical line dividing the paper in two. In the left-hand column, write down the conversation. Note each speaker's turn on a separate line. In the right-hand column, next to each message write down what you think is the underlying reason for that message. Think about the key assumptions each conversational partner is making and the reasons that guided his or her interaction. How could you change the conversation to make the outcome better? How would the key assumptions need to change?

2. Find an opinion piece or an editorial in a magazine or a newspaper. Read the editorial and highlight the key words and phrases that the author uses. Focusing on these key words and phrases, how would you describe the way the author perceives his or her community?

3. Consider the following list of labels we use to describe some of the roles that people can play in society and organizations: When a person is labeled in a certain way (for example, as an AIDS activist), what kinds of communication are permitted? What does the label allow the person to do? Given how a person is labeled, what kinds of communication are prohibited? What does that label prohibit the speaker from doing? In what ways could these labels liberate these communicators?

professor	CEO
student	construction worker
AIDS activist	lawyer
mother	doctor
politician	

4. Using InfoTrac College Edition type in the keywords *communication* and *community*. Examine the articles that have been written about communication and community during the last 2 years. Given what you learned from these articles, generate a list of questions that you think communication scholars are trying to answer.

Group Activities

1. Form small groups of four to five students. Take a blank piece of poster board and draw a picture of a model that captures your view of the communication process. As a group, discuss what features need to be included in the communication model

and why. Compare your communication model with those created by other groups in the class.

2. As an individual, complete the following statement: "I dream of a community where . . ." In groups of four to five other students, share your dreams for your community. As a group, construct a vision for what an ideal community would look like. Then discuss the kinds of communication that need to happen to make that vision a reality. Who needs to talk to whom? About what? How?

3. Form small groups of five to six students. The communication discipline has several national organizations, including the National Communication Association (**http://www.natcom.org**) and the International Communication Association (**http://www.icahdq.org**). Split up and visit each site, and write a one-page summary of the way that site portrays the communication discipline. Then compare each subgroup's finding on the sites. What is the purpose of communication according to each site? What kinds of issues are studied in communication?

 ## References

Barge, J. K. (in press). Dialogue, conflict, and community. In J. Oetzel & S. Ting-Toomey (Eds.), *The SAGE handbook of conflict communication: Integrating theory, research, and practice.* Thousand Oaks, CA: Sage.

Eisenberg, E. M., & Goodall, H. L. (2004). *Organizational communication: Balancing creativity and constraint* (4th ed.). Boston: Bedford/St. Martin's.

Frey, L. R., Botan, C. H., & Kreps, G. L. (2000). *Investigating communication: An introduction to research methods* (2nd ed.). Boston: Allyn & Bacon.

Frey, L. R., Pearce, W. B., Pollock, M. A., Artz, L., & Murphy, B. A. O. (1996). Looking for justice in all the wrong places: On a communication approach to social justice. *Communication Studies, 47,* 110–127.

Gottman, J. M., & Silver, N. (1999). *The seven principles for making marriage work.* New York: Crown.

Hatch, G. L. (1996). *Arguing in communities.* Mountain View, CA: Mayfield.

Katzenbach, J. R., & Smith, D. K. (2001). *The discipline of teams.* New York: Wiley.

Kayes, D. C. (2002). Proximal team learning: Lessons from United Flight 93 on 9/11. *Organizational Dynamics, 32,* 80–92.

Lasswell, H. (1964). The structure and function of communication in society. In L. Bryson (Ed.), *The communication of ideas* (pp. 37–51). New York: Cooper Square. (Original work published 1948)

Littlejohn, S. W., & Foss, K. A. (2005). *Theories of human communication* (8th ed.). Belmont, CA: Wadsworth.

O'Hara, L. S. (2001). Service-learning: Students' transformative journey from communication student to civic-minded professional. *Southern Communication Journal, 66,* 251–266.

Pearce, W. B. (1994). *Interpersonal communication: Making social worlds.* New York: HarperCollins.

Pearce, W. B., & Pearce, K. A. (2004). Taking a communication perspective on dialogue. In R. Anderson, L. A. Baxter, & K. N. Cissna (Eds.), *Dialogue: Theorizing difference in communication studies* (pp. 39–56). Thousand Oaks, CA: Sage.

Shannon, C. E., & Weaver, W. (1949). *The mathematical theory of communication.* Urbana: University of Illinois Press.

Spano, S. (2001). *Public dialogue and participatory democracy: The Cupertino Community Project.* Cresskill, NJ: Hampton.

Watzlawick, P., Beavin, J. H., & Jackson, D. D. (1967). *Pragmatics of human communication: A study of interactional patterns, pathologies, and paradoxes.* New York: W. W. Norton.

Wuthnow, R. (1994). *Sharing the journey: Support groups and America's new quest for community.* New York: Free Press.

© Leland Bobbé/Corbis

LEARNING OBJECTIVES | After studying this chapter, you should be able to

1. Describe how competence viewed as an impression is different from competence viewed as an ability.

2. Balance appropriateness and effectiveness goals in how you communicate in different communication contexts.

3. Construct an inventory of your own areas of communication competence and incompetence.

4. Apply the standards of appropriateness and effectiveness to your personal ethics of communication.

5. Identify and describe the major components of the communication competence model.

6. Distinguish among the types of contexts and identify communication events in terms of contexts.

7. Identify the features that distinguish among the levels of context.

8. Illustrate how perception influences a communicator's competence.

A Model of Communication Competence

C ambria was a transfer student at a prestigious, small fine arts university. Shortly after leaving her hometown community college and moving into a small apartment, she was invited to a social for communication majors. She got back to her apartment from a day hike just in time to quickly clean up and get dressed. Upon arriving at the event, she saw she was dressed less formally than the others attending the social. The gathering was in a large carpeted room with marble columns and fine art on the walls. About 40 people were there, faculty and students from freshmen to seniors.

Cambria joined a small group of students conversing about the program, the courses, the professors, and the major. She repeatedly felt like she couldn't keep up with the conversation. She was not accustomed to conversing with people from cultures so different from her own and with such strong dialects. She would occasionally make a general comment but avoided saying much. She really wanted to let her peers and professors know how excited she was to be attending the college but wasn't quite sure how to do this in the context of these discussions.

About an hour into the social, the department chair asked everyone to form a large circle. After some introductory remarks, he asked everyone to take turns introducing themselves. As chance would have it, Cambria was asked to start. Cambria mumbled her name and that she was from California and said the first thing that came to her mind: she felt "out of place" that evening.

Tired from her day's hike, self-conscious about how she was dressed and how uninformed she was compared with her peers, Cambria was suddenly cast into the spotlight. As the evening wore on, she felt nervous, unclear about what she was doing there, or simply unable to communicate well. ■

Your success or failure when communicating depends on many factors. As Cambria's story suggests, three—motivation, knowledge, and skills—are especially important, though sometimes to differing degrees. Cambria was tired, nervous, and at times unclear about why she was at the social, so her motivation was less than ideal. She wasn't familiar with many of the topics being discussed, so she wasn't very knowledgeable and thus could not contribute much to the conversations. Finally, she introduced herself in an overly quiet voice and didn't have anything interesting to say when the opportunity came. She did not have the skills to overcome her tiredness and communicate in the way she would have liked. This chapter examines these three factors of communication—motivation, knowledge, and skills—and their implications for improving communication in everyday situations.

How Competent Are You? _____

Answer the following questions:

- How many animals of each species did Moses take aboard the ark?
- Divide 30 by one-half and add 10. What do you get?
- Read the following sentences out loud:

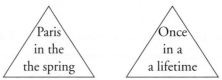

For the first question, did you answer 2? One question more—what was *Moses* doing aboard the ark? For the second question, did you answer 25? If so, you probably multiplied by ½ rather than divided by ½. If you followed instructions properly, you got the answer 70. In the third item, did you pronounce the redundant "the" and "a" in each triangle?

Many people get these items wrong, despite almost everyone who can read them being sufficiently competent to get them correct and the information necessary to do so is clearly there in black and white. This illustrates a very basic principle of learning about communication—much of what we will talk about in this book, like the three items above, will *seem* like common sense or something intuitively obvious, and yet, it is easy to overlook our own incompetence at actually communicating in situations that seem simple or obvious.

This is not surprising. There is ample evidence that although most of us communicate "okay" in everyday life, many people face serious difficulties in their communication, and most of us do not communicate nearly as competently as we could *if we were communicating optimally.* Most of us think we communicate acceptably because we spend most of our waking life communicating in one way or another—speaking, listening, reading, writing, or processing information of some sort. This fact is made more apparent in today's media-saturated society. A study by the Kaiser Family Foundation (Rideout, Roberts, & Foehr, 2005) found that the average person between 8 and 18 years of age spends 45.5 hours a week interacting with or through electronic media, compared with an average of just more than 2 hours with parents and only 1.5 hours in physical activity (and only 50 minutes spent on homework!).

Research shows that the more deficient a person is in communication skills, the more likely he or she is to experience problems with educational performance, loneliness, depression, divorce, drug abuse, dysfunctional conflicts with others, risky sexual activity, and even physical illness and premature death (Spitzberg & Cupach, 2002). Furthermore, studies indicate that somewhere between 7% and 25% of the population experiences communication problems serious enough to interfere with their quality of life. In some areas, such as public speaking anxiety or shyness, this figure often reaches 40% (Spitzberg & Cupach, 2002). So before you conclude that learning about communication is just common sense, it might be a good idea to consider how many of life's problems, perhaps including your own, could be avoided or reduced by engaging in more competent communication. Let's start by thinking about what we mean by this term.

What Is Communication Competence?

We have been talking a lot about competent communication but have yet to provide a specific definition of the concept. **Communication competence** is the extent to which persons achieve desired outcomes through communication acceptable to a situation (Spitzberg, 2000). In other words, competence means how effective and appropriate a person is in a given context. We will arrive at a more formal definition later, but for our current purposes, this definition can already lead us to examine certain issues, such as "How do we know whether something has been accomplished?" and "How do we know whether a communication behavior fits a situation?" To better answer such questions, we need to examine what impressions people form about communication.

Competence as an Impression

People reach a virtually infinite number of impressions about communication. For example, when a friend asks to see your notes the night before an exam, you may evaluate your friend's request in a variety of ways, such as "How inconsiderate!" "How nice that she thought of me first." "What nerve!" "I'm flattered that she thinks that highly of my academic abilities." "Her timing is awful!" We can't begin to predict all the possible impressions people make of our communication. In the Luann cartoon Diane's date is making a wide variety of assumptions about what kind of impression his behavior is making, or might make, on Diane. Diane, it turns out, has a different impression altogether. It's not always easy to know what impression we're creating.

Even if our impressions about communication are almost infinite, some are more important for our communication success than others. In the cartoon, as in most situations, what seems to matter is whether your behavior seems appropriate and whether you achieved what you were trying to accomplish. Let's look at each of these.

Appropriateness

Appropriateness describes communication that fits a given context, which means that behavior is considered legitimate, acceptable, or suitable to a situation. An important way of determining whether behavior fits is to ask whether it seems to follow the implicit or explicit rules or norms relevant to the situation. **Rules** are prescriptions you can follow for what should or should not be done in a given type of situation (Shimanoff, 1980). Sometimes they are explicit: "Don't call someone names when arguing." Sometimes they are

LUANN by GREG EVANS

© Merrim / Monkmeyer Press

What we think we're communicating and what we're actually communicating are often entirely different.

People generally communicate their displeasure at inappropriate actions with subtle verbal and nonverbal sanctions, or symbolic punishments.

more implicit: "You should arrive at parties 30 minutes to an hour after the stated beginning time." Despite the importance of being clear or understandable, some rules even call for ambiguous types of messages. For example, rules of polite behavior typically suggest that in response to a question such as "How do you like my new hair style?" rather than say, "It really sucks!" if you don't like it, you will be better off saying something like "Wow, that's a different look for you" or "That's interesting."

In general, you know a rule exists when you have violated it. Rule violation typically evokes a feedback behavior called a **sanction,** a negative evaluation ranging from a raised eyebrow or a scowl to a slap on the face that lets you know you did something inappropriate. In general, appropriate communication tends to be somewhat invisible to the interactants. Only when communication is inappropriate do you elicit sanctions, which tell you that a rule has been violated.

Effectiveness

Effectiveness describes the extent to which communication accomplishes valued outcomes. We all pursue goals, objectives, intentions, and outcomes in our interactions with others. You may call someone to see whether you can borrow their notes, ask someone for a date, interview for a job, or speak to a group to persuade them to support a proposal. In this way, communication is functional (see Chapter 1)—it serves to get things done. Culture, society, politics, religion, business, conflict, and relationships are accomplished through interaction, through the behavior of communication. Clearly, to be competent requires that a person be able to accomplish the basic communicative tasks and goals of everyday life (Berger, 2002). In this sense, competence is the extent to which people are effective in accomplishing what they want through communication.

We defined effectiveness in terms of valued outcomes. However, this does not mean that effective communication is always satisfying. Sometimes we have to choose the lesser of two evils. For example, people may dislike having an argument with someone over an important issue. But would you rather a person scream at you and criticize you or calmly identify the problems with your position? Even though you may feel uncomfortable with either, most of the time in North American culture a calm discussion is likely to be viewed as less dissatisfying than screaming and yelling. Thus effectiveness sometimes means choosing the least problematic course of action, even if all available courses of action are negative.

How do you know when you have been effective? Usually you consider yourself effective when you obtain (1) something you value, (2) something you set as a goal to accomplish (regardless of how conscious that goal was), and (3) something you expend some effort to obtain (Spitzberg, 2003). Unlike appropriateness, which is judged by others, effectiveness is something that generally only you determine for yourself. Only you know when you have obtained a preferred outcome.

The Competence Grid

Now you've considered two possible standards of competence: appropriateness and effectiveness. In theory, these are separate and independent features of how we evaluate our own and others' communication. That is, a person's behavior can be either appropriate or inappropriate, and either effective or ineffective, and various degrees in-between of either. However, in actual interaction, each standard tends to depend on the other. That is, in practice, when we behave in inappropriate ways, we tend to make it more difficult to get what we want. A person who dresses inappropriately for a job interview jeopardizes the prospect of getting the job. Conversely, people who are consistently ineffective are often viewed as inappropriate. A candidate who consistently loses elections eventually may be viewed as inappropriately wasting the electorate's time by running. If we consider the possibility that someone can be perceived as inappropriate or appropriate, and ineffective or effective, there are four possible combinations for communication: A person can be inappropriate and ineffective, inappropriate and effective, appropriate and ineffective, or appropriate and effective. Each of these communication possibilities is examined next.

The first possible way to communicate is both inappropriate and ineffective. This represents a **minimizing communication,** in which a person not only fails to achieve any personally desired outcomes in interaction but also alienates other people through his or her behavior. Consider someone frustrated by waiting in line and then yelling at the person working behind the counter, only to be told that nothing can be done. Indeed, by creating a scene this person may even be escorted out of the room by a security guard, forfeiting any chance to attain his or her goal. This person gets minimum results out of the interaction.

The appropriate but ineffective person interacts with **sufficing communication,** which enables him or her merely to get by. Although this person's behavior is not inappropriate, it doesn't accomplish much of anything either. For example, Cambria spent most of the early part of the social merely standing silently in groups while other people talked. Her behavior did not break any rules or norms, but she probably did not get much out of the social, such as making new friends, finding out about upcoming activities, or getting to know faculty members.

The inappropriate and effective type of communicator engages in a **maximizing communication.** A person maximizes when he or she is assertive or aggressive without concern for other people's sense of appropriateness. From a maximizing perspective, winning is all that matters, and lying, cheating, stealing, coercing, exploiting, hurting, and abusing are all fair game if they help you win. But the inappropriateness of such activities is destructive to the communicator's relationships.

The communicator who achieves preferred outcomes in a way that preserves the relationship and respects the rules of the situation has chosen **optimizing communication.** This person achieves success through means that others consider acceptable and recognizes the importance of self-satisfaction in communication situations. He or she also understands that such satisfaction should not come at the expense of others' satisfaction (Figure 2.1).

learning link

How do clarity, appropriateness, and effectiveness differ?

• • •

learning link

What are the types of competence and incompetence? How do they differ?

• • •

Figure 2.1

The Communication
Competence Grid

The competence grid al-
lows you to map your
communication behavior
and to analyze your most
important communica-
tion goals in any given
situation.

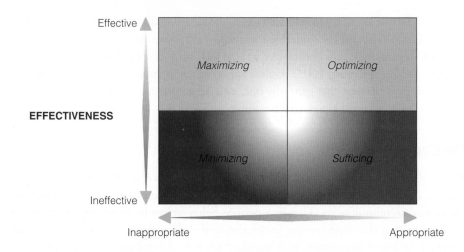

Communication and communicators are judged on many characteristics, such as satisfaction, clarity, attractiveness, efficiency, and emotional warmth. However, such characteristics matter only to the extent that they contribute to the appropriateness and effectiveness
of the encounter. The key challenge of competent communication in most situations is finding the delicate balance between the need for appropriateness and the desire for effectiveness
(Spitzberg, 2000; Spitzberg, Canary, & Cupach, 1994). Failures to attain that balance are
likely to call competence into question. One of the issues that results from failures of
appropriateness or effectiveness is the ethics of our behavior. We examine this question next.

Ethics and Communication Competence

Communication ethics, debated for centuries, were first outlined by the ancient Greeks.
According to Plato, communication should serve the truth, otherwise it can be used to ex-
ploit people and lead them away from the truth. Plato's student Aristotle cleverly countered
this argument, claiming that the best defense against such exploitation is to be informed
about the ways in which communication can be misused. In a sense, the more competent
you are as a communicator, the less likely you are to be exploited because you understand
the techniques of exploitation.

Many people since Plato and Aristotle have argued for ethical standards with which to
evaluate communication. For example, the National Communication Association (NCA)
developed a credo, or statement of belief, in ethical communication (Table 2.1). This credo
illustrates a set of beliefs in the value of freedom of expression, openness of access, accuracy of content, diversity of representation, and respect of persons and opinions.

Ethical codes are sets of principles for guiding behavior in ways considered good or
moral in nature. Most ethical codes emphasize the nature of the conduct itself, the purposes the conduct serves, or the particular considerations of the context in which the conduct occurs. These three emphases represent means-oriented, ends-oriented, or context-
oriented code.

Means-oriented codes define what behaviors are considered moral or immoral, regardless of their outcomes. For example, if a code says that lying is immoral regardless of the
liar's motive, then it is a means-oriented code. In contrast, if it is not the behavior itself, but

THE COMPETENCE GRID IS A PARTIAL ATTEMPT TO provide an ethical framework for understanding communication. Appropriateness and effectiveness are not just impressions—they can be ethical judgments as well. If effectiveness is primarily an orientation of self-interest, we can view appropriateness primarily as an orientation of interest in the other person. Optimizing competence, therefore, means locating the best course of interaction for the relationship and the people with whom you are interacting while pursuing your own interests.

Let's look at three examples of interpersonal communication. In the first, a friend of yours has a terminal disease and you know she doesn't have much time left to live. But at her bedside, you tell her you believe she will find a way to beat the disease. In the second example, your best friend tells you she is cheating on her boyfriend but asks you to keep it secret from her boyfriend. In the third example, on a second date a student begins unbuttoning his date's blouse without warning and she slaps him hard. These examples illustrate deception, secrecy, coercion, and violence. Each instance also opens small windows into the world of communication ethics.

In the first example, lying to a dying person is generally viewed as appropriate because it is motivated by a sincere desire to help the other person. If this communication were more selfish in nature, such as lying to avoid dealing with the discomfort of facing reality, then we would tend to view it as less appropriate. In short, deception is generally considered competent to the extent that it is intended to benefit others rather than the self.

In the second example, being asked to cover for a friend's unethical behavior creates a number of ethical problems. You are likely to choose your course of action by weighing the importance of various goals in this relationship against the appropriateness of your behavior. If your effectiveness in maintaining your relationship with the girlfriend outweighs the importance of being appropriate in the boyfriend's eyes, then you would be likely to keep the secret. If, however, your standards of appropriateness are independent of the relationship, for example, if you believe infidelity is simply wrong regardless of context, then you would be less likely to keep the secret. In this case, the result might well be that you and the girlfriend would view each other's responses as incompetent.

Even though we generally view violence as inappropriate even when it is effective, in the third example most people would view the slap as an act of self-defense and thus appropriate, because it is guarding against an inappropriate and coercive behavior. In other words, the man's coercion is inappropriate in the context because the woman did not provide a clear indication that such assertive behavior would be appropriate. In turn, the slap would be viewed as appropriate because it stops another person's inappropriate behavior.

These three examples illustrate that the ethics of communication conduct is a constant balancing of our own goals and effectiveness with others' sense of what is appropriate and legitimate in a situation. In addition, ethical communication sometimes means balancing our own sense of appropriateness with what would be effective. Lying, cheating, and coercing may be effective, but they tend to be appropriate only when they are countering others' unethical conduct or when they are intended to benefit the other persons. Even under these circumstances, however, there are times when you will find that the benefit of others or protection of the self still do not justify such behavior.

Ethics define our morals, values, and standards of conduct or potential conduct. If asked, most people would probably claim that deception and violence are unethical no matter what the circumstances. Yet when their everyday lives are examined in detail, most people would also discover a host of questionable practices. The white lie, the use of physical force in self-defense, the use of an ambiguous response to avoid an awkward issue, and other such dark forms of communication are common practices (Cupach & Spitzberg, 1994). Their frequency raises the question of their ethics. To the person engaging in such behaviors, these actions can be rationalized as ethical, but to the person on the receiving side, such a judgment might be far less likely.

the purpose or outcome of the behavior that is considered moral or immoral, then the code is an **ends-oriented code.** Under an ends-oriented code, lying to help others, for example, might be viewed as ethical, but lying for selfish reasons would not. Finally, **context-oriented codes** claim that the morality of communication behavior depends on the specific circumstances of the situation. For example, when some Jews lied to Nazis about

Table 2.1

NCA Credo for Ethical Communication

- We advocate truthfulness, accuracy, honesty, and reason as essential to the integrity of communication.
- We endorse freedom of expression, diversity of perspective, and tolerance of dissent to achieve the informed and responsible decision making fundamental to a civil society.
- We strive to understand and respect other communicators before evaluating and responding to their messages.
- We promote access to communication resources and opportunities as necessary to fulfill human potential and contribute to the well-being of families, communities, and society.
- We promote communication climates of caring and mutual understanding that respect the unique needs and characteristics of individual communicators.
- We condemn communication that degrades individuals and humanity through distortion, intimidation, coercion, and violence, and through the expression of intolerance and hatred.
- We are committed to the courageous expression of personal convictions in pursuit of fairness and justice.
- We advocate sharing information, opinions, and feelings when facing significant choices while also respecting privacy and confidentiality.
- We accept responsibility for the short- and long-term consequences of our own communication and expect the same of others.

SOURCE: http://www.natcom.org.

their religious beliefs during World War II to escape internment and later death, they did so to help themselves, but given the extreme nature of the consequences and the immorality of the opposing forces, lying under those circumstances may be viewed as ethical.

The concepts of appropriateness and effectiveness provide a hybrid ethical code of communication conduct. The appropriateness standard is typically a means standard because, within most groups and cultures, certain behaviors tend to be considered ethical and other behaviors are considered unethical. The effectiveness standard is more of an ends-oriented code because it specifies behavior that accomplishes valued outcomes as ethical. In the context of an actual communication event, the participants determine how to balance and evaluate the importance of the two standards.

Applying the competence grid as a code of ethical communication conduct is not simple. For example, in a study in which people were asked to keep a diary of their lies each day, persons in the general community reported an average of one lie a day and college students reported about two lies a day. Many of these lies were self-serving, but many others were motivated by a desire to make things easier or better for someone else (DePaulo, Kashy, Kirkendol, Wyer, & Epstein, 1996). Thus in any given situation, determining whether a communication behavior is ethical will require our taking into account the means, the ends, and the context. Nevertheless, the more you can optimize a communication situation by achieving desired personal goals while preserving the sense of appropriateness others apply to the context, the more likely your communication is to be considered ethical.

Basic Components of the Communication Competence Model

The competence grid shows that competence in communication is a delicate balance of both appropriateness and effectiveness. It illustrates what we need to accomplish, but it doesn't show us how. Learning how requires us to consider factors that allow us to be more appropriate and effective. These are motivation, knowledge, and skills, and they form the basic model of communication competence we will apply to the communication contexts we cover throughout this book.

Shakespeare tells us that all the world is a stage and we are merely actors on it. Thinking about life as drama is very useful in understanding communication (Goffman, 1974). In this metaphor, our everyday communication is not viewed as acting in the sense of "pretending" but instead as behaving with an awareness of performing for, or at least with, an audience. For the purposes of understanding competence, we can ask, "What makes for a competent acting performance?" Certain factors are likely to enhance a person's ability to communicate appropriately and effectively. So the question for us is, which factors increase the chances that an actor will be viewed as competent by a given audience? The model of communication competence identifies these factors as motivation, knowledge, and skills (Spitzberg & Cupach, 1984).

Motivation

For an actor to communicate competently, it is important first to *want* to give a competent performance. That is, the actor must be motivated to be competent. **Motivation** has both positive and negative sides.

Negative motivation is the experience of anxiety about a course of communicative action or the perception of low reward potential, in a real or imagined communication situation. **Positive motivation,** in contrast, is the perception of potential reward value in pursuing a course of communicative action. It is the result of efforts and desires that drive your performance toward excellence. People find the motivation to act competently from such sources as the situation itself and their own goals in it. Some situations simply offer greater rewards. For example, you will probably be much more motivated to perform competently on a job interview or a first date than when sitting next to a stranger on an airplane. The stakes for the first two situations are much higher.

So situations vary in their reward potential. People also vary in the degree to which they seek rewards in situations. Some people are more likely than others to set and pursue their own communication goals. The booming business of motivational speaking is based on the simple notion that those who actively motivate themselves and consciously search for goals to pursue and develop plans to serve those motives will achieve more than those who merely follow their natural motivational tendencies without conscious analysis and planning. Because everything starts with motivation, it is important to spend an extra moment considering its role in communication competence.

The first key to communicating more competently is finding the motivation to communicate better than you currently do. People are motivated to communicate in either of two ways—by approach or by avoidance. That is, people want to approach certain communication situations, and they want to avoid others. Sometimes people experience both approach and avoidance motivations in the same context. For example, most people are nervous or anxious about a formal job interview, but they also are motivated to go through with it and get a better job by performing well. Most people don't like engaging in conflict with a loved one, but we often do it anyway because the issues being discussed are too important to avoid.

Our motives to avoid communication situations are usually based in some way on anxiety or apprehension about the implications of the anticipated communication encounter. Such anxieties represent the most common type of negative motivation. In particular,

communication apprehension is the fear or anxiety an individual experiences as a result of either real or anticipated communication with another person or persons (Beatty, McCroskey, & Heisel, 1998). Common signs of apprehension include shaky hands, sweaty palms, or just a squeamish feeling in the pit of your stomach. The result is a tendency to either avoid communication or suffer from feelings of yet more anxiety when forced to communicate.

There are people who are generally apprehensive, but most people are anxious about only certain situations. You may be afraid of spiders but not snakes. You may like heights but not confined spaces. Similarly, people are often afraid of some contexts but not others. **Context apprehension** is anxiety about communicating in a particular context such as interpersonal, small group, or public speaking. For example, many of us are fine talking one on one but experience some anxiety about public speaking. There is not sufficient research as yet to know just how much, if any, of a person's apprehension is instinctive and how much is learned. However, one research study found that whether it is inborn or not, even people with high levels of apprehension can learn to manage and control it (Ellis, 1995).

One of the most problematic, and most common, forms of context apprehension is public speaking anxiety, commonly referred to as stage fright. **Public speaking anxiety** refers to a person's fear or anxiety associated with a real or anticipated public speaking event. Although public speaking apprehension is perhaps the most common fear, anxiety in interpersonal situations, or **social anxiety,** is very common as well. Social situations can seem very threatening because we derive so much of our self-concept from what we think others think of us.

When anxiety occurs across a wide variety of social situations over an extended period, it generally results in **shyness,** a tendency to withdraw from social activities. Shy people may not appear very different from others in a given situation, but they are less likely to initiate or actively participate in conversation. It is important to remember that some societies, such as Asian cultures, value unassertiveness, and there, conversational shyness does not necessarily reflect incompetence. On the contrary, "nonassertiveness and nonargumentativeness are probably more socially desirable" (Kim, 1999, p. 62), making shyness in interpersonal communication competent within that particular culture. However, it is possible to be shy even by the standards of a relatively unassertive culture. Communication anxiety can be a challenge in any context or culture. We will discuss the various types of context-specific anxiety in greater detail in the later chapters.

In contrast to avoidance and apprehension as the negative side of motivation, there is a positive side. Communicative **goals** are the outcomes, objectives, or purposes being sought through communication. They represent "some desired state in other people" (Berger, 1997, p. 19). Goals are the specific outcomes a person intends to bring about through his or her interpersonal communication.

Goals are particularly relevant to communication competence because they are a way of assessing your effectiveness. An interpersonal communicator who achieves his or her goals is effective and, therefore, more competent. Goals, in turn, help guide communication behavior. It is much easier to know what to do and how to do it if you are clear about the social goals you intend to bring about.

Perhaps like Cambria in the opening vignette, you have found yourself at a social event in which you looked at people talking comfortably among themselves and thought, "I want to join in the conversation, but I don't know how to break the ice and capture the interest of people I don't know." You have the motivation to communicate, but you don't know what to say or do. Motivation alone is not enough—you also need knowledge to communicate competently. We now turn to the second component of the competence model: knowledge.

Knowledge

Shakespeare's "life is but a stage" metaphor also applies to knowledge. Motivation alone is often not enough to make you a competent actor. To be competent, an actor also needs to know the script, something about the type of audience, the stage or set, the lines of the other actors, the playwright's intentions, and his or her own acting strengths and weaknesses. Returning to everyday communication, the audience is the person or persons to whom you are speaking, the stage and set make up the communication situation, the lines are others' responses, and the playwright's intentions correspond to the goals of the situation. A competent communicator needs to be knowledgeable about all these elements in communication situations. **Knowledge** in communication guides us about what to say and do and tells us the procedures by which we can do it.

In the Chickweed Lane cartoon, the woman experiences the precise problem of communicative knowledge that is the topic of our discussion. Most of us encounter situations in which we realize only some time later what we wish we had said. We generally can think of what to say and do but not always when and in what way that would be most competent.

Knowledge can be roughly broken down into the what and the how of communication, known as content and procedural knowledge, respectively. **Content knowledge** is an understanding of the topics, words, meanings, and so forth, required in a situation. **Procedural knowledge** tells us how to assemble, plan, and perform content knowledge in a particular situation. When you get a driver's license, you take a written test on traffic laws and practices (content knowledge) and a driving test of your ability to apply that content knowledge in a car while driving (procedural knowledge). For most of us, the bottom line of a person's driving ability is his or her actual driving performance. The same is true of communication. Performance depends on motivation and knowledge, but ultimately, it is a person's behavior, his or her skill, that we judge as competent or incompetent.

We all experience situations in which we are at a loss for what to say or do.

Skills

You may have witnessed both terrible and terrific acting performances. Even the worst actors are motivated to perform well, and they probably know their scripts inside and out. So what makes some performances bad? The simple answer is that the actors lack the acting skills to apply their motivation and knowledge.

Skills, the third part of the communication competence model, are repeatable, goal-directed behaviors. They must be repeatable, because anyone could accomplish something by accident, but if it can't be accomplished again, it is not a skill the person possesses. You might give a very funny introduction to a speech, but if you can't ever get a laugh again, you can't say you have the skill of creating humorous introductions. Skills are also goal directed, because they must be designed to accomplish something. If they don't, they are just behaviors, rather than skills.

Communication skills have both general and specific levels. At the general level, for example, regardless of culture, people need to be able to ask questions, display certain facial expressions such as anger, sadness, happiness, and perform greeting rituals (such as handshaking, bowing, waving in greeting). All people in all cultures develop routines they use in certain situations. Yet, at the specific level, within each situation every communication event represents a unique interaction. Small talk probably always seems like small talk, yet every episode of small talk is a unique event different from what you have experienced before. Thus some skills are used across almost all situations, and others are reserved for very particular situations.

learning link

What are the components of the communication competence model and how do they differ?

• • •

Thus to communicate competently, we must be motivated, knowledgeable, and skilled. We can use these three key components to analyze why a communicator, whether ourselves or someone else, was or was not competent in any situation. When communicating, we apply these components in an actual situation, toward some kind of audience, which brings us to context, the fourth component of our model. Any performance, or communication behavior, occurs in a particular place and time, and with some audience in mind. That is, communication takes place in a context, and it is in that context that its competence is evaluated. Therefore context becomes an essential part of the model of communication competence.

Context

The communication **context** is the frame within which action occurs. At a museum, you look at a painting and often don't notice the frame. But it provides a set of boundaries to define what is in the frame and what is not. It defines what you should consider as the art itself. In communication, the context consists of the boundaries we perceive that help us know what the communication is and what it is supposed to be.

So far, we've been using the terms *context* and *situation* almost interchangeably. But context can be viewed in a number of different ways. For some people, context is the climate, or feel, of a situation; for others, context is the physical location in which communication occurs. For still others, it includes everything in the surroundings, physical and psychological. We define *context* as consisting of two sets of factors.

Context consists of both types and levels. **Context types** are routine ways in which you think about and respond to the communication episode. **Context levels** refer to the number of communicators in the episode and the direction of communication among them. The most common context levels are interpersonal, small group, and public communication, which are the subjects of the main sections of this book.

Context Types

The most common context types are cultural, chronemic, relational, situational, and functional (Spitzberg & Brunner, 1991).

Culture consists of the enduring patterns of thought, value, and behavior that define a group of people (Samovar & Porter, 1995). Culture encompasses people's beliefs and attitudes about the world, their spirituality, their sense of status and hierarchy, their use of time and physical space, and their relationships to one another. It represents a collection of these mental and behavioral patterns that give people a sense of belonging to a group or community viewed by its members as distinct from other groups. Culture is always present as a backdrop to whatever we do and however we see ourselves and others.

Although culture is commonly thought of as the same as ethnicity, race, and nationality, it is not. *Ethnicity* refers "to a wide variety of groups who might share a language, historical origins, religion, identification with a common nation-state, or cultural system" (Lustig & Koester, 1993, p. 47). Similarly, *nationality* simply refers to people born, raised, or with citizenship in a given nation-state. In contrast, *race* implies a group of people with common genetic or physical characteristics. Many people have expanded the notion of culture to include organizations, chat rooms, and even eras, gender, and sexual preference. Thus we can speak of Microsoft or Barnes & Noble as having different corporate cultures from Apple or Amazon.com, respectively. Culture is also described as the mood of a time, such as "the culture of narcissism" or "the culture of complaint." So culture may include ethnicity, race, and nationality, but it usually implies more, including belief systems and ways of thinking and behaving.

One facet of context is always with us yet often unnoticed. Chronemics is the experience and perception of time in communication events. If time is money in North America, then every minute that ticks by on the clock while a contract is not signed is money lost. But if time is viewed as more natural and cyclical, then there is less rush to push the natural order of things. Time is the collective and individual perception of the sequence and progression of events. Some cultures, such as Germanic cultures, are known for their strict punctuality and precise organization of time. Others, such as Mediterranean and Pacific Islander cultures, are much more relaxed when defining time and punctuality. In North America, New York is a fast-paced city, whereas San Diego is considered slower paced. Individually, some people believe rapid development of physical intimacy is appropriate in romantic relationships, whereas other people believe physical intimacy should progress very slowly. Time is a context that weaves its way into everything we experience, and it is a primary dimension along which we make sense of both our own and others' communicative behavior.

Context types can also be understood by their **relational content.** At the most general level, **relationship** is the implication your behavior has for your continued connection with another person or a group of people. To have a relationship with someone is to be **interdependent,** which means that each person depends on the other to achieve desired outcomes. In collectivistic, or group-oriented cultures, for example, family relationships are more important than personal goals. Divorce in Japan, for example, tends to be viewed as selfish if pursued merely because the relationship is loveless. Preserving the family is more important than pursuing individual goals. In North America, however, personal happiness and individual pursuit of love are considered reasonable bases for breaking off a relationship.

We can understand the relational aspects of contexts according to two dimensions: power and affiliation. **Power** refers to the status relationship of the people involved—who has the ability to influence whom? Most relationships contain some form of power. For example, relationships between boss–employee, parent–child, professor–student, older sibling–younger sibling, therapist–client, and doctor–patient all imply some hierarchy among the participants, with one person higher in status than the other. In any one of these pairs, however, interaction over time may redistribute the power to make the relationship quite different.

Affiliation is the emotional and evaluative dimension of relating to others; that is, the degree to which you like and are drawn toward someone or dislike and want to avoid this person. Determining whether you like or dislike someone, and in what way, is one of the most fundamental evaluations you can make about a person. For example, most people perceive communication as becoming more competent as intimacy increases in relationships (Knapp, Ellis, & Williams, 1980). But affiliation can be viewed along several dimensions, including intimacy, kinship, and enmity.

On a continuum of *intimacy,* relationship types vary from strangers to acquaintances, friends, close friends, best friends, boy- and girlfriends, lovers, fiancés and fiancées, spouses, and everything in-between. Culture affects where people place relationships on a continuum of intimacy. For example, Japanese students tend to view acquaintance (*chijin*), roommate (*doshukusha*), and best-friend (*ichiban no shinyu*) relationships as more intimate than U.S. students do, whereas U.S. students tend to view boy- or girlfriend (*otoko* or *onna tomodachi*), lover (*koibito*), and fiancé (*konyakusha*) relationships as more intimate than Japanese students do (Gudykunst & Nishida, 1986).

Another continuum is *kinship,* ranging from parents to siblings, grandparents, aunts, uncles, cousins, nieces and nephews, and so forth. Again, culture affects the way people experience these affiliations. Japanese students view uncle (*oji*) as a more intimate relationship than U.S. students do, but the reverse is true of son (*musuko*) and daughter (*musume*) relationships (Gudykunst & Nishida, 1986). Still another continuum, *enmity,* ranges from friends to enemies, including social, romantic, and even political enemies. Someone who deceives you, exploits you, threatens you, or takes something (or someone) you value is affiliated with you in terms of an "enemyship" rather than friendship.

The fourth type of context consists of the situational aspects of the communication event, what most people think of as the environment or physical surroundings. The **situational context** includes all the physical characteristics that are present—temperature, lighting, amount of space permitted for movement, objects in the space, and the media through which we communicate. Some public speakers discover the difficulty of keeping an audience's attention if there is background noise in the environment or if the temperature is uncomfortable. Group leaders often find themselves challenged when projectors or teleconference links fail to work. Surroundings can also help communication, as in the early stages of a romantic relationship in which a participant tries to get the lighting, privacy, and music to match the couple's feelings.

The final type of context describes the functional aspects of communication. The **function** of communication is what the communication behavior attempts to accomplish or actually accomplishes. A funeral is functionally different from an inauguration. A labor negotiation's function is different from that of a team-building meeting. The function of communication on a date is different from that in a class lecture. Contexts in each of these situations are different, independent of the culture, time, relationship, and place in which they occur. Communicators are attempting to accomplish something different in each context. Different communication goals help define the function of communication in the context and thereby influence the types of behavior considered appropriate and effective.

In the opening vignette, Cambria's competence was challenged by each of these context types. The mix of cultures was alien to her. She felt rushed and therefore somewhat anxious when she arrived. She didn't know anyone well enough to have established a comfortable relationship. The situation was more formal than she anticipated and she didn't realize that one of the functions of the gathering would be to introduce herself to the entire group. In other words, had she been better able to analyze and anticipate the context types, she could have communicated much more competently.

Context Levels

The levels approach to context helps us understand context in terms of the number of people involved. The four levels of context are interpersonal, group, public speaking, and mediated, and they differ according to whether a person is communicating on a one-to-one, one-to-several, or one-to-many basis and whether some technological medium is involved.

The levels are not entirely distinct, however. A communication event may fit more than one level of context. Is a family discussion an interpersonal or a group context? Is a weekly presentation by a department head to middle management a group or public speaking context? Is sending an e-mail via an intranet a form of group or mediated communication? The answer in each case is both. Although context levels frequently overlap, the levels do suggest that the number of people in a context makes a difference in your communication. As the number of people increases, the potential number of meanings attributed to a message increases and the number of audience characteristics to be considered increases. You don't need a podium or microphone in a small group context, and you don't cast votes on a proposed decision in an interpersonal situation. In other words, the level of context affects your communication choices and thus your communication competence.

In this book, we concentrate on the most common levels of contexts (Powers, 1995). We present the **interpersonal context** as an informal interaction among people in social or personal relationships. Social relationships are most often defined based on informal, social-emotional roles (family, friends, lovers,). However, other communications, such as when you speak to a salesperson about a product or service or to another student about an assignment, are also considered interpersonal, even though they are more formal and task based.

The complexity of connections differentiates the interpersonal from a group encounter. When dealing with only one or two other people, you make far fewer communication exchanges and target messages to one particular person, rather than to a general group. **Group contexts** include a larger number of people, typically 3 to 12, and usually take place in a more formal, task-oriented context. Although messages may sometimes be directed to specific individuals in the group, there is an understanding that the entire group is the appropriate audience, and other members of the group may respond to the messages. Also, the group usually meets to accomplish some predetermined purpose through its interaction. For example, when the senior management of a human resources department meets to determine its response to a prospective Equal Employment Opportunity Commission investigation of their organization, it constitutes a group meeting for a specific purpose, its comments tend to be meant for its participants, but have implications for a subsequent report to the organization, and the meeting occurs in a meeting room (or rooms if through teleconferencing media) of the organization.

In **public speaking contexts,** typically one person or a small group of people will speak to a larger number of people who have little or no speaking role. This does not mean they don't communicate, however. Even if audience members do not address the speaker

New media offer more options than ever to communicate with others whenever and wherever we are.

or the rest of the audience with a particular message, they may ask questions and provide feedback at the end of the speech, and their bodies and demeanors provide feedback, such as when they nod, laugh, look distracted, or make eye contact.

The **mediated context** is capable of communication from one to one or one to many. It is distinguished from the other contexts by the fact that the medium through which communication occurs is technologically facilitated. During much of the 20th century, mediated communication was the same thing as mass communication. However, with the development of the World Wide Web and the Internet, as well as the rapid evolution of digital and wireless technologies, the differences between interpersonal, group, and public speaking contexts are being dissolved by communication media. Is blogging, a collective process of back-and-forth e-mailing in virtual real time, a form of interpersonal, group, public, or mass communication? Are entries on a personal website or a personal advertisement on an online dating site a form of interpersonal, group, public, or mass communication? For now, communication professionals think it is best to treat mass and mediated communication as a separate context defined by the reliance on media to transmit the message.

People communicate in these four contexts throughout their lives. As you can imagine, almost everyone communicates interpersonally every day of their life. The success of educational systems, civic and religious organizations, private and public organizations, athletic institutions, special interest clubs and organized hobbies, and social events (for example, concerts or chat rooms), is based in large measure on group interactions. Finally, many people in business or politics or even those attending community events speak publicly with surprising frequency.

The Process Model of Communication Competence

Models tend to be static—that is, they stop a process in the same way a photograph provides a still image of something that was ongoing. It is a limitation of models. However, it is important not to lose sight of how the ongoing aspects of the competence model work. In this section we discuss the model of communication competence in terms of its ongoing process.

The model of communication competence we've discussed thus far consists of motivation, knowledge, skills, and context. The more motivated, knowledgeable, and skilled we are, in ways that are appropriate and effective to each type and level of context, the more likely that we will be perceived as competent communicators. Each part of this text examines the skills relevant to its context level: interpersonal, small group, and public speaking. Before we get to those individual contexts, let us understand those processes common to all contexts: verbal communication, nonverbal communication, perceptions, expectancies, and impressions.

Verbal and Nonverbal Communication

Communication, in any context, occurs in two basic forms: verbal and nonverbal. **Verbal communication** is linguistic and can be written, spoken, or otherwise behaviorally or visually transmitted, as in the case of American Sign Language (ASL). All verbal communication uses language, a symbol system consisting of letters and words.

Nonverbal communication is all forms and aspects of communication that are not based on language. It consists of physical behavior commonly referred to as body language as well as gestures, use of space, and use of voice. We discuss verbal and nonverbal communication in more detail in Chapters 4 and 5.

Perception, Expectations, and Impressions

Any behavior, whether verbal or nonverbal, must make an impression if it is to communicate a message. The behavior must be observed, interpreted, understood, and evaluated through a process called **perception,** which is the way we make sense of the infinite amount of information provided by the world around us. We examine perception in more detail in Chapter 3.

Over time, people learn to categorize certain types of situations and people as similar to better understand them. They develop **expectations,** or mental pictures of what ought to be, about the types of situations and individuals that call for certain behaviors. Thus the competence of a person's communication performance is strongly influenced by the way it fulfills others' expectations in a given situation.

Competent communication requires the use of verbal and nonverbal behavior. However, these behaviors are not competent in and of themselves. Rather, as discussed earlier, competence is an impression we form about the behavior. This impression is based on how well the behaviors fulfill our expectations of competence in a given situation (Spitzberg, 1994). Returning to the opening vignette, Cambria was concerned that she was not able to fulfill expectations as competently as those around her. If the faculty and the other communication students had expectations that communication majors are articulate and outgoing, especially at a social, their impressions of Cambria's communication behaviors would probably be that they were less than competent.

learning link

How does perception influence a communicator's competence?

● ● ●

The Competence Model in Action

Communication competence is the use of verbal and nonverbal behavior to accomplish preferred outcomes in a way that is appropriate to the context. Behavior that accomplishes preferred outcomes is effective. Behavior that is both effective and appropriate optimizes the potential of creating desired impressions of competence in the context.

Figure 2.2 displays the components of communication competence in action. It shows that motivation and knowledge are internal to individuals, but both influence the individual's skills. These skills, or behaviors, are displayed in communication events with others. Each communicator forms an impression of these behaviors based on the context and the process of perception. The other's judgments of these behaviors, in terms of their appropriateness and effectiveness, then influence the self's motivation and knowledge, which in turn influence his or her skills, and the process continues.

This general model of communication competence touches on all the pieces of the process a person goes through to communicate competently (Spitzberg, 1997). However, as you saw in this chapter, context plays a substantial role in competent communication. Most of the remainder of this text is concerned with specific contexts, and we discuss the model described in this chapter as it applies to each type of context. Although motivation, knowledge, and skills are important in all contexts, each context may differ in terms of what constitutes motivation, or what knowledge is needed, or which skills are ideal.

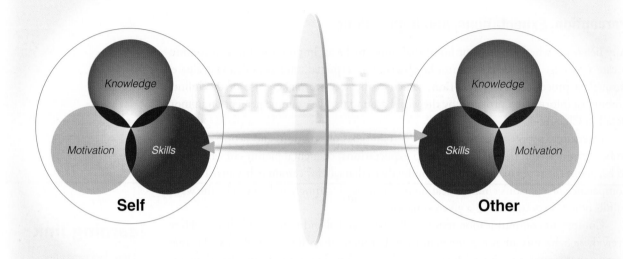

 Figure 2.2

The Communication Competence Model

Achieving competent communication requires the interplay of two or more communicators using their motivation, knowledge, and skills in a given context to create impressions of their appropriateness and effectiveness.

Source: Adapted from Spitzberg, 1997.

Chapter Summary

Competent communication depends on both the self and others' perception of its appropriateness and effectiveness. Achieving the perception of competence in communication is more likely if a person is motivated, knowledgeable, and skilled in a given context. Motivation can be negative, as in anxiety and shyness, or positive, as in recognizing the goals that a context potentially provides. Knowledge can be content based, as in knowing what to say and do, or it can be procedurally based, as in knowing how to say and do something. The more motivated and knowledgeable a person is, the more likely he or she will be able to enact the specific appropriate verbal and nonverbal behaviors, or skills, in the pursuit of preferred outcomes. Finally, motivation, knowledge, and skills occur in a context. What is competent in one context is not necessarily competent in another.

Context types include cultural, chronemic, relational, situational, and functional features. The competence of a person's communication depends on what culture the behavior is enacted in, the timing of the behavior, the relationship and physical space in which the behavior occurs, and the purpose the communication is intended to serve. Context levels refer to the three most commonly recognized communication contexts: interpersonal, small group, and public speaking. These levels differ in the number of communicators involved and, therefore, the formality and complexity of the communication process.

Study and Review

The premium companion website for *Human Communication* offers a broad range of resources that will help you better understand the material in this chapter, complete assignments, and succeed on tests. The website resources include

- Interactive self-assessments, competency grids, and other tools
- Web links, practice activities, self-quizzes, and a sample final exam

For more information about this text's electronic learning resources, consult the *Guide to Online Resources for Human Communication* or visit **http://communication .wadsworth.com/morreale2.**

 ## Key Terms

The key terms below are defined in the chapter on the pages indicated. They are also presented alphabetically with definitions in the Glossary, which begins on page 467. The book's website includes flashcards and crossword puzzles to help you learn these terms and the concepts they represent.

communication competence 29
appropriateness 29
rule 29
sanction 30
effectiveness 30
minimizing communication 31
sufficing communication 31
maximizing communication 31
optimizing communication 31
means-oriented code 32
ends-oriented code 33
context-oriented code 33
motivation 35
negative motivation 35
positive motivation 35
communication apprehension 36
context apprehension 36
public speaking anxiety 36

social anxiety 36
shyness 36
goal 36
knowledge 37
content knowledge 37
procedural knowledge 37
skill 38
context 38
context types 38
context levels 38
culture 39
relational content 39
relationship 39
interdependent 39
power 39
affiliation 40
situational context 40
function 40

Building Motivation

This self-assessment resource begins on page 49. An interactive version of it is also available on the book's website.

 ## Building Knowledge

The questions below are among the practice activities on the book's website.

1. Is clarity the best way of defining competent communication? If not, why?
2. What are the implications of defining competence as an impression rather than an ability?
3. Are there situations in which either appropriateness or effectiveness (but not both) should be considered more important in determining a person's communication competence? If so, under what circumstances? Why?
4. How do the standards of appropriateness and effectiveness provide an ethical system for communication?
5. Provide an example of each type of competence and incompetence (that is, minimizing, sufficing, maximizing, optimizing).
6. Think back on your own communication experiences. Identify a difficult communication situation you have encountered. Describe how motivation, knowledge, skills, or all three helped your competence in the context.
7. Describe a communication situation in which the culture, time, relationship, place, function, or any mixture of these influenced your competence.
8. How do people's expectations of you influence their impression of your competence? Describe an example in which your expectations have influenced your view of someone else.

 ## Building Skills

The exercises below are among the practice activities on the book's website.

Individual Exercises

1. Identify some recent communication encounters that you feel did not go as well as they could have. Describe these situations in terms of who was involved, what you were hoping to get out of the encounter, what you might have said or done differently, and why you thought the encounter did not go well. Then analyze each encounter in terms of the communication competence model. Were you simply not motivated to make a good impression? Did you lack specific knowledge or say the wrong thing (that is, lack skills)? Does the model provide a useful basis for understanding what happened? Why or why not?

2. Describe some recent communication encounters that went better than you expected, and then analyze them in terms of the communication competence model. Does the model provide a useful basis for understanding what happened? Why or why not?

3. Locate an example of a communication event that exists in both a video-recorded and written-text format, such as Martin Luther King Jr.'s "I have a dream" speech, Shakespeare's Macbeth, the president's State of the Union speech, a Woody Allen movie and its script, or Thomas Harris's *Silence of the Lambs* (see, for example, **http://www.script-o-rama.com/snazzy/dircut.html**). Obtain both versions. First read a segment of the written form. Evaluate the communicator's competence. Now view or listen to the recorded version. What does the nonverbal dimension add to the verbal communication? What, if anything, does it take away from the verbal format? Is one better than the other? Why or why not?

4. Go to the websites for Coldstone (**http://www.coldstonecreamery.com/main/index.asp**) and Ben & Jerry's (**http://www.benjerry.com/our_company/index.cfm**). Assume you are applying for a job in the ice cream industry. Based on your research of these websites, how would you characterize the similarities and differences in context of a job interview with these companies? For example, could you treat your relationship to the interviewer as more or less formal in both contexts? Would you expect one company to engage in more group rather than individual interviews? Knowing these differences in their contexts, how might this affect your communication behavior if you were to get a job interview?

5. Strike up a conversation with someone from a culture significantly different from your own. Afterward, identify the difficulties in communicating competently, such as any anxiety about approaching the person, maintaining the conversation, knowing what to talk about, and so forth.

6. Using InfoTrac College Edition, search for "communication competence." Locate an article by Robert Duran and Brian Spitzberg on cognitive communication competence. After reading the article, find the self-report questionnaire assessing your tendency to plan, think about, and analyze your communication situations, that is, your tendency to develop and use communicative knowledge. Answer the questionnaire items, and then reflect on your level of communicative knowledge. How competent are you at developing and using your communicative knowledge? In which of the areas of knowledge covered by the questionnaire are you best, and in which areas do you need the most improvement?

Group Activities

1. Form groups of three to five students. Each group should identify a public speaking current event that is making news, such as a politician holding a press conference, a sports figure answering charges of cheating or drug use, or a person who engaged in some heroic action giving interviews. Analyze the event in terms of the person's motivation, knowledge, and skills in the context. How applicable is the model?

2. Go to the National Communication Association's ethics credo website (**http://www.natcom.org/conferences/ethicsconferencedo99.htm**), scroll halfway down the page, and read its ethical guidelines. Individually, come up with an exception to each ethical principle. Then form groups of three to five students and share your exceptions. How do your exceptions differ from those of the other group members? What kinds of ethical principles do the exceptions suggest? What do the

exceptions tell you about the relationship between appropriateness, effectiveness, and ethics?

3. Form groups of three to five students. As a group, brainstorm about the contexts in which you have the most difficulty communicating competently in terms of motivation. Repeat the process for knowledge, then for skills. As a group, rank the contexts from most to least difficult. To what extent did you find that others perceive the same or different types of contexts as most challenging? Speculate as a group why these similarities or differences exist and how they might best be overcome from the perspective of the communication competence model.

 ## References

Beatty, M. J., McCroskey, J. C., & Heisel, A. D. (1998). Communication apprehension as temperamental expression: A communibiological paradigm. *Communication Monographs, 65,* 197–219.

Berger, C. R. (1997). *Planning strategic interaction: Attaining goals through communicative action.* Mahwah, NJ: Erlbaum.

Berger, C. R. (2002). Goals and knowledge structures in social interaction. In M. L. Knapp & J. A. Daly (Eds.), *Handbook of interpersonal communication* (pp. 181–212). Thousand Oaks, CA: Sage.

Cupach, W. R., & Spitzberg, B. H. (Eds.). (1994). *The dark side of interpersonal communication.* Hillsdale, NJ: Erlbaum.

DePaulo, B. M., Kashy, D. A., Kirkendol, S. E., Wyer, M. M., & Epstein, J. A. (1996). Lying in everyday life. *Journal of Personality and Social Psychology, 70,* 979–995.

Ellis, K. (1995). Apprehension, self-perceived competency, and teacher immediacy in the laboratory-supported public speaking course: Trends and relationships. *Communication Education, 44,* 64–78.

Goffman, E. (1974). *Frame analysis: An essay on the organization of experience.* Cambridge, UK: Harvard University Press.

Gudykunst, W. B., & Nishida, T. (1986). The influence of cultural variability on perceptions of communication behavior associated with relationship terms. *Human Communication Research, 13,* 147–166.

Kim, M-S. (1999). Cross-cultural perspectives on motivations of verbal communication: Review, critique, and a theoretical framework. In M. E. Roloff (Ed.), *Communication yearbook 22* (pp. 51–90). Thousand Oaks, CA: Sage.

Knapp, M. L., Ellis, D. G., & Williams, B. A. (1980). Perceptions of communication behavior associated with relationship terms. *Communication Monographs, 47,* 262–278.

Lustig, M. W., & Koester, J. (1993). *Intercultural competence: Interpersonal communication across cultures.* New York: HarperCollins.

Powers, J. H. (1995). On the intellectual structure of the human communication discipline. *Communication Education, 44,* 191–222.

Rideout, V., Roberts, D. F., & Foehr, U. G. (2005, March). *Generation M: Media in the lives of 8–18 year-olds: Executive Summary.* Kaiser Family Foundation: Menlo Park, CA. Retrieved May 28, 2005, from http://www.kff.org/entmedia/loader.cfm?url=/commonspot/security/getfile.cfm&PageID=51805.

Samovar, L. A., & Porter, R. E. (1995). *Communication between cultures* (2nd ed.). Belmont, CA: Wadsworth.

Shimanoff, S. B. (1980). *Communication rules: Theory and research.* Beverly Hills, CA: Sage.

Spitzberg, B. H. (1994). The dark side of (in)competence. In W. R. Cupach & B. H. Spitzberg (Eds.), *The dark side of interpersonal communication* (pp. 25–50). Hillsdale, NJ: Erlbaum.

Spitzberg, B. H. (1997). A model of intercultural communication competence. In L. A. Samovar and R. E. Porter (Eds.), *Intercultural communication: A reader* (8th ed., pp. 379–391). Belmont, CA: Wadsworth.

Spitzberg, B. H. (2000). What is good communication? *Journal of the Association for Communication Administration, 29,* 103–119.

Spitzberg, B. H. (2003). Methods of skill assessment. In J. O. Greene & B. R. Burleson (Eds.), *Handbook of communication and social interaction skills* (pp. 93–134). Mahwah, NJ: Erlbaum.

Spitzberg, B. H., & Brunner, C. C. (1991). Toward a theoretical integration of context and competence inference research. *Western Journal of Speech Communication, 56,* 28–46.

Spitzberg, B. H., Canary, D. J., & Cupach, W. R. (1994). A competence-based approach to the study of interpersonal conflict. In D. D. Cahn (Ed.), *Conflict in personal relationships* (pp. 183–202). Hillsdale, NJ: Erlbaum.

Spitzberg, B. H., & Cupach, W. R. (1984). *Interpersonal communication competence.* Beverly Hills, CA: Sage.

Spitzberg, B. H., & Cupach, W. R. (2002). Interpersonal skills. In M. L. Knapp & J. A. Daly (Eds.), *Handbook of interpersonal communication* (pp. 564–612). Thousand Oaks, CA: Sage.

Building Motivation _____

Self-Assessment: Rate each of the following communication situations, indicating the typical level of competence you feel you can or do achieve. Use the scale of 1–4 provided, with 1 being minimal competence and 4 high competence. Rate one component (motivation) through all the situations, and then rate the next component (knowledge), and then the third (skills).

Motivation	Knowledge	Skills
1 = Anxious, nervous, or no motivation to be competent	**1** = Completely inexperienced and ignorant about how to behave	**1** = Completely incapable of behaving competently in the situation
2 = Somewhat nervous, but some motivation to be competent	**2** = Minimal experience and knowledge about how to behave	**2** = Barely capable of behaving minimally competently
3 = Somewhat confident and motivated to be competent	**3** = Somewhat experienced and knowledgeable about how to behave	**3** = Fairly capable of behaving competently
4 = Highly confident and motivated to be competent	**4** = Highly knowledgeable about all aspects of how to behave	**4** = Highly capable of behaving competently

For example, if you think you are very knowledgeable and skilled at meeting new people in a business context but a little nervous when you do so, you might respond to the following item thus:

Communication Situations:	Motivation	Knowledge	Skills
Meeting new people in a business context	2	4	4

INTERPERSONAL CONTEXT

Communication Situations:	Motivation	Knowledge	Skills
1. Interacting socially with people from very different cultures			
2. Asking someone for a date			
3. Refusing a date with someone			
4. Asking some people to not cut in a line in front of you or telling them so			
5. Discussing safe sex with someone you are considering sexual relations with			
6. Telling a subordinate that she or he has done something wrong			
7. Telling a boss she or he has done something wrong			

Communication Situations:	Motivation	Knowledge	Skills
1. Reintroducing a topic you think is important after a group has moved on			
2. Making a spontaneous joke or quip in the middle of a serious group discussion			
3. Correcting a group leader's minor error in summarizing the group's discussion			
4. Making an argument for what you believe in even though you know everyone in the group is against your position			
5. Telling a group member that he or she interrupted you and should wait			
6. Explaining to a group that you haven't prepared adequately for this meeting			
7. Becoming the leader of a group			

Communication Situations:	Motivation	Knowledge	Skills
1. Giving a simple, prepared, informative speech in front of a classroom			
2. Presenting a prepared technical report to a group of employees			
3. Making an elaborate toast to a large, formal wedding party			
4. Introducing a political candidate you support to a large crowd			
5. Giving a persuasive speech at a city council meeting on a proposal the members oppose			
6. Giving an impromptu speech at a political rally			
7. Giving an interview on stage after being picked from a live television audience			
Total Scores			

Interpreting Your Scores: For each context level, total your ratings for each column (motivation, knowledge, skills). You should end up with three scores. The possible range of scores per column is 7–28. Scores 7–14 indicate you are minimizing your competence and have significant room for improvement in this area of competence. Scores 15–21 indicate you think you are average in your competence. You may be sufficing or maximizing your competence and still have room for improvement. Scores 22–28 indicate you think you are nearing optimizing competence. Although you may still improve, you have a good grasp of the competence process.

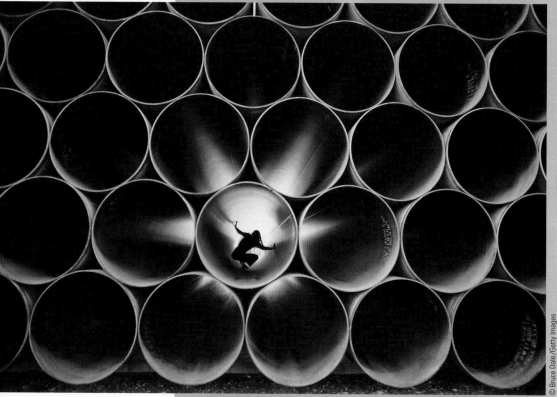

Chapter 3

© Bruce Dale/Getty Images

LEARNING OBJECTIVES

After studying this chapter, you should be able to

1. Define perception and explain how noticing, organizing, and interpreting constitute perception.

2. Explain how mindfulness, expectations and the self-fulfilling prophecy, and language influence the way people notice other people, situations, and events in any culture.

3. Use prototypes, stereotypes, and scripts effectively to organize information into impressions.

4. Demonstrate how implicit personality theory and attribution

theory can help us understand individuals' personalities as well as their motives for behavior.

5. Anticipate how culture influences perception during conversation.

6. Describe how the self is constructed through communication with others.

7. Identify the challenges to perception and self and demonstrate your ability to manage them.

Perception and Culture

Ann-Chinn and Loern are both enrolled in an introductory political science class. Ann-Chinn has noticed that Loern comes to class very well prepared. She saw that he always highlighted sections of his text and prepared two or three questions about the assigned reading that he asked in class. Ann-Chinn was surprised because she did the same thing and thought that no one else did. When the instructor asked Loern questions, Ann-Chinn was impressed with how thoughtful and detailed his answers were. Although others in the class perceived Loern as trying to get on the professor's good side, Ann-Chinn thought of him as a very serious, thoughtful, and dedicated student.

One day Ann-Chinn walked out of class with Loern and they began talking. As they walked out into the parking lot, Ann-Chinn noticed several bumper stickers on Loern's truck. Two that stood out were "Earth first, we'll log the other planets later" and "A little nukie never hurt anyone." Ann-Chinn was startled by these messages and asked Loern what those bumper stickers were doing on his truck.

Loern's eyes flashed with passion. "Well, honestly, I'm just sick of these fanatical environmentalists who are trying to halt our economic development. As for nukes, sure, nuclear energy has some problems, but it is a very important energy source for the future."

"But what about a responsibility to our environment?" Ann-Chinn asked in shock. "If we log the old forests, people in the future will never have an opportunity to see a towering redwood tree or hike in a rain forest."

Loern responded, "But what about a responsibility to the economic well-being of future citizens? Sure, seeing old trees would be nice, but we need the lumber. Besides, trees are a renewable resource. If we just have a solid reforesting plan, we can keep the environment going."

Ann-Chinn was bewildered, "I feel I don't know who you are. You're not the same person I take political science with!" ■

Many times we form an initial impression of a person only to have that impression disconfirmed later. Ann-Chinn noticed Loern's attention to detail and level of class preparation, and given that she focused on her studies in the same way, she assumed he was similar to her in other ways—including attitudes about the environment. When her expectations were violated, she felt she didn't really know the true Loern.

Like Ann-Chinn's, our sense of identity influences what we notice about others and how we interpret phenomena. This chapter first examines how we process the wide variety of information cues we receive and how we interpret them. We then discuss how culture influences our perceptions of others. We next highlight how our personal identity is created, its influence on perceptions, and the way we express ourselves. The chapter concludes with some practical tips on how to manage challenges arising from perception.

What Is Perception?

Perception is the process of noticing, organizing, and interpreting data about people, events, activities, and situations. It is an active process in which we use the senses of touch, taste, sight, hearing, and smell to gather data about both our external environment and our internal experiences and subsequently try to make sense of these sensations. To understand perception, we need to understand the activities of noticing, organizing, and interpreting.

Perception Means Noticing

What moved Ann-Chinn to notice Loern's behavior in class? What caused her to notice and subsequently be surprised about his beliefs regarding the environment? Three major factors influence our ability to notice data within a situation: (1) mindfulness, (2) expectations and the self-fulfilling prophecy, and (3) language use.

Mindfulness

Imagine that you have just shown up for class the first day. What do you notice? Most likely, your senses are fully engaged and you probably observe every small detail in the classroom. You may hear who talks to whom. You may note what people wear, and so on. **Mindfulness** is paying close attention to the task at hand, absorbing each bit of detail that you possibly can (Langer, 1997). Typically, people become mindful of their own behavior and the situation in which they find themselves when the situation is somewhat novel. But the more others behave in routine ways and the more situations unfold predictably, the more people gloss over the details of the person or the situation.

Expectations and the Self-Fulfilling Prophecy

As we say in Chapter 2, expectations are the standards and guides by which we anticipate what people will do. Expectations function in two different ways. On the one hand, they create a type of self-fulfilling prophecy. A **self-fulfilling prophecy** occurs when you make assumptions about yourself or another person and then behave or interact with the person as if these assumptions were true. Our expectations guide our inquiry into a situation as we seek out information and details that confirm these expectations. In employment interviews, as in many social situations, the interviewer forms an impression about the interviewee and then seeks out information that confirms the impression, rather than disconfirming information (Judge, Higgins, & Cable, 2000). Similarly, if you believe you are unqualified for a job or that you will botch the interview, often the interview will not go well, confirming your expectations.

On the other hand, when our expectations have been violated, we engage in a more extensive information search within the situation (Burgoon, Stern, & Dillman, 1995). In this situation, we may ask questions such as these:

We become mindful of our surroundings when they are relatively novel. In a new job, we may hang on to every word that's uttered in a weekly staff meeting but lose such mindfulness when we experience the meetings as routine. When they become regular, we tend to gloss over the details of situations and events.

- How is the situation different from what I expected?
- What has caused this change in the situation?
- In what ways is the person behaving differently than I expected?
- What is motivating this person to behave differently?

In this situation we feel a need to understand events in more detail; we seek out what is causing the change and what is motivating people to act in unexpected ways.

Language Use

Language influences our perception because words are pointers; they direct our attention toward certain aspects of people and situations. Take, for example, the debate about whether to refer to a person as "Indian" or as "Native American." What do you notice when you call someone "Indian"? You notice ethnicity. What do you notice if you refer to someone as Native American? You notice that in the United States Europeans are not native to North America and that several tribal peoples were the first inhabitants of the country. Even though the terms *Indian* and *Native American* are similar in that they both gloss over differences between tribal nations, such as the Lakota, the Sioux, the Cherokee, the Navajo, and the Hopi, they point your attention to two different elements of the tribal experience in the United States.

Words are so important in influencing our impressions that we need to be careful not to engage in **linguistic tyranny,** which occurs when people use one set of words that have a certain value or connotation to describe and control the outcome of a situation, instead of playing with different words to describe the situation (Pearce, 1994). Politicians typically engage in linguistic tyranny to influence citizens' interpretations of particular events. Consider the words that U.S. politicians used to promote the war on terrorism in Iraq. They spoke of "weapons of mass destruction," or WMDs, words that closely paralleled the description of another major international threat recently confronted by the United States, the former Soviet Union's possession of nuclear weapons. These words were particularly potent in influencing the American public to see the invasion of Iraq as just, necessary, and

BIZARRO   **By Dan Piraro**

Although all communication involves labels, we struggle as a society to use labels that do not tyrannize the groups to which these labels are applied.

urgent. Linguistic tyranny also happens at the interpersonal level, such as when we struggle to find appropriate terms or labels for people with certain characteristics. In the *Bizarro* cartoon, the characters are struggling over what constitutes a restrictive label, all realizing that some label is required to talk about anything.

Perception Means Organizing

Cognitive psychology suggests that people use schemas to make sense of and organize incoming information. A **schema** is a framework that helps people organize information and place it into a coherent and meaningful pattern. Imagine that you walked into an art museum and saw a painting by Picasso. Unless you had a schema that included information about cubism and surrealism, you might have difficulty recognizing the various elements in the painting or even finding it beautiful. A variety of schemas help organize our impressions around people, events, situations, and activities: (1) prototypes, (2) stereotypes, and (3) scripts.

Prototypes

In the *Dilbert* cartoon, Dogbert has grouped all people into one of four basic categories, making fun of our general tendency to view people as types. These categories help us place people, events, activities, and situations into categories called prototypes. A **prototype** is the best example of some concept. For example, your prototype of a luxury car might be a Lexus or any car with the following characteristics: roomy inside, large, powerful, constructed of superior materials, and very expensive. Most people have developed a prototype for the competent communicator as someone who is intelligent, articulate, confident, outgoing, well dressed, and a good listener (Pavitt & Haight, 1985). Prototypes are useful perceptual schemas that help us determine the kinds of people, situations, or activities we are experiencing.

Stereotypes

Prototypes provide a general example of a category, whereas **stereotypes** are schemas that connect a variety of characteristics we believe to be true of a category to a given person or situation we see as a member or example of that category. For example, we may develop stereotypes about tourists as people running around in tennis shoes, plaid shorts, and uneven sunburns, with cameras hung around their necks. You might predict they will buy cheap trinkets to give as gifts to friends and family back home. Similarly, we may develop stereotypes about how people look or act on the basis of their ethnicity, sexual orientation, gender, age, religion, and level of education.

Stereotypes can impair communication by bolstering our belief that people have a single self or identity. This belief is the assumption of **allness,** the conclusion that what we

We often categorize people based on our concept of the best possible example, or prototype, of a type of person. The same behavior may be viewed differently if people use different prototypes.

believe to be true of one part is true of the whole. If we encounter a rude traffic cop, we may conclude that all traffic cops are rude. In addition, if this traffic cop is also female, we might then start making assumptions about all females in positions of power. Stereotypes simplify complex situations. We cannot notice everything, so we seek to group as many things as possible into categories that make them understandable and familiar. However, we need to recognize that stereotypes can't capture the whole person or situation.

Scripts

A **script** is an expected sequence of events that is coherent to the individual (Abelson, 1976). Take the following random list of questions and statements a server in a restaurant might say to you. Reorder them as you would anticipate them to be asked.

- Would you like dessert?
- Would you like a little more time to make your selections?
- What would you like to order as your appetizer?
- Good evening.
- What entrée would you prefer?

Most likely, you reordered the questions as follows:

- Good evening.
- Would you like a little time to make your selections?
- What would you like to order as your appetizer?
- What entrée would you prefer?
- Would you like dessert?

As schemas, scripts provide us with guides for interpreting events and organizing our communication. In a restaurant, if asked, "Would you like a little more time to make your selections?" we know that we are to answer either yes or no. But if a member of the wait staff came up to us and said, "I've had a lousy day—I don't even know why I came to work," we would be confused and not know how to act. Such statements don't follow the typical script we have created for ordering food at a restaurant. We usually don't become aware that we are using scripts to guide our interpretations and actions until someone violates the plotline.

Perception Means Interpretation

Once we have noticed something and organized it according to a cognitive framework using prototypes, stereotypes, or scripts, we interpret what we have noticed. That is, we attempt to make sense of the information to draw conclusions about the kind of person with whom we are interacting or the type of situation in which we find ourselves. There are two ways to look at how we draw such conclusions: implicit personality theory and attribution theory.

Implicit Personality Theory

Implicit personality theory suggests that we use one or a few personality traits to draw inferences about what people are like (Wegner & Vallacher, 1977). A continuum of dimensions, or traits, that make up people's personalities is called a construct; constructs can include traits such as happy–sad, strong–weak, close–distant, and so on. Implicit personality theory suggests that certain constructs are central to our determining what a person is like. For example, you may focus on a single construct such as gender (male–female), economic status (rich–poor), or educational status (grade school–college) and draw inferences about the person based on that construct.

Implicit personality theory also examines how traits are clustered together and how certain central traits trigger associations with others. For example, you may associate the construct of being college educated with being artistic and elitist. However, other people may associate the construct of a college education with prosperity and friendliness. In the opening vignette, Ann-Chinn associates the construct of "good student" with preparation and class participation.

Implicit personality theory helps explain why first impressions of others are so powerful. **First impression bias** means that our first impression sets the mold by which later information we gather about this person is processed, remembered, and viewed as relevant. For example, based on observing Ann-Chinn in class, Loern may have viewed her as a stereotypical Asian woman and assumed she is quiet, hard working, and unassertive. Having reached these conclusions, rightly or wrongly, he now has a set of prototypes and constructs for understanding and interpreting Ann-Chinn's behavior. Over time, he fits the behavior consistent with his prototypes and constructs into the impression he has already formed of her. When he notices her expressing disbelief over his selection of bumper stickers, he may simply dismiss it or view it as an odd exception to her real nature because it doesn't fit his existing prototype.

Attribution Theory

Attribution theory provides people with a framework for determining the motives underlying others' behavior (Spitzberg, 2001). We tend to make such attributions about people based on the principles of consistency and distinctiveness, and we draw conclusions about their importance based on the principles of locus and controllability (Seibold & Spitzberg, 1982).

The **principle of consistency** suggests that we make attributions about people based on the similarity of their characteristics or actions across time and space. If a student has a history in both high school and college of getting teachers to accept late assignments, you are likely to attribute persuasiveness to this student. This particular behavior is said to be high in consistency. However, if you saw that this student persuaded one professor to permit a late assignment but had no success in convincing two other professors, you have no consistent pattern to use in attributing persuasiveness to this student.

The **principle of distinctiveness** suggests that we make attributions about people based on whether their particular characteristics and actions are associated with specific outcomes unique to the situation. Distinctiveness is the extent to which things occur only with each other and not with other things. For example, if the student with the late assignments seems well liked by peers and professors but is clearly treated harshly by one of the professors, then the student seems to evoke a distinctive reaction from this professor. If the professor in question is consistently harsh with many other students, then the behavior is not distinctive to the late-assignment student; rather it is low in distinctiveness, and you will tend to consider the professor a harsh person. If instead, you see this professor being friendly with all students except the student with the late assignments, then the student seems to be unique or distinctive in eliciting this response from the professor. In this case, the professor's behavior is high in distinctiveness and you are more likely to attribute the cause to the late student having done something to upset this professor.

The **principle of locus** states that we attempt to determine whether a cause of some outcome is internal or external to a person. Is the student who asks permission to turn in assignments late working two jobs, a single parent, and taking 10 courses? If so, many would assume the student is late with assignments not so much out of laziness, an internal condition, but out of the external demands of that student's life. In contrast, if you frequently see this student on campus throwing Frisbees and chatting with friends at the student union, you are more likely to attribute the student's late assignments to laziness, a quality inherent to that particular student.

The **principle of controllability** means we try to determine not only whether the cause of a particular action is internal or external but the extent to which a person is able to alter or change the outcome. Whether you feel sympathy or dislike for the student depends in large part on whether your attribution is one of laziness or excessive external demands. But notice that even with the attribution of excessive demands, you could still blame the student for taking too much on or failing to prioritize properly. The more you perceive an outcome, such as lateness, to be controllable, the more likely you are to hold that person responsible for his or her outcomes, whether positive or negative.

How do these principles become important in communication? The way you feel and act toward people depends on how you attribute outcomes to their actions. Table 3.1 shows how attribution principles might work in the courtroom where decisions of guilt and innocence are being decided. Consider the communication predicament attorneys might face in dealing with a student accused of acquaintance rape. To influence the judge or jury, the attorneys base their stories on attribution principles to construct a coherent argument regarding the defendant's guilt or innocence.

As you can see, the principles of consistency, distinctiveness, locus, and controllability describe the way attributions are likely to be made if people are rational. However, research shows that people tend to be biased in applying these attribution principles (Nisbett & Ross, 1980). The most consistent biases are the fundamental attribution error and the self-serving bias. The **fundamental attribution error** occurs when we assume other people's behavior is due to internal characteristics such as their personality, whereas we view our own behavior as a result of factors in the context or situation (Jones & Nisbett, 1971). The **self-serving bias** states that we tend to attribute positive outcomes to ourselves, which is an internal attribution, and negative outcomes to others or to the situation, which are external attributions (Nisbett & Ross, 1980). Consider students discussing the

learning link

How does implicit personality theory help explain the role perceptions play in the development of communication competence discussed in Chapter 2?

• • •

Table 3.1

Attribution Theory in the Courtroom

A student accuses a fellow student she had been dating of engaging in date rape. How might the attorneys attempt to use attribution theory to make their respective cases for their clients?

Attorney	Consistency	Distinctiveness	Locus	Controllability	Specific Attribution
Definition	How often does one event occur when the other event occurs?	To what extent does one event occur *only* when the other event occurs?	Is the cause of the event "inside" the person or "outside" the person?	To what extent is the person able to change or control what happens?	What caused this person to do what he or she did?
Defense	Low: My client never tried this before with this person.	Low: My client never tried this with any of his other dating partners.	External: The plaintiff teased and led my client on. She didn't say "please don't" until they were undressed, and then only feebly.	Uncontrollable: Both my client and the defendant had had a lot to drink that night.	My client is not a coercive person; he simply got carried away by the context due to mixed signals from the plaintiff (i.e., he should not be held responsible).
Prosecution	High: My client claims that the defendant consistently persisted in pressuring her for sexual relations.	Low: Previous dating partners testify that the defendant was sexually aggressive with them.	Internal: The defendant talked and talked about how much he wanted to have sex with my client.	Controllable: The defendant said to her: "I know what you need and I'm going to give it to you whether you want it or not."	The defendant clearly *intended* to have sex with my client, forcing himself on her against her will (i.e., he should be held responsible).
	High: The defendant has a reputation for being very sexually persistent and aggressive.	High: The defendant was clearly uniquely obsessed with my client; he was more aggressive with her than with previous partners.	Internal: The defendant bragged to friends about how he was going to score with my client.	Controllable: Actions on the date—going to a party, to his place drinking, threatening to leave her stranded if she didn't have sex—reveal the defendant's intentions.	The defendant clearly had *planned* to have sex with my client, regardless of her consent, and he did things to assure this outcome (i.e., he should be held responsible).

NOTE: Attribution theory explains how we determine what caused some event, but it also guides how we make explanations in everyday arguments. What other types of arguments could be made about either the defendant's or the plaintiff's actions, motives, or background that are based on consistency, distinctiveness, locus, or controllability?

grades they received on a recent exam. You will find that most people seem to earn A's but are given D's. That is, an A is achieved through the internal characteristics of effort and ability on the part of the student, but a D is a product of the external situation such as not having enough time to study or having an overly difficult or demanding professor.

How Does Culture Affect Perception?

We are born into preexisting and ongoing cultures. As defined in Chapter 2, a *culture* encompasses people's beliefs and attitudes about their world, their spirituality, their sense of status and hierarchy, their use of time and physical space, and their relationships to one another (Samovar & Porter, 2003). Our understanding of culture is not limited to differences among national cultures associated with particular countries. Rather, it can refer to any group of people who have created an enduring pattern of thought, value, and behavior that defines them. Culture can characterize societal institutions such as organizations (Eisenberg & Riley, 2001), as well as differing groups of people based on individual characteristics such as gender (Wood & Reich, 2003) and physical ability or disability (Braithwaite & Braithwaite, 2003).

Whether you use it to refer to a nation, an organization, or a specific group of people, culture influences how you perceive people, situations, and events. Culture has an effect on the kinds of schemas people employ to make judgments about the appropriateness and effectiveness of a person's communication. For example, in the West silence is typically viewed as an empty space devoid of meaning and people become uneasy when silence dominates a conversation. However, in Asia where silence is valued, people may sit side by side for long periods without talking and not experience discomfort (Lim, 2002).

Culture and Beliefs, Attitudes, and Values

Cultures are characterized by their beliefs, attitudes, values, and behavior patterns. The most widely used model for characterizing different cultures' beliefs, attitudes, and values has been offered by Hofstede (1980, 2001, 2004). In his original study, Hofstede (1980) collected data from 117,000 employees in a large multinational corporation in 66 countries. He found four dimensions that characterized cultural differences regarding work cultures:

1. Power distance: the difference in interpersonal power and influence between managers and subordinates.
2. Uncertainty avoidance: the degree to which individuals are tolerant of uncertainty and prefer ambiguous situations.
3. Individualism: the degree to which people value the individual or the collective.
4. Masculinity: the degree to which the country emphasizes assertive or nurturing behavior.

Hofstede (2004) has suggested that a fifth dimension, long-term versus short-term orientation, may also be used to characterize national cultures. A long-term orientation emphasizes values such as thrift and perseverance, whereas a short-term orientation emphasizes meeting social expectations.

Researchers often use the individualism–collectivism dimension to distinguish cultures. **Individualistic cultures** stress personal goals and achievements over the collective's goals and achievements (Haslett & Ruebush, 1999). For example, North American students of all ages express concern about working in groups because they feel the group's result may not adequately reflect their contributions or that they will be forced to do the majority of the work. In **collectivist cultures,** collective goals take priority over individual goals. People in collectivist cultures such as Japan, China, and Korea may find it hard to speak up and offer their opinions in a group setting, especially if those views are contrary to the group's majority opinion. Their sense of loyalty precludes them from voicing dissenting opinions and disrupting the group. Take a moment and assess your level of individualism and collectivism using the scales provided in the Test Your Cultural Orientation box.

Perceptions Vary by Culture

Culture influences the way we perceive situations, events, and people. For example, is it appropriate to talk about one's children and family during a business lunch? In the United States bringing up the topic of family may be viewed negatively; however, in Mexico, bringing out pictures of one's family and talking about them at length is viewed positively. Mexico is a relationship-based culture, and talking about one's family suggests that the person is responsible and takes his or her obligations seriously (Hooker, 2003).

Cultural influences can affect our perceptions in two ways. First, culture influences our ability to understand and interpret people's communication from another culture. For example, persons in individualistic cultures view confrontational conflict management styles as more appropriate than do people from collectivist cultures (Lustig & Koester, 1999). This can lead to relational misunderstanding because a person from an individualistic culture using confrontation to manage conflict would view this style as normal whereas a person from a collectivist culture would likely view it as inappropriate. Even if there is some shared meaning regarding particular cues across culture, people may still have difficulty accurately interpreting their meaning given their unique cultural perspective. For example, though nonverbal expressions such as frowns and smiles seem to be associated universally with specific emotions, persons are more likely to recognize accurately the emotions of another person from their own culture than those of a member of a different cultural group (Elfenbein & Ambady, 2003). Second, culture can also influence the attribution process. The fundamental attribution error occurs within all cultures.

Test ✓ Your
Cultural Orientation

Are you more individualistic or collectivistic? Complete the scales to see where you fall.

INSTRUCTIONS: The purpose of this questionnaire is to help you assess your individualistic and collectivistic tendencies. Respond by indicating the degree to which the values in each phrase are important to you on a scale of 1 to 5: "opposed to my values" is 1, "not important to me" is 2, "somewhat important to me" is 3, "important to me" is 4, and "very important to me" is 5.

_____ 1. Obtaining pleasure or sensuous gratification

_____ 2. Preserving the welfare of others

_____ 3. Being successful by demonstrating my individual competency

_____ 4. Restraining my behavior if it is going to harm others

_____ 5. Being independent in thought and action

_____ 6. Having safety and stability for people with whom I identify

_____ 7. Obtaining status and prestige

_____ 8. Having harmony in my relations with others

_____ 9. Having an exciting and challenging life

_____ 10. Accepting cultural and religious traditions

_____ 11. Being recognized for my individual work

_____ 12. Conforming to social norms

_____ 13. Being self-directed

_____ 14. Being benevolent (and kind to others)

_____ 15. Having power

_____ 16. Being polite to others

_____ 17. Being ambitious

_____ 18. Being self-controlled

_____ 19. Being able to choose what I do

_____ 20. Enhancing the welfare of others

Answers: To find your individualism score, add all your numerical responses to the odd-numbered items. To find your collectivism score, add your responses to the even-numbered items. Both scores will range from 10 to 50. The higher your scores, the more individualistic or collectivistic you are. Equal scores in both areas reflect a balance between individualist and collectivist tendencies.

SOURCE: Gudykunst (1998), p. 67

However, in collectivist cultures people tend to attribute behavior to factors in the situation or context rather than to the individual (Stephan & Stephan, 2002).

How Do We Develop Self-Concept?

Like culture, our self-concept influences our perceptions of people, places, and events. The idea of having a self suggests that people are different from one another and that to understand a person's self you need to understand the uniqueness of that particular person. However, understanding one's self also requires us to understand what we share with others within our culture.

Communication and Self

In the cartoon, Amos experiences what many of us experience in less dramatic, if equally powerful, ways in our everyday communication: a significant change in how we feel about ourselves based on the messages that others communicate to us. The meanings and interpretations that we create for ourselves and others result from our interactions with other people. The importance of the other in constructing the self was noted by Cooley (1922), who explicitly argued that the self is a **social self.** According to Cooley, the self comes into being through interaction with others and can be determined only through relationships with other people. Cooley (1922) coined the term the *looking-glass self* to demonstrate how our relationships with other people form the self. The **looking-glass self** assumes people imagine the perception that others hold of them, and it is this act of perceiving the self as an object through the eyes of others that creates the self. The looking-glass self consists of three principal elements: (1) the imagination of one's appearance to another person, (2) the imagination of the other person's judgment of that appearance, and (3) a resulting feeling such as pride or shame.

learning link

How might your cultural background influence your perception of another person's communication competence?

• • •

Mead (1934) also argued that the self arises from communication with others and that it comprises both an "I" and a "Me." The "I" represents the impulsive and unpredictable part of the self. The "Me" represents the norms of a community and reflects the generalized expectations for what patterns of behavior are allowed within a community. The "I" serves as the driving force for performing an act but is quickly controlled and guided by the "Me." For example, a mischievous aspect of the "I" may encourage you to shout, "Fire!" impulsively in a crowded movie theater; the "Me" controls this impulse because it knows that shouting such words in a crowded movie theater could not only injure people as they stampede for the exits but also lead to your arrest. For Mead, the "Me" serves an important function in regulating behavior in society.

The "Me" is associated with the generalized other. Mead (1934) states that to develop the fullest sense of self we need to consider the attitudes of the **generalized other**—the entire social group or community to which we belong. **Significant others** are specific people who influence our life such as parents, partners, friends, and teachers, whereas the generalized other is the general class, category, or group of people we use to assess our actions. The term *generalized other* implies the communal rules and guidelines that determine how people who belong to a particular social group or community should view situations and act. Assume you are a volunteer for a women's shelter that provides assistance and support to abused women. A new woman comes to the shelter and presents you with a problem you have never encountered before. You ask yourself, "What should a volunteer at this

9 CHICKWEED LANE By Brooke McEldowney

How you communicate yourself to others often depends on how they communicate your self to you.

shelter do?" Rather than asking what a specific person such as another volunteer or volunteer coordinator should do, you have asked what the general community of volunteers would do. When we ask questions that evoke the generalized other, we can begin to coordinate our actions more successfully because we are drawing on a common base of shared assumptions and beliefs.

We form the generalized other through the use of **significant symbols,** verbal or nonverbal messages that have shared meaning. Take the preceding example of the significant symbol "Fire!" When you use a significant symbol, you can assume the listener's role and empathize with the perception of your message. This process is called **role taking.** As you've seen so far, Mead suggests that people experience themselves through the perceptions of others. He further suggests that the way we begin to understand others is through using significant symbols.

We also have conversations with ourselves, or **self-talk.** Through these internal conversations we reflect on what we are doing well or what we are doing poorly; we reflect on how we have done in the past and what we anticipate doing in the future. The power of self-talk to help people accomplish their goals has been demonstrated (Hollenbeck & Hall, 2004). For example, when you are preparing for a speech you may visualize a successful performance. When a speaker thinks positive thoughts, such as "I can see what I need to do" as opposed to negative thoughts such as "I hope I don't freeze up," he or she is more likely to perform the desired behavior.

The Postmodern Self

The notion that the self comprises an "I" and a "Me" is the basis for the idea of the **modern self** (Giddens, 1991), the classic Western tradition of viewing people as having a core single self whose character and personality are stable over time. The common expression "just be yourself" reflects this philosophy, implying there is a true self that others can perceive accurately or inaccurately.

The concept of a **postmodern self,** in contrast, rejects the notion of a single true self and suggests that the self is actually made up of many different selves. For example, on any given day, you might face interactions that include the following: You log on to your computer and download a dozen e-mail messages, some from friends, some from colleagues or fellow students. You reply to people and then enter a couple of chat rooms where you chat for a while with one person about your hobby and with another about romance. You call your parents to let them know about your plans to visit. You go to campus and attend a couple of afternoon classes and afterward meet with a couple of students in your study group. Before you leave campus, you talk to a librarian about an overdue fee. You go home, but not before doing some grocery shopping. You call your romantic partner to see about getting together that night with some mutual friends at a club.

During the course of this day, you have been an acquaintance, a friend, a counselor, a romantic partner, an instructor, a hobbyist, a student, a patron, and a son or daughter, and yet, in the end, you remain yourself. As the world offers more and more opportunities and avenues for communication, the ways we present ourselves to the world, and to ourselves, have become more complex. The postmodern self is a product of this increasing complexity.

The postmodern self is multiple, adaptable, and socially constructed (Gergen, 1991). The first of these characteristics, the **multiple self,** means that we create many different versions of self across contexts. Some of your friends might know you primarily as an athlete, others through your shared hobbies, as a fraternity or sorority member, or as a work colleague. We give certain faces more prominence in some relationships and in some contexts than in others (Rosenberg & Gara, 1985). All these faces are true and yet each gives people a different view of us. These faces also reveal the very complex nature of self. You may easily see your multiple selves as parts of a whole, but the fact that you can be polite in one context, aggressive in another, passive in one context, and powerful in another, suggests just how many different selves you are capable of revealing.

The second characteristic of the postmodern self is that it is adaptable. Not only do we reveal different selves across contexts but we show different faces of ourselves within contexts and across time (Zurcher, 1977). That is, we adapt. Think about the last complicated and serious conflict you had with someone close to you. You might have had to play the role of confidant, advocate, friend, counselor, competitor, and victor or loser, all within a single communication episode. Over time, you may also discover that you have become more competitive or less forgiving, more expressive or less confident. These adaptations result from life experiences such as marriage, children, divorce, loss of a parent or close friend, or job changes. Such adaptations occur not only in a person's behavior but in the conception of self. Adaptations can even be specific to particular contexts. Look back at yourself in high school—are you the same person you were then? Chances are, you're not. One study found that even victims of childhood sexual abuse sometimes find silver linings in such dark experiences, including a more cautious view of others, greater determination not to repeat the experience with their own children, and a toughened personality (McMillen, Zuravin, & Rideout, 1995). The self often finds ways of adapting to the most severe and varied experiences.

Finally, the postmodern self is socially constructed, which means that the way you see and create yourself depends in large part on how others perceive you. Consider the very simple question of how physically attractive you are. Most of us have some idea of our level of physical attractiveness. But where does this idea come from? Is there some objective, universal set of characteristics that defines attractiveness according to a continuum? No. Some characteristics are universally considered more attractive than others (such as a good complexion or facial symmetry); however, our view of our own attractiveness is based on the communications we receive from our social and cultural worlds. There is no self-concept of physical attractiveness without others to help define what is and what is not attractive.

The postmodern self is multiple, adaptable, and socially constructed. Through our interactions with many different people and institutions, we find ourselves adapting our self to these experiences and to the expectations that others have of us. These interactions provide many opportunities for us to define ourselves as we most want to be seen, but how

learning link

What are the similarities and differences between the modern and postmodern self?

● ● ●

Close Up *on Community*
Managing Multiple "Me's" in a Diverse Society

GEORGE HERBERT MEAD VIEWED THE "ME" AND THE generalized other as the glue that holds society together. With a common set of values, beliefs, and assumptions, people were able to communicate clearly with one another because they had a shared understanding of what various symbols mean. At the time of his writing in the 1930s, the notion of a single "Me" and a generalized other made sense as many people within the United States viewed the country as having a homogeneous set of values and beliefs.

In light of this shared value and belief system, the dominant way of talking about significant public issues was debate. Debate worked well as long as there was a shared identity among community members. However, today, there is great diversity within society, and people have differing values, beliefs, and assumptions about which kinds of behaviors are acceptable and moral and which are not. In such a pluralistic society, the traditional form of debate may actually divide and polarize communities instead of uniting and integrating them.

Consider, for example, the proposal to extend health benefits to the partners of gays and lesbians. For some people, their view of the proposal is rooted in morality and goes against their religious beliefs. For others, the policy rightly extends equal rights to gay and lesbian couples. Because these two different groups use different standards to judge the acceptability of the proposal, it is not surprising that they have difficulty reaching agreement. There is no common standard with which to judge the validity of the proposal.

One of the ways that community members can begin to manage the multiple "Me's" and generalized others of a community is to engage in dialogue. Dialogue is a process of standing one's ground while being profoundly open to other perspectives (Pearce & Pearce, 2004). The characteristics of dialogue include the following:

- We try to understand one another's perspectives.
- We accept that listening is as important as speaking.
- We speak from personal experience.
- We discover differences even among those with whom we agree.
- We discover shared concerns among those with whom we disagree.
- We ask questions out of true curiosity and the desire to know more.
- We try to work collaboratively.

The notion of dialogue in public life has taken on added importance. A number of groups such as the National Issues Forum, Study Circles, the Public Conversations Project, and the Public Dialogue Consortium are devoted to developing ways of communicating that promote dialogue. Understanding one another's unique perspective is an important first step in managing the identity of a community.

SOURCE: Pearce & Littlejohn (1998).

we want to be seen often varies across time, context, and relationship. Communication, therefore, is not just a situation in which you reveal yourself but a process in which you co-create yourself with others. The ability to co-create multiple selves that adapt to changing circumstances can be a liberating experience. However, as the Close-Up on Community box highlights, the existence of multiple "I's" and "Me's" within society can make it challenging for people to work together.

Expressing Self to Others

Every communication event gives us an opportunity to express ourselves. In doing so, we reveal something about who we are and who we view ourselves as being. If we reveal too much, we risk offending others or making ourselves vulnerable. If we reveal too little, others may not know who we are or how to interact with us. Competent interaction means finding an appropriate and effective balance. The process by which we reveal ourselves to others is self-disclosure.

Self-Disclosure

Self-disclosure is the process of intentionally and voluntarily providing others with information about yourself that you believe is honest and accurate and unlikely to be discovered elsewhere. To be considered self-disclosure, a message must be intentional. If Loern is staring at Ann-Chinn while she is talking about her vacations and responds, "What great lips, uh, I mean trips," Ann-Chinn may think he has disclosed something about his thoughts. But if he had no intention and his comment was purely accidental, then it is not self-disclosure.

To be considered self-disclosure, a message must also be voluntary. It can hardly be considered self-disclosure if someone is brainwashed, tortured, or coerced to provide information. We come to know someone not only by what she or he chooses to tell us, but by the fact that she or he chooses to tell us at all. The choice is as informative as the information.

Self-disclosure provides information about the self. If a student sitting next to you tells you she thinks the class is boring, you might consider this information relevant to who she is. But is it about her? Certainly it reveals information about her attitudes, and this gives you information about her. She may not consider it self-disclosure, but attitudes, beliefs, and values make up a significant part of our self-concepts, and disclosing them, in effect, is disclosing who we think we are.

Finally, self-disclosure reveals information that is unlikely to be discovered through other means. If your professor states on the first day of class, "I'm your professor," it is not self-disclosure. You are not revealing anything about yourself if you tell someone something he or she already knows. In contrast, if you tell someone something that can only be known because you say it, you have truly opened yourself up to that person.

Types of Openness

We can understand how we open ourselves through a concept known as the **Johari Window.** Johari is pronounced "Joe Harry," after the scholars who first developed the ideas, Harry Ingham and Joseph Luft (Luft, 1969). The window is defined by two dimensions: the self-dimension and the other dimension (Figure 3.1). The self-dimension identifies what is or is not revealed or known to one's self. The other dimension of openness identifies information about the self that is or is not revealed or known to others. When these dimensions are crossed, they form a window with four areas, called the open, blind, hidden, and unknown selves.

The **open self** is what is known to the self and to others, the part of you that you are aware of and show to people around you. Your hobbies, your major, your career objectives, whether or not you are married, and the like, are often very open. The **blind self** consists of those aspects of yourself that others know but you don't know yourself. You may not be aware that you come across as overly aggressive or critical, but others know this. The **hidden self** is known to you but not to others. This area represents those aspects of yourself that you intentionally keep to yourself. Perhaps you did something cruel to a person or animal when you were young that you choose not to reveal to others. Finally, the **unknown self** is the part of you that neither you nor those around you know. You might be terrified of scuba diving deep underwater, but if you have not had the experience, you might not be aware of this reaction. You may want children but may not realize it at this point in your

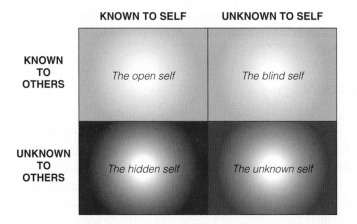

Figure 3.1

The Johari Window

The Johari Window illustrates that, by revealing different degrees of who we are to ourselves and to others, we constantly create different versions of ourselves.

KNOWN TO SELF   UNKNOWN TO SELF

KNOWN TO OTHERS   *The open self*   *The blind self*

UNKNOWN TO OTHERS   *The hidden self*   *The unknown self*

life because the idea may simply not be very relevant. However, once you experience something in the unknown self, it moves to either the hidden self or the open self.

People vary considerably in their self-disclosure. Some people disclose very little, regardless of the person with whom they are communicating. Others seem to disclose almost everything. In the Test Your Self-Disclosure box, you can assess your level of self-disclosure. Take a moment and complete the self-test before continuing.

An important part of any communication situation is to determine the appropriate type of disclosure for the situation. Not only does this depend on how open or private you are as a person but it also depends on the characteristics of the disclosure itself.

Dimensions of Self-Disclosure

Information about the self is not simply there or not there in a message. The process of self-disclosure is more like a faucet than a light switch. With the typical light switch, the light is either on or off. But with a faucet, we can vary temperature, pressure, direction, amount, and so forth. So it is with self-disclosure. There are several dimensions along which information about the self varies. In particular, we alter our messages about the self in terms of breadth, depth, valence, reciprocity, and relevance.

The vast number of topics we may choose to disclose about ourselves is referred to as the **breadth** of disclosure. People may disclose information about their hobbies, family background, religious beliefs, political beliefs, romantic history, fears, hopes, and so on. Some people like to disclose a lot about some relatively specific aspect of their life, such as their exercise regimen or their current romantic relationship but choose not to talk about their family or their religion. Others may disclose less about more areas of their lives.

Depth of self-disclosure is the importance and relevance of information to our core sense of self. Whether you want to get married may be a fairly superficial piece of information. Disclosing the type of person you want to marry may be more personal and central to your conception of self. At the deepest levels might be types of information such as the meaning of marriage in your life, including your image of your parents' marriage, your fears about marriage, and your dreams of happiness in a marital relationship. The closer the information to your most intimate sense of who you are, the deeper the disclosure.

Controlling the depth of disclosure is only one way in which we are selective about disclosing information. Another way is by controlling the positive or negative implications of the information we disclose. **Valence,** derived from the same root as *value,* represents whether a disclosure casts the disclosing person in a positive or negative light. Because

Test ✓ Your
Self-Disclosure

INSTRUCTIONS: Some of us are very open people. Some of us are very private. Several situations in which you might find yourself communicating are described. The five columns list people with whom you might be communicating in each situation. Using a scale from 0 to 2, where 0 is "I would never disclose something of a private or personal nature," 1 is "I would occasionally disclose something of a private or personal nature," and 2 is "I would usually disclose something of a private or personal nature," rate how you would self-disclose according to each situation and audience.

SITUATION	AUDIENCE				
	BEST FRIEND	RECENT ACQUAINTANCE	ROMANTIC PARTNER	FAMILY MEMBERS	COMPLETE STRANGERS
1. In your dorm or apartment					
2. Over lunch in a restaurant					
3. In a classroom before lecture					
4. In a study group					
5. In a speech to a volunteer group					
6. In a job interview					
7. On a long airplane trip					

Generally, a person who discloses everything to anyone (one who answered almost all 2s here) is viewed with caution and distrust. If this person has no sense of privacy, perhaps he or she also has no sense of secrecy and would tell others anything you reveal about yourself. We often have a negative image of the person who is always talking about himself or herself. We may not trust a person such as this because his or her motives seem self-serving.

Although you generally don't disclose everything to anyone (if you scored all 1s here), consider a phenomenon known as the "stranger on the plane." On a plane, train, or bus you don't expect to see the person sitting next to you again, and so you may feel little risk in disclosing personal information. However, in most situations, if you think you may encounter a person again, you are concerned with what he or she might think of you or do with the information you disclose. In contrast, people who never disclose almost all 0's here) are often viewed with distrust, but for another reason. Trust implies that we know what a person will do. If a person doesn't disclose anything to us, we may find it difficult to know this person and, thus, difficult to trust.

people generally want to be viewed as attractive, they tend to disclose information that enhances their valence rather than detracts from it. Thus when negative information is disclosed, it tends to carry more weight in our impressions of others.

Another selective aspect of disclosure is **reciprocity,** the degree to which the communicators match each other's levels of disclosure. In early stages of relationships, whether between friends, romantic partners, or colleagues, disclosure tends to be highly reciprocal. People tend to disclose at similar rates and similar levels of breadth and depth as others disclose to them. This helps regulate the appropriate unfolding of interpersonal knowledge and understanding. If you disclose your life's story on a first date, but your date discloses virtually nothing to you, you may feel disappointed because you took risks and engaged in trusting behavior whereas your date didn't.

Finally, self-disclosure varies in how closely related the information is to the topic being discussed, or its **relevance.** If during your first date you have just finished talking about your hobbies and your date starts disclosing his or her most embarrassing moment in high school, it would probably seem like an overly abrupt shift of topics. Not only do irrelevant disclosures knock the conversation off track when you make them but, if you make them, you may appear as though you aren't listening or simply aren't sensitive to the other person's concerns.

The dimensions of self-disclosure reveal that letting others get to know us is very complex. Even so, self-disclosure represents a relatively small proportion of our total daily communication with others (Duck, 1994). However, its significance is not in the frequency with which we disclose, but in the depth, breadth, valence, reciprocity, and relevance of our disclosures. The more competently we disclose, the more comfortable people will be opening up to us, and the more satisfying the progress of the ongoing interaction is likely to be. In short, the better we are at letting others understand us, the better we become at understanding others and ourselves.

Challenges to Perception and Self

learning link

What are the main challenges to perception?

• • •

In an old *Peanuts* cartoon, Lucy asks Linus what he wants to be when he grows up. Linus simply replies, "Outrageously happy." Ultimately, people want to live lives that are meaningful and bring them joy. The challenge to creating meaningful lives depends, in part, on how we perceive others and express the self to others. Three choices can be particularly challenging: (1) how to manage perceptions and disclosures, (2) how to develop complete and more accurate perceptions, and (3) how to change the self for the better.

Which perception is most important at a particular moment? For example, when meeting a person for the first time, is it most useful to perceive the person as a potential date, a business partner, or a friend? What information is useful to disclose to this person? The answer will depend on the person you are talking to and the situation. What and how much you disclose will affect your competence.

The second challenge is to develop rich and detailed perceptions. People have a tendency to form judgments that are not only based on limited information but also reflect certain biases. For example, the fundamental attribution error suggests that we tend to attribute our success to external factors and we attribute others' success or failure to internal factors. One of the key challenges to forming rich, detailed, and accurate perceptions is to guard against such biases.

Third, how do we manage to develop our self? As the theory of the postmodern self suggests, the self is adaptable—it can change and grow. In what direction do we wish to grow and develop? Significant others play an important role in the development of the self. Yet it is important to be proactive in developing the self and not let others dictate who we are to become.

Managing the Challenges to Perception and Self

Three possible strategies can help you manage these challenges: (1) using multiple perspectives to create descriptions of situations and people, (2) anticipating the consequences of perceptions and disclosures, and (3) envisioning the future.

Using Multiple Perspectives to Create Descriptions

We all tend to have certain prejudices that shape the way we perceive people and events. One way to develop a richly detailed perception of a person or situation is to challenge our prejudices and view a person or an event from a variety of different perspectives.

First, slow down the perception process and explore other ways to interpret the person's actions or the event. This may mean delaying or suspending a judgment until later. Ask yourself a variation of the simple question why (Senge, Kleiner, Roberts, Ross, & Smith, 1994). If you ask this question five times before forming an impression, you can begin to unpack the reasoning and assumptions you used to make this inference. Consider the following example:

I perceive this person as lazy.	Why?
Because he or she didn't turn in his or her assignment on time.	Why?
Because he or she doesn't know how to manage his or her time well.	Why?
Probably no one has told him or her how to manage his or her time well.	Why?
Because the high school he or she attended probably didn't assign homework.	Why?

Asking why helps develop an understanding of the assumptions we use to make inferences. Perhaps the professor associates turning in an assignment late with a lack of time-management skills and infers that these skills have not been developed because the student was not assigned homework in previous educational experiences. Having explored this chain of reasoning, the professor might approach the student differently by asking, "What led you to turn in the assignment late?"

Another way to slow down the perception process is to step outside your frame of reference and explore your perceptions of people and events from different points of view. For example, the professor might explore how the tardy assignment situation feels from the student's standpoint. The professor might imagine how other colleagues as well as other students might view this situation.

Anticipate Consequences

Suppose a person in a romantic relationship has a history of infidelity and feels that, for the present relationship to work, he or she must come clean and be honest with his or her new partner. Should this person disclose information about his or her relational history? To answer this question, the person would need to consider the short-term consequences

One way to create useful impressions is to challenge any pre-existing prejudices we may hold. What are the prejudices you may hold of people who are from different countries or have differing religious beliefs?

of the disclosure. He or she might attempt to answer the following questions: "Is my partner ready for this type of disclosure? What will my partner do with this information? Will he or she break off the relationship or let it continue?" The person should also consider the long-term consequences of this disclosure: "Will this disclosure strengthen our relationship over time? By being open and honest, can we build a trusting relationship, or will the disclosure make me untrustworthy in the eyes of my partner?" Many times there are no clear-cut answers to these types of questions. However, by thinking through the consequences of the disclosure, you can gain a better sense of whether it will help or hurt the development of positive relationships.

Envision the Future

As you assess your behaviors, attitudes, and values, you may realize that you are acting in ways that aren't as effective or appropriate as possible. How can you best change your behaviors, attitudes, and values? Two strategies are useful.

First, focus on what you have done well in the past as well as on what you are currently doing well. By focusing on your successes instead of your problems, you can more quickly accomplish the results you desire (Cooperrider & Whitney, 1999). For example, golfers such as Tiger Woods or Annika Sorenstam are able to ignore hostile crowds, challenging weather conditions, and their competition. They focus their energy on accomplishing the task—striking the golf ball cleanly. Similarly, when people are depressed or anxious about their communication ability, they can lessen these feelings by focusing on situations where they have succeeded in not being depressed and anxious.

A second strategy for changing the self is to set reasonable goals for change. If you make small changes in your behavior, these changes accumulate over time and yield bigger results (Wheatley, 1994). For example, say that you want to become friendlier and perceived as more sociable by others. To accomplish this you might set a goal of greeting everyone with a smile. Over time, these seemingly insignificant changes in your behavior may result in a positive story about your friendliness among your friends and acquaintances.

To set reasonable goals, consider the following guidelines:

1. Identify small changes that can lead to big results if carried through over time.
2. Specify concrete behaviors that are within your control to perform.
3. Know the contexts in which these behaviors need to be performed.
4. Determine the standards you will use to measure whether you have performed the behaviors well.

By exploring the multiple perspectives of people, events, and situations and anticipating the consequences of your actions, you can begin to develop ways of acting that allow you to achieve desirable goals.

Chapter Summary

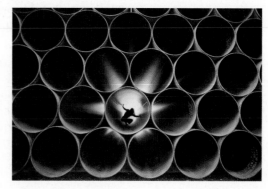

Perception is a process of noticing, organizing, and interpreting data about people, events, activities, and situations. Our ability to notice bits of data is directly influenced by how mindful we are within situations, the kinds of expectations and self-fulfilling prophecies we create for situations, and the way we use language. The way we organize the data depends on the kinds of cognitive schemas such as prototypes, stereotypes, and scripts we use. When we interpret data and form impressions, we must be aware of the role that our first impressions play in creating perceptions and how we go about making attributions of whether particular behaviors are internally or externally motivated.

Our interpretations of people, events, activities, and situations influence how we choose to respond in situations and regulate our behavior. Different people interpret events differently. Understanding the root causes of perceptual differences can facilitate our understanding and avoid miscommunication and conflicts.

One of the major reasons we have different perceptions of people and events is that our perception is influenced by culture. Cultures differ according to a number of dimensions, such as individualism–collectivism, and the differences affect how we perceive situations and the kinds of attributions we make regarding people's behavior.

A person's unique self-concept also influences perception. As we interact with people and groups that influence our lives—significant and generalized others—we begin to form our personal identity. Contemporary thought highlights the notion of a postmodern self—an idea that we have multiple selves and who we become, our identity, changes according to whom we are talking to in particular situations.

Our self-concept not only influences the way we perceive situations but also what information we disclose to others. As the Johari Window illustrates, in any situation parts of our self are open to others such as the open and blind self, and parts of our self are not open to others, such as the hidden and unknown self. The degree to which we choose to self-disclose depends on the dimensions of breadth, depth, valence, reciprocity, and relevance.

The primary challenge to perception is finding ways to manage our perceptions so that we can grow and develop personally. Three strategies can foster an ability to grow and develop: (1) using multiple perspectives to create descriptions, (2) anticipating consequences, and (3) envisioning the future.

Study and Review

The premium companion website for *Human Communication* offers a broad range of resources that will help you better understand the material in this chapter, complete assignments, and succeed on tests. The website resources include

- Interactive self-assessments, competency grids, and other tools
- Web links, practice activities, self-quizzes, and a sample final exam

For more information about this text's electronic learning resources, consult the *Guide to Online Resources for Human Communication* or visit **http://communication .wadsworth.com/morreale2.**

 **Key Terms** _____

The key terms below are defined in the chapter on the pages indicated. They are also presented alphabetically with definitions in the Glossary, which begins on page 467. The book's website includes flashcards and crossword puzzles to help you learn these terms and the concepts they represent.

perception 56
mindfulness 56
self-fulfilling prophecy 56
linguistic tyranny 57
schema 58
prototype 58
stereotype 58
allness 58
script 59
implicit personality theory 60
first impression bias 60
attribution theory 60
principle of consistency 60
principle of distinctiveness 61
principle of locus 61
principle of controllability 61
fundamental attribution error 61
self-serving bias 61
individualistic culture 63
collectivist culture 64
social self 65

looking-glass self 65
generalized other 65
significant other 65
significant symbol 66
role taking 66
self-talk 66
modern self 66
postmodern self 66
multiple self 67
self-disclosure 69
Johari Window 69
open self 69
blind self 69
hidden self 69
unknown self 69
breadth 70
depth 70
valence 70
reciprocity 72
relevance 72

 Building Motivation _____

This self-assessment resource begins on page 81. An interactive version of it is also available on the book's website.

 Building Knowledge _____

The questions below are among the practice activities on the book's website.

1. What is the role of perception in understanding people and situations? How do you see the relationships among noticing, organizing, and interpreting data about people and events? Does noticing influence how we organize data or vice versa? Do the interpretations we draw about people and events at one time influence what we notice at a later time?

2. In what kinds of situations are people more likely to become mindful of their surroundings?

3. What is first impression bias? How might a competent communicator guard against first impression bias?

4. Think of a recent argument you had with someone. How might the attribution theory principles of consistency, distinctiveness, locus, and controllability help explain the positions that were taken?

5. Consider the last time your romantic relationship with someone broke up. In what ways did the fundamental attribution error play a role in how you interpreted why the relationship ended?

6. What communication challenges might people who have a strong individualistic orientation face if they accept a job with a company that moves them to a foreign country with a highly collectivist culture?

7. Do you think there is a single self or multiple selves? Why? What influences how you create and present yourself?

 ## Building Skills _____

The exercises below are among the practice activities on the book's website.

Individual Exercises

1. How well do you know yourself? Review the following scenarios. Put yourself in each situation described and then answer the following questions.

   Situation A: Your best friend tells you that he or she is having an affair and then asks you not to tell his or her spouse about it, even though you consider yourself a close friend to the spouse as well. What do you do?

   Situation B: A friend and classmate asks if you want to study the answers he purchased from someone who stole them for the upcoming examination. How do you answer?

   Situation C: Someone you are really attracted to has just asked you out to a social event, but you had already agreed to do something with a friend that evening. How do you answer?

   Situation D: You are purchasing an item that costs $5, for which you gave the cashier a $10 bill. The cashier apparently thought you presented a $20 bill, and you get $10 more back than you should have. Do you call the mistake to the cashier's attention? Why or why not?

   Situation E: You have been waiting in line for 35 minutes to get tickets to a hot concert and three people cut in front of you when they see someone they know in line two people ahead of you. What do you do?

   Reflect on how easy or difficult it was to respond to the situations. What role did your self-concept play in your responses? What role did others' possible impressions of your behavior play in your responses?

2. Return to the situations in question 1, and predict what a good friend of yours would do. Is it easier to predict your behavior or your friend's? Why? Who looks better in their responses to the situations, yourself or your friend? Review the implicit personality theory and fundamental-attribution-error principle covered in this chapter. How might they account for your responses to this question?

3. On a blank sheet of paper, describe your best friend. Next, review what you have written to see if there is anything you would add or change. Go through your

description very carefully; looking for any constructs you have used to describe your friend. Remember, a construct is any dimension along which you understand the concept of "friend." Thus if you described your friend as thin, tall, dark-haired, and attractive, these all represent a single construct of "physical characteristics." Count the number of constructs you use to understand the concept of your best friend. How well do these constructs describe friendship? What constructs might you include if you wanted to describe friendship more completely? How might a simpler or smaller set of constructs result in different behavior with your friend than a more complex or larger set of constructs?

4. Using InfoTrac College Edition, look up articles that have appeared within the last five years with the term *personal identity* in the title. Using the titles and abstracts as guides, make a list of those factors that influence people's personal identity.

5. Briefly describe your most prominent impressions of yourself using each of the following areas:
   Personality
   Physical characteristics
   Morality
   Activities or hobbies
   Career (or career objectives)
   Intelligence
   Select a parent (or parent figure), best friend, present or former romantic partner, professor, and the student sitting next to you in some class. Ask these people to answer the same question about yourself (such as "How would you describe my key or most prominent characteristic in terms of the following concepts?"). To what extent did these people mention the same things? To what do you attribute their similarities or differences to each other's and to your own answers?

Group Activities

1. Pair off with another person. Each person in your dyad should write down a common emotion or adjective on each of 5 separate note cards, such as happy, sad, boring, angry, intelligent, and so on. Collect the 10 cards and shuffle them. Each person should select a card without revealing the card to the other person. Have a conversation with each person acting in ways that are consistent with the emotion or adjective provided on the card. After the conversation, each person should guess the emotion or adjective the other person is acting out. After guessing, reveal the emotions that were being performed. Discuss what cues were used to make judgments about the emotions performed. How accurate were the guesses? Discuss what principles of perception might have influenced your abilities to assess each other's emotion.

2. Form a group of four to five people. Each group member should write a brief personal advertisement describing themselves to prospective dates and then share the personal advertisement with the group. Each person should answer the following questions: "Why did you decide to feature certain aspects of yourself and not others?" "How did the 'other' in the form of the prospective date influence how you wrote the advertisement?" Compare each group member's answers.

3. Form a group of four to five people and locate the website for Kids in Crisis (**http://www.geocities.com/Heartland/Bluffs/5400**), which focuses on challenges children and teenagers face in daily living. As you examine the website, list

all the challenges that youth face as they are developing their personal identity. What challenges do you perceive as significant that are not included on the website? Why are these challenges significant? What suggestions does the website offer for developing a healthy self-concept?

 References _____

Abelson, R. (1976). Script processing in attitude formation and decision-making. In J. S. Carroll & J. N. Payne (Eds.), *Cognition and social behavior* (pp. 33–45). Hillsdale, NJ: Erlbaum.

Braithwaite, D. O., & Braithwaite, C. A. (2003). "Which is my good leg?" Cultural communication of persons with disabilities. In L. A. Samovar & R. E. Porter (Eds.), *Communication between cultures* (4th ed., pp. 165–176). Belmont, CA: Thomson/ Wadsworth.

Burgoon, J. K., Stern, L. A., & Dillman, L. (1995). *Interpersonal adaptation: Dyadic interaction patterns.* Cambridge, UK: Cambridge University Press.

Cooley, C. H. (1922). *Human nature and the social order* (rev. ed.). New York: Scribner's.

Cooperrider, D. L., & Whitney, D. (1999). *Appreciative inquiry.* San Francisco: Berrett-Koehler.

Duck, S. (1994). *Meaningful relationships: Talking, sense, and relating.* Thousand Oaks, CA: Sage.

Eisenberg, E. M., & Riley, P. (2001). In F. M. Jablin & L. L. Putnam (Eds.), *The new handbook of organizational communication* (pp. 291–322). Thousand Oaks, CA: Sage.

Elfenbein, H. A., & Ambady, N. (2003). Universals and cultural differences in recognizing emotions. *Current Directions in Psychological Science, 12,* 159–164.

Gergen, K. K. (1991). *The saturated self: Dilemmas of identity in contemporary life.* New York: Basic Books.

Giddens, A. (1991). *The consequences of modernity.* Stanford, CA: Stanford University Press.

Gudykunst, W. B. (1998). *Bridging differences: Effective intergroup communication* (3rd ed.). Thousand Oaks, CA: Sage.

Haslett, B. B., & Ruebush, J. (1999). What differences do individual differences in groups make? In L. R. Frey, D. S. Gouran, & M. S. Poole (Eds.), *The handbook of group communication theory and research* (pp. 115–138). Thousand Oaks, CA: Sage.

Hofstede, G. (1980). *Culture's consequences.* Beverly Hills, CA: Sage.

Hofstede, G. (2001). *Culture's consequences: Comparing values, behaviors, institutions, and organizations across nations.* Thousand Oaks, CA: Sage.

Hofstede, G. (2004). Business cultures. In F. E. Jandt (Ed.), *Intercultural communication* (pp. 8–12). Thousand Oaks, CA: Sage.

Hollenbeck, G. P., & Hall, D. T. (2004). Self-confidence and leader performance. *Organizational Dynamics, 33,* 254–269.

Hooker, J. (2003). *Working across cultures.* Stanford, CA: Stanford Business Books.

Jones, E. E., & Nisbett, R. E. (1971). The actor and the observer: Divergent perceptions of the causes of behavior. In E. E. Jones & R. E. Nisbett (Eds.), *Attribution: Perceiving the causes of behavior* (pp. 70–94). Morristown, NJ: General Learning Press.

Judge, T. A., & Higgins, C. A., & Cable, D. M. (2000). The employment interview: A review of recent research and recommendations for future research. *Human Resource Management Review, 10,* 383–406.

Langer, E. J. (1997). *The power of mindful learning.* Cambridge, MA: Perseus Books.

Lim, T. (2002). Language and verbal communication across cultures. In W. B. Gudykunst, & B. Mody (Eds.), *Handbook of international and intercultural communication* (2nd ed., pp. 69–88). Thousand Oaks, CA: Sage.

Luft, J. (1969). *Of human interaction.* Palo Alto, CA: National Press Books.

Lustig, M. W., & Koester, J. (1999). *Intercultural competence: Interpersonal communication across culture* (3rd ed.). New York: Longman.

McMillen, C., Zuravin, S., & Rideout, G. (1995). Perceived benefit from child sexual abuse. *Journal of Consulting and Clinical Psychology, 63,* 1037–1043.

Mead, G. H. (1934). *Mind, self, and society.* Chicago: University of Chicago Press.

Nisbett, R., & Ross, L. (1980). *Human inference: Strategies and shortcomings of social judgment.* Englewood Cliffs, NJ: Prentice-Hall.

Pavitt, C., & Haight, L. (1985). The "competent communicator" as a cognitive prototype. *Human Communication Research, 12,* 225–241.

Pearce, W. B. (1994). *Interpersonal communication: Making social worlds.* New York: HarperCollins.

Pearce, W. B., & Littlejohn, S. W. (1998). *Moral conflict: When social worlds collide.* Thousand Oaks, CA: Sage.

Rosenberg, S., & Gara, M. A. (1985). The multiplicity of personal identity. In P. Shaver (Ed.), *Self, situations, and social behavior* (pp. 87–114). Beverly Hills, CA: Sage.

Samovar, L. A., & Porter, R. E. (2003). Understanding intercultural communication: An introduction and overview. In L. A. Samovar & R. E. Porter (Eds.), *Intercultural communication: A reader* (10th ed., pp. 6–17). Belmont, CA: Thomson/Wadsworth.

Seibold, D. R., & Spitzberg, B. H. (1982). Attribution theory and research: Review and implications for communication. In B. Dervin & M. J. Voight (Eds.), *Progress in communication sciences* (Vol. 3, pp. 85–126). Norwood, NJ: Ablex.

Senge, P. M., Kleiner, A., Roberts, C., Ross, R. B., & Smith, B. J. (1994). *The fifth discipline fieldbook.* New York: Currency Doubleday.

Spitzberg, B. H. (2001). The status of attribution theory qua theory in personal relationships. In V. Manusov & J. H. Harvey (Eds.), *Attribution, communication behavior, and close relationships* (pp. 353–371). Cambridge, UK: Cambridge University Press.

Stephan, C. W., & Stephan, W. G. (2002). Cognition and affect in cross-cultural relations. In W. B. Gudykunst, & B. Mody (Eds.), *Handbook of international and intercultural communication* (2nd ed., pp. 127–142). Thousand Oaks, CA: Sage.

Wegner, D. M., & Vallacher, R. R. (1977). *Implicit psychology: An introduction to social cognition.* New York: Oxford University Press.

Wheatley, M. J. (1994). *Leadership and the new science.* San Francisco: Berrett-Koehler.

Wood, J. T., & Reich, N. M. (2003). Gendered speech communities. In L. A. Samovar & R. E. Porter (Eds.), *Communication between cultures* (4th ed., pp. 144–154). Belmont, CA: Thomson/Wadsworth.

Zurcher, L. A., Jr. (1977). *The mutable self: A self-concept for social change.* Beverly Hills, CA: Sage.

Building Motivation _____

Self-Assessment: Indicate the degree to which you agree or disagree with the following statements, using the following scale:

Scale		
0 = Disagree (D)	1 = Neutral (N); neither agree nor disagree	2 = Agree (A)

BELIEFS ABOUT SELF

D	N	A	
0	1	2	**1.** I must be loved by others to like myself.
0	1	2	**2.** If I am anything less than perfect, I am not worthwhile.
0	1	2	**3.** If I do something wrong, I deserve the blame for it, regardless of why.
0	1	2	**4.** I have no control over my happiness or unhappiness.
0	1	2	**5.** I worry about how things might go wrong.
0	1	2	**6.** I prefer to avoid difficult situations rather than face them.
0	1	2	**7.** I prefer to find someone stronger than myself to rely on.
0	1	2	**8.** My present is entirely a product of my past.
0	1	2	**9.** For all communication problems there is a single correct or best solution.
0	1	2	**10.** If I think I might make a mistake, I choose not to do something.

TOTAL SCORE:

BELIEFS ABOUT OTHERS

D	N	A	
0	1	2	**11.** I often worry about what others will think of me.
0	1	2	**12.** I think others are watching me to find fault with me.
0	1	2	**13.** When others criticize me I feel terrible for a long time afterward.
0	1	2	**14.** I am nervous when I have to perform a complicated task in front of others.
0	1	2	**15.** When in a group situation, I focus on how the other members view me.
0	1	2	**16.** I am constantly thinking about what kind of impression I am making.
0	1	2	**17.** I would be more outgoing if I weren't so worried about what others think of me.
0	1	2	**18.** Even when I know they can't make a difference, I am anxious about others' opinions of me.
0	1	2	**19.** Other people's impressions of me make more of a difference than my own impression of myself.
0	1	2	**20.** When in social situations, I can't help but wonder what others are thinking of me.

TOTAL SCORE:

FEELINGS

D	N	A	
0	1	2	**21.** I get nervous in a new social situation.
0	1	2	**22.** I am anxious when meeting new people.
0	1	2	**23.** I worry about making a fool of myself when I have to speak in public.
0	1	2	**24.** I am nervous in group situations.
0	1	2	**25.** I can't seem to relax when I have to make a good impression on others.
0	1	2	**26.** I lack confidence in public speaking situations.
0	1	2	**27.** I am generally afraid to speak up in group meetings.
0	1	2	**28.** I get tense when I'm about to introduce myself to someone.
0	1	2	**29.** I can't stop shaking when I communicate in public.
0	1	2	**30.** I am nervous when conversing with someone for the first time.

TOTAL SCORE:

Interpreting Your Scores: The statements here are divided into sections—"Beliefs about Self," "Beliefs about Others," and "Feelings." Total the scores for each section.

"Beliefs about Self" refer to beliefs you may have that create unrealistic expectations for yourself. The more irrational beliefs you have about yourself, the more difficult it is for you to develop a competent self in interacting and communicating with others. The score for this section ranges between 0 and 20. A score of 15 or greater indicates that you agree with half or more of these beliefs, and you should examine the reason you perceive yourself and the situations you face in these ways.

The "Beliefs about Others" score reflects the extent to which you fear others' opinions and attitudes. The more concerned you are about others' evaluations, the more anxious you will be and the less competence and confidence you will be able to display in interactions with others. The score for this section varies between 0 and 20 and any score of 15 or greater indicates that you are overly concerned with what others think. If you have scored above 15, reexamine why your opinion of yourself depends so much on others' opinions.

Finally, the "Feelings" section measures your anxiety level in communication situations. To the extent that you score 15 or greater, you perceive communication situations as threatening. If so, pay close attention to the motivation chapters throughout this textbook, and perhaps talk to your instructor to see if there are classes in the curriculum devoted to students with communication anxiety.

LEARNING OBJECTIVES | After studying this chapter, you should be able to

1. Describe language and its nature.

2. Explain the arbitrary nature and meaning of symbols.

3. Clarify the two roles of rules in language.

4. Outline the importance of language and its three functions.

5. Identify challenges to language and how to overcome them.

Language

Ernesto is enrolled in an introductory communication course. Before each class, the communication professor e-mails a discussion question to all the students and has them post their responses on the class website. Ernesto downloads the following message on Monday evening when he opens his mailbox:

Date: 3 October 05 09:12:18 AM
From: Professor Bateux <bateux@univ.edu>
Subj: Assignment for October 5, 2005
To: Comm 101 <comm101@univ.edu>

Please consider the following question on language for Wednesday's class discussion: how can language marginalize certain groups of people and perpetuate their minority status? Please send me your responses by Tuesday night no later than 9 p.m.

Ernesto scratches his head and asks himself, "What in the world is Professor Bateux asking for?" He calls one of his classmates for assistance.

"Sylvia? Hi, this is Ernesto. Did you get the discussion question from Professor Bateux?"

"Yeah, I did. It looks pretty easy."

"Easy? I didn't see it that way. What did you write about?"

"What I said is that sometimes minority groups like African Americans, Hispanics, or gays and lesbians develop their own jargon and use it to talk among themselves. Because they are the only ones who use the language, they set themselves up as different and exclude others from participating in their discussion. I mean, if you don't know the slang, how can you talk with them?"

"So you think when the professor uses the term *minority* he means a minority like an ethnic group?"

"Of course. Isn't it obvious?"

"I don't know, Sylvia. In my psychology class we talked about 'minority opinion.' That's when a small number of people in a large group have opinions different from the majority of the group. I think Professor Bateux wants us to talk about how people who are in the minority according to their opinions use language—not ethnic minorities."

"Well, go ahead and send your answer in—but I think you're going down the wrong track."

In the next class, Ernesto and Sylvia sit together, anxious to find out who's right. Professor Bateux opens the lecture by saying, "What really pleased me was how each of you picked up on the notion that there are multiple meanings for the term *minority*. So let's start there and discuss how you all used the term *minority*." Ernesto and Sylvia looked at each other in confusion. Why wasn't the professor going to give them the correct definition and meaning of *minority*? ■

How we make sense of the meaning of words influences how we respond to others in conversation. Until Ernesto could grasp what the word *minority* meant to him he was unable to formulate a response to the professor's question.

Making sense of the words people use during conversation can be difficult because of the complexity of language. Words mean different things to different people. For Sylvia, *minority* referred to a minority status based on ethnicity, religion, or sexual orientation. For Ernesto, *minority* referred to a small group of people with a set of opinions different from those of the majority group. Both meanings are entirely appropriate depending on the context. When talking about race relations within the United States, *minority* may take on the meaning associated with race, ethnicity, or religion. When talking about decision making in organizational work teams, *minority* may be more closely associated with a difference of opinion. The meaning of words and language is fluid and changes depending on the situation.

This chapter focuses on the complex nature of language and the challenges it presents. Competent communicators recognize that words take on different meanings depending on how they are used in specific contexts, as well as on who utters them. Competent communicators are able to spot the unique meaning of a word as it is being used in a particular situation and determine the most appropriate and effective use of language to respond.

What Is Language?

Language is a complex phenomenon whose meaning depends on where and when it is used. But this does not prevent us from making decisions about what people mean given the language they use or anticipating the possible effects our language has on others. As Chapter 1 discusses, **language** is a verbal symbol system that allows us to take messages and utterances, in the form of words, and translate them into meaning. Competent communicators need to understand the rules and resources that people use to interpret the meaning of words and anticipate the consequences of their words on others.

Language Is a System of Symbols

A **symbol** is a sign or word used to define a person, idea, or object. The symbols we use every day in speech are arbitrary—they are not inherently connected to the things they represent. We could just as easily call your cell phone a communicator; however, we have arbitrarily decided to call this piece of wireless technology a cell phone. In their classic model called the semantic triangle, Ogden and Richards (1946) suggest that human beings have thoughts, or what they call **references,** about the object they observe. They called the actual objects people perceive **referents** and viewed referents as having a direct relationship with thoughts. They also argued that thoughts have a direct **relationship** with the symbols that people use to represent their thoughts. Referents and symbols, however, are indirectly connected. For example, in Figure 4.1, the top of the triangle represents the thoughts you might have about a referent, in this case a bear. You think of the bear as ferocious and strong, and your thoughts are directly connected to the symbol "bear." The solid lines between thought and referent and between thought and symbol represent direct connections. The dotted line between symbol and object represents the imputed relationship people make between the two. What this model suggests is that people may have trouble managing meaning because they can use the same word to talk about two different animals, use different words to talk about the same animal, or use the same symbol but have different thoughts about what that symbol means.

Over time, people in a community create a set of agreements that specify the arbitrary relationship between symbols and referents. New speakers entering into the community are socialized into that set of agreements. Part of understanding a language, therefore, is grasping the set of arbitrary connections between symbols and referents. For example, in English-speaking cultures we use the symbol "bear" to describe "any of various usually omnivorous mammals of the family Ursidae, having a shaggy coat and short tail" (*The American Heritage Dictionary,* 2004, p. 123). Depending on the particular culture we belong to and the language we speak, we could easily have developed another word to describe this animal. Arabic speakers call "bear" *dubab;* Danish speakers, *bjorne;* Finnish speakers, *karhu;* Mandarin

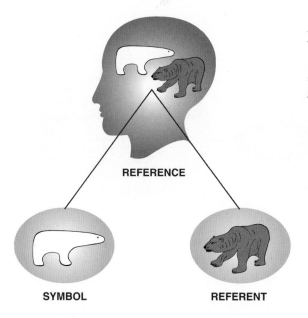

Figure 4.1

The Semantic Triangle

Each person attributes the relationship between symbols and the objects they represent.

REFERENCE

SYMBOL

REFERENT

Chinese speakers, *xíong;* and Spanish speakers, *oso.* Although the relationships between the symbols and referents are arbitrary, competent communicators must learn them if they are to communicate effectively and appropriately.

Learning a language requires more, however, than simply understanding the set of connections among symbols and referents. You need to understand the entire symbol system, which includes the set of relationships among symbols as well. Poststructural philosophers such as Derrida (1978) use the terms **signifier** for symbol and **signified** for referent. If you are to understand what a signifier means, you also need to look at other signifiers associated with it at a specific time and place (Derrida, 1978). If we stopped our understanding of the meaning of the word *bear* with the relationship between the signifier and the signified, we would know only that *bear* is associated with a specific kind of animal. However, much more is associated with *bear*—perceptions, feelings, and attitudes—which we can grasp only if we explore the other words linked to it. Figure 4.2 illustrates how different signifiers associated with *bear* are interrelated. In the English language, the signifier *bear* has become linked with the words *wild animal* and *ferocious.* At the same time, English speakers associate *bear* with the qualities strong and protective because bears often attack humans and other animals if they perceive them as threatening their cubs. Finally, we may also think of endangered species because many types of bears, such as giant pandas and North American grizzlies, are in danger of becoming extinct.

Examining the relationships among signifiers is important because even when people within a community agree on the arbitrary relationship between a signifier and a signified, they each may still hold different meanings for that signifier because they associate it with other, different signifiers. This is the reason people can agree about the denotative meaning of symbols but not their connotative meaning. **Denotative meaning** refers to the dictionary definition of words; for example, the symbol "chair" typically means a seat that has four legs. **Connotative meaning** refers to the personal associations people make for a symbol, and depending on the web of relationships among the signifiers, they may have different meanings.

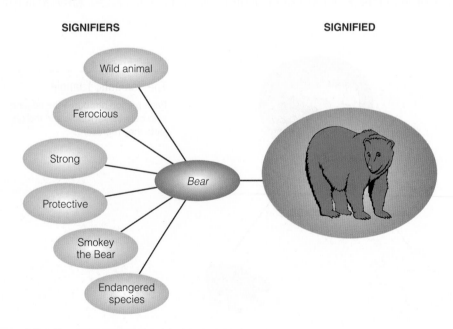

► Figure 4.2

Relationship among Signifiers

The words *wild animal, strong, ferocious, protective,* and *endangered species* are signifiers that may be related to the word we use in English to signify the animal we call a bear. The signifier *bear* takes on slightly different meanings when associated with each of the words *wild animal, strong, ferocious, protective,* and *endangered species.*

SIGNIFIERS

SIGNIFIED

Wild animal

Ferocious

Strong

Protective

Smokey the Bear

Endangered species

Bear

Language Is Guided by Rules

People use **constitutive rules** to help sort out what certain words or phrases mean and **regulative rules** to determine what they should say next in an ongoing conversation (Cronen, 1999).

Constitutive rules take the basic content of the message, its words, and tell us what they mean and how we are to make sense of them. They connect signifiers and signifieds to one another. Consider, for example, the following words and phrases. What do they have in common?

"Hi!"	"What's happening?"
"How are you doing?"	"Haven't seen you in a while."
"Hello!"	"It's good to see you!"

You probably have heard these millions of times and you correctly interpret them as greetings. Whether consciously or unconsciously, you apply constitutive rules to them to determine their meaning and function in conversation. Figure 4.3 shows how constitutive rules help us understand how we interpret and use language when we greet one another. Constitutive rules take the string of words "How are you doing?" and tell us that these words count as a greeting in the context of a greeting situation.

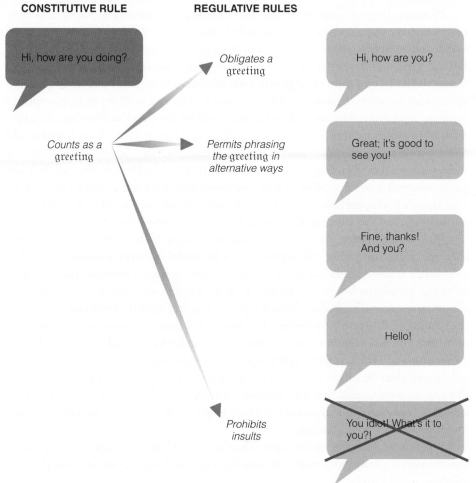

CONSTITUTIVE RULE

Hi, how are you doing?

Counts as a greeting

REGULATIVE RULES

Obligates a greeting

Permits phrasing the greeting in alternative ways

Prohibits insults

Hi, how are you?

Great; it's good to see you!

Fine, thanks! And you?

Hello!

You idiot! What's it to you?!

Figure 4.3

The Rule-Guided Nature of a Greeting

Constitutive rules help us interpret words and phrases; regulative rules guide our response. In this case, the phrase on the left is interpreted as a greeting and four of the five responses on the right are judged as acceptable. The last response is inappropriate because the regulative rule prohibits insults.

Regulative rules help you determine the appropriate response given your interpretation of a message. These rules usually take the form "If X happens, then Y follows." Regulative rules are moral in the sense that they tell you what you should or shouldn't do during an interaction. They create opportunities for action—what we can do—as well as constraints for our actions—what we can't do. Using our previous example, once we have assigned the meaning "greeting" to the words, in most cases regulative rules obligate us to respond with a greeting in kind that we can phrase in a variety of ways. At the same time, we are prohibited from insulting or ignoring the person after the initial greeting.

How Is Language Important?

learning link

What is the difference between constitutive and regulative rules?

• • •

People have traditionally viewed language as important because it is our primary vehicle for getting a point across and expressing thoughts and ideas. This is why effective public speakers such as Colin Powell, Ronald Reagan, Barack Obama, and Maya Angelou devote attention to using vivid and poetic language that makes their points memorable and persuasive. It is also why lawyers use concrete and specific language when writing legal briefs. They want to make sure their reasoning is clear to the judges who will evaluate their case.

However, language does more than make messages memorable or transfer information. Language plays another important role in our lives by helping us create our social worlds and by labeling the meanings we ascribe to people, issues, and events. In the 1950s, Edward Sapir and Benjamin Lee Whorf developed the **Sapir-Whorf hypothesis.** This theory was based on a form of **linguistic determinism,** which means that language determines what we see in the world and how we think. Take the word *key* as an example. In German, *key* is masculine, and when German speakers are asked to describe a key, they tend to use words such as "hard," "heavy," and "jagged." In Spanish, *key* is feminine and Spanish speakers choose words such as "golden," "intricate," and "lovely" when describing a key. German and Spanish speakers see *key* differently as a function of whether their language conceives it as a masculine or feminine phenomenon ("Continental divide," 2002). The Sapir-Whorf hypothesis maintains that reality is already implanted in the structure of our language and this structure determines how we perceive our world.

Many contemporary theorists and researchers take a different approach to the way language creates our reality; this approach is called **social constructionism.** Rather than assume that reality is implanted in the structure of our language, social constructionist theorists and researchers believe that people create their reality, and relationships, in the process of interaction. Think about what happens when you label the emotions you experience during an interaction by saying, "I'm angry!" Labeling your emotion as "anger" not only helps you make sense of your emotions, it also provides you with cues about how to subsequently act. For example, angry people may be expected to show their anger through yelling and attacking others verbally. Angry people may have some latitude to say things in the heat of the moment that they normally wouldn't say. The words and language we choose to characterize our experience not only help us make sense of a situation, they also foreshadow future ways of acting.

Whether we subscribe to the Sapir-Whorf theory of linguistic determinism or social constructionist theory, both emphasize that language and language use are critical to creating our social worlds.

Functions of Language

Language is an active force in our lives that shapes the way we live together as human beings and the kinds of communities in which we live. Language performs three key functions: (1) it makes us notice things, (2) it creates opportunities and limitations for identities and relationships, and (3) it facilitates social coordination.

Language Makes Us Notice Things

Language organizes our perceptions of people, events, and issues and directs our attention to certain aspects of situations. It also informs our understanding of what those aspects mean. Moreover, the words we use to label a situation highlight certain possible actions that are appropriate to take in the future. Words tell us not only how we make sense of a situation (what we view as important) but also how we will act in the future (where we need to go).

Imagine you are a consultant and have been called in by a hotel to solve the problem of guest complaints about slow elevators. What would you recommend? Instead of reducing the long wait time by replacing the elevators' motors with faster ones or installing more elevators, the real consultant in this situation diagnosed it as a "people problem" not a mechanical one and recommended simply placing mirrors on each floor by the elevators (Mitroff, 1978). Although the wait was just as long, the guests stopped complaining because the mirrors gave them something to do as they waited, such as fixing their hair or adjusting their clothing, and the problem was economically solved. Labeling it a mechanical problem would not have led to such a quick and simple solution, which demonstrates the power of language to make us notice certain things more than others.

What does this sign make you notice that you otherwise might not have?

As another example of the ability of language to direct our attention, think about the term **politically correct, or PC, language.** Its proponents argue that we can rid our minds of discriminatory thoughts by removing from our language any words or phrases that could offend people by the way they reference differences and handicaps. Los Angeles County in California asked suppliers to stop using the terms *master* and *slave* on computer equipment, even though these are commonly used terms that refer to primary and secondary hard disk drives, because of cultural sensitivity ("'Master' and 'slave'," 2003). Other substitutions, such as *police officer* for *policeman,* are intended to highlight that such positions are held by both men and women.

Using PC language and being PC have come to be viewed negatively, however, and even lampooned and satirized because they overcompensate for others' sensitivities. One reason that PC language is fairly easy to lampoon is that its political agenda is not always connected to large social and cultural institutions (Fairclough, 2003). For example, it is one thing to say that we need to rid the workplace of sexist language in an effort to create equal relationships between men and women, but unless this directive is connected to a broader agenda of fostering gender pay equity and equal opportunity for promotions and advancement, merely ridding the workplace of sexist language may not generate the hoped-for effect. People now tend to use the label "PC" as a pejorative term to silence critical discussion (Banning, 2004). Critics of using indigenous people as sports team names, for instance, are frequently labeled as "PC" and their concerns are dismissed as overly sensitive (Strong, 2004). Rather than address issues of equity and justice, labeling those who oppose using Indian mascots and logos as "PC" tends to write off their real concerns.

Language Creates Opportunities and Limitations

To understand how language can create opportunities as well as constraints for interaction, take the example of what it means to be "just friends." Let's say you have developed a close relationship with someone. When people ask you about your relationship, you both reply, "We're just friends." If you label your relationship with this person as "just friends," what opportunities does that create for you in terms of what you say to and do with one another? Some of the regulative rules that offer opportunities might look like this:

If we are "just friends," we can talk about our personal lives—including our love lives.

If we are "just friends," we can offer advice and counsel to the other person when he or she is having difficulties.

If we are "just friends," we can do things together such as go to a party or have dinner.

Though the status of "just friends" creates certain opportunities like the ones just listed, it also prohibits certain actions. Some of the regulative rules that impose limitations may look like this:

If we are "just friends," we should not make any sexual advances toward each other.

If we are "just friends," we should not lie to each other.

If we are "just friends," we should not reveal each other's personal confidences to others.

The language we use to characterize our relationship influences what we can say and do with one another as well as what we cannot say and do.

The idea that language creates opportunities and limits possible actions underscores the important role it plays in structuring our communication as well as in shaping our relationships and identities. The patterns of communication you engage in sculpt your identity, and in turn, your identity affects your subsequent communication. We see this connection between communication and identity in two types of language: gender communication and hate speech.

The dominant view connecting language and gender has been labeled the **gender-as-culture hypothesis** or, more recently, the different-cultures thesis (Maltz & Borker, 1982; MacGeorge, Graves, Feng, Gillilahan, & Burleson, 2004). The basic idea underlying the **different-cultures thesis** is that language shapes the way girls and boys perceive themselves as they are socialized into a feminine or masculine culture. Girls and boys receive subtle but different kinds of messages as they grow up:

Parents discuss emotions more with girls than with boys.

Mothers with daughters focus on the daughter's emotional state itself, whereas mothers with sons focus more on causes and consequences of the son's emotional state. For example, if a girl falls down and skins her knee, the mother may ask, "How much does it hurt?" But if a boy gets hurt, she may focus on the action rather than the emotion and ask, "Did you fall down and go boom?"

Parents encourage girls to be more socially oriented.

Girls receive rewards and reinforcements to be nurturing and obedient; boys are pressured to be independent and self-reliant. (Adapted from Guerrero & Reiter, 1998, p. 325)

These messages socialize girls to emphasize building harmonious relationships and being cooperative whereas boys are socialized to be more individualistic, focused on the self, assertive, and more competitive (Eagly & Koenig, in press).

This initial set of socializing experiences creates gender roles that move women and men toward certain patterns of language use. Women and men are believed to share a common vocabulary but to use that vocabulary in stylistically different ways (Mulac, in press). For example, some researchers have found that (1) men use more direct language styles using directive statements ("Write that down") whereas women are more indirect and tend to use uncertainty verbs ("It seems to be . . ."), questions ("What's that?"), and hedges ("kind of"), and (2) men are more succinct in their use of language and use elliptical sentences ("Great posture.") whereas women are more elaborate in their language use and use adverbs that intensify feeling and emotion ("really," "so"), begin sentences with adverbs ("Actually, it's . . ."), and use longer sentences (Mulac, Bradac, & Gibbons, 2001). In general, women use language to gain approval and reinforce intimacy, and men use language to maintain or increase their status and establish independence (Sagrestano, Heavey, & Christensen, 1998). This pattern of language use subsequently reinforces each gender's sense of identity. If women prove successful in using language that creates approval and intimacy, they create and maintain an identity that emphasizes cultivating close personal relationships. Recently, some theorists and researchers have questioned this thesis and suggest that the particular function of communication is what accounts for differences in language use, not gender (MacGeorge et al., 2004).

Whether it is radio shock jocks making racist and sexist remarks, white supremacist groups verbally attacking ethnic minorities, neo-Nazi groups demeaning Jews, Catholics, African Americans, and Hispanics, or rap music artists advocating the killing of cops or the rape and brutalization of women, hate speech has become a part of our social fabric. **Hate speech** has been defined as "speech that (1) has a message of racial inferiority, (2) is directed against a member of a historically oppressed group, and (3) is persecutory, hateful, and degrading" (Nielsen, 2002, p. 266).

Although many people believe freedom of speech is a civil liberty guaranteed by the Constitution, hate speech is viewed negatively and as an exception to the Bill of Rights. One reason is that the effects generated by hate speech are overwhelmingly negative. Hate speech can produce negative emotions in the aggressor, hurt feelings in those targeted, and changes in the victims ranging from psychological to physical, brought on by severe emotional distress. Hate speech solidifies the aggressor's identity by reinforcing hateful attitudes and beliefs and making them almost impossible to overcome. In response, the targets of hate speech internalize a negative image of themselves as individuals and as a group (Calvert, 1997). This relationship is mediated by people's perception of whether a particular hate message is viewed as harmful. European Americans typically perceive racist messages as more harmful than do Asian, African, or Hispanic Americans. However, Asian Americans are more likely to perceive indirect racist speech as more harmful than are

European, African, or Hispanic Americans. These results are due to historically oppressed groups being desensitized to hate messages because they have heard them before and to the role that culture plays in interpreting racist messages (Leets, 2001, 2003).

The murder of James Byrd Jr. highlights the potential consequences of hate speech. Hate speech has the power to shape people's personal identities in ways that perpetuate negative stereotypes and feelings of inferiority for the targeted group.

Racial, sexual, and religious epithets perpetuate an atmosphere of inequality. Moreover, hate speech constructs intolerance—the culture targeted by such language is not viewed as worthy of existence. Hate speech directed at certain groups of people labels them as inferior and deserving of hate crimes directed toward them, justifying the words and actions of the aggressors. It dehumanizes the target in the eyes of the aggressor and incites and justifies violence toward a group of people.

Language has the ability to create opportunities and constraints for interaction. As a result, organizations such as the American Psychological Association have created guidelines for reducing bias in language. The Close-Up on Diversity box has some examples. Competent communicators must make judgments about the consequences of their language use and determine what kinds of identities and relationships are appropriate and effective in different situations.

Language Facilitates Social Coordination

The way you use language can either enhance or hurt your ability to organize your actions and work with others. When you use language that is sexist or racist, you reduce your ability to collaborate with others because people may become offended by your speech and refuse to cooperate. Language that promotes coordination does not insult or demean others or place them in a defensive position. Your ability to work with others also depends on the level of abstraction in your language. Coordinating your actions with others requires you to select language that is appropriately clear and direct for the situation.

One tool for selecting language that is appropriately clear and direct is Hayakawa's Ladder of Abstraction. S. I. Hayakawa (1964), a noted linguist, placed language on a continuum from the very concrete to the more abstract. He devised a **Ladder of Abstraction** on which he placed the most concrete words on the lower rungs and arranged words on higher rungs as they increased in abstraction. Figure 4.4 shows an example. Low-level abstractions or descriptions of concrete phenomena, placed on the lowest rung of the ladder, are the most descriptive and clear because they refer to specific instances and behaviors. The middle rung of the ladder is more abstract because it includes words that draw general inferences about a person or situation based on concrete phenomena. Finally, the highest level includes abstract generalizations about the person, issue, or event that gloss over specific instances.

Looking at Figure 4.4, at the lowest rung and lowest level of abstraction, we see that the concrete description of the behavior is that Madison did not turn in the final term paper on time. On the middle rung of the ladder, an inference is drawn about Madison's behavior in this specific context: "Madison is lazy when it comes to class assignments." At the highest level of abstraction, the inference is generalized across situations and used to label Madison's behavior as lazy in general.

CloseUp on Diversity
Reducing Bias in Language

BEING POLITICALLY CORRECT, OR PC, HAS BEEN described as going to ridiculous lengths to rid language of any potential bias due to gender, sexual orientation, race or ethnicity, disability, or age. Critics of PC language attribute the creation of such new terms as an excess of sensitivity to the feelings of particular classes of people. Yet if language does create identity, then we need to take seriously the notion that the words we use may perpetuate negative stereotypes and demeaning attitudes about certain classes of people.

The *Publication Manual of the American Psychological Association* (2001) provides a guide for avoiding bias in language, consisting of useful suggestions for treating fairly individuals and groups when we write and speak about them. Here are some examples:

1. Describe individuals and groups at an appropriate level of precision: Describing all human beings as *man* or *mankind* is not as precise as using the phrase *men and women*. When describing the sexual orientation of a group of men and women, the term *gay* can be interpreted to refer to men and women or only men. To provide a greater specificity, use the phrase *gay men and lesbians*.

2. Be aware of labels: Classes of people may have preferences for what they prefer to be called, and these preferences change over time. For example, the term *Hispanic* covers a number of nationalities and regions from Central or South America. Using terms such as *Mexican American* or *a person of Colombian descent* may be more specific and appropriate. When in doubt, ask people what designation they prefer.

3. Avoid labeling people: Using labels deprives people of their individuality and objectifies them. When you make statements about the handicapped, the elderly, youth, and so on, your language labels

them in terms of one characteristic they possess, not as individuals. In the case of labels such as *handicapped, mentally retarded,* and so on, this language equates the condition with the person. Strategies to counter the use of labels include placing the descriptive adjective in front of a noun (*handicapped people, elderly man, young woman*) or put the person first and follow with a descriptive phrase (people with AIDS).

4. Avoid using one group as a standard against which others are judged: When you portray one group as superior or normal and use this group as the standard to judge others, your language creates bias and possibly justifies discrimination. The following statements contain some level of judgment that can breed bias:

- When African American student scores are compared to those of the general public . . . (Are African American students not part of the "general" public?)
- The comparison between lesbians and normal women . . . (Are lesbians not "normal"?)
- Women are not as competitive as men . . . (Is being "competitive" a desired characteristic?)

Each of these statements implicitly or explicitly contains an idea that one group sets the standard for other groups. Using words that emphasize difference as opposed to level of sophistication or progress ("Women are different from men . . .") or using a more even-handed comparison ("The comparison between lesbians and heterosexual women . . .") will help reduce this bias.

The following list presents examples of biased language associated with several human characteristics, as well as corresponding examples of unbiased language that are preferred substitutes. This list is based on information found in the *Publication Manual of the American Psychological Association,* 2001, pp. 61–76.

Characteristic	Biased Language	Unbiased Language	Rationale
Gender	man, mankind	people, humanity, human beings, humankind, human species	Use words that explicitly include both genders.
	to man a project	to staff a project, to hire personnel, to employ staff	Specific nouns reduce the possibility of stereotypic bias and often clarify discussion.

Characteristic	Biased Language	Unbiased Language	Rationale
Gender (cont'd)	man–machine interface	user–system interface, person–system interface, human–machine interface	
	manpower	work force, personnel, workers, employees, human resources	
	woman doctor, lady lawyer, male nurse, woman driver	doctor or physician, lawyer, nurse, driver	Specify sex only if it is relevant to the discussion.
Sexual orientation	Most homosexuals feel . . .	Most gay male adolescents feel . . . Most lesbians feel . . .	Avoid a general use of homosexual, and specify gender. Use *gay* to refer to men and *lesbian* to refer to women.
	Some gays think . . .	Some gay men . . . Some lesbians . . .	
	the gay designer, the lesbian mechanic, the homosexual activist	designer, mechanic, activist	Avoid specifying the sexual preference of people where it is irrelevant.
			Avoid lumping all gays and lesbians together.
			As with anybody, many gays and lesbians do not necesarily share the same opinions simply because they are gay or lesbian.
Racial and ethnic identity	black person, Hispanic	African American, Mexican American, Latino/Latina, Nicaraguan, Peruvian	As appropriate, provide additional information about national racial origin.
	American Indian	Choctaw, Hopi, Navajo, Seminole	
	the Jewish lawyer, the African American doctor, the Mexican farm worker	the lawyer, the doctor, farm worker	Avoid noting a person's race, ethnicity, or religion when it's not relevant to the discussion. This can signal a perceived "exception" or a stereotype.
Disabilities	disabled person	person with (who has) a disability	Put people first, not their disability.
	defective child	child with a congenital disability child with a birth impairment	
	mentally ill person	person with mental illness	
	depressives	people who suffer from depression	Avoid equating the person with the disability by separating the two concepts.
	epileptics	individuals with epilepsy	
	AIDS patient	person with AIDS (or HIV), a person who is HIV positive	
	retarded adult	adult with mental retardation	

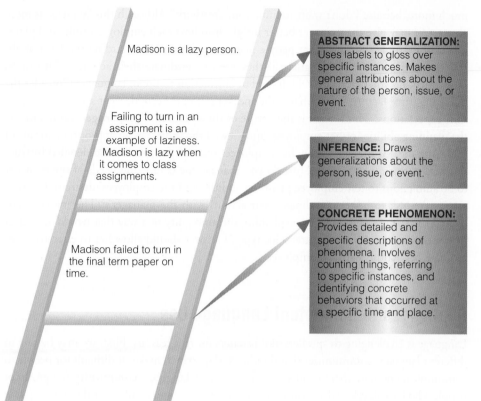

Madison is a lazy person.

ABSTRACT GENERALIZATION: Uses labels to gloss over specific instances. Makes general attributions about the nature of the person, issue, or event.

Failing to turn in an assignment is an example of laziness. Madison is lazy when it comes to class assignments.

INFERENCE: Draws generalizations about the person, issue, or event.

Madison failed to turn in the final term paper on time.

CONCRETE PHENOMENON: Provides detailed and specific descriptions of phenomena. Involves counting things, referring to specific instances, and identifying concrete behaviors that occurred at a specific time and place.

◄ Figure 4.4

Hayakawa's Ladder of Abstraction

The Ladder of Abstraction moves from concrete language, such as "failed to turn in the final term paper on time," on the lowest rung to inferences on the next rung, "Madison is lazy when it comes to class assignments," and abstract generalizations on the top rung, "Madison is a lazy person."

To motivate Madison to improve his performance, you would use language that is low in abstraction and concrete: "You failed to turn in the final term paper by Friday at 5 p.m. when it was due." Stating a problem with concrete language that explicitly describes the performance difficulty clearly indicates the specific actions necessary to remedy this problem. Telling Madison, "You are a lazy person and must stop that," however, is very ambiguous. Madison may not understand what is prompting you to make this assessment or what now needs to be done so as not to be viewed as lazy. In this situation, language at a low level of abstraction is viewed as more accurate and clear, and as a result, it is more effective.

Can we assume that concrete specific language is always the best language to use? Indeed, in some situations using concrete language is very useful in helping people coordinate their actions, such as in the previous example. Using more abstract language is useful in other cases. For example, consider a new manager who wants to test her employees' planning skills. She may ask her employees to develop a written plan for a particular project. The manager could use very concrete and specific language to describe the assignment: "I want you to develop a five-page plan for this proposed project. First, make sure you include an overview of the project in the introduction. Second, I want a section that highlights your analysis of why we have embarked on this project. Third, I want a solutions section in the report. Finally, I want a description of the criteria and benchmarks for assessing the success of your proposed solution." This request uses very concrete and specific language, but does it meet this manager's needs? By outlining the length and format for the project proposal, the manager clearly specifies what she wants, and in doing so, she reduces her chances to assess her employees' planning abilities. She could have made her request more ambiguous: "Please develop a proposal for this project. I don't want to tell you too much more, because I don't want to limit your creativity." Although this language is more abstract, it may give the manager better insight into how each employee thinks and plans.

Our example illustrates that people need to make choices regarding the level of abstraction they use in their language if they are to coordinate their activity with others. How, then, do you determine which level of abstraction to use in language? Consider the following three factors: First, what is the speaker's intent? Second, what are the other person's expectations? Third, what is the nature of the situation? The manager wanted to test the planning abilities of her employees and viewed the project as an appropriate means of achieving this. At the same time, her employees may ask for specific and detailed instructions for performing the task. How do you manage the competing needs of the manager to be ambiguous to test employee planning abilities and the employees' desire to be given a concrete task to better coordinate their actions with the manager's? The manager answered the request ambiguously, explaining the ambiguity in a way that would also meet the employees' need for structure. This type of answer should allow her to effectively coordinate her actions with her employees'.

Challenges to Competent Language Use

Language is challenging to speakers and listeners for two reasons. First, we may belong to different language communities that do not overlap, which makes it difficult for people to communicate because there is no shared language. A **language community** is a group of people who have developed a common set of constitutive and regulative rules, which guide the meaning of words and the appropriate reactions, based on interpreting those words. Even within the same language, such as English, there are many different language communities. Some of these are based on work, gender, religion, race, ethnicity, political affiliation, and so on. Although the language we use may be understandable to others within a particular language community, it may be incomprehensible to those outside—and those people may interpret our language in ways other than we intend. Luckily, our language communities frequently overlap, making it possible for us to communicate with one another. Second, even if there is overlap between language communities, we may interpret language through the filter of those communities that are not shared, resulting in misunderstanding. This is a real challenge to language use because it makes it difficult to predict how other people will interpret your language.

Take, for example, the challenges associated with public participation in determining the appropriate use of public lands. Multiple stakeholders such as developers, home builders, campers and hikers, off-roaders, business owners, and environmentalists have an interest in the way the land is developed. These stakeholders are normally invited to meetings designed to solicit their input and make decisions regarding how the land should be used. However, each stakeholder represents different interests and positions. Land developers may be primarily concerned about building homes and subdivisions and use the language of economic development to further their interest. Campers and hikers may be more concerned with environmental preservation, keeping the land pristine for the use of future generations, than with finding ways to leverage the land for building a stronger local economy.

BIZARRO   By DAN PIRARO

Men and women belong to different language communities.

They use the language of environmental preservation. These stakeholders belong to different language communities and talk about land use in distinct ways. Therefore they may end up talking past each other. As a result, many participation projects now emphasize working with stakeholders to cultivate a common language for all to use (Barge, in press). By developing a common language, participants in such projects can develop a shared focus and better coordinate their actions.

Strategies for Overcoming Challenges to Language

Using language competently requires developing abilities that allow us to make sense of the unique characteristics of a situation and determine the most useful language choices. Such abilities include being sensitive to a situation, the people involved and their expectations, and adjusting our language to fit the situation. Three strategies are very useful in developing these abilities: (1) inviting curiosity about the meaning of words, (2) anticipating possible interpretations before we speak, and (3) trying different phrasing possibilities.

Be Curious about the Meaning of Words

As the *B.C.* cartoon illustrates, different words have different meanings in different contexts. For a musician a *gig* is positive, but for a frog a *gig* means having a metal spike inserted into the brain stem to scramble the brain. We develop personal meanings for words that differ from others' given our unique background and experiences. Yet we sometimes forget this simple fact and assume that others have the same meaning for words. This leads to ethnocentric communication (Pearce, 1989). **Ethnocentric communicators** recognize as valid only their own meanings for words and reject alternative meanings as wrong. When we acknowledge the existence of a number of different, valid meanings for words, in contrast, we become cosmopolitan communicators. **Cosmopolitan communicators** recognize that the meanings they have created for certain words are unique to them and not shared by others. They are curious about the unique meanings other people have for words, and they know that if you have a closed and rigid opinion about the "right" meaning of words, you might miss the distinctive meaning of the other person's message.

A word's meaning depends on context.

The most basic way to invite curiosity is to ask questions. Three types of questions are most useful: clarifying questions, showing questions, and comparing questions. A **clarifying question** invites the other person to elaborate on his or her meaning. Imagine you are in a meeting and one of the group members accuses you of "slacking off." You are shocked because you feel that you have performed at a high level and contributed to the group. If you are curious about your colleague's criticism, you might ask the following kinds of clarifying questions: "What exactly do you mean when you say I am 'slacking off'?" "What do you mean by that?"

Showing questions are based on the idea that meaning is revealed by the way the words are used and the kinds of actions associated with them (Wittgenstein, 1953). Asking showing questions invites the respondent to focus on specific actions or activities they associate with the word. Returning to our meeting example, you might ask questions such as "When I 'slack off,' what does that look like?" "How does my 'slacking off' show itself?" "How might someone outside the group notice that I was 'slacking off'?"

Finally, comparing questions invite the respondent to point to words that are similar in meaning to the word in question as well as to list words that carry different meanings. By understanding how the word or phrase you have in mind differs from other words or phrases, you can begin to gain a better understanding of its meaning. To probe what it means to slack off, you might ask **comparing questions** such as "What other phrases could you use besides 'slacking off' to describe my performance?" "If I weren't 'slacking off,' what would you use to describe my performance?"

By asking questions such as these that come from a genuine curiosity to learn about the other person's point of view, you can begin to fully understand what people mean in their language and avoid miscommunication. If you use such questions as a technique to prove your superiority or point of view, similar to how an attorney questions witnesses during a trial, you will make the other person defensive and will not fully comprehend other people's unique use of language.

Anticipate Possible Interpretations before You Speak

Whether you are in an interpersonal, group, or public speaking situation, to communicate competently you need to anticipate how people will make sense of your language. By anticipating how others might interpret your message, you will be able to construct messages that are coherent and understandable. Three strategies help anticipate how people may interpret your language: examining your wording from different perspectives, understanding the larger context, and exploring the historical background for the message.

The first strategy involves taking account of the multiple perspectives of different audiences. What are the different audiences to whom you are presenting your message? How might each interpret your language? Do they hold similar or different interpretations of your message? If different audiences have different interpretations, you have to develop a message that evokes a common set of meanings across the different audiences. Or you'll need to state your message in several different ways to ensure that all your listeners interpret the message correctly.

The second strategy is to examine the larger context in which the message occurs. The meaning of a word or phrase depends on the context in which it is uttered (Barge & Pearce, 2004; Bateson, 1972). Three contexts are of particular importance: (1) episodes, (2) relationships, and (3) culture. An **episode** is a sequence of messages that has a clear beginning and end and a set of constitutive and regulative rules. For example, in greeting episodes, we know that statements such as "Hi, how are you?" count as greetings and we are expected to respond with a similar message (see Figure 4.1). However, the phrase "Hi, how are you?" may be interpreted differently if it occurs in a gossip episode where the initiator of the conversation wants to obtain information about your private life. This message may function not as a greeting, but as an attempt to collect information. In this context, the message may put recipients on the defensive because they perceive the meaning of the message as snooping into their private lives. Understanding the episodic context of your message helps you anticipate how people will interpret your message.

The term *commitment ceremony* (or *civil union,* where legal) is used as the equivalent of *marriage.* The term *marriage,* in particular, has become the center of conflict because same-sex couples increasingly want the privileges and responsibilities of full marriage, whereas their opponents belonging to language communities outside the gay and lesbian community want to reserve the term for opposite-sex unions.

The relationship also serves as an important context for anticipating how your message may be interpreted by others. What relationship do you have with your audience? How does that relationship influence how your audience may interpret your message? For example, if your boss said, "I am disappointed in your performance," you may interpret the message as a criticism or warning. If a co-worker uttered the same message, you might interpret it as sarcasm or a joke. Understanding how your relationship with the receivers of the message influences their perception of the message will help you anticipate how they will make sense of your language.

Messages also occur in a cultural context. As you'll recall from Chapter 2, **culture** refers to the enduring set of beliefs, values, and norms held by a social group. We can have group cultures, organizational cultures, national cultures, ethnic cultures, and so on. Examine the cultural context in which your message is sent. How does that influence audience interpretation? For example, what does it mean to introduce someone as your partner? In the United States, introducing someone as your partner typically refers to a business relationship you have with that person. However, in European countries and gay and lesbian subculture, the term *partner* means you are romantically involved with that person. Your audience may interpret the word *partner* differently than you intend depending on its culture.

Finally, the third strategy for anticipating possible interpretations is to examine the historical background to your message. Messages and language are communicated over time. What happened in the past before you spoke? How might these events influence the language that you use? For example, if in the past a manager has been criticized by his employees for "not giving clear directions" then he would likely avoid using high-level abstract language to communicate to his employees.

Experiment with Possible Phrasings

Using language competently not only means anticipating your audience's interpretations of what you are saying but it also entails steering listeners' behavior in ways you prefer. Playing with the phrasing of your messages can shape people's interpretations and actions. Indexing and experimenting with pronouns are two strategies for playing with your phrasing.

Indexing uses language that places an issue, event, or person in a specific time or in a specific context. For example, if you were to index according to time, instead of saying, "Dr. Smith is a poor teacher," you would say, "When I had Dr. Smith 4 years ago, I thought he was a poor teacher." If you were indexing to place a person in a particular context, you would say, "When we discussed affirmative action, I found Kwan's views offensive," instead of "Kwan's views are offensive."

By highlighting the time and circumstances under which certain events occur, indexing uses language that is more specific and lower in abstraction. Using indexing allows people to make specific observations about themselves and others and avoid using language that leads to unwarranted generalizations. Indexing thus may be appropriate when you want to be specific and clear in your communication, when the person you are talking to requires specificity and clarity to understand your communication, or when the successful completion of a task requires clear, specific language.

Experimenting with pronouns is another way to play with different phrases and see how they work within a situation. Consider the following three statements:

1. You are angry.
2. I think you are angry.
3. We are angry with one another.

What differences can you detect among these messages? They use different pronouns to describe anger. The first message is called a **you-message,** a statement that labels another person and involves some evaluation of that person's behavior. The second message is an **I-message,** a statement that labels the speaker's own behavior. The third message is a **we-message,** which labels and describes the joint behaviors of two or more people. These messages differ in where they place the anger emotion. The first message locates the anger in the other person, and the second message identifies the anger as the speaker's perception of anger. The third message places the anger in the relationship shared by two people.

Using different pronouns in language opens up different ways of talking (Harre, 1989, in Pearce, 1994). For example, when you use a you-message you imply that the other person is acting a certain way. You-messages can put people on the defensive because they are evaluative and imply the person needs to change. As a result, the subsequent conversation in this example may become focused on the target of the message denying the label "angry." But when you use an I-message you own the statement and acknowledge it as your perception of the other person's behavior. In this way, the subsequent conversation can focus on why you perceived the person as "angry" and whether the perception is accurate, without labeling the person. Finally, when you use a we-message the emphasis is on what you and the message receiver have done jointly to create the situation. Responsibility is placed not on one individual or the other, but on both. The conversation subsequent to the we-message is in many cases the most constructive of all because it focuses on how both parties can deal with the situation instead of debating the label or the perception.

To communicate competently, you need to anticipate how the receiver will respond to your use of you-, I-, or we-messages. Will the person you're talking to view a you-message as an accusation or as an accurate description of his or her behavior? Will your use of I-messages be viewed by others as an honest attempt to acknowledge that your perceptions may be faulty or will it be viewed as condescending? Will the use of a we-message be interpreted as a justified call to share the responsibility for an event or will it be construed as an attempt to shift the blame? Experimenting with different phrasings to understand how others may respond contributes to your grasp of the uniqueness of the situation and person you are addressing and, in turn, to your overcoming challenges to competence in using language.

learning link

How does using I-, you-, and we-messages change the relationships people create with others?

• • •

Chapter Summary

Language is a rule-guided system of symbols that allows you to take words and phrases and translate them into meaning. Constitutive rules help determine what particular words mean and regulative rules help you decide how you will respond given the meaning you have assigned a word or phrase. The meaning of a symbol is determined by the arbitrary relationship between a signifier (the symbol) and the signified (the referent) as well as the signifier's relationship with numerous other signifiers (symbols).

Language defines who we are and how we perceive our reality. The Sapir-Whorf hypothesis suggests that our world is linguistically determined: our language shapes how we see the world and what we perceive as real. Although emphasizing the connection between language and social reality, social constructionism believes that reality emerges through interaction.

Language serves three key functions. First, it directs our attention to particular aspects of our social worlds and away from others. Second, language creates opportunities and limitations for identities and relationships. Some forms of communication such as hate, racist, or sexist speech are problematic because they have the potential to create negative images and identities. Third, language facilitates social coordination when we avoid making people defensive and manage the level of abstraction appropriately.

Each language community may have a unique way of using language. Because we belong to multiple language communities, determining which language community is important for the person you are talking to will help you communicate competently.

Competent communicators can develop several strategies for overcoming these challenges to language: (1) inviting curiosity about the meaning of words by using clarifying, showing, and comparing questions; (2) anticipating possible interpretations before you speak by examining your wording from different perspectives, understanding the larger context in which your message occurs, and exploring the historical background for your message; and (3) playing with possible phrasings through the use of indexing and pronoun use. Indexing allows you to place an issue, event, or person in a specific time or context to make your communication more specific and avoid labeling. Experimenting with pronouns enables you to use you-, I-, and we-messages to better understand how your audience will respond to the phrasing.

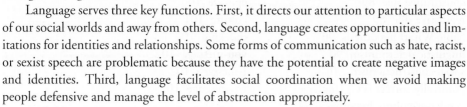

The premium companion website for *Human Communication* offers a broad range of resources that will help you better understand the material in this chapter, complete assignments, and succeed on tests. The website resources include

- Interactive self-assessments, competency grids, and other tools
- Web links, practice activities, self-quizzes, and a sample final exam

For more information about this text's electronic learning resources, consult the *Guide to Online Resources for Human Communication* or visit **http://communication .wadsworth.com/morreale2.**

Key Terms _____

The key terms below are defined in the chapter on the pages indicated. They are also presented alphabetically with definitions in the Glossary, which begins on page 467. The book's website includes flashcards and crossword puzzles to help you learn these terms and the concepts they represent.

language 86
symbol 87
reference 87
referent 87
relationship 87
signifier 88
signified 88
denotative meaning 88
connotative meaning 88
constitutive rule 89
regulative rule 89
Sapir-Whorf hypothesis 90
linguistic determinism 90
social constructionism 90
politically correct (PC) language 91
gender-as-culture hypothesis 92

different-cultures thesis 92
hate speech 93
Ladder of Abstraction 94
language community 98
ethnocentric communicator 99
cosmopolitan communicator 99
clarifying question 100
showing question 100
comparing question 100
episode 100
culture 101
indexing 101
you-message 102
I-message 102
we-message 102

Building Knowledge _____

The questions below are among the practice activities on the book's website.

1. Why is it important to see how words or signifiers relate to other words or signifiers? For example, why is it important to know whether the word *execute* relates to words such as *computer* and *program* as opposed to *prison* and *justice?*

2. Describe a situation in which the language someone used caused you to notice something about the situation that you might not normally have noticed. What language did the person use to focus your attention on that aspect of the situation?

3. In what ways do language and labeling create opportunities or constraints? Give an example of language that does both.

4. Is clear language always the best language to use? Under what conditions is it competent to use clear language? Under what conditions might it be better to use ambiguous language?

5. Recall a situation in which you used very abstract language that might have caused a misunderstanding. Using the Ladder of Abstraction, what could you have said that would have been more concrete and facilitated understanding?

6. If you are not sure of the meaning of what a person is saying, what kinds of questions would you ask to help make sense of his or her meaning?

7. Consider a situation in which you felt your language was misunderstood by another person. In what other ways could you have phrased your message to be better understood?

The exercises below are among the practice activities on the book's website.

Individual Exercises

1. Write down as many bumper sticker messages as you can recall. Next write a list of the different kinds of people you know. How would each of them interpret the meaning of each bumper sticker?

2. Consider the following kinds of conversations: job interview, greeting a friend, greeting a professor, and asking someone out for a date. For each conversation write down as many constitutive rules as you can. For each constitutive rule, try to draw a regulative rule using Figure 4.3 as a guide. How can understanding the rules of language make you a more competent communicator in each type of communication?

3. Take a word and place it in the center diagram here. List five words associated with that word. For each of the five words you generate, list four words associated with that word. What does your diagram tell you about the related nature of words? What would happen to the meanings of the other words if you changed one of the words in your diagram?

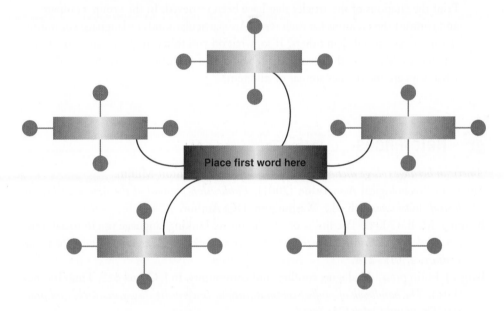

Place first word here

4. The three major national political parties in the United States have websites: American Reform Party (**http://www.americanreform.org**); Democratic Party (**http://www.democrats.org**); Republican National Committee (**http://www .rnc.org**). Look at each website and examine the language used to describe the party that sponsors the site. What kind of language is used to describe the views of opposition parties? How do the words and phrases used to describe the parties differ?

Group Activities

1. Form groups of four to five students. Using the following list of words, compare what the words mean to each member of the group. Discuss how the meaning of a word changes depending on the language community to which a group member belongs.

family values family planning
happiness freedom
liberal success
welfare

2. Form groups of four to five students. Have one of the group members answer the following question: "What does it mean to be a good friend?" Each group member then asks a question of the first person that adds to the understanding of the meaning the first person has for "good friend." After each question has been asked and answered, go to the next person. Repeat this process for each person in the group. Discuss the kinds of questions that help you understand the meanings that people have for words.

3. Form groups of four to five students. Each person should select one of the following terms:
African American communication
Asian American communication
gay or lesbian communication
gender communication
Latino (Hispanic) American communication

4. Using InfoTrac College Edition each person should look up their selected term. Print the citations of the articles that have been retrieved. In the group, compare and contrast the citations for each term. Are particular kinds of language communities more researched than others? If so, what do you think might account for these differences? What are the themes that characterize the articles for each group? In what ways are the themes similar or different?

 ## References

American heritage college dictionary. (2004). Boston: Houghton-Mifflin.

American Psychological Association (2001). *Publication manual of the American Psychological Association* (4th ed.). Washington, DC: Author.

Banning, M. E. (2004). The limits of PC discourse: Linking language use to social practice. *Pedagogy: Critical Approaches to Teaching Literature, Language, Composition, and Culture, 4,* 191–214.

Barge, J. K. (in press). Dialogue, conflict, and community. In J. Oetzel & S. Ting-Toomey (Eds.), *The handbook of conflict communication: Integrating theory, research, and practice.* Thousand Oaks, CA: Sage.

Barge, J. K., & Pearce, W. B. (2004). A reconnaissance of CMM research. *Human Systems, 15,* 13–32.

Bateson, G. (1972). *Steps to an ecology of mind.* New York: Ballantine.

Calvert, C. (1997). Hate speech and its harms: A communication theory perspective. *Journal of Communication, 47,* 4–19.

"Continental Divide." (2002, March 18). *Report/News Magazine* (Alberta Edition), 29 (6), p. 4.

Cronen, V. E. (1999). Coordinated management of meaning: Practical theory for the complexities and contradictions of everyday life. In J. Siegried (Ed.), *The status of common sense in psychology* (pp. 185–207). Norwood, NJ: Ablex.

Derrida, J. (1978). *Writing and difference.* Chicago: University of Chicago Press.

Eagly, A. H., & Koenig, A. M. (in press). Social role theory of sex differences and similarities: Implication for prosocial behavior. In D. J. Canary & K. Dindia (Eds.), *Sex differences and similarities* (2nd ed.). Mahwah, NJ: Erlbaum.

Fairclough, N. (2003). "Political correctness": The politics of culture and language. *Discourse & Society, 14,* 17–28.

Guerrero, L. K., & Reiter, R. L. (1998). Expressing emotion: Sex differences in social skills and communicative responses to anger, sadness, and jealousy. In D. J. Canary & K. Dindia (Eds.), *Sex differences and similarities in communication* (1st ed., pp. 321–350). Mahwah, NJ: Erlbaum.

Hayakawa, S. I. (1964). *Language in thought and action* (2nd ed.). New York: Harcourt, Brace, & World.

Leets, L. (2001). Explaining perceptions of racist speech. *Communication Research, 28,* 676–706.

Leets, L. (2003). Disentangling perceptions of subtle racist speech: A cultural perspective. *Journal of Language and Social Psychology, 22,* 145–168.

MacGeorge, E. L., Graves, A. R., Feng, B., Gillilan, S. J., & Burleson, B. R. (2004). The myth of gender cultures: Similarities outweigh differences in men's and women's provision of and responses to supportive communication. *Sex Roles, 50,* 143–175.

Maltz, D. N., & Borker, R. A. (1982). A cultural approach to male-female miscommunication. In J. J. Gumperz (Ed.), *Language and social identity* (pp. 196–216). Cambridge, UK: Cambridge University Press.

"'Master' and 'slave' computer labels unacceptable, officials say." (2003). Retrieved February 2005 from CNN.com.

Mitroff, I. I. (1978). Systemic problem solving. In M. M. Lombardo & M. W. McCall, Jr. (Eds.), *Leadership: Where else can we go?* (pp. 129–144). Durham, NC: Duke University Press.

Mulac, A. (in press). The gender-linked language effect: Do language differences really make a difference. In D. J. Canary & K. Dindia (Eds.), *Sex differences and similarities* (2nd ed.). Mahwah, NJ: Erlbaum.

Mulac, A., Bradac, J. J., & Gibbons, P. (2001). Empirical support for the gender-as-culture hypothesis: An intercultural analysis of male/female language differences. *Human Communication Research, 27,* 121–152.

Nielsen, L. B. (2002). Subtle, pervasive, harmful: Racist and sexist remarks in public as hate speech. *Journal of Social Issues, 58,* 265–280.

Ogden, C. K., & Richards, I. A. (1946). *The meaning of meaning.* New York: Harcourt, Brace, & World.

Pearce, W. B. (1989). *Communication and the human condition.* Carbondale: Southern Illinois University.

Pearce, W. B. (1994). *Interpersonal communication: Making social worlds.* New York: HarperCollins.

Sagrestano, L. M., Heavey, C. L., & Christensen, A. (1998). Theoretical approaches to understanding sex differences and similarities in conflict behaviors. In D. J. Canary & K. Dindia (Eds.), *Sex differences and similarities in communication* (1st ed., pp. 287–302). Mahwah, NJ: Erlbaum.

Strong, P. T. (2004). The mascot slot: Cultural citizenship, political correctness, and pseudo-Indian sports symbols. *Journal of Sports & Social Issues, 28,* 79–87.

Wittgenstein, L. (1953). *Philosophical investigations.* Oxford: Blackwell.

© Mark Romine/Stone/Getty Images

LEARNING OBJECTIVES

After studying this chapter, you should be able to

1. Define nonverbal communication and appreciate its importance.

2. Outline and discuss four functions of nonverbal communication.

3. Apply your understanding of physical appearance and first impressions, body communication, touch, voice, and time and space in various communication contexts.

4. Identify the major challenges to nonverbal communication.

5. Demonstrate strategies to overcome the challenges.

Nonverbal Communication

Bookstore cafés are popular meeting places for college students. One Saturday afternoon right before the beginning of fall semester, Samantha drove to campus to visit the bookstore and pick up books for her classes. She also hoped she might meet a few other students taking the same classes that fall.

For this outing, Samantha wore a somewhat conservative tweed jacket and turtleneck with a nice pair of jeans. Upon entering the bookstore café, Samantha spotted Steve having a cup of coffee at a small table. Steve's clothes, hairstyle, and even personal mannerisms looked hip and cool. At a glance, Samantha decided she liked how he looked so she grabbed a latte and sat down at a table near him. Finding Samantha attractive despite her tweedy appearance, Steve moved over to her table and struck up a conversation.

As Samantha became attracted to Steve, she changed the way she communicated very slightly without even realizing it. Her voice became a little softer and lower and she leaned toward Steve, smiling and making direct eye contact. As their conversation continued, Steve sat up taller and spoke with a little more authority in his voice.

After an hour of conversation, Samantha glanced nervously at her watch. Noticing that nonverbal cue, Steve leaned across the table, touched Samantha lightly on the arm, and asked if she would like to see him again. She agreed to a date the next Friday, and Steve said he would pick her up at her apartment at 7 p.m. sharp. As she left the bookstore, Samantha wondered how she would ever control her tendency to arrive late. She was about to miss a movie date with a friend and she was already worried about being ready at seven on Friday when Steve arrived.

During this first meeting, Steve and Samantha reacted to an array of nonverbal cues of the kind that play a critical role in shaping people's first impressions of one another. At first glance, Samantha appeared conservative and Steve more casual and cool. However, both students overcame these differences in appearance by using nonverbal communication to help them get better acquainted. Whenever people communicate, in addition to using words, they continually send, receive, and react to nonverbal cues. The effectiveness and appropriateness of nonverbal communication, in addition to what is said verbally, add to the competence of communication. ■

The first step to achieving competence in nonverbal communication is to be motivated to pay attention to the vast number of nonverbal cues that surround each of us every day. It's also important to understand what nonverbal communication is and how it works. Finally, competence depends on the skill with which you send and receive nonverbal messages. Let's begin by defining nonverbal communication and considering its importance to you as a communicator.

Defining Nonverbal Communication

Scholars' opinions differ about the definition of nonverbal communication. Some describe it as all communication other than words. Others prefer to distinguish between nonverbal behaviors, which contain no meaning, and **nonverbal cues,** which are nonverbal behaviors or objects to which meaning is assigned. The intentional assignment of meaning by a sender, receiver, or social group to any nonverbal behavior or object makes that behavior or object into a nonverbal cue, which is what creates nonverbal communication (Burgoon, Buller, & Woodall, 1989).

For instance, the behavior of scratching your head unintentionally may tell others you're confused. Or if you wear a unique piece of jewelry or a tweed jacket as Samantha did, that may become a nonverbal cue when someone notices it and assigns meaning to it. When Steve reached across the table and touched Samantha on the arm, that nonverbal cue communicated that he wanted to get better acquainted (O'Neil, 1998b).

Taking the approach that it's the intentional assignment of meaning to behavior or an object, nonverbal cues to which meaning is assigned constitute nonverbal communication just as words constitute verbal communication or language. Nonverbal communication often takes place at the same time as verbal communication, yet it is not language. Some researchers even claim that human beings used nonverbal communication before they developed language, and language emerged out of humans' ability to use nonverbal cues (Brook, 1997).

We now can define **nonverbal communication** as all behaviors, attributes, and objects of humans—other than words—that communicate messages and have shared social meaning. This definition includes any aspect of physical appearance, body movements, gestures, facial expressions, eye movements, touching behaviors, the voice, and the way people use objects, time, and space to communicate.

Appreciating Nonverbal Communication

An early summary of various studies on the importance of nonverbal communication found that 65% of the conversational meaning in most interpersonal interactions comes from nonverbal cues (Philpot, 1983). Figure 5.1 highlights this summary. More recently, an authority on nonverbal communication confirmed the critical role nonverbal cues play in our interpersonal interactions (Burgoon & Le Poire, 1999). Burgoon says that nonverbal cues are crucial to effectively communicating messages about involvement and pleasantness in

learning link

Is verbal or nonverbal communication more essential to communication competence in the interpersonal context? In small groups? In public speaking?

• • •

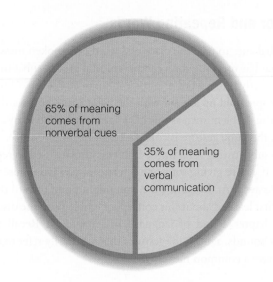

65% of meaning comes from nonverbal cues

35% of meaning comes from verbal communication

Figure 5.1

The Dominance of Nonverbal Communication

How much of a message is communicated nonverbally? A summary of research studies finds that a surprising 65% of the meaning of conversational messages is communicated using nonverbal cues.

Adapted from Philpot (1983).

any relationship. Other researchers confirm that extroverted individuals make very effective use of expressive forms of nonverbal communication (LaFrance, Heisel, & Beatty, 2004).

Indeed, research demonstrates that children who lack the ability to communicate non-verbally develop fewer friendships and often have feelings of incompetence, resulting in depression and negative feelings about themselves (Duke & Nowicki, 1995; Nowicki & Carton, 1997). Students who receive training and practice in nonverbal communication increase their confidence and speaking performance (Costanzo, 1992). Teachers expressed stronger liking for students who were effective nonverbally (Baringer & McCroskey, 2000). For adults, the effective use of nonverbal cues contributes to satisfying intimate and romantic relationships (Manusov, 1995) and helps reduce stress in life (Ryan, 1995). For married couples, accuracy in interpreting the nonverbal messages of a partner is associated with greater marital satisfaction (Koerner & Fitzpatrick, 2002). Professionally, good non-verbal skills help lawyers win cases in court and psychologists interact better with their clients (Hall, Harrigan, & Rosenthal, 1995; Klein, 1995).

Given the importance of nonverbal communication, you would expect most people to be well aware of the role of nonverbal cues in their everyday lives and skilled at figuring out the meaning of nonverbal messages. That is not the case. In fact, nonverbal communication happens at a low level of awareness and frequently goes unnoticed. Let's now consider how we all use nonverbal cues daily to accomplish various communication goals.

learning link

In what communication situations is nonverbal communication most critical and why?

• • •

Functions of Nonverbal Communication

People use nonverbal cues to accomplish many communication goals. Nonverbal cues sub-stitute for and repeat words, complement and accent words, contradict words, regulate ver-bal interactions, and perhaps most important, define the social and emotional aspects of many interactions and relationships. Let's take a closer look at these five functions.

Substituting for and Repeating Words

People use nonverbal cues to take the place of a word or a spoken message. An **emblem** is a nonverbal cue that has meaning for a certain cultural group, substitutes for a word, and translates almost directly into a word or phrase (Ekman & Friesen, 1969). For example, in North America, people hold up a hand with the palm turned outward to say "stop where you are." Although an emblem such as this has a meaning agreed to by a majority of people in North America, the same gesture is considered an insult in Greece.

In addition to substituting for a word, emblems also are used to repeat a spoken word or verbal message. If you're giving someone directions, you would use words to say that a street is three blocks away. At the same time, you might point toward the street or hold up three fingers. You first learned about this concept of emblems in the discussion of messages and symbols in Chapter 1 and of language in Chapter 4. Recall that symbols were identified as words, sounds, actions, or gestures that arbitrarily refer to something else and that people agree have a common meaning.

learning link

How might you use nonverbal messages to enhance communication competence in interpersonal and group and public speaking situations?

• • •

Complementing and Accenting Words

Nonverbal cues can also enhance spoken messages. An **illustrator** is a nonverbal cue that complements and accents the verbal message (Ekman & Friesen, 1969). People use illustrators such as tone of voice and rate of speech, facial expressions, and gestures to bring their spoken words to life. Good public speakers use gestures as illustrators to add excitement to speeches.

Some cultures use illustrators more frequently than others. Most Americans make extensive use of illustrators when they're excited or emotionally aroused or when they need to explain a difficult concept or idea. People from Mediterranean cultures and South America often use illustrators even in simple and everyday conversation.

Contradicting Words

On some occasions, a nonverbal message may contradict the verbal message. When a nonverbal cue contradicts a verbal message, you send what is called a **mixed message.** Interestingly, when nonverbal and verbal messages contradict one another, most of us tend to believe the nonverbal message. For instance, in interpersonal situations when you are already suspicious about what someone might say, you are more likely to rely on the person's nonverbal cues to determine whether they are lying (Hubbell, Mitchell, & Gee, 2001). Instead, before judging others as liars or truth tellers, collect more information, both verbally and nonverbally.

When relying on nonverbal cues to detect deception, most people are not very effective. In fact, most people fail miserably when tested for their ability to detect deception (Goode, 1999). A review of 120 research studies on deception found only 2 in which subjects scored higher than 70% accuracy at detecting deceit. The people who stood out as expert lie detectors didn't rely on any single nonverbal cue, such as lack of eye contact; rather, they noticed and interpreted clusters of both verbal and nonverbal cues.

In one study, prison inmates (considered more expert) and college students (less expert) were tested to see who was better at judging whether a witness was lying or telling the truth about an event (Hartwig, Granhag, Stromwall, & Andersson, 2004). The inmates did outperform the students in detecting lies, at an accuracy level higher than chance. But

"I knew the suspect was lying because of certain telltale discrepancies between his voice and non verbal gestures. Also his pants were on fire."

Nonverbal cues sometimes serve as indicators of deception—even if they are not as dramatic as the liar's pants being on fire!

in a study of three groups of presumed expert lie catchers—police officers, prosecutors, and judges—the experts' beliefs about deception were notably wrong and not supported by scientific literature and studies on deception (Stromwall & Granhag, 2003).

Regulating Interactions

People can use nonverbal cues to manage the flow of conversations. A **regulator** is a nonverbal cue that helps regulate and coordinate communication interactions among people (Ekman & Friesen, 1969). For example, we use regulators when we want to ask for a turn in a conversation or yield a turn to the other person. If you want to ask for a turn to speak, you might lean forward toward the speaker and use direct eye contact. If someone is about to interrupt you, you might suppress the interruption by speaking faster and avoiding pauses.

In the chapter's opening story, Samantha's glance at her watch served as a regulator that sent the message "I need to end this conversation." Steve responded by setting a date for their next meeting.

Defining Social and Emotional Relationships

Finally, people use nonverbal cues to define the social and emotional nature of their relationships and interactions (Burgoon & Le Poire, 1999). A **socioemotional regulator** is a nonverbal cue that lets others know your feelings and communicates roles in the relationship or particular situation. We communicate nonverbally to tell others whether we like them, just as Steve and Samantha did in the opening vignette. We may indicate who is most important in a situation by asking that person to sit at the head of the table, for instance. We even use nonverbal cues to make statements about who we are and what we believe, as Steve did by what he wore to the bookstore that Saturday afternoon.

learning link

Which type of nonverbal message plays the biggest role in communication in interpersonal and group contexts and in public speaking?

• • •

As you now can see, people use nonverbal cues to accomplish many different communication goals in their daily lives. As a result, we assign meaning to an array of human behaviors and objects, sending and receiving many different types of nonverbal messages.

Types of Nonverbal Messages

We send and receive nonverbal messages by making use of physical appearance, body communication (which includes movement and posture, gestures, facial expression, and eye contact), touch, voice, and even time and space. As you learn more about these different types of nonverbal messages, you will recall that several were discussed in Chapter 2. When you learned about the model of communication competence and types of communication contexts, we referred to *time* and *place* as critical aspects of context, both of which are discussed here as well.

Physical Appearance and First Impressions

Physical appearance includes everything you notice about a person, including how attractive or unattractive the person is to you, the person's race and ethnicity, age, gender, height, weight, body shape, clothing, and even how the person smells. Based on this physical appearance, you quickly form a first impression about the person's education level, social status, economic background, trustworthiness, and moral character. For instance, in a study of nonverbal behavior and initial impressions of instructors in videotaped distance-education courses, instructors who were considered nonverbally effective—more expressive, warm, and involved based on their nonverbal cues—also were judged as highly competent and their course content was judged more favorably (Guerrero & Miller, 1998).

Based on first impressions and nonverbal cues, interviewers claim to know within 1 to 2 minutes whether a job applicant is a winner and people decide in 30 seconds whether a blind date will be a success (Berg & Piner, 1990). Recall that when Samantha noticed Steve in the bookstore café, her reaction to him was typical of how quickly people form first impressions.

One aspect of physical appearance that sends powerful nonverbal messages is clothing and personal artifacts, which include hairstyle, jewelry, and any other personal decorations. Our clothes and artifacts make personal statements about our status, position in life, and even our beliefs and values. For instance, college students and members of various social groups sometimes distinguish themselves by wearing particular sweatshirts, T-shirts, or other adornments such as jewelry, tattoos, and body piercings.

learning link

Why are nonverbal cues and first impressions a challenge to communication because of the postmodern self?

• • •

If you are giving a speech or interviewing for a job, remember how quickly you may be judged based on nonverbal cues and your personal appearance. Furthermore, when judging others, be sensitive to how their physical appearance affects your reactions to them. As discussed in the chapter on perception, when you attribute certain characteristics to others, you may be incorrect in the impressions you form. Although we often send messages by our choice of apparel and artifacts, those messages may not always accurately represent who and what we are.

Body Communication

In addition to appearance, the human body itself sends strong nonverbal cues. Body communication, or **kinesics,** focuses on how people communicate through movement and

Body language can clearly communicate your feelings.

posture, gestures, and expressions of the face and eyes. The power of these nonverbal cues is illustrated in a study of communication between mothers and their young adult children (Trees, 2000). Mothers who used these cues to indicate conversational involvement were perceived as more supportive during a conversation about a relationship problem.

Body Movement and Posture

Whether you intend to send a message or not, the way you stand, sit, and walk communicates strong nonverbal messages to others. Body movement and posture, also called body language, communicate three things in any situation: how people see power operating, how they feel about themselves in the situation, and how they feel about the topic of discussion. If you feel powerful in a situation, you may communicate that power nonverbally by expanding your body into the space around you or gesturing more expansively. When you feel self-confident, you communicate a sense of immediacy and involvement by facing people directly, sitting in an erect but relaxed posture, and maintaining an open body posture. You communicate positive feelings about a topic of discussion by sitting up fairly straight and looking at or leaning toward the speaker.

As in most types of nonverbal messages, researchers have identified gender differences in the use of body language (Wood, 1994). An open body posture, using both the arms and legs, is adopted by men to communicate power (Cashdan, 1998). By comparison, when women feel they have less power, they tend to be less expansive and restrict the amount of space their bodies take up. One study found that a woman executive's intelligence and competence would be overlooked if she communicated weakness through her body language (Mindell, 1996). Weak nonverbal cues for women include slouching, sitting with stooped shoulders, and clutching the arms around the torso.

Here are some suggestions for using body movement and posture competently:

- Be aware of how you stand, sit, walk, and take up space to make statements about power relationships with others and about your own self-esteem.
- Be mindful of how other people use these subtle cues—consciously and unconsciously.
- When appropriate, modify your body language to be sure you are sending the message you intend.

Gestures

Another important aspect of body communication is **gestures**—large and small movements of the hands and arms that communicate meaning. These nonverbal cues are used differently depending on the culture (Samovar & Mills, 1998). For example, people from

learning link

Do you agree or disagree that body communication is important to communication competence in contemporary life?

• • •

Mediterranean cultures tend to use large gestures that are more animated than the gestures of people from the British Isles and eastern Asia.

Gestures are so effective that public speakers such as politicians are now being trained in their use (Ratcliffe, 1996). Even more impressive is a study that found that when blind children speak, they use gestures at precisely the same rate as those who can see (O'Neil, 1998a).

Used appropriately, gestures can enhance the verbal message, but they also can detract from it (Brittan, 1996). A public speaker who fiddles with a pencil or plays with the buttons on a jacket communicates nervousness or a lack of confidence. Limited gesturing on the part of a speaker may communicate a lack of enthusiasm for the presentation topic. Speakers who don't gesture at all—who keep their hands in their pockets or clasped together in front or back—seem insecure and uncertain.

Here are a few suggestions for using gestures positively and competently:

- Be sure your gestures match your verbal message. If you're talking about an expansive or important topic, use bigger gestures. If you're involved in a quiet discussion, avoid such large gestures.
- When speaking, gesture freely and naturally with both hands. Don't clasp your hands together nervously or leave them in your pockets while speaking.
- Don't allow another person's gestures to divert your attention from the message.

Facial Expressions

Movements of the face—facial expressions—convey feelings and the emotional meaning of messages. Facial expressions, also called **affect displays,** communicate the six universal and basic emotions that the human face is capable of displaying: sadness, anger, disgust, fear, surprise, and happiness (Ekman & Friesen, 1975). Frequently, people blend two or more of the affect displays into one facial expression, resulting in what is called an **affect blend.** Typical affect blends are fear–anger and surprise–happiness.

Researchers have studied the kinds of judgments based on facial expressions people make about others. Not only do we judge emotions but we also form opinions about a person's interpersonal traits, such as their tendency toward being a dominating kind of person or kind and warm—all based on facial expressions (Knutson, 1996). We perceive a person with a relaxed facial expression as more powerful than someone who has a nervous look (Aguinis, Simonsen, & Pierce, 1998). We even think that "baby faced" people, whose faces resemble those of children, are more truthful than other people (Masip, Garrido, & Herrero, 2004). Preschoolers think that adults who smile more when reading to them are more trustworthy and likable (Rotenberg, Eisenberg, Cumming, Smith, Singh, & Terlicher, 2003).

Accurately identifying emotions and other aspects of a person, based on facial expressions alone, is not always easy (Fernandez-Dols, Sanchez, Carrera, & Ruiz-Belda, 1997). Although people usually know when they are reacting to someone's expressions, they sometimes also react to a **micromomentary facial flash**—an expression that flashes across the face so quickly it is imperceptible. In the blink of an eye, in about 2 seconds, your mind jumps to a conclusion about what was observed (Gladwell, 2005). When you have an intuitive sense that something is wrong and you aren't sure why, you may be reacting to a micromomentary facial flash.

To complicate matters, the way people use facial expressions varies based on gender and cultural background (Samovar & Mills, 1998; Wood, 1994). In North America,

learning link

Why are some people better than others at concealing their feelings and not revealing them through their facial expressions?

• • •

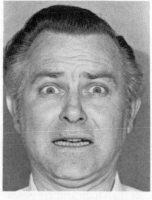
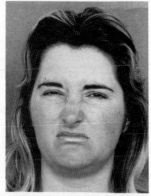
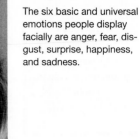

The six basic and universal emotions people display facially are anger, fear, disgust, surprise, happiness, and sadness.

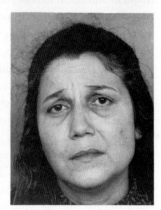

women tend to be more facially expressive and smile more than men, even when they are not genuinely happy. Men tend to display less emotion on the face and smile less. The Chinese and Japanese don't show emotion freely on their faces in public. In fact, in these cultures, the face is sometimes used to conceal rather than reveal feelings. By contrast, people from Latin American and Mediterranean cultures often display emotions on the face more freely.

Here are a few suggestions for communicating through facial expressions:

- Be aware of what your face is communicating, particularly in a heated or emotional discussion.
- Avoid a deadpan expression, which can happen when you're involved in a situation of little interest to you.
- Be alert and sensitive to differences in the way people use facial expressions as a result of individual, gender, or culturally based differences. Although the six affect displays are universal, timing and appropriateness for different facial expressions varies by culture.

Eye Contact

The eyes send powerful nonverbal messages. The appropriate and effective use of eye contact, also called **oculesics,** helps you to be seen as credible, dynamic, believable, likable, and persuasive (Aguinis, Simonsen, & Pierce, 1998). People generally use eye contact — or

learning link

In which context is eye contact most important— interpersonal, small group, or speaking in public?

● ● ●

the lack thereof—to accomplish two goals: to communicate interest and intimacy or to express dominance, power, and control. The person with the most power often engages in less eye contact and looks away from the other person. The person with less power maintains eye contact and watches the dominant person more closely to figure out what that person is thinking and feeling.

At an interpersonal level, we communicate sincerity, trustworthiness, and friendliness using eye contact. In team situations, we use eye contact to communicate understanding and build a sense of community in the group. Effective public speakers make frequent eye contact with the audience, and good listeners demonstrate interest and respect by maintaining eye contact with the speaker.

The use of eye contact varies based on gender and culture. Women engage in more frequent and sustained eye contact than men and are generally more visually attentive than men (Bente, Donaghy, & Suwelack, 1998). In one study of happily married couples, wives looked at their husbands significantly longer, as if listening attentively; husbands used shorter glances at their wives, suggesting they were monitoring the situation (Weisfeld & Stack, 2002). Both sexes communicate interest and involvement with others using eye contact, but men also use it to challenge others or to assert their status and power.

In Western cultures, such as North America and western Europe, direct eye contact communicates interest and respect and indicates that the channels of communication are open. In contrast, people in many Asian, Native American, and Latin cultures are made uncomfortable by too much eye contact. In Japan, people may look away from one another almost completely, and in China, Indonesia, and rural Mexico, the eyes are lowered to communicate deference (Samovar & Mills, 1998).

Consider the following suggestions for using eye contact competently:

- Use eye contact to communicate interest and attention, but remember that some people are comfortable with direct eye contact whereas others are not.
- Eye contact can be misunderstood, so be sensitive to the other person's reactions to avoid miscommunication.
- Pay attention to any unspoken cultural rules for eye contact and adapt your behaviors accordingly.

Touch

Touch, physical contact between people, is another powerful form of nonverbal communication, which social scientists call **haptics.** Touch when used appropriately communicates support, power, and the intimacy level of a relationship. Touching behaviors and physical contact are considered essential to human social development and to encouraging communication (Jones & Brown, 1996; McDaniel & Andersen, 1998).

learning link

How does touch help to develop self-concept and a high level of self-esteem?

● ● ●

One research study on interpersonal communication found that touching a person encourages self-disclosure and makes people far more cooperative (Remland & Jones, 1994). If you recall from the opening story, Steve leaned across the table and touched Samantha lightly on the arm when he asked her for a date, a nonverbal cue that marked the beginning of their relationship. In the same way, a defense lawyer in court might purposefully touch a client to send a message to the jury that the person is likable enough to touch.

Finally, people use touch as a social ritual, saying hello and goodbye with handshakes, hugs, and kisses. Social and cultural groups have unique forms of ritualistic touching. In

North America, if two people agree or are excited about something, they'll hold a hand up in the air, palm forward, and clap it against the other person's upraised hand. This salutation originated with the African American use of "Gimme five!" and then permeated North American culture as the "high five." The high five is being replaced with the knuckle-to-knuckle fist bump greeting shown in the photo here.

The amount of touching that occurs among people varies culturally. A study compared touching behaviors in low-contact cultures of northern Europe and high-contact cultures of southern Europe (Remland, Jones, & Brinkman, 1995). Italians and Greeks involved in casual conversations touched far more than the English, French, and Dutch, and people with a Jewish cultural background touched a great deal.

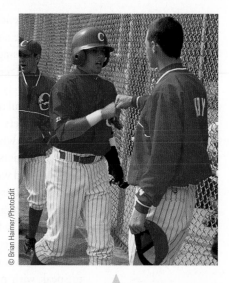

The knuckle-to-knuckle fist bump, a quick one-move greeting, has replaced the high five among members of hip hop culture and for athletes.

In addition to knowing how much touch is appropriate in any culture, it's also essential to be aware of culturally based touching taboos. Muslims in Arab cultures, for example, eat and engage in socially acceptable touching with the right hand, reserving the left hand for use in the toilet. To touch an Arab Muslim with the left hand is considered a social insult (Samovar & Mills, 1998).

Finally, gender differences in touching behaviors also exist (Wood, 1994). Women are more likely to hug and use touch to express support and affiliation. Men use touch to assert power or express sexual desires, and men tend to touch females more than females touch males. Interestingly, higher status individuals, regardless of gender, touch lower status individuals more than vice versa (Hall, 1996).

Here are a few suggestions for using touch to communicate with competence:

- Be sure the touching behavior is appropriate to the relationship and the situation.
- Realize that your intention in touching someone could be misunderstood, not just by the person being touched but by others watching you.
- Pay attention to how the other person reacts to being touched. If a person reacts negatively, acknowledge his or her feelings and apologize.

Voice

The human voice itself adds a significant nonverbal dimension to communication. **Paralanguage,** also called **vocalics,** includes all the nonverbal elements of the voice that contribute to communication competence. These elements are **rate,** or the speed at which you talk; **pitch,** or the highness or lowness of your voice; and **intensity,** or your volume. Most communication instructors agree that variety in the use of these elements is essential to being perceived as persuasive, competent, and dynamic.

To examine the importance of the voice, one research study compared the influence of vocal intensity and touch on getting people to cooperate (Remland & Jones, 1994). The researchers asked strangers to mail a postcard for them. In one situation, the subject was touched on the forearm. In another situation, there was no touch but vocal intensity varied and was low, medium, or loud. Increased vocal intensity was more effective than touch in getting people to mail postcards. By speaking more loudly and without hesitation, within reason of course, you will appear more confident, as well as more attractive (Kimble & Seidel, 1991; Zuckerman & Driver, 1989).

learning link

Does a speaker's rate, pitch, or intensity affect you more in an interpersonal context, in groups, or when listening to a public speech?

• • •

The absence of voice, or silence, also communicates nonverbal messages. In an age where we are surrounded by constant sound and stimulation, strategic silence can send powerful messages (Leira, 1995; Martyres, 1995). A silent pause can underscore the importance of a remark and allow listeners to reflect on what was said. Furthermore, using silence effectively will help you avoid **nonfluencies,** those distracters that slip out when you speak, particularly when you're nervous (*uh, um, y'know,* and *OK*). A study of radio talk show "ummers" (people who use lots of *ums*) found that too many *ums* had a negative influence on what audiences thought of the speaker (Christenfeld, 1995). This may occur because listeners assume a speaker who uses lots of *ums* is anxious or unprepared.

Men and women use paralanguage differently (Wood, 1994). In general, women use a softer voice, less volume, and more vocalic inflection when they speak, as Samantha did in the café when talking to Steve. Men use their voices to be assertive and take command of a conversation, which results in a lower pitch, more volume, and somewhat less inflection.

Not surprisingly, culture affects the use of vocalics (Samovar & Mills, 1998). Members of cultures that have strong oral traditions, such as African Americans and Jews, tend to speak with more gusto and enthusiasm. Italians and Greeks also are noted for using more volume, whereas the Thai and Japanese may speak with quieter voices. In many Asian cultures, people talk less and appreciate silence more.

Here are some suggestions for using paralanguage competently:

- Use vocal variety to reinforce meaning and add emotion to what you say to hold listeners' attention.
- Incorporate silent pauses at strategic points in conversations and control nonfluencies that distract listeners from your message.
- Anticipate cultural differences in paralanguage and modify your vocalics appropriately.

Time and Space

"Time is money." "Don't keep me waiting." "Give me some space." "I feel crowded by this relationship." These expressions illustrate a final set of nonverbal cues that you may not at first consider to be nonverbal communication. People exchange meaningful messages with one another using time—the clock—and space—the environment and distance.

The Clock

The intentional and unintentional use of time to communicate is called **chronemics.** The way people structure and use time in a society communicates messages about their valuation of time, whether they value each other, and the status and power of those communicating. In a society where a high value is placed on time, such as North America, people try to accomplish as much as possible within a given amount of time. When time is highly valued, respect for others is communicated by not "wasting" their time, by arriving promptly for appointments, and replying to their phone calls or e-mail messages promptly. Finally, in such time-sensitive cultures, people with higher status and power often control the use of time by deciding whether and when meetings take place. They can also communicate by making those with less status wait, as their time is considered less valuable.

Chronemics is complicated because its use varies significantly from one culture to the next and from one person to the next. Every culture and each individual has his or her own pace and rhythm and way of valuing time (Levine, 1997). In the opening story, Samantha was immediately aware that her tendency to be late could have a negative impact on her relationship with Steve who mentioned arriving at 7 p.m. *sharp*.

When people from cultures with different orientations to time interact, problems can arise (Samovar & Mills, 1998). People from the United States, Germany, and Switzerland place a high value on time and avoid "wasting" it, which often results in rushing, multitasking, impulsiveness, and making quicker decisions. By contrast, people from Mexico, Japan, China, and Korea favor a slower pace, giving fuller attention to the moment, which results in more reflection and less impulsiveness. As a result, people from clock-bound societies and backgrounds may move more quickly to solve a problem, whereas those who are less clock-bound may favor a slower, more deliberative approach to interacting and solving problems.

In societies that place a high value on time, people sometimes find themselves rushing from one task to the next, driven by constant deadlines, appointments, and other commitments.

Here are some suggestions for communicating competently using chronemics:

- Make sure your use of time matches your intentions. If a friend values promptness, the message you send by arriving late or not returning phone calls or e-mails is a negative one.
- When communicating with someone whose culture values and uses time differently, respect his or her chronemic behaviors and preferences.
- If a person of higher status, such as a supervisor, appears to control or take advantage of your time, try to understand it as a result of some of our unspoken cultural rules.

learning link

How might you use time and space to shape the perceptions and impressions that others form of you?

• • •

The Environment

In addition to time, people send nonverbal messages through their use of space. One important aspect of space is the physical environment in which communication occurs. Physical environments affect how people feel and therefore how they communicate.

Architects and home builders are well aware of how the physical structure of an environment affects communication. Designed communities and public buildings contain gathering spots such as club rooms and recreation facilities. Private homes often have conversation pits; large, open kitchens; and great rooms that bring families together in conversation. At an individual level, every physical environment reflects and provides insights into what its owner likes and is like. In fact, in one research study, students were able to accurately describe people's personalities based on only photos of the interiors and exteriors of their homes (Sadalla, 1987).

Two elements in any environment significantly affect communication—spatial arrangement and the use of artifacts and objects. **Spatial arrangement** is the way spaces are laid out and relate to one another, as well as how objects and furniture are placed in the spaces. The positioning of rooms and furniture in rooms can promote or hinder communication.

For example, in homes, communication is encouraged by positioning couches and chairs at slight angles to one another and at a comfortable distance apart for easy conversation. In the workplace, spatial arrangement sends a message about the power of various

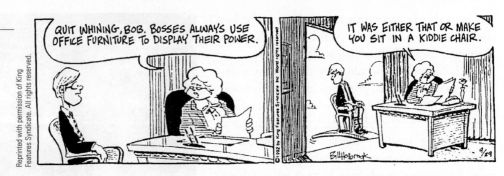

Office furniture communicates messages about power relationships at work.

employees. Upper level executives often get corner offices with walls of windows. High-ranking managers occupy the offices right next door, which allows them easy access to the boss, an advantage sometimes denied to lower level employees. Also, in many contemporary offices, workspaces are designed to give people privacy in which to work. The result is a working environment that is not very conducive to communication except in common areas such as a lunch room.

Artifacts are the objects in the environment that make nonverbal statements about the identity and personality of their owner. These include furniture, wall hangings, books, houseplants, art, or any other items used for practical or decorative purposes. Artifacts make statements about status and position in life and reveal what the room's owner thinks is important or attractive. Of course, money affects what a person has, so artifacts are not always accurate indicators of personal taste. They may indicate only what a person can afford at the time.

There is continuing interest in the U.S. in a practice that suggests artifacts have unique powers when arranged in a certain way in a room. **Feng shui** (pronounced fung shway), a 3,000-year-old Chinese approach to spatial arrangement and the use of artifacts, is gaining popularity in North America and around the world. Practitioners of feng shui claim to be able to affect many facets of people's lives simply by rearranging their homes and offices (Too, 1996). They believe blessings and good fortune result from the correct positioning and use of artifacts such as furniture, plants, mirrors, or lighting.

Distance

How much space you take up, how close you stand to others, and even how you identify your personal territory, communicate as loudly as words. **Proxemics** is the study of how people move around in and use space to communicate. Proxemics includes **personal space,** which is how people distance themselves from one another, and **territoriality,** which describes how people stake out space for themselves.

Anthropologist Edward T. Hall (1969) thought that people prefer to maintain comfortable distances from others based on how they feel about them, the situation they're in, and their goal for communicating. Each person is at the center of a personal bubble in which he or she is surrounded by intimate, personal, social, and finally public space. Figure 5.2 illustrates Hall's concept of how people use the space surrounding them.

Intimate space starts at the skin and extends out 18 inches around you. Typically, we allow only those with whom we have intimate relationships to get this close. Exceptions are crowded situations or professional relationships, such as with doctors, dentists, and hairdressers. Personal space extends outward, from 18 inches to 4 feet, and is reserved for people we know fairly well. If someone moves into your personal space, you may feel a little

A sunbather with an exaggerated sense of personal space.

Cowles Syndicate, Inc. © 1987.

Different people have different needs regarding personal space. We use movable markers to stake out our territory.

uncomfortable. **Social space** extends from 4 feet to about 12 feet and it is where more formal interactions occur, such as most conversations at work. In the opening story, recall that Steve quickly moved from a social distance into Samantha's personal space. Beyond social space is **public space,** which extends outward from 12 feet and beyond. Public speakers usually maintain this amount of distance from audience members.

In addition to personal preferences for distance, as described by Hall, unspoken cultural norms and rules dictate the amount of space people need and how closely they interact (Samovar & Mills, 1998). In eastern European, Middle Eastern, and Latin cultures, people tend to sit and stand closer together than in North America or northern Europe. In the United States, people feel comfortable with more personal space, and when this distance is intruded on, cultural norms are violated.

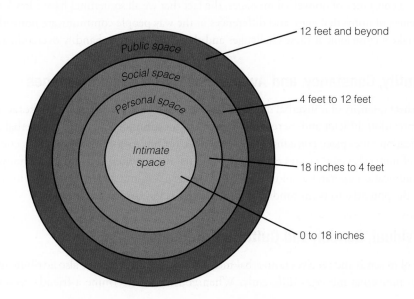

12 feet and beyond

Public space

Social space

Personal space

Intimate space

4 feet to 12 feet

18 inches to 4 feet

0 to 18 inches

Figure 5.2

E. T. Hall's Concept of Space

Each of us is at the center of a space bubble that extends outward from our bodies. We are surrounded by intimate, personal, social, and then public space. When someone invades our intimate or personal space, it makes us uncomfortable.

Adapted from Hall (1969).

How people use personal space also can make nonverbal statements about status, privilege, and power. Powerful people are usually given more personal space and allowed to encroach on the personal space of those lower in status (Wood, 1994). Nonetheless, invading a person's personal or intimate space may be considered intrusive and therefore not appropriate, regardless of status.

Closely linked to the idea of personal space is the concept of territoriality. Whereas personal space refers to the space around you and your body, territoriality relates to fixed space, such as a room, a house, a yard, a city, or even a country and its borders. Because people become uncomfortable when their space is invaded, they stake out and mark what they consider their territory using fixed or movable markers of various sorts. Fixed markers include fences around houses or even a regular seat at the dinner table, as well as the borders that mark where one country ends and another begins. Movable markers are the things you take with you into public spaces, such as clothing or books, that you use to stake out your territory. For instance, you might leave your jacket on the seat at a movie or a water bottle on the floor at your aerobics class. At an extreme, invading others' territory can result in a fight or even a war. But if you're in the library and someone sits down in your territory, you can just pick up your books and move.

Suggestions for using environment and space to communicate competently include the following:

- Be sensitive to the way physical environments, spatial arrangement, and artifacts affect the way you and others communicate.
- Recognize any unspoken rules for using personal space and respect other people's personal and cultural preferences.
- Respect the territory of others and understand when others unintentionally invade your territory.

learning link

How can individual, gender, and cultural differences in nonverbal communication be used to your advantage, rather than your disadvantage, as a competent communicator?

• • •

Challenges to Nonverbal Communication

As you can see by now, nonverbal communication can be an effective way to communicate, but it also presents some challenges to competence. These challenges stem from the quantity and constancy of nonverbal messages, the fact that we all sometimes have a low level of awareness of nonverbal cues, and differences in the way people communicate nonverbally. Let's take a close look at these challenges and then some ways to handily overcome them.

Quantity, Constancy, and Awareness of Nonverbal Messages

The sheer quantity of nonverbal messages people send and receive every day makes accurate interpretation difficult and increases the potential for misunderstanding. Nonverbal communication takes place constantly, even when we try not to communicate. This constant flow of nonverbal cues creates even more potential for misinterpretation. Also, nonverbal communication operates at a low level of awareness. Without awareness of the nonverbal cues, the potential to be misunderstood or viewed as less competent is great.

Individual, Gender, and Cultural Differences

Each of us sends and receives nonverbal messages in a unique way. We also attribute meaning to nonverbal messages differently. When you try to determine a friend's reason for

CloseUp on Gender

Female and Male Nonverbal Communication—Nature or Nurture?

RESEARCHERS HAVE FOUND THAT WHEN WOMEN communicate, they engage in very different nonverbal communication behaviors than men. They make more frequent and sustained eye contact and they smile and nod their heads in agreement more than men. They often lean toward the person talking and make positive sounds of agreement. All these nonverbal cues suggest women are more concerned with relationships than men.

Observing these gender differences, you may ask whether they are the result of how we are nurtured—sociology and psychology—or nature—biology and genetics. This is not a trivial question. In fact, the president of Harvard University recently set off a national controversy by publicly suggesting that fewer women in engineering and science fields may be due to inherent differences in the intellectual abilities of the sexes and that their brains function differently (Crenson, 2005).

Scholars tend to answer this nature versus nurture question differently, depending on their field, as it applies to nonverbal communication. Sociologists say we're conditioned to use the nonverbal cues our society deems appropriate for our gender. We learn to communicate nonverbally based on observing the behaviors of male and female role models in our families and in society. Another group of researchers takes a different view. The field of sociobiology studies how evolution shapes behavior in animals, as well as in humans. For example, sociobiologists studying human courtship behaviors examine innate behaviors, such as the instinct to search for a mate with the best qualities for procreation to ensure the survival of the species. According to sociobiologists, men value women who display a variety of nonverbal cues that reflect fertility and are associated with youth and health—full lips, clear skin, lustrous hair, a bouncy and youthful gait, and animated facial expressions. Women value men based on their physical size and strength and the display of nonverbal cues that communicate they will be ambitious, dependable, stable, and in good health, all traits that suggest a potential good provider for a family. Opponents to sociobiology state that this approach to understanding human behavior discounts the impact of the environment.

Can sociobiology be used to explain at least some human communication behaviors? McCroskey (1997), a prominent communication scholar, argues that people have innate predispositions to communicate in certain ways as a function of their biology; however, he doesn't rule out the influence of learning on communication. According to McCroskey, genetics (nature) and learning (nurture) interact to influence the way we communicate. We are born with genetic traits or tendencies to communicate in certain ways, such as being "naturally" shy or apprehensive about communicating with others. Then, life's experiences reinforce or restructure these tendencies to communicate in a certain way. Simply stated, nature and nurture are intertwined and both affect the way people use nonverbal cues and communicate nonverbally.

We don't yet know which of these factors—nature or nurture—has the most influence on communication behaviors. But we do know that nothing is true of all people all the time. So when researchers say women tend to communicate in one way and men another, these generalizations should be seen as just that—generalizations that aren't true of all people all the time.

SOURCES: Crenson (2005); Kenrich & Trost (1998); McCroskey (1997); Walsh (1995).

---

behaving in some way, if you base your interpretation solely on nonverbal cues, you are more likely to make a mistake.

Gender also plays an influential role in the way people send and interpret nonverbal messages. All gender-based nonverbal differences related to body communication, touch, and voice represent challenges to communication and can lead to misunderstandings. Take a look at the Close-Up on Gender box for one possible explanation of gender differences in nonverbal communication.

Culture also is a challenge because few of us are aware of the rules and expectations for nonverbal communication in cultures outside our own. This lack of knowledge of culturally based nonverbal differences can present a real challenge. The inability to communicate nonverbally with persons of other cultural backgrounds can limit how well people coordinate their activities, from something as simple as getting directions in a foreign country to determining appropriate seating arrangements at an international meeting.

Now that you are aware of the three challenges to nonverbal communication, let's consider how, through use of a competence model, they can be easily overcome.

Overcoming Challenges to Nonverbal Communication

A competence approach is a perfect framework for becoming a more effective and appropriate nonverbal communicator.

First, you want to be motivated to become more aware and mindful of nonverbal cues and messages. This starts with being mindful of the array and constancy of the messages you send—with your face, eyes, gestures, body movement, and so forth. Be mindful of the nonverbal cues you receive from others, too, but without overreacting or giving too much weight to any one message. Instead, look for similar messages that are expressed in various nonverbal channels. Avoid jumping to conclusions, ask for clarification, and listen to what the speaker is saying with an open mind.

Second, you need to be knowledgeable about how other people communicate nonverbally based on individual, gender, and cultural differences. As you learn about individual differences, avoid judging other people's nonverbal cues as wrong, and don't expect the other person's nonverbal messages to mirror yours. If you are uncertain about what nonverbal cues are appropriate, exercise restraint and avoid nonverbal behavior that could be misinterpreted. If you anticipate an interaction with someone from a culture different from yours, educate yourself about that culture's customs, including nonverbal behavior. Most important, give everybody respect, regardless of any nonverbal behavior they exhibit that may be new to you.

Third and finally, you need to develop and practice skills for sending and receiving nonverbal messages, integrated with verbal messages. Many of the challenges just discussed arise when verbal and nonverbal messages conflict with one another. If you are to communicate competently, it's essential that your verbal and nonverbal cues work together and complement one another. One way to integrate verbal and nonverbal messages effectively is to bring the nonverbal message to a verbal level. If there is any potential for misunderstanding as the result of a misleading or unclear nonverbal cue, ask the speaker to clarify the message instead of guessing what it means. This process will introduce mindfulness and respect for the communicators involved and effectively integrate the verbal and nonverbal messages.

In the opening story to this chapter, Steve and Samantha used nonverbal cues effectively and appropriately to communicate their interest in one another. When Samantha realized that she found Steve attractive, she sat at a table near him. When they began to talk, she lowered her voice, leaned toward Steve, smiled, and made direct eye contact. In response to Samantha's quick glance at her watch, Steve leaned forward, touched Samantha gently on the arm, and asked her for a date. Steve and Samantha used nonverbal cues to send and receive subtle messages to one another and accomplish their communication goals. You can improve your communication competence by the mindful use of nonverbal cues, by respecting differences in how people communicate nonverbally, and by skillfully integrating verbal and nonverbal communication.

Chapter Summary _____

Nonverbal communication includes all behaviors, attributes, and objects of humans—other than words—that communicate messages and have shared meaning. Nonverbal cues provide 65% of the meaning of conversational messages, signaling that nonverbal communication is crucial in people's personal and professional lives.

People use nonverbal cues to substitute for and repeat words, to complement and accent words, to contradict words, to regulate interactions and conversations, and to define the socioemotional aspects of interactions and relationships. The types of nonverbal messages that achieve these five functions include physical appearance, body communication, body movement and posture, gestures, facial expressions and eye contact, touch, voice, and time and space.

Physical appearance, which includes clothing and artifacts, significantly impacts first impressions. Body movement and posture communicate how people see power operating, how they feel about themselves, and how they feel about a discussion topic. Natural gestures that match the verbal message enhance it, but negative gestures, such as fidgeting, or the lack of gestures detract from the message. Facial expressions, including the universal affect displays of sadness, anger, disgust, fear, surprise, and happiness, convey feelings and the emotional meaning of messages. The effective and appropriate use of eye contact affects credibility; communicates interest and intimacy; and expresses dominance, power, and control. Touch encourages self-disclosure and is used to communicate support, power, and the intimacy level of the relationship. Vocal variety, or paralanguage, is achieved by varying rate, pitch, and intensity and using silence effectively, including avoiding vocal nonfluencies. The way people use time communicates messages about their value of time itself, their valuation of one another, and the status and power of the people communicating. Physical environments and how people use and fill up space also send important nonverbal messages.

Challenges to nonverbal communication include the quantity and constancy of nonverbal messages, the low level of awareness of nonverbal cues, and individual, gender, and cultural differences in how people communicate nonverbally. These challenges can be overcome by being more mindful of nonverbal messages, learning about and respecting differences in nonverbal communication, and integrating verbal and nonverbal messages skillfully.

Study and Review

The premium companion website for *Human Communication* offers a broad range of resources that will help you better understand the material in this chapter, complete assignments, and succeed on tests. The website resources include

- Interactive self-assessments, competency grids, and other tools
- Web links, practice activities, self-quizzes, and a sample final exam

For more information about this text's electronic learning resources, consult the *Guide to Online Resources for Human Communication* or visit **http://communication .wadsworth.com/morreale2.**

Key Terms _____

The key terms below are defined in the chapter on the pages indicated. They are also presented alphabetically with definitions in the Glossary, which begins on page 467. The book's website includes flashcards and crossword puzzles to help you learn these terms and the concepts they represent.

nonverbal cue 110	vocalics 119
nonverbal communication 110	rate 119
emblem 112	pitch 119
illustrator 112	intensity 119
mixed message 112	nonfluency 120
regulator 113	chronemics 120
socioemotional regulator 113	spatial arrangement 121
kinesics 114	artifact 122
gesture 115	feng shui 122
affect display 116	proxemics 122
affect blend 116	personal space 122
micromomentary facial flash 116	territoriality 122
oculesics 117	intimate space 122
haptics 118	social space 123
paralanguage 119	public space 123

 Building Motivation _____

This self-assessment resource begins on page 133. An interactive version of it is also available on the book's website.

 Building Knowledge _____

The questions below are among the practice activities on the book's website.

1. Discuss the five functions of nonverbal communication as they relate to the three levels of communication (interpersonal, group, public speaking). For each level of communication, which function do you think is most important and why?
2. Explain to someone from another planet who just landed on earth why humans have two communication systems, verbal and nonverbal.
3. Misunderstandings can result from cultural differences in the use of nonverbal cues. Discuss the advantages and disadvantages of those differences and what can be done to change a communication problem into a positive experience for individuals from different cultures.
4. Of the various types of nonverbal messages, which is the most powerful and meaningful in North American culture? Offer a description and examples to support your choice. If you are familiar with another culture, describe which types of nonverbal messages are important in that culture.
5. If you had to choose only one type of nonverbal communication to use, which type would it be and why?

6. Knowing how to use nonverbal cues effectively could give people an unfair advantage and help them manipulate, mislead, or deceive others. What are the ethical implications of becoming a better nonverbal communicator?

 Building Skills _____

The exercises below are among the practice activities on the book's website.

Individual Exercises

1. On a single sheet of paper, list the types of nonverbal messages described in this chapter. Next to each type of message, describe how competently you use it and how you could improve.
2. Go to Exploring Nonverbal Communication at **http://zzyx.ucsc.edu/~archer/ intro.html**. Using the photos at that site, determine how good you are at identifying emotions displayed on the face and the meaning of gestures from different countries. What steps might you take to correct for your weak areas?
3. Observe several environments in which you communicate: at school, work, and home. How does the spatial arrangement in those environments affect communication? Are there unspoken rules about the way space is used?
4. If you are using InfoTrac College Edition, enter *nonverbal communication* as a search topic. You'll find periodical articles on subjects such as eye contact and even hugging. Choose a type of nonverbal communication and read what's available in InfoTrac about it. Write a short paper summarizing what you've learned.

Group Activities

1. Form small groups of four to six students. Select two students to act out either of the following scenarios for about 5 minutes using both verbal and nonverbal communication. Others in the group observe the role play and take notes about how the two actors use nonverbal cues to substitute, repeat, complement, accent, or contradict words, regulate their interactions, and define relationships. Discuss the role play with the student actors.
   Scenario 1: A student asks a professor to change a grade on an essay exam. The student first approaches the professor right after class, and a second discussion takes place during the professor's office hours.
   Scenario 2: An employee approaches his or her boss to ask for a day off to attend to a personal matter not covered by the sick leave or vacation policy of the company.
2. Form a group of six students. Write each of the basic emotions and affect blends identified in this chapter on a piece of paper. Have each student choose a slip of paper from a hat. Each student should demonstrate the selected emotion and other group members guess which emotion is portrayed and identify parts of the face used to display it. Discuss which basic emotions and affect blends are the most difficult to identify and why.
3. With a partner, visit The Nonverbal Dictionary of Gestures, Signs, and Body Language Cues website at **http://members.aol.com/nonverbal2/diction1.htm**. Test each other to see how many of the definitions of different nonverbal cues you know.

References

Aguinis, H., Simonsen, M., & Pierce, C. (1998). Effects of nonverbal behavior on perceptions of power bases. *Journal of Social Psychology, 138*(4), 455–470.

Baringer, D. K., & McCroskey, J. C. (2000). Immediacy in the classroom: Student Immediacy. *Communication Education, 49*(2), 178–186.

Bente, G., Donaghy, W., & Suwelack, D. (1998). Sex differences in body movement and visual attention: An integrated analysis of movement and gaze in mixed-sex dyads. *Journal of Nonverbal Behavior, 22*(1), 31–58.

Berg, J., & Piner, K. (1990). Social relationships and the lack of social relationships. In S. W. Duck & R. C. Silver (Eds.), *Personal relationships and support* (pp. 104–221). London: Sage.

Brittan, D. (1996). Talking hands. *Technological Review, 99*(3), 10.

Brook, D. (1997). On nonverbal representation. *British Journal of Aesthetics, 37*(3), 232–246.

Burgoon, J. K., Buller, D. B., & Woodall, W. G. (1989). *Nonverbal communication: The unspoken dialogue.* New York: Harper & Row.

Burgoon, J. K., & Le Poire, B. A. (1999). Nonverbal cues and interpersonal judgments: Participant and observer perceptions of intimacy, dominance, composure, and formality. *Communication Monographs, 66*(2), 105–125.

Cashdan, E. (1998). Smiles, speech, and body posture: How women and men display sociometric status and power. *Journal of Nonverbal Behavior, 22*(4), 209–228.

Christenfeld, N. (1995). Does it hurt to say um? *Journal of Nonverbal Behavior, 19*(3), 171–186.

Costanzo, M. (1992). Training students to decode verbal and nonverbal cues: Effects on confidence and performance. *Journal of Educational Psychology, 84*(3), 308–313.

Crenson, M. (2005, February 28). Brainy Battle of the Sexes. *The Washington Post Express,* p. 4.

Duke, M., & Nowicki, S. (1995). Children who don't fit in need help. *The Brown University Child and Adolescent Behavior Letter, 11*(4), 1.

Ekman, P., & Friesen, W. (1969). The repertoire of nonverbal behavior: Categories, origins, usage and coding. *Semiotica, 1,* 49–98.

Ekman, P., & Friesen, W. (1975). *Unmasking the face.* Englewood Cliffs, NJ: Prentice-Hall.

Fernandez-Dols, J., Sanchez, F., Carrera, P., & Ruiz-Belda, M. (1997). Are spontaneous expressions and emotions linked? *Journal of Nonverbal Behavior, 21*(3), 163–178.

Gladwell, M. (2005). *Blink: The power of thinking without thinking.* New York: Little, Brown.

Goode, E. (1999, May 11). To tell the truth, it's awfully hard to spot a liar. *New York Times,* p. F1.

Guerrero, L. K., & Miller, T. A. (1998). Associations between nonverbal behaviors and initial impressions of instructor competence and course content in videotaped distance education courses. *Communication Education, 47*(1), 30–43.

Hall, E. T. (1969). *The hidden dimension.* Garden City, NY: Doubleday.

Hall, J. A. (1996). Touch, status, and gender at professional meetings. *Journal of Nonverbal Behavior, 20*(1), 23–44.

Hall, J., Harrigan, J., & Rosenthal, R. (1995). Nonverbal behavior in clinician-patient interaction. *Applied and Preventive Psychology, 4*(1), 21–27.

Hartwig, M., Granhag, P., Stromwall, L., & Andersson, L. (2004). Suspicious minds: Criminals' ability to detect deception. *Psychology, Crime and Law, 10*(1), 83–95.

Hubbell, A. P., Mitchell, M. M., Gee, J. C. (2001). The relative effects of timing of suspicion and outcome involvement on biased message processing. *Communication Monographs, 68*(2), 115–132.

Jones, S. E., & Brown, B. C. (1996). Touch attitudes and behaviors, recollections of early childhood touch, and social self-confidence. *Journal of Nonverbal Behavior, 20*(3), 147–163.

Kenrich, D. T., & Trost, M. R. (1998). Evolutionary approaches to relationships. S. Duck (Ed.), *Handbook of personal relationships* (pp. 151–177). West Sussex, UK: Wiley.

Kimble, C. E., & Seidel, S. D. (1991). Vocal signs of confidence. *Journal of Nonverbal Behavior, 15,* 99–105.

Klein, R. B. (1995). Winning cases with body language: Moving toward courtroom success. *Trial, 31*(7), 82.

Knutson, B. (1996). Facial expressions of emotion influence interpersonal trait inferences. *Journal of Nonverbal Behavior, 20*(3), 165–182.

Koerner, A. F., & Fitzpatrick, M. A. (2002). Nonverbal communication and marital adjustment and satisfaction: The role of decoding relationship relevant and relationship irrelevant affect. *Communication Monographs, 69*(1), 33–51.

LaFrance, B. H., Heisel, A. D., & Beatty, M. J. (2004). Is there empirical evidence for a nonverbal profile of extraversion? A meta-analysis and critique of the literature. *Communication Monographs, 71*(1), 28–48.

Leira, T. (1995). Silence and communication: Nonverbal dialogue and therapeutic action. *Scandinavian Psychoanalytic Review, 18*(1), 41–65.

Levine, R. (1997). *A geography of time.* New York: Basic Books.

Manusov, V. (1995). Reacting to changes in nonverbal behaviors: Relational satisfaction and adaptation patterns in romantic dyads. *Human Communication Research, 21*(4), 456–477.

Marin, R. (1999, September 9). Hug-hug, kiss-kiss: It's a jungle out there. *New York Times Sunday Styles,* sec. 9, pp. 1–4.

Martyres, G. (1995). On silence: A language for emotional experience. *Australian and New Zealand Journal of Psychiatry, 29*(1), 118–123.

Masip, J., Garrido, E., & Herrero, C. (2004). Facial appearance and impressions of credibility: The effects of facial babyishness and age on person perception. *International Journal of Psychology, 30*(4), 276–289.

McCroskey, J. C. (1997). *Why we communicate the way we do: A communibiological perspective.* The Carroll C. Arnold Distinguished Lecture. Presented at the annual convention of the National Communication Association, Chicago, IL.

McDaniel, E., & Andersen, P. (1998). International patterns of interpersonal tactile communication: A field study. *Journal of Nonverbal Behavior, 22*(1), 59–75.

Mindell, P. (1996). The body language of power. *Executive Female, 19*(3), 48.

Nowicki, S., & Carton, E. (1997). The relation of nonverbal processing ability of faces and voices and children's feelings of depression and competence. *Journal of Genetic Psychology, 158*(3), 357.

O'Neil, J. (1998a, November 24). Thinking with a wave of the hand. *New York Times,* p. F8.

O'Neil, J. (1998b, December 8). That sly 'don't-come-hither' stare. *New York Times,* p. F7.

Philpot, J. S. (1983). *The relative contribution to meaning of verbal and nonverbal channels of communication: A meta-analysis.* Unpublished master's thesis, University of Nebraska.

Ratcliffe, M. (1996). Gesture, posture and pose: Everybody's acting nowadays. *New States-man, 26,* 41.

Remland, M. S., & Jones, T. S. (1994). The influence of vocal intensity and touch on compliance gaining. *Journal of Social Psychology, 134,* 89–97.

Remland, M., Jones, T., & Brinkman, H. (1995). Interpersonal distance, body orientation, and touch: Effects of culture, gender, and age. *Journal of Social Psychology, 135*(3), 281–298.

Rotenberg, K., Eisenberg, N., Cumming, C., Smith, A., Singh, M., & Terlicher, E. (2003). The contribution of adults' nonverbal cues and children's shyness to the development of rapport between adults and preschool children. *International Journal of Behavioral Development, 27*(1), 21–30.

Ryan, M. E. (1995). Good nonverbal communication skills can reduce stress. *Law Office Management, Trial, 31*(1), 70.

Sadalla, E. (1987). Identity and symbolism in housing. *Environment and Behavior, 19,* 569–587.

Samovar, L., & Mills, J. (1998). *Oral communication: Speaking across cultures.* Boston: McGraw-Hill.

Stromwall, L., & Granhag, P. (2003). How to detect deception? Arresting the beliefs of police officers, prosecutors and judges. *Psychology, Crime and Law, 9*(1), 19–36.

Too, L. (1996). *The complete illustrated guide to feng shui.* Rockport, ME: Elements Books.

Trees, A. R. (2000). Nonverbal communication and the support process: Interactional sensitivity in interactions between mothers and young adult children. *Communication Monographs, 67*(3), 239–261.

Walsh, A. (1995). *Biosociology: An emerging paradigm.* Westport, CT: Praeger.

Weisfeld, C. C., & Stack, M. A. (2002). When I look into your eyes: An ethological analysis of gender differences in married couples' nonverbal behaviors. *Psychology, Evolution & Gender, 4*(2), 125–147.

Wood, J. T. (1994). *Gendered lives: Communication, gender, and culture.* Belmont, CA: Wadsworth.

Zuckerman, M., & Driver, R. (1989). What sounds beautiful is good: The vocal attractiveness stereotype. *Journal of Nonverbal Behavior, 13,* 67–82.

Building Motivation

Self-Assessment: Rate each of the eight communication situations described here, indicating your own typical level of nonverbal competence. Rate each situation for motivation, knowledge, and skills. Use a 1–4 scale, with 1 being minimal competence and 4 high competence. Rate one component (motivation) all the way through for all eight situations, then rate the next component (knowledge), and then the third (skills).

Motivation	Knowledge	Skills
1 = Distracted, disinterested, or simply no motivation to be competent **2** = Somewhat distracted or disinterested, but motivated to be competent **3** = Somewhat interested and motivated to be competent **4** = Highly interested and motivated to be competent	**1** = Completely inexperienced and ignorant about what to do and how to do it **2** = Minimal experience and sense of what to do and how to do it **3** = Somewhat experienced and knowledgeable about what to do and how to do it **4** = Highly knowledgeable about all aspects of what to do and how to do it	**1** = Completely incapable of behaving competently **2** = Barely capable of behaving minimally competent **3** = Fairly capable of behaving competently **4** = Highly capable of behaving competently

Communication Situations:	Motivation	Knowledge	Skills
1. Visiting a foreign country for the first time			
2. Going on a blind date with a person from a different culture			
3. Meeting a homeless person and chatting for a few minutes			
4. Accompanying a close friend to a therapy group discussion about drug abuse			
5. Presenting a project to a work team at your job or to your class at school			
6. Presenting the commencement speech at your school graduation			
7. Discussing a problem with your boss who is of the opposite sex			
8. Attending a party by yourself where you know hardly anyone			

TOTAL SCORES

Interpreting Your Scores: Total your score separately for each component (motivation, knowledge, and skills). The possible range of the score per component is 8–32. If your total score for any of the three components is 14 or less, you see yourself as less competent than you should be. A score of 15–28 means you are average at sending and receiving nonverbal messages. A score of 29–32 indicates you have a high level of nonverbal competence.

© Richard Lord/PhotoEdit

Chapter 6

LEARNING OBJECTIVES

After studying this chapter, you should be able to

1. Define listening and explain how the listening process works.

2. Describe the three types of listening.

3. Use the three types of listening appropriately and effectively in various communication contexts.

4. Explain how physical, psychological, and interaction barriers are challenges to listening.

5. Demonstrate your ability to overcome the challenges to listening.

Listening

Marie and Jesse met at the computer lab where they both worked while going to school. They went on a date the first day they met and spent plenty of time together from then on. Because they worked at the same place and were students on the same campus, they had a great deal in common. When they first met, they were curious to learn more about each other. They would listen attentively and tune in to each other's verbal and nonverbal messages. Even though Marie talked rather fast and sometimes left out important details, this was not a problem for Jesse. After listening closely to what Marie said, he would try to figure out exactly what she meant. Then he would describe what he thought he had heard and ask whether he was right. Likewise, when Jesse told Marie what happened during his shift in the computer lab, she would listen attentively and express genuine interest in his daily activities.

However, as time went on, Marie and Jesse began to take each other for granted. During this cooling-off period in the relationship, their excellent listening skills began to fade. In contrast to the early days, now there were times when they didn't listen to each other at all. When Jesse complained about a tough assignment in his calculus class, Marie found her attention wandering from Jesse's problem to matters of more importance to her. When Jesse asked for advice on how to approach the calculus professor about his concern, Marie faced a typical listening dilemma—she had no answer to his question because she hadn't even listened to Jesse's problem. Over time, poor listening skills began to have a negative influence on what had been a good relationship. ■

Have you ever found yourself in a similar situation? Your friend or partner or coworker is talking away and suddenly looks to you for a response. You have nothing to say because you weren't really listening. Your mind was far away and you haven't a clue about

learning link

How can competent listeners become more sensitive and alert when they are hearing what is said but not really listening?

● ● ●

what was just said. Or you are multitasking—talking on the phone and processing e-mail at the same time—and the person on the phone asks you a pointed question. Such listening dilemmas are not unusual in today's busy world.

In interpersonal contexts, we often fail to listen when it's most important to do so, during disagreements and heated arguments. In small groups, sometimes we don't listen to the opinions of other group members; instead we listen for an opening in the discussion to present the best idea: ours! In public speaking situations, such as lectures or training sessions, our attention often wanders. In fact, you've probably sat through more than your share of dull lectures and failed to listen to what was being said.

Although such bad listening habits are the norm, most people, including college students such as Marie and Jesse, spend more time listening than using any other communication skill (Barker, Edwards, Gaines, Gladney, & Holley, 1980). Figure 6.1 illustrates this surprising fact. In light of how much time you spend listening as a student, you might benefit considerably by listening more effectively (Ford, Wolvin, & Chung, 2000).

Listening is also important at work, particularly in the communication-technology-rich 21st century and regardless of your career or job (Bentley, 2000). Leaders in a wide variety of fields, including accounting, management, medicine, and engineering, link success on the job to competent listening (Campbell & Inguagiato, 1994; Darling & Dannels, 2003; Harris, 1997; Tan, Fowler, & Hawkes, 2004). In helping professions, listening is equally important. Researchers find that good listening skills are crucial for helpline volunteers, mental health care providers, and of course, teachers (Graves, 1995; Paukert, Stagner, & Kerry, 2004; Rea & Rea, 2000). Even the clients in a welfare-to-work job-training program found that fundamental elements of communication, such as listening skills, are a good antidote for welfare dependence (Waldron & Lavitt, 2001).

Given this value of listening, we can apply the model for communication competence presented in Chapter 2 to improving how we listen. Competent listening relies on knowledge, skills, and motivation, that is, a willingness to listen in a variety of situations.

learning link

Which context—interpersonal, group, or public speaking—represents the greatest challenge to competent listening and why?

● ● ●

▶ **Figure 6.1**

Communication Activities of College Students

Although college students spend the majority of their communication time listening, listening skills are often overlooked.

Source: Barker, Edwards, Gaines, Gladney, & Holley (1980).

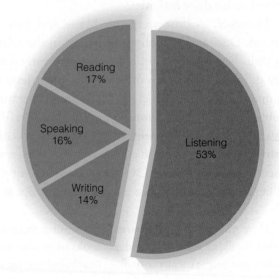

What Is Listening?

Competent listening begins with knowing and understanding what listening is and how it works. The following definition of listening reflects the best thinking of leading researchers and experts in the field: "**Listening** is the process of receiving, constructing meaning from, and responding to spoken and/or nonverbal messages" (International Listening Association, 1995).

Receiving means tuning in to the speaker's entire message, including both its verbal and nonverbal aspects, and consciously paying attention to it. This means making critical choices about paying attention to some things and ignoring others (Wolvin & Coakley, 1996). **Constructing meaning** involves assigning meaning to a speaker's message and mentally clarifying your understanding of it. This step is made more difficult because the meanings that listeners assign to messages reside in themselves, not in the words they are listening to (Bohlken, 1995). Listeners often don't construct the same meaning as the speaker intends. **Responding** completes the interaction between the listener and speaker and is the step in which the listener lets the speaker know the message, its verbal and nonverbal aspects, has been received and understood. This step, if overlooked or poorly done, leads to misunderstandings between the listener and speaker. Figure 6.2 illustrates these three steps in the listening process.

In the opening vignette, Marie followed a process opposite to these three steps. She failed to receive the message and pay attention to Jesse; in fact, she tuned him out almost completely. She couldn't construct any meaning out of his message because she hadn't listened to him. She found herself with only bad choices for responding to Jesse: guess what he said, fake a response, or admit to not listening. By contrast, Marie could have engaged in competent listening, which includes the willingness to listen in a variety of situations, even when the situation is not personally appealing or intriguing (Roberts, 1998; Wolvin & Coakley, 1994).

A **competent listener** applies motivation, knowledge, and skills during all three steps in the listening process—receiving, constructing meaning, and responding. If you want to be a good listener, you must be motivated to listen, knowledgeable about the listening process, and able to use listening skills throughout the three steps. The diagram in Figure 6.3 clarifies this important concept.

learning link

Which step in the listening process challenges communication competence the most? During which step is listening ineffectively most likely to occur?

● ● ●

LUANN *by GREG EVANS*

Receiving the message is a crucial first step in the listening process!

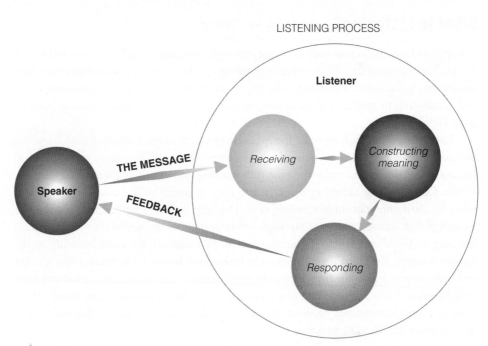

▲ **Figure 6.2**

Listening: A Three-Step Process

The listener receives the message in the first step of this process. During step 2, the listener constructs meaning out of the message that is received. In step 3, the listener responds to the speaker.

To learn to listen more competently, let's now learn about the types of listening, as well as how to integrate them in different situations.

Types of Listening

We can categorize types of listening by their purpose (Wolvin & Coakley, 1996). We listen for any one of three reasons: to learn and comprehend, to evaluate and critique messages, and to empathize with and understand others (Table 6.1).

Listening to Learn and Comprehend

Listening to learn and comprehend includes a search for facts and ideas and a quest for information. This type of listening often occurs during public presentations, when technical subjects are explained, or new information is presented. The listener's purpose is to receive a message that is as similar as possible to the speaker's intended message. Here people listen because they need to know something, such as the meaning of ideas or events, or because they want to keep up with the world.

A good example of listening to learn is the classroom lecture. The professor's purpose is for as many students as possible to receive and comprehend the message being presented. A training event or similar experience at work is another situation where listening to learn

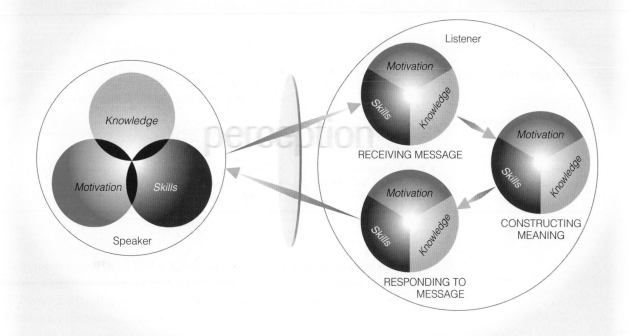

Figure 6.3

A Competence Model of Listening

Motivation, knowledge, and skills are essential to competence at each step in the listening process.

and comprehend is crucial. Attendees need to know the material presented to perform their jobs well, which is accomplished by concentrating on the speaker's message.

A challenge to listening to learn and comprehend is the vast amount and complexity of information that bombards us everyday through broadcast, print, and electronic media. Although you might not think of reading computer-mediated messages as a form of listening, the steps of receiving, constructing meaning, and responding apply to e-mail, instant messaging, and even to chat-room conversations. By carefully selecting which messages to attend to and then giving them your full attention, you can listen to learn and comprehend more competently, both in traditional settings and on the Internet.

Listening to Evaluate and Critique

In addition to comprehending a message, **listening to evaluate and critique** calls for critically analyzing the meaning and merit of a speaker's message. The purpose of evaluative listening is to critique the speaker's facts, opinions, and assumptions. When Jesse told Marie about the problem he was experiencing in his calculus class, he might have been

learning link

Is any one of the three types of listening more valuable than another for communicating interpersonally, in groups, or in public situations? Explain each.

• • •

Table 6.1

Types of Listening

Each of the three types of listening encompasses a particular set of challenges. The solutions to each challenge are shown in the right-hand column.

Listening Types	Description	Challenges	Solutions
To learn and comprehend	▪ Involves searching for facts, ideas, and information	▪ Large amount of information available ▪ Complexity of information	▪ Discriminate among available messages ▪ Attend to message carefully
To evaluate and critique	▪ Focuses on critically assessing and analyzing the speaker's message	▪ Speaker biases ▪ Listener biases	▪ Be open-minded ▪ Postpone judgment
To empathize and understand	▪ Entails concentrating on the speaker's feelings and attitudes	▪ Disagreement with speaker ▪ Discomfort talking about feelings	▪ Try to understand the message ▪ Respect the speaker

looking for her to listen in an evaluative manner and give him some advice about managing the workload in the course.

As you may suspect, because listening to evaluate means critiquing the speaker's message, it entails critical thinking: that is, examining the speaker's reasoning processes and logic, sifting through the ideas and evidence presented, and forming your own conclusions of what was said. This is not a negative process. Rather, it's important to remain positive and open-minded and postpone judgment until you've listened to the entire message.

Evaluative and critical listening skills are crucial in a variety of situations. You may find yourself attending an important presentation at work where you will be expected to comment and provide feedback to the speaker. Or you may be listening to a politician's speech on an issue of importance to you and your neighbors. In each of these situations, as a judge and jury does, you first must listen carefully to the evidence and information presented and give it your full attention. Then you analyze and critically evaluate it, before formulating your opinion or decision.

As a juror, your most important task is to listen to evaluate and critique, no matter how emotional the defense, prosecution, or defendant become. Every juror's duty is to cut through all distractions and focus on the very important task of listening.

The main challenge to evaluative and critical listening is biases, both your own and the speaker's. These biases affect the way you perceive a message, as well as the way the speaker presents it. Interestingly, we all tend to critique a message more severely when we disagree with the speaker and less severely when we agree with what is said. So when listening to evaluate, listen critically to all messages, even those that agree with your opinions and biases on the topic. Furthermore, if the speaker appears biased in a way that influences the way the message is presented, try to separate the speaker's biases from the message itself. If the message is intended to persuade or if the speaker has considerable emotional involvement in the topic, the likelihood of personal bias is increased. By remaining open-minded and postponing judgment, and above all, by listening in an evaluative manner and critically, you can side-step any tendency toward bias.

Listening to Empathize and Understand

Listening to learn and listening to evaluate concentrate our attention on the *content* of the message. By contrast, in **listening to empathize and understand** we focus more on the speaker's *feelings and attitudes* while gaining information. But we're not trying to gain information for our own purposes or to form judgments of what is said. Rather, the interests, opinions, and feelings of the other person override our own. The empathic listener's purpose is to see and feel the world as the other person does and offer two things—understanding and support.

There are two types of empathic responses. A **nonjudgmental empathic response** from a listener helps both people better understand and probe what is going on. A **judgmental empathic response** provides support but also helps to interpret and evaluate the speaker's situation (Rogers, 1986). At the beginning of this chapter, when Jesse shared his worries about the calculus class, he might have wanted Marie to listen empathically, understand his frustration with the course and professor, and provide a judgmental empathic response.

Because empathetic listening helps you understand other people, it's a useful skill in building and maintaining healthy relationships as well as helping other people. If a friend or a partner comes to you with a serious problem, listening to empathize is crucial to understanding the other person's point of view. Listening, and then expressing your impression of the speaker's feelings and attitudes, will help your friend feel better and strengthen your relationship.

One of the main challenges to empathetic listening is to avoid criticizing even when you disagree with the speaker. Overcoming this challenge requires that we suppress the desire to argue about what the person is saying or jump in to offer solutions too soon. Instead, try to just listen to all that the speaker has to say and use nonverbal and verbal feedback to let him or her know that you understand and respect the message.

Another challenge to empathic listening is finding your own level of comfort in talking about feelings and emotions. Although this level of comfort differs from person to person, many researchers say that gender is a factor, with women favoring such talk more than men. In fact, women often express dissatisfaction with the listening behaviors of their male partners when it comes to discussing emotional topics (Borisoff & Merrill, 1998). Whether you are male or female, different communication situations call for the use of different types of listening. Read the Close-Up on Gender box to understand how gender affects how you listen.

Integrating the Types of Listening

For the sake of clarity, we have discussed the three types of listening separately. However, thinking about them as if they were unconnected to one another is misleading. There are times when you want to use more than one type of listening during the same conversation. Suppose you're talking with a good friend about an important life decision, such as deciding whether to change careers, get married, or even get a divorce. In addition to empathizing with how difficult some decisions in life can be, you also want to listen critically to evaluate your friend's choices and offer advice if asked.

CloseUp on Gender

Gender-Based Stereotypes and Expectations for Listening

To learn to listen more competently, start with an awareness of your own listening style. You may find it surprising, but the way you listen is influenced by your gender.

Have you ever noticed that when men listen to a message, they tend to focus more on its content, on the words and tangible details of what is said? For this reason, men are sometimes called action-oriented listeners. Women, in contrast, consider content but also attend more to the relationship and personal aspects of what is said, the feelings and attitudes underlying the message. Women are sometimes referred to as people-oriented listeners. Imagine a couple discussing a problem. Typically, the man listens for an opportunity in the conversation to offer advice to solve the problem—to take some action. The woman listens to empathize and understand the feelings of the speaker to offer support, not just solutions. Because men listen to offer solutions, they may tune out what they can't solve right away. Or they may not listen as attentively if there isn't clearly a problem to solve. Because women tend to listen empathetically, they may delay offering a solution to a problem while trying to understand its complexities.

Cynthia Langham, a listening instructor at the University of Detroit, says that men fall short at remembering details of personal conversations and women may not be as good at remembering facts. This might explain why a man may forget a discussion about a planned social event but recall all of the details of a major news event. When asked why these gender differences exist, Langham points to socialization. Other communication researchers such as Deborah Borisoff and Lisa Merrill agree. They say that society predisposes men and women to use gender-based communication behaviors. What they mean is that society imposes expectations based on gender stereotypes for appropriate behaviors on both men and women, and people tend to conform to those expectations.

Although it sounds as though these gender-based expectations present a challenge, researchers who evaluate listening skills say they can be handled effectively by listening and then responding in a socially desirable way. That means you should remember the three types of listening—listening to learn and comprehend, to evaluate and critique, and to empathize and understand. A competent listener, whether male or female, considers the listening situation he or she is experiencing and decides which type of listening is most appropriate.

Sometimes listening to learn is the right thing to do. For example, you want to listen for content and details at work when you're getting instructions for operating a new computer program or being briefed about new corporate goals. If a candidate for public office wants your vote, you'll need to listen critically, evaluate the facts, detect biases, and then form your opinion. And when a friend or significant other speaks to you about a concern in your relationship, listening to understand the other person's feelings and viewpoints is the right thing to do. Some researchers claim that men listen for facts and women for feelings, but a competent listener adjusts his or her listening style to the demands of the situation and the needs of the other person.

SOURCES: Lawson & Winkelman (2003); Ivy & Backlund (1999); Borisoff & Merrill (1998).

If you're participating in a group discussion about a new project at work, listening both to learn and to critically evaluate others' ideas are equally important. But if your co-workers start worrying aloud about not liking the task or how much time it will take, listening to empathize may be helpful, followed by a nonjudgmental empathic response.

Challenges to Listening

We've seen that integrated use of the three types of listening has many benefits. If that is true, why haven't we all become better listeners? The reason is that every day we encounter challenges to competent listening: physical barriers, psychological barriers, and interaction barriers that affect all three steps in the listening process—receiving, constructing meaning, and responding.

Physical Barriers

The world in which we live and communicate is full of **physical barriers** to listening, including interferences from the physical environment and distracting characteristics or behaviors of the speaker, the listener, or both.

Physical Environment and Noise

An environment does not have to be loud to be distracting. Any interfering sounds or noises, however minor, can become obstacles to competent listening. Even mild distractions such as voices from a nearby discussion or traffic in the street outside can become barriers. An uncomfortable chair, a bad view of the speaker, or a hot and stuffy room can easily distract you from listening.

Speaker and Listener Characteristics and Behaviors

Physical characteristics or behaviors of a speaker can also serve as barriers to listening. A slight accent, a lisp, or even nervous pacing on the part of a speaker may be enough to distract a well-intentioned listener. Physical barriers sometimes also exist in listeners. Feelings of physical fatigue, hunger, or thirst can easily distract any of us from listening. Other physiological limitations, such as hearing problems, also act as physical barriers.

Because physical barriers to listening are common, in some cases you may need to plan ahead to be ready to listen. Whenever possible, you want to avoid opening yourself up to physical distractions. For example, arrive early and take a seat near the front of the class in any course that you find challenging or unappealing. At an interpersonal level, if you and a friend need to have an important conversation, choose a quiet restaurant, not a noisy bar. And if you need to attend an important training or meeting at work, be as well rested as possible.

Closely linked to physical barriers are **psychological barriers** to competent listening. This set of barriers resides within the listener and includes mental and emotional distractions to listening such as boredom, daydreaming, and thinking about personal concerns. If you're not interested in the topic of a message or if some aspect of it offends you, you

learning link

How might a competent communicator use language or nonverbal communication to overcome the barriers to listening?

• • •

Psychological barriers to listening may cause even competent listeners to become distracted.

may succumb to psychological distractions. In our opening story, Marie was already losing interest in Jesse when she gave in to psychological distractions while listening to him talk about his problems with calculus.

These psychological distractions to competent listening often occur as a result of several other factors: the difference in speaking and listening rate, message overload, and message complexity.

Speaking Versus Listening Rate

The difference between the rate at which people speak and the rate at which they can listen causes a psychological distraction. Taking an average of the findings from different studies, people in today's world now speak at approximately 200 words per minute but can listen at about 500 to 600 words per minute, a vast difference (Wolvin, personal communications, 1999). This wide discrepancy leaves considerable mental downtime during which your mind wanders and psychological barriers such as daydreaming begin to occur.

Message Overload and Complexity

Two other causes of psychological distractions are **message overload**—the sheer quantity of messages—and **message complexity**—the extent to which messages are detailed and complicated. Most people spend a large amount of time listening to all kinds of messages

Message overload is a challenge to competent listening in today's information-intensive workplace.

and, as a result, they experience message overload. We listen to teachers, friends, salespeople, and even radio and television personalities. At our workstations, we sift through piles of postal mail, voice mail, and e-mail messages. Who wouldn't tire of listening, given the number of messages we are exposed to every day? Message complexity adds to message overload. We tend to tune out messages we perceive to be too complex or complicated, particularly if we think we can't figure them out. Have you ever attended a lecture that was hard to understand or contained an overwhelming amount of complicated new information? In such situations, even the best listeners become distracted, lose interest, and begin to daydream.

Psychological barriers present even more of a challenge than physical barriers, because they often go unnoticed as they divert our attention from listening (Roberts, 1998). Furthermore, when your attention wanders, you may deny that a psychological barrier has affected you. When someone says you aren't listening, you may automatically deny your negative listening behavior.

One remedy for overcoming the psychological obstacles of message overload and complexity is to listen more selectively and attentively. Consider your typical day. As a college student, you may attend several lectures a day. At work, you spend plenty of time listening to your co-workers. Outside school and work, you listen to your friends and family. It's not surprising that by the end of the day you may experience message overload and complexity. Among all these messages, you need to make decisions about which are most important. Once you consciously decide to listen to a message, give it your full attention and concentration.

Calvin and Hobbes

by Bill Watterson

Listening is an excellent way to overcome interaction barriers between good friends.

Interaction Barriers

Although physical and psychological barriers primarily occur within ourselves, other obstacles to listening result from our interactions with other people. **Interaction barriers** may arise as a result of engaging in verbal battles and using inflammatory language or because of cultural differences between the speaker and listener.

Verbal Battles and Inflammatory Language

When people become entangled in heated arguments, they often fail to listen to one another. In a variety of situations—at home, school, or work—discussions that begin as conversations about opinions and preferences sometimes spiral into disagreements and verbal battles, and little or no listening occurs. While one person is speaking, the other is preoccupied with planning a counterattack, rather than listening. During these verbal battles, speakers often use **trigger words,** words or phrases that cause emotional reactions, intensify the conflict, and further discourage listening. Such words or phrases, particularly in a heated discussion, stop competent listening and foster prejudgment.

You can address this obstacle to listening by making a conscious effort to control verbal battles and your own use of inflammatory language. You also have to learn to handle such language when you are on the receiving end. When a verbal battle is intensifying, try to refocus the discussion on how you and the other person can communicate more competently. Counselors often use this method of stepping outside the conversation and focusing on the process of communication to defuse and deal with conflict situations.

Cultural Differences

Another interaction barrier to competent listening may occur when communicating with people from other cultures and cultural subgroups, which encompasses characteristics such as race, ethnicity, gender, and age.

Culture, which is extensively discussed in Chapter 4, becomes an interaction barrier to listening in two ways. Cultural differences in listening styles are real, so you need to recognize and respect them. Also, people from other cultures may speak or send messages in ways that are different from what you're used to. This means you need to listen more competently, despite the fact that the different speaking or presentation style may tend to distract you from listening.

According to an expert in intercultural communication, the general rules for communicating in a culture predispose members of that culture to favor particular listening styles (Wood, 2003). For example, in Nepal, it's considered impolite to make vocal sounds of any kind while listening. In contrast, in the United States and other Western cultures, sounds such as *um-hmm* indicate the listener is paying attention. In Western cultures, it's considered polite for the listener to make frequent, but not constant, eye contact with the speaker. In some Eastern and Middle Eastern cultures, however, it's considered disrespectful for a listener to look directly at a speaker. In some Asian cultures, periods of silence during conversations are considered desirable opportunities to reflect on key ideas being discussed. In most Western cultures, if a speaker pauses, the listener may rush in to fill a silence that seems awkward and uncomfortable. Although you need to adjust to culturally based differences in listening styles, don't pretend to prefer the listening style of another culture because that may appear condescending. That said, you can communicate respect for the speaker by being aware of the cultural differences. And if a person from another culture is listening to you, don't expect them to display the listening styles of your culture.

Just as listening styles differ, the ways people send and present messages differ from culture to culture. A competent listener is aware of cultural differences in the way messages are presented and adjusts to the speaker's style by putting aside personal or cultural expectations. To listen competently, be patient with the way the other person communicates and avoid being distracted by cultural differences. For instance, if you are listening to a speech or lecture and the speaker's remarks are organized in a way you can't easily follow, make an extra effort to understand or ask politely for some clarification.

Overcoming Challenges to Listening

Table 6.2 summarizes the three challenges to listening just discussed. Although the barriers to listening may seem overwhelming, adopting a competence approach will simplify these challenges and help you overcome them. Let's now examine listening competence at each step in the listening process—receiving, constructing meaning, and responding.

Receiving Competence

Receiving competence means the listener is motivated, knowledgeable, and skilled at tuning in to the speaker's message and attending to it. When Jesse told Marie about his problem, she did not receive his message competently—she tuned him out and failed to pay attention. Instead, Marie could have set aside her own interests for the moment to listen to Jesse's concerns. A competent listener would have demonstrated motivation by being open and receptive to the message and showing a willingness to adjust his or her listening style to the speaker. A competent listener also demonstrates knowledge and understanding of the various factors that influence the way a message is received. With such understanding, Marie would have realized that her own interests were taking priority and that she had to consciously make an effort to pay attention. Even if you have the motivation and knowledge to listen to a message, without skills you cannot receive that

Table 6.2

Challenges to Listening		
Challenges to Listening	**Barriers**	**Causes of Barriers**
Physical Barriers	▪ Environment and noise	▪ Peripheral conversations, uncomfortable furniture, bad view, crowds, heat, cold, noise
	▪ Distracting speaker characteristics	▪ Accent, lisp, pacing, tics, unusual clothing
	▪ Distracting listener characteristics	▪ Fatigue, hunger, thirst, uncomfortable clothing, hearing problems
Psychological Barriers	▪ Speaking versus listening rate	▪ Boredom ▪ Daydreaming ▪ Worry about personal concerns
	▪ Message overload and complexity	▪ Quantity of messages ▪ Message delivery in multiple media ▪ Complexity of messages
Interaction Barriers	▪ Verbal battles and inflammatory language	▪ Trigger words and phrases ▪ Emotional reactions
	▪ Cultural differences	▪ Different cultural listening styles ▪ Different cultural speaking styles

message competently. Here are some receiving skills to help you become a more competent listener:

- Prepare yourself to listen mentally, physically, and emotionally. Be well rested and well fed (but not too well fed!).
- Clarify your purpose for listening—to learn, evaluate, or empathize. Set a specific but flexible listening goal for yourself in a given situation. Decide exactly what outcome you hope to achieve by listening to the speaker.
- Identify barriers to listening and eliminate distractions so you can concentrate on the message.
- Focus your attention on listening in the moment. Concentrate on the speaker and the message, not on your own thoughts and feelings.
- Postpone evaluation of the message until the speaker has finished.

This list of skills may be hard to recall if a situation arises suddenly and you are called on to listen more competently. However, simply remembering that you have a responsibility to attend to and receive a speaker's message will help you receive that message more competently when it matters most.

Constructing Meaning Competence

Constructing meaning competence calls for the listener to be motivated, knowledgeable, and skilled when it comes to assigning meaning to a speaker's message. Marie was not able to attribute meaning accurately to Jesse's message, primarily because she had failed to even receive it. Had Marie *received* Jesse's message, she then might have realized that his perceptions of the meaning of the message differed from her own. She could have demonstrated knowledge and understanding of any biases influencing how she or Jesse constructed meaning out of the message. Remember, as discussed in Chapter 1, real meaning—objective meaning—is not in words but is individually constructed by both the speaker and the listener. In addition to motivation and knowledge, here are some constructing meaning skills that will help you listen more competently:

- Set aside personal biases and prejudices as you attribute meaning to the message: make a conscious effort to listen as impartially as possible before you decide what the message means.
- Repress any tendency to respond emotionally or negatively to the message: Don't overreact or listen for flaws in the message. Set aside your emotional reactions until you've listened to the entire message and clarified your perception of it.
- Analyze objectively what the speaker is saying: Listen for both the global meaning of the message and the speaker's evidence or argument. Mentally construct a picture of the speaker's message and examine and evaluate its meaning and worth, based on its own merits.

As with the receiving skills, these constructing meaning skills may not come readily to mind when you need them most. If you find yourself in a heated argument, you probably won't take this list from your pocket, read it, and repress any tendency to respond emotionally. However, you can and do have a responsibility as a competent listener to remember that the meaning you and the speaker construct for the same message may be quite different and that you should respect those differences.

Responding Competence

Responding competence means the listener is motivated, knowledgeable, and skilled when communicating to the speaker that the message has been received and understood. Returning to the opening story, Marie was unable to respond competently to Jesse because she had failed to both receive and construct meaning out of his message. A competent listener demonstrates motivation by showing interest and responding appropriately and effectively. Marie, for instance, should have listened to Jesse, and then she would have been able to respond to his concerns. Competent listeners also demonstrate knowledge and understanding of the importance and roles of verbal and nonverbal feedback and paraphrasing for overcoming barriers to listening. In addition to motivation and knowledge, here are some responding skills you should use as a competent listener:

- Identify and remember the main points of the message: use memory devices such as taking notes to help you accurately recall the message.
- Strive to understand and clarify the meaning of the message by asking questions to clear up anything you don't understand.
- Demonstrate interest in the speaker's message by providing appropriate verbal and nonverbal feedback: Provide verbal feedback to clarify your understanding of and reactions to the message. Let the speaker know you're listening by using nonverbal cues.
- Paraphrase the message to achieve full comprehension and clarity: describe the meaning you have attributed to the message, without evaluating it or presenting your point of view.

Feedback and paraphrasing obviously are central to responding and competent listening. These two processes are now described in a bit more detail but, before going on,

Table 6.3

The Listening Process		
Motivation	**Knowledge**	**Skills**
Receiving Competence A competent listener is motivated to - be open and receptive to the message - adjust his or her listening style to the speaker - overcome physical barriers and bridge differences	A competent listener understands the influence on receiving of - culture, values, communication styles, and preferences - speaking and listening rates - message overload and complexity	A competent listener - prepares to listen - clarifies the purpose for listening - identifies barriers and eliminates distractions - focuses attention on listening - postpones evaluation of the message
Constructing Meaning Competence A competent listener is motivated to - respect differences in perception between speaker and listener - acknowledge that biases distort how meaning is attributed to the message	A competent listener understands the influence on constructing meaning of - perceptual differences of meaning on the message - personal experiences, opinions, and attitudes - personal biases	A competent listener - sets aside biases and prejudices - listens impartially - represses emotional or negative responses - analyzes the message objectively
Responding Competence A competent listener is motivated to - show interest and respect for what is said - avert misunderstandings by clarifying the message	A competent listener understands the influence on responding of - feedback and paraphrasing - verbal and nonverbal feedback - interrupting the speaker	A competent listener - identifies and remembers main points - provides verbal and nonverbal feedback - clarifies meaning by asking questions - paraphrases the message - controls interruptions

you may want to review the succinct summary of the motivation, knowledge, and skills for listening in Table 6.3.

Feedback and Paraphrasing

Feedback is the process a listener uses to communicate to the speaker his or her understanding of the message, reactions to it, and any effects it might have had on the listener. Feedback, which can be sent verbally and nonverbally, is the listener's way of informing the speaker that the message has been received.

Paraphrasing is a technique for providing verbal feedback to the speaker by summarizing and restating the meaning of the speaker's message in his or her own words. Because both the verbal and nonverbal aspects of a message are important, listeners may need to paraphrase both. To provide such feedback, you would summarize the content of the message—the speaker's opinions, ideas, and attitudes—and the way the speaker appears to feel about the message. For example, Marie could have paraphrased her impression of Jesse's calculus situation in this way: "I think you seem to be having a real problem keeping your head above water in the calculus class, and that is very upsetting to you. Am I correct?"

In a group meeting at work, paraphrasing can clarify your understanding of a new concept or solution to a problem being presented. Paraphrasing allows the speaker and other group members to know what you have understood as well as what you haven't, and it gives the speaker a chance to clear up any misconceptions. In addition to paraphrasing and sending feedback, which are verbal techniques, you could send nonverbal feedback to

learning link

Is verbal or nonverbal feedback more essential to communication competence when communicating interpersonally, in groups, or in public?

• • •

the speaker in the group by nodding your head in agreement or smiling in reaction to the presentation. Or you might furrow your brow or shake your head in disagreement if you don't think the idea is a good one.

A concept discussed in Chapter 4 provides an important key to paraphrasing and sending feedback competently. By the way you use language you can establish your ownership of the response you send to the speaker. The goal is to indicate clearly that you are communicating only *your* perception of the message. To do this, begin the paraphrase statement with an "I" statement and end it with a perception-checking statement. "I think that I heard you say this or that. Am I right? Is that what you meant?" This ownership of your perception of the message is important because you may not be correct in your perception. Also, by indicating that it is only your perception, not reality, the speaker can feel comfortable about amending your perception. The perception-checking question gives the speaker an opportunity to clarify if his or her message has been misunderstood.

Another key to paraphrasing and sending feedback with competence relates to the way feedback messages are worded. In a study of college students in a public speaking class, students exhibited a greater number of preferred speaking behaviors and improved more when they received feedback that was low in intensity and not perceived as direct, personal criticism (Smith & King, 2004). The use of "I" messages is one way to appear less critical of the speaker.

Despite the value of feedback and paraphrasing in interpersonal and small group communication situations, these skills should be used cautiously in intimate relationships. Research suggests that using paraphrasing to check understanding and express empathy isn't always as effective as previously thought (Gottman, Coan, Carrere, & Swanson, 1998). Gottman and other researchers have found that hearing this kind of feedback too often from an intimate partner can become annoying and have a negative effect on the discussion. This caution aside, feedback and paraphrasing are important skills for a competent listener to use, based on the following guidelines:

Paraphrasing and feedback help intimate relationships thrive when those skills are used appropriately.

- Feedback should be fairly immediate (King, Young, & Behnke, 2000). The sooner the speaker receives feedback, the more valuable it is, because people pay more attention to information about recent events.
- The paraphrased message should represent your honest impression and feelings, without being unnecessarily cruel. To avoid offending the other person, you can sometimes preface negative feedback with positive feedback. The positive message predisposes the other person to pay attention to any negative feedback.
- The feedback you provide to the speaker should be clear, informative, and unbiased. Think through what you intend to say to make sure it's a fair and objective interpretation of the speaker's message. Then, be open to corrections to your feedback.

In summary, competent listening draws on three sets of competencies that relate to the three stages in the listening process. In the story at the beginning of this chapter, if Marie had received Jesse's message and accurately assigned meaning to it, she would have been able to respond and provide feedback to him.

Table 6.4

A Model of Competent Relational Listening		
Before Interaction	**During Interaction**	**After Interaction**
Hear	Just listen	Remember the conversation
Put own thoughts aside	Respond	Act on it
Be open-minded	Don't interrupt	
Be there	Talk freely	
Make conscious effort	Be together	
Take time	Acknowledge	
Do it even if don't want to	Give input	
Sit down	Share	
Willingness	Attend to verbal cues	
	Interact	
	Participate	
	Attend to nonverbal cues	
	Be involved	

SOURCE: Halone & Pecchioni (2001).

A group of 13 college students, much like Jesse and Marie, were asked to identify the listening competencies that would be most useful before interacting, during an interaction, and afterward (Halone & Pecchioni, 2001). Compare your own ability to listen competently with their list, presented in Table 6.4.

The next three main parts of this book focus on interpersonal communication, small group communication, and public speaking. The motivation, knowledge, and skills necessary for competent listening discussed in this chapter are essential to competence in each of these three communication contexts.

 ## Chapter Summary

Listening is the process of receiving, constructing meaning from, and responding to spoken or nonverbal messages or both. Receiving is tuning in to the speaker's verbal and nonverbal message; constructing meaning involves assigning meaning to the message; and responding is the process the listener uses to let the speaker know the message is received and understood.

Achieving competence in listening is crucial—in college, at work, and in relationships and society. A competent listener is highly motivated to listen well across a variety of these situations.

Listening to learn and understand requires a search for facts and ideas and a quest for information. Listening to evaluate and critique focuses on critically analyzing the meaning and merit of a speaker's message. Listening to empathize and understand entails concentrating on the speaker's feelings and attitudes.

Challenges to listening competence result from physical, psychological, and interaction barriers. Physical barriers include distractions in the physical environment and distracting characteristics or behaviors of the speaker or the listener. Psychological barriers include mental and emotional distractions to listening and can result from the discrepancy between speaking and listening rates and from message overload and complexity. Interaction barriers arise when people engage in verbal battles and use inflammatory language or because of culturally based differences in listening or speaking styles.

A competence model for listening calls for the listener to apply motivation, knowledge, and skills to the three steps in the listening process and thus overcome the challenges to listening. A competent listener is motivated, knowledgeable, and skilled when it comes to tuning in to the speaker's message, assigning meaning to it, and letting the speaker know the message is received and understood. Feedback communicates the listener's understanding and reactions to the speaker's message, as well as effects it might have had on the listener. The listener uses paraphrasing to restate verbally the meaning of both the verbal and nonverbal content of the speaker's message.

Study and Review

The premium companion website for *Human Communication* offers a broad range of resources that will help you better understand the material in this chapter, complete assignments, and succeed on tests. The website resources include

- Interactive self-assessments, competency grids, and other tools
- Web links, practice activities, self-quizzes, and a sample final exam

For more information about this text's electronic learning resources, consult the *Guide to Online Resources for Human Communication* or visit **http://communication.wadsworth.com/morreale2.**

Key Terms

The key terms below are defined in the chapter on the pages indicated. They are also presented alphabetically with definitions in the Glossary, which begins on page 467. The book's website includes flashcards and crossword puzzles to help you learn these terms and the concepts they represent.

listening 137
receiving 137
constructing meaning 137
responding 137
competent listener 137
listening to learn and comprehend 138
listening to evaluate and critique 139
listening to empathize and understand 141
nonjudgmental empathic response 141
judgmental empathic response 141
physical barrier 143

psychological barrier 143
message overload 144
message complexity 144
interaction barrier 145
trigger word 145
receiving competence 146
constructing meaning competence 147
responding competence 148
feedback 149
paraphrasing 149

Building Motivation

Go to the book's website to complete an interactive self-assessment similar to the other Building Motivation Self-Assessments in the text. The online Listening Self-Assessment asks you to consider eight communication situations and rate your listening competence in each.

 Building Knowledge _____

The questions below are among the practice activities on the book's website.

1. If listening improves the quality of life in society, what can you do to encourage more people to listen better?

2. Which of the three steps in the listening process (receiving, constructing meaning, responding) is most important and why? Which step causes the most misunderstandings? Explain.

3. Of the three types of listening (to learn, to evaluate, and to empathize), which do you find most difficult to do and why? How can you address that personal challenge?

4. Of the three types of barriers to listening (physical, psychological, and interaction), which causes you the most problems as a listener? Why and what can you do about it?

5. Motivation to listen in a variety of communication situations is important to competent listening. What can you do to become more motivated in less appealing situations?

6. Research suggests that paraphrasing and feedback in intimate conversations can be annoying, but we know it helps prevent misunderstandings. How can we provide feedback in the most acceptable way in intimate discussions?

 Building Skills _____

The exercises below are among the practice activities on the book's website.

Individual Exercises

1. Ralph Nichols, a notable scholar of listening, constructed a list, Top 10 Bad Listening Habits. Evaluate yourself based on the list. Go to **http://www .dartmouth.edu/~acskills/docs/10_bad_listening_habits.doc**.

2. Identify a communication situation in which it's important to listen to learn. List the reasons for that importance. Then identify communication situations in which listening to evaluate and listening to empathize are crucial and list the reasons why.

3. At the beginning of the next meeting you attend at work or a lecture at school, identify possible barriers to listening in that situation. Decide how you can overcome these barriers and listen more competently. Set a goal to listen attentively throughout the lecture or meeting. Afterward, do a self-check to see if you retained more information than you usually do.

4. On the Internet, go to **http://www.listen.org/pages/quotes.html**, an award-winning site containing many quotations about listening. Choose several quotations that particularly appeal to you and write a short explanation of why they are meaningful.

5. Watch an interview on television, perhaps one of the late-night or Sunday morning talk shows. Observe the listening skills of the interviewee and interviewer. Critique each person's listening, feedback, and paraphrasing skills. Who is the better listener and why?

6. If you are using InfoTrac College Edition, enter *listening* as a search topic. In various articles, you'll find a variety of hints for improving listening skills. Review the suggestions and prepare your own list of things to do to become a better listener.

7. Analyze a listening situation in which you were recently involved and develop an action plan to develop and refine your listening skills.

Group Activities

1. Form a small group and have each group member think of a person who is a good listener. Each member then writes a description of what that person actually does and why he or she is a good listener. Compare the descriptions and produce a summary list of characteristics and behaviors of good listeners. Then have each group member self-evaluate based on the list.

2. In a small group, have each group member list several trigger words that can provoke an emotional reaction. Share the words in the group and try to come up with alternative words that won't trigger an emotional response. Compile a list of trigger words and their alternatives and share them with other groups.

3. Form groups of four with people you don't already know. Each group member should choose a number, from 1 to 4. For 3 minutes, person 1 tells person 2 about herself or himself. Then for another 3 minutes, person 2 tells person 1 about himself or herself. Persons 3 and 4 observe. Then person 1 paraphrases and provides feedback to person 2 about what was said. In the same way, person 2 paraphrases and provides feedback to person 1. Give each person a chance to speak, listen, and observe. Neither person should interrupt the other while the paraphrased message is being presented. The observers (persons 3 and 4) should comment on how accurate the feedback was. Finally, persons 1 and 2 are given time to clarify any misunderstandings. Switch pairs so persons 3 and 4 speak and listen while persons 1 and 2 observe.

References

Barker, L., Edwards, R., Gaines, C., Gladney, K., & Holley, F. (1980). An investigation of proportional time spent in various communication activities by college students. *Journal of Applied Communication Research, 8,* 101–109.

Bentley, S. (2000). Listening in the 21st century. *International Journal of Listening, 14,* 129–142.

Bohlken, B. (1995). *The bare facts about the listener's responsibility in understanding semantic meaning.* Paper presented at the annual meeting of the International Listening Association, Little Rock, AR.

Borisoff, D., & Merrill, L. (1998). *The power to communicate: Gender differences as barriers* (3rd ed.). Prospect Heights, IL: Waveland.

Campbell, T., & Inguagiato, R. (1994). The power of listening. *Physician Executive, 20*(9), 35.

Darling, A., & Dannels, D. (2003). Practicing engineers talk about the importance of talk: A report on the role of oral communication in the workplace. *Communication Education, 52*(1), 1–16.

Ford, W., Wolvin, A., & Chung, S. (2000). Students' self-perceived listening competencies in the basic speech communication course. *International Journal of Listening, 14,* 1–13.

Gottman, J., Coan, J., Carrere, S., & Swanson, C. (1998). Predicting marital happiness and stability from newlywed interactions. *Communication Education, 60,* 5–22.

Graves, D. H. (1995). Teacher as listener. *Instructor, 105*(2), 36.

Halone, K. K., & Pecchioni, L. L. (2001). Relational listening: A grounded theoretical model. *Communication Reports, 14,* 59–71.

Harris, R. M. (1997). Turn listening into a powerful presence. *Training & Development, 51*(7), 9.

International Listening Association. (1995, March). An ILA definition of listening. *ILA Listening Post, 53,* 1–4. Milwaukee, WI: Alverno College.

Ivy, D., & Backlund, P. (1999). *Exploring genderspeak: Personal effectiveness in gender communication* (2nd ed.). New York: McGraw-Hill.

King, P. E., Young, M. J., & Behnke, R. R. (2000). Public speaking performance improvement as a function of information processing in immediate and delayed feedback interventions. *Communication Education, 49*(4), 365–375.

Lawson, M., & Winkelman, C. (2003). The social desirability factor in the measurement of listening skills: A brief report. *Counseling Psychology Quarterly, 16*(1), 43–45.

Paukert, A., Stagner, B., & Kerry, H. (2004). The assessment of active listening skills in helpline volunteers. *Stress, Trauma, and Crisis: An International Journal, 7*(1), 61–76.

Rea, C., & Rea, D. (2000). Responding to user views of service performance. *Journal of Mental Health, 9*(4), 351–363.

Roberts, C. (1998, March). *Developing willing listeners: A host of problems and a plethora of solutions.* Paper presented at the International Listening Association Convention, Kansas City.

Rogers, C. R. (1986). Reflection of feelings. *Person-Centered Review, 1,* 375–377.

Smith, C. D., & King, P. E. (2004). Student feedback sensitivity and the efficacy of feedback interventions in public speaking performance improvement. *Communication Education, 53*(3), 203–217.

Tan, L., Fowler, M., & Hawkes, L. (2004). Management accounting curricula: Striking a balance between the views of educators and practitioners. *Accounting Education, 13*(1), 51–67.

Waldron, V., & Lavitt, M. (2001). "Welfare-to-work": An analysis of the communication competencies taught in a job training program. *Communication Education, 50*(1), 15–33.

Wolvin, A., & Coakley, C. (1994). Listening competence. *Journal of the International Listening Association, 8,* 148–160.

Wolvin, A., & Coakley, C. (1996). *Listening* (5th ed.). Dubuque, IA: Brown & Benchmark.

Wood, J. (2003). *Communication mosaics* (3rd ed.). Belmont, CA: Thomson Learning.

Listening Competence Skills Grid _____

To help you understand how to use this grid, the skills displayed by Marie and Jesse in the opening vignette of this chapter have been analyzed below. Examine that analysis and then think about a recent listening situation and what you could have done more competently. First, describe the context of the listening situation in the spaces provided. Next, analyze your listening skills based on the skills explained in this chapter for each step in the listening process. In the first column, briefly describe and give examples of how your skills may have been less than competent. Using these less competent skills as a point of comparison to fill in the second column, describe the skills you think would have been perceived as more competent in the particular context. With practice, you will find you can use this grid to help develop your listening skills for future listening situations, as well as to analyze listening situations you have already experienced.

ANALYZING MARIE AND JESSE'S LISTENING SKILLS

Context

CULTURE: College campus in the United States

TIME: Evening after work and school

RELATIONSHIP: A girlfriend and boyfriend in an intimate relationship

PLACE: At the home of one of the two students

FUNCTION: To exchange information about each other's experiences of the day

LISTENING SKILLS	LESS COMPETENT	MORE COMPETENT
RECEIVING SKILLS	Marie tuned Jesse out completely, and her attention wandered from what he was saying to matters of more personal importance to her.	Jesse needs to talk to Marie at a time when she is more ready to listen. Marie should eliminate any barriers to listening that are distracting her, so she can focus her attention on what Jesse has to say.
CONSTRUCTING MEANING SKILLS	Because Marie failed to receive Jesse's message, she was unable to accurately assign meaning to it.	Marie needs to analyze Jesse's messages objectively, listening for his global meaning.
RESPONDING SKILLS	Marie was unable to respond competently because she had neither received nor constructed meaning out of Jesse's message.	When Marie realized that she had not listened to Jesse, she could have responded honestly and asked him to repeat his concerns and problem, perhaps at another time.

ANALYZING YOUR LISTENING SKILLS

Context

CULTURE:

TIME:

RELATIONSHIP:

PLACE:

FUNCTION:

LISTENING SKILLS	LESS COMPETENT	MORE COMPETENT
RECEIVING SKILLS		
CONSTRUCTING MEANING SKILLS		
RESPONDING SKILLS		

© Marc Dolphin/Stone/Getty Images

LEARNING OBJECTIVES

After studying this chapter, you should be able to

1. Demonstrate the difference between knowing "what" and knowing "how" to communicate.

2. Distinguish among repertoires, scripts, and rules.

3. Formulate goals in communicative plans and subplans.

4. Diagnose factors that can interfere with action assembly of communicative behavior.

5. Explain the role of positive and negative expectancies in the perception of competence.

6. Describe how empathy and perspective taking assist in learning how to be a competent communicator.

7. Describe how information-gaining strategies assist in learning how to be a competent communicator.

Interpersonal Competence: Building Knowledge

E liah was a young, attractive college student tending bar in the campus pub. Preston, a recent graduate, was visiting with his friends, Greg and Jeff, who had decided to meet him at the pub to discuss their recent job-finding experiences and catch up with each other. After some discussion, one of them mentioned how attractive he found Eliah. All three guys agreed, and their conversation turned to the awkwardness of asking someone out for a date. They talked about various ways of introducing themselves to women, various pickup lines they had used, and the general strategies of directness and indirectness, serious and humorous approaches, and so on. After some heated discussion about their respective "theories" about pickup lines, Preston excused himself for a moment while Greg and Jeff continued debating the merits of their favorite approaches to the initial courtship ritual. A few minutes later, Preston returned to the table and announced that he was able to get Eliah's number and she would be expecting a call from him the following week!

Thoroughly surprised, Greg and Jeff asked how he had managed to get her number. Preston explained that he had approached the bar with a big smile on his face, placed his personal data assistant on the bar, and asked her which day she would like him to call her. At first she had seemed a little flustered, but regaining her composure, she gave him the excuse of a busy schedule. Preston realized that

159

Eliah experienced some embarrassment about being put on the spot, so he made small talk about how busy the bar looked, sympathizing that she must have a lot of responsibility at work. He then suggested he would adapt his schedule to hers, and asked if there was any time on his schedule that would work for her. After the initial awkwardness had been smoothed over by chatting with her, she looked over his appointment book and wrote her number on a date on which Preston had nothing scheduled. Greg and Jeff looked at each other in disbelief, and after a long moment passed, Jeff simply said, "There goes my theory." ■

This situation illustrates several important features about the role of knowledge in interpersonal communication. First, people often have theories about how things are supposed to work, and what things work better than others. These theories are based on all types of notions. In the vignette, notice that Preston, Greg, and Jeff were operating on the assumption that men are supposed to do the asking. Greg and Jeff assumed further that the asking should be ornamented or disguised as a strategy.

Second, people's theories are not always correct in a given situation. It is possible that any of Greg's, Jeff's, or Preston's strategies would have worked. However, there are several other possibilities. Eliah may already be in an exclusive relationship. She may only go out with people of a given religion or ethnic group. Eliah might be a lesbian. She might even prefer to do the selecting and asking, rather than letting the man do it. In short, people's working theories of communication are just that: theories. They may do a fair job of accounting for things much of the time, but they are rarely right in all cases.

Third, sometimes people overanalyze. Preston had the same chance of being competent or incompetent as Greg or Jeff. But rather than thinking through the situation in all its possible variations, while Greg and Jeff were debating the fine points of their strategies, he took the chance and acted creatively on his instinct and experience. It is possible to overanalyze communication, and often the best solution is to follow your instincts.

This chapter examines the role of knowledge in the development of relationships. When you interact with someone, you are developing a relationship. Over time, you come to consider a person a "stranger," "acquaintance," "friend," "best friend," "lover," "colleague," "sibling," "parent," "kin," or even an "enemy." Other relationships, such as with parents and siblings, evolve significantly over time even if the basic label for the relationship does not. All these labels represent mental models of people in your world and how you are supposed to behave toward them. They suggest a type of relationship with someone, and they all imply that you have interacted, or might interact, with this person. How any of these relationships unfold, whether they are successful or unsuccessful, brief or enduring, depends in large part on how you use your knowledge of communication to influence their course.

Knowledge underlies all communication. Yet most of the time you are unaware of how you know what to say and do. You simply "know" or you "don't know." To communicate more competently, it is important to understand the mystery of what we know and how we know it. The first step is to understand the difference between the two basic types of communicative knowledge introduced in Chapter 2: content and procedural knowledge. As you recall, content knowledge is what you know and procedural knowledge is your understanding of how to use content knowledge.

How We Learn

Most of us take pride in what we have learned to do in our lifetime. When it comes to your communication competence, you probably assume you have acquired it by being a keen observer of the social world and by developing a social intelligence through careful application and attention to the effects of your behaviors. Certainly, much of what we know about what and how to communicate is learned. Yet a surprising amount of what we know of communication is based on our genetic inheritance. For example, studies of twins suggest that a third to half of our communication anxiety, general friendliness, and interpersonal aggressiveness is genetic (Beatty, Heisel, Hall, Levine, & La France, 2002). It is likely that our inherited tendencies are significantly shaped and enabled by our experiences in the world, both as a developing infant and as a child, as well as our experiences throughout our lifetimes.

When our general inherited tendencies are significantly shaped and influenced by our experiences, we can view the result as a type of learning process. Specifically, **learning** is the internalization of a new way of understanding and behaving such that it can be produced on demand. That is, learning translates experiences into information, principles, or ability, any of which we can produce as needed. Obviously, what we can learn, we can unlearn as well. You learn someone's phone number and then promptly forget it after entering it into your cell phone's speed dial. You might have learned how to make papier-mâché in third grade and forgotten how by now.

Throughout our lives, we tend to learn things through two basic modes: direct and indirect. **Direct learning** is the internalization of understanding or behaviors through your individual action and experience in the world. You touch a hot stove and rapidly learn to touch glowing objects with considerable caution in the future. You misuse a word and are corrected, and you learn to not use it that way again. You crack a joke in class and other students laugh, and you learn that you can achieve social rewards through humor, and you are more likely to seize opportunities to make jokes in the future.

Direct learning tends to occur through reward and punishment processes. When behaviors produce rewards or satisfying states of experience, we are more likely to engage in those behaviors in relevant situations in the future. Sometimes these behaviors are positively reinforcing, as when a joke elicits laughter, which increases the likelihood of our making jokes in subsequent interactions. Other times these behaviors are negatively reinforcing, such as when we try to change the topic to avoid the frustration of arguing or getting into a conflict with a loved one. Finally, some behaviors we learn through punishment, such as when we are disciplined for "talking back" to our parents, which may extinguish our tendency to engage in such insolence in the future.

We are able to learn only a fraction of all the communication behaviors we use in our lifetimes through direct learning. There simply is not enough time to engage in all the situations we would need to directly learn everything we need to know. For example, the first time you attend a school dance, you may never have been in that exact type of situation before. So how do you figure out how to behave competently? You think back to similar types of situations you have observed, and you observe what people are doing once you get there. You can draw upon any number of models of competent (and incompetent) behavior. You can recall movies, novels, stories, wedding receptions you have attended, and so forth. Your observation of relevant examples of behavior for the internalization of understanding or behavior is **indirect learning.**

During indirect learning, also called "social learning" (Bandura, 1977), we observe how other people, whether real or fictional, behave. These others serve as models for our own behavior. We consider whether their behaviors appeared to be rewarded or punished, and we formulate mental conceptions of what can be done, what to do, and what not to do. Because you observe many instances and models, you may construct mental amalgams of behaviors. For example, by the time you went on what you would consider your first date, you had probably indirectly experienced dozens, if not hundreds, of models for how to behave on a first date. You had seen such dates in movies, read about them in magazines, heard about them from your friends, and perhaps even observed others in your own social network who were on a first date. From all these observed experiences, for any given situation you pick and choose those behaviors, types of statements, and patterns of activity that seem most competent, and that becomes a working mental plan. Some behaviors may be ignored because they don't seem like you, and others may seem beyond your ability. Once in the situation, you may make any number of adjustments to your working plan. Finally, once you actually engage in these behaviors, you then experience direct learning, and adjust your indirect learning accordingly.

Ultimately, what we know about what and how to communicate in any given situation is a product of the gifts we were born with and all the myriad direct and indirect experiences we have had along the way. Our knowledge of communication informs what we do and what we believe we are able to do. When we believe we are able to communicate competently in a given situation, this belief reflects our **self-efficacy** (Bandura, 1977). For example, when you feel anxious about whether you have sufficient information in a situation to behave competently, whether you remain in the situation to reduce your uncertainty depends on whether you believe you can find out what you need to know (Afifi & Weiner, 2004). Instead of going to a school dance, some people lacking sufficient self-efficacy avoid going for fear of not knowing what to do. Much of the value of course work in communication is to enhance your self-efficacy in various contexts you may encounter.

Finally, as illustrated by any performance activities and assignments in your communication courses, deliberate practice is a common technique for refining your knowledge. As your knowledge and learning improve, the speed, accuracy, and flexibility of your skills will increase and you can better apply those skills (Greene, 2003).

Content Knowledge: Knowing What to Communicate

Superstars and geniuses are often asked what makes them so much better than their peers. Whether in science, sports, acting, writing, or another field, such stars often are unable to answer this question. Of course they study under good teachers or coaches, work hard, and use established methods of their trade. But their peers can claim the same. So what makes these superstars more successful?

This is one of the enduring mysteries of knowledge. We often know something without really knowing *how* we know it. You remember learning how to drive or calculate percentages, but do you remember learning how to communicate a compliment or have an argument? When another person says something, do you take time to interpret each word separately and then add up all these meanings, based on your knowledge of syntax, or do you just have an instinctive sense of the person's overall meaning? Do you reflect back on all the similar statements you have ever heard, run through all the possible responses you have learned, select one, and then decide how to deliver it with a particular style of inflection and nonverbal nuance? There may be situations in which you do, but in general, conversation simply happens, without our giving much conscious attention to how it is happening at the moment.

To the extent we have learned bad communication habits, we may not only fail to recognize these bad habits in ourselves but be unaware of how to change these habits. Clearly, the first step to improving our communication competence is to learn about how we learn and how we know what we know in communication.

Understanding how communicative knowledge works requires first an understanding of how we build a mental library of concepts. This library of our mind is a repository of what we know. It is our content knowledge, the "what" of knowledge. It represents the ideas and words we use to construct messages. A recipe first lists the contents needed to make a dish before it tells you what to do with the contents. Likewise, when you tell a joke, your content knowledge is the actual words or lines of the joke.

We send many signals when we communicate, but are we always sure of what those signals are and how they are interpreted? Are any of the people in the picture flirting, or are they merely being friendly? How do you know? What cues do you use to determine whether these people are flirting or being friendly?

In a large bookstore, the books are organized in two very different ways. In the sales tables or bins, books are often shelved with no attention to type of book, author, or subject matter. On the retail shelves however, books are typically arranged according to subject matter. Fiction is divided into adventure, romance, suspense, science fiction, and horror. Nonfiction may be divided into reference, travel, current events and politics, social sciences, self-help, and so forth. Although you may doubt it at times, our minds are almost never organized like the sales bins.

People often do not have readily available information on what to communicate or how to communicate it. In the cartoon, the suitor on a first date finds himself at a loss for what to say, and instead of locating appropriate topics in his store of communicative knowledge, he brings notes along to guide his conversation. Clearly, he would be more competent were he to have better organized knowledge of the communication context.

To be useful, knowledge must be organized, and to be organized, it must be categorized. Like books, knowledge is rarely generic. There is little you could say that is equally relevant to all situations. In the context of interpersonal communication, three categories of communicative knowledge comprise the library of the mind.

Repertoires

A **repertoire** is the set of all roles a person is capable of playing, or enacting, along with behaviors, or actions, that comprise those roles. **Roles,** in turn, are the patterns and style of statements and behaviors a person is able to perform across contexts. Thus a repertoire consists of the various characters, or persons, you can perform.

The idea of a repertoire is derived from the theatrical metaphor we discussed in Chapter 2. In their careers, most actors play many different roles with many different characters and types of plot lines. Similarly, you may have a repertoire of many different roles in your everyday communication with others. To one person you're a friend, to another a classmate, to another a sibling, to another a person who stops to help change a tire, to another an employee, and to still another a romantic partner. When registering for classes, you are a student, and the person behind the counter is an administrator. But if you and the administrator meet later at an intramural baseball game and go to a celebration afterwards,

Doonesbury

Competent communicative knowledge is not always as accessible as it seems it ought to be.

you both engage in a completely different set of activities that in part define who and what you are to each other and what behaviors are viewed as competent.

Repertoires vary in both breadth and depth. **Breadth** is the number of different types of roles a person can play. The actors Johnny Depp and Kate Winslet have played very different types of roles. Most Elvis impersonators, in contrast, probably know only one role—Elvis. **Depth** is the level of familiarity a person has with any given role in a repertoire. A typical singer may know a few Elvis songs, but a professional Elvis impersonator is likely to know all of them.

Roles are defined by a set of behaviors that can be chosen to enact the roles. Any given role may have an almost infinite number of behaviors, but most roles specify a particular set of appropriate behaviors, as well as prohibited or inappropriate behaviors. For example, consider the nonverbal behaviors listed in Table 7.1. The entries in the second through fourth columns reveal that appropriate behaviors differ slightly from one role to another, depending on whether the person intends to play the role of a flirt, a friend, or a seducer. Most people prefer to have all three roles in their repertoire and to be expert in them all. In other words, it is generally advantageous to have both breadth and depth in one's repertoire.

In general, the broader and deeper a communicator's repertoire, the higher a communicator's competence level. Broader repertoires allow a person to select from a wider set of roles and achieve the most competent enactment in a given situation. Greater depth in a repertoire results from greater experience and expertise in performing any given role. However, at the same time, too much breadth or depth can be detrimental to one's competence.

For example, being too familiar with a role often leads a communicator to fall back on that role rather than find another more appropriate one. A lawyer who lapses into legalistic styles of arguing with her spouse may find that her lawyerly role is inappropriate in that context. In the opening vignette, Eliah may get approached for a date so often in her role as an attractive bartender that her rejection routine may become second nature to her. Clearly, however, there may be times when she needs to resist the familiar routine and consider the merits of the person making the approach. Thus, as the breadth and depth of a communicator's repertoire increase, the person is more likely to communicate competently, but only up to a point. Beyond that point, breadth and depth are likely to limit competence.

Table 7.1

Repertoires of Behaviors in Different Types of Roles

Different roles require different types (breadth) and amounts (depth) of behavior, as illustrated by the roles of friendly, flirtatious, and seductive communication.

Channel	Friendly	Flirtatious	Seductive
Kinesics (use of body)	Small amount of smiling; body relaxed	Moderate amount of smiling; head tilted; open mouth/pout	Frequent amount of smiling; body relaxed exposed skin
Haptics (use of touch)	Little/no touch	Moderate touch (arm, shoulder)	Touch hand/leg
Proxemics (use of space)	Farther away from each other while talking	Moderately close; cross legs toward each other	Very close
Oculesics (use of eyes)	Little/moderate eye contact	Moderate eye contact with occasional glances downward	Constant eye contact
Vocalics (use of voice)	Neutral voice tone; less fluency/more silences	Animated voice tone; decreased silences/latencies	Intimate voice tone: greater fluency/fewer silences

SOURCE: Adapted from Koeppel, Montagne-Miller, O'Hair, & Cody (1993). Reprinted by permission of Liana Koeppel.

Scripts

A repertoire is a set of various roles a person may perform. Kate Winslet has played a wide variety of roles and therefore has a broad repertoire of roles she can play. Jackie Chan, in contrast, plays almost exclusively action roles and therefore has a relatively narrow repertoire of acting roles. Roles, in turn, imply scripts that define those roles. A **script** is a sequence of actions intended to achieve some form of narrative sense. In essence, a script is a story that needs to occur in a given sequence. If the actions are taken out of sequence, the story falls apart.

Roles and scripts are related yet distinct. In the opening vignette, Eliah plays the role of bartender. Within this role, she may occasionally need to enact the script of dealing with difficult patrons who flirt with her, being a good listener when someone wants to talk about personal problems, and so on. However, when she goes out with Preston, she will need to play a different role and use a different script than being a bartender. Furthermore, Preston's role of pursuing a relationship with Eliah started with one script of getting her to say yes to a date. Once on their date, there are many different scripts he could play to further develop the relationship. Roles and scripts are distinct concepts, yet neither is fully defined without the other.

Scripts are rarely exact in social interaction. Wedding vows, greeting rituals, and some teasing routines become highly scripted. Most scripts, however, take the form of general sequences of types of actions. For example, Table 7.2 illustrates typical scripts for the types of relationship stages romantic relationships typically progress through. Several characteristics of scripts are apparent from these stages.

First, scripts vary in their complexity and detail. As shown in Table 7.2, some steps in developing a romantic relationship, such as getting to know one another, rely on a wide variety of specific communication activities, including self-disclosure, asking questions, storytelling, and so on. Women reveal somewhat more complex date scripts than men, and

learning link

What is the relationship between a person's repertoire and the various selves constructed in our postmodern life discussed in Chapter 3?

• • •

Table 7.2

Scripting the Story of Romantic Relationships

Research has shown that different stages of relationships are represented by different scripts for the behavior that should occur and in what sequence. In the table, when sex differences have been found, these are noted by italics. In later stages of the relationship, there are few consistent sex differences in the way behavior unfolds.

Acquaintance: Getting a Date

Woman's Script	Man's Script
Notices the other	Notices the other
Get caught staring at each other	Get caught staring at each other
Smile	Smile
Find out about the other person from friends	Find out about the other person from friends
Manipulate ways to "accidentally" run into him	Manipulate ways to "accidentally" run into her
Get introduced by a friend	Get introduced by a friend
Say hello	*Begin the conversation*
Attempts in conversation to find common interests	Attempts in conversation to find common interests
	Asks for her phone number
	Phones later to ask her out
	Makes arrangements by beginning small talk

Developing Dating

Woman's Script	Man's Script
Groom and dress	*Pick up date*
Feel nervous	*Meet parents or roommates*
Man picks up	*Leave to pick up woman*
Introduce to parents or roommate	*Pick up friends*
"Courtly behavior" (e.g., man opens doors)	Discussion to confirm plans
Leave	Talk, joke, laugh
Discussion to confirm plans	Go to movies, show, party
Get to know or evaluate date	Eat or drink
Talk, joke, laugh	*Initiate sexual contact*
Go to movies, show, party	*Make out*
Eat or drink	*Take date home*
Talk to friends	*Ask for another date*
Have something go wrong	*Initiate kiss goodnight*
Be taken home	Go home
Be asked for another date	
Man says he'll call	
Respond to goodnight kiss	
Go home	

Developing: Becoming More Intimate

Meet for the first time (party, class, bar, and so on)
Ask for other's phone number and call later
Small talk (discuss weather, school, and so on)
Show physical affection (kiss, hug, touch, and so on)
Formal dating (dinner, movie, and so on)
Self-disclosure of intimate information
Overcome relational crisis (jealousy, uncertainty)
Meet parents

Table 7.2 (cont'd)

Talk about future plans as a couple
Verbal expression of love
Bonding rituals (give gifts of flowers, gifts, jewelry)
Verbal commitment (stating a desire for an exclusive relationship)
Sexual intercourse
Cohabitation (living together)
Other-oriented statements (stating interest in each other's goals)
Marriage

Dissolution: Decline and Dissolution

Display lack of interest
Notice other people
Act distant
Try to work things out
Increase physical distance/avoidance
Display lack of interest
Consider breaking up
Communicate feelings
Try to work things out
Notice other people
Act distant
Date other people
Get back together
Consider breaking up
Move on and recover
Break up

SOURCES: Adapted from Battaglia, Richard, Datteri, & Lord (1998), Honeycutt, Cantrill, & Greene (1991), Pryor & Merluzzi (1985), Rose & Frieze (1993).

they view the man's actions as part of their script. In contrast, men show somewhat simpler scripts, which are entirely made up of the actions they initiate.

Second, scripts can vary according to role and context. In the acquaintance and development stages of Table 7.2 there are some sex differences because dating in our culture is still influenced by traditional gender stereotypes, such as who should plan and initiate the date. However, in the relationship developing and dissolution stages, gender is less relevant to the roles that partners enact.

Third, scripts are flexible. In Table 7.2 the breakup script reveals several loops in which the partners rekindle the relationship and then leave it again. Apparently relationships, and therefore their scripts, are relatively fluid and often get several chances to revive. Despite their flexibility, many of these script elements would not make sense if they occurred out of sequence. Obviously it makes no sense to "pick up date" in the middle of a date.

Scripts give coherence and meaning to what would otherwise be random strings of actions. They cannot generally go in random directions or tell whatever story people want them to. Scripts, like virtually all communication, are constrained by social preferences known as rules.

learning link

In what ways could scripts function as challenges to listening as discussed in Chapter 6?

• • •

Rules

Rules are "followable" prescriptions for behavior in a given context. *Followable* means it must be possible to avoid violating the rule. It makes no sense to make a rule that is not followable. "Defy gravity" or "Recite the entire Constitution of the United States from memory" are not followable and therefore make no sense as rules. But "Don't use foul language when referring to the other person" or "Don't yell when having an argument" specify behaviors most of us can avoid.

learning link

How might rules relate to the creation and maintenance of community discussed in Chapter 1?

• • •

Rules are prescriptions. They specify what behavior is or is not allowable. "Be nice" is advice many people give, but it is not a rule because it is not clear what it means in any particular situation. In contrast, "When having an argument, let the other person finish what he or she is saying before starting to speak" is a prescription that is specific about what is allowed. Prescriptions can indicate what to do or what *not* to do, and sometimes both. For example, the rule just stated is really another way of saying "Don't interrupt the other person when having an argument." In both instances the rule specifies what is allowable.

Finally, rules are context specific. "Don't interrupt" is in fact not a very useful rule in all communication contexts. Many interruptions are actually appropriate. Many of them signal involvement, such as when you excitedly give reinforcing feedback in the form of "yeah," "OK," or "no kidding." Other interruptions help the speaker, such as filling in a desired word when the speaker can't think of the right phrase. However, in given contexts, interruptions are highly inappropriate, such as in many conflict encounters where they signal a lack of respect for the other's position or right to express a position. Table 7.3 illustrates a number of typical communication rules for two contexts, friendship and conflict. The Close-Up on Culture box describes how conversational rules vary across cultures.

Together, repertoires, scripts, and rules constitute the content knowledge of communication. They provide a communicator with a sense of what can and should be communicated. But when you tell a joke, only part of your competence is in knowing what to say. Much of the competence of the joke lies in how you tell it, which relies on your procedural knowledge.

Procedural Knowledge: Knowing How to Communicate ___

From the time you are an infant, you add more and more behaviors, roles, scripts, and rules to your content knowledge. But merely having such knowledge does not mean it is useful to you as a communicator. For this knowledge to be useful, you need to know how to access and use it. Two processes allow us to do this. **Planning** is the process of anticipating and formulating possible strategies for achieving some goal or goals (Duran & Spitzberg, 1995). Action assembly is the process by which you put behaviors together in an actual performance in the pursuit of those goals.

Planning

A **plan** is an intentional description of the actions and means needed to achieve a goal. A plan is meant to accomplish some goals or outcomes. However, it does not have to be entirely conscious or immediate. When you flirt with someone, you may be fulfilling a plan to initiate a romantic relationship, but you may also be facilitating a larger plan to get

Table 7.3

Relationship Rules

Research reveals that communicators are aware of many rules in two common interpersonal contexts.

Rules of Friendship

Exchange:	Share news of success with the other
	Show emotional support
	Volunteer help in time of need
	Strive to make other happy while in each other's company
	Repay debts and favors
Intimacy:	Trust and confide in the other
Third Parties:	Stand up for the other person in his or her absence
	Be tolerant of the other's friends
	Don't criticize each other in public
	Keep each other's confidences and secrets
	Don't be jealous or critical of the other's relationships
Coordination:	Don't nag the other
	Respect each other's privacy

Rules for Conflict

Understanding:	Say you're sorry when you have transgressed
	Support and praise other when he or she deserves it
	Listen to the other
	See the other's viewpoint
	Be honest and say what is on your mind
	Look at each other
Rationality:	Don't get angry
	Don't raise voice
	Avoid combative issues
	Don't lose temper or be aggressive
	Try to remain calm and not get upset
Conciseness:	Get to point quickly
	Be specific; don't generalize
	Be consistent
	Keep to the main point
	Avoid rash judgments
Consideration:	Don't talk too much
	Don't make other feel guilty
	Don't push your view as the only view
	Don't mimic the other or be sarcastic
	Don't talk down to the other

SOURCE: Adapted from Argyle & Henderson (1984); Honeycutt, Woods, & Fontenot (1993).

married someday. For example, in the opening vignette, Preston's first goal was getting Eliah's phone number, which in turn was a step in getting a first date, which in turn is a step in the plan of achieving an intimate relationship.

Most plans are made up of smaller plans, or **subplans,** which are the steps that need to be taken to achieve a given stage of the larger plan. You may not want to get married

CloseUp on Culture
Conversational Rules

RULES HAVE BEEN DESCRIBED AS CONTEXT-specific prescriptions for behavior. Given that culture is one of the main types of context, it follows that rules are often culture specific. Violating rules increases the likelihood of being seen as incompetent, so following rules is one of the more important ways of communicating competently. But how do you know what rules to follow when interacting with someone whose cultural rules may be different from your own?

Some rules are likely to be fairly common across cultures. For example, rules regarding behaving politely, such as being courteous, speaking the appropriate language, being considerate of the other, and listening to the other, are likely to be important regardless of the other person's culture. However, certain other rules may vary from one ethnic or cultural interaction to another. In one study, for example, African American, Mexican American, and European American college students were asked to recall recent conversations that were either appropriate or inappropriate. When researchers analyzed the recollections, they found certain rules to be relevant to competence throughout the conversations (Collier, 1988):

- Politeness: speaking proper English, being verbally courteous, using appropriate nonverbal style, asking for feedback, listening actively.
- Roles: acknowledging ethnic identity, avoiding stereotyping, behaving consistently with gender role, following job or student roles.
- Content: using proper reasoning in statements, staying relevant to the conversation topic, keeping criticism constructive.
- Expressiveness: speaking assertively without violating other person's rights, being open-minded, speaking directly to the point.
- Relationship: expressing appropriate dominance or submissiveness, expressing appropriate friendliness or hostility, feeling comfortable, seeing other's behavior as predictable, showing trust.
- Goals: gaining information, achieving personal goals.
- Understanding: being appropriately empathic, being understood.
- Self-validation: confirming each other's statements, feeling good about the self.
- Cultural validation: feeling pride in one's own cultural identity, avoiding embarrassment.

Collier found that politeness and following rules were fairly commonly identified as important across interactions. In contrast, European Americans tended to emphasize politeness and roles more when interacting with other European Americans than when interacting with African Americans or Mexican Americans. Mexican Americans recalled conversations being affected by relationship rules more among themselves than when interacting with European Americans. African Americans tended to recall interactions as affected by roles when interacting with European Americans more than when interacting with each other.

These kinds of differences may help explain why somewhat different characteristics of communication are viewed as satisfying by different ethnic groups (Hecht & Ribeau, 1984). Compared with European Americans and African Americans, Mexican Americans tend to be most satisfied in conversations in which the look on the other person's face indicates the interactants want the same thing and that neither is "talking down" to the other. African Americans, compared with Mexican Americans and European Americans, were more satisfied when there was no misunderstanding in the interactions.

Culture also affects what interactants consider the most competent way to repair or improve conversations when rules are violated. One study (Martin, Hecht, & Larkey, 1994) shows that, although both European Americans and African Americans try to avoid inappropriate topics or ignore rule violations and involve the other person more in the conversation, there are differences in the extent to which they demonstrate these tendencies in conversation. African Americans are more likely to use strategies that involve the other person in the conversation or avoid unpleasant topics, whereas European Americans are more likely to not go along with what the other person is doing or saying or expect the other person to apologize. In other words, African Americans tend to engage in more relational-focused forms of conversational repair by adapting to the other person, and European Americans tend to use more individual-focused forms of conversational repair by pursuing their own ideas persistently.

All cultures value competent conversation. Thus when interacting with someone from another culture or ethnicity, knowledge of possible rule differences may be essential to being viewed as competent.

right now, but you realize that at some point you may meet the right person and flirtation with a person now is part of the same step that will eventually lead to meeting the right person. You are unlikely to get married without flirting with someone, so flirting to establish a romantic relationship becomes a subplan to the larger "parent" plan of getting married, even if fulfillment of the parent plan seems far off.

Plans are oriented toward goals (Berger, 2003). Goals, like plans, have subgoals. A **subgoal,** like a subplan, is a goal formulated as part of defining and achieving a larger goal. If flirting is a subplan, establishing a romantic relationship is this subplan's goal. But this goal is a bridge to the larger goal of getting married. At the same time, if this relationship doesn't lead to marriage, it is not necessarily viewed as a loss, because the subgoal can be a desirable goal itself.

Figure 7.1 reveals how complex a potential mental map of a plan may be. This map represents a composite of college students' conceptions of what goes into asking someone for a date. It is clear that there are many different pathways in these plans. If one gets blocked, there may be adaptations that can be made. There are subgoals that have to be met for other goals to be achieved. You may not be particularly conscious of all these plans and subgoals, but as you look over the elements of Figure 7.1, you probably also recognize most of them as potentially relevant behaviors in the date-request script. The importance of developing better and more complex plans is illustrated by the fact that students who were found to have simpler plans tended to be higher in loneliness than those with more complex or complete plans (Berger, 2003).

As we indicate in Chapter 2, goals are an essential part of communication motivation. They also serve to trigger and guide knowledge processes, such as searching for and retrieving appropriate rules, roles, scripts, and so forth. Communicators do not spend all their time thinking through every possible message they could be communicating at any point in time. Such an overload of information processing would be disabling. Instead, communicators process information efficiently by selecting what they will think about. They make these choices based on their communicative goals.

Goals are transactional; they are interdependent with the goals of others and they evolve over time. Their interdependency means that for you to achieve your goals you have to adapt your goals to the goals of the other persons in the interaction, and in the process, you exchange symbols and meanings so as to change or refine existing goals and develop new goals. In the opening vignette, Preston did not know he would be pursuing the goal of flirtation when he went to the pub to meet his friends. Indeed, had his discussion with Jeff and Greg not ventured into the topic of flirtation, he might never have thought to attempt his bold move. But the context provided the right opportunity for him to redefine his goals in that encounter.

The flexibility and adaptation of goals illustrates a key to the process of communicative planning. Planning is generally efficient (Berger, 2003). **Efficiency** refers to the amount of effort invested in developing and performing a plan. Given two plans to get a date with someone, assuming both plans would succeed, people generally choose the plan that requires less effort to think through and enact. To achieve efficiency in plans, communicators tend to process plan-based information according to certain principles.

The first principle of plan efficiency is the **competence principle.** We select plans on the basis of their efficiency in competently achieving the goals to which the plans are directed. Efficiency generally serves the major concerns of appropriateness and effectiveness. Given two plans equal in efficiency, we tend to choose the one most likely to be viewed as competent. In the opening vignette, Preston's immediate goal was to get a date with Eliah.

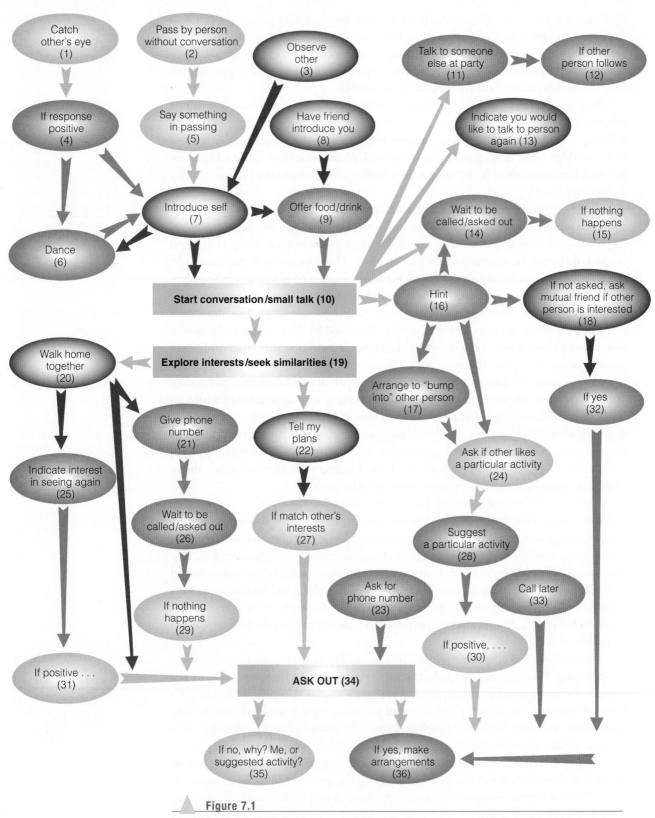

Figure 7.1

Planning to Ask Someone Out on a Date?

Plans can represent complex mental maps through which we organize our communication behavior.

One plan would be to start small talk with her, try to achieve some rapport, and leave a good first impression so that at some later time he could come into the pub and continue the conversation and ask her out. Another plan would be to make the bolder approach that he used. The second plan was far more efficient. But a plan is very inefficient if it fails, and in this case, Preston was betting that the more efficient plan would not be so inappropriate that it would make him look incompetent in Eliah's eyes. Communicators want to accomplish their goals, but only rarely do they choose the most efficient plan if that plan could make them look incompetent. Goal accomplishment is most likely to occur when behavior is appropriate to the context in which the goal is being pursued.

The second principle of planning efficiency is the **prior success principle:** we base plans on previous plans when those seem effective and apply to the present situation (Berger, 1997). When a goal arises for a communicator, the communicator could spend an enormous amount of energy analyzing the roles, rules, and script options of the context. Or the communicator may realize that he or she has already faced this goal context before and was able to achieve the desired goal by using a plan available from memory. A question interviewers often ask during a job interview is "What are your weaknesses?" This question throws many an interviewee into a panic, but a person who has been asked this difficult question previously will have plans for answering it more competently and so should be able to recall the answer and deliver it fluently in the future.

The third efficiency principle is the **simplicity principle:** all things being equal, communicators are likely to simplify their plans or make only slight alterations rather than complicate them (Berger, 1997). If a communicator can think of two plans to achieve a goal, the simpler one tends to be chosen. Furthermore, once a person has begun enacting a plan, he or she tends to make changes sparingly rather than shifting radically to an alternative plan. Major alterations of plans require a radical shift of behavior and may appear too wild and unpredictable to observers.

Communicators highly experienced in a given area are likely to develop more complex plans over time because they understand all the factors in the situation. For such knowledgeable communicators, producing more involved plans is efficient because they don't need to put much effort into analyzing the plans. A good salesperson has heard all the reservations that potential customers may have. With this experience, this salesperson is likely to have developed not only a wide variety of responses, but also a complex set of plans for combining these responses in the most persuasive ways. This combining of plans results from the process of action assembly.

Action Assembly

Action assembly is the mental process of putting behaviors together in the pursuit of goals (Greene, 1993). When Preston opened up his calendar planner in the opening vignette and asked Eliah for a date, from where did this action originate? Had he performed this tactic before? If not, how did he know how to enact it? What vocal inflection should he use? Should he be smiling or not? Should he ask it as a teasing command? Should he try to seem shy while asking his bold question, or should he act assertive and confident? Preston resolved all these questions and many more in a split second. He did not entirely know what he would say or do—but when he got to the bar it all fell into place almost as if it had been planned. Like the employee in the *Real Life Adventures* cartoon, we often make any number of interpretations of any given message, and on the basis of these interpretations, we almost simultaneously construct and enact our responses.

REAL LIFE ADVENTURES by Gary Wise and Lance Aldrich

The remarkable computer called the human brain is capable of playing out multiple scenarios in milliseconds.

Reprinted by permission of Universal Press Syndicate.

We are able to process extensive knowledge while communicating.

Action assembly is activated when a particular goal becomes relevant to a communication context. This goal stimulates a mental search of a person's repertoire of applicable roles, scripts, and rules. These action sequences can be viewed as packets of behaviors and their associated goals.

Action assembly starts with a goal. The goal is sometimes presented by a situation, such as when Preston saw Eliah in the pub. At other times a person generates and plans around the goal that leads to the situation, which would happen if Eliah decides where Preston and she should go on their first date. When presented with the goal, a communicator searches his or her memory for examples of similar situations and goals to see whether certain communication behaviors have worked before to achieve a goal similar to the current one. It may be that Preston had previously used this particular approach, or something similar, and decided it might work again.

If there are no previous examples of the present goal or situation in memory, the communicator searches for those situations and goals that are most similar and then searches for communication behaviors that worked for those situations and goals. Preston might not have tried to flirt with a bartender before but he might have flirted with a waitress, and he views the situations and goals as similar. Having located situations and goals that are similar, the communicator then examines the behaviors he or she used in those situations and determines which ones most competently achieved the goals. Here the other principles of efficiency help the communicator choose the particular behaviors that will be assembled for performance.

Having mentally collected a set of behaviors, we must assemble them in a way that makes sense in the context. In some cases this means applying memories of role, script, or rule information. For example, Preston probably realizes it is generally the male's role to ask for the woman's telephone number. Although the normal cultural script is to spend some time conducting small talk before asking for the person's number, Preston perceives that this script may not apply when the other person is engaged in work activities and has only a brief time to talk. Finally, among the rules that would guide the assembly of action in this situation is to avoid being too pushy or aggressive.

Research has shown that 40 to 50 behaviors or behavior sequences may be associated with flirtation in U.S. culture (Egland, Spitzberg, & Zormeier, 1996). Although a person may have all these behaviors in repertoire memory, it is not likely that he or she will remember them all as equally competent. Furthermore, as a flirtation episode unfolds some flirtation routines may appear more effective than others depending on whether the other person seems disinterested, distracted, interested but reluctant, and so forth. We store not only actions but also their consequences in our memory.

The action assembly process can fail in a variety of ways. You may lack the motivation necessary to engage in an adequate search and assembly process. If you are physically exhausted, you may not care if you appear competent, and thus you may not go to the trouble of searching out the most competent actions for a given situation. You may have the actions in memory, but lack the appropriate plan or knowledge of the role, script, or rules for combining the actions. While Preston walked right up to Eliah and asked her out, his friends Greg and Jeff were still wondering how to best go about the task.

Further, a communicator may have the actions in memory but not make the connection to the present context because he or she had previously used the actions in another type

The best laid plans often go astray.

of context. If you meet someone who had been a friend years earlier, you may continue to search only for friendship actions rather than flirtation actions, even though under the present circumstances the latter may now be relevant.

People may activate less competent actions because they are more familiar or of more recent use, or because they seem to be the best match at the time. You may occasionally find yourself in the midst of saying something even while you realize that you could be saying something else much more appropriate to the situation. You probably simply went with what first came to mind, which means it had the best initial match, even if it wasn't the most competent action to call forth.

Finally, plans may fail because the other interactants in the episode make a plan irrelevant or incompetent in that context. The cartoon *Cathy* illustrates this common problem. Despite careful anticipation and planning, all it takes is someone else working on a different plan to suddenly shift the relevance of initial plans.

Thus far we have examined what communicators know how to say and do and how they organize this knowledge. Throughout we have considered some of the ways this knowledge is processed to increase, and occasionally decrease, a person's communication competence. Competence depends not only on having knowledge but also on knowing how to apply it. For full understanding of the role of knowledge, we need to discuss the relationship between knowledge and others' impressions of competence.

Challenges to Competence in Relationships

Competent communication does not appear out of thin air as though conjured by a magic trick. People learn how to be competent over long periods, and this learning process is represented in the communicator's knowledge. But knowledge is not always as useful or as accessible as we need it to be. We now examine some of the specific challenges that knowledge presents to competent performance and ways we can overcome these challenges.

Empathy and Perspective Taking

Few characteristics have so consistently challenged interpersonal communication competence as self-centeredness. Self-centered communicators think primarily of their own goals, needs, communication behaviors, and ways of doing things. They are more likely to pursue topics of conversation they find interesting, direct the conversation to their own topics of interest, and interrupt others' topics of conversation. Any attention they pay to the other person in the interaction tends to focus on their own needs and how to get that person to do what they want. Furthermore, self-centered communicators often tend not to see things from the other's perspective, resulting in simplistic ways of thinking about the world. They may believe their way of doing things is best or be closed to other alternatives.

Self-centeredness weakens your interpersonal communication competence in several ways. Others tend to view you as narcissistic or uncaring because you do not include them in the conversation. Further, if your effectiveness depends on getting the other person to do what you want, that person is less likely to comply to the extent that he or she views you as incompetent or only interested in yourself. Finally, a large part of what makes a relationship is sharing. If you are self-centered in your communication, you do not get the benefit of what the other person has to offer to you and the relationship.

Empathy is the ability to experience feelings similar to or related to those of another person. It is often confused with sympathy but is quite different. **Sympathy** is a desire to offer support for another, generally when that person is in a predicament. Empathy does not imply that you feel sympathy or vice versa. If you see a person on the news who just lost a loved one in a home fire, you may sympathize by feeling sorry for that person but you may not feel what that person is feeling. If you see an expectant father in a hospital waiting or delivery room, you may feel excited empathy for him even if you have never been a father, and there may be little reason for you to feel sympathy in this context.

In contrast to empathy and sympathy, **perspective taking** means seeing the world as the other person sees it. In the examples just described, you may not feel the loss or the excitement but you can visualize what the people are experiencing, the thoughts they might be thinking, and you can imagine what it might be like to lose a loved one or be about to gain a loved one. So empathy primarily elicits emotions, whereas perspective taking primarily elicits thoughts and perceptions.

Both empathy and perspective taking are important methods to overcome some of the challenges to competent interpersonal communication. Empathy helps you feel the other person's joys and sorrows, moods and rages, and even quiet reflections. It promotes sympathy, and perhaps more importantly, gives credibility to offers of sympathy and support. Perspective taking lets you see the world from another person's point of view and discover another way of thinking. It helps you anticipate the other person's actions and adapt your own behaviors accordingly. Both empathy and perspective taking therefore facilitate plan adjustment by providing better information about how the other person would react to changes in your communication plans.

Knowledge-Gaining Strategies

Not all knowledge is based strictly on emotional and mental processes. One of the ways people acquire knowledge is through active and interactive **knowledge-gaining strategies** (Berger & Bradac, 1982), which are behaviors we use to obtain information about others. The most common strategies for gaining information relevant to interpersonal communication are questioning, contextual alteration, and self-disclosure.

Questioning is the explicit or implicit use of verbal or nonverbal behavior to request information from another person. If you need more information about someone, one of the best ways to get it is to ask the person. Instead of assuming that Patricia would like to be called "Pat" or "Patty," you can simply ask her. You can also apply this strategy less directly, such as when you ask someone else for information about that particular person.

learning link

Considering again the Chapter 3 concept of the postmodern self, is perspective taking becoming more or less difficult? Why?

• • •

For example, you can ask a friend or associate of Patricia whether she likes to be referred to by a nickname.

Contextual alteration changes something about a situation so we can see how a person reacts. The person's reaction can reveal a lot about that person's personality or thought process. For example, you may clean up your roommate's mess because it is bothering you. But if the roommate does not notice you cleaned up his or her mess, it tells you something about how attentive this person is.

A third strategy, self-disclosure, is somewhat counterintuitive. As discussed in Chapter 3, we generally use self-disclosure as a strategy for making ourselves known to others. But by making yourself known to another you also tend to make it easier for you to know the other. As a relationship progresses people tend to reciprocate each other's disclosures, creating a context in which each increasingly feels safe disclosing information about himself or herself.

Acquiring knowledge of communication is not simply about reading tactics in a book—it is about trying them out. What you *think* you know and what you know are often quite different, and what you can get your mind to do and what you *want* it to do are also quite different. For example, DO NOT THINK ABOUT A FLAMINGO! Oops. You just thought about a flamingo. We tell ourselves to communicate better, but it is important to have a more specific set of strategies for achieving better knowledge.

 ## Chapter Summary

Communicative knowledge comes in two forms: content and procedural. We store content knowledge in the form of repertoires, scripts, and rules. Repertoires are the various roles that we perform in interpersonal interaction. Scripts are the sequences in which we learn to enact behaviors, and rules are the guidelines that help us discern what communication is appropriate and inappropriate in given contexts. Procedural knowledge is our understanding of how to implement our content knowledge. We understand the procedures of interpersonal communication when we are able to engage in planning and action assembly. Planning is the anticipation and intentional description of actions that can achieve a goal. Action assembly is the process of putting these planned  actions into a complete package that can be performed. We can overcome challenges to competent use of communicative knowledge through the use of empathy, perspective taking, and knowledge-gaining strategies.

Study and Review

The premium companion website for *Human Communication* offers a broad range of resources that will help you better understand the material in this chapter, complete assignments, and succeed on tests. The website resources include

- Interactive self-assessments, competency grids, and other tools
- Web links, practice activities, self-quizzes, and a sample final exam

For more information about this text's electronic learning resources, consult the *Guide to Online Resources for Human Communication* or visit **http://communication .wadsworth.com/morreale2.**

Key Terms

The key terms below are defined in the chapter on the pages indicated. They are also presented alphabetically with definitions in the Glossary, which begins on page 467. The book's website includes flashcards and crossword puzzles to help you learn these terms and the concepts they represent.

learning 161
direct learning 161
indirect learning 161
self-efficacy 162
repertoire 163
role 163
breadth 164
depth 164
script 165
rule 168
planning 168
plan 168
subplan 169

subgoal 171
efficiency 171
competence principle 171
prior success principle 173
simplicity principle 173
action assembly 173
empathy 176
sympathy 176
perspective taking 176
knowledge-gaining strategies 176
questioning 176
contextual alteration 177

Building Knowledge

The questions below are among the practice activities on the book's website.

1. Of the two types of knowledge, content and procedural, which one are you least likely to be aware of? Why?

2. Identify a situation that you think is relatively well scripted. How flexible is that script? What factors might influence changes in that script? Why?

3. Identify a situation that you think has a lot of rules associated with it and a situation that has very few rules associated with it. What is different about these situations in terms of their goals, their scripts, their complexity, and the efficiency with which you would communicate in them?

4. Explain the influence of positive and negative expectancies on impressions of competence. Have you had any encounters that illustrate both types of expectancies? Explain.

5. Think of a recent interpersonal communication encounter in which you did something differently than you usually do. Describe the action assembly of your behavior by identifying what similar situations you might have used as examples or analogues from which to develop your actions.

Building Skills _____

The exercises below are among the practice activities on the book's website.

1. The following six problems concern familiar or everyday scripts. Answer each of them, and do not read any farther until you do so.
   a. If you had only one match, and entered a room in which there was a kerosene lamp, a wood-burning stove, and a gas fireplace, which would you light first?
   b. How many outs are in an inning of baseball?
   c. A patient is wheeled into the emergency room and the surgeon, looking at the patient, says, "I can't operate on this patient—he's my son!" The surgeon is not the patient's father. How is this possible?
   d. You have a dime in an otherwise empty wine bottle. The bottle is corked. How do you get the dime out without removing the cork or damaging the bottle in any way?
   e. Connect the following nine dots using only straight lines, without removing your pen from the paper.

   These questions seem simple enough. But people often answer them incorrectly, or cannot answer them at all. This is in part because each of them leads you to expect a script that is not actually the appropriate script, or because each leads you to focus on the wrong part of the script. In each case, discuss what led you to apply the wrong script. What situations in everyday communication encounters might you experience in which you could apply the wrong script?
   Answers:
   a. The match. We are led to think of lighting the sources of warmth, rather than the item we use to light these sources.
   b. Six. We tend to think of baseball in terms of how many outs there are for our team. But there are two teams.
   c. The surgeon is the patient's mother. We still tend to think of surgeons as men.
   d. Push the cork in. We tend to think of wine bottles only in terms of removing the cork.
   e. Follow along as illustrated. This problem tends to frustrate people because they think the nine dots form a square. We are accustomed to seeing squares and therefore think "inside the box." The only way to solve the problem is to think "outside the box."

2. Think through some of the situations you have experienced (student–professor discussion about a grade, job interview, negotiating the price of a car, and so on). Choose one and write out the script for this situation. What factors might influence changes in that script? How rigid is this script? Why? How detailed is your script compared with those identified in this chapter?

3. The chart on the next page identifies several types of behaviors and several types of situations. In the spaces provided, use the scale to rate the appropriateness of each behavior for each situation.

4. For a week keep an interaction diary. After each conversation more than 10 minutes long, whether face to face or mediated, take notes on the following aspects: When

	CLASS-ROOM	FIRST DATE	INTERVIEW	ELEVATOR	OWN ROOM	TOTAL
Talk						
Kiss						
Argue						
Cry						
Laugh						
Total						

If you add across each row, and then down each column, you will get a number ranging between 5 and 25. The higher the row sum, the more rule bound the behavior. The higher the column sum, the more rule bound the situation. What is it about these behaviors and situations that make them differ in terms of their rules?

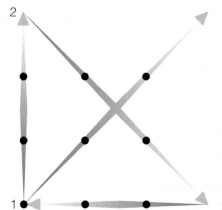

did it occur? Where did it occur? How long did it last? What was your relationship with the other persons? What were the main themes or topics of the conversation? What were your goals in the conversation? What rules would you say were most important in the situation? What cues best informed you of how to behave in the conversation? How competent were you and the other person? After the week of diary entries has been completed, look them over for patterns. Compared with before the diary assignment, how well did you engage in empathy and role taking in your conversations? To what extent did you find yourself differently empathizing and perspective taking as you got more accustomed to making diary entries? How can empathy and perspective taking improve your interpersonal competence in everyday conversation?

5. Think of an important conflict you have had with another person. Remember it in as much detail as you can. Go to the International Online Training Program on the Intractable Conflict Web site at **http://www.colorado.edu/conflict/peace/**. On the menu bar of topics, under "Conflict Problems" click on "Communication." Review the types of communication problems the site identifies. Return to the menu bar and under "Treatments" click on "Communication." You will see a list of strategies for "Treating Communication Problems." Review the techniques listed, occasionally clicking on any technique that seems particularly relevant to the communication problems you might have experienced in the conflict encounter you have recalled. How might you have behaved differently in the conflict to have been a more competent interpersonal communicator, using the conflict management techniques discussed in this website?

6. In InfoTrac College Edition, enter *communicator competence*. Retrieve and review the following article: The funny people: A source-orientation to the communication of humor. (1995). Wanzer, M., Booth-Butterfield, M., & Booth-Butterfield, S. *Communication Quarterly, 43*(2) p. 142–155. The competency of being humorous requires two types of communicative knowledge. First, humor requires content knowledge, that is, the joke or humorous idea. Second, humor requires procedural knowledge, or the way the humor needs to be delivered. Identify procedural types of knowledge needed to be competent at being humorous. Which of these types of knowledge do you think are most important? Why?

Group Activities

1. One of the indirect ways we learn how to communicate is by playing roles. We often look to others to tell us what role we should play. These persons are role models. Our role models include mothers, fathers, movie stars, rock stars, and historical figures such as Mother Teresa or Amelia Earhart. One way of developing your knowledge in any given situation is to imagine what your role models would do in that situation. List three problematic communication situations you have experienced recently, and list the role model you would most want to follow as an example for how to behave in that situation. What would the model's response have been in each situation? Now compare your list of situations, role model, and responses with those of another classmate. What are the similarities and differences between your lists? Discuss factors you think might have led to these similarities and differences.

2. Form groups of four students. Each member should write down three strategies for gaining information on a first date. There should be one question, one contextual alteration, and one self-disclosure strategy for each member. Compare your list with those generated by the other members in the group. How competent do you think these strategies would be? Would any of them violate the rules or the scripts of the first-date situation? Why?

3. Form a dyad with someone in your class you don't know very well.
   a. The chart on the next page lists several questions. Conduct a get-acquainted conversation, making sure you don't directly ask the other person any of the questions that are listed in the chart. After the conversation each member of the dyad should provide answers to questions, even if they are guesses.
   b. Compare your answers about your partner with your partner's answers regarding you. How accurate are they? What kinds of information can you reasonably expect to get about a person from casual conversation? If the kinds of information you can get from a person in a casual conversation are limited, how do you make decisions on such information about deeper or more important goals, such as what kind of relationship you would like to have with this person?

4. Form groups of three to five students. Identify an interpersonal communication context of interest to the group. For example, your group might select an intimacy situation in which you ask someone to marry you, a confrontation situation in which you try to get a roommate to change a personal habit, or a negotiation situation in which you are bargaining for a better deal on a car or computer system. Each member of your group should then individually construct his or her rules and script for the competent person involved (for example, a potential mate, roommate, or negotiator). As a group, compare, discuss, and combine your answers to

a. What is the person's religious affiliation, if any?	**f.** Are or were the person's parents divorced?
b. Does the person have or want to have children?	**g.** Is the person in a satisfying romantic relationship?
c. Is the person basically happy most of the time?	**h.** Is this person a political liberal, conservative, independent, or politically disinterested?
d. Where would the person most like to visit or travel to?	**i.** What is this person's favorite food or cuisine?
e. Would the person rather go to a formal ball or a casual party at someone's apartment?	**j.** What career does this person want after college?

construct a new script and set of rules. To what extent did other members come up with script elements similar to yours? To what extent and in what ways is the group product more complete than your individual answers? Why?

 ## References

Afifi, W. A., & Weiner, J. L. (2004). Toward a theory of motivated information management. *Communication Theory, 14,* 167–190.

Argyle, M., & Henderson, M. (1984). The rules of friendship. *Journal of Social and Personal Relationships, 1,* 211–237.

Bandura, A. (1977). *Social learning theory.* Englewood Cliffs, NJ: Prentice-Hall.

Battaglia, D. M., Richard, F. D., Datteri, D. L., & Lord, C. G. (1998). Breaking up is (relatively) easy to do: A script for the dissolution of close relationships. *Journal of Social and Personal Relationships, 15,* 829–845.

Beatty, M. J., Heisel, A. D., Hall, A. E., Levine, T. R., & La France, B. H. (2002). What can we learn from the study of twins about genetic and environmental influences on interpersonal affiliation, aggressiveness, and social anxiety? A meta-analytic study. *Communication Monographs, 69,* 1–18.

Berger, C. R. (1987). Planning and scheming: Strategies for initiating relationships. In R. Burnett, P. McGhee, & D. Clarke (Eds.), *Accounting for relationships: Explanation, representation, and knowledge* (pp. 158–174). London: Methuen.

Berger, C. R. (1997). *Planning strategic interaction: Attaining goals through communicative action.* Mahwah, NJ: Erlbaum.

Berger, C. R. (2003). Message production skill in social interaction. In J. O. Greene & B. R. Burleson (Eds.), *Handbook of communication and social interaction skills* (pp. 257–290). Mahwah, NJ: Erlbaum.

Berger, C. R., & Bradac, J. J. (1982). *Language and social knowledge: Uncertainty in interpersonal relations.* London: Edward Arnold.

Collier, M. J. (1988). A comparison of conversations among and between domestic culture groups: How intra- and intercultural competencies vary. *Communication Quarterly, 36,* 122–144.

Duran, R. L., & Spitzberg, B. H. (1995). Toward the development and validation of a measure of cognitive communication competence. *Communication Quarterly, 43,* 259–275.

Egland, K. L., Spitzberg, B. H., & Zormeier, M. M. (1996). Flirtation and conversational competence in cross-sex platonic and romantic relationships. *Communication Reports, 9,* 105–118.

Greene, J. O. (1993). An action assembly perspective on social skill. *Communication Theory, 3,* 26–49.

Greene, J. O. (2003). Models of adult communication skill acquisition: Practice and the course of performance improvement. In J. O. Greene & B. R. Burleson (Eds.), *Handbook of communication and social interaction skills* (pp. 51–92). Mahwah, NJ: Erlbaum.

Hecht, M. L., & Ribeau, S. (1984). Ethnic communication: A comparative analysis of satisfying communication. *International Journal of Intercultural Relations, 8,* 135–151.

Honeycutt, J. M., Cantrill, J. G., & Greene, R. W. (1991). Memory structures for relational escalation: A cognitive test of the sequencing of relational actions and strategies. *Human Communication Research, 16,* 62–90.

Honeycutt, J. M., Woods, B. L., & Fontenot, K. (1993). The endorsement of communication conflict rules as a function of engagement, marriage, and marital ideology. *Journal of Social and Personal Relationships, 10,* 285–304.

Koeppel, L. B., Montagne-Miller, Y., O'Hair, D., & Cody, M. J. (1993). Friendly? Flirting? Wrong? In P. J. Kalbfleisch (Ed.), *Interpersonal communication: Evolving interpersonal relationships* (pp. 13–32). Hillsdale, NJ: Erlbaum.

Martin, J. N., Hecht, M. L., & Larkey, L. K. (1994). Conversational improvement strategies for interethnic communication: African American and European American perspectives. *Communication Monographs, 61,* 236–255.

Pryor, J. B., & Merluzzi, T. V. (1985). The role of expertise in processing social interaction scripts. *Journal of Experimental Social Psychology, 21,* 362–379.

Rose, S., & Frieze, I. H. (1993). Young singles' contemporary dating scripts. *Sex Roles, 28,* 499–509.

© Dex Images, Inc./Getty Images

Chapter 8

LEARNING OBJECTIVES

After studying this chapter you should be able to

1. Distinguish among skills and actions.

2. Explain the link between skills and impressions.

3. Identify and use the key behaviors that constitute the skills of attentiveness, composure, coordination, and expressiveness most likely to be viewed as competent.

4. Identify differences in contexts that would lead to differences in how coordination, composure, expressiveness, and attentiveness are performed.

5. Competently balance your use of selectivity with flexibility.

6. Competently balance your use of adaptability with consistency.

Interpersonal Competence: Developing Skills

Dipak, an international student from India, roomed with Chad in an apartment near campus. One Sunday morning, during a particularly busy weekend of homework, Dipak woke up and walked into the common space to brew some coffee. The chaos of their living area shocked him. He had difficulty seeing the floor because everything was covered by books, wadded-up paper, empty pizza boxes, soda cans, blankets, and potato chip bags. Chad was sprawled on the sofa covered by an old sleeping bag. As Dipak struggled to get to the kitchen, in frustration he yelled, "This place is a disaster zone!" waking Chad from his 2 hours of sleep.

Chad groggily made some excuses about having an exam the next day and having invited some friends from class over to study after Dipak had gone to bed. The exchange quickly spiraled into a shouting match, and Dipak said he couldn't live like this—the place was like a pigsty. Escalating the argument, Chad retorted, "Are you implying I'm a pig?" Furious, Dipak replied, "Yeah, that's exactly what I'm implying!"

"Well, what would you know about pigs, given how your culture worships animals?" Chad angrily accused.

Dipak began to shake visibly. "At least I believe in something! You're nothing but a typical godless American with no values and—"

Chad interrupted midsentence, "You don't like the way I am? Find someone else crazy enough to live with you someplace else. Just get out of my face and let me get some sleep for once."

Conflicts and arguments often bring out the worst in people (Spitzberg, Canary, & Cupach, 1994). One reason is many of us have never learned or had the opportunity to refine competent skills for managing conflict. Dipak and Chad are well-intentioned people who are usually socially skilled and polite. However, they come from family backgrounds and cultural contexts that gave them different ways of handling conflict. Dipak has learned to conform when possible or to otherwise avoid conflict. Chad has learned to be competitive and internalized the belief that to withdraw from conflict is a sign of weakness. Dipak's style of conflict management works well when the issues are not too serious or ongoing, but it leads him to bottle up his dissatisfactions. In this confrontation, they boiled over and he exploded. Chad's style of conflict, in contrast, leads him to refuse to let someone else "win," which in turn leads him to try to always get the last word in. The concepts of rational argument clarifying each other's concerns and interests and calmly discussing possible solutions simply did not occur to either of them. ■

This chapter examines interpersonal communication skills in conversations. Conversation is the primary mechanism through which we create, maintain, cause problems for, and end our relationships. It is also the primary vehicle through which we negotiate our activities and achieve our goals in everyday life, whether mundane or vital, tangible or intangible. Ultimately, all we know of any communicator is what he or she shows us through behavior. Because we cannot know exactly what people are thinking or feeling, our only choice is to infer these things from their actions. This behavior, in turn, is a reflection of their communication skills.

The Nature of Communication Skills

Much practical information about communication competence comes across as intuitive or common sense. Yet, as we have shown (Chapter 2), it is easy to overlook even the most basic challenges. For example, if you were asked to explain how to get someone else to laugh, you might say, "say something funny." But this raises the question, How do you say something funny? If you were asked to explain how to take a speaking turn away from someone who is speaking, you might say, "interrupt them." But this raises the question, How do you successfully interrupt someone so that you get your speaking turn? Where in the other person's speaking turn do you interrupt to do that?

We get through everyday conversations using common sense and intuition, but we are not very good at articulating the principles or behaviors underlying such activities. If we are not aware of the principles, it makes it difficult or even unlikely that we will improve our competence. This chapter examines the skills through which we interact in conversations. Some of them do rely on intuition and common sense, but many of the principles of competent interpersonal skills are far from intuitive. The fact that most people cannot provide specific answers to the questions about how to be funny or interrupt shows that most of us have significant room to improve our interpersonal communication competence.

Characteristics of Skills

A **skill** is a repeatable, goal-oriented action sequence enacted in a given context (Spitzberg, 2002). As explained in Chapter 2, *skills* are behaviors directed toward the achievement of preferred outcomes in a given context. Several key concepts help build this simple notion.

Skills Are Actions

First, **actions** are the behaviors performed by a person. They are not the same thing as motivation, knowledge, or ability. You do not enact all the behaviors you are able to perform. You select which behaviors to enact on the basis of motivation and knowledge. At the very specific level, our goals unconsciously influence how we select the actual phonemes and syllables that make words and the relationships of these words within sentences (Samp & Solomon, 2005). The more motivated you are, the more consciously you search your knowledge for the best possible behaviors to select. The more knowledgeable you are, the broader and deeper your repertoire of behaviors from which to select. Finally, when we speak of skills, it refers to the actions you have enacted as a product of these motivation and knowledge processes.

People commonly use the word *skills* to refer to either or both of two things. First, the person is able to perform certain behaviors necessary to accomplishing some goal, and second, the person enacts these behaviors at a high level of quality. These two meanings of the concept of skill are often confused. For our purposes, we reserve the first meaning for *skills* and the second for *competence*. Thus to say that someone is "skilled" is to say this person is able to perform a series of behaviors repeatedly in pursuit of a goal. To say this person is "competent" is to say he or she performs these behaviors in a high-quality manner, that is, in a manner perceived by self or others as relatively appropriate and effective.

learning link

Recalling Chapter 2, what role do goals play in linking motivation with skills?

● ● ●

Skills Are Goal Oriented

A skill is a set of behaviors directed toward achieving some particular outcome. The more of your goals you achieve through your communication, the more effective you are. Goals generally define the skill itself. For example, *conflict skills* refer to achieving your goal of resolving conflict. Assertiveness skills refer to the goal of asserting your rights. *Argumentation skills* refer to the goal of constructing arguments. So skills achieve some outcome. The effectiveness with which they achieve these outcomes determines the quality of the skill itself, and in large part, your effectiveness. Dipak and Chad displayed rather poor-quality conflict management skills because neither seemed to achieve their desired goals.

Skills Are Repeatable

A third characteristic of skills is that they are repeatable. You might tell a joke with all the right inflections and delivery one time but not the next time. Such subtleties can make all the difference in telling a joke, and the skill of telling it is in the ability to perform it the same way, or better, as the context calls for that performance.

Skills Are Sequential

As you saw in Chapter 7, most of what we know about communicating can be formulated into scripts. Scripts, in turn, are always sequential; that is, certain behaviors need to occur before others for the action sequence to be competent. Skills are not performed in random sequences—they have to follow a sequence and script for them to make sense. Skill sequences may have great flexibility, but they also have at least some sequential order (Kellermann, 1991). When we initiate a conversation with someone, we tend to begin with a greeting ("Hi, how are you?"), move to topics of health ("I've had the flu"), reason for presence ("I have an appointment"), where we live ("I'm currently living downtown"), persons known in common ("Oh, do you know Misty Shatto who works there?"), what we do ("I'm working in HR there"), interests ("I work out at that gym"), family ("My family recently visited me"), near-future activities ("I'm going skiing next month"), and then begin to move toward topics of evaluation of the encounter ("It was great to see you"), reason for terminating the encounter ("I've gotta run, I'm late for my appointment"), and a goodbye ("Bye, see you later"). It makes little sense to introduce the reason to terminate the encounter and then discuss the weather. Yet there is considerable flexibility in whether discussion of the weather precedes or follows discussion of what you do.

Skills Are Contextual

Skills are also contextual in that they, and the goals they are intended to achieve, depend on the context in which they are performed. A person seeking social or emotional support is performing communication in a different context than a person seeking to persuade someone to clean their shared dorm room. The goals in these examples define different contexts to which the communicators' skills are directed.

Abstractness of Skills

Skills exist at many different levels. These levels reflect their **abstraction dimension,** in which communication behaviors range from specific-level skills to general-level skills. Atoms make up molecules, and molecules make up substances, which make up things like the chair you are sitting on. Similarly, communication skills consist of the very specific units of behavior that, when performed in larger sequences, become the more general types of communication. Phonemes become words, words become sentences, sentences become speaking turns, speaking turns become conversations, which become contexts. **Specific-level skills** include such behaviors as gestures, eye contact, smiling, vocabulary, articulation, vocal variety, and so forth. **General-level skills** represent the assembly of specific-level skills to create the performance of general skills such as assertiveness, self-disclosure, social support, conflict management, deception, and wit.

If specific-level skills are the bricks and mortar, general-level skills are the actual rooms built from the bricks and mortar. But these rooms serve different purposes. Living rooms are different from kitchens. Much of communication competence depends on selecting the right specific-level skill for the relevant general-level skill. Thus if you use loud volume to express how serious you are about the context but do so in offering social support to a friend at a traditional solemn funeral, the specific skill of volume is not well adapted to the general skill of support. Later in this chapter we identify the general skills of interpersonal communication competence along with the types of specific skills that are the basis of those more abstract skills.

Impressions and Skills

Most of us at some point have had a job interview in which we used a variety of communication skills—we made eye contact, used humor, answered questions, avoided interruptions, and so forth—and yet we did not get the job because there was just something the interviewer didn't like about us. This illustrates one of the most important lessons about skills—they are not the same thing as competence. Skills are behaviors, but any given behaviors can be viewed as competent by some and incompetent by others. As you saw in Chapter 2, motivation, knowledge, and skills make you more *likely* to be perceived as competent, but they do not guarantee your competence (Canary & Spitzberg, 1990). Competence is the *perception* that skills have been performed appropriately and effectively. Optimizing competence will require you to find the skills that will achieve the perception of appropriateness and effectiveness you desire or else conclude the other person's view of your competence is less important than other goals you may have in that encounter.

This distinction between impressions and behaviors is central to the model of interpersonal competence we introduced in Chapter 7. A given set of behaviors comprises a skill. But the competence of this skill still depends on how it is perceived, interpreted, and evaluated. Fortunately, such impressions are rarely arbitrary. In a given culture certain types of skills and behaviors are more likely to be viewed as competent than are others. The question then is, which skills are most likely to be viewed as competent? The following section addresses this question.

learning link

How does attribution theory help explain the relationship between impressions of competence and communication skills?

● ● ●

Types of Interpersonal Skills

If competence varies from context to context, how can you hope to develop a set of skills that helps you communicate competently across these contexts? Consider that the rules of sports differ widely, but most still require eye-hand coordination, fast reflexes, endurance, and so forth. Similarly, even though communication contexts vary considerably, certain skills are important across these contexts.

The communication skills we discuss here represent four general-level skills useful in all interpersonal contexts. The specific-level skills we'll discuss within each general skill are a bit like building blocks. A box of building blocks may give you pictures of basic models you can build from the pieces, but you can build an infinite number of models from the blocks provided. Similarly, the skills of coordination, composure, expressiveness, and attentiveness discussed here are pictures of key models you can build from the building blocks of interpersonal skills (Spitzberg, 1994b; Spitzberg & Cupach, 2002), but you should not limit yourself to only these models or the illustrations within each general skill. Figure 8.1 shows how some specific skills make up more than one general skill. Expression of personal opinions, for example, is clearly an aspect of a communicator's expressiveness. In addition, expressing personal opinions also reveals a person's sense of composure and confidence in speaking up for himself or herself. Although seeing the skills displayed in so straightforward a way may make them seem simple, there are many challenges to their competent use. We discuss these challenges later in the chapter.

Attentiveness

Attentiveness is the skill of showing interest in, concern for, and attention to the other person or persons in the interaction. It is the ability to involve the person with whom you're communicating in the interaction and to demonstrate your own involvement with that person and his or her contribution to the conversation.

Attentiveness significantly overlaps with listening, the topic of Chapter 6, but it is also distinct in many ways. The goal of attentiveness is not to decode exactly what the other person is saying; rather it is to behave in ways that support and involve the other person in the interaction. As suggested by the *Drabble* cartoon, we often are able to behave attentively without actually listening. Such attentiveness can take many forms, only some of which include listening skills.

learning link

Given your understanding of empathy discussed in Chapter 7, how does empathy help make assertive behavior more competent?

● ● ●

COMPOSURE

- Vocal confidence (neither tense nor nervous sounding)
- Posture (neither too closed/formal nor too open/informal)
- Shaking or nervous twitches (weren't noticeable)
- Fidgeting (with rings, hair, fingers)
- Speaking rate (neither too slow nor too fast)
- Speaking fluency (avoided pauses, silences, "uh")
- Use of eye contact
- Expression of personal opinions (neither passive nor aggressive)

COORDINATION

- Initiation of new topics
- Maintenance of topics and follow-up comments
- Interruption of partner's speaking turns
- Speaking rate (neither too slow nor too fast)
- Use of eye contact
- Initiation of new topics
- Maintenance of topics and follow-up comments
- Interruption of partner's speaking turns

ATTENTIVENESS

- Leaning toward partner (neither too far forward nor too far back)
- Asking questions
- Encouragements or agreements (encouraged partner to talk)
- Speaking about partner or partner's interests
- Speaking about self (didn't talk too much about self/own interests)
- Nodding of head in response to partner's statements
- Use of eye contact
- Use of time speaking relative to partner

EXPRESSIVENESS

- Facial expressiveness (neither blank nor exaggerated)
- Use of gestures to emphasize what was being said
- Smiling and/or laughing
- Use of humor and/or stories
- Articulation (language clearly pronounced and understood)
- Vocal variety (avoided monotone voice)
- Volume (neither too soft nor too loud)
- Expression of personal opinions (neither passive nor aggressive)

▲ **Figure 8.1**

The Four General Skills

The four basic general skills of interpersonal communication are made up of smaller specific skills, some of which make up more than one general skill.

Even if conversations aren't contests, people often treat them as if they were.

Two closely related aspects of attentiveness that can greatly improve or impair the skill of attentiveness are topic development and time management. **Topic development,** which typically is used after topic initiation, is the management of the subject under discussion in a conversation. Topic development progresses in two basic ways: topic shifts and questions. A **topic shift** is illustrated in the following example:

Mary: My summer place has been such a blessing this year.
John: I know, I sure would like a place like that, the way I've been feeling, but I've got to earn the bread first, you know?
Mary: Yeah.
John: I figure that if I work enough this year and next, I'll be able to check out that place in Vermont again and maybe . . . (Derber, 1979, p. 26)

Here John develops the topic into an area of interest to himself. This skill, when used carefully, can show competence because it requires careful attention to the topic of the other person to make the transition smoothly. However, most people want to talk about a topic of interest to themselves, and this is where the second skill of topic development is relevant: questioning.

Questions, by verbally soliciting information, invite the other person to determine where the topic goes. But you can also influence that topical development through the types of questions you use. Questions come in two forms. **Open-ended questions** permit the other person wide discretion in how to answer. They contrast with **closed-ended questions,** which give the respondent very limited options in answering. For example, "What's your major?" and "Where were you born?" are closed ended. They generally call for one-word answers and do not supply topical materials for the respondent to elaborate on. In contrast, consider the following questions: "What got you interested in your major?" and "What, if anything, do you miss about where you were born?" These concern the same topics as the closed-ended questions but direct the respondent to become much more involved in the process of developing the topic.

The second aspect of topic development that can improve or impair attentiveness is **time management,** the skill of balancing the relative proportion of time each communicator gets to speak during a conversation. Achieving the right balance between speaking time and attentiveness is crucial to competent communication. On the one hand, the skill of expressiveness requires taking time in a conversation to reveal your feelings and interests. On the other hand, using the skill of attentiveness allows the other person to express himself or herself and shows interest through listening and openness. Research shows that people are perceived as more competent the more time they spend speaking relative to the other person, but only up to a point. When someone begins talking 70%, 80%, or 90% of the time rather than letting others take their turn at conversation, this person tends to be viewed as egotistical and manipulative and thus less competent (Wheeless, Frymier, & Thompson, 1992).

Composure

Composure is the skill of appearing in control of the course of one's communication behavior. The most common challenge people face in managing their composure is anxiety. Virtually everyone has experienced communication anxiety in public speaking contexts. However, anxiety in interpersonal situations is very common as well. **Social anxiety** is the real or imagined fear of interacting in an interpersonal encounter. Fear is the result of a

learning link

Considering the discussion of listening in Chapter 6, what is the connection between listening and attentiveness?

• • •

perceived threat. Social situations can be very threatening to self-concept because we derive so much of our self-concept from what we think others think of us. Thus social anxiety occurs not only during actual communication situations but also in anticipation of an actual situation or even when imagining a situation.

Generally speaking, the more formal and the more unfamiliar the situation, the larger the audience, and the more important the goals, the more nervous people become. Most people would feel more nervous interacting with their state's governor than their best friend because of the formality of the situation. Likewise, most people would experience more anxiety interacting with their family on a televised talk show than in their living room because of the unfamiliarity of the situation and the size of the audience.

When someone experiences anxiety across a wide variety of social situations over an extended period, it generally is known as **shyness,** a tendency to withdraw from social activities. Shy people may not appear very different from others in a given situation, but they are less likely to initiate or actively participate in conversation. It is important to remember that some cultures, such as many Asian cultures, value more unassertive public communication styles and their members may seem shyer than others. In these cultures, conversational shyness does not necessarily reflect incompetence. On the contrary, here "nonassertiveness and nonargumentativeness are probably more socially desirable" (Kim, 1999, p. 62), making shyness in interpersonal communication competent within that particular culture. However, it is possible to be shy even by the standards of a relatively unassertive culture. Thus shyness can be a challenge to competence regardless of a communicator's culture.

Social anxiety and shyness challenge interpersonal communication competence by making it more difficult for people to meet their needs and goals in interactions. Generally speaking, you don't get a date if you don't ask or accept, you don't get a job if you don't interview for it, and your partner doesn't know how much you love him or her if you don't communicate it. If you are anxious about such activities, it is difficult to fulfill your needs and goals.

The behaviors resulting from negative interpersonal motivation are probably familiar. Avoiding eye contact, fidgeting, tripping over words, speaking quietly with a quavering voice, initiating speaking turns less often, and displaying an impression of nervousness are all behaviors that result from negative motivation. In comparison, positive motivation is associated with confidence and assertiveness. People who are strongly motivated and knowledgeable tend to be more forceful, dynamic, and charismatic in their communication style. Such people are more fluent, speak with a steadier vocal tone and louder volume, use more confident and expressive gestures, and engage in eye contact. Positively motivated communicators initiate more speaking turns, spend more time talking, and appear more in control of their behavior as well as the course the conversation takes.

The communication skills that manage negative motivations and show positive motivation reflect the general skill of composure in conversation. A lack of composure typically produces an impression that a communicator is anxious, nervous, shy, or apprehensive. A person skilled at projecting composure is more likely to be viewed as competent, confident, focused, motivated, and assertive. Specifically, the skill of composure can best be understood in terms of its more competent form of performance: assertiveness. When composure occurs in excess, it is more likely to appear as aggressiveness. When composure is lacking, it is more likely to appear as passiveness.

Assertiveness is the skill of expressing one's rights or views without violating another's rights or views. It is the ability to give voice to your interests, position, needs, desires, and opinions in a way that is appropriate to the context. Assertiveness is different from its alternatives, aggression and passivity. **Aggressive communication** is the expression of your rights or views in a way that violates other's rights or views. It generally represents an excess of composure in that all you care about are your own motives. Finally, **passive communication** is the avoidance of self-expression or the accommodation to others' concerns over your own. In the opening vignette, when Chad made an excuse about the mess being due to late-night studying, it was a passive attempt to deal with the accusation that it should have been cleaned up. When the interaction degraded into name calling, it became more aggressive. Neither Chad nor Dipak found a more assertive manner in which to discuss the issue of the neatness of their shared space.

To better differentiate these three concepts, consider the following situations:

1. You have been standing in line for hours to buy tickets to a popular concert, and several people walk up to someone they know in line in front of you and start up a conversation as if they are now part of the line.

2. You are up studying late for a final exam to be held the next day. The people in the apartment next to yours are partying and playing loud distracting music at 1 a.m.

3. You are at a family dinner, meeting your romantic partner's parents and siblings for the first time. Your partner's father expresses an opinion that you find offensive, and no one at the table seems to take notice of the comment as anything unusual.

In each of these situations, you have an opinion you would express in an ideal world. Indeed, if you found yourself in these situations you probably would have a planned response. Interestingly, however, research shows clearly that most people "think" a better game than they actually play (Spitzberg & Cupach, 1984). That is, in the abstract it's easy to believe you would say something in these situations, but most people don't. People are often nervous about causing trouble or disrupting the situation. Many think that if they assert themselves, they will be seen as rude or aggressive. Indeed, when assertiveness is performed with abruptness and intensity, it is often interpreted as aggressive. Some of the distinctions among assertive, aggressive, and passive communication are illustrated in the Close-Up on Conflict box.

Composure is important, but it can be demonstrated in very different ways. Typically the most competent form is **empathic assertion**, the attempt to recognize and grant legitimacy to others in a situation while simultaneously expressing your own rights or views. In our examples, your assertive response would first attempt to acknowledge the other people's reasons for their actions ("I know you are all having fun, but . . ."), but then assert your position in the situation. In this way, you are not invalidating their rights in the process of trying to achieve your own. In essence, you are aiming to be effective and at the same time appropriate.

Coordination

Coordination is the skill of managing the flow of the interaction. It regulates whose turn it is to speak, development of topics for discussion, how to maintain the conversation, and the manner for entering and exiting conversations. The skill of coordination generally is considered competent when people engage in conversation that is viewed as smooth rather than awkward. Smoothness, at least in North American cultures, implies that uncomfortable silences, in which people are wondering what to say next or whose turn it is to speak, are rare.

CloseUp on Conflict

Conflict, Assertiveness, and Competence

As portrayed in the cartoon, Cathy and Irving are motivated and knowledgeable about how to engage in disagreements and conflicts. However, they lack the skills to apply their motivation and knowledge. One of the reasons is that conflict tends to bring the worst out in people. Conflict is difficult to manage in part because it pits the key competence dimensions against one another. You are trying to be effective by achieving your goals. However, the other person considers these goals inappropriate. Thus in the attempt to pursue your effectiveness, you are likely to be perceived as inappropriate, and the other person's attempts at keeping you from achieving your goals will in turn seem inappropriate to you. In a conflict situation, to the extent that the other person is effective, you are likely to be ineffective. In short, it is very difficult for people involved in a conflict to be competent, that is, both appropriate and effective.

Research on competence in conflict has identified three general conflict skills. **Avoidance skills** function to displace conflict. You postpone the conflict to another time or place to avoid dealing with the issue at a particular moment, or you sidetrack the interaction so it is forgotten or redirected. Avoidance often means shifting the topic of discussion, postponing the discussion until later, or simply leaving the situation when the conflict seems ready to get out of hand. In the opening vignette, Chad could have asked to talk with Dipak later that morning, or

Chad might have started talking about how his exam was coming up soon and how he had to get ready. Avoidance is commonly assumed to be an incompetent approach to conflict, but some classic research showed it sometimes helps communicators avoid the type of escalating conflict that enveloped Dipak and Chad (Raush, Barry, Hertel, & Swain, 1974).

The second conflict skill is distributive interaction. **Distributive skills** attempt to divide, that is, distribute, the outcomes of the conflict so that you win more than the other person. It is a maximizing and aggressive approach to communication. Deception, competition, persistent argumentation, yelling, criticizing, complaining, and refusing to admit fault are all forms of distributive communication. We generally don't think of these as "skills" of conflict management, but these are repeatable goal-oriented behaviors that we learn to perform, regardless of whether others view such behavior as competent. There are times when we need to behave in very competitive ways, and some communicators are clearly better than others in using them, even though, generally speaking, the more communicators use these skills, the more incompetently they are perceived (Olson, 2002). Certainly Dipak and Chad engaged in their share of distributive communication in the opening vignette and viewed each other's approaches to the disagreement as incompetent.

The final conflict skill is integrative communication. Whereas distributive skills attempt to divide the

cathy®

by Cathy Guisewite

Being motivated and knowledgeable in conflict management is not enough if you don't also have the skills to manage conflict.

outcomes of the conflict, **integrative skills** attempt to bring your goals and the other person's goals together so both of you can achieve what you want. It requires careful interaction that uncovers both persons' goals, clarifies the importance of these goals, identifies possible options, and develops a plan to achieve everyone's interests. Had Dipak and Chad calmed down and discussed how Chad might get the room cleaned up if Dipak gave him another 24 hours, until after the exam, it would have illustrated an integrative approach to the conflict.

Research on conflict has made three things clear about these skills (Spitzberg, Canary, & Cupach, 1994). First, in any given situation or context, any one of these skills can be competent (Gross, Guerrero, & Alberts, 2004). Sometimes it is best to avoid a conflict rather than let your anger loose (Canary, Spitzberg, & Semic, 1998). Sometimes distributive skills are the only way to escape being exploited by someone who is determined to be distributive, such as in negotiating for the best price on a car.

Second, it is the competence with which you engage in these skills that determines their impact on your relationship with the other person (Cramer, 2002). It is not as important which skill you use as it is how competent the skill is perceived to be in the context in which you use it. Thus if distributive skill is viewed as the most competent form of conflict in a given relationship, then it will tend to lead to a satisfying, trusting, and pleasant relationship. If in contrast, avoidance skill is viewed as most competent, then it is the behavior most likely to lead to a satisfying and trusting relationship.

Finally, across most situations, competing behavior, particularly aggressive competitive behavior, tends to be viewed as relatively incompetent. Conversely, across most situations, collaborative behavior tends to be viewed as competent (Gross et al., 2004).

Smooth conversation also implies that interactants don't interfere excessively with each other's efforts to contribute to the interaction. Like most people, you might think this means avoiding interrupting others, which most of us believe to be a general rule of conversation. However, this rule's inaccuracy illustrates just how fallible people's intuitions about communication can be. When we study everyday conversations word by word and turn by turn, we find that interruptions are both complex and common. They also tend not to be disruptive; on the contrary, they are even considered competent most of the time (Kennedy & Camden, 1983).

Interruptions occur in many forms. The two most common forms are talkovers and deep interruptions. **Talkovers** are instances in which you say something during someone else's turn to talk, typically during internal natural pauses or near the end of the other speaker's sentences. Most of these interruptions are reinforcers in which the listener provides feedback to the speaker that his or her words are understood or need clarification. As you saw in Chapter 6 in the discussion of responding skills, expressions such as "Hm-hm," "yeah," "uh-huh," "Really?" "You're kidding," and so on, are common expressions inserted while another person is speaking to display listener involvement. Other types of talkovers are competent forms of assistance, such as when the listener supplies the right word that allows the speaker to continue speaking. These types of talkovers are competent when the speaker struggles to find the right word and thereby risks introducing an uncomfortable pause in the speech.

Deep interruptions are interruptions that take over a speaker's turn in the middle of that person's statement. This is what most people mean when they warn not to interrupt when others are speaking. However, even deep interruptions are sometimes neither disruptive nor incompetent. In lively group interactions, members are often so excited by the topic of conversation and working toward a common goal that they build on each others' thoughts before the speaker is even finished expressing the idea. In group interactions, deep interruptors are perceived as less appropriate but more dynamic, and they tend to be effective in gaining their turns at talk (Hawkins, 1991).

One of the reasons for interruptions is that silences and pauses, even extremely short silences, are the doorways through which people generally get to take a turn in conversation. Most communicators don't need much of an opening to take a turn at speaking. One of the world's foremost scholars of conversation claims that any pause of 1 second or more is universally seen as representing some kind of problem in the conversation (Jefferson, 1989). That is, the vast majority of the time, a second is all the time needed to pick up the next turn at talk.

Avoiding silence, an important aspect of coordination, implies that the communicators are able to find a topic to talk about. This reflects the skill of **topic initiation,** introducing topics for discussion. Competent topic initiation typically means the development of topics relevant to all interactants as well as to the context at hand that permit all interactants to participate in the conversation. Competent topic initiation also continues threads of topics from previous conversations, adding a dimension of cohesiveness. This cohesiveness of topics over the course of conversation is highly flexible. You may frequently wonder how you got from the beginning topic of the conversation to the topic you are currently discussing. Yet if you were to trace the turn-by-turn shift of topics, you would see that each turn represents a reasonable and relevant extension of the previous topics.

learning link

Looking back at Chapter 2, what is the impact of negative motivation on a communicator's composure skills?

- - -

Expressiveness

Expressiveness is the skill of animating verbal and nonverbal communication. Expressiveness makes communication behavior lively, varied, and colorful. It serves as the primary avenue for displaying affect and emotion in interaction, as well as getting across particular shades of meaning and intention. Expressive communication relies heavily on facial displays, gestures, vocal variety, and word choices. If you have experienced a conversation with someone with an emotionally flat vocal tone, or who is extremely monotonic, you quickly realize that such a voice detracts from the communication.

As you saw in Chapter 5, the voice provides an important window into expressiveness (Scherer, 1986). The voice has three basic forms of expressiveness: wide–narrow, tense–lax, and full–thin. The **wide–narrow dimension** describes a range from lower frequency tones produced by a relaxed vocal tract to higher frequency tones produced by tense vocal tracts. Generally, people using wider voices are viewed as more competent and those with narrow voices as less competent.

The **tense–lax dimension** refers to a range from the harshness of a metallic or piercing voice to a continuous more muffled and relaxed voice. Generally, people using lax voices are viewed as more competent than those using tense voices.

Finally, the **full–thin dimension** of vocal expressiveness describes a vocal range from deep and forceful resonance, voices that communicate strong energy, to more rapid and shallow resonance and low-energy voices. Generally, people with fuller voices are viewed as more competent than those with thin voices.

The skill of expressiveness is also evident in nonverbal messages sent though facial expressions and eyes. The face, particularly the eyes, is considered a window into a person's true feelings. Despite this assumption, we learn early in life to control or edit our facial expression so as not to reveal feelings we don't want others to see. This interpersonal skill of managing facial expressions becomes vital to competent communication in a variety of situations. Many situations call for polite responses that mute true feelings. For example, a friend may ask you what you think of her new hairstyle. Although it may make you want to laugh out loud, you are more likely to express a toned-down response. Rather than being deceptive, such responses are representative of the nature of social interaction and the roles we play and the roles that society requires of us to function smoothly.

The range of facial expressiveness is also important to competence. In most contexts, people who are more facially expressive are perceived as more competent and attractive (Sabatelli & Rubin, 1986), and the resulting interactions are judged as more satisfying (Friedman, DiMatteo, & Taranta, 1980). Even something as simple as a smile can positively affect people's impressions of a communicator (Harwood & Williams, 1998). In short, facial expressiveness generally enhances a communicator's competence.

Collectively, the expressiveness skills of using your voice and face have a great influence on whether people find you interesting or not. However, there are other things that influence others' interest. One way of thinking about the value of expressiveness is to think of how you might describe a boring communicator. Boring communicators are passive, tedious, sometimes distracting, unemotional, and self-focused and seem to engage only in small talk or trite sayings (Leary, Rogers, Canfield, & Coe, 1986). Every one of these characteristics refers to some aspect of expressiveness. If a lack of expressiveness leads to boredom, it follows that expressiveness in communication leads to excitement, all other things being equal. Indeed, communicating in an animated style has a powerful effect on people's tendency to remember you and view you as competent (Norton, 1984).

Challenges to Managing Interpersonal Skills

We use four general communication skills in all our interpersonal interactions. Each one of these skills is made up of many more specific skills. In every instance of interpersonal communication, we attempt to manage these skills so we effectively achieve our goals in a way that is appropriate to the context. Given the number, subtlety, and complexity of these interpersonal communication skills, it is not surprising that we face several challenges to our competence. The four major challenges are managing habit and routine; balancing adaptability and consistency; balancing the quantity, or amount, of certain behaviors we use to enact skills; and balancing self-interests versus other-interests in our communication.

Habit and Routine

Often when we say something we regret, we ask ourselves, "What in the world was I thinking when I said that?" This question assumes that thinking before communicating makes us more competent, whereas mindlessness makes us incompetent. This assumption is far from accurate. **Mindlessness** is a state of engaging in activities without consciously monitoring the operations or process of that activity. If you commute using a given route to school each day you may occasionally arrive at your destination only to realize that you don't remember how you got where you are! This is an example of mindless activity. You drove, biked, or walked a route, changed your pace, made turns, saw traffic go by, and generally reached your destination without mishap. Yet you may not recall a single specific perception of the trip itself.

So was your commute incompetent? Not really. Mindlessness is truly a double-edged sword. Learning a new skill or concept for the first time is a very mindful process. For

learning link

What kind of context is created by a communicator who speaks too much of the time versus too little of the time?

• • •

example, in learning how to speak a foreign language or how to drive, the early learning stages are difficult because, among other things, they are extremely mindful. However, over time, with practice and experience the mind becomes so fluent at calling forth the required actions that it has forgotten how it knows to do these things. If you have tried to explain to someone how to drive a car you recognize the difficulty of putting your knowledge into a form the other can use. Your knowledge of how to drive is so deeply embedded in your mind, you find it difficult to articulate what you know. It has become **overlearned,** or learned to the point that it is no longer very consciously accessible.

As efficient as mindlessness sometimes is, it creates challenges for interpersonal communication competence when you rely on it too much in situations in which your ordinary ways of doing things don't work. The challenge therefore is to become mindful of what you are doing wrong and how to improve your competence. However, once you have the appropriate knowledge, this knowledge too needs to become relatively mindless in its application to achieve competence. This communication course, therefore, may occasionally make you feel less competent in the process of trying to improve your communication competence, because communication routines that were mindless in the past will have become mindful. Although mindless routines are efficient, they are not necessarily competent. We often continue with them not because they are competent, but because it would involve effort, and perhaps temporary incompetence, to change them. In addition, given that these routines are mindless, you may not even realize you are doing them incompetently.

Mindlessness can be particularly problematic in ongoing relationships with others. You develop routines and rituals of interaction, ways of greeting each other, typical arguments, and patterns of bickering. To change your behavior would require a great deal of conscious reflection in situations that demand spontaneity. Over the short term, a person trying to communicate more competently in his or her relationships may seem awkward or even manipulative. This person may need to pause, reflect, experiment with new behaviors, and generally respond with less fluency than before. But over time, if the new behaviors become routine and therefore mindless and if the new routines are selected on the basis of their appropriateness and effectiveness, their mindlessness is likely to improve competence.

Once a skill has been overlearned it becomes harder to recognize when the actions no longer work. Overlearned skills become habitual and routine. Habit and routine are very efficient means of getting through life. However, they also let you run on autopilot until something goes very wrong. We often don't become aware anything is wrong with our communication until we violate a social rule. Consequently, we cannot either accurately monitor feedback or adapt our behavior to changes in the communication situation.

Balancing Adaptability and Consistency

learning link

Referring back to Chapter 3, does mindlessness always result in habit and routine, and why or why not?

• • •

Our tendency to rely on habit and routine creates a related challenge: excessive consistency. If we become too predictable, we may become boring. To overcome this challenge, people need to balance adaptability with consistency in their communication skills (Spitzberg, 1993, 1994a). **Adaptability** is the ability to alter skills appropriately as contexts and conversations evolve and change. **Consistency** means maintaining similar ways of behaving across contexts and conversations. Although these skills are the opposite of one another, they are both essential to interpersonal communication competence.

We rely on others to be at least somewhat predictable. We trust that people generally speak the truth as they know it; they will respond to our statements with statements that aren't always just what we want to hear; and if they have generally been outgoing or shy, they are likely to continue to be so. This consistency in our conversational partner's communication skills permits us to concentrate on conversational goals without second-guessing every aspect of the encounter. In other words, because we predict certain things about each interaction, we are able to concentrate on those aspects that are not predictable and the content and goals of the conversation itself. If nothing were predictable, every interaction would require a huge amount of effort just to coordinate basic communication activities.

To a large extent, therefore, each new communication context brings with it a variety of old and a variety of new behaviors and experiences. Competence in interaction requires a constant balancing of adaptability and consistency, in which a communicator portrays a performance consistent with his or her past performances while simultaneously altering his or her behaviors to be appropriate to the situation at hand. Competence, in short, means changing your behaviors against a backdrop of constancy.

learning link

Examining Chapter 3 again, in what way does the skill of adaptability help explain the postmodern self?

● ● ●

Balancing the Amount of Skills

Interpersonal skills are performed in amounts. You engage in eye contact a certain proportion of the time in a conversation. You ask a certain number of questions. Consider each of the following examples for the skills discussed in this chapter: coordination, composure, expressiveness, and attentiveness. Some communicators are too coordinated. If you have ever been approached by a professional salesperson or telemarketer, they often practice the skill of coordination to the detriment of all others. They speak in clichés and jargon that seem as though they have been repeated thousands of times, and they are too quick to offer immediate canned answers to all your responses. In this way, their communication lacks spontaneity and genuineness because they come across as too smooth and practiced.

Some communicators are too composed. They display a brash overconfidence and an air of unflappable self-control. In any social situation, things could go wrong in an almost infinite number of ways. A display of composure that seems disconnected to such risks can appear out of touch with the actual situation. Furthermore, overly composed people may be so caught up in their own goals that they may not adapt their behavior to others. Finally, there is often a thin line between extreme confidence and aggressiveness or arrogance.

Other communicators are overly expressive. Every emotion is a flood of expression. When the situation calls for a grin, the person lets out a loud laugh. When a loud laugh seems appropriate, this person bellows in a fit of outrageous laughter. Every facial expression is made as if on a stage and every vocalization as if the recipient needs an exaggerated version of the emotion being expressed. Such excesses can create a sense of insincerity, exhaust the senses of the recipients, and leave little room for interpreting subtleties that certain messages may require.

Finally, attentiveness when overdone can lose its competence as well. As much as we like to feel attended to, in the extreme it can become unnerving. Too much attentiveness forces you into the spotlight by placing the responsibility of the entire conversation on your shoulders. Too much attentiveness may also detract from a person's competence because he or she may be perceived as lacking anything to say.

A general principle of the relationship between communication skills and competence is the **moderation principle:** as use of attentiveness, composure, coordination, and expressiveness skills increase, impressions of competence increase, *to a point,* after which the behaviors become excessive and detract from competence. Too little of something, such as talk time, tends to be viewed as incompetent. But too much of the same thing, in this case talking all the time in a conversation, is also likely to be perceived as incompetent.

In short, much of the challenge of using interpersonal skills competently is in implementing the moderation principle by finding the optimal balance for producing those skills in a given context. In most situations, displaying coordination, composure, expressiveness, and attentiveness will enhance the impression of competence that others have of you. However, each skill has its breaking point, such that producing more of that skill will detract from your competence. Too much of a skill is often just as incompetent as too little.

Balancing Self-Interests and Other-Interests

When communicating, most of us have something we want to achieve, and in the process, we often pay little attention to what others are trying to achieve. The person in the cartoon is simply expressing what many of us sometimes feel, but would rarely admit. Some skills are directed toward satisfying your goals, whereas other skills are directed toward satisfying others' goals. Balancing the pursuit of self and other goals is a key challenge to competent interaction. Too much self-satisfaction becomes narcissistic, whereas too much satisfaction

You're a fascinating conversationalist, but totally useless as far as my career is concerned, so I think I'll move on.

of others becomes submissive or passive. The challenge is whether to value effectiveness over appropriateness or appropriateness over effectiveness.

Composure and expressiveness are largely self-focused skills. Composure is the control of your own behavior. When you engage in expressiveness skills, you are giving voice to your own inner experience, your feelings, and your thoughts. Extremes of these behaviors risk **conversational narcissism,** which is the appearance in your communication of caring only about yourself (Vangelisti, Knapp, & Daly, 1990). Conversational narcissism is displayed through self-aggrandizing or defensive statements, interruptions and other attempts to control a conversation, minimal uninvolved responses to others' statements, overly lengthy and frequent speaking turns, excessive self-disclosure, and showy or exhibitionist behavior (Leary, Bednarski, Hammon, & Duncan, 1997).

In contrast, coordination and attentiveness are more other-focused skills. Coordination depends on adapting one's own actions to those of another person. Successful coordination requires orienting toward the other's actions so your collective behavior meshes smoothly. Attentiveness, in turn, is a skill almost entirely focused on the other person. However, extremes of these skills can appear ingratiating. **Ingratiating communication** behavior in interaction makes the person appear to be only interested in seeking favor from the other person. Frequent compliments, offering of favors, constant agreement, and ongoing attention focused on the other person all reflect forms of ingratiating behavior.

Consequently, one of the challenges of interpersonal skills is not just applying each skill in the right amount, but balancing all four skills. If you concentrate too much on expressiveness and composure, you may appear narcissistic or self-focused. But if you display the skills of coordination and attentiveness too much, you may be perceived as lacking individuality. Indeed, this is the challenge of relationships in general, which are a constant balance of managing our own versus others' needs and interests (Spitzberg, 1993).

We have examined several challenges to interpersonal skills in relationships. So what can be done to avoid excessive use of skills, unbalanced use of skills, and habitual inattention to our skills? There are no simple answers, but becoming aware of such challenges is the first step.

 ## Chapter Summary

Communicative competence depends on our subtle use of communication skills. Skills are repeatable, goal-oriented actions that vary along a dimension of abstraction, from specific skills, such as gesturing or giving a compliment, to general skills, such as being supportive or engaging in conflict. The more skilled you are, generally the more likely it is that you are perceived, by yourself and others, as a competent communicator. We adapt our skills to various contexts, but certain sets of skills are used across most interpersonal communication situations. The four general skills most common across communication encounters are attentiveness, composure, coordination, and expressiveness. Attentiveness consists of behaviors that display interest in and concern for others. Composure skills display confidence and self-control. Coordination skills manage the flow and timing of interaction, and expressiveness skills reveal animation and variability in communication.

There are four common challenges to the competent use of these skills: managing habit and routine, balancing adaptability with consistency, balancing the amount of skills, and balancing self- with other-interests.

Study and Review

The premium companion website for *Human Communication* offers a broad range of resources that will help you better understand the material in this chapter, complete assignments, and succeed on tests. The website resources include

- Interactive self-assessments, competency grids, and other tools
- Web links, practice activities, self-quizzes, and a sample final exam

For more information about this text's electronic learning resources, consult the *Guide to Online Resources for Human Communication* or visit **http://communication .wadsworth.com/morreale2.**

Key Terms

The key terms below are defined in the chapter on the pages indicated. They are also presented alphabetically with definitions in the Glossary, which begins on page 467. The book's website includes flashcards and crossword puzzles to help you learn these terms and the concepts they represent.

Building Knowledge _____

The following questions are among the practice activities on the book's website.

1. What are the relationships and distinctions among skills, abilities, behaviors, and impressions of competence?
2. How are general skills (empathy, assertiveness, and so on) related to specific skills (facial expressiveness, asking questions, and so on)?
3. How can conversational interruptions be competent?
4. What are the four major skill areas of interpersonal communication competence? How do they differ from one another? Give examples for each type of skill.
5. In what ways do the four skill areas of interpersonal communication competence relate to self-concern and other-concern?
6. Distinguish among assertive, aggressive, and passive communication behavior.
7. Describe the process of balancing adaptability with consistency.
8. Describe the process of balancing appropriateness with effectiveness.

 Building Skills _____

The exercises below are among the practice activities on the book's website.

Individual Exercises

1. Skills examined in this chapter are listed in the Skills/Levels of Competence chart on page 204, grouped by skill area. Select one skill in each skill area, describe the skill you have chosen, and define five levels of competence for each skill. The first two skill areas have been completed as examples.
2. Go to the Conflict Resolution Network and their component on the twelve skills of conflict management (**http://crnhq.org/twelveskills.html**). Think of two communication situations you have faced recently, one in which you responded too aggressively and one in which you responded too passively. Briefly describe the contexts: who you were talking to, what your relationship was with that person, where you were, and so on. Then, as accurately as you can remember the conversation, write down a statement or response you provided that was too aggressive in the first situation and too passive in the second situation. Now, using the information in this website's description of "I statements," reformulate your statements to be more appropriately assertive. To what extent could these "I statements" help resolve conflicts in which you find yourself in everyday encounters? Why?
3. Following are several potentially problematic situations. For each situation, describe an aggressive, a passive, and an assertive response.
   a. A week ago you and your steady dating partner of a year broke up. You still have strong feelings for this person, but you need to move on. A week later, your best friend calls and says, "Guess what? I'm going to a party with your ex-partner. I hope you don't mind."
   b. Despite having agreed to buy food separately to avoid disputes over who can eat which snacks, you come home to find your roommate eating the last of your microwave popcorn.

SKILLS/LEVELS OF COMPETENCE (QUESTION 1)

	LEVELS OF COMPETENCE
VOCAL CONFIDENCE *A display of vocalic firmness, calmness, forcefulness, and steadiness of expression*	1. Vocalizations are almost constantly nervous, shaky, breaking in pitch, or equivocal in tone or volume 2. Vocalizations are frequently nervous, shaky, breaking in pitch, or equivocal in tone or volume 3. Vocalizations are occasionally nervous, shaky, breaking in pitch, or equivocal in tone or steadiness of volume 4. Vocalizations are generally calm or forceful, or both, and firm and composed 5. Vocalizations are consistently calm or forceful, or both, and firm, composed, and assertive
FACIAL EXPRESSIONS *A facial display of a range of emotion, animation of face, and normal facial expressions compatible with verbal content and partner statements*	1. Constant display of blank, uninterested, or hypnotic gaze or highly exaggerated, cartoonish expressions, or expressions inconsistent with verbal content of discussion, or both 2. Frequent display of blank, uninterested, or hypnotic gaze or highly exaggerated, cartoonish expressions, or expressions inconsistent with verbal content of discussion, or both 3. Occasional display of blank, uninterested, or hypnotic gaze or highly exaggerated, cartoonish expressions, or expressions inconsistent with verbal content of discussion, or both 4. General display of variation in facial emotion consistent with subject matter and partner 5. Consistent displays of variation in facial emotion consistent with subject matter and partner
ATTENTIVENESS Leaning toward partner Eye contact Asking of questions Use of time when speaking	
COORDINATION Speaking fluency Topic initiation Topic maintenance Interruptions of partner	
COMPOSURE Posture Nervous twitches Expression of personal opinion Volume	
EXPRESSIVENESS Speaking about self Vocal variety Use of gestures Smiling or laughing	

c. Someone you have been dating exclusively for a while says, "I think we're getting a little stale. Maybe we should start seeing other people for a while."

d. You take someone you have been dating exclusively to a local pub. Soon after arriving, you go up to the bar to order something, and when you turn around, you see your partner flirting with someone else.

4. Here are several situations in which you might find yourself. For each situation, write three possible statements you might make to open up conversation.

a. You are at the veterinarian and you see another person with a pet like yours.

b. You are discussing an essay with a professor in his or her office.

c. You are at the park watching people throw a Frisbee and an elderly person sits next to you on the bench.

d. You see a friend at a shopping mall.

e. You are at a party and an attractive person asks you what time it is.

5. Here are some examples of closed-ended questions. For each question, write three open-ended questions that are related to the same topic area.

a. Where are you from?

b. How long have you been in or out of school?

c. What is or was your major?

d. Where do you work? What is your position?

e. What are your hobbies?

f. Where do you live?

Group Activities

1. Here is a list of terms and topics. In this activity you will be asked to show creativity in topic development. Choose a partner. The first person to volunteer should select a topic from the list and make a comment related to the topic. For example, if the first topic selected was gun control, you might start by saying something like, "I can't believe the government hasn't banned assault rifles yet." The person to the right of the person who went first will then select another topic from the list and make a statement that is topically relevant to both the topic selected and the previous statement made by the other person. Thus following our example, if the next topic was abortion, the next person's statement might be something like, "Yeah, if they don't start controlling guns better, they'll keep having these nuts go out and attack abortion clinics or whatever else they disagree with." Each person sequentially to the right of the person who spoke before in the group continues by making a comment that is topically relevant to both the previous comment and the next topic he or she selects from the list. Continue until all topics have been exhausted. See whether you can continue without the list once you have finished all its topics.

Topics

Equal rights	Auto safety
Terrorism	The economy
Welfare	AIDS and HIV
Drunk driving	Foreign language education
Hunting and poaching	Media violence
Sports	Genetic engineering
Separation of church and state	Sex education
Right to die	Illegal aliens
Family values	The environment

When the conversation ends, discuss the skill of topic maintenance and development. What distinguished competent from incompetent follow-up comments?

2. Go on InfoTrac College Edition and enter the search term *interpersonal skills*. Among the entries you will find an article by Virginia Anderson, Janet Reis, and Yvonne Stephens on interpersonal skills and sexual coercion, published in *Adolescence* in 1997 (article A196119422). The authors examine how confident adolescents are in asserting themselves in sexual situations. Form a dyad and discuss the items in the article's Table 1. Are there situations college students face that were not identified in this list? What are they? Are college students more competent at asserting themselves in these situations than high school students? Why? Finally, which general and specific interpersonal skills would be helpful in these kinds of situations?

3. Choose someone to work with whom you don't know very well. Conduct a get-acquainted conversation. For the first 3–5 minutes, both parties should engage in zero eye contact. For the next 3–5 minutes, both of you should engage in total eye contact. For the final 3–5 minutes, engage in conversation as you normally would. Afterward, discuss the three conditions (no eye contact, total eye contact, normal eye contact) in terms of how they made you feel, how they affected the conversation, and what they suggest about the role of eye contact in conversation management.

4. Choose a partner in class whom you don't know very well. Conduct a get-acquainted conversation. Throughout the conversation, both parties should wait 5 seconds before responding to the other's previous statement. You can do this by mentally counting off the seconds before saying anything. After about 10 minutes, discuss the effects of the delays in affecting the flow of the conversation.

5. Select five emotions from the list here. List them in the chart in the blanks provided. Form a dyad, making sure neither person can see the other's list. Take turns expressing each of the five emotions on your lists. First express the emotion using only your face. Then express the same emotion by using only vocalics, or the nonverbal aspects of your voice such as pitch, tone, volume, pace, and so on, when saying the phrase: "We take these truths to be self-evident, that all people are created equal." After each facial expression and each vocal expression, have your partner write down the emotion from the list he or she thinks you are expressing. Afterward, compare the emotions you intended to express with those that your partner thought you were expressing. Discuss the implications of the results for being interpersonally competent.

Emotions

Anger	Happiness
Anticipation	Hate
Attraction	Hopefulness
Confidence	Hopelessness
Depression	Impatience
Despair	Love
Disgust	Pessimism
Eagerness	Sadness
Embarrassment	Solitude
Excitement	Surprise
Fatigue	Tension
Fear	Terror

EMOTIONS EXPRESSED	PARTNER'S INTERPRETATION

References

Canary, D. J., & Spitzberg, B. H. (1990). Attribution biases and associations between conflict strategies and competence outcomes. *Communication Monographs, 57,* 139–151.

Canary, D. J., Spitzberg, B. H., & Semic, B. A. (1998). The experience and expression of anger in interpersonal settings. In P. A. Andersen & L. K. Guerrero (Eds.), *Handbook of communication and emotion: Theory, research, and applications* (pp. 189–213). San Diego, CA: Academic Press.

Cramer, D. (2002). Linking conflict management behaviors and relational satisfaction: The intervening role of conflict outcome satisfaction. *Journal of Social and Personal Relationships, 19,* 425–432.

Derber, C. (1979). *The pursuit of attention: Power and individualism in everyday life.* Cambridge, MA: Schenkman.

Friedman, H. S., DiMatteo, M. R., & Taranta, A. (1980). A study of the relationships between individual differences in nonverbal expressiveness and factors of personality and social interaction. *Journal of Research in Personality, 14,* 351–364.

Gross, M. A., Guerrero, L. K., & Alberts, J. K. (2004). Perceptions of conflict strategies and communication competence in task-oriented dyads. *Journal of Applied Communication Research, 32,* 249–270.

Harwood, J., & Williams, A. (1998). Expectations for communication with positive and negative subtypes of older adults. *International Journal of Aging & Human Development, 47,* 11–33.

Hawkins, K. W. (1991). Some consequences of deep interruption in task-oriented communication. *Journal of Language and Social Psychology, 10,* 1–20.

Jefferson, G. (1989). Preliminary notes on a possible metric which provides for a "standard maximum" silence of approximately one second in conversation. In D. Roger & P. Bull (Eds.), *Conversation: An interdisciplinary perspective* (pp. 166–196). Philadelphia: Multilingual Matters.

Kellermann, K. (1991). The conversation MOP, II: Progression through scenes in discourse. *Human Communication Research, 17,* 385–414.

Kennedy, C. W., & Camden, C. T. (1983). A new look at interruptions. *Western Journal of Speech Communication, 47,* 45–58.

Kim, M.-S. (1999). Cross-cultural perspectives on motivations of verbal communication: Review, critique, and a theoretical framework. In M. E. Roloff & G. D. Paulson (Eds.), *Communication yearbook 22* (pp. 50–89). Thousand Oaks, CA: Sage.

Leary, M. R., Bednarski, R., Hammon, D., & Duncan, T. (1997). Blowhards, snobs, and narcissists: Interpersonal reactions to excessive egotism. In R. Kowalski (Ed.), *Aversive interpersonal behavior* (pp. 111–131). New York: Plenum.

Leary, M. R., Rogers, P. A., Canfield, R. W., & Coe, C. (1986). Boredom in interpersonal encounters: Antecedents and social implications. *Journal of Personality and Social Psychology, 51,* 968–975.

Norton, R. (1984). *Communicator style: Theory, applications, and measures.* Beverly Hills, CA: Sage.

Olson, L. N. (2002). "As ugly and painful as it was, it was effective": Individuals' unique assessment of communication competence during aggressive conflict episodes. *Communication Studies, 53,* 171–188.

Raush, H. L., Barry, W. A., Hertel, R. J., & Swain, M. A. (1974). *Communication, conflict, and marriage.* San Francisco: Jossey-Bass.

Sabatelli, R. M., & Rubin, M. (1986). Nonverbal expressiveness and physical attractiveness as mediators of interpersonal perceptions. *Journal of Nonverbal Behavior, 10,* 120–133.

Samp, J. A., & Solomon, D. H. (2005). Toward a theoretical account of goal characteristics in micro-level message features. *Communication Monographs, 72,* 22–45.

Scherer, K. R. (1986). Vocal affect expression: A review and a model for future research. *Psychological Bulletin, 99,* 143–165.

Spitzberg, B. H. (1993). The dialectics of (in)competence. *Journal of Social and Personal Relationships, 10,* 137–158.

Spitzberg, B. H. (1994a). The dark side of (in)competence. In W. R. Cupach & B. H. Spitzberg (Eds.), *The dark side of interpersonal communication* (pp. 25–49). Hillsdale, NJ: Erlbaum.

Spitzberg, B. H. (1994b). Instructional assessment of interpersonal competence: The Conversational Skills Rating Scale. In S. Morreale, M. Brooks, R. Berko, & C. Cooke (Eds.), *Assessing college student competency in speech communication* (1994 SCA Summer Conference Proceedings, pp. 325–352). Annandale, VA: Speech Communication Association.

Spitzberg, B. H., Canary, D. J., & Cupach, W. R. (1994). A competence-based approach to the study of interpersonal conflict. In D. D. Cahn (Ed.), *Intimates in conflict* (pp. 183–202). Hillsdale, NJ: Erlbaum.

Spitzberg, B. H., & Cupach, W. R. (1984). *Interpersonal communication competence.* Beverly Hills, CA: Sage.

Spitzberg, B. H., & Cupach, W. R. (2002). Interpersonal skills. In M. L. Knapp & J. R. Daly (Eds.), *Handbook of interpersonal communication* (3rd ed., pp. 564–611). Newbury Park, CA: Sage.

Vangelisti, A. L., Knapp, M. L., & Daly, J. A. (1990). Conversational narcissism. *Communication Monographs, 57,* 251–274.

Wheeless, L. R., Frymier, A. B., & Thompson, C. A. (1992). A comparison of verbal output and receptivity in relation to attraction and communication satisfaction in interpersonal relationships. *Communication Quarterly, 40,* 102–115.

Interpersonal Communication Competence Skills Grid

To help you understand how to use this grid, the skills displayed by Dipak and Chad in the opening vignette of this chapter have been analyzed below. Examine that analysis and then think about a recent interpersonal communication situation you were in and what you could have done more competently. First, describe the context of the interpersonal communication situation in the spaces provided. Next, analyze your interpersonal communication skills based on the skills explained in this chapter for each step in the listening process. In the first column, briefly describe and give examples of how your skills might have been less than competent. Using these less competent skills as a point of comparison to fill in the second column, describe the skills you think would have been perceived as more competent in the particular context. With practice, you will find you can use this grid to help develop your skills for future interpersonal communication situations, as well as to analyze situations you have already experienced.

ANALYZING DIPAK AND CHAD'S INTERPERSONAL COMMUNICATION SKILLS

Context

CULTURE: An Indian and North American student in a U.S. apartment

TIME: Weekend morning

RELATIONSHIP: Roommates, friends, and fellow college students

PLACE: In a shared apartment

FUNCTION: Dipak: to get Chad to clean up the apartment

GENERAL SKILL	LESS COMPETENT	MORE COMPETENT
ATTENTIVENESS	Accusing the other person; using insulting language (e.g., "pigsty" and "disaster zone"); giving ultimatums (e.g., "Find someone else. . . .")	Describing the situation; using more neutral language (e.g., "very cluttered" or "messy"); being flexible (e.g., "Can we find some way to resolve this?")
COMPOSURE	Aggressiveness (e.g., "Find someone else. . . ."); passiveness (e.g., making excuses when you are to blame); escalating unnecessarily by yelling back	Empathetic assertiveness (e.g., "I think you may want to consider finding another roommate"); responsibility (e.g., "I will clean it up later today"); remaining calm
COORDINATION	Interrupting the other person in midsentence; waking someone by yelling	Letting the other person finish his or her turn speaking; waiting until a person is ready to talk to begin conversation
EXPRESSIVENESS	Exaggeration (e.g., "pigsty" and "typical godless American"); yelling louder and louder	Reasonable description (e.g., "The room is a mess" and "I don't see what you believe in"); speaking in an animated but not screaming voice

ANALYZING YOUR OWN INTERPERSONAL COMMUNICATION SKILLS

Context

CULTURE:

TIME:

RELATIONSHIP:

PLACE:

FUNCTION:

GENERAL SKILL	LESS COMPETENT	MORE COMPETENT
ATTENTIVENESS		
COMPOSURE		
COORDINATION		
EXPRESSIVENESS		

© Bob Daemmrich / The Image Works

LEARNING OBJECTIVES

After studying this chapter, you should be able to

1. Define small group communication.

2. Explain how perception, interdependence, and communication function in groups of three or more people.

3. Distinguish between group problem solving and decision making.

4. Define questions of fact, conjecture, value, and policy.

5. Highlight which types of communication are important to

high-quality decision making maintained by a functionalist approach to group communication.

6. Use vigilant interaction, decision acceptability, collaboration capability, and personal development to assess decision quality.

7. Avoid the pitfalls associated with groupthink.

8. Apply procedures and processes that enhance divergent and convergent thinking.

Small Groups and Decision Making: Building Knowledge and Skills

S tudent enrollment at National University has risen dramatically, provoking concerns about the faculty's ability to provide high-quality instruction and conduct cutting edge research. National University's president has appointed a task force comprising students, faculty, and administrators to generate recommendations for managing the student enrollment problem. She appointed Eva, a faculty member, to chair the task force.

Eva began the first meeting by providing an overview of the president's charge to the task force, "The committee's charge is to make a recommendation to the president on how to manage future student enrollment. There is a concern that our recent growth is causing problems."

Bob, the vice president for Finance, immediately responded, "As far as I'm concerned, this isn't a problem. More students mean more tuition dollars and revenue for the university. We should continue to enroll more students each year."

Sally, the president of the Faculty Senate, jumped in. "What I hear from faculty is that they are seeing 20% more students in class. Moreover, the overall quality of students has gone down and faculty find they are having to spend a lot more time covering basic material in their classes. This is a huge problem!"

Nilam, president of the student body, stated, "I know there is a lot of over-crowding in the classes and the students don't feel they're receiving enough attention from the faculty." Eduardo, the Alumni Association president, chipped in, "Our alumni have also been quite vocal in their opinions. If we decrease the number of students we admit each year by raising entrance requirements, they worry that some of their kids won't be able to get in."

The discussion quickly erupted into a heated debate with some of the task force members arguing that a decrease in student enrollment would provide better instruction for students. They argued that raising entrance standards would allow National University to be more selective and admit only the most qualified students, so that professors could teach more challenging material. Other task force members contended that increased student enrollment was the only way to bring in enough money to keep the university running. The president had said she wanted to keep tuition low, so significantly decreasing student enrollment while raising tuition was not an option—which left increasing student enrollment at National. Other task force members voiced concern that a decision had already been made by the regents and that this task force was simply spinning its wheels.

Eva sat there quietly trying to figure out what to do. There were so many different issues to manage for the task force to make a decision. When another task force member mused out loud that perhaps this was a time to reconsider the university's mission, because the size of the university depended on its mission, she sighed heavily and knew it was going to be a long afternoon.

Small groups are increasingly being used to make decisions and solve problems. The issues confronting organizations, governments, and societies, such as the environment, health care, stem cell research, globalization, and terrorism, are growing in complexity and require the coordinated efforts of many people to make wise decisions. When issues grow more complex, knowledge and information become fragmented, because some people possess unique facts regarding issues that others do not. People may also perceive issues in radically different ways given their personal backgrounds. For example, National University's enrollment task force faces a very complicated issue in that students, faculty, administrators, and alumni each have a different understanding of what the enrollment crisis means and divergent ideas about how to manage it. ■

The key to making effective decisions in groups is communication. When small group members communicate in ways that facilitate sharing information, pooling knowledge, rigorously analyzing a problem, and critically evaluating possible solutions, it is more likely they will make a high-quality decision. In the opening vignette, Eva failed to create a process to facilitate the sharing of information by task force members; instead, members simply broadcast their own views to other committee members without listening critically to the input or insights others had to offer. The group's ability to analyze the problem and evaluate possible solutions quickly became sidetracked when committee members failed to explore each unique perspective.

This chapter focuses on a specific collection of people known as a small group. Small groups have a set of distinctive qualities that separate them from other collections of people. In this chapter, we explore what makes a small group and the role communication plays in promoting high-quality small group decision making and problem solving. Part of making high-quality decisions is having knowledge about the general qualities of group tasks and how effective decisions are made, as well as possessing the skill to communicate messages that facilitate defining and analyzing a problem, generating solutions, evaluating solutions, and thereby establishing an effective group process.

What Is a Small Group?

In the chapter-opening vignette, Eva was placed in charge of the enrollment management task force. Do you view this task force as a small group? List the criteria you used to decide whether the task force was a small group. Although a great many criteria exist for classifying a collection of people as a group, four criteria determine a small group: (1) the collection must be made up of three or more people, (2) every group member must have the perception of belonging to this particular group, (3) each group member's behaviors and goals must be interdependent and the group must be interdependent with its larger context, and (4) there must be communication between group members. Using these four criteria, a **small group** can be defined as three or more people who perceive themselves to be a group, who are interdependent, and who communicate with one another. Let's look more closely at these criteria.

Includes Three or More People

Using the criterion that small groups must consist of at least three people, Eva's task force would be considered a small group. When you move from a dyad to a group of three or more people, possibilities for majority rule, minority opinion, coalitions, and voting emerge. Because Eva's group consists of more than three people, several task force members can formulate a majority opinion by agreeing on the need for an enrollment increase. It is also possible that a few task force members hold a minority opinion that enrollment should be decreased and actively try to build a coalition with undecided members to overturn the majority opinion.

If the lower boundary for any small group is three people, you may wonder, "How large can a group be and still be called a small group?" Do you consider a large lecture class of 250 people a small group? You'll find that most people would not, but what is the criterion we use to distinguish small groups from large groups? One rule that's been used in the past says that small group members should have some reaction about each of the others as an individual person, even if it is only to recall that the other was present (Bales, 1950, p. 33). This suggests that the ability to be aware of all the other people in a group and to recall what a particular group member was like or what he or she did sets the upper limit for people in a small group.

Includes Shared Perception

If you asked a collection of people standing at a bus stop if they thought they belonged to a group, how do you think they would answer? You might assume correctly that their answer would probably be no. This was a random group of people assembled at a bus stop to get

transportation to go home, to work, or to some other location. They didn't know one another because they had never met before. If you asked members of a study circle if they were a group, they would probably answer yes. Members of study circles have worked together over time and know each other, which would lead them to characterize themselves as a group.

People can be said to belong to a group if they perceive themselves as belonging to it. If they label themselves as group members, then they have met the second criterion. Using this perception criterion, it is likely that Eva's task force would count as a group. The people at the bus stop are waiting together and they interact with one another, but they would not perceive themselves as belonging to a small group. The criterion of perception is important for defining small groups because it cautions us to avoid the mistake of thinking that people who interact with each other necessarily form a group.

Emphasizes Interdependence

The third criterion for a small group is interdependence. Three or more people who are interdependent make up a small group. **Interdependence** means that two elements are related to and mutually affect one another. Small group interdependence can appear in three ways: (1) goal interdependence, (2) behavioral interdependence, and (3) context interdependence. These forms of interdependence are not mutually exclusive; they can be simultaneously present within a small group.

The first way in which group members can be interdependent, **goal interdependence,** is accomplished by sharing goals. Goals are the ends to which effort is directed. For example, consider Eva's task force members. Their goal is to develop a way to manage future student enrollment that reflects the needs of important stakeholders such as students, faculty, administrators, and alumni. Although the goals of individual groups are different, each has a primary group goal that all members share. When individuals share a common goal, we can say they are interdependent. Table 9.1 lists several different types of groups, each of which performs a particular kind of activity associated with a specific goal.

A second form of interdependence is **behavioral interdependence,** which means that an individual's messages affect and are affected by other people's messages. Consider the following conversation from a small group:

Rasheed: What do you think we should do for our class project?

Mei: That's a good question. I think we should do something that the professor would like.

Al: I agree. It's best to choose a topic that Professor Barge would like. When he lectured on small group decision making, he became much more animated and passionate. I think he really loves that topic. What about doing something on small group decision making?

Mei: That's an excellent idea! I also noticed that he cited a lot of his own research when he discussed decision making. Let's do something on decision making for the project.

Table 9.1

Type of Groups by Activity and Goal

Groups can be categorized according to the activities and goals they share. A person can belong to more than one of the groups. How many do you belong to?

Activity and Goal	Small Groups
Commercial	Consumer groups, food cooperatives, investment groups, real estate boards
Educational	Work groups in preschool, ability-level groups in elementary and secondary school, study groups in college and graduate school, occupational-training groups
Familial	Immediate family, extended family, orphanages, foster care groups, day-care groups, communal-living groups, assisted-living home groups, senior residential-facility groups, convents, rectories, abbeys
Health and welfare	Therapy groups, support groups, rehabilitation groups, residential-care facility groups
Occupational	Quality circles, management teams, research-and-development teams, committees, corporate boards of directors, work teams
Political/civic	Zoning boards, planning boards, political party committees, protest groups, boards of directors for charities, civic leagues
Recreational	Sports teams, fraternal associations, lodges, scout troops, musical bands, choirs
Social	Friendship groups, groups of acquaintances, gangs, clubs
Spiritual	Church groups, Sunday school classes, synagogues, mosque congregations, cults, covens

SOURCE: Adapted from Socha (1996), p. 14.

In the conversation, you can see how each message incorporates some piece of information from the message immediately preceding it. Behavioral interdependence is characterized by a flow of messages in which each message is influenced by the messages preceding it and affects the messages following it.

Finally, group members can be interdependent through context. **Context interdependence** occurs when a group's environment affects and is, in turn, affected by a group's actions. Groups and group members do not exist in a vacuum; they exist in a web of relationships with other stakeholder groups in a larger environment. In the chapter-opening vignette, the enrollment management task force is affected by a number of environmental influences—alumni preferences, the university president's goals, and the tuition rates of other universities. These environmental influences affect the way the members interact with one another as they take them into account to make their decisions. At the same time, it is also possible for a small group to influence the environment, in this case, the task force may try to alter alumni opinion against limiting enrollment.

learning link

What are the differences among goal, behavioral, and context interdependence?

• • •

Requires Communication

As discussed in Chapter 1, communication is a process of managing messages and meaning. The last criterion for a small group to exist is that three or more people need to communicate with one another. Eva's task force would be considered a group because the task force members communicate with one another.

The primary channel Eva's task force uses is face-to-face communication. The explosion of information technologies such as e-mail, videoconferencing, and audioconferencing now allows group members to communicate through mediated channels; they no longer need to be face to face. But regardless of what channel of communication they use, to be considered a group, members need to communicate with one another.

To summarize, a collection of people can be classified as a small group if (1) it includes three or more people, (2) the people perceive themselves as belonging to a group, (3) the people share a set of goals and their actions are interdependent with one another, and (4) they communicate with one another. These criteria help distinguish small group communication from interpersonal and public communication as well as from collections of three or more people who are randomly put together. For a comparison of groups with teams in organizations, see the Close-Up on Teams and Teamwork box.

Knowing How to Make Group Decisions

Competent small group communicators need to be knowledgeable about several areas regarding group communication: (1) the relationship between decision making and problem solving, (2) the types of group decision-making tasks, (3) the process of group decision making, and (4) the criteria for high-quality decisions.

Distinguishing between Problem Solving and Decision Making

A **problem** exists when there is a gap between an ideal state and the current state of events. For example, school board members may find that local teen pregnancy rates are significantly higher than the national average and decide they must develop solutions to reduce this difference.

Problem solving is a group process in which members assess problems and formulate solutions to resolve the problems. Central to the notion of assessing problems is Kurt Lewin's (1951) idea of a **force field analysis,** a process for analyzing the reasons for a problem as well as what is preventing the problem from being eliminated. Figure 9.1 illustrates a force field analysis. The problem—the gap between an ideal and current state of affairs—is at the center of a force field analysis. The key questions are (1) What is causing this problem? and (2) What is preventing the resolution or management of the problem?

The first question focuses on the **drivers,** or the causes (sources) of a particular problem, and the second question introduces the idea of **restraining forces,** or forces that prevent the resolution of the problem. For example, what is creating the gap between the local and national rates of teen pregnancy? Drivers for this particular problem may include the lack of appropriate sex education for teenagers, low self-esteem on the part of teenagers, poor communication between parents and their children, or a lack of constructive role models for teenagers (Figure 9.1).

The second question introduces the concept of restraining forces in the force field analysis. Restraining forces are those factors that prevent groups from addressing and solving the problem. Conservative lobbyists may try to prevent changes in the sex education curriculum. School board officials may try to squash discussion about the problem because it is such a controversial issue. The state school board may set limits on the content of the sex education curriculum.

To understand a problem fully it is important to assess the drivers and restraining forces. Then you can proceed to solve the problem by addressing the drivers and removing

CloseUp on Teams and Teamwork

Teams and Teamwork

TEAMS AND TEAMWORK HAVE BECOME POPULAR terms to describe the work of small groups. Particularly in businesses and corporations there has been an emphasis on creating team-based organizations as a way of tapping into the knowledge and abilities of employees and responding quickly and efficiently to challenges emerging from a rapidly changing business environment. The question is whether the terms *small group* and *team* are synonymous or whether teams are qualitatively different from small groups.

A broad definition of *team* is "a distinguishable set of two or more people who interact, dynamically, interdependently, and adaptively toward a common and valued goal/objective/mission, who have been assigned specific roles or functions to perform, and who have a limited life-span of membership" (Salas, Dickinson, Converse, & Tannenbaum, 1992, p. 4). In many ways this definition parallels several of the qualities for the definition of small group that we created by emphasizing a small number of people who interact with each other and are linked by a common goal. However, the key difference between small groups and teams is the high level of interdependence among team members that leads to high performance.

Team members' individual activities are highly interdependent. Teams produce collective work products that reflect team members working together, whereas groups may produce individual work products, where the sum of the individual contributions equals the group's total work output (Katzenbach & Smith, 2003). Synergy occurs in teams where the collective team output is greater than the sum of the individual contributions. For example, in a cardiac surgical team, cardiac surgeons, anesthesiologists, nurses, and technicians who run the heart-lung bypass machine must work together seamlessly to perform the surgical procedure (Edmondson, 2003). The collective work product, a successful surgical procedure, depends on team members being able to work well together—the actions of each team member influence the performance of the others. This requires teams to communicate so that information is easily shared among team members, make decisions so that everyone's voice is heard, value learning, and experiment with different ways to address problems (Kayes, 2002).

What are the conditions that facilitate teamwork? In a study that examined more than 600 teams and 6,000 team members in organizations, Frank LaFasto and Carl Larson (2001) identified five key factors that foster teamwork and collaboration:

1. Team members: Effective team members have experience in the profession they are engaged in and are excellent problem solvers. They are also open in their communication, able to share their views with others, supportive of other group members and the group task, action-oriented, and have a positive outlook.

2. Team relationships: Effective team relationships depend on being open to feedback from group members, making a commitment to build constructive relationships, creating a safe environment for people to share their insights, and appreciating each other's perspectives.

3. Team problem solving: Effective team problem solving depends on teams maintaining a clear focus in their work, knowing what needs to be accomplished at a particular moment in the discussion, and fostering a supportive climate. Through open communication, team members can share information and critically analyze the causes of problems and possible solutions.

4. Team leadership: Effective team leaders are able to help a team focus on the goal by articulating the goal in a clear, elevating way and helping team members see how they can contribute to accomplishing the goal. Effective team leaders are able to build a collaborative climate and the confidence of their fellow teammates. Effective team leaders also have the required technical knowledge to solve the problem.

5. Organizational environment: For teams to prosper, the organizational environment must be supportive. A good environment requires management to set priorities and give clear direction, manage resources in a way that allows the team to do its work, and establish clear operating principles.

By recruiting competent team members, establishing constructive relationships, developing problem-solving capacity, fostering effective leadership practice, and creating a supportive organizational environment, high-quality teamwork is possible.

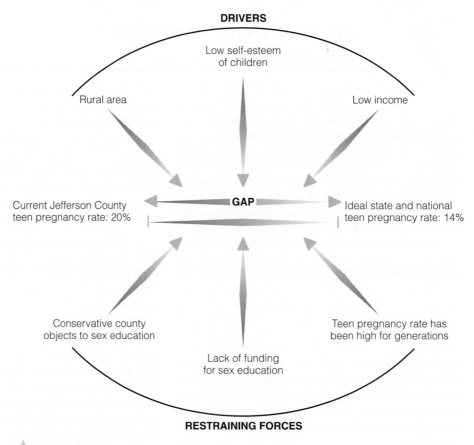

DRIVERS

Low self-esteem
of children

Rural area

Low income

Current Jefferson County
teen pregnancy rate: 20%

GAP

Ideal state and national
teen pregnancy rate: 14%

Conservative county
objects to sex education

Teen pregnancy rate has
been high for generations

Lack of funding
for sex education

RESTRAINING FORCES

▲ **Figure 9.1**

Force Field Analysis

The teen pregnancy rate in Jefferson County is 20% and the ideal state at the national level is 14%—a gap of 6%. Geography, low self-esteem of children, and income may be driving the gap, and political groups, lack of funding for sex education, and historical factors may be restraining decision makers from making decisions that reduce the gap.

restraining forces to close the gap. How might the enrollment task force manage the gap between the current enrollment of National University and where it needs to be? Task force members might begin by asking, "What is driving this gap?" Some possible drivers include the university's need for tuition revenue dollars, a lack of rigorous admission policies, and a low student-to-faculty ratio. They may also ask, "What is preventing the problem from being solved?" Possible restraining forces could include the alumni's resistance to making National more selective, a university mission that emphasizes giving access to a wide variety of students, and financial issues. The task force members could propose two solutions: (1) hiring additional faculty to meet student demand, or (2) establishing more selective enrollment policies. The former solution removes a significant driver for the problem, and the latter removes a key restraining force.

Decisions are distinct from problems. A **decision** is the selection among alternative explanations or proposals. Alternatives may be competing explanations for what causes a problem. Is the gap in health care coverage caused by the high cost of health care insurance or by the high costs of medical procedures? Alternatives may include competing proposals for solving a problem. Which alternative is better for reducing health insurance costs—capping fees and charges for selected medical procedures or limiting access to high-cost experimental procedures? **Decision making** may be used to solve problems, but it is not the same as problem solving. A decision is simply a choice. For example, suppose the U.S. Congress is trying to determine which causes are most important in sustaining the health care crisis. At this stage of discussion, they are not solving a problem; they are making choices of which causes are more or less important.

Defining Group Decision-Making Tasks

Groups perform a wide variety of tasks such as manufacturing products, providing services, creating strategic plans, developing marketing campaigns, and so on. Each of these tasks requires making choices. One way to define a decision-making task is to identify the kinds of choices groups make given the specific question that a group must discuss. The most frequently used typology suggests there are four kinds of questions that small groups may discuss: (1) questions of fact, (2) questions of conjecture, (3) questions of value, and (4) questions of policy (Gouran, 2003).

Questions of fact focus on whether a particular claim regarding an event is accurate or true. Juries are a prime example of small groups that focus on questions of fact. In jury trials, the prosecution presents evidence and testimony from witnesses to make its case against the defendant. The defense attorneys present information supporting the innocence of their client and attempt to persuade the jury that their client is innocent.

Returning to the chapter-opening vignette, the enrollment management task force may need to consider the following questions of fact:

- What is the optimal number of incoming students given our facilities? Number of faculty?
- Do we have a sufficiently large pool of potential applicants from which to select?
- Are our student recruitment strategies attracting a qualified pool of applicants?

Although each question is designed to surface important facts, what counts as a legitimate, nonbiased, factual answer to the question depends on how people define key terms. For example, the optimal number of incoming students may vary depending on how you define *facilities*.

Questions of conjecture ask what might happen in the future. They can be projections about events or possibilities that might occur. For example, private investors in the stock market are continually asking questions of conjecture about the future. What will happen if new companies enter the market? What will happen if the stock takes a dip? Will it bounce back to its former level? Although their decisions may be informed by statistical evidence, trend data, history, and expert opinion, the decision is ultimately based on conjecture.

Returning to the enrollment management committee, it may ask a variety of questions of conjecture:

- How will faculty respond to increased numbers of students?
- What are the possible positive or negative consequences of increasing enrollment? Decreasing enrollment?
- How will the culture of the university be influenced if we change entrance requirements?

learning link

What are the differences among questions of fact, conjecture, value, and policy?

● ● ●

Questions of value explore issues of the intrinsic importance; worth; utility; and desirability of objects, attitudes, and beliefs. They revolve around fundamental moral and ethical questions: Is it important? Is it right? Is it desirable? Is it worthwhile? For example, the U.S. Departments of Agriculture and Interior constantly deal with questions of value when they determine land-use policy. Should economic values be privileged and more forests opened to timber and mining development? Should environmental values be elevated and recreational use of the parks be limited to preserve the environment? Value judgments are inherently subjective. Depending on whom you ask, you will receive different answers regarding what values should be given priority.

Questions of value at National University could assess the relative importance of varied stakeholder interests and questions about the kind of community the university would like to create, including the following:

- What kinds of students best fit the kind of community we would like to create?
- What is more important to us—quantity of students or quality of students?
- Are we serving our community if we limit our enrollment?

By answering questions such as these, the enrollment management committee may be able to develop a workable enrollment plan that reflects the university's values.

Questions of policy focus on actions that should be taken to solve a problem, such as to increase literacy, reduce illegal drug use, or decrease domestic violence. In the example of the enrollment management committee, the central question of policy is, "What actions should the university take regarding enrollment?"

It is rare that any group will make a decision based on the answer to only one question of fact, conjecture, value, or policy. Rather, the resolution depends on making decisions regarding a variety of other issues first. This is called **nested decision making,** which requires decision makers to prioritize the questions they ask. Questions they ask early in the process serve as the foundation for subsequent questions, which in turn lead to the answer of the major question. It is difficult to answer the central question in a nested decision that your group is responsible for without answering those questions that serve as its foundation.

To answer the central policy question, "What should the university's policy be regarding enrollment?" the enrollment management committee must answer a number of other questions of fact, conjecture, and value. If the committee is not clear on the factual economic impact of varying levels of student enrollment, it will make a poor policy decision. If the committee has not explored the possible consequences of varying levels of student enrollment on facility issues, again, the decision may be a poor one. Finally, if the committee does not clarify what key values the university and key stakeholder groups maintain, the decision may be inappropriate. The ultimate quality of the policy decision depends on the ability of the group to identify and answer subquestions that are nested beneath the major question, as shown in Figure 9.2.

Communication and Group Decision Making

If a group desires to make effective and appropriate decisions, then it is important for small group members to be aware of those processes associated with high-quality decision making. In the early 1900s, John Dewey (1910), a scholar in philosophy, interviewed hundreds of students and asked them to describe the processes they used to make decisions. From

QUESTIONS OF FACT
- What is the optimal number of incoming students given our facilities? Number of faculty?
- Do we have a sufficiently large pool of potential applicants from which to select?
- Is the applicant pool qualified?
- Are our student recruitment strategies attracting a qualified pool of applicants?

QUESTIONS OF VALUE
- What kind of university community do we desire? What kinds of students best fit the kind of community we would like to create?
- How important is limiting enrollment to us?
- What is most important to us—quantity of students or quality of students?
- Are we serving our community if we limit our enrollment?

QUESTIONS OF CONJECTURE
- What will happen to the university if we raise enrollment?
- How will faculty respond to increased numbers of students?
- What are the possible positive or negative consequences of increasing enrollment? Decreasing enrollment?
- How will the culture of the university be influenced if we raise entrance requirements?

QUESTIONS OF POLICY
- What actions should the university take regarding enrollment?

 Figure 9.2

A Flow Chart for a Nested Decision

The answers to the enrollment management task force's questions of fact, value, and conjecture, in this order, will prepare them to answer their question of policy.

the information he gathered in these interviews, he created the **reflective thinking model,** which profiles a series of steps that decision makers follow to make high-quality decisions. The steps are the following:

1. Recognize that a problem exists.
2. Define the scope and nature of the problem and identify factors that cause the problem.

3. Generate a number of solutions that may solve the problem.
4. Develop criteria for choosing among alternative solutions and evaluate those solutions using those criteria.
5. Select the best solution.
6. Assess the solution to see whether it is the right one.

The reflective thinking model assumes that these steps need to be followed in the prescribed sequence to analyze problems logically and make decisions.

Dewey's reflective thinking model has become the basis for a perspective called the **functionalist approach.** A functionalist approach to group decision making assumes that particular decision-making functions can be identified that when performed will lead to high-quality decision making. Dennis Gouran and Randy Hirokawa (Gouran, 1999; Gouran & Hirokawa, 2003; Wittenbaum, Hollingshead, Paulus, Hirokawa, Ancona, Peterson, Jehn, & Yoon, 2004), the chief proponents of this approach, argue that four key decision-making functions need to be performed if a group is to make a high-quality decision:

1. Assess the problem situation.
2. Establish evaluation criteria.
3. Generate a range of alternatives.
4. Evaluate the alternatives in light of positive and negative consequences.

Early research using the functional approach contended that groups that fail to fulfill these key functional requisites will make poor decisions (Gouran & Hirokawa, 1996). For example, if a group fails to assess the problem accurately, it may generate solutions that do not address that particular problem. Similarly, if group members do not identify a wide range of alternatives and generate only one alternative, a systematic evaluation of alternatives cannot be undertaken and the most appropriate alternative may be overlooked.

Recent research suggests that certain functions are more important in promoting high-quality decision making than others and that their importance may change depending on the situation. Communication that assesses the problem and evaluates the negative consequences of alternative solutions is more likely to generate high-quality decisions than communication that generates alternatives without assessing their consequences (Orlitzky & Hirokawa, 2001). What this suggests is that small groups need to evaluate critically the kind of question they are discussing, the context in which the group is performing, and the potential disadvantages of decision alternatives if they want to make a good decision.

learning link

How does performing the four key decision-making functions lead to higher-quality decisions?

• • •

BLONDIE

Effective decision-making groups rigorously evaluate the consequences of possible ideas and proposals.

Group members need to devote time and energy evaluating the negative consequences of alternatives when the task is equivocal if they are to make a good decision (Hirokawa, 1990; Orlitzky & Hirokawa, 2001). Equivocal tasks are characterized by the existence of several possible alternatives, unclear criteria for selecting among competing alternatives, and difficulty in judging the appropriateness of the solutions. When a task is equivocal, the need to assess critically the information and arguments during discussion, or evaluation demands, increases. **Evaluation demands** are the need to assess the information and arguments that emerge in the group discussion.

How does a functional approach to decision making relate to the task force in the chapter-opening vignette? The task is high in evaluation demands because many possible solutions exist and the evaluation criteria for solutions are unclear. It is not surprising, therefore, that the task force members spent much of their time analyzing the task they were given and the causes for the student enrollment problem. Given that task force members were a mix of students, faculty, and administrators, they more than likely had differing perspectives on the problem they were charged with resolving. Therefore they will need to spend more time sharing the unique knowledge and information they possess. To make a wise choice, however, functional theory suggests that the task force will also have to devote a good amount of time to assessing the negative consequences of the task given the high evaluation demands. As a result, the task force may have to spend time looking at the negative consequences of possible actions such as raising admission standards.

Assessing the Quality of Decision Making

It is tempting to say that groups have made a high-quality decision when it is "correct." However, this assumes that there is really an objectively correct decision, much as there is a right answer to a true or false question on an objective test and it is immediately knowable. Yet much of group decision making does not lend itself to judging decisions by their correctness. Suppose a group of city supervisors makes a policy decision to annex a piece of property adjoining the city to manage growth. They won't know whether this is the correct decision until they have actually annexed the property, waited 2 or 3 years, and looked at whether their decision did or did not control growth.

Similarly, when groups make decisions about questions of value, correctness is not a useful criterion. Questions of value, by definition, do not have right or wrong answers. You may think that correctness is the most useful criterion when deliberating questions of fact. However, with some exceptions, even questions of fact are open to debate. In jury trials, jurors are asked to determine a question of fact: is the defendant guilty or innocent? Even the answer to this question of fact is not truly about the correctness of facts. Rather, in jury trials, the jurors are instructed to vote to convict only if the prosecution's case has been proven beyond a reasonable doubt. By law in the United States all defendants are innocent until proven guilty. In this case, correctness, although important, is less important than the notion of reasonable doubt.

If correctness is not a standard for differentiating between effective and ineffective decisions, then what is? Four criteria are used for evaluating decision-making effectiveness: (1) vigilance, (2) decision acceptability, (3) collaboration capability, and (4) personal development.

First, *vigilance* is a process-oriented criterion that evaluates whether group members are committed to assessing the problem rigorously, developing goals for the decision-making process, and generating and evaluating alternatives. Process criteria focus on the type and quality of communication that needs to occur during group discussion. The criterion of **vigilant interaction** is the idea that the group communicates in ways that uncover needed information and subsequently analyzes it in a critical fashion. Vigilant interaction emphasizes the need for group members to be mindful of performing key decision-making functions, including the following:

- Exploring a wide range of alternative courses of action.
- Asking members to elaborate the data and underlying assumptions that inform their position.
- Maintaining a position of openness to differing ideas.
- Soliciting input from all members.
- Searching for information that confirms and disconfirms existing viewpoints.
- Reviewing critical decision alternatives (Gouran & Hirokawa, 2003).

Unlike the first criterion, which is process oriented, the next three criteria for evaluating decision-making effectiveness are outcome oriented. They focus on the consequences of the decision-making process rather than the process itself (Hackman, 2002). **Decision acceptability** reflects the degree to which the decision meets the standards of quality, quantity, and timeliness set by the people who will use or be affected by the decision. Returning to the chapter-opening vignette, will the decision of the enrollment committee be acceptable to students, faculty, administrators, alumni, and the community the college serves?

Collaboration capability reflects the ability of group members to work interdependently in the future. Decisions that increase the likelihood that members will collaborate in the future are more effective. When group members leave a meeting enthused about the next meeting, the criterion of collaboration capability has been met. Such positive outward signs reflect a positive group experience and a willingness for group members to work together in the future.

The **personal development** criterion refers to decision processes that enhance the personal well-being of group members and facilitate their growth and development. When group members leave a meeting believing they have acquired new skills and abilities that enhance their communication competence, the decision processes have facilitated their personal development.

It is possible for group members to decide that only one or two of the criteria described here are important to determine whether a decision is high quality. However, those decisions that use vigilant interaction, produce a high level of decision acceptability by others, build collaboration capability among group members, and allow individual members to grow and develop are more effective. Such decisions are more effective because they pay attention to the process used to make the decision as well as the consequences of the decision. Last, but not least, they focus on the needs of group members as well as on the needs of people who will be affected by or use the decision. The ethical use of groups to make decisions is considered in the Close-Up on Group Decision Making box.

Task Skills for Making Decisions

A **task skill** is a message a person performs that helps the group make a decision. Five central task skills, based on ideas contained in the reflective thinking model, the functionalist approach, and vigilant interaction, are key to making effective decisions: (1) defining the

Close Up on *Group Decision Making*

When to Use Groups to Make Decisions

USING GROUPS TO MAKE DECISIONS WITHIN THE public and private sectors has grown dramatically over the last 20 years. Federal, state, and city governments increasingly use citizen task forces and committees to help them make decisions about public policy (Barge, in press). In the private sector, business and industry are using team-based decision making as a means of improving productivity and effectiveness. Giving team members decision-making responsibility is believed to enhance performance because they are more attuned to the challenges and issues confronting their team than are higher level managers who do not face these issues daily (Katzenbach & Smith, 2003).

Given this increased use of groups to make decisions, the ethical use of groups to make decisions and create recommendations must be considered. For example, is it ethical for a manager to create a team to make a decision or a recommendation if he or she has no intent of following the team's recommendation? Many of you would answer no. Yet many teams face the demoralizing situation in which the group makes a decision or recommendation that conflicts with the manager's desires, and as a result, he or she ignores the committee's recommendation. Is it ethical to charge a group with making a decision when it is the manager's responsibility? Again, you would probably respond no. Yet managers sometimes set up committees to make unpopular decisions so they can scapegoat the committee for the decision and avoid taking the blame.

When a group devotes time and energy to making a decision or developing a recommendation that has no chance of being implemented or adopted or when a group is positioned to take the blame for an unpopular decision, we would be inclined to say that using groups to make decisions in these circumstances is unethical. When then is it ethical and appropriate to use groups to make decisions?

Group leaders have five considerations to explore for using groups ethically:

1. Explore your motivation for using a group to make a decision or develop a recommendation. It is ethical to use groups when you need a diversity of opinions on a particular issue. Bringing in people from a broad spectrum of backgrounds introduces unique insights and experiences into the decision-making process. Conversely, if the motivation for assembling a group is simply to avoid accountability for a decision, it is unethical to use groups.

2. Determine the scope of the group's responsibility. Is the group simply to serve in an advisory role or does it have the authority to implement the members' suggestions? Is the group to be held accountable if its recommendations produce negative outcomes or is another individual or group accountable? It is unethical to hold a group accountable if members do not have the authority to implement their recommendations.

3. Clearly communicate the task to the group. When groups meet for the first time, it is critical for the group leader creating the group to provide a clear orientation to the task. As long as the group knows what its responsibilities are, who will accept or reject its final decision, and how it will be implemented, the manager has ethically appointed this group to the task. One strategy for conveying the task is to explain how the group task fits into the overall process, as well as who will consider the final decision.

4. Provide periodic feedback to the group as it performs the task. A common mistake is to assign the group a task and then never check back with the group until it has come to a decision or completed the task. By keeping the communication lines open with a group as it completes a task, a manager can keep the group on track and provide new information that might assist the group in achieving its goal. Managers who behave ethically check in with the group periodically to provide information and ensure that group members and the manager have a shared understanding of the group's task.

5. Provide feedback on the implementation of the group's decision. Many times, group members make decisions and recommendations to others only to never find out what has been done with their work. Providing feedback on how the work has been used not only provides a group closure on a project but also communicates valuable information about what members may need to consider the next time they are given a group task. If the recommendation has been rejected, for example, they can explore the reasons for the rejection and this information may help them construct future recommendations that may be more likely to be accepted.

Using groups to make decisions is a trend that will continue in the 21st century. The question, therefore, is not "Will we use groups to make decisions?" but rather "How do we use groups ethically to make decisions?"

Understanding the motivation for using groups as well as providing clear ongoing communication about the task and expectations are strategies that make use of groups ethically.

problem, (2) analyzing the problem, (3) identifying criteria for solving the problem, (4) generating solutions or alternatives, and (5) evaluating solutions. Using the vignette that opened the chapter, let's explore what kinds of messages may facilitate groups making high-quality decisions.

Defining the Problem

Developing an answer to the question, "What appears to be the problem?" can be difficult. Group members can send many messages to facilitate defining the problem. They include the following:

- Developing a problem statement: messages that propose a specific definition of the problem.
- Modifying the problem statement: messages that combine competing definitions of the problem or slightly alter an existing problem statement.
- Detailing assumptions: messages that examine the assumptions made about the nature of the problem and the people who are either involved in the decision-making process or who will be affected by the group's decision.
- Changing perspectives: messages that highlight how different people or stakeholders perceive the problem.

Each of these messages further clarifies the definition of the problem.

If Eva, the task force chair, had sent these types of messages, she might have stated the problem this way: "I think our problem is we don't have enough faculty and staff to meet the increased enrollment." Or she might have asked each member of the task force for a problem statement: "What do you see as the problem facing National University?" She might have detailed the assumptions regarding the problem statement: "One of the assumptions I make when looking at enrollment trends is that providing high-quality instruction to our students is key to our future success." She might have used other people's perspectives to explore the problem statement: "What do you think our alumni would view as the problem?" or "If some of the town's community leaders were here at this meeting, what might they say is our problem?" In the event that multiple problem statements surfaced during the discussion, Eva might have modified the problem statements: "It sounds as if the problem is both declining revenues and limited faculty resources." Group members and leaders who want to facilitate constructing a useful problem definition need to be skilled at performing these kinds of messages.

learning link

What kinds of messages characterize the five task skills associated with making effective decisions?

• • •

One important task skill that leads to making high-quality decisions is collecting data to help define the problem

Analyzing the Problem

The next skill necessary for effective decision making is analyzing the causes, obstacles, history, symptoms, and significance of the problem the group is attempting to solve. Statements that analyze a problem explore a variety of issues:

- Symptoms: How do we know there is a problem? What signs point to this?
- Drivers: What is driving the problem? What is the basis for the problem?
- Restraining forces: What is preventing us from solving the problem? What forces are restraining our ability to manage the problem?
- Significance: How important is the problem? To whom?
- History: What is the history of this problem? When did it begin? Who was the first to determine it was a problem?

These kinds of statements help flesh out the rich detail inherent in any problem.

To lead the task force, Eva could have asked several questions to analyze the problem: "How do we know there is a problem?" "Who was the first to notice the problem?" and "When did the problem start?" Asking about the symptoms of the problem would allow her to guide the discussion toward exploring the problem's significance and history. For example, she could offer a statement of the significance of the problem: "If we are unable to raise money through increased grant-proposal writing by our faculty, we will have to explore other means of generating revenue, including raising enrollment." She may offer an account of what led to the problem: "This problem really began 5 years ago when we lost our vice president for development. Since then contributions by alumni and business and industry have decreased." To set up the discussion for generating solutions, she may guide the meeting into a discussion of drivers and restraining forces. She may articulate a driver for the problem, such as "The reason we've enrolled too many students is that we are not selective enough in our admissions policy," or solicit board members' opinions regarding possible drivers, such as "What do you think are the major reasons for too high enrollment?" Questions such as "What is preventing us from solving these problems?" or "How can we overcome this problem caused by lax admissions policy?" may help the task force identify the restraining forces that prevent solution of the problem.

Identifying Criteria for Solving the Problem

Groups need to identify criteria for assessing the quality of alternatives for solving the problem. The following statements facilitate the establishment of criteria:

- Propose criteria: What are the criteria or standards we need to use when evaluating solutions?
- Modify criteria: How can these criteria be combined to create a useful standard for evaluation? How can we alter a criterion to make it more appropriate in light of the group's task?

For example, the task force members on student enrollment could identify criteria by asking questions or making comments, such as "What criteria do we need to use when selecting among plans for raising tuition?" or "Any action that helps provide high-quality student instruction must take faculty resources into account." Questions and comments that help modify criteria include "I agree that any proposal we put forth must recommend a decrease in admissions, but it also needs to suggest that the Development Office be more involved in generating revenue" or "I understand that we need to decrease student enrollment significantly, but could you quantify what you consider to be an acceptable decrease?" Proposing and modifying decision criteria will enable the group to make higher quality decisions.

Generating Solutions or Alternatives

Two types of messages that generate alternatives are those that solicit solutions and those that propose a solution. For example, to focus the task force on the issue, Eva could have solicited solution proposals by asking, "What can we do to resolve this problem?" She could also have proposed solutions by providing the group a list of her recommendations. When a solution is proposed, however, it is often modified by other group members. For example, Eva might have proposed higher admissions requirements as a strategy for reducing student enrollment. During the group discussion, another committee member might have introduced exceptions for the children of alumni. This committee member might have offered the rationale that a higher enrollment of children of alumni will encourage their parents to make bigger donations. These skills of proposing alternatives and openness to modifying the alternatives help groups make high-quality decisions.

Evaluating Solutions or Alternatives

Statements and questions that address the consequences and test the appropriateness of particular alternatives facilitate decision making. Specifically, group members need to investigate the following areas:

- Positive consequences: What advantages are gained from adopting this solution?

- Negative consequences: What disadvantages are created from adopting this solution?
- Problem-solution fit: Does the solution meet the criterion established at the beginning?
- Reality testing: Does the solution make sense? Is the solution possible? Will people support the solution?

Together these areas facilitate a well-rounded analysis of the strengths and weaknesses of various alternatives under consideration by the group.

Returning to the opening vignette, how might Eva have helped the committee to look more closely at the opportunities and difficulties of each proposed solution? Certainly she could have asked broad open-ended questions such as "What do we gain or lose if we adopt this alternative?" or made statements to communicate her assessment of the advantages and disadvantages of various alternatives: "If we adopt X, what I am afraid will happen is Y." Alternatively, she could have tied the discussion of alternatives back to the criterion set by the group and discussed how this solution would work in real life: "How well does this alternative meet our goal of managing student enrollment?" On the other hand, she could have asked a series of questions to help the group test the reality of their solution:

- If we adopted this alternative, what would be the next step?
- Who would be in charge of the next step?
- What would we do if the next step failed?
- Who would be supportive of this alternative? Who would oppose it?
- Given the level of support and opposition, can we realistically expect this solution to work?

In reality testing, Eva would be trying to help the group identify what specifically will need to be done in the future and to examine whether those steps are realistic. Asking questions that probe the support or opposition of those affected by the decision allows a group to foresee the challenges associated with implementing a decision, making it more acceptable to those who will use it.

Challenges to Competent Decision Making

One of the primary explanations for poor decision making is groupthink (Ahlfinger & Esser, 2001; Park, 2000). **Groupthink** occurs when group members establish a norm that makes consensus the highest priority and diminishes the vigilant appraisal of the reasons for and consequences of possible alternatives to their final decision (Janis, 1972, 1982; Janis & Mann, 1977). Groupthink results from pre-existing conditions that lead to ineffective decision-making behavior, as shown in Figure 9.3.

Causes of Groupthink

Three major pre-existing conditions lead to groupthink. First, groups that are moderately or highly cohesive tend to suffer from groupthink. As the group becomes more cohesive and members share more similar values, the danger increases that each individual will stop thinking critically to maintain a strong sense of affiliation with other group members and group spirit.

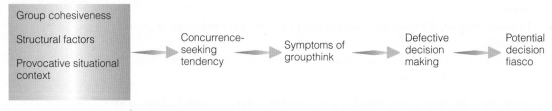

Concurrence-seeking tendency → Symptoms of groupthink → Defective decision making → Potential decision fiasco

Figure 9.3

Janis's Model of Groupthink

Janis's groupthink model explains how potential decision fiascoes are created. Three major pre-existing conditions propel groups to seek concurrence regarding an issue. The concurrence-seeking tendency of groups can lead to groupthink, which can cause defective decision making.

Second, several structural factors may influence a group's likelihood to engage in groupthink:

Insulated group. When groups begin to feel cut off from their larger environment, they are more likely to engage in groupthink. A classic example of insulated groups are cults that are isolated from society at large. In fact, this is one explanation for the tragedy of David Koresh and the Branch Davidians in Waco, Texas.

Lack of impartial leadership. When group leaders express strong opinions about solutions to problems, the group members may be more prone to engage in groupthink. In this situation, group members may try to please the leader by following his or her opinions without evaluating alternatives.

No methodical procedures. Groupthink is more likely to occur when the group does not have procedures in place to encourage a rigorous analysis of the problem and possible solutions.

Members with similar backgrounds. The more people share attitudes, values, and beliefs, the more likely they are to engage in groupthink. Given the similarity of experience, group members may take certain things for granted and neglect to evaluate alternatives.

Third, a provocative situational context may propel groups toward groupthink. Two key situational factors are particularly provocative: stress and self-esteem. High stress is positively linked to groupthink. When group members are placed under pressure, they tend to short-circuit the decision-making process. They may conclude that they do not have enough time to analyze the problem, generate solutions, or evaluate alternatives. Similarly, when group members have low self-esteem they are more likely to engage in groupthink. Members suffering from low self-esteem lack the confidence to articulate an individual viewpoint, particularly one that challenges the larger group.

Concurrence Seeking and Decision Making

High levels of cohesion, structural factors such as biased leadership, and highly provocative situational contexts lead to **concurrence seeking,** in which groups try to achieve a consensus regarding their decision. The tendency for concurrence seeking is not inherently problematic; after all, most groups try to come to a consensus on the actions that need to be taken regarding a problem. However, when this tendency goes too far, it produces symptoms of groupthink and defective decision making.

Here are several symptoms of groupthink:

- Group members possess an illusion of invulnerability. They feel they are invincible and cannot make a poor decision.
- There is an unquestioned belief in the group's inherent morality. As a result, the ethical implications of decisions are not fully explored.
- Members make collective rationalizations or justifications for their decisions and ignore warning signs that signal a flawed decision.
- Group members who disagree, raise concerns, or oppose the decision are negatively stereotyped and characterized as wrong, weak, unintelligent, or unimportant. Their claims or critiques are not viewed as legitimate.
- Members pressure those who dissent from the majority opinion to reconsider their views and conform. Dissenting group members may find their opinions attacked and their positions in the group threatened.
- As direct pressure is leveled against dissenters, other group members may censor their own dissenting opinions to maintain an illusion of unanimity.
- Some group members assume the role of protecting the group from dissenting opinions and maintaining the majority argument.

When groups fall prey to groupthink, the decisions they make may have extremely negative consequences. In the case of Abu Ghraib, one explanation for this tragedy is that group members became insulated from their larger environment and failed to question the assumptions and beliefs that informed their decisions.

These symptoms of groupthink lead to defective decision making. The group suffers from informational problems because groupthink prevents it from collecting relevant and necessary information and seeking expert opinion on the issue under consideration. Instead, it suppresses all information that exposes or disconfirms the preferred solution. The group also is hurt by an inability to engage in rigorous and open analysis of the decision. Key objectives are not thoroughly analyzed, the full range of alternatives is not examined, preferred alternatives are not reexamined for pitfalls, and dismissed alternatives are not reexamined. Finally, in the event that the decision is faulty, the group does not create contingency plans.

Overcoming Challenges to Competence

How can groups overcome challenges such as group members' low self-esteem, high levels of group cohesion, and members with similar backgrounds to make high-quality decisions? One answer suggested by the theory of groupthink is that competent small group members need to employ group procedures methodically. A **group procedure** is a process for performing a function that is central to the group. It can serve important functions such as keeping the group focused on central decision-making functions and maintaining a sense of order and coherence within the group (Sunwolf & Siebold, 1999). Group procedures can be used to (1) stimulate divergent thinking, and (2) initiate convergent thinking.

Stimulating Divergent Thinking

One of the major challenges small groups face is to explore fully the nature of the problem and generate a number of possible solutions. The first description of the problem or the first solution offered is typically not the most effective or creative, yet small group members tend to latch on to their first problem description or the first solution suggested. **Divergent thinking** generates multiple ideas and alternatives about issues, problems, and solutions. It is particularly useful when groups need to survey the broad variety of possible causes of and solutions to a problem and want to avoid focusing on only one or two. Brainstorming and brainwriting are two group procedures that enhance divergent thinking.

Brainstorming is a group procedure in which each individual in a group generates ideas and adds them to the group discussion. It is guided by three rules:

- The "no criticism rule": Group members are not allowed to evaluate the quality of other group members' ideas.
- The "hitchhiking rule": Group members are allowed to develop their ideas based on other ideas from the group. For example, in a discussion on how to address teen violence in a community, one member may suggest developing boot camps for first-time offenders. Another member may "hitchhike" off this idea and suggest establishing activity camps where kids could learn about art, music, and drama.
- The "quantity breeds quality rule": The first ideas generated are usually the most obvious or simple; by generating lots of ideas, group members increase the chances that high-quality and creative ideas will emerge.

Brainstorming is typically done orally within a group with a member assigned to record each of the ideas on a laptop computer or a flip chart.

To use brainstorming effectively, group leaders need to pay close attention to two issues. First, is every group member participating? Group brainstorming works best when each member feels free to contribute ideas. Yet some group members do not feel comfortable volunteering their ideas in large group settings. One way to address this concern is to have members first silently brainstorm ideas and then state them out loud in the group. Giving the members some time to prepare an answer silently may make them less anxious about volunteering their ideas. Another way to enhance member participation is to divide the group into two or more subgroups. Each subgroup then can brainstorm and subsequently share the resulting ideas in the larger group. Decreasing the size of the group increases the likelihood that a quieter member will participate in the brainstorming. Moreover, splitting and mixing up group members into smaller subgroups enables each subgroup to generate as many ideas as the larger group might. In fact, when the ideas generated by two subgroups are combined, they generally total more than if the large group had simply brainstormed without splitting.

A procedure known as **brainwriting** also allows each group member's voice to be heard in the discussion. In brainwriting, a written method for brainstorming, a grid is created on a sheet of paper and passed along for each member to contribute an idea while reviewing what previous group members have written (Wycoff, 1995). Brainwriting is used in groups that rely on oral communication as well as for groups whose primary mode of communication is written, such as groups linked through email.

Effective brainstorming requires people to suspend
judgment.

A second issue is the degree to which a group focuses on only one idea as opposed to multiple ideas. One of the drawbacks to brainstorming is that group members may be so heavily influenced by one idea that the subsequent ideas they generate are simply variations on it. For example, if a person had volunteered the idea of boot camps as a solution for dealing with juvenile crime and subsequent ideas only covered different kinds of camps—arts camps, computer camps, sports camps—the range of ideas will be limited. Other possible solutions such as after-school programs, tutoring in the schools, and neighborhood youth centers are neglected. The creativity of brainstorming may be preserved if each individual silently generates or initially writes down a few ideas before sharing them with the group. This method prevents group members from being influenced by others in their thinking.

Initiating Convergent Thinking

Whereas divergent thinking generates lots of ideas, **convergent thinking** is concerned with evaluating the ideas and selecting the one most appropriate to the task at hand. Procedures that narrow the range of alternatives to be considered and explore the strengths and weaknesses of each alternative help promote convergent thinking. Two procedures are particularly useful in stimulating convergent thinking: nominal group technique and fishbone diagrams.

Nominal group technique (NGT) is a procedure in which group members generate ideas individually, share these ideas with the group, and then evaluate them as a group. This technique assumes that idea generation is best done individually and idea evaluation is best done as a group. Nominal group technique uses the following steps:

1. Each member silently generates and writes down as many ideas as possible on the selected topic.
2. Each person volunteers one idea, which is recorded on a flip chart set before the group. This process is repeated until each member has volunteered all his or her ideas.
3. Using the list of ideas written on the flip chart, the group evaluates the strengths and weaknesses of each idea.
4. Group members individually rank the ideas. Another group member tallies up the individual rankings and produces an overall group ranking of the ideas.

learning link

What are the differences
between convergent and
divergent thinking?

• • •

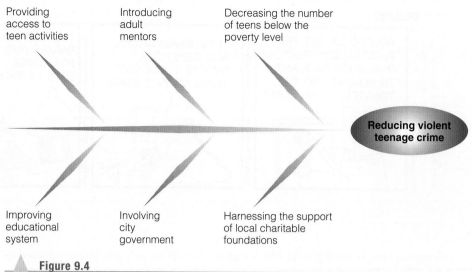

Providing access to teen activities

Introducing adult mentors

Decreasing the number of teens below the poverty level

Reducing violent teenage crime

Improving educational system

Involving city government

Harnessing the support of local charitable foundations

Figure 9.4

A Fishbone Diagram

Activities that will allow the group to achieve the goal are placed along the bones, with the most important placed closest to the head. In this diagram, decreasing the number of teenagers who live below the poverty line is more likely to decrease violent teenage crime than involving city government.

5. The group selects the most highly ranked ideas (say, the top three), and the subsequent discussion focuses on those top ideas.
6. Steps 3–5 are repeated until the group reaches a decision.

Another tool that can help group members examine the strengths and weaknesses of ideas is **fishbone diagrams,** illustrated in Figure 9.4, which are visual maps of the important causes and drivers that influence the outcomes group members wish to pursue. At the head of the fish, you write down the desired outcome. Continuing the earlier example, the desired outcome is reducing violent teenage crime. Along the bones branching off the fish spine, with the most important placed closest to the head, you note the various causes and drivers that would lead to a decrease in violent teenage crime such as access to after-school teen activities and the presence of adult mentors. Once groups have generated their fishbone diagram, discussion then centers on which of the bones, or actions, is most likely to bring about the desired outcome.

Convergent thinking works best when it helps group members see differing perspectives on an issue. As you saw earlier in the chapter, groups that make high-quality decisions are vigilant in their interaction; they explore the problem from a variety of perspectives. One of the dominant approaches that is typically used to bring in the perspectives of others and rigorously explore their implications is the devil's advocate procedure.

In the **devil's advocate procedure,** the group assigns an individual to question the assumptions and the processes it uses to make the decision. This person, the devil's advocate, challenges the group's thinking by introducing contrasting viewpoints and ideas. The more that minority opinion is included in the final decision, the higher the quality of the decision (Schwenk & Valacich, 1994). Devil's advocate procedure is effective only when group members are open to criticism and value contrasting ideas. If a group is not open to hearing divergent views, no matter how hard the devil's advocate tries, the minority views will not be heard. Even if a minority opinion is present in the discussion, if it is not heard or valued by the majority of the group, it will not lead to high-quality decisions.

The devil's advocate procedure is designed to foster contrived dissent, not genuine dissent. **Contrived dissent** occurs when individuals hold similar opinions regarding an issue but adopt a protocol such as the devil's advocate procedure to reality test their decision. **Genuine dissent** occurs when individuals truly hold differing opinions regarding an issue. Recent research has suggested that genuine dissent is a stronger predictor of high decision quality than contrived dissent (Schulz-Hardt, Jochims, & Frey, 2002). One explanation for this result is that groups whose members hold different views may be less confident about their decision and use a more balanced information search than groups whose members share similar beliefs. Another explanation is that group members who take a devil's advocate position may not subscribe to the position and as a result do not present convincing and persuasive counterarguments to the group. This suggests that, when possible, decision-making groups should be constructed that emphasize heterogeneous versus homogeneous member opinions.

Chapter Summary

Small groups are central to helping get work done by weighing competing alternatives and making informed choices. Decision making means selecting among competing alternatives, whereas problem solving is about reducing a gap between a current and an ideal state. Conducting a force field analysis can help you understand what is causing the problem and restraining the problem from being solved.

Groups make decisions about a variety of issues, using questions of fact, conjecture, value, and policy. Beginning with Dewey's reflective thinking sequence and continuing with functionalist theory, effective groups need to (1) assess the problem situation, (2) specify the goals of the decision-making process, (3) identify a range of alternatives, and (4) evaluate the alternatives in light of positive or negative consequences. Effective decisions are those that are acceptable to key stakeholders, help promote group members' future collaboration, and enhance the group members' personal development.

Knowing how to make decisions must be paired with task skills for competent small group communication. Five task skills are key to effective decision making: (1) defining the problem, (2) analyzing the problem, (3) identifying criteria for solving the problem, (4) generating solutions or alternatives, and (5) evaluating solutions or alternatives.

Groupthink short-circuits the decision-making process by moving group members toward a superficial analysis of the problem and potential solutions. A number of factors can move the group toward groupthink: cohesiveness, structural factors, and provocative situational contexts. Group members in a cohesive group may decrease critical thinking to maintain affiliation. Groups that are insulated from the larger environment, lack impartial leadership and methodical procedures, and have members who share values, beliefs, and assumptions have a tendency for groupthink. Finally, the situational factors of high stress and low self-esteem among group members can lead to groupthink.

Group procedures can help determine whether ideas need to be generated (divergent thinking) or evaluated (convergent thinking). Brainstorming and brainwriting are two procedures that can be used to enhance divergent thinking. Nominal group technique (NGT), fishbone diagrams, and devil's advocate procedure are tools used to narrow down competing alternatives in a process called convergent thinking.

Study and Review

The premium companion website for *Human Communication* offers a broad range of resources that will help you better understand the material in this chapter, complete assignments, and succeed on tests. The website resources include

- Interactive self-assessments, competency grids, and other tools
- Web links, practice activities, self-quizzes, and a sample final exam

For more information about this text's electronic learning resources, consult the *Guide to Online Resources for Human Communication* or visit **http://communication.wadsworth.com/morreale2.**

 ## Key Terms

The key terms below are defined in the chapter on the pages indicated. They are also presented alphabetically with definitions in the Glossary, which begins on page 467. The book's website includes flashcards and crossword puzzles to help you learn these terms and the concepts they represent.

Building Motivation _____

This self-assessment resource begins on page 243. An interactive version of it is also available on the book's website.

 Building Knowledge _____

The following questions are among the practice activities on the book's website.

1. How do the criteria for classifying a small group (three or more people, perception, interdependence, and communication) connect? Is it possible to have a small group that perceives itself to be a small group but whose members do not talk or communicate with one another? Is it possible for two people who perceive themselves as a group, who are interdependent, and who communicate with one another to be classified as a group? Why or why not?

2. What are the differences between a small group and a team? What are the most important factors for helping build a high-performing team?

3. What are the differences between problem solving and decision making? Is it possible to solve a problem without making a decision or make a decision without solving a problem?

4. Are all decisions nested? Do all decisions inherently involve questions of fact, conjecture, value, and policy? Can you have a question of fact that does not involve a question of value? Can you have a policy question that does not involve questions of fact?

5. What kinds of communication do the reflective thinking model and the functionalist approach to decision making suggest are important for effective decision making?

6. How does groupthink influence decision making? Are there ever times when a group leader may want to encourage groupthink?

7. When should group members engage in divergent and convergent thinking? What strategies can they use to generate and evaluate ideas?

 Building Skills _____

The exercises below are among the practice activities on the book's website.

Individual Exercises

1. Ask four or five friends how they define small group communication. Do their definitions of small group communication reflect the four characteristics of small groups: three or more people, perception, interdependence, and communication? Why do you think your friends defined communication in the way that they did?

2. Select and interview two or three individuals who participate in small groups. Use the following questions for your interview:
   a. What has been your best experience in group decision making?
   b. What made it such a good experience?
   c. What factors make it possible to make a good decision?

    d. What criteria do you feel should be used to evaluate whether a group has made a good decision?

Compare the answers you get from your interviews to the material in the chapter. In what ways are your interviewees' answers similar to or different from the material in the chapter? Why do you think that is?

3. Brainstorm a list of problems that concern you. Starting with the most important problem, do a force field analysis on this problem. What is the gap that represents the problem? What are the drivers? What are the constraining forces?

4. Imagine you are a member of an organization. You have been assigned to write a memo about effective decision making that will be distributed to all members. What are five rules for effective decision making you would include in the memo?

5. Log on to the Internet and search for sites that discuss decision-making procedures. Enter the keywords *decision-making procedures* and identify two sites that discuss ways to coordinate group decision-making activity. Compare the procedures they highlight to the procedures identified in the chapter that facilitate divergent thinking, convergent thinking, developing reflective ability, and creating a common focus. In what ways are they similar to and different from the procedures discussed in the chapter?

Group Activities

1. Form groups of four to five people. Using the following list of group topics, brainstorm the kinds of ground rules you would set up for a constructive discussion on a controversial topic such as affirmative action or extending health benefits to partners of gays and lesbians:

attendance	end-product orientation
discussion	constructive confrontation
confidentiality	contributions
analytic approach	

2. As a group of four to five people, watch the 1950s movie *12 Angry Men*. Focus on the character played by Henry Fonda. Using Fonda as an example, what is it that allows a person to create effectively the role of devil's advocate? As a group, generate a list of rules for being an effective devil's advocate.

3. Using InfoTrac College Edition, look up an article using the key words *team building*. Read through the article. Using the information contained in the article, prepare a presentation for your class that addresses the following question, "What processes are important for building high-performing teams?"

 References _____

Ahlfinger, N. R., & Esser, J. K. (2001). Testing the groupthink model: Effects of promotional leadership and conformity predisposition. *Social Behavior and Personality, 29,* 31–42.

Bales, R. F. (1950). *Interaction process analysis: A method for the study of small groups.* Reading, MA: Addison-Wesley.

Barge, J. K. (in press). Dialogue, conflict, and community. In J. Oetzel & S. Ting-Toomey (Eds.), *The SAGE Handbook of Conflict Communication: Integrating Theory, Research, and Practice.* Thousand Oaks, CA: Sage.

Dewey, J. (1910). *How we think*. Boston: D. C. Heath.

Edmondson, A. C. (2003). Speaking up in the operating room: How team leaders promote learning in interdisciplinary action teams. *Journal of Management Studies, 40,* 1419–1452.

Gouran, D. S. (1999). Communication in groups: The emergence and evolution of a field of study. In L. R. Frey, D. S. Gouran, & M. S. Poole (Eds.), *The handbook of group communication theory and research* (pp. 3–36). Thousand Oaks, CA: Sage.

Gouran, D. S. (2003). Reflections on the type of question as a determinant of the form of interaction in decision-making and problem-solving discussions. *Communication Quarterly, 51,* 111–126.

Gouran, D. S., & Hirokawa, R. Y. (1996). Functional theory and communication in decision-making and problem-solving groups: An expanded view. In R. Y. Hirokawa & M. S. Poole (Eds.), *Communication and group decision making* (2nd ed., pp. 55–80). Thousand Oaks, CA: Sage.

Gouran, D. S., & Hirokawa, R. Y. (2003). Effective decision making and problem solving in groups: A functional perspective. In R. Y. Hirokawa, R. S. Cathcart, L. A. Samovar, & L. D. Henman (Eds.), *Small group communication* (pp. 27–38). Los Angeles, CA: Roxbury.

Hackman, J. R. (2002). *Leading teams*. Boston: Harvard Business School Press.

Hirokawa, R. Y. (1990). The role of communication in group decision-making efficacy: A task-contingency perspective. *Small Group Research, 21* (2), 190–204.

Janis, I. L. (1972). *Victims of groupthink: A psychological study of policy decisions and fiascoes* (2nd ed.). Boston: Houghton Mifflin.

Janis, I. L. (1982). *Groupthink: Psychological studies of policy decisions and fiascoes* (2nd ed.). Boston: Houghton Mifflin.

Janis, I. L., & Mann, L. (1977). *Decision-making: A psychological analysis of conflict, choice, and commitment*. New York: Free Press.

Katzenbach, J. R., & Smith, D. W. (2003). *The wisdom of teams: Creating the high performance organization*. New York: HarperBusiness.

Kayes, D. C. (2002). Proximal team learning: Lessons from United Flight 93 on 9/11. *Organizational Dynamics, 32,* 80–92.

LaFasto, F., & Larson, C. (2001). *When teams work best*. Thousand Oaks, CA: Sage.

Lewin, K. (1951). *Field theory in social research*. New York: Harper & Row.

Orlitzky, M., & Hirokawa, R. Y. (2001). To err is human, to correct for it divine: A meta-analysis of research testing the functional theory of group decision-making effectiveness. *Small Group Research, 32,* 313–341.

Park, W. (2000). A comprehensive empirical investigation of the relationships among variables of the groupthink model. *Journal of Organizational Behavior, 21,* 873–887.

Salas, E., Dickinson, T. L., Converse, S., & Tannenbaum, S. I. (1992). Toward an understanding of team performance and training. In R. W. Swezey & E. Salas (Eds.), *Teams: Their training and performance* (pp. 3–29). Norwood, NJ: Ablex Publishing.

Schulz-Hardt, S., Jochims, M., & Frey, D. (2002). Productive conflict in group decision making: Genuine and contrived dissent as strategies to counteract biased information seeking. *Organizational Behavior and Human Decision Processes, 88,* 563–586.

Schwenk, C. R., & Valacich, J. S. (1994). Effects of devil's advocacy and dialectical inquiry on individuals versus groups. *Organizational Behavior and Human Decision Process, 59,* 210–222.

Socha, T. (1996). Group communication across the life span. In L. R. Frey & J. K. Barge (Eds.), *Managing group life: Communicating in decision-making groups* (pp. 1–28). Boston: Houghton-Mifflin.

Sunwolf, & Siebold, D. R. (1999). The impact of formal procedures on group processes, members and task outcomes. In L. R. Frey, D. S. Gouran, & M. S. Poole (Eds.), *The handbook of group communication theory and research* (pp. 395–431). Thousand Oaks, CA: Sage.

Wittenbaum, G. M., Hollingshead, A. B., Paulus, P. B., Hirokawa, R. Y., Ancona, D. G., Peterson, R. S., Jehn, K. A., & Yoon, K. (2004). The functional perspective as a lens for understanding groups. *Small Group Research, 35,* 17–43.

Wycoff, J. (1995). *Transformation thinking.* New York: Berkley Books.

Building Motivation _____

Self-Assessment: Rate each of the following tasks associated with group communication competence, indicating the typical level of competence you feel you can or do achieve. Use the scale of 1–4 provided, with 1 minimal competence and 4 high competence. Rate one component (motivation) through all the situations, and then rate the next component (knowledge), and then the third (skills).

Motivation	Knowledge	Skills
1 = Anxious, disinterested, or no motivation to be competent	1 = Completely inexperienced and ignorant about how to behave	1 = Completely incapable of behaving competently in the situation
2 = Somewhat nervous, but some motivation to be competent	2 = Minimal experience and knowledge about how to behave	2 = Barely capable of behaving minimally competently
3 = Somewhat confident and motivated to be competent	3 = Somewhat experienced and knowledgeable about how to behave	3 = Fairly capable of behaving competently
4 = Highly confident and motivated to be competent	4 = Highly knowledgeable about all aspects of how to behave	4 = Highly capable of behaving competently

Small Group Communication Competencies:	Motivation	Knowledge	Skills
1. Define and analyze a problem that confronts the group.			
2. Participate in establishing the group goal and identify criteria for assessing the quality of the group outcome.			
3. Generate solutions or alternatives to the problem.			
4. Evaluate the solutions or alternatives identified by group members.			
5. Help the group stay on the task, issue, or agenda item under discussion.			
6. Manage disagreements and conflict among group members.			
7. Provide supportive comments and encouragement to other group members.			
8. Manage the group interaction and invite other members to participate.			

Total Scores

Interpreting Your Scores: Total your score for each column (motivation, knowledge, and skills). You should end up with three scores. The possible range of scores per column is 8–32. Scores 8–14 indicate you are minimizing your competence and have significant room for improvement. Scores 15–21 indicate you think you are average in your competence. You may be sufficing or maximizing your competence, and you still have room for improvement. Scores 22–28 indicate you think you are nearing optimizing competence. Although you may still improve, you have a good grasp of the competence process. If your score for the motivation component is lower than you like, pay close attention to the content and suggestions in Chapters 9 and 10. To improve your scores in the knowledge component, study the knowledge sections in both Chapters 9 and 10. To improve your scores in the skills component, study the skills and overcoming challenges sections in both chapters.

© Bob Daemmrich / The Image Works

Chapter 10

LEARNING OBJECTIVES

After studying this chapter, you should be able to

1. Explain how leadership, as a communication process, involves performing task and relational functions to help groups adapt to changing situations.

2. Articulate the relationships among change, adaptive work, and team learning.

3. Describe how the concepts of interaction, interdependence, and incompatibility inform a definition of conflict.

4. Distinguish among affective, ideational, and procedural conflict.

5. Identify group situations where the avoidance, distributive, and integrative styles of conflict management are superior.

6. Use the skills of acknowledging and reflecting to help manage conflict and create a supportive group climate.

7. Demonstrate how creating a supportive climate, explaining positions, and using issue framing can help manage relationships within groups.

Leadership in Small Groups: Challenges and Overcoming Them

Rob is the newly hired executive director for the Arlen Arts Company (AAC), a local nonprofit group that sponsors a wide variety of adult and children's theatrical programs. The theater has flourished over the years, expanding its initial programming to now include a children's theater program and summer productions. During the last 5 years, however, season ticket sales have plummeted, the talent pool of actors has dwindled, and volunteer support for building the sets and helping at the box office has fallen. The board of directors hired Rob to reverse the pattern of falling ticket sales and to increase community involvement with the theater.

Rob quickly conducted an analysis of the theater's operating budget and created a set of recommendations for the board of directors to consider. When he presented his ideas to the board a heated discussion erupted in the board meeting. Some board members strongly disagreed with Rob's recommendation and verbally attacked him, calling him "young and inexperienced." These board members had voted for another candidate for executive director and had difficulty accepting Rob. Other board members didn't want to talk about Rob's recommendations at all; they had great difficulty moving beyond the theater's financial difficulties to actions that could address its problems. Still other members wanted to talk about the theater's history. They had belonged to the theater for more than 20 years and wanted to focus on how good things had been in the past. Any new idea that Rob presented was met with the refrain of "that's not how we've done it in the past." Other board members were open to Rob's ideas and tried to keep the discussion focused on his recommendations. And some board members sat there in silence trying to make sense of the discussion.

Rob had problems leading the discussion. He believed that some board members were out to get him and no matter what he said they were going to disagree. He thought other board members were out of touch and so focused on the past that they failed to recognize that times had changed and what worked well in the past doesn't work today. Although he appreciated the efforts of those group members who were receptive to his ideas, he knew they were a minority on the board. He was confused and getting angry. Rob thought to himself, "They hire me to help straighten out the theater, and yet they fight me when I want to make changes."

Just as Rob thought the discussion couldn't get any worse, one of his staff members, the director of the Children's Theater, entered the discussion and criticized Rob's recommendations as not being sensitive to his department's needs. At that point, Rob suggested that the board table his recommendations until the next board meeting and adjourn.

Part of the difficulty that Rob faced during the meeting emerged because multiple groups of board members were each pursuing their own agenda. It is not surprising that the meeting became chaotic and unproductive given such a diverse set of people, goals, and expectations. Although Rob believed quite correctly that he had been hired to change the theater's operations to generate increased ticket sales and community involvement, when he tried to be proactive and make recommendations to change the theater he met resistance. This highlights a common dilemma for group leaders. They are commonly charged with creating change and innovation within a group, yet the groups they work with deny that change is needed or desired. ■

Is it fair to blame Rob for this meeting's failure? As the formally appointed leader of the group, Rob does share some responsibility for the disintegration of the meeting. Yet the individual board members also made choices about their participation in it. Some chose to pursue their political agenda and sabotage Rob's authority. Others chose to abdicate their responsibility to think about the future and chose to remain focused on the past. Others chose to work toward making changes in the theater that could lead to increased ticket sales and community involvement. Although it was Rob's responsibility to manage the board of directors meeting, that does not absolve group members of the responsibility to participate constructively. Members of any group make choices, consciously or unconsciously, about how they are going to position themselves during the discussion.

This chapter focuses on the issue of leading small groups and managing group member participation. In any group we belong to, we make choices regarding the way we coordinate people's actions, and these choices have consequences for the way group members work together. We can choose to establish cooperative or competitive relationships with other group members. We can choose to foster conflict and create defensive climates, or we can select ways of communicating that manage conflict and create supportive relationships.

Let's begin by examining the kinds of knowledge that leaders require to coordinate group activity competently.

Knowing How to Lead Groups

When you think of leaders, who comes to mind? Whom do you perceive as group leaders? Organizational leaders? Community leaders? National leaders? International leaders? As you think about your list, what characteristics do these leaders share? In Western culture, leaders are typically associated with people who manage crises and problems effectively (Kouzes & Posner, 2003). For example, Martin Luther King Jr. confronted the problem of racial inequality in the United States. Susan B. Anthony advocated voting rights for women. As mayor of New York City, Rudy Giuliani managed the aftermath of the World Trade Center attack. Jaime Escalante became an educational leader at East Garfield High School in Los Angeles as he worked to educate lower income children in mathematics. In each of these cases, the individual was charged with managing a crisis and managed it well.

Although there appears to be some agreement that leadership is associated with managing difficulties and problems, there is much disagreement about what leadership is and what counts as effective leadership. Let's examine three questions: (1) What is leadership? (2) How can leaders change a group, organization, or community? and (3) How do leaders manage conflict?

Understanding Leadership

What is leadership? This is a difficult question to answer because more than 300 definitions of leadership have been recorded (Bennis & Nanus, 1985). Some people associate leadership with formal positions of authority, such as a manager in an organization or an

© Kim Kulish /Corbis

elected official; others view leadership as a process involving informal authority. Some people view leadership as an elite process that can be performed only by people born with particular personality, physical, or cognitive traits, whereas others contend that leadership is an ability that anyone can develop and be taught.

For purposes of our discussion, we define **leadership** as a communication process that helps groups organize themselves to achieve desirable goals. **Leaders** are individuals within a group who guide and direct the group's activities. Our definition of leadership has four important implications.

Leadership Is a Communication Process

Early leadership research focused on the traits that individuals were born with that enabled them to emerge as leaders with groups, organizations, and society (Stogdill, 1948). A variety of traits such as intelligence, motivation, drive, social competence, assertiveness, and communication anxiety were examined to see whether they allow individuals to emerge as leaders. However, researchers discovered no uniform correlation between personality traits and leadership. What happened next was that people began to view leadership as a behavioral process. The focus shifted from the question, "What are leaders like?" to "What do leaders do?" This latter question is about communication. How do leaders talk? What do they say? How do they use nonverbal communication to get their point across? Contemporary leadership theory views leadership as a communication process that is directly tied to what leaders say and do.

Leadership Means Performing Task and Relational Functions

The task–relational dimension surfaced in early research regarding the **equilibrium problem** (Bales, 1970). The equilibrium problem is the challenge small groups face in maintaining a constructive tension between getting the task done and maintaining a positive group environment. The answer for some groups has been to share the leadership responsibilities, with one person taking primary responsibility for keeping the group on task and another person maintaining a positive group climate. The former are **task functions** that require instrumental behavior aimed at goal achievement and emphasize clarifying the purpose and scope of the group's task, maintaining the group's focus on the task, and managing the way the group collects, structures, and uses information in problem solving and decision making. The latter reflects **relational functions** that emphasize the importance of building a positive group culture and managing conflict (Barge, 2003; Galanes, 2003). Both types of functions must be performed if a group is to be successful. For example, leaders of creative teams such as marketing and advertising teams must simultaneously develop a stimulating social environment that facilitates working relationships to keep the creative juices flowing but must also keep the team focused on its task.

Leadership Is a Situated Process

Leadership cannot be defined by generic responses to situations that are prescribed; rather, response will vary according to the situation. Early leadership work emphasized the importance of identifying the one best style that characterizes leadership (Lewin, Lippitt, & White, 1939). For example, many contend that effective leaders are democratic in nature regardless of the situation. **Democratic leadership** uses two-way communication among leaders and followers who have equal status and collectively determine the direction of the group. **Autocratic leadership** is about leaders having more power than followers and using one-way communication to direct and guide the actions of followers. Autocratic leaders unilaterally make decisions and use communication to command followers to execute their decisions. For many years, leadership researchers have argued that democratic leadership is superior because group members feel more included in the decision-making process and are more committed to adhere to the decisions that have been made. Moreover, having more people participating in decision making brings more diverse views into the process and increases the likelihood of making high-quality decisions. However, democratic leadership also takes time to perform and during crisis situations autocratic leadership may provide a more rapid and timely response. Gender has another influence on leadership, as discussed in the Close-Up on Gender box.

The difficulty of identifying the one best style of leadership has led many researchers to believe that a key skill for leaders is an ability to read a situation and adapt their behavior according to the particular constraints of the situation (Bolman & Deal, 2003; Morgan, 1997). From this perspective, effective leadership is about acting in ways that are appropriate given the situation.

What kinds of situational factors influence how a leader should act? Here are some of the key situational factors that influence leadership behavior:

learning link

What are the advantages
and disadvantages of
democratic leadership?

• • •

Task structure: When the nature of the task is very clear and the steps that group members need to take to complete the task are unambiguous, effective leaders need to be supportive and encourage group members to complete the task. When the nature of the task is unclear and there are many ways to complete the task, effective leadership helps clarify the nature of the task and lay out the pathway to achieve the goal.

Group maturity: If group members have the necessary knowledge or expertise to perform a task and are highly motivated to perform the task, leaders may delegate the task to the group members. If group members are not knowledgeable about how to perform a task and are not motivated to learn or perform it, leaders need to tell group members precisely what to do.

Group commitment and acceptance: If the ability to implement a decision depends on the commitment and support of the group, it is better to use a democratic style of leadership. If the ability to implement a decision is independent of the group's acceptance, a leader can use an autocratic style of leadership.

Information requirements: If each group member has unique information and insights about the task, democratic leadership should be used in order to pool the information of the different group members. If all group members have the same level of task knowledge, it may be appropriate to employ autocratic leadership.

Ambiguity: If the nature of the task is ambiguous, leaders may need to clarify the scope and nature of the task. If the nature of the task is very structured and clear, a leader may need to introduce some ambiguity into the discussion to prompt creative thinking.

Effective leaders need to examine the situations and groups they are leading and determine what needs to be done to keep the group moving forward. They need to pay attention to factors such as the task structure and group commitment to determine what course of action will best propel the group toward success.

It is tempting to think that leaders simply need to pay attention to one or two of these factors when they choose how to respond to situations. Yet each situation is unique given

CloseUp on Gender
A Feminine Advantage?

WHEN YOU THINK OF THE TERM LEADER, WHO comes to mind? Are most of the leaders you listed males or females? Historically, leadership has been viewed as a predominantly masculine activity. Yet recently, with the influx of women into the work force and more and more women occupying leadership positions in the public and private sectors, there has been a renewed interest in examining the relationship between gender and leadership. An important current question is "How is the leadership performance of men and women the same, and how is it different?"

Several researchers contend there is a distinct difference between men and women and the way they lead groups and organizations. Consider some of the research findings relating gender and leadership:

- Male leaders are perceived as more task oriented and female leaders are more relationship oriented.
- Male leaders tend to employ styles that are more directive and autocratic in nature and women use styles that are more democratic and participatory in nature.
- Female leaders' styles are intended to intellectually stimulate and inspire their followers to a larger degree than male leaders'.
- Male leaders tend to wait longer for problems to become serious before intervening than do female leaders.
- When women adopt autocratic styles of leadership, they are viewed less positively than men who adopt an autocratic style.
- Male leaders receive higher evaluations than female leaders when performing in positions usually filled by men (Eagly & Carli, 2003).

Such research draws a clear line between the way most men and women lead. In fact, people argue that the feminine way of leading with its emphasis on participation and relationship is more effective in today's society (Helgesen, 1995). Given that organizations are increasingly moving to team-based styles of management, it is important for leaders to be able to develop and cultivate strong working relationships among team members.

Yet other researchers argue that no significant and consistent differences exist in the leadership performance of men and women. They claim that men and women use the same kinds of styles to lead. There is no behavioral difference in the ways that men and women lead (for example, see Thompson, 2000). Rather, the way a leader performs depends more on the nature of the situation than the gender of the leader.

This split in the research poses a potential problem for leaders: does my gender make a difference in the way I lead and the way I am perceived? To be an effective leader means you have to pay attention to the nature of the situation, and part of the situation is the gender of the leader. Therefore effective leaders need to answer the following kinds of questions to ensure they have addressed gender issues:

- At what stage of development is the group? If the group is in the early stages of development, group members will evaluate leaders in terms of gender stereotypes (Eagly & Johnson, 1990). This means male leaders are expected to be autocratic, independent, and competitive and female leaders are expected to be democratic, dependent, and cooperative. At this stage of development, if a leader wants to be viewed as competent, he or she needs to either (1) conform to the stereotypical expectations for male or female leadership or (2) provide an explanation for why he or she is deviating from these expectations. As groups enter later stages of development, the situation, rather than gender, will be the dominant criterion for evaluating competence.
- What does the situation require of the leader? In more developed groups, the nature of the situation influences the type of leadership required. Issues of task structure, information requirements, and acceptability become important.

Although it is unclear whether gender exercises a significant influence on leadership performance, leaders need to be flexible in their behavior. The nature of the situation is critical in determining what kinds of leadership behavior are required. The competent leader therefore needs to be able to master both so-called masculine leadership styles such as being more autocratic and competitive and so-called feminine leadership styles, which are more democratic, participatory, and cooperative in nature.

the particular combination of people, context, and task. The question leaders need to ask is "What needs to be done in this specific situation?" (Zaccaro, Rittman, & Marks, 2001). Leadership is not as simple as following a predetermined script or looking for the one or two factors that typically characterize a situation and basing your response on those factors. Rather, leadership means constructing detailed descriptions of situations and, given the unique opportunities and constraints of the situation, determining what needs to be done to keep the group moving forward (Barge & Oliver, 2003).

Leadership Is a Social Process

Leadership is the give-and-take, the communication, among leaders and followers. To be a leader, you must have people who are willing to follow. *Leadership* is the process of communication that occurs between leaders and followers. To understand leadership, you need to look at what leaders say and how followers respond, as well as what followers say and how leaders respond.

learning link

What factors may influence your choice of a particular leadership style?

• • •

How do positions of group leadership get created? One way is for leaders to be appointed to the group by some external authority. For example, managers are often appointed to be leaders of work teams within an organization. Upper-level managers appoint lower-level managers to guide and direct work teams. Another way positions of leadership get created in groups is that leaders emerge from the interaction among group members. An individual may emerge as a leader in a group if he or she participates a great deal within the group, demonstrates expertise that other group members do not have, and collaborates with other group members (Barge, 1996).

Is one way better than the other? No. Both approaches have strengths and weaknesses. Appointed leaders may be viewed favorably by other group members particularly if the people doing the appointing are well respected. Being appointed by high-status people can give a leader credibility. At the same time, if group members do not perceive the process of appointing leaders as legitimate, the appointed leader may be viewed as incompetent or not deserving the position. Leaders who emerge in the course of the group discussion tend to be viewed as more credible. At the same time, individuals who are unqualified may emerge as leaders. For example, people who participate a great deal in the discussion tend to emerge as leaders (Barge, 1996). Other group members take this high level of participation as a sign of commitment and concern for the group and allow this person to emerge as the leader. Yet does talking a lot in a group discussion guarantee that a person has the knowledge and expertise needed to guide the group? The answer is a resounding no.

The chapter-opening vignette illustrates several of these important ideas concerning leadership. Viewing Rob's leadership from a communication perspective means we focus on how he managed the board meeting: what he said or did during the meeting. Rob had to perform both task and relational functions during the meeting. He needed to help the group accomplish the task of developing a strategy for making the company financially viable and simultaneously had to manage his relationships with other board members. Rob also had to respond to the unique emerging situation. His initial hope for the meeting was to have the board make some decisions regarding what to do about the company's shaky finances; but given the resistance in the meeting from board members and members of his staff, he decided to postpone the decision. Finally, Rob may need to find ways to legitimate his authority during meetings. Even though Rob was appointed to be the leader of the AAC, some people resist his authority, and this is a challenge that Rob will need to manage in the future if he is to succeed.

Table 10.1			
Distinguishing Technical and Adaptive Work			
Type of Work	**Problem Definition**	**Solution and Implementation**	**Primary Locus of Responsibility for the Work**
Technical	Clear	Clear	Leader
Adaptive	Requires learning	Requires learning	Group members, leader

Adapted from Heifetz (1994), p. 76.

Leadership and Change

Perhaps the biggest responsibility a group leader faces is creating change within the group. As group tasks become more complex in rapidly changing environments, leaders must help groups adapt to and meet environmental challenges (LaFasto & Larson, 2001). The kind of leadership needed to create change within a group depends on the type of work a group is doing and what needs to be changed.

There are two kinds of work that small group leaders and followers do (Heifetz & Linsky, 2002; Table 10.1). In **technical work,** the problem the group is working on is clearly defined as are the solution and implementation. If a doctor has a patient with an infection, the problem is clear—the patient has an infection—and the solution is clear and easy to implement—the doctor tells the patient to take antibiotics.

In technical work, the leader is most responsible for the change. It is up to the leader to tell the group what needs to be done and how to do it. For example, suppose you are a leader of a sales team for a pharmaceutical company and you have been told your team needs to report their sales data to the headquarters in a new way. The problem is clear—change the way the data is reported. The solution is clear—as the leader, you have the new format for reporting data to headquarters. You also have the authority to make the change. To implement it, you simply need to inform the team about the change and ask them to make it.

However, not all group work is technical. Would you classify the kind of work Rob was doing with the board of directors for the AAC as technical work? Probably not. The problem Rob is dealing with is not clearly defined, nor are the solution and its implementation. Such work is better labeled adaptive work. **Adaptive work** has problems and solutions that are not clearly defined and that place the responsibility for change on the group members. Given the ambiguity and complexity of the problem, group members need to learn about the nature of the problem and about possible solutions and ways of implementing them. In adaptive work, the role of the leader is to facilitate the group's learning so they can make the change. Consider a doctor working with a terminally ill cancer patient. The doctor and the patient know death is imminent. Yet there is a great deal of learning the patient needs to do. How do you talk to friends and family about your disease? Are the finances in order? If the patient has dependent family members, how will they be cared for? These are problems that do not have simple and clear answers. The doctor's role in this instance is to raise important questions that help create an environment in which the patient can learn and develop definitions and solutions for the problem. It is the patient who is responsible for the change, not the doctor. In the case of the AAC, as much as Rob wants to change the board, it is up to the board to learn and to make the changes. It is Rob's responsibility to create an environment in which the board takes responsibility for understanding the problem and generating solutions.

To help the group begin the process of doing adaptive work, leaders need to create an environment in which group members can first investigate what is causing the distress or problem. At this point, leaders need to get the group to engage with questions such as these:

- What is causing the problem?
- What perspectives do key stakeholders in the group or organization hold that are now in conflict?
- What is the history of the problem?
- How do people respond to the problem?
- In the past, when has the problem reached a breaking point and people have begun to engage in self-destructive patterns?
- How have people in the past tried to address the problem?

These questions focus the group members on the tensions that are creating the problem so they can learn about the details of the problem and how the problem has been addressed in the past.

Leaders may then focus the group on the issues that need attention. What are the issues that we need to focus on in light of our problem analysis? Which issues are ripe for working with? For example, if Rob had worked with the board of directors on defining the problem, the group might have generated a list of problems, ranging from poor audience attendance to unmotivated board members. The group may then decide the issue most ripe for change is the audience attendance issue. They may believe that talking about poor board-member motivation may simply aggravate the situation and not help. In the process of discussing these various issues, they may reach an understanding that one of the reasons the board wants to avoid working on the problems is that if they did, they would be forced to confront their lack of motivation. By exploring the past and identifying issues that are ripe for working with, leaders can facilitate new understandings about a situation that can lead to change. Such work is not easy and may generate conflict within the group. As a result, leaders must also be skilled at managing conflict within groups if they are going to create change.

Group Conflict

Although many definitions have been offered, **conflict** is typically defined as interaction among interdependent people who perceive each other as opposing their goals, aims, or values and having the potential to frustrate them in achieving these goals, aims, or values (Putnam & Poole, 1987, p. 552). This definition contains the three "i's" of conflict: (1) interaction, (2) interdependence, and (3) incompatibility.

It is through interaction that people become aware of the differences among their goals, aims, or values and begin to manage these differences. People are not telepathic (at least most of us are not!), and the exchange of verbal and nonverbal cues is the way we become aware of the differences that separate us. The notion of interdependence also is central to understanding conflict. We can disagree over a variety of issues. You might vote for a particular political candidate and I might vote for another. You might think the welfare system should be overhauled and I don't. These disagreements, however, are not necessarily conflicts. People can disagree but not be in conflict with one another. Conflict emerges when one party in the conflict can interfere with the realizations of the other party's goals, aims, and interests. For example, if Rob wants to pursue a particular recommendation for the AAC and the board does not, Rob and the board are in conflict. Rob's ability to pursue a recommendation depends on the board, and the board depends on Rob to follow the board's wishes. At the heart of conflict is the third "i"—incompatibility. There needs to be a real or perceived opposition to one party's interest for conflict to exist.

Types of Conflict

Reflect on your past group experiences. What kinds of conflicts have you had within groups? What were the conflicts over? Who did you have the conflicts with? Make a list of your answers and you will see there is a great variety of topics and issues that group members may find themselves in conflict about.

Three types of conflict typically emerge in groups. **Affective conflict** results from the interpersonal relationships formed among group members and the group's emotional climate. It can occur when two members don't like one another or there is a power struggle between people. In the first case, members may begin sniping during group meetings and insulting one another. In the second, they may fight over who will be the leader of the group. Part of a group's success depends on its ability to manage disagreements and conflict appropriately. By staying focused on issues rather than on personalities and by finding ways to blend the talents of group members, group leaders and members can help move a group from being paralyzed by different styles of conflict to using conflict as a resource for greater productivity. Affective conflict may occur when two group members don't like one another or there is a power struggle between people. In the former, people who don't like one another may begin sniping during the group meetings and insulting one another. In the latter, two group members may fight over who will be the leader of the group.

Many times affective conflict occurs over what group roles people perform. One classic typology of group roles, offered by Benne and Sheats (1948), is based on the type of behavioral function performed by the individuals playing the role. A **group role** is made up of a set of prescribed behaviors that individuals are expected to perform. Table 10.2 identifies three general classes of roles as well as specific examples for each type:

Task roles help the group achieve its task or objective. They include behaviors that orient the group to the task at hand, manage the exchange of ideas and opinions, and encourage the group to complete the task.

Relational roles include behaviors that function to maintain the interpersonal climate within the group. They provide harmony to the group, create openness for sharing information, convey the feelings of group members, and help manage the relational environment of the organization.

Ego-centered roles emphasize the individual's personality and thereby favor the needs of the individual over the group. Such roles are typically viewed as destructive to a group because they hinder the organization's ability to achieve a task.

Table 10.2

Typology of Group Roles

There are three categories of group roles: task, relational, and ego centered. Within each category, group members may select among several distinct roles to play.

Role	Function
Task Roles	
Initiator	Provides direction and guidance to a group. Proposes definitions of problems, suggests solutions, gives ideas, and suggests operating procedures.
Information seeker	Recognizes the need for additional information. Requests clarification of ideas and relevant facts about the group's task.
Information giver	Provides relevant facts about the group's task.
Opinion seeker	Solicits people's feelings and views about any aspect of the group's task. Tests for the group opinion.
Opinion giver	Offers personal views and evaluation of the group's work. May comment on the value of certain group procedures, the solutions under consideration, or the nature of the group's task.
Clarifier	Eliminates confusion by identifying points of agreement or restating ideas or viewpoints.
Elaborator/coordinator	Extends information and clarifies relations among various viewpoints, ideas, and solutions within the group.
Problem identifier	Proposes definitions of a problem and its related causes or antecedents.
Procedure developer	Proposes and identifies the procedures a group should use when making a decision; includes setting and proposing an agenda.
Orienter-summarizer	Focuses the group on the task and summarizes its discussion by reviewing the relationships among solutions, facts, and opinions.
Information recorder	Records group discussion.
Tester of agreement	Checks to see how close the group is to reaching an agreement.
Energizer	Motivates the group and prods it toward action.
Relational Roles	
Supporter	Recognizes others' contributions and encourages them to participate.
Harmonizer	Attempts to balance and manage conflict within the group. Serves to maintain and restore a positive interpersonal climate. Includes helping the group express its feelings to relieve tension.
Tension reliever	Through joking and humor, attempts to relieve group stress.
Compromiser	Seeks to maintain group cohesion by compromising his or her own ideas that are in conflict with the group's. Admits error to the group.
Gatekeeper	Manages and directs the flow of communication and participation within the group.
Feeling expresser	Highlights for the group its feelings, emotions, and attitudes. Shares feelings with other group members.
Standard setter	Articulates the standards the group must achieve. Refers to these standards when evaluating the group's progress.
Follower	Accepts the ideas and views of other group members without question.
Ego-Centered Roles	
Blocker	Inhibits group discussion by refusing to cooperate. Rejects other group members' ideas.
Aggressor	Tries to gain power within the group by criticizing other group members' ideas and competence.
Deserter	Withdraws from group participation.
Dominator	Monopolizes group discussions.
Recognition seeker	Seeks personal recognition and praise from other group members by boasting about past accomplishments.
Confessor	Distracts the group from its task by using the group as a means of solving personal problems.
Playboy	Uses cynicism, humor, and horseplay to distract the group from its task.
Special interest pleader	Pursues a personal agenda or the agenda of an outside group.

SOURCE: Adapted from Benne and Sheats (1948). *Note:* This table appeared in J. K. Barge (1994).

Affective conflict can occur when people fight over performing the same role or feel that the role another person is performing is inappropriate.

Ideational conflict centers on the different opinions people may have about how to define problems, generate solutions, set and apply criteria, and select among competing alternatives. People may disagree about what counts as appropriate data and assumptions to base decisions on or how to define the problem or which criteria are acceptable.

Procedural conflict is differences of opinion about what procedures to use during group discussion. Disputes can arise over how to structure the agenda or whether to use a specific procedure such as nominal group technique or the devil's advocate procedure to enhance convergent thinking.

Conflicts come in many different forms. For leaders, an important choice is deciding how best to respond to the conflict in a way that facilitates accomplishing the group's task.

Conflict Management Styles

One way to manage conflict is to adopt a style appropriate for the situation. **Conflict management styles** are distinguishable patterns of behavior that represent different forms of managing disputes. Although many typologies of conflict management styles exist, three styles are typically identified in group communication theory and research: (1) avoidance, (2) distributive, and (3) integration (Folger, Poole, & Stutman, 2001; Jarboe & Witteman, 1996).

An **avoidance style** is low in both assertiveness and collaboration. Rather than engage in disputes, conflict avoiders do not want to expend energy to advocate their own view or to collaborate with others. They may ignore the conflict or shift the conversation to a different topic. When people say, "I don't want to get into it with you" or "Let it be," they are indicating they don't want to get involved with the conflict.

The **distributive style** is a "win-lose" approach to conflict. Group members who employ such a style are high in assertiveness—they want to achieve their goals—and low in cooperativeness—they are relatively unconcerned whether the other disputant achieves his or her goals. The most important goal is to achieve your own goals and needs no matter the cost. Such a style emphasizes confrontation and attempting to control the conversation by persistently arguing for your own position.

An **integrative style** is high in both assertiveness and collaboration. Collaboration necessitates that both disputants be creative in finding ways that allow each to achieve personal goals (high assertiveness) while still allowing the other to achieve personal goals (high cooperation). For example, suppose a person is sitting in a library with a friend and asks permission to open the window in the room. The friend refuses it. If these two parties use a collaborating style, they may try to find a way to meet each other's needs. Upon exploring the issue, the two parties learn that the person who made the request did so because she was hot and the friend who refused the request did so because she was afraid the draft from the open window would blow their papers around. They collaboratively come up with a solution by opening the door to the room, which allows fresh air to enter and cool the room but without a draft (Fisher & Ury, 1991). Collaboration is about inventing creative "win-win" solutions to conflict.

It is tempting to think that an integrative style is the best way to manage conflict within a small group. However, each of these styles can be appropriate depending on the situation. Several factors such as the importance of the issue to self and other, the importance of maintaining a positive relationship, time pressure, and the level of trust can dictate what

Integrative conflict management means group members are willing to collaborate with one another.

style may be appropriate for a situation (Folger et al., 2001). A person may want to use the avoidance style if the issue is unimportant and if the other disputant has the power to punish the person if he or she disagrees. For example, suppose Rob in the opening vignette believed that certain recommendations were less important than others, and these less important recommendations were adamantly opposed by certain board members. Rob may avoid getting into a conflict over these relatively unimportant proposals to achieve his more important proposals.

On the other hand, say you have special knowledge or expertise about the problem or issue that the group is addressing or you will be held accountable for the consequences of the decision. In such circumstances, a distributive style may be appropriate. Finally, integration may be very useful when group members trust one another. Trust allows members to share information and engage in joint problem solving to work through a conflict. However, if low levels of trust exist, one may protect his or her power by adopting a distributive style.

Conflict styles have typically been studied as an individual characteristic, which means the focus has been on how an individual manages conflict within a group setting. However, it is important to examine the way conflict is collectively managed by group members because their interaction is likely to have important consequences for the way they perform their task. Over time, groups develop norms for how they will manage conflict and this influences how they perform a variety of activities such as decision making. Groups that use integrative conflict management style tend to make better decisions than groups that use avoidance or distributive styles (Kuhn & Poole, 2000). This may occur because groups are able to share information and engage in a rigorous debate over their

learning link

What are the differences among avoidance, distributive, and integrative conflict management styles?

▪ ▪ ▪

positions and issues. Examining conflict management as a collective group effort suggests the superiority of an integrative style, yet future research needs to be conducted that examines whether certain tasks or other situational variables influence its effectiveness.

What conflict management style should Rob select to manage the current problems at the AAC? Given the severity of financial issues, Rob cannot use avoidance; the financial issues are important and must be addressed. Given that his success at addressing these issues will depend on his working with the other board members in the future, a distributive style will not work because it would continue to separate Rob from the board. An integrative style seems most appropriate, but Rob is working with a highly fragmented and resistant board. To make an integrative style work in this situation, Rob may need to devote time in the immediate future to building trust with the other board and staff members, so they feel that a supportive climate exists for working through the conflict collaboratively.

Challenges to Leadership

As highlighted earlier in the chapter, group members have multiple motivations for entering a group, and these influence the way they go about creating relationships with other group members. For example, think of a time when your instructor or professor assigned a group project for a class. Many times such group projects are difficult because members have different expectations regarding the outcome. Some want to put out great effort to get an A because they feel it is important to do good work. Others may be satisfied with a C because the class is not in their major and not viewed as important. Similarly, part of Rob's difficulty in the chapter-opening story may have emerged from the different expectations of Rob held by different board members. Some wanted him to maintain the status quo and others desired change. A key challenge to small groups is to identify people's expectations, and if they are different, to learn how to work with them.

A second challenge that small groups face is the stability of membership in the group. Although it is possible for a small group to remain intact from its beginning until its end, it is more likely that group members will drop out and new members will join. For example, take a university department. Over time, some instructors and professors will stay and others will leave. When faculty leave, they are typically replaced by new instructors and professors. Why does this pose a challenge? On one hand, it may not. Group turnover can provide an opportunity for renewal and rejuvenation. New instructors and professors may provide fresh ideas, insights, and programs and foster innovation. On the other hand, faculty who have been in the department for a while may be resistant to change.

A **group phase** is a stage in the group's life span when there is a clearly defined purpose and theme for the group activity. Just as people sometimes go through a phase, when they constantly perform some activity, so do groups. Several models that identify phases of group development exist (Bales & Strodtbeck, 1951; Fisher, 1970; Tuckman and Jensen, 1977), yet most researchers share the belief that the following phases are important in group life:

> Orientation: Group members orient themselves to the task and the ways they should relate to one another. Discussion of roles, leadership, and guidelines for interaction characterize the orientation phase.
>
> Conflict: Group members offer their opinions regarding the task. Typically these opinions polarize the conversation, and disagreement and debate may occur. It is not unusual for members to try to persuade other members to adopt their way of thinking.

Emergence: Group members offer suggestions on how to perform the task. A collaboration among group members begins to develop a workable solution to the task.

Each of these phases suggests that group members create different kinds of relationships with each other. During the orientation phase, group members do not know and have not established relationships with each other. Therefore it becomes important to have conversation within the group that orients its members to one another and articulates how they will relate to one another and what kinds of roles each will assume. During the conflict phase, relationships among group members were created, and those relationships are put to the test as group members argue over how the task can best be accomplished. At this stage, group members need to talk in ways that resolve their conflicts and maintain their existing relationships. During the emergence stage, group members feel comfortable with their relationships and focus on the task at hand. They are able to reach a consensus on what solutions should be selected and implemented.

The impact of fluctuating group membership depends on the stage of development the group is in. If the group is in the orientation phase, shifting new members into that group may not pose a problem because the group is still in the process of developing an understanding of the task and their relationships with one another. Similarly, if the group is in the conflict phase there may be little impact when new members join the group. Because the group is in the middle of hashing out differences, adding new differences may not pose any difficulty. However, group turnover during the emergence phase may be problematic. By this time the group has established norms about how to act and developed policies and procedures for group behavior. New members at this stage of group development have the potential to disrupt the group.

Managing Leadership Challenges

Managing the complexity of group life can be difficult. Being able to keep the discussion on track, analyze problems and solutions in depth, manage a variety of conflicts, and have the ability to lead change in a group are difficult tasks. These tasks are made even more problematic when we recognize that group members may have different expectations and values and that group turnover can require groups to constantly revisit their norms and operating agreements. As you can see in the vignette that opened the chapter, Rob did not have the skills to manage the AAC board meeting. Three major communication skills allow competent leaders to address these challenges: (1) creating a supportive group climate, (2) exploring positions, and (3) framing the issue in a way that all group members can engage with.

Creating a Supportive Group Climate

Among the qualities of successful teams is that team members are highly motivated, have clear elevating goals, and are supportive of one another (LaFasto & Larson, 2001). Whether a team of championship professional athletes such as football's New England Patriots or a high-performing work team such as the design team that created the iPod or Microsoft's Xbox, successful groups have supportive member relationships. Group members are able to offer support to other members and motivate them to higher levels of group performance. Central to constructing supportive member relationships is the creation of a group environment. A **group environment** is the social climate in which group members communicate; it is informed by the feelings and emotions of group members.

Recognizing a group's current environment allows a competent communicator to select messages that either affirm constructive feelings and emotions or transform negative hostile environments.

Two different kinds of group environments exist (Gibb, 1961). A **supportive group environment** exists when group members collaborate with each other to achieve group goals jointly. The following types of communication are typical of supportive environments:

- Communication that describes, rather than evaluates, situations or feelings.
- A problem orientation, indicating a mutual interest in solving the problem rather than controlling or manipulating other group members' actions.
- Spontaneous openness and honesty, not a preconceived strategy that is disguised as being unpremeditated.
- Communication that conveys empathy and concern, not a neutrality or a lack of concern.
- Equal value assigned to all members and ideas, rather than assigning power, status, and values to a few members and ideas.
- An open give-and-take of ideas rather than an inflexibility about new and different ideas. (Lumsden & Lumsden, 1993, pp. 207–208)

Defensive group environments, in contrast, are characterized by a lack of trust and cooperation among group members. Such environments create competition among group members, arouse negative emotions between group members, and frustrate achieving group goals. They are created when group members negatively evaluate situations and feelings, manipulate others' actions, use ambiguity to gain control, demonstrate a lack of concern and caring, act as if their ideas are superior to others', and communicate that they are certain they are right in their thinking and others are wrong. Other group members typically view such behaviors as ineffective and inappropriate.

Competent small group communicators understand how constructing supportive group environments can generate positive results. For example, supportive environments can help groups accomplish work by creating feelings of affirmation among group members. On the other hand, defensive environments can frustrate group members and prevent them from accomplishing their task. Returning to the opening vignette, one reason Rob may have difficulty with the AAC board is that they have created a hostile group environment. Board members acted in ways that conveyed superiority and voiced their opinions in ways that indicated certainty that they knew the correct answer. Such communication arouses negative feelings for other group members and feeds the conflict among them. Success in transforming defensive group environments into supportive ones depends on how group members are able to manage conflict.

Two skills are particularly useful in creating supportive climates within groups: acknowledging and reflecting. **Acknowledging** helps members indicate that they understand one another, their situation, their process, and their actions. Group leaders and members can acknowledge a variety of issues, feelings, and attitudes during a group meeting, such as the following:

learning link

What are the differences between supportive and defensive group climates?

● ● ●

- problems and difficulties ("It sounds as though one of the problems you perceive is . . . ")
- what people want and need ("For you to feel we have arrived at a good solution, you need . . . ")

- differences and issues ("Where we in the group differ over this issue is . . . ")
- hard work and positive contributions ("I appreciate the hard work you have put in on this task.")
- positive, respectful interaction ("It really helps the discussion when we keep personal attacks out of it.")
- recognition of others ("Bob has done a tremendous job on this project.")
- progress on the task ("We've come a long way since we started. Let's summarize what we've done so far.")
- shared concerns and common ground ("What we share is . . . ")
- areas of consensus ("It sounds as though most of us agree that . . . ")
- decisions that have been made ("So, what we have decided is . . . ")

Acknowledgment serves two important functions. First, by highlighting points of difference and consensus, as well as progress and decisions that have been made, group members keep track of where they are in the discussion. Thus they are better able to participate and control their environment to bring about desirable goals. Second, acknowledgment can heighten motivation. When the contributions of group members are recognized, when positive moments during the interaction are praised, and when hard work is acclaimed, group members know what is expected and will be more likely to exert the effort to accomplish the task.

A second skill, **reflecting,** means repeating someone's feelings about what they have said. It helps check understanding, helps participants feel confirmed and acknowledged, and helps group members understand the emotional dimension of what others are saying. Here are some possible reflections one could offer during a group meeting:

- Reflect strong expressions of emotion: "You seem very upset."
- Reflect feelings that are especially pertinent to a member's position, interest, values, or perspective: "I see you really feel that all group members need to give the same level of effort to completing the project."
- Reflect feelings that may not be heard by other members of the group: "So Sandra, you feel pretty happy that Bri got her work in on time."
- Reflect feelings that come across better nonverbally than verbally: "This can be kind of stressful, huh?"

Reflecting recognizes the validity of a member's feelings and beliefs. It allows people to feel they have been heard, which helps build supportive climates.

Explaining Positions

Whether you are managing diverse points of view or conflict within a group, it is important to articulate your viewpoints in ways that are heard and understood by other group members and to inquire into the expressed viewpoints of other group members. Two skills are particularly useful to help you articulate and understand your own and others' views: (1) exploring people's interests and (2) giving accounts and explanations for your viewpoints as well as exploring other members' accounts of their viewpoints.

The ability to explore a person's interests requires you to distinguish between an individual's position and his or her interest (Fisher & Ury, 1991; Stone, Patton, & Heen, 2000). A **position** is a stated course of action that the person wants to see pursued in the

All group members have positions and interests that influence they way they work together in groups. Competent small group communicators are curious about and use communication to identify other members' positions and interests.

group. An **interest** is the underlying motivation or reason the person wants to pursue a particular position. For example, take the following statements of position:

- We need a clear timeline for completing the project.
- I just want to make sure this project is doable.
- I don't want to work on this project. It's a boring idea.

What interests underlie the positions taken in each of these statements? For the first statement, perhaps the group member's interest is to feel safe about being able to complete the project, and one way to achieve this is to have clear-cut timelines. Alternatively, perhaps the person's interest is efficiency—he or she may be involved in balancing a number of other projects. For the second statement, perhaps the group member's interest is self-esteem—the person wants to achieve success and feels this is possible only by taking on projects that are doable. Or the underlying interest might be the amount of effort devoted to the project—a doable project requires less effort than a demanding project. For the third statement, the interest underlying the position could be self-actualization; this group member may not want to work on the project because it will not allow a chance to grow and develop.

Why is listening for someone's interest important? Remember that people in groups may have hidden agendas; by listening for their interest and differentiating it from their position, you may be able to discern it. This strategy also better allows you to identify the multiple motivations of group members and to avoid the bad habit of mistaking a group member's position for his or her motivation.

Providing an explanation and using inquiry rest on your ability to delve into the assumptions, values, and beliefs used to form an opinion, explore the data used to arrive at the conclusion, and understand the way context influences people's conclusions. The Ladder of Inference presented in Figure 10.1 provides one way to articulate your position and inquire into other group members' positions in a rich and detailed manner (Senge, Kleiner, Roberts, Ross, & Smith, 1994). The **Ladder of Inference** is a tool that helps people articulate their reasoning processes. This same process can also help people explore others' reasoning.

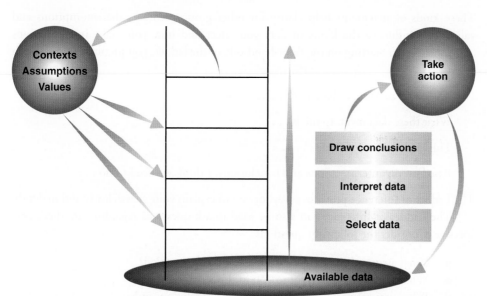

Figure 10.1

The Ladder of Inference

Group members can better articulate their own views and reasoning and inquire into those of others by using the Ladder of Inference.

Starting at the right-hand side of the figure, the Ladder of Inference suggests there is a wealth of information people can draw on when making conclusions. Given the large amount of information, we select only bits of the data and interpret it. From these interpretations, we draw conclusions that move us toward action. For example, suppose you are at a group meeting with a number of people for the very first time. You notice that Jose is talking a great deal. However, one thing that Jose said stands out in your mind: he used some incorrect statistics to make his point. You interpret that to mean he was not adequately prepared for the meeting and you conclude he is not going to be a productive team member. You then decide to ignore him for the rest of the meeting. This approach to drawing conclusions follows the Ladder of Inference. From all the available data that you could focus on regarding Jose, you selected his misuse of statistics. From this selected data, you interpreted that to mean he was unprepared. That led to the conclusion that Jose would be a poor team member, which led you to take the action of ignoring him during the rest of the discussion.

What influences your perception of what data is important or how to draw inferences? The Ladder of Inference suggests that context, assumptions, and values influence what data you select and the way you draw inferences and make conclusions. For example, suppose the meeting you and Jose attended had been scheduled for a long time and that it had been stressed that everyone was to be prepared. This might explain why you focused on the misstatement of statistics. Alternatively, perhaps you have made the assumption that all team members should be prepared for the meeting or have as a key personal value the importance of preparation. This may account for why you focused on that particular data and drew the conclusions you did.

The Ladder of Inference can help you explain your position clearly and inquire into others' positions and perspectives. Starting with the left-hand side of the ladder, you might say things such as these:

I think the situation calls for . . .

One of the assumptions I am making . . .

It is important to me because . . .

These kinds of statements help clarify for other group members the assumptions and values that influence the kinds of data you select and how you make interpretations and conclusions. Starting on the right-hand side of the ladder, you might say things such as this:

The data I'm using to base my inferences on are . . .

What these data mean to me is . . .

This leads me to conclude . . .

Based on my interpretations and conclusions, I think we need to do . . .

The Ladder of Inference provides a way for you to explain your views clearly and in depth.

The Ladder of Inference can also be used to ask questions regarding another's perspective. Consider the following questions:

- What assumptions are you making about this situation?
- What values are important to you in this situation?
- What data are you using to base your interpretations on?
- Why are you focusing on this data and not other data?
- How does it make sense for you to interpret the data in the way that you have?
- How do your interpretations influence what conclusions you are making?
- Why are you taking the actions you are, given your conclusions?

By asking these kinds of questions, you can gain a more detailed understanding of other group members' perspectives.

learning link

How do creating a supportive group climate, exploring positions, and framing help leaders manage situations?

· · ·

Framing the Issue

The foundation for most group work is the group's task, or the problem that is assigned. For groups to engage in a thoughtful and appropriate selection of alternatives, they must be focused on the key issues confronting them. Moreover, the issue needs to be framed in a way that allows group members to relate and connect with each other in a productive manner. **Issue framing** is a thoughtful way to define and clarify important questions and choices. Just as a photographer frames, or arranges, a picture to highlight certain features in the photograph and not others, groups frame, or formulate, discussion questions that they will deliberate. If the discussion question is not framed appropriately, the discussion will not address the concerns of the group and may result in unwanted conflict. Issue framing consists of a number of steps aimed at refining the discussion question for the group. The group may begin with a fuzzy statement of the problem and then develop a more precise wording of the problem. The group then identifies their choices to solve the problem.

Group members and leaders can help the group go through this process by doing the following:

1. Select a concern shared by most of the members of the group. Explore what is important to the group. What matters to them? Do not worry if participants disagree about this. The most controversial issues are often the most important concerns.
2. State the issue as a neutral open question with several possible answers. Do not state or propose a solution.

3. Word the question so that more than two options are possible. Avoid either-or questions. Leave open several possible choices for answering the question.

4. Find a wording that everyone can live with.

How might Rob have used issue framing to work with the board of directors? First, he might have asked what group members thought was their primary concern. They might have agreed it was low audience attendance. Second, Rob might have had the group play with the wording of the question. The group might have discussed the viability of the following three questions:

- Will a new advertising campaign increase audience attendance?
- Is a new advertising campaign or are lower ticket prices better?
- What opportunities do we have for increasing audience attendance?

The first question violates the rule of embedding a solution into the question. The second question not only embeds a solution into the question, it also phrases the question as

Table 10.3

Reframing Strategies

Reframing allows you to reinterpret what an event or issue means for people. Reframing can get people to think about an event or issue in creative and constructive ways.

Reframing Strategy	Example	Purpose
Reframe from past to future	*Member:* I'm tired of people not putting out enough effort. *Leader:* So you want to see more effort in the future, right?	Focusing on the future may open up new ways of viewing the present
Reframe from negative to positive	*Member:* I feel overworked. *Leader:* It sounds as if the group really respects the quality of work you do and gives you a lot of work.	Focusing on the positive can be motivating and encouraging
Reframe from personal attack to problem definition	*Member:* People are just not following through on their assignment. They are just so incompetent and inconsiderate. *Leader:* So part of the difficulty is failing to complete the assignment in a timely fashion.	Focusing on the problem versus the person can diminish feelings of defensiveness
Reframe from a demand to a goal or need	*Member:* If I don't get some help with this work, I quit! *Leader:* It sounds like you need some assistance to get your work done.	Focusing on what needs to be done as opposed to issuing demands opens up the space for creative solutions
Reframe from an individual concern to a group concern	*Member:* I'm just worried that I don't have the skills to do the work I've been assigned. *Leader:* So it would help if the group could work together to make sure you are assigned work that makes sense.	Placing the concern on the whole group takes pressure off the individual
Reframe from a concern to a vision	*Member:* I just don't want to do this project. It's too boring. *Leader:* So you would like to have a project that's exciting and interesting.	By focusing on a vision, people begin identifying what they like and what motivates them

an either-or: the group can select only one or the other option. The third question is the best because it provides enough focus for the group but does not prescribe the final solution. Moreover, it invites all group members to engage with the issue and to work collaboratively with one another.

Sometimes group members become stuck in their thinking. The way they have described or framed the issue may be continuing the conflict. One way to refocus the group is to reframe the discussion topic or issue. Reframing is restating something in a new, constructive way. It helps soften and neutralize hostile comments, encourage progress, clarify the issue, and introduce creative possibilities. For example, a work team may be having conflict over the men's treatment of the women on the team. The way the group might have framed the conflict is in terms of sexual harassment. Yet each time the group talks about sexual harassment, its members get into major conflict—the men deny they are engaging in sexual harassment and the women maintain they are. No amount of explaining viewpoints or inquiring into other members' viewpoints is going to help the group get beyond the conflict. The more group members explain their position or the more they inquire into the views of other group members, the more they come into conflict.

In this instance, the group could reframe the topic to one of creating positive working relationships instead of ending sexual harassment. This reframe may allow the group to talk about the issue more productively as it shifts the responsibility for maintaining a good working relationship to all group members. Reframing can be accomplished in a variety of ways (Table 10.3). The power of reframing lies in its ability to enable group members to see situations in new ways and represents a useful leadership tool for creating change and managing conflict.

 ## Chapter Summary

The increasing complexity of group tasks and a rapidly changing environment have heightened the need for effective leadership in small groups. Small group leadership requires a working knowledge of (1) managing change in small groups and (2) managing conflict. Managing change means recognizing whether the group is engaged in technical or adaptive work. When it is technical work, the leader may adopt a more autocratic style and inform the group members of what needs to be accomplished. When the work is adaptive work, the group leader may need to work more collaboratively and democratically with group members to foster innovation. Group conflicts can occur over interpersonal relationships and the group's emotional climate (affective conflict), the group's task or issues (ideational conflict), and the procedures that should be employed during group discussion (procedural conflict). Managing these various conflicts means mastering a variety of conflict management styles, including avoidance, distributive, and integrative styles.

Small group leaders face two significant challenges to their competence: (1) differing goals, expectations, and needs of group members and (2) the stability of group membership.

These challenges can be met by engaging in three important communication skills. First, providing social support through the skills of acknowledgment and reflecting allows group members to feel their voices have been heard, which in turn can help create supportive group environments. Second, explaining positions using the Ladder of Inference can help articulate the reasons and motivations of group members that may lead them into conflict or resisting leadership. Third, framing issues in ways that allow group members to work collaboratively helps build supportive group environments and manage conflict.

Study and Review

The premium companion website for *Human Communication* offers a broad range of resources that will help you better understand the material in this chapter, complete assignments, and succeed on tests. The website resources include

- Interactive self-assessments, competency grids, and other tools
- Web links, practice activities, self-quizzes, and a sample final exam

For more information about this text's electronic learning resources, consult the *Guide to Online Resources for Human Communication* or visit **http://communication .wadsworth.com/morreale2.**

Key Terms

The key terms below are defined in the chapter on the pages indicated. They are also presented alphabetically with definitions in the Glossary, which begins on page 467. The book's website includes flashcards and crossword puzzles to help you learn these terms and the concepts they represent.

Building Knowledge

The following questions are among the practice activities on the book's website.

1. How does the nature of the group task influence the type of leadership that small groups need? What are the different skills associated with technical and adaptive work?
2. What are the defining characteristics of conflict? Under what conditions would group members engage in affective, ideational, or procedural conflict?

3. Is using an integrative style the best way to manage group conflict? When might it be desirable to use avoidance and distributive conflict management styles?

4. What are the differences between supportive and defensive group environments? What kinds of communication can help create supportive group environments?

5. What components make up the Ladder of Inference? How might you use the Ladder of Inference to explain your reasoning to other people? To inquire into other people's views?

6. How does framing contribute to constructing a supportive group environment? What are the different strategies leaders can use to frame and reframe issues and problems?

 ## Building Skills

The exercises below are among the practice activities on the book's website.

Individual Exercises

1. Consider a group you belong to in which you have made arguments or stated conclusions during discussion. List two or three arguments or conclusions that you made. Using the Ladder of Inference, evaluate each and answer the following questions:
   a. What assumptions was your conclusion based on?
   b. What data did you select to make your conclusion?
   c. What inferences did you draw from these data?
   d. What kind of future actions did you take based on your conclusion?
   Consider arguments or conclusions you have heard in the discussion that didn't make much sense to you. Using the Ladder of Inference, draw up a list of questions you could use to explore the reasoning the person used to draw the conclusion.

2. Draw two columns on a piece of paper. In the left-hand column, list the typical kinds of conflict you have in groups. In the right-hand column, describe the kind of conflict management style you use to solve the conflict. Go back to the left-hand column and classify the conflict as either an affective, ideational, or procedural conflict. Analyze the data in the two columns. Does your conflict management style vary according to the type of conflict?

3. Identify a leader who has recently instituted some change in a group. Interview that group leader and explore what he or she did to create the change. What techniques or strategies did he or she employ? Did the leader view the change as involving technical or adaptive work?

4. Identify an issue or topic that is important to a group you belong to. Using the steps in issue framing, generate three acceptable discussion questions that could guide the group discussion.

5. Go to the leadership website for the Jepson School of Leadership Studies at the University of Richmond at **http://oncampus.richmond.edu/academics/ leadership/courses/index.html.** Examine the course offerings for the school. Given the information on the website, prepare a presentation for your class on the important knowledge and skills effective leaders may need to possess.

1. In a group of four to five people, generate a list of common statements people make that can disrupt a discussion. Using Table 10.3 as a guide, develop three re-frames. What kinds of openings do the reframes create to get the discussion back on track?

2. With four to five people, select a conflict that might emerge in a small group. Have members play roles using the avoidance, distributive, and integrative conflict management styles to explore how that conflict would be managed. How does communication differ according to each style? What kinds of roles do different group members take when they perform a particular style? Which conflict management style best manages this conflict? Why?

3. In a group of four to five people, select an important issue or problem currently being discussed on your campus. Would you characterize this issue as being a technical or adaptive problem? If you were to lead an effort to address the problem, what steps would you take?

4. Using InfoTrac College Edition, look up the article "Leadership for a new age," *Nation's Business,* May 1997, *85*(5), pp. 18–25, by Sharon Nelton. Read the article. Prepare a presentation for your class that answers these two questions: (1) Why will more democratic leadership styles be more prominent in the future? (2) What allows individuals to become more democratic and participative in their leadership style?

References

Bales, R. F. (1970). *Personality and interpersonal behavior.* New York: Holt, Rinehart & Winston.

Bales, R. F., & Strodtbeck, F. L. (1951). Phases in group problem-solving. *Journal of Abnormal and Social Psychology, 46,* 485–495.

Barge, J. K. (1996). Leadership skills and the dialectics of leadership in group decision making. In R. Y. Hirokawa & M. S. Poole (Eds.), *Communication and group decision making* (2nd ed., pp. 301–344). Thousand Oaks, CA: Sage.

Barge, J. K. (2003). Leadership as organizing. In R. Y. Hirokawa, R. S. Cathcart, L. A. Samovar, and L. D. Henman (Eds.), *Small group communication* (pp. 199–214). Los Angeles: Roxbury.

Barge, J. K., & Oliver, C. (2003). Working with appreciation in managerial practice. *Academy of Management Review, 28,* 124–142.

Benne, K. D., & Sheats, P. (1948). Functional roles of group members. *Journal of Social Issues, 4,* 41–49.

Bennis, W. G., & Nanus, B. (1985). Leaders: *The strategies of taking charge.* San Francisco: HarperCollins.

Bolman, L. G., & Deal, T. E. (2003). *Reframing organizations: Artistry, choice, and leadership* (2nd ed.). San Francisco: Jossey-Bass.

Eagly, A. H., & Carli, L. L. (2003). The female leadership advantage: An evaluation of the evidence. *The Leadership Quarterly, 14,* 807–834.

Eagly, A. H., & Johnson, B. T. (1990). Gender and leadership style: A meta-analysis. *Psychological Bulletin, 108,* 233–256.

Fisher, B. A. (1970). Decision emergence: Phases in group decision making. *Speech Monographs, 37,* 53–66.

Fisher, R., & Ury, W. (1991). *Getting to yes* (2nd ed.). New York: Penguin.

Folger, J. P., Poole, M. S., & Stutman, R. K. (2001). *Working through conflict* (4th ed.). New York: Longman.

Galanes, G. J. (2003). In their own words: An exploratory study of bona fide group leaders. *Small Group Research, 34,* 741–770.

Gibb, J. R. (1961). Defensive communication. *Journal of Communication, 11,* 141–148.

Heifetz, R. A. (1994). *Leadership without easy answers.* Cambridge, MA: Belknap.

Heifetz, R. A., & Linsky, M. (2002). *Leadership on the line: Staying alive through the dangers of leading.* Boston: Harvard Business School Press.

Helgesen, S. (1995). *Web of inclusion: A new architecture for building great organizations.* New York: Doubleday.

Jarboe, S. C., & Witteman, H. R. (1996). Intragroup conflict management in task-oriented groups: The influence of problem sources and problem analysis. *Small Group Research, 27,* 316–338.

Kouzes, J. M., & Posner, B. Z. (2003). *The leadership challenge: How to get extraordinary things done in organizations* (2nd ed.). San Francisco: Jossey-Bass.

Kuhn, T., & Poole, M. S. (2000). Do conflict management styles affect group decision making? Evidence from a longitudinal field study. *Human Communication Research, 26,* 558–590.

LaFasto, F., & Larson, C. (2001). *When teams work best.* Thousand Oaks, CA: Sage.

Lewin, K., Lippitt, R., & White, R. K. (1939). Patterns of aggressive behavior in experimentally created "social climates." *Journal of Science Psychology, 10,* 271–299.

Lumsden, G., & Lumsden, D. (1993). *Communicating in groups and teams: Sharing leadership.* Belmont, CA: Wadsworth.

Morgan, G. (1997). *Images of organization* (2nd ed.). Thousand Oaks, CA: Sage.

Putnam, L. L., & Poole, M. S. (1987). Conflict and negotiation. In F. M. Jablin, L. L. Putnam, K. H. Roberts, & L. W. Porter (Eds.), *Handbook of organizational communication* (pp. 549–599). Thousand Oaks, CA: Sage.

Senge, P. M., Kleiner, A., Roberts, C., Ross, R. B., & Smith, B. J. (1994). *The fifth discipline fieldbook.* New York: Currency Doubleday.

Stogdill, R. M. (1948). Personal factors associated with leadership: A survey of the literature. *Journal of Psychology, 25,* 35–71.

Stone, D., Patton, B., & Heen, S. (2000). *Difficult conversations: How to discuss what matters most.* New York: Penguin.

Thompson, M. D. (2000). Gender, leadership, orientation, and effectiveness: Testing the theoretical models of Bolman & Deal and Quinn. *Sex Roles, 4,* 969–992.

Tuckman, B. W., & Jensen, M. (1977). Stages of small-group development revisited. *Group and Organization Studies, 2,* 419–427.

Zaccaro, S. J., Rittman, A. L., & Marks, M. A. (2001). Team leadership. *The Leadership Quarterly, 12,* 451–483.

Leadership Competence Skills Grid _____

To help you understand how to use this grid, the skills displayed by Rob in the opening vignette of this chapter have been analyzed below. Examine that analysis and then think about a recent leadership situation you were in and what you could have done more competently. First, describe the context of the leadership situation in the spaces provided. Next, analyze your leadership skills based on the skills explained in this chapter. In the first column, briefly describe and give examples of how your skills might have been less than competent. Using these less competent skills as a point of comparison to fill in the second column, describe the skills you think would have been perceived as more competent in the particular context. With practice, you will find you can use this grid to help develop your listening skills for future leadership situations, as well as to analyze leadership situations you have already experienced.

ANALYZING ROB'S LEADERSHIP SKILLS

Context

CULTURE: Theater staff and board of directors in North American context

---

TIME: Weekday evening

RELATIONSHIP: Executive director-board member, staff-board member, executive director-staff

---

PLACE: In the meeting room of the theater

FUNCTION: Rob must manage the conflicts that are surfacing due to proposed changes

---

LEADERSHIP SKILLS	LESS COMPETENT	MORE COMPETENT
EXPLAINING POSITIONS	Not providing the reasons why the meeting was necessary; not using data to base one's inferences or conclusions; not explaining the reasoning process behind one's conclusion	Stating values or assumptions that inform your position (for example, "The reason I think this is important is because ..."); explaining one's reasoning (for example, "I'm basing my position on ... "); inquiring into the reasoning other group members use
FRAMING THE ISSUE	Focusing on the past problem without consideration of the group's dreams; framing issues in ways that privilege one side over another in a group discussion; framing issues in ways that fragment and divide the group	Focusing on the future (for example, "In the future you'd like to see ... "); focusing on the positive elements of the situation (for example, "One of the strengths of this group is ... "); focusing on the problem not the person (for example, "The challenge we are facing ... "); focusing on group versus concern (for example, "When we as a group focus on ... ")
CREATING A SUPPORTIVE CLIMATE: ■ **ACKNOWLEDGING COMMENTS** ■ **REFLECTING COMMENTS**	Ignoring people's needs; criticizing or diminishing the significance of others' ideas and feelings; recognizing only one side of the issue without giving others' opinions consideration	Acknowledging difficulties or differences among issues (for example, "It sounds as though one of the problems ... " and "Where we disagree in the group is ... "); acknowledging people's needs and wants (for example, "It sounds that for you to feel good about this, you need ... "); acknowledging consensus on concerns (for example, "What we agree on ... "); reflecting other group members' emotions and feelings (for example, "You seem really upset.")

ANALYZING YOUR LEADERSHIP SKILLS

Context

CULTURE:

TIME:

RELATIONSHIP:

PLACE:

FUNCTION:

LEADERSHIP SKILLS	LESS COMPETENT	MORE COMPETENT
EXPLAINING POSITIONS		
FRAMING THE ISSUE		
CREATING A SUPPORTIVE CLIMATE: ■ **ACKNOWLEDGING COMMENTS** ■ **REFLECTING COMMENTS**		

© David Greenwood/Taxi/Getty Images

LEARNING OBJECTIVES | After studying this chapter, you should be able to

1. Explain the history of public speaking in rhetoric.

2. Define public speaking and describe the types of speeches and types of delivery.

3. Analyze the audience and situation and adapt your speech to what you learn.

4. Choose and narrow a speech topic.

5. Develop a speech purpose and thesis statement.

6. Gather support materials to accomplish your speech purpose.

7. Select an organizational pattern and create an outline for your speech.

8. Plan an introduction, body, transitions, and conclusion for your speech.

Speech Preparation: Building Knowledge

Althea approached speech preparation the way many students do, facing a blank computer screen the night before her speech. She had chosen a topic and done a little research for the speech she had to give in her marketing class on Tuesday morning. But when she got home from school at 8 o'clock Monday night, she hadn't yet organized her support materials or prepared an outline for the speech. She found herself with a mountain of information that lacked organization and focus. By midnight, she had sifted through her research material and achieved some semblance of a speech outline but had no energy left to practice the presentation. So she went to bed, planning to arrive early enough at school to practice with her friend Zachary, who no doubt was well prepared for his presentation.

Zachary was ready to present his speech. When the assignments were given out, he took the time to get acquainted with other students in the class before choosing his speech topic. He was surprised to learn that most of his classmates were interested in job skills needed in the marketplace, but they were not well informed about the need for on-the-job communication and public speaking skills. Based on that bit of information, Zak chose the importance of public speaking in a business setting as his speech topic. The purpose of his speech would be to motivate other business majors like himself to think about the benefits of public speaking skills and continue to improve theirs beyond graduation. He interviewed his manager at work and also the developer of a website about the importance of public speaking in the work setting. He located several good sources of information on the Internet and in the campus library and prepared an outline for presenting the speech. He had even practiced ahead of time using a computerized presentation as a visual aid. You can probably guess what happened in the marketing class the next morning. Not only did Zachary get a higher grade than Althea, his speech was better received and he felt more confident presenting it. Zak presented his speech competently, because he understood the importance of speech preparation. ■

Competent speech preparation actually begins with knowledge, with an understanding of the roots of public speaking in rhetoric, the various types of speeches, and the different ways that you can deliver a speech.

Rhetoric and Public Speaking

When you present your next speech, you are participating in the age-old tradition of rhetoric. **Rhetoric**—the art of influencing an audience through words—dates back many centuries, having roots in the Greek and Roman periods of history.

The Greek Period

Long ago, before 500 BC, a teacher and his student, Corax and Tisias, taught ordinary citizens on the island of Sicily how to organize arguments in their own defense for presentation in court. The work of Corax and Tisias led to the early tradition of rhetoric in ancient Greece. In 481 BC, a group of Greek philosophers called sophists began to teach about thinking and speaking persuasively. Other Greek writers later criticized the sophists for focusing too much on technique and not enough on the content of a speech. As a result, like rhetoric, the term *sophistry* is sometimes used today to refer to empty or meaningless use of language. One sophist, Protagoras—still known today as the father of debate—required his students to first speak in favor of an issue and then argue against it, to develop an understanding of the reasoning on both sides. Isocrates, the father of eloquence, carried on the traditions of the sophists. He had his students learn about a variety of subjects and form political, social, and ethical judgments, so they would become better citizens and more eloquent public speakers.

Plato, one of the most famous Greek philosophers, stressed participation in **dialectic,** a question-and-answer process used to examine all sides of an issue in search of the truth. Another famous Greek philosopher and writer, Aristotle, saw logic as essential to understanding any subject. He was the first to describe a system of persuasion for Western culture based on logic, emotion, and speaker credibility. That system is still used today to help students understand persuasive speaking (see Chapter 13).

The Roman Period

The Romans continued the tradition of public speaking that began with the Greeks. In the 2nd century BC, Cicero combined rhetoric and philosophy in his writings about public speaking. Like the Greeks, he believed good public speakers needed a well-rounded education, but his unique contribution was a refined process for analyzing issues and developing a speech.

Public speaking can trace its roots back to the rhetorical traditions of ancient Greece and Rome.

In the 1st century AD, another Roman, Quintilian, extended the Roman tradition of public speaking by developing a series of questions to encourage creative and critical thinking on important social and philosophical issues. Quintilian is credited with a concern for public speakers being ethical as well as effective. If you recall from Chapter 2, competent communication is described as containing both these elements. In his early writings, Quintilian described the ideal speaker as a good person who spoke well. By that, he meant that an effective speaker is also ethical and of good character.

The basic ideas about rhetoric introduced centuries ago by the Greeks and Romans have endured until the present day. Those **rhetorical canons** represent five activities that all public speakers engage in when preparing and presenting a speech.

- **Invention** is identifying—or inventing—the materials that will make up your speech, including a topic and information to support it.
- **Arrangement** is organizing—or arranging—what you have invented in a logical and effective manner to accomplish the goal of the speech.
- **Style** is the manner and way you give the speech, most particularly the way you use language.
- **Delivery** is the presentation of the speech itself, how it is actually delivered to the audience.
- **Memory**—memorizing your speech—is a rhetorical canon of less importance today because speeches typically are not memorized by public speakers.

The ability of citizens in contemporary society to use these canons to debate logically and argue effectively in public continue to be important. And recent studies tell us that it is possible to develop these skills. Public speaking training, like you are now getting, prepares

learning link

How might ordinary citizens in the 21st century use public speaking skills to contribute to their communities and to a better society? What are the challenges in today's society to speaking ethically?

• • •

student speakers to participate effectively in civil, robust, and effective public discourse (Gayle, 2004). Given this possibility, let's now think about what public speaking is and how it works.

What Is Public Speaking

Public speaking is communication from one to many. A single person—or sometimes a group of people—presents a message to a larger number of people, who usually do not have speaking roles except sometimes asking questions. These speeches can be categorized according to the type of speech—its purpose—and how the speech is delivered or presented.

Types of Speeches

Although in the future you may be asked to give a speech to entertain an audience or commemorate a special occasion, the two types of speeches covered in most public speaking classes are informative and persuasive. An **informative speech** has the purpose of communicating something new or a new perspective to an audience and moving listeners to greater understanding or insight. A **persuasive speech** has the purpose of influencing an audience's attitudes, beliefs, values, or behaviors and moving listeners to change or to action of some kind.

Your success at work may depend in part on how competently you can present informative and persuasive speeches.

learning link

Is the ability to present an informative speech or to present a persuasive speech a more valuable skill for most people?

• • •

Types of Delivery

Both types of speeches—informative and persuasive—can be presented using any one of four different methods of delivery: impromptu, extemporaneous, manuscript, or memorized. Each type of delivery involves a different amount of preparation time and is appropriate to use in different public speaking situations.

The **impromptu speech** is delivered with the least amount of preparation, usually with little or no time to plan your remarks. Your first speech in a public speaking class could be an impromptu, perhaps a speech of self-introduction or on another topic assigned by your instructor. If that happens, you can borrow some hints from debaters who are trained to prepare remarks quickly during fast-paced debates (Davis & Dickmeyer, 1993; Voth, 1997). Here is a quick summary of their good advice:

- First, keep your composure and try to relax.
- Before you speak, jot down quick notes to focus and organize what you will say.
- Quickly figure out your single most important point and something to illustrate and support it. Keep your remarks organized around that central theme or idea.
- Decide on a simple introduction, middle, and conclusion to organize what you will say.
- When you get to your conclusion, say it and stop speaking. The biggest mistake impromptu speakers make is talking on and on.

THE WIZARD OF ID *by BRANT PARKER and JOHNNY HART*

Listeners appreciate brevity in impromptu speeches.

Unlike the impromptu, an **extemporaneous speech** is carefully planned and prepared ahead of time. It is delivered in a conversational tone of voice using note cards or a presentational outline to remember key ideas and information. Because your note cards or outline contain only key words to remind you of what to say, the wording of the speech varies each time it is presented, creating an illusion of spontaneity. Extemporaneous speaking is a popular type of delivery in college classrooms, as well as in businesses and organizations. Despite its advantages, this type of delivery makes it difficult to keep within a time limit. You can remedy this problem by including less information and practicing the speech ahead of time to be sure you can cover what is on your note cards.

Speech instructors agree that students who practice before presenting give better speeches and get better grades. Another problem with extemporaneous speeches, researchers have discovered, is that your anxiety may be higher than if you are reading your speech aloud to the audience (Feldman, Cohen, Hamrick, & Lepore, 2004). Again, practicing before presenting will help to handle this anxiety.

A **manuscript speech** is written out ahead of time and read word for word to the audience. If you were to write out the content of each note card or item from the speech outline for an extemporaneous speech, it would become a manuscript speech. This type of delivery is called for when complete accuracy is necessary, such as a keynote address at an important conference or a business meeting.

Although accuracy and formality are advantages, a problem with this type of delivery is a lack of spontaneity—speakers sometimes make less eye contact and gesture less as they read the speech. You can handle this problem in the following ways: When preparing the manuscript, use more adverbs and adjectives to liven up the speech, and use shorter paragraphs, which are easier to come back to after looking up. Type the manuscript in a large typeface for ease of reading. And practice with the manuscript, so you memorize some parts and can say them to the audience instead of just reading them.

A **memorized speech** requires the most preparation because it is fully written out and memorized ahead of time, then spoken to the audience word for word. Like a manuscript speech, this type of delivery is used when accuracy is crucial. This type of delivery is the most time-consuming and frequently the least effective because it can appear rehearsed and insincere. Furthermore, if the speech is interrupted for some reason, you may lose your place in the text. These problems can be avoided by practicing the speech so much that you can convey spontaneity and sincerity to the audience when you deliver it.

Preparing with Competence

In addition to understanding the types of speeches and delivery, competent speech preparation involves following the same steps that Zachary used to develop his speech for the marketing class.

1. Carefully analyze the audience and the speaking situation and adapt your speech to what you learn.
2. Based on that analysis, choose and narrow a topic for your speech.
3. Develop a clear and specific purpose for your topic and a thesis statement, a central idea, for your speech.
4. Gather support materials to help accomplish the speech purpose and link those materials clearly to your central idea.
5. Organize the information in an outline that includes an introduction, body, transitions, and conclusion.

learning link

Are all the speech preparation steps equally essential to competence? Which are the most important?

• • •

Researchers provide evidence of how important these preparation steps are. One research study, involving 119 public speaking students, investigated the relationship between preparation and public speaking performance (Menzel & Carrell, 1994). The quality of the students' speech performances, as indicated by their grades, was directly proportional to total preparation time, including the amount of time spent conducting research, time spent preparing a visual aid, the number of times the speech was rehearsed before an audience, and the amount of time spent rehearsing silently and out loud. The lesson is clear: speech preparation is a crucial part of public speaking competence. Let's now consider each of the speech preparation steps in more detail.

Analyzing the Audience and Situation

As you learned in Chapter 2, the context in which communication takes place influences and shapes any communication event. Therefore competence in public speaking calls for carefully preparing and adapting your speech to the particular context.

Like Zachary and Althea, the context in which you present speeches in college probably will be a public speaking course or a class that requires individual or group presentations. Outside school, you will give presentations at work, at community gatherings, on special occasions, or at various social events. To adapt your speeches to these as well as other contexts, you must consider two critical components of the context—the audience or listeners and the particular speaking situation.

Analyzing the Audience

Experts in public speaking say the number one reason a speech fails to achieve its goal is because the speaker does not know his or her listeners well enough (St. John, 1995). **Audience analysis** is the process a speaker uses to ascertain relevant facts and information about the listeners that then shape how the speech is prepared and delivered. The key word here is "relevant." You do not need to find out everything about the audience, but you do need to be aware of anything about them that will affect how they perceive and react to you and your speech.

In Chapter 3, you learned how differences in perception result in people interpreting communication events and messages quite differently. By engaging in audience analysis, you anticipate these differences in perception and adapt your speech to what you learn. Three sets of characteristics about the listeners are important to know: (1) personal (demographic) characteristics, (2) cultural characteristics, and (3) psychological characteristics (Morreale & Bovee, 1997).

As you analyze these characteristics, it is helpful to think about the audience on a scale ranging from highly similar (the audience members are much like one another) to highly diverse (the audience members are not very much alike). If there is a high level of similarity, it will be easier to choose a topic that will appeal to the majority of your listeners. Greater diversity in personal, cultural, or psychological characteristics represents a greater challenge as you choose a topic and adapt it to the particular audience.

learning link

What characteristics of the audience are most important to consider if you are speaking to an audience that is highly diverse? How should you adapt a speech to that diversity?

• • •

Personal Characteristics

Personal characteristics include objective demographic information about the audience members. Most relevant are the listeners' ages, household types, education, occupation, and income levels.

Age is often an indicator of the concerns or interests of listeners. For example, you can assume that most college students are less interested in the details of a retirement plan than a group of adults in their 50s or 60s. Age also tells you what major historical events the listeners may or may not be aware of. If your audience is fairly similar in age, be sure your topic is one that appeals to the average age of the listeners. If they are diverse in age, provide background information for any ideas with which they may be unfamiliar.

Household type—a description of who is living in the household—is another personal characteristic that may affect audience reactions. At one time, households in the United States were characterized by a higher level of similarity than they are today. For instance, in 1970, households of married couples with only one wage earner and with children were the most common household arrangement (49%); in 1998, only 26% of homes were constituted in this way; in 2003, only 23% (U.S. Census Bureau, 2003). Today's diverse household types include many people living alone, households with two working parents, single-parent families, stepfamilies, intergenerational families with grandparents and grandchildren living under the same roof, and gay and lesbian households. If you reference any aspect of home life in your speech, allow for the fact that your listeners may live in different household types. Choose a topic and develop your speech so it is equally appealing and respectful of all the listeners.

Knowing the educational level of your listeners will also help you prepare a speech they will relate to and find engaging. Although education sometimes shapes what people are interested in, keep in mind that education and intelligence are not the same. Many highly intelligent and successful people have not attained high levels of academic achievement, but they do have inquiring and quick minds and are interested in a wide variety of topics. Let the educational background of your listeners guide how you develop your topic. If the topic is one the audience would know about only through more education, fill them in so they can appreciate it.

What audience members do for a living and how much they earn can also provide insights into what they will find interesting. Occupational choices sometimes indicate people's likes and dislikes, and their income may shape what they are able to do in life and what they want to hear about in a speech. If there is a high level of occupational similarity, choose a topic with appeal to those similarities. If there is a high level of economic diversity, be sure your topic will be interesting, regardless of income level.

*"Good God! He's giving the
white-collar voters' speech to the blue collars."*

Audience analysis is essential whether you're running for public office or giving a speech in class.

Cultural Characteristics

Some communication scholars say that culture—defined in Chapter 2 as enduring patterns of thought, value, and behavior that define a group of people—affects and shapes everything listeners perceive, learn, understand, and know. Therefore, cultural characteristics of audience members influence what they expect from a speech and how they will react to it.

Cultural characteristics of importance to public speaking come from two kinds of groups that listeners belong to: those they are born into or grow up in—such as their biological sex, race, and ethnicity—and groups they may choose to belong to—such as their religion, clubs, political parties, or other sorts of organizations. By becoming aware of the groups your listeners belong to, you can prepare a more effective speech that appeals to and respects their culturally diverse experiences and perspectives.

This is particularly important in contemporary society, because today's audiences often represent a rich mix of interests and racial and ethnic backgrounds (Nolan, 1999). Indeed, statisticians tell us that the United States is becoming increasingly multicultural and multiracial. Table 11.1 presents projections on diversity in the United States to 2050.

The Close-Up on Diversity box provides some concrete guidelines for analyzing a diverse audience and adapting your speech so it is appropriate for the listeners and effective in the particular context.

Psychological Characteristics

The audience's **psychological characteristics** that must be analyzed include their needs and motivation and their attitudes, beliefs, and values. These characteristics represent subjective information that frequently is more difficult to determine than objective, personal characteristics. At a glance, you can estimate the average age and even income of an audience, but ascertaining what they might need or value is far more difficult.

Communication experts agree that it is essential to assess and understand an audience's needs and keep those needs in mind to develop meaningful messages and effective speeches (Langham, 1994; Monroe & Nelson, 2004). The reason is that most people are motivated to listen more attentively if the information presented relates to a topic they need to know about. Human needs can be divided into five categories: physiological, safety and security, love, self-esteem, and self-actualization (Maslow, 1954). If your speech focuses on satisfying one of these needs, such as ensuring public safety in the troubling times since September 11, 2001, or achieving a higher level of self-esteem or self-actualization through one's work, the audience is more likely to be motivated to pay attention to what you say.

Along with listeners' needs, their attitudes, beliefs, and values affect their reactions to a speech. Figure 11.1 illustrates how these characteristics are embedded in a person's

Table 11.1

Diversity in the United States by 2050

By the year 2050, the racial and ethnic demographics of United States society will shift significantly. A competent and ethical public speaker prepares and presents with sensitivity to the diversity of contemporary audiences.

Race/Ethnicity	July 1, 2005	July 1, 2015	July 1, 2025	July 1, 2050
White	199,802	205,019	209,117	207,901
Minorities	86,179	105,115	125,933	186,029
Hispanic	36,057	46,705	58,930	96,508
Black	35,485	39,512	43,511	53,555
American Indian	2,183	2,461	2,744	3,534
Asian	2,454	16,437	20,748	32,432

U.S. DIVERSITY

SOURCE: U.S. Bureau of the Census (2000), Population Projections.

psychological makeup, with values at the core or center of the person, overlaid by the person's beliefs and then attitudes. For the purpose of audience analysis, the following descriptions clarify these three psychological aspects of a person.

Attitudes are psychological reactions to another person, object, or concept that affect people's behaviors. Our attitudes represent what we like or dislike, our positive or negative inclinations, ranging on a continuum from favorable to neutral to hostile. For instance, if you have a generally positive attitude toward work, most days you go to your job cheerfully. **Beliefs** are people's basic convictions about what is true or false, based on their own knowledge and experience. Beliefs represent what we have learned or come to know as a result of our exposure to others and to our culture. If you hold the belief that people should work hard to get ahead, you will apply yourself at work and give your all to your job. **Values** are deeply rooted clusters of attitudes and beliefs that reflect what a person considers important or unimportant, worthy or unworthy. Our values act as the criteria we often use for making big choices and judgments in life (Johannesen, 2001). If you highly value professional success and achieving status in the workplace, that value will shape your

CloseUp *on Diversity*

Analyzing and Adapting to a Diverse Audience

MOST STATISTICIANS AGREE THAT THE UNITED States is becoming increasingly diverse. What's more, they predict that one of the most important social trends that will directly affect most people in the future will be changes in the racial and ethnic makeup of the nation. The prediction is that the overall proportions of white and nonwhite populations in the United States will shift significantly by the middle of the 21st century (see Table 11.1). Whites are currently a majority, but by or before 2050, they will account for only about half the total population, and the other half will be made up of a mix of other racial and ethnic groups—African Americans, Asian Americans, Hispanic Americans, and so forth.

Given how diverse society is becoming, competent public speakers are ethically bound to prepare and present their speeches with sensitivity to diverse audiences. One way to accomplish that is through culturally sensitive audience analysis. The following suggestions can guide public speaking in a more diverse society:

- Avoid stereotyping. Despite the need to consider similarities in the personal and psychological characteristics of the listeners, don't assume any characteristic is always true of all of your listeners simply because they belong to a certain group. Remember, no matter what group they belong to, people are individuals, and they prefer to be treated that way.

- Avoid ethnocentric communication. Ethnocentric communicators, as you learned in Chapter 4, think their own meanings for words are right and they reject other meanings as wrong. Don't use your own culture or group as the standard against which the communication of others is measured and evaluated. To avoid ethnocentrism as a public speaker, do not assume that your culture and subculture's attitudes, opinions, or behaviors are right or better than those of your listeners. Do not suggest there is one right or normal way to do things that is reflected by your

group but not by a group to which your listeners belong.

- Avoid racial and ethnic bias, as well as gender bias. Don't make judgments about listeners' preferences, interests, abilities, or knowledge of certain topics based on their race, ethnicity, or gender. In any society, including a highly diverse one, individuality transcends culturally based characteristics.

- Show an interest in other cultures. Your listeners will appreciate it if you include in your speech the contribution of diverse opinions or observations from members of other cultures. Become well informed about the cultural background of the listeners and communicate your interest in them without appearing condescending or insincere.

- Respect differences in how other cultures communicate. Adapt your communication style to the audience, but do so without offending your listeners. If you know the audience prefers a certain communication style, either more relaxed or more formal, use that approach when giving your speech. People from Kenya, for example, tend to prefer a very ceremonial public speaking style and place importance on publicly recognizing people of status in a speech (Miller, 2002). Without knowing it, your speech could fail to impress and might even offend listeners from Kenya.

- Respect how different cultures organize and present information. Some cultures prefer organizing ideas linearly, coming directly to the point, presenting the speech purpose, and moving quickly from one point to the next. Other cultures prefer a less direct approach and consider directness impolite and even aggressive. Respect such cultural differences, whether preparing and presenting a speech or listening to someone from another culture give a speech.

SOURCE: Miller (2002); Nolan (1999).

behaviors and choices. When offered a promotion, regardless of any marginal negative consequences, you will accept the offer.

Your speech will be more effective if you carefully analyze your listeners' attitudes, beliefs, and values (Figure 11.2). They are more likely to listen to and remember information that supports or is at least compatible with their existing attitudes. Because beliefs are

Figure 11.1

Attitudes, Beliefs, and Values

Because values are at the very core of a person, surrounded by his or her beliefs and then attitudes, people's values are the hardest to influence or change.

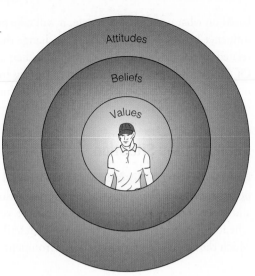

PUBLIC SPEAKING CONTEXT

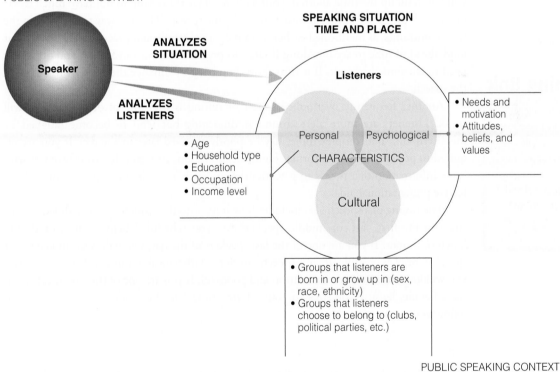

Figure 11.2

Competence and Audience Analysis

A competent speaker adapts to any public speaking context by analyzing both the listeners and the speaking situation to learn relevant facts and information that are used to prepare and deliver the speech.

based on what people think is true, it will take presenting facts and persuasive evidence to influence beliefs. Values are harder to change than attitudes or beliefs. However, a speech related to your audience's values will hold their attention because they really care about it. Of course, this recommendation for adapting to the audience does not mean you should misrepresent your own attitudes, beliefs, or values in your speech, which would be unethical as a public speaker.

Analyzing the Situation

Besides analyzing the listeners' personal, cultural, and psychological characteristics, a competent speaker also analyzes the speaking situation. **Situation analysis** includes both time and place. **Timing** involves how much time you have to speak and when the speech is scheduled to be presented. **Place,** as we describe in Chapter 2, relates to the context in which the speech is presented, the environment, and the physical surroundings.

Time

When you consider how much time you have to present your speech, remember that two of the worst things you can do as a public speaker is run overtime or rush to cover everything. If your speech runs too long and you seem to be rambling on and on, you will lose your audience's attention and appear disorganized. But if your speech runs too short and you fail to fill up the time allotted, your audience may think you do not have much to say or you did not gather sufficient information for the speech. The best way to stay within the time constraints, as mentioned earlier, is to prepare carefully and practice your speech out loud ahead of time to see how long it takes to present. If it runs overtime, you obviously need to cut something out. If it runs short, you need to enhance the content to lengthen the speech.

learning link

How can the suggestions described here for analyzing time and place be applied to communicating in interpersonal and group contexts?

● ● ●

Another frequently overlooked aspect of timing is the time of day when you will speak. Listeners are more alert around midmorning but tend to become fatigued by midafternoon, so a complex topic may be poorly received later in the day. If you are required to present complex information in the afternoon, enliven it for your listeners with some information that is easy to pay attention to, such as stories or examples, or with effective presentational aids.

The timing of a speech also includes how it fits into the sequence of scheduled events. Are you the first, last, or middle speaker? Are you scheduled before, after, or during lunch or dinner? If you are one of the last speakers of the day, you will want to keep your speech as brief as possible. If your speech interferes with a meal or causes a class to run over, you will lose your audience's attention and goodwill. If you are one of the first speakers on the schedule, be sure you stick to your allotted time out of consideration for those who follow you.

Place

Place includes the arrangement of furnishings and seating for the listeners, audiovisual equipment being used, and any other incidental physical factor, such as lighting, that could affect your speech.

Experienced public speakers often visit the place where they will speak ahead of time to reduce the possibility of last minute surprises. They check out the location of the speaker's podium, where the listeners are seated, and where they will be seated before and after the speech. Most important, they examine the audio or visual equipment to be sure it will work well during the actual presentation. They examine the lighting in the room to be sure the listeners will be able to see their visual aids while taking notes.

When you familiarize yourself with the speaking place, consider doing a practice session in the real environment. As a result, you will encounter fewer problems later and you also will feel and appear more confident when the time comes to present the speech.

As you now can see, analyzing the context—time and place—for your speech, as summarized in Figure 11.2, is essential to public speaking competence. Based on that analysis, a competent speaker next turns her or his attention to the speech topic.

Choosing and Narrowing a Topic

The next preparation step is choosing and narrowing a speech topic. While this step is critical to preparing your speech competently, many speakers overlook its importance. Reflect on everything you have learned about the speaking context. With that information in mind, use the following guidelines to find a good topic and then adapt and narrow it to the interests of your listeners and the limitations of the situation.

learning link

How could brainstorming rules—no criticism, hitchhiking, and quantity breeds quality—be applied to brainstorming ideas for a speech topic?

● ● ●

Finding a Good Topic

First, it is important to understand the difference between a general subject area and a speech topic. A **subject area** is a general area of knowledge such as the American Civil War, college or work life, contact sports, or organic chemistry. A **topic** is a specific facet or aspect of a subject area. For example, the subject area of Zachary's speech was public speaking. On the basis of an analysis of his audience's needs and interests, he chose as a topic the importance of presenting speeches effectively in a business setting.

The best place for you to start is with a subject area you find interesting or know something about. A good topic is one that appeals to you; if you're interested in it, you'll prepare and present a much better speech. Explore your own experiences for a possible topic by using an approach that marketing experts call personal brainstorming (Rubel, 1995). Think imaginatively about your own interests and write down everything that comes to mind. Then examine the list for a subject area of interest and a topic within it. You also could organize a meeting with a group of your classmates to brainstorm possible topics.

Besides searching your own mind and experiences for a topic, you could browse through newspapers, magazines, and books at the local bookstore or library for ideas. Or try using the Internet to find a topic. Go to one of several websites that include an idea generator (for example, **http://www.lib.odu.edu/libassist/idea/index.php**). You use an idea generator to search main categories or subject areas such as arts and humanities, business and public administration, sports, and recreation and leisure. For each category, the idea generator provides an extensive list of possible speech topics.

Adapting and Narrowing the Topic

After choosing a topic, you must adapt and narrow it so it's appropriate for the audience and speaking situation. On the basis of your audience analysis, decide on an approach to the topic that will appeal to the listeners. Then narrow and limit what you'll cover in the speech. You narrow the topic by getting more and more specific about what you will cover until it reaches a manageable level. Think about what the audience really needs or wants to know about it. Also consider the level of explanation and background description that will be necessary for them to understand it.

A common mistake is preparing a speech that contains too much information. If your speech is fairly narrow in its focus, your listeners will find it easier to understand and follow. And narrowing the topic simplifies the preparation process. A speech topic that is too broad is difficult to research.

Developing a Speech Purpose and Thesis Statement

Once you're satisfied with your speech topic, the next step is to clarify what you hope to accomplish by speaking. All successful speeches are built around a general and a specific purpose and they contain a thesis statement, or central idea. Without these, your listeners will not understand why you are speaking and they won't be able to follow what you say (Leeds, 1995).

General Purpose

Speeches can have any one of several **general purposes,** or goals, as discussed earlier in this chapter under types of speeches: *to inform* the listeners and extend their understanding of something; *to persuade* them to change an attitude, belief, value, or behavior; or to entertain the listeners or commemorate a special event. The two main types of speeches we explore in this book are speeches to inform (covered in detail in Chapter 13) and speeches to persuade (covered in Chapter 14).

Specific Purpose

In addition to a general purpose, every speech also has its own **specific purpose,** or specific goal, a statement of the response the speaker would like from the audience. The specific purpose, written as a single infinitive statement, summarizes what you want the audience to know, do, or feel as a result of listening to your speech. Zachary's speech, from the opening story in this chapter, provides this example of a specific purpose:

> To persuade the audience to continue to develop and improve their public speaking skills beyond graduation and for the benefit of their careers in the business world.

learning link

How could suggestions for clarifying the specific purpose of a speech be used to improve a person's communication competence in other contexts?

• • •

As this example illustrates, a good specific purpose is clear, realistic, and focused on the audience. Because it's clear, it can guide your work throughout the entire preparation process, letting you know exactly what to research and what to include or exclude from the speech. By being realistic, the specific purpose limits the goal of your speech to what can be accomplished in the amount of time allowed. By being audience focused, it describes exactly what you want to accomplish with the audience.

Table 11.2

Understanding Subject, Topic, Purpose, and Thesis Statement

In the opening story, Zachary used this process to narrow and focus what he would cover in his speech.

Speech Detail	Explanation
Subject area	Public speaking
Narrowed topic	Public speaking in business settings
General purpose	To persuade

Specific purpose

To persuade the audience to continue to develop and improve their public speaking skills beyond graduation and for the benefit of their careers in the business world.

Thesis statement

Today, by highlighting the value of public speaking skills in business and at work and by providing specific resources for continued skills development, I hope to persuade you to continue to improve your skills beyond this class and after graduation.

Thesis Statement

Building on the specific purpose, the next step to competence is to formulate a thesis statement, which is said out loud to the audience when you deliver the speech. The **thesis statement,** in one or two sentences, outlines the specific elements that support your speech goal. A good thesis tells the audience exactly what you want them to know, understand, and remember when your speech is done. Write it as a simple, declarative sentence (or two) that restates the speech purpose and states the main points that support the purpose. Although you may formulate a thesis statement early in the speech development process, you may revise and reword it as you research your topic.

Zak's speech provides the following thesis statement:

Today, by highlighting the value of public speaking skills in business and at work and by providing specific resources for continued skills development, I hope to persuade you to continue to improve your skills beyond this class and after graduation.

The examples in Table 11.2 of the subject area, topic, general purpose, specific purpose, and thesis statement from Zachary's speech clarify these aspects of speech development.

Gathering Support Materials

After you choose and narrow a topic and develop a purpose and thesis statement, the next step in competent speech preparation is to find information to support and accomplish the speech purpose. To help you with this step, we now discuss various sources of information, including personal observations, experiences, interviews, the Internet, and the library. This discussion provides you with solid suggestions for locating the best support materials to make your speech effective.

Personal Observations, Experiences, and Interviews

Information you gather firsthand, from your own observations and experiences, lends support and credibility to factual information. Moreover, telling a story or recounting an experience helps you relax and relate better to your listeners. To come up with a personal experience for your speech, think about your topic and whether you have done something, known someone, or witnessed something that relates to it. Tell the audience that story, and because it's personal to you, you'll tell it well. That said, if you decide to use observations or personal experiences, don't make any ungrounded claims based on the story that you tell. Any story represents only your viewpoint, so acknowledge that fact and do not draw generalizations about others from your own experiences.

Interviewing is another effective way to gather information for your speech, either from an expert or from someone whose life experience relates to your topic. An informational interview can help you gather testimony and convincing evidence such as a quotation. For example, Zachary interviewed his manager at work to get her viewpoints on the importance of public speaking skills in a business setting.

Before you decide to use an interview to gather information, determine whether this method will provide the kind of evidence you need. Do you have sufficient factual information but need the opinion of an expert or the testimony of someone experienced in your topic? If so, can you arrange an interview with a person who would be a credible source? After you've identified someone to interview, contact that interviewee and offer a choice of several ways for the interview to occur—in person, by phone, or by e-mail—and then choose a mutually satisfactory time. Definitely consider the possibility of an electronic interview, a skill in which some students are receiving specialized training (Crawford, Henry, & Dineen, 2001). You could locate an expert on your speech topic using the Internet and submit your interview questions to him or her by e-mail, which Zachary did with an expert he found on a website on public speaking in business.

Preparation is the key to a successful interview, so plan carefully what you'll ask and how you'll ask it (Stewart, 1991; Yaskin, 1990). Develop interview questions ahead of time, ranking them according to how much you need the information. Include open-ended questions that the interviewee cannot answer with a simple yes or no, and prepare several follow-up questions for each open-ended question.

During the interview itself, be prepared to skip questions if the discussion moves in an unexpected direction. Above all, be flexible, polite, and respectful of the interviewee's time and tape-record the interview only if you have permission to do so. Review your notes immediately after the interview, looking for themes or major ideas that support your thesis. Is there a meaningful quotation that will enliven your speech? If so, be sure to contact the interviewee and ask for permission to use it.

An interview with an expert or a person with experience relative to your topic can yield useful information for your speech.

Using the Internet

In addition to personal experiences and interviewing, the Internet can be either a great resource for researching a speech or a frustrating waste of time (McBride & Dickstein, 1998). Used effectively, the Internet provides avenues for researching your speech that include e-mail and electronic discussion lists, newsgroups and chat rooms, and websites on the World Wide Web.

E-mail is useful for communicating directly with people who can help you research your speech. People often go to great lengths to help others looking for information. If you locate an e-mail discussion list of a group of people interested in the subject area of your speech, you can send an inquiry about your topic to many people at once. Also you can participate in a newsgroup or electronic chat room that discusses your subject area or speech topic and ask questions in real time of people who are potential experts on your topic.

The addresses of expert individuals, e-mail lists, and chat rooms are often available from associations or organizations interested in a subject area. On the Internet itself, some sites provide search tools to help locate electronic discussion groups. Meta-List (**http://www.meta-list.net**) is a search engine you can use to search a large and varied array of public e-mail lists and newsletters by keyword or category.

The World Wide Web is a collection of an overwhelming number of websites, any of which may contain useful information for your speech. The web is seen as such a viable tool for preparing speeches that a debate program now incorporates its use in a forensic event titled "Electronic Extemporaneous Speaking" (Voth, 1997). Students on both sides of a debate topic are given access to the Internet for 30 minutes to help construct a 7-minute speech immediately before presenting it. The event is said to have a positive impact on students' research, organizational, critical thinking, and speaking skills.

To help you use the World Wide Web for speech research, there are many search engines to choose from, which are not all alike and won't conduct the same kind of search (Berkman, 2000). You can choose among hierarchical indexes, standard search engines, alternative search engines, and meta search engines.

A hierarchical index, such as Yahoo (**http://www.yahoo.com**), is extremely selective. People trained to categorize information examine websites and put them in categories and subcategories. When you do a search, it is much more likely that what you find will be relevant to your topic.

Standard search engines, such as Google (**http://www.google.com**), Yahoo (**http://www.Yahoo.com**), AltaVista (**http://www.altavista.com**), Excite (**http://www.excite.com**), Go Network (**http://infoseek.go.com**), and Hotbot (**http://www.hotbot.com**), use software "spiders" that act as personal minisearch engines that search the entire web and calculate mathematically how relevant the pages are to your search terms. They return a long, ranked list of sites that represent the best match to what you request. You may not want to use a standard search engine when you have a very broad subject, because of the sheer number of sites the search will yield. Instead, use a hierarchical index to find more relevant, well-catalogued sites. AllTheWeb.com (**http://www.alltheweb.com**) is a good and current engine that you may find helpful.

Some alternative search engines take other individual approaches to searching the Web. For example, with the alternative engine Ask Jeeves (**http://www.askjeeves.com**) you don't enter keywords. Rather, you type a question in plain English, such as "Is there life on Mars?" Jeeves has recorded millions of questions that users ask and supplies you with websites to answer that particular question.

Search engines that search other engines are called meta engines. ProFusion (**http://www.profusion.com/index.htm**) offers links to more highly targeted search sources instead of just hundreds or thousands of web pages. The meta engine Dogpile (**http://www.dogpile.com**) searches the best known and lesser known search engines. SearchEdu is a meta engine that indexes and searches more than 20 million websites in the educational

learning link

Since most interviews involve interpersonal communication, what skills outlined in Chapter 8 would enhance your ability to communicate in the interviewing context for a speech?

• • •

learning link

What unique ethical challenges does the use of the Internet for research introduce that are not as much of a problem when using the library for research?

• • •

domain (**http://www.searchedu.com**). SearchGov is a meta engine for governmental sites (**http://www.searchgov.com**).

Finally, sites linked to universities and colleges (*.edu) are good places to look for scholarly research. Nonprofit organizations (*.org) can be an additional source of information because they have access to large volumes of research data in a particular field. Some sites serve as portals to other sites and sources of information. For example, the Librarians' Index to the Internet (**http://lii.org**) is a trustworthy portal to information on many academic topics. And Firstgov.gov (**http://www.firstgov.gov**) is the U.S. government's official website with links to governmental agencies, organizations, reports, and statistics.

Zachary in the opening story used the Internet to search for information on his speech topic. He first entered the phrase "public speaking" using the search engine AltaVista, shown in Figure 11.3. The result was 70,000,000 possible hits, or sites that he could visit to research his topic. Obviously, his topic was too broad but he knew how to narrow it while still using AltaVista. He narrowed the search by using the Boolean operand + and entering "public speaking+career success+business environment" and came up with 952,000 hits. By using + between the words, Zachary had asked the search engine to use the phrases together to create a combined search and thus narrow and focus it. Zachary didn't have time to research all 738,000 hits returned via his Boolean search. However, after reviewing the top 20 websites listed, he found several that related directly to his topic of public speaking in businesses. Let's look at what Zak found:

■   He went to the website of an organization called the CEO System for Public Speaking, which provides public speaking training for businesspeople.

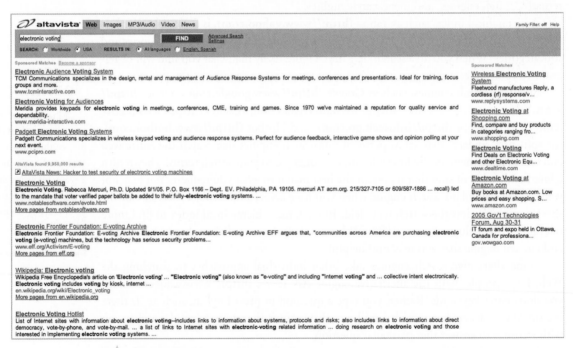

▲   **Figure 11.3**

Using the Internet to Gather Support Materials

Using a search engine such as AltaVista, enter search terms using Boolean operators, for example, a plus sign (+), to locate websites of relevance to your speech topic. Sometimes it takes trying different combinations of key terms before you come up with the right combination for your topic.

The site had just been updated, and the credentials of its developers were impressive. Zachary sent an e-mail message to Brent Filson, one of the owners of the company, and then conducted an online interview with him about the importance of public speaking skills and how to improve them (**http:// theceopublicspeakingsystem.com**).

■ He visited the website of the U.S. Department of Labor and found a government document on career projections for the 21st century that said that college graduates need more training in communication and public speaking skills (**http://www.dol.gov**).

■ Zachary also found two websites that could help students continue to improve their public speaking skills in business after graduation. Seminar-Master.com provides training in public communication as part of a self-growth program (**http://www.selfgrowth.com/public.html**). Sandra Schrift is a personal success and business coach who provides executive speech coaching online (**http://www.schrift.com**).

Evaluating Internet Sources

Zachary not only found interesting information on the Internet, he also made sure the websites were credible sources. It is your responsibility as a competent public speaker to validate the authenticity of any electronic source you include in your speech. If you are using a website as a source of information, begin with its home page to determine what you can about its authors or developers. Ask yourself the following questions, which are typical of what college librarians ask, as you evaluate an Internet source (University of Colorado, 2005):

■ What is the goal of the site and is it stated anywhere? Who is the audience?

■ How accurate and reliable is the information on the site compared with similar information from other sources?

■ Are sources for the information provided? Is the origin of the content documented and are facts verifiable?

■ Is the information on the site current and is there an indication of when it was posted or updated?

■ How broad is the coverage of the topic and is it explored in depth?

■ Is the information on the site presented objectively or does it appear to be biased? Is the information fact, opinion, or propaganda?

■ Finally, who are the developers of the site and what are their credentials? How reputable is the organization or institution with which the site is associated? Is it clear who is responsible for the site and can the author be contacted?

In sum, apply the same stringent criteria to evaluating a website as a source of information that you would when finding support materials for your speech in the library.

Using the Library

While the Internet provides some sources of support materials for your speech, much excellent information can be accessed in printed form and computerized databases in the library on your campus.

© Tom Rosenthal/SuperStock

The multitude of different sources of information in the library will supply a wealth of support materials for your speech.

Computerized Databases

A **computerized database** contains abstracts and full-text versions of documents and publications or indexes to information that is located elsewhere. Such online databases are housed on the library computer system or accessed using the Internet, and they typically are fully and easily searchable. Some databases also are available and can be accessed on CD-ROMs or DVDs. Most school libraries can provide detailed lists of the computerized databases that they have available.

Libraries also contain an array of other resources, including reference books, newspapers and periodicals, and government documents.

Reference Books

The library houses many diverse reference works such as almanacs, biographies, dictionaries, directories, encyclopedias, statistical reports, and collections of quotations—most of which are available in print, online, and on CD-ROM and DVD.

Almanacs are compilations of statistics and other facts about nations, politics, the labor force, natural phenomena, and so on. The *Statistical Abstract of the United States,* an annual publication of the Department of Commerce, contains information about life, work, and government in the United States. Best known almanacs are the *Information Please Almanac,* the *World Almanac and Book of Facts,* and the *Universal Almanac.*

If you want information about a famous person, living or dead, you could check a biographical reference book. *Who's Who in America* and *Who's Who in the World* are available in print and on CD-ROM and DVD. Two indexes to biographical books, the *Biography Index* and *Current Biography,* will direct you to short biographies or whole books about famous people.

You can use dictionaries to not only clarify unfamiliar terminology but also provide the definition of a word in the speech itself. The 20-volume *Oxford English Dictionary* is available in print and on CD-ROM and DVD, and specialized dictionaries are available for technical and professional fields.

Directories contain information about various professions, special interest groups, and organizations. Organizations listed in a directory often will provide information for your speech or the name of a person to contact about it. For example, you could use the *Encyclopedia of Associations* to find an organization whose members are experts on your speech topic and then contact that organization directly for more information or a referral.

Encyclopedias also can serve as good starting points for research because they cross-reference subjects and list additional readings and names of experts in a field. Single-volume encyclopedias such as the *Columbia Encyclopedia* and the *Random House Encyclopedia* provide quick but brief introductions to subject areas; useful multiple-volume encyclopedias are the *New Encyclopedia Britannica* and the *Encyclopedia Americana.* Specialized encyclopedias cover particular subject areas like art, philosophy, religion, technology, and ethnic studies.

Books of quotations, organized by subject, topic, or source, could provide a clever or meaningful quote for your speech. Most popular are *Bartlett's Familiar Quotations* (**http://www.bartleby.com/100**) and the *Oxford Dictionary of Quotations* (**http://www.askoxford.com/dictionaries/quotation_dict**). Retail bookstores often carry lesser known collections of quotations.

Newspapers and Periodicals

Newspapers and periodicals are good sources of current information about politics, business, media, crime, fashion, weather, and the many events that shape and influence society. Past issues of these publications can provide historical perspectives on many topics and events. This vast source of information includes daily, weekly, and other newspapers, as well as regularly published periodicals. Periodicals include popular magazines, trade journals, business magazines, and academic journals. Indexes to newspapers and periodicals can be searched by topic or keyword to find an article on practically any speech topic. The popular *New York Times Index* can be searched in print volumes and online to locate current or historical articles that can then be read in full text on microfilm or online. The *Reader's Guide to Periodical Literature* indexes many popular magazines such as *People* and *Newsweek*. There are also specialized indexes in subject areas like communication, education, or psychology. If you're interested in a historical and academic perspective on your topic, the *Cumulative Contents Index* provides indexing to more than 3,000 academic journals dating back to the 19th century. Most popular indexes are available in print, online, or on CD-ROM and DVD, or you can go directly to print newspapers and periodicals or their electronic version on the World Wide Web.

learning link

Which library source is potentially the best for support materials, and which is the best starting point for researching a speech?

. . .

Government Documents

Most U.S. government departments and offices regularly collect and publish information and data to keep the public informed. The subjects covered in governmental publications are endless, ranging from college enrollment to the unemployment rate, census data, population projections, and economic forecasts. Like other large sources of information, indexes and catalogs are available in the library to simplify the process of searching for the right government document.

All of this governmental information is in the public domain, which means it can be easily accessed on the Internet by visiting the website for the governmental department such as the Departments of Education, Justice, or Labor. Also, at the websites of the U.S. Senate (**http://www.senate.gov**) and the House of Representatives (**http://www.house .gov**), you'll find information on bills being debated and passed in Congress that may provide valuable information for your speech.

Zak visited the library to find support materials for his speech. Heeding the advice of a helpful librarian, he used a computerized database to research communication literature and found a journal article and a book that talked about how important communication and public speaking skills are to professional success. In the book, he discovered quotations by well-known business leaders on the value of public speaking and communication in contemporary organizations. In the *Encyclopedia of Associations* he learned about the National Speakers Association, an organization that provides information about experts in a variety of industries who work as trainers, consultants, and public speakers in addition to their regular jobs in business.

Support Materials and Critical Thinking

As you examine the wide array of sources of information—from other people, from the Internet, and from the library—you use critical thinking skills to evaluate and determine which support materials are most useful for your speech. **Critical thinking** involves evaluating evidence, assumptions, and ideas, which is precisely what you must do as you prepare your speech. If you do this job well, your ability to think critically about your topic will be obvious to your listeners and they will judge you and your speech to be highly credible. The Close-Up on Critical Thinking provides suggestions.

Organizing and Outlining

The last step in competent preparation is to organize the support materials and develop an outline for your speech. The importance of this step was emphasized by the Roman rhetorician Quintilian, referenced earlier in this chapter, who said, "In speaking, however

CloseUp on Critical Thinking

Thinking Critically during Speech Preparation

RESEARCHERS HAVE LEARNED THAT CRITICAL thinking and communication are inextricably intertwined (Allen & Berkowitz, 1999). A summary of research studies found that training in public speaking, discussion, and debate has a significant positive impact on critical thinking abilities. Students learn more, and their critical thinking skills improve. In fact, even beginners in a problem-based public speaking course improved their critical thinking skills with regard to both the depth and breadth of the content of their speeches (Sellnow & Ahlfeldt, 2005).

Critical thinking has several advantages for you as a public speaker. As you prepare a speech, you research support materials, examine the evidence, and then form opinions about it. As a result, you become well informed on the topic. When you present your evidence, the listeners recognize that you know what you're talking about and that you examined the topic with an open mind. Your well-informed judgments will promote respect from the audience, thus enhancing your credibility. Furthermore, thinking critically while researching your speech enables you to present your ideas with more confidence, because you know you can support your claims and defend your opinions. This confidence also enhances your credibility. Here are some suggestions for improving your critical thinking skills:

- Seek to understand new ideas by examining all the information and evidence.
- Consider all ideas, whether your own or someone else's, from different viewpoints.
- Probe and examine assumptions by questioning and challenging them.
- Understand the difference between a fact and an opinion—you can verify a fact but not an opinion.
- Explore contradictions and differences in opposing viewpoints.
- Weigh all the evidence before forming a judgment.
- Draw conclusions only after examining all alternatives and possibilities.
- Question unsupported claims or assertions.
- Be mindful that not all information posted on the Internet is authoritative and reliable.

SOURCE: Allen & Berkowitz (1999); Sellnow & Ahlfeldt (2005).

abundant the matter may be, it will merely form a confused heap unless arrangement be employed to reduce it to order and to give it connection and a firmness of structure" (Butler, 1950).

To give your speech connection and structure, we first consider various ways to organize the support materials. Then we discuss how you can use several types of outlines to both prepare and present your speech.

Organizational Patterns

A variety of organizational patterns can be used to organize the body of your speech. The most common patterns are topical and chronological, which are very effective for informative speeches. **Topical speech organization** arranges information according to subtopics or subcategories of the speech subject. Although the subtopics do not have to occur in any particular order, often a preferred order becomes obvious as you organize your materials. **Chronological speech organization** presents information based on time, so it is important to order the subtopics in the sequence they might occur. Other patterns, such as problem solution and a technique called the motivated sequence, lend themselves more to persuasive speeches. Table 11.3 provides a preview of the various organizational patterns that are covered in detail in Chapters 13 and 14. For now, we discuss a basic approach to organizing and outlining that will work for any speech and with any organizational pattern.

Table 11.3	
Types of Organizational Patterns	

An organizational pattern is used to structure the main part or body of your speech. Certain patterns lend themselves more easily to informative speeches and others to persuasion, but this is not an absolute rule. Your job is to choose the right organizational pattern to accomplish the purpose of your speech.

Organizing the Informative Speech

1. *Topic:* Divides information about the topic into subtopics or subcategories
2. *Chronology:* Describes changes or developments in any situation or circumstance, historical or sequential
3. *Space:* Organizes information based on the positioning of objects in physical space or relationships among locations
4. *Comparison and contrast:* Describes or explains how a subject is similar to or different from something else
5. *Cause and effect:* Examines why something happens or happened and the results

Organizing the Persuasive Speech

1. *Problem-solution:* Identifies a problem and then proposes a solution to solve it
2. *Motivated sequence:* Moves through a sequence of five steps designed to motivate and persuade listeners psychologically
3. *Refuting the opponent:* Dismantles the opponent's argument to indicate the superiority of the speaker's argument
4. *Comparing alternatives:* Examines two or more alternatives, and then makes an appeal for the speaker's preferred choice

Basics of Outlining

Most outlines look much like the basic structure for a speech presented in Figure 11.4. They contain an introduction, a body, and a conclusion. This approach to organizing speeches dates back to the Greek orators Corax and Tisias, mentioned earlier, who taught citizens how to organize arguments for presentation in court. That centuries-old model contained a prologue, an argument or proof, and an epilogue, which parallel the introduction, body, and conclusion approach still used today. Remember that the organizational pattern you choose—topical, chronological, and so on—is used to structure the *body* of your speech outline and not the introduction and conclusion.

The outline itself should be based on the simple structure of introduction, body, and conclusion and resemble the standard outline format presented in Figure 11.5. This format makes use of an alphanumeric system with a consistent pattern of numbers and letters to indicate subordination of ideas. Indented headings and subheadings indicate how the points in the outline relate to each other, with main points to the extreme left and subpoints indented in a consistent manner throughout the outline.

Here are a few suggestions to help you develop your outline. Always have at least two main points labeled by a Roman numeral in any speech. And for each main point, have at least two subpoints labeled by a capital letter. So if you have "I," you always have "II"; if you have "A," you always have "B," and so on. Also, the main parts of the speech—the introduction, body, and conclusion—are not identified with Roman numerals. Examine the

Figure 11.4

Basic Structure for a Speech Outline

When you organize a speech, fit your ideas into a structure for a speech outline that contains an introduction, a body, and a conclusion.

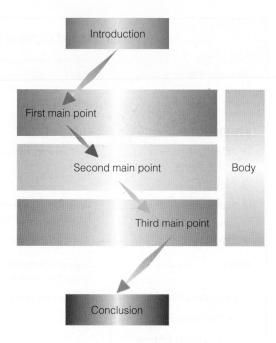

standard outline format in Figure 11.5 very carefully for further clarification of this outlining process.

Types of Outlines

As you go through the process of developing your speech, you will do a far better job of organizing it if you make use of three different types of outlines: a working outline, a formal outline, and a presentational outline.

A **working outline** contains brief references to the support materials, gathered through your research efforts and arranged in the order you plan to use them in your speech. This outline acts as a vehicle for organizing and reorganizing your main ideas and support materials. As you develop the working outline, you identify the main points and decide on the best way to organize them to accomplish the purpose of the speech. This outline is, in essence, a very preliminary, rough draft of your speech. You'll change it often as you experiment with different ways of organizing the information, and then it will serve as the foundation for creating a more formal outline. In Figure 11.6, Zachary's working outline for his speech shows how he began the process of organizing his support materials.

A **formal outline** contains all of the information from the final version of your working outline, organized and presented in more detail using the alphanumeric system for main and subpoints in the standard outline format in Figure 11.5. Use this formal outline to examine your main points visually, to check whether you have enough but not too many subpoints under each main point, and to review the logic of how your ideas are arranged and relate to one another. Orderliness, neatness, and logic are essential, and often professors require this outline to include references for the sources of information used in the speech.

Zachary's formal outline is presented in Figure 11.7. Make particular note of how Zak quickly captures his audience's attention in the introduction with a quote from a well-known business and financial leader. Then he establishes his credibility by referencing his extensive research on the speech topic.

Figure 11.5

Standard Outline
Format

All speeches can be orga-
nized using a standard
outline format such as this
one that contains all of the
components essential to
an effective speech.

Standard Outline Format

Speech Title .... Indicates the speech topic (Piques curiosity)
General Purpose .... Type of speech—to inform, to persuade, or to entertain
Specific Purpose .... Statement of the response the speaker would like from the
audience

INTRODUCTION

I. Attention-getting or .... Motivates listeners to pay attention
   lead-in device

II. Establish credibility

III. Thesis statement .... Restates in a sentence or two the speech purpose and the main
points supporting that purpose

IV. Preview of main points .... Alerts listeners to what to expect

BODY .... Supports central claim by presenting a series of main points and
supporting material

I. First main point .... Key idea that proves claim and supports thesis statement

   A. First subpoint

      1. Support material

      2. Support material

   B. Second subpoint

      1. Support material   } ... Supports main point

      2. Support material

TRANSITION .... Word, phrase, or sentence that demonstrates how the main points
relate to each other

II. Second main point .... Key idea that proves claim and supports thesis statement

   A. First subpoint

      1. Support material

      2. Support material

   B. Second subpoint   } ... Supports main point

      1. Support material

      2. Support material

TRANSITION .... Word, phrase, or sentence that demonstrates how the main points
relate to each other

CONCLUSION .... Signals to listeners speech is ending and reminds them of the thesis
statement or central idea

I. Review of main points .... Summarizes speech meaning and purpose through review of
content

II. Restatement of thesis .... Restates the speech purpose and refers back to the introduction

III. Closing device or .... Leaves listeners with a memorable idea and message
   attention-getter

Figure 11.6

Zachary's Working Outline

Zachary's working outline contains the support material he gathered from the Internet, the library, and from an interview at work.

Introduction

- Charles Schwab on importance of public speaking
    - Quote from Schwab on paying people more who speak better
    - Improving public speaking skills equals business success

Body

- Importance of public speaking skills related to business:
    - U.S. Department of Labor career projects
    - Journal article of annotations of 100 studies and reports—manager's opinion
- How to continue to improve skills after graduation
    - Brent Filson's advice
    - National Speakers Association
    - Two websites: SeminarMaster.com and the CEO System for Public Speaking

Conclusion

- Review
- Inspiring quote from CEO of Pier One Imports about correlation between ability to express ideas and getting ahead in business

A speaking, or **presentational, outline** is what you use when you give your speech. It contains only enough information to remind you of what to say at a glance. You prepare it from the formal outline, selecting out just enough details to jog your memory. This outline could take the form of a brief keyword outline on a single sheet of paper, or you could put notes on one side of a 3-by-5-inch note card. Using either method, including too much information won't allow you to see key points at a glance and may cause you to lose your place in the speech. You also want to avoid becoming **note dependent**—meaning that you refer to your notes too often and lose contact with the audience when giving the speech. A presentational outline for Zachary's speech is provided in Figure 11.8.

As these three types of outlines confirm, most speeches do have three main parts: an introduction, body, and conclusion—with main points and subpoints supporting each section. We now discuss these three main parts of any speech.

Introduction

The **introduction** sets the tone for the speech and motivates the audience to become involved in what is about to be presented. The main functions of the introduction are to capture your listeners' attention, establish speaker and support material credibility, present your main claim and say why it's important, and preview what the speech will be about.

An attention-getting device for the introduction could be a startling statement, a question, a quotation, a personal experience, a story, or a reference or compliment about the audience or speaking occasion. In Zachary's speech, he used a quotation from a well-known industrialist and financial leader, Charles Schwab, as an attention getter.

I'll pay more for a man's ability to speak and express himself than for any other quality he might possess.

Figure 11.7

Zachary's Formal Outline

This formal outline for Zachary's speech on public speaking in business evolved from his working outline.

SUCCESS SPEECH

Speech Title: Speaking Your Way to Success in Business
General Purpose: To persuade
Specific Purpose: I want to persuade the audience to continue to develop and improve their public speaking skills beyond graduation and for the benefit of their careers in the business world.

Introduction

I. *Attention getter:* Many people know Charles M. Schwab as the CEO of the major financial and investment company that bears his name. But did you know that Charles Schwab is a business leader who highly values public speaking skills? According to Schwab, he'll "pay more for a man's [or woman's] ability to speak and express himself than for any other quality he might possess."

(Source: Filson, 1991)

II. *Establish credibility:* Schwab's statement reinforces what I have learned through extensive research on the importance of public speaking skills to professional success.

III. *Thesis statement and preview of main points:* Today, by highlighting the value of public speaking skills in business and at work and by providing specific resources for continued skills development, I hope to persuade you to continue to improve your speaking skills beyond this class and after graduation.

Body

I. Numerous national studies and surveys have identified public speaking skills as crucial to a person's professional success in life.
   A. U.S. Department of Labor Career Projections to 2005
      1. Communication and public speaking skills most needed in fastest growing careers well into 21st century
      2. Communication skills most in demand across occupations

(Source: U.S. Department of Labor website)

   B. Academic article "Why communication is important: A rationale for the centrality of the study of communication."
      1. Annotations of nearly 100 national articles, commentaries, and publications, all of which call attention to the importance of communication in contemporary society
      2. Development of the whole person; growth as a responsible citizen, both socially and culturally; and most important, success in one's career and in the business enterprise

(Source: *Journal of the Association for Communication Administration,* 2000)

   C. Statement from manager at work on the value of public speaking skills on the job

(Source: Zachary's manager, personal communication, April 23, 2005)

Transition: Now that we have seen how important public speaking is in the business world, I'd like to share some ideas about how to improve your public speaking skills beyond graduation.

II. There are a variety of opportunities for improving your public speaking skills once you leave college and begin or continue gainful employment.
   A. E-mail interview with Brent Filson
      1. Developer of website CEO System for Public Speaking
      2. Filson's statement on importance and suggestions for continued growth as a speaker

(Source: B. Filson, personal communication, April 30, 2005)

   B. National Speakers Association: Represents individuals in a variety of industries and disciplines who, in addition to their jobs in business, work in their respective fields as trainers, consultants, and public speakers

(Source: *Encyclopedia of Associations* and National Speakers Association website)

    C. Websites that provide resources for improving public speaking skills of those in business
        1. Sandra Schrift, a personal success and business coach, provides executive speech coaching for business leaders

        (Source: http://www.schrift.com)

        2. SeminarMaster.com provides links to many other sites on improving public speaking skills

        (Source: http://www.selfgrowth.com/public.html)

Conclusion

I. Review and restatement of thesis: Now we clearly see how beneficial public speaking skills are to professional success in life. As Brent Filson said, "The one indispensable skill that leaders must possess is the ability to communicate, the ability to inform, persuade, convert, and compel." Plus, you now know how many opportunities are available to continue to grow as a public speaker well beyond the confines of this classroom.

II. Closing device/attention getter: Take the advice of Clark Johnson, CEO of Pier One Imports, who said: "As I moved up in business, starting at the bottom as a lumber salesman, I watched how successful executives dressed and behaved. I saw that there was a strong correlation between their ability to express ideas [publicly] and to get ahead!"

(Source: Filson, 1991)

References

Filson, B. (April 1, 2005). The CEO System for public speaking [11 pages]. Retrieved April 30, 2005, from http://theceopublicspeakingsystem.com.

Filson, B. (1991). *Executive speeches: 51 CEOs tell you how to do yours.* Williamstown, MA: Williamstown Publishing.

Morreale, S., Osborn, M., & Pearson, J. (2000). Why communication is important: A rationale for the centrality of the study of communication. *Journal of the Association for Communication Administration, 29,* 1–25.

National Speakers Association (1999). In T. E. Heets (Ed.), *Encyclopedia of associations* (35th ed., p. 1126). Farmington Hills, MI: The Gale Group.

Schrift, S. (2005). Sandra Schrift: Personal success and business coach [10 pages]. Retrieved April 30, 2005, from http://www.schrift.com.

U.S. Department of Labor Career Projections to 2005: Fastest Growing Careers. (2000). [30 pages]. "Communication skills in demand across occupations well into the 21st century." Retrieved April 30, 2005, from http://www.dol.gov.

Wheeler, W. (2005). SeminarMaster.com, Inc. [8 pages]. Retrieved April 30, 2005, from http://www.selfgrowth.com/public.html.

learning link

Which part of the speech—introduction, body, or conclusion—is most critical to preparing and presenting effectively?

• • •

The thesis statement, the central idea of the speech, follows the attention-getting device in the introduction. In addition to stating the single most important idea of the speech, a good thesis tells the audience why the speech is important.

After you capture the listeners' attention, establish credibility, and present the thesis, you then provide a preview of the content of the speech. The purpose of the preview is to indicate what your listeners should anticipate and be listening for. Sometimes the preview specifically states the main points of the speech that are to follow; in other speeches this is not a good idea. If your speech is designed to build to a suspenseful conclusion or if you

1

Speaking Your Way to
Success in Business

Introduction

– Charles Schwab, CEO of major company

– Quote: "I'll pay more for a man's ability
to speak . . ."

– Value of public speaking in business and
at work

– Resources for continued improvement

2

Body

– Importance

– Dept of Labor career projections

– 100 national studies and reports

– Manager's opinion

3

How To's

– Brent Filson's advice

– National Speakers Association

– Websites: Sandra Schrift and
SeminarMaster

4

Conclusion

– Review

– Pier One CEO

Quote: "As I moved up in business, starting
at the bottom . . ."

▲ **Figure 11.8**

Zachary's Presentational Outline

Zachary's outline for giving his speech is written on 3-by-5-inch cards and contains only the key-words necessary to keep him on track and remember what to say. If this outline contained too much information, he would end up referring to it too much and losing the spontaneity essential to extemporaneous speaking.

Telling a lie is not an ethical way to get the audience's attention.

first want to impress a hostile audience with your evidence, you may not want to mention your main points in the preview.

Body of the Speech

The **body of the speech** supports your central claim through the presentation of a series of main points. The **main points** are key ideas that, when taken together, prove the claim and support the thesis statement. They are ordered based on the speech organizational pattern you selected for the body of the speech—for instance, topically, chronologically, or problem solution. An effective speech contains at least two main points but no more than five, because listeners can pay attention to only a limited amount of information at one time. All main points should contain approximately the same amount of information and number of subpoints.

Within the body of the speech, the main points are connected using **transitions**—words, phrases, or sentences—that demonstrate how the points relate to each other. Transitions are also used to connect the introduction to the body of the speech and the body to the conclusion. Transitions, like couplings between train cars, connect main points and let listeners know you're ending one idea and going on to the next. They also can serve as an internal summary telling the audience what you've covered so far. A transition could be something as simple as saying: "Next, I'd like to describe . . ." or "Having examined the problem of . . . , let's consider a solution."

Conclusion

The **conclusion** lets the listeners know your speech is ending and reminds them of your central idea. An effective conclusion brings a sense of finality to your speech and emphasizes the significance of your message. Its main functions are to review the content of the speech and summarize its meaning and purpose, refer back to the introduction and reinforce the thesis, and leave the audience with a final attention-getting message. Like the opening statement in the introduction, the closing device can be a question, a short story, a quotation, or an inspirational appeal. In closing his speech, Zak called on his classmates to continue to improve their public speaking skills and he used a quotation from the CEO of Pier One Imports as an impressive closing device.

> As I moved up in business, starting at the bottom as a lumber salesman, I watched how successful executives dressed and behaved. I saw that there was a strong correlation between their ability to express ideas (publicly) and to get ahead!

There are a few pitfalls to avoid while preparing and presenting a conclusion. Try not to start your conclusion with a phrase such as "Now, in conclusion . . ." or "To wrap up . . ." Instead, just begin your concluding story or comments and the audience will immediately know that you are ending the speech. Avoid presenting new information in the conclusion because the conclusion should end the speech and not expand it, and don't apologize or make excuses for anything you said. When you've finished the conclusion, just stop talking; avoid comments such as "Well, I guess that's all I have to say." Finally, if you plan to take questions, pause briefly after the conclusion and then ask if anybody has questions or comments.

The steps to competent speech preparation just outlined in this chapter helped Zachary successfully prepare and present a speech, unlike his friend Althea's efforts. Preparation is the key to effective presentation. Like Zak, you should now be motivated to prepare a good speech; you should understand how to prepare a speech effectively; and you should possess the skills necessary to competent speech preparation. Chapter 12 discusses the skills essential to presenting a speech with competence.

Chapter Summary

Research studies support the importance of speech preparation to public speaking competence. Competent speech preparation starts with an understanding of the roots of public speaking in rhetoric, the various types of speeches, and the different ways to deliver a speech. A competent speaker begins preparation by analyzing the speech context—the listeners and the speaking situation—and then chooses or adapts a speech topic based on that analysis. A good topic is found in personal experiences and interests, outside sources, or on the Internet. The speaker adapts and narrows the topic, identifies a general and specific purpose for the speech, and then writes a thesis statement, the central idea or claim of the speech. To accomplish the purpose and support the thesis, support materials are gathered from personal observations and experiences, interviews, the Internet, and the library.

The next step in speech preparation is organizing the support materials in outline form. Organizational patterns order information in the most effective way for the informative or the persuasive speech. A working outline serves as a vehicle for organizing and reorganizing the support materials into main points. A formal outline contains all the information from the final version of the working outline, organized and presented using an alphanumeric system to label main points and subpoints. The presentational outline contains only enough information to remind the speaker of what to say at a glance, when presenting the speech. Most speeches have three main parts: an introduction, body, and conclusion. The introduction sets the tone for the speech, motivates the audience to become involved, and previews what is about to be presented. The body of the speech supports the central claim through the presentation of a series of main points that, taken together, prove the central claim and support the thesis. Within the body of the speech, transitions indicate how the main points are related to each other. The conclusion lets the listeners know the speech is ending and reminds them of the central idea of the speech.

Study and Review

The premium companion website for *Human Communication* offers a broad range of resources that will help you better understand the material in this chapter, complete assignments, and succeed on tests. The website resources include

- Interactive self-assessments, competency grids, and other tools
- Web links, practice activities, self-quizzes, and a sample final exam

For more information about this text's electronic learning resources, including Speech Builder Express, consult the *Guide to Online Resources for Human Communication* or visit **http://communication.wadsworth.com/morreale2.**

Key Terms

The key terms below are defined in the chapter on the pages indicated. They are also presented alphabetically with definitions in the Glossary, which begins on page 467. The book's website includes flashcards and crossword puzzles to help you learn these terms and the concepts they represent.

rhetoric 276
dialectic 276
rhetorical canon 277
invention 277
arrangement 277
style 277
delivery 277
memory 277
public speaking 278
informative speech 278
persuasive speech 278
impromptu speech 278
extemporaneous speech 279
manuscript speech 279
memorized speech 279
audience analysis 280
personal characteristics 281
household type 281
cultural characteristics 282
psychological characteristics 282
attitudes 283
beliefs 283

values 283
situational analysis 286
timing 286
place 286
subject area 287
topic 287
general purpose 288
specific purpose 288
thesis statement 289
computerized database 294
critical thinking 296
topical speech organization 297
chronological speech organization 297
working outline 299
formal outline 299
presentational outline 301
note dependent 301
introduction 301
body of the speech 305
main point 305
transition 305
conclusion 305

Building Motivation

This self-assessment begins on page 311. An interactive version of it is also available on the book's website.

Building Knowledge

The following questions are among the practice activities on the book's website.

1. Why is the history of rhetoric of any relevance to public speakers in the 21st century?
2. If a speaker uncovers a source of information that contradicts the claim in his or her thesis statement, what should be done and why? What is the ethical thing to do?
3. Based on how diverse the United States is becoming, what are the ramifications for a speaker when gathering evidence and support materials for a speech?
4. How apparent should the speaker's organizational pattern be to the listeners? How can a speaker effectively let the audience know how the speech is organized?

5. How might an introduction or conclusion be inappropriate or offensive? What kinds of introductions and conclusions should a speaker avoid?

6. Some speakers prefer to write out their speeches in manuscript form and then develop a speaking outline. Is that a good idea? Explain your answer.

Building Skills

The exercises below are among the practice activities on the book's website.

Individual Exercises

1. Develop a list of speech topics by using personal brainstorming. Take three sheets of paper and label the sheets with these subject areas: Work Life and Academics, Leisure Activities, and Social Concerns and Issues. Then write one word or phrase under each subject area. Under Academics, you might write psychology; under Leisure Activities, maybe music or sports; under Social Concerns, perhaps the environment. Next, list five possible speech topics for each subject area.

2. Using InfoTrac College Edition, enter a keyword or phrase that represents the topic of your next speech. Locate a minimum of three sources of information for your speech, at least one of which was published in the last 2 years.

3. Locate a site on the Internet that contains support materials that appear useful for your next speech. Evaluate the quality of that site using the evaluative criteria at **http://www.library.cornell.edu/olinuris/ref/research/webeval.html.**

4. Locate support materials for your speech topic by searching with a keyword at **http://www.infoplease.com,** which is a website that searches almanacs and dictionaries, a thesaurus, and an encyclopedia.

5. Take the sources of information gathered from activities 2, 3, and 4, and organize them for the body of a speech using the standard outline format described in this chapter.

6. Sharpen your ability to evaluate websites with the online exercise for evaluating electronic information at **http://www.lib.calpoly.edu/infocomp/modules/ 05_evaluate.**

7. Locate a source of support materials for your next speech using Meta-List, which is a search engine for electronic mailing lists. Find a discussion list or newsletter relevant to your next speech topic and contact that source for information at **http://www.meta-list.net.**

Group Activities

1. Break into small groups of three to four students. Choose a controversial speech topic such as Do violent video games cause users to commit violent acts? Should we make it legal to copy for private use any music that is accessible on the Internet? Have each team gather support materials to support or refute the topic. Establish a time limit (one class period or the week between class meetings) for gathering information. Have each team present its findings and vote on whose support materials are most effective.

2. In small groups, discuss the next speech you'll present in class. Exchange ideas about your possible topic, speech purpose, thesis statement, possible major points, support materials, and organizational pattern.

3. In small groups, discuss your next speech and the introduction and conclusion you plan to use to make it effective.

 ## References

Allen, M., & Berkowitz, S. (1999). A meta-analysis of the impact of forensics and communication education on critical thinking. *Communication Education, 48,* 18–30.

Berkman, R. (2000, January 21). Searching for the right search engine. *Chronicle for Higher Education,* B6.

Butler, H. E. (Trans). (1950). *The institutio oratoria of Quintilian,* 3(7), 2–3. Cambridge, MA: Harvard University Press.

Crawford, M., Henry, W., & Dineen, F. (2001). Developing interviewing skills of accounting students on the Web. *Accounting Education, 10*(2), 207–218.

Davis, M. J., & Dickmeyer, S. G. (1993, November). Critical thinking pedagogy: Opportunities to take limited preparation beyond the realm of competition. Paper presented at the 79th annual meeting of the National Communication Association, Miami, FL.

Feldman, P., Cohen, S., Hamrick, N., & Lepore, S. (2004). Psychological stress, appraisal, emotional and cardiovascular response in a public speaking task. *Psychology and Health, 19*(3), 353–368.

Gayle, B. (2004). Transformations in a civil discourse public speaking class: Speakers' and listeners' attitude change. *Communication Education, 53*(2), 174–185.

Johannesen, R. L. (2001). *Ethics in human communication* (5th ed.). Prospect Heights, IL: Waveland.

Langham, B. (1994). Speaking with style. *Successful Meetings, 43*(7), 94–96.

Leeds, D. (1995). People shouldn't wonder, "what was that about?" *National Underwriter, 99*(11), 12–13.

Maslow, A. H. (1954). A theory of human motivation. *Psychological Review, 50,* 381.

McBride, K., & Dickstein, R. (1998, March 20). The Web demands critical reading by students. *The Chronicle of Higher Education,* B6.

Menzel, K. E., & Carrell, L. J. (1994). The relationship between preparation and performance in public speaking. *Communication Education, 43*(1), 17–26.

Miller, A. N. (2002). An exploration of Kenyan public speaking patterns with implications for the American introductory public speaking course. *Communication Education, 51*(2), 168–183.

Monroe, M., & Nelson, K. (2004). The value of assessing public perceptions: Wildland fire and defensible space. *Applied Environmental Education and Communication: An International Journal, 3*(2), 109–117.

Morreale, S., & Bovee, C. (1997). *Excellence in public speaking.* Fort Worth, TX: Harcourt, Brace, Jovanovich.

Nolan, R. W. (1999). *Communication and adapting across cultures: Living and working in the global village.* Westport, CT: Bergin & Garvey.

Rubel, C. (1995). Out of ideas? Try thinking "out of the dots." *Marketing News, 29*(23), 19.

Sellnow, D., & Ahlfeldt, S. (2005). Fostering critical thinking and teamwork skills via a problem-based (PBL) approach to public speaking fundamentals. *Communication Education, 19*(1), 33–38.

St. John, S. (1995). Get your act together. *Presentations, 9*(8), 26–33.

Stewart, C. J. (1991). Teaching interviewing for career preparation. Bloomington, IN: ERIC Document Reproduction Service No. ED 334 627.

University of Colorado. (2005). Evaluating web resources. Colorado Springs: Author.

U.S. Census Bureau. (2003). America's families and living arrangements [20 pages]. Retrieved April 30, 2005, from **http://www.census.gov/population/www/socdemo/hh-fam.html.**

Voth, B. (1997). Catching a wave in the Internet surf: Electronic extemporaneous speaking. *Argumentation and Advocacy, 33,* 200–206.

Yaskin, S. (1990). Interviews: Are you prepared? *School Press Review, 66*(1), 10–16.

Building Motivation _____

Self-Assessment: Rate each of the following public speaking situations, indicating the typical level of competence you feel you can or do achieve. Use the scale of 1–4 provided, with 1 being minimal competence and 4 high competence. Rate one component (motivation) through all the situations, and then rate the next component (knowledge), and then the third (skills).

Motivation	Knowledge	Skills
1 = Distracted, disinterested, or no motivation to be competent **2** = Somewhat nervous, but some motivation to be competent **3** = Somewhat confident and motivated to be competent **4** = Highly confident and motivated to be competent	**1** = Completely inexperienced and ignorant about how to behave **2** = Minimal experience and knowledge about how to behave **3** = Somewhat experienced and knowledgeable about how to behave **4** = Highly knowledgeable about all aspects of how to behave	**1** = Completely incapable of behaving competently in the situation **2** = Barely capable of behaving minimally competently **3** = Fairly capable of behaving competently **4** = Highly capable of behaving competently

Public Speaking Situations:	Motivation	Knowledge	Skills
1. Presenting a speech to a group of people from cultures very different from your own			
2. Talking to a group of senior citizens to convince them to support your favorite cause			
3. Presenting the toast to the bride and groom at a wedding			
4. Presenting a group project to your class at school and serving as the main speaker for the group			
5. Presenting a project summary at your new job to all of upper management			
6. Presenting the student speech at your college graduation			
7. Giving an impromptu speech at a political meeting to gather support for a cause you really believe in			
8. Interviewing for a job and presenting a speech about your background and why you are right for the job			

Total Scores

_____

Interpreting Your Scores: For each context level, total your ratings for each column (motivation, knowledge, skills). You should end up with three scores. The possible range of scores per column is 8–32. A score of 8–14 indicates you are minimizing your competence and have significant room for improvement in this area of competence. A score of 15–28 means you think you are average at speaking in public. A score of 29–32 indicates a perceived high level of competence.

© Jon Feingersh / Masterfile

LEARNING OBJECTIVES | After studying this chapter, you should be able to

1. Establish and maintain credibility as a public speaker.

2. Use language and words clearly, vividly, and appropriately in a speech.

3. Vary the rate, pitch, and volume of your voice to heighten and maintain audience interest.

4. Apply appropriate pronunciation, articulation, and grammar in the delivery of your speech.

5. Support and enhance your speech using nonverbal cues including appearance, posture and body movement, gestures, facial expression, and eye contact.

6. Develop and use various presentational aids, including computerized presentation tools to enhance your speech.

7. Understand the challenge of public speaking anxiety and use the right strategies to overcome it.

Speech Presentation: Developing Skills

Wen Shu and Sergio were pleased when the chancellor of their campus invited them to accompany her on a speaking tour around the state to promote the university and encourage students from rural areas to come to the city to attend their school. At every stop on the tour, Wen Shu and Sergio would present 5-minute speeches about their positive experiences at the university. After the excitement of the invitation subsided, Wen Shu and Sergio started to prepare what they would say. When their speeches were fully outlined, they practiced together and critiqued each other's performances. Then they revised their outlines based on each other's reactions and presented the revised speeches to their public speaking course instructor.

The professor said that Sergio projected his voice extremely well, but she had a few concerns with language and word choice—how he said what he said. Sergio used fancy words and jargon that might be unfamiliar to the students to whom he would be speaking. Furthermore, he mispronounced some words, didn't articulate sounds correctly, and tended to use some *uhms* and *uhs* without knowing it. The professor told Sergio to rework several parts of the speech and practice it more with Wen Shu before embarking on the tour.

The professor liked Wen Shu's use of language and commended her excellent pronunciation and use of grammar, particularly because English was not her first language. Wen Shu chose her words carefully and spoke at just the right level for the students in the audience. Despite those strengths, the professor said that Wen Shu communicated nervousness and a lack of confidence nonverbally. She rocked from one foot to the other, and unlike Sergio, she spoke quietly and kept looking down and doodling nervously on her speech outline. In addition, no matter what content she presented, her face was almost expressionless, even when she told an emotional story about being the first in her family to leave China to go to college in the United States. The professor told Wen Shu to videotape her speech and concentrate on improving several of the nonverbal cues she found most challenging.

Both Wen Shu and Sergio did a great job on the tour. Sergio watched the students' reactions to his speech and when he thought something he said was unclear, he modified his remarks right then and there. Wen Shu succeeded in using nonverbal cues much more effectively. Their public speaking skills training had paid off and both students were pleased with a job well done. ■

Perhaps you have experienced some of the same difficulties as Sergio and Wen Shu when giving a speech. If so, you are not unique—until they receive training in public speaking, most people have no way of knowing how to present a speech effectively. It's like any other skill—skiing, playing tennis, or even using a computer—training and practice are essential to developing effective skills. In fact, researchers have found that formal training in public speaking is the best way for people in the workplace and students to improve their public speaking skills.

In one study, employees from all different kinds of organizations—manufacturing, service, production, and research companies—received presentation skills training (Seibold, Kudsi, & Rude, 1993). A significant number of the trainees reacted positively to the training, reporting that they believed they had improved their public speaking skills a great deal. In addition, their co-workers said the 194 training participants improved significantly in 12 of 16 presentation skills. Those skills encompassed all the verbal and nonverbal aspects of giving a speech covered in this chapter. In two other studies, college students just like you who took a public speaking course exhibited significant gains in overall public speaking competence and in the skill with which they used language, their voices, their ability to speak correctly, and nonverbal cues (Ellis, 1995; Morreale, Hackman, & Neer, 1995).

This research provides solid evidence that, through training, you can improve your ability to give an effective speech. When you're faced with the challenge of presenting a speech—at school, at work, or in your public life—you'll know how to present it competently and confidently.

Presenting with Competence and Credibility _____

Competent speech presentation today involves what the Roman orator Cicero centuries ago described as style and delivery (May, 1988). By **style,** Cicero meant the distinctive way a speech is presented that makes it memorable, which is achieved primarily through the speaker's use of language. Wen Shu's instructor was giving her stylistic advice when encouraging her to use language more effectively. By **delivery,** Cicero was referring to the actual presentation of the speech to the audience. A skillful delivery involves the effective use of the voice and all the nonverbal cues that Sergio incorporated in his presentation.

The presentation skills described in this chapter are similar to the principles introduced by Cicero centuries ago, and they are crucial to being perceived as competent and credible by your listeners.

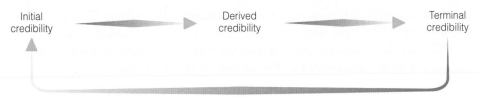

Initial credibility ➤ Derived credibility ➤ Terminal credibility

Building your credibility over the course of time

Figure 12.1

How Speaker Credibility Develops Over Time

Your initial credibility is what you bring with you to the speaking situation. You develop derived credibility as you speak, and your terminal credibility is what the audience takes away with them.

Becoming a Credible Speaker

Speaker credibility is the impression listeners form of a speaker in a given public speaking context and at a given time. These impressions can change over time, as Figure 12.1 illustrates.

Your **initial credibility** is based on what the audience knows about you before hearing you speak. If they've heard you are well informed on your topic, your initial credibility is higher than if it is based on their first impression of you. That is why the introduction to your speech is key to your credibility. **Derived credibility,** based on what you say and how you behave, develops as the audience listens to you speak. The credibility of the information you present, as discussed in Chapter 11, and your presentational skills, discussed in this chapter, both affect derived credibility. Finally, **terminal credibility** is the long-term impression you leave behind—what happens after the listeners go home and think about your speech. As they reflect on what you said and how you said it, their impressions of your credibility and competence as a speaker will change and solidify.

Becoming a Competent Presenter

Some communication experts say that perceptions of a speaker's competence, trustworthiness, dynamism, and credibility are highly influenced by dynamics of verbal communication such as volume, pitch, rate, and pronunciation, as well as postural movements, gestures, facial expression, and eye behavior (Fatt, 1999). In one experimental study, college teachers used what are called immediacy behaviors in the classroom: smiling frequently, using vocal variety and gestures, and walking in a relaxed manner around the room. As a result, these teachers were

The New Yorker Collection 1988. Donald Reilly from cartoonbank.com.

"Let's run through this once more—and, remember, you choke up at Paragraph Three and brush away the tear at Paragraph Five."

How would you rate this speaker's credibility?

perceived as significantly more credible and competent by students (Thweatt & Mc-Croskey, 1998). Obviously, what worked for those teachers could work for you.

What are the specific presentation skills that will enhance your credibility and competence as a speaker and ensure the effective delivery of your speeches?

1. Use language and words that are clear, vivid, and appropriate.
2. Vary the rate, pitch, and volume of your voice.
3. Apply correct and appropriate pronunciation, articulation, and grammar.
4. Incorporate a variety of nonverbal cues in your presentation: appearance, posture, body movement and gestures, facial expression, and eye contact.
5. Develop and use presentational aids to enhance your speech.

Let's now consider each of these key presentation skills in detail with the goal of presenting your next speech most competently.

Using Words

© Central Press/Getty Images

▲

The great impact of the "I Have a Dream" speech by Martin Luther King Jr. is due partly to the way he used language to deliver his message of peace and equality for all races.

The importance of language and the spoken word is a topic that has been studied and discussed extensively (Dance, 2002). By changing the way he used language, Sergio communicated better with the future college students in his audience.

Martin Luther King Jr.'s celebrated 1963 "I Have a Dream" speech is an excellent example of using words competently and effectively (Logue, 1997). In fact, when *USA Today* identified the top 100 speeches of the 20th century, King's speech before a crowd of 200,000 gathered at the Lincoln Memorial in Washington, D.C., was in the number one slot. Just reading the following section of the speech will give you an idea of how he used language:

Let freedom ring from the prodigious hilltops of New Hampshire. Let freedom ring from the mighty mountains of New York. Let freedom ring from the heightening Alleghenies of Pennsylvania! Let freedom ring from the snowcapped Rockies of Colorado! Let freedom ring from the curvacious peaks of California! But not only that; let freedom ring from Stone Mountain of Georgia! Let freedom ring from Lookout Mountain of Tennessee! Let freedom ring from every hill and molehill of Mississippi. From every mountainside, let freedom ring.

Competent language, such as King demonstrated, enhances the listeners' understanding and enthusiasm for a speech by the use of words that are clear, vivid, and appropriate. Although most people could not deliver the "I Have a Dream" speech as well as King did, the use of clear, vivid, and appropriate language is nonetheless essential for all competent speakers.

Clarity

Clear language uses words in such a way that the listeners understand and can easily comprehend the meaning of the speaker's message. If your listeners have to try to figure out what you mean, they'll be distracted from listening to your speech. You achieve clarity by being sensitive to how the meanings of words and phrases vary from one person to another and by using words that are concrete and familiar to your listeners.

Meaning

Chapter 4 states that language and words (as symbols) can mean different things to different people and different things in different situations. When you present a speech to an audience of 20 people, there are 20 opportunities for what you say to mean something different. For example, suppose you use a simple term such as *partner* in your speech. If you tell the audience that you are sharing your partner's opinion with them, some listeners could think that you mean your business partner, whereas others might imagine that they are hearing the opinion of your loved one. One effective way to avoid this sort of confusion and achieve clarity is to use words that are unambiguous and less open to various interpretations.

Concreteness

To help your listeners interpret your words as you intend them, use language and words that are more concrete than abstract. As Chapter 4 demonstrates, the Ladder of Abstraction categorizes language by placing concrete words lower on the ladder and abstract ones on higher rungs (Hayakawa, 1964). A concrete word refers to something specific your audience can visualize, such as an object, person, or specific place. Apple, for instance, is a concrete word and easily visualized, whereas fruit—a category of objects—is more abstract.

In the introduction to "I Have a Dream," notice the combination of concrete terms that set the stage and one abstract word, "free": "Five score years ago, a great American, in whose symbolic shadow we stand, signed the Emancipation Proclamation. . . . But one hundred years later, we must face the tragic fact that the Negro is still not free." Later in the speech, King clarified the meaning of "free" by providing concrete examples.

learning link

How can a public speaker discover what a particular audience will or will not perceive as a credible presentation?

• • •

Familiarity

Every field of knowledge has its own jargon and specialized or technical terms, but the use of unfamiliar words clouds rather than clarifies the meaning of a speech. If you use slang or regionalisms, such as surfer slang, cowboy slang, or homeboy slang, the meaning of your message will not be clear to all your listeners. Even a phrase such as "it's raining cats and dogs" or "the ball is in your court" may be confusing to people from other countries. Unfamiliar terms also can stump people from different cities or even social groups.

Although it may be tempting to use elaborate language to impress your audience, you run the risk of mispronouncing or misusing a fancy word, which would damage your credibility. Furthermore, if you make a point clear the first time, you then can pay attention to using vivid language later that will enliven your speech.

Vividness

Vivid language promotes enthusiasm for a speech by bringing the speaker's message to life and moving the audience emotionally. It makes a speech and its main points memorable, engaging, and real for the listeners. In fact, researchers have found that the powerful use of language affects perceptions of a speaker's dynamism, status, and credibility, as well as the listeners' attitudes toward what the speaker is recommending (Haleta, 1996; Sparks, Areni, & Cox, 1998). Powerful language can be achieved through the use of imagery, figures of speech, and other techniques.

learning link

Of the five public speaking skills, does one stand out as more essential to communication competence? If so, which skill and why?

• • •

Imagery

Imagery is the creation of mental pictures and imagined sensory experiences through description. When listeners can almost see, feel, taste, smell, or hear something, they're much more likely to be impressed by it and remember it. For example, when Wen Shu described leaving China to come to college in the United States, she might have talked about her feelings on the very first day on a new campus, including details about how big the campus seemed at first and how she sat nervously in the back of the room on the first day of class.

learning link

Is it always a good idea to present a speech that uses language eloquently?

• • •

Figures of Speech and Other Rhetorical Techniques

In addition to imagery, several **figures of speech,** such as simile, metaphor, and analogy, and other rhetorical techniques, such as the rhetorical question, alliteration, and repetition, bring the style Cicero talked about to your speech. These figures of speech and rhetorical techniques help the listeners visualize, identify with, or really think about the points you're trying to make. You probably use these in everyday conversation without realizing it, but their intentional use in a speech is quite effective.

A **simile** is an explicit comparison that compares two unlike things using *like* or *as*. Wen Shu could have used a simile by saying that stepping on to the new campus on the first day of class was like a Broadway star stepping on to the stage for the first time on opening night. Here are a few more simple examples of similes:

The pond is as dirty as dishwater.

You eat like a bird.

The winner of the race ran like greased lightning.

A **metaphor** also implies a comparison between two unlike things, but it does so without using *like* or *as* (Ausmus, 1998). Here's an example: "Communication apprehension can be either the anchor that weighs you down or the shoulder you stand on to reach new heights in public speaking."

An **analogy** is an extended simile or metaphor that asks the listeners to accept that things that seem alike in most respects will be alike in the respect being discussed. Here's an example: "Overcoming public speaking anxiety is like taking a journey to an unknown place. The first step is always the hardest and perhaps a bit scary. But as you travel along and become familiar with the new terrain, your anxiety subsides. And when you reach your destination, you think it wasn't so hard getting there after all."

A **rhetorical question** is asked for effect rather than to get a real answer from the listeners. When you ask a rhetorical question in your speech, you're inviting your listeners to answer silently to themselves and then continue thinking about the question while you speak. Speakers frequently use this technique as the attention-getting device in the introduction to a speech. Here are two different ways Sergio or Wen Shu could have used a rhetorical question directed at potential students to start their speeches on the tour:

Have you begun to ask yourself where you want to be 10 years from now?

As you sit here today, are you satisfied with the plan you now have for achieving your goals after you graduate? Are you ready to hear about another plan?

Alliteration is the repetition of the same consonant sound in a series of words or phrases to draw attention to certain ideas and help listeners remember what is said. When you use alliteration, the sounds add a subtle but memorable dimension to your message.

Sergio might have appealed to the students to get started planning for college by saying, "The key to *prosperity* is *preparing, planning,* and *placing* yourself in the front row of class this fall."

When the speaker repeats the same word or phrase several times in a section of a speech, it is called **repetition.** This repetition helps emphasize or tie several ideas together so your audience remembers and understands the connections you've made. It also helps to reinforce your point and make it memorable. King's "I Have a Dream" speech is full of repetition. Here is but one example:

> Go back to Mississippi, go back to Alabama, go back to South Carolina, go back to Georgia, go back to the slums and ghettos of our northern cities, knowing that somehow this situation can and will be changed.

Anyone can use vivid language in a speech. You could write out a rhetorical question and use it to open your speech or use a simple simile or metaphor to illustrate any point you want to make. If you choose to use a simile or metaphor, try to personalize it for the audience by using personal pronouns such as *you, us, we,* or *let's* (Harris, 1994). For instance, it would be more effective to say, "Most of us experience opening-night jitters during our first speeches," rather than, "Many students experience anxiety during their first speeches."

Appropriateness

In Chapter 4 we point out that language is guided by rules and expectations that govern what we must, may, or cannot say—more simply, what is appropriate. In a public speaking situation, **appropriate language** presents information in a way that respects and treats

Using language that celebrates diversity in the 21st century is quite a challenge.

all audience members as equals without being condescending or using biased language and stereotypes.

Condescending Language

To be respectful and treat your audience members as equals, adapt what you say to their knowledge of your topic and avoid the use of **condescending language** that speaks down to them. If your audience is unfamiliar with the topic, provide details about anything they may not understand, but do so without setting yourself up as the only expert on the topic. If information is presented in a condescending manner, you risk the audience members not listening to what you have to say because it communicates disrespect and negatively impacts their attitude toward your message and you as a speaker.

Biased Language

Another way to present your speech appropriately is to avoid the use of **biased language,** words or phrases that derive their meaning from stereotypes based on gender, race, ethnic group, age, sexual orientation, or disability. Most people know to avoid overt racial slurs, but they may hold certain stereotypes that will subtly influence what they say and thus insult others. By contrast, the use of unbiased language makes a positive statement about your credibility and serves to bring audiences together and encourage open discussion of even the most controversial topics.

Gender-biased language, for instance, can result from something as simple as referring to *he* more often than *she,* which may suggest the speaker respects men more than women. Gender bias also results from using words that designate certain occupations or professions as male and others as female. You can avoid that by saying *flight attendant* rather than *stewardess, firefighter* rather than *fireman, chairperson* rather than *chairman,* and *people* rather than *mankind.* Moreover, rather than refer to someone as a woman lawyer or a male nurse, leave off the gender descriptor, unless it's really necessary to understand your point. Table 12.1 provides a checklist of specific suggestions for using gender-neutral language in your speech.

The guidelines for avoiding gender-biased language apply equally to other types of bias. Stereotypically pairing certain professions or occupations with certain races or ethnic groups or remarking on the race or ethnic background of a person in a certain profession is a form of subtle language bias. For example, to refer to an African American doctor may somehow communicate that an African American doctor is an unusual occurrence.

Unless your audience needs to know the gender, race, or age of the person you're talking about, omit that information from your speech. Likewise, leave out references to a person's disability unless that information is relevant. Eliminate from your speech any words or phrases that categorize people on the basis of stereotypes or that patronize people in any way.

The Close-Up on Diversity box describes a way of using language that is free of bias and honors diversity in contemporary society. An approach to using language called **multicodality** is similar to being multilingual in that speakers retain their unique way of using words and language while learning to use some of the language codes and patterns of their listeners. When you are multicodal, you engage in a communication behavior known as **code switching,** which means you switch from your own way of encoding a message and encode it the way another person would (Huspek, 2000).

At this point, you may be thinking that it is quite a challenge to use language effectively in your speech. However, by developing a few well-planned and effective phrases or

Table 12.1

Checklist for Avoiding Gender-Biased Words and Phrases

Simple changes in language will help you become a gender-neutral public speaker.

1. Replace phrases that contain *man* or *woman* with gender-neutral terms.

Instead of	*Substitute*
policeman	police officer
manpower	labor force
waitress	waitperson
workman	laborer

2. Restructure sentences to eliminate sexist language.

Instead of	*Substitute*
The fabric in the dress is man-made.	The fabric in the dress is synthetic, not natural.
What are the average man-hours it will take to do the job?	How many hours will it take to do the job?
When will a new chairman be assigned?	When will someone be appointed to the chair's position?

3. Use plurals to avoid gender-specific pronouns.

Instead of	*Substitute*
When a staff member arrives, tell him to sit in the front row.	As staff members arrive, tell them to sit in the front row.
A public speaker should plan the handouts he will use ahead of time.	Public speakers should plan the handouts they will use ahead of time.

4. Mention women first as often as men.

Instead of	*Substitute*
Men and women experience public speaking anxiety in the same way.	Women and men experience public speaking anxiety in the same way.
He or she will help us out.	She or he will help us out.

SOURCE: Detz (1992).

sentences ahead of time that draw mental pictures and evoke emotions, you can improve your speech immensely. By carefully wording and writing out these parts of your speech ahead of time, you will ensure that you say them just as you intend. Use the checklist in Table 12.2 for using language competently to decide which techniques suit you and your speech the best.

Using Your Voice

A popular communication axiom—a self-evident truth—states that it isn't what you say but how you say it that counts (Fatt, 1999)! As a competent speaker, you use **vocal variety** to heighten and maintain audience attention and interest in your speech, varying the rate (fast versus slow), pitch (high versus low), and volume (loud versus soft) of your voice.

Rate

Rate is the speed at which a speaker delivers a speech. Good public speakers vary their rate, sometimes talking fast and sometimes slower, but always speaking at a pace that allows the audience to understand the words. Adjust your rate to the topic of the speech. A serious

Language in a Multicultural World

INTERCULTURAL COMMUNICATION EXPERTS AGREE that communicating with people of cultural backgrounds different from your own can be challenging for a variety of reasons, including differences in verbal and nonverbal communication patterns and communication preferences (Martin, Hecht, & Larkey, 1994; Samovar & Porter, 2004).

Bicultural and bilingual people use code switching as a solution to these culturally based communication differences. They switch back and forth from one language to another within one conversation (Auer, 1998). Sometimes code switchers switch only a word or two to clarify meaning. For instance, in Canada, French–English bilinguals use the English word *fun* because the French language lacks a good counterpart. When two people of different cultures first meet, they often code switch to learn what language will be most comfortable for talking with one another.

Code switchers also switch from one dialect to another within the same language. One researcher, on a trip to Italy, overheard an Italian friend switch from standard Italian into a regional dialect, Genovese. By peppering his language with the regional dialect, the speaker quickly established rapport and a sense of informality and community with a stranger.

As public speakers we can learn by observing what people who share multiple cultures are doing naturally. If code switching helps build rapport and understanding, we could first become familiar with any distinctive verbal or nonverbal cultural codes or language patterns of our listeners. Then we can use those codes or patterns in the speech to build rapport and to communicate that we are aware of and value the listeners' culture.

Of course we should not forsake our own way of communicating to embrace the code of our listeners nor should we use the other code in an insincere or condescending manner. Rather, we want to incorporate aspects of the listeners' codes within the message to communicate interest and respect.

SOURCES: Auer (1998); Huspek (2000); Martin, Hecht, & Larkey (1994); Samovar & Porter (2004).

Table 12.2

Checklist for Using Clear, Vivid, and Appropriate Language

Use clear, vivid, and appropriate language to promote understanding and avoid offending your listeners.

1. Clear language promotes understanding and comprehension of meaning.

- Be sensitive to variations in meaning
- Use concrete rather than abstract words
- Use familiar words

2. Vivid language promotes enthusiasm, brings the message to life, and moves the audience emotionally.

- Use imagery to create visual pictures
- Use figures of speech
  Simile compares unlike things using *like* or *as*
  Metaphor compares dissimilar things without using *like* or *as*
  Analogy extends a simile or metaphor

3. Appropriate language respects and treats listeners as equals and avoids biased language and stereotypes.

- Adapt language to listeners' knowledge base but avoid being condescending
- Avoid biased words or phrases based on stereotypes about gender, race, ethnic group, age, or disability

subject deserves a slower and more deliberate rate; less serious subject matter can be delivered a bit faster. Rate also creates mood; for example, talking faster creates a sense of excitement.

Many beginning public speakers tend to talk too fast because they're nervous, which makes it difficult for their listeners to absorb what they say. By contrast, a speaker who talks too slowly bores listeners and gives them time to shift their attention away from the speech. A speech delivered at the same rate throughout sounds monotonous and the listeners may tune out.

The key to avoiding these problems is variety in rate. Change the length of the silent pauses that fall naturally between words, phrases, or sentences. Even while speaking fairly quickly, pause to emphasize a point and allow your listeners a moment to think about it (Clair, 1998). Pauses also act as silent transitions from one thought to the next, letting the listeners know that you've completed one idea and you're moving on to another.

One benefit of pausing silently is that it helps you reduce your use of **vocalized pauses,** which are the meaningless sounds or words a speaker utters, such as *like, uh, you know,* and *OK.* These filled pauses, which usually result from nervousness, interrupt the flow of a speech and can be distracting to the listeners. The easiest way to learn to substitute a silent pause for a vocalized pause is to record yourself giving a speech. Once you become aware of the vocalized pauses you tend to use, you can train yourself to take a quick breath instead.

learning link

How could guidelines for vocal variety help improve communication in interpersonal situations and in small groups?

● ● ●

Pitch

Pitch is the highness or lowness of the speaking voice. All speakers have a natural pitch at which they usually speak, but competent speakers try to achieve a more effective pitch by adjusting it to a slightly lower or higher timbre (Wolff, 1998). A change in pitch, called an **inflection,** reveals the emotional content of the message. Raising your pitch at the end of a sentence, for example, indicates it is a question. Sometimes inexperienced speakers do this at the end of their sentences even when they don't intend to ask a question.

Anxiety may cause a speaker's vocal pitch to rise to a squeak, giving away the fact that the speaker is nervous. Equally distracting is a speaker who uses a monotone pitch or stays in a narrow, unchanging range for an entire speech. By varying your pitch, you keep your listener's attention and emphasize important points in your speech. Experienced speakers determine an optimal pitch for their voices and vary it with control when speaking publicly.

© CNN

Volume

Volume is the intensity, the loudness or softness, of the speaker's voice. Competent public speakers vary their volume based on the size of the audience, the size of the room, and the amount of background noise they may be speaking against. Being heard is so important that experienced speakers often arrive early for speaking engagements to test audio equipment and acoustics so that all audience members will able to hear them without straining. They speak loudly enough so everyone can hear, but they are also careful not to overpower the listeners with a booming or loud voice. When a speaker's

Use the most effective rate, pitch, *and* volume for the particular speaking situation to ensure that everyone hears and appreciates your speech, not just those in the front row.

Figure 12.2

Public Voice vs. Private Voice

Public voice makes full use of variety in rate, pitch, and volume and is more appropriate for public speaking situations than your private voice.

volume is too loud, the listeners may feel their space is being vocally invaded, making the speech an unpleasant experience.

In the opening story, Wen Shu had a problem with volume that many beginning speakers have. From lack of confidence in themselves and their voice, new public speakers either don't talk loudly enough or let their voices quietly fade out at the end of a thought. As a public speaker, you can use volume and vocal variety most effectively by developing the use of your public voice (Figure 12.2).

Public Voice and Private Voice

A **public voice** makes use of increased variety in rate and pitch and increased volume, so your words are easily heard and understood by the entire audience. Your private voice is the one you use in interpersonal conversations or small groups. Although your private voice seems quite natural, you need to become accustomed to a louder public voice for giving speeches, even though it may sound strange at first.

To achieve a public voice, make use of the full range of rate, pitch, and volume when you are practicing your speech. As you do that, use your voice to call attention to important parts of your speech. The faster and louder you say something, the more emotion and excitement you assign to it. By slowing down, dropping your pitch, or decreasing your volume, you can call attention to an idea in a more subtle way.

The three aspects of vocal variety are briefly summarized in the checklist in Table 12.3 to help you remember what to do.

Speaking Correctly and Appropriately

Another factor in public speaking competence is speaking correctly and appropriately for the context. Your listeners may not understand what you're saying if, for example, you mispronounce a word. An error in pronunciation, articulation, or grammar calls attention to itself, distracts the listeners from your message, and damages your credibility as a speaker. **Pronunciation** means stressing and accenting the right syllables in a word. **Articulation** is forming individual speech sounds correctly with your mouth, so they combine to produce an understandable word. **Grammar** is the rules and structure for putting words together in sentences.

Table 12.3	
Checklist for Varying Rate, Pitch, and Volume of the Voice	
By varying the rate, pitch, and volume of your voice, you can maintain the listeners' attention and interest in what you're saying.	

1. Vary rate.

- Vary rate by talking fast and then talking more slowly (but be sure you can be understood).
- Talk more slowly and more deliberately for a serious subject.
- Talk faster for less serious subject matter.
- Use silent pauses.
- Avoid vocalized pauses.

2. Vary pitch.

- Adjust pitch to a slightly lower or a slightly higher timbre.
- Use inflections to reveal emotional content.
- Don't raise pitch at the end of a sentence, except to ask a question.

3. Vary volume.

- Vary volume but speak loudly enough to be heard.
- Don't overpower listeners with a loud voice.
- Develop a public voice for presenting speeches.

Pronunciation

Most speakers try to pronounce words correctly and appropriately for the given audience. But people grow up pronouncing words as others around them do; plus, regional and ethnic dialects affect pronunciation patterns. As a result, without knowing it, we may mispronounce many familiar words, saying, for instance, "lyberry" for *library,* "ax" for *ask,* or "jis" for *just.* If you have any doubt about how to pronounce a word, look it up in the dictionary to see which syllables should be accented.

Articulation

Besides pronunciation problems, speakers frequently fail to articulate speech sounds correctly. Most people know that "awtuh" should be *ought to.* They know the right way to pronounce it, but they may not bother to articulate it correctly. Clear and correct articulation depends on how the speaker's mouth forms sounds, which could be affected by factors such as chewing gum while speaking or even wearing braces. More often, poor articulation results from simply not paying attention to how you form sounds when you speak. Common articulation problems are errors of omission, substitution, addition, and slurring.

- **Omission** means leaving out and not saying part of a word. The most common omissions are word endings, such as when *working* becomes "workin" and *speaking* becomes "speakin." Sometimes we omit parts from the middle of a word, so *listening* becomes "lis-ning," and sometimes we leave out the end, so *grand* becomes "gran" and *appointment* becomes "appointmin."

■ **Substitutions** occur when the speaker replaces part of a word with an incorrect sound. At the beginning of a word, the "d" sound may be substituted for the "th" sound. The result is that people say "dese," "dem," and "dose" instead of *these, them,* and *those*. Sometimes the ending of *th* is replaced by just *t,* and the word *with* becomes "wit."

■ **Additions** occur when a speaker adds extra parts to a word. An *athlete* becomes an "athalete"; *regardless* becomes "irregardless," which is a nonstandard word and not generally accepted.

■ **Slurring,** or running sounds and words together, is caused by the speaker's saying two or more words at once, or overlapping the end of one word and the beginning of the next. Pairs of words that end with *of* or *to* are often slurred together: *sort of* becomes "sorta"; *want to* becomes "wanna," and *must have* becomes "musta." Try alternative phrasing; instead of saying "alotta" something, refer to *many, quite a few,* or an *array of*.

Grammar

Finally, correct language calls for avoiding grammatical errors. If listeners are distracted by a mistake in grammar, their attention turns from what you are saying to the error itself. Moreover, if you commit an error in grammar, the listeners will think, perhaps wrongly, that you don't know enough about the topic to be talking about it.

Most people pay close attention to the grammatical structure of sentences when they are writing, but they are less careful about grammar when they speak in public. The typical kinds of errors most people make are simple ones such as the erroneous use of the verb *to be:* "All of them was there" and "Sergio and Wen Shu was late for class" are incorrect uses of the verb *to be*. *All* is a plural noun, so it should take the plural form of the verb. "All of them were there" and "Sergio and Wen Shu were late for class" are grammatically correct.

Less obvious but equally mistaken is the incorrect use of pronouns such as *self, me,* and *I*. *Self* is a reflexive pronoun used to reflect on a noun or another pronoun to add emphasis. "I myself accept the invitation to speak" is correct. "Wen Shu and myself accept the invitation" is wrong; it should be "Wen Shu and I accept the invitation."

I and *me* play specific roles. When used as the subject in a sentence, *I* is correct; when used as the object, *me* is correct. "Wen Shu and me accept the invitation" is wrong; "Wen Shu and I accept the invitation" is correct. "Thanks for inviting Wen Shu and I" is wrong; "Thanks for inviting Wen Shu and me" is correct.

Subject–verb agreement errors often happen when a word is confusing in regard to its plural and singular forms. *Data* and *media* are good examples. *Datum* and *medium* are the singular forms of these nouns; *data* and *media* are the plural forms. So an example of the correct subject–verb agreement is "The data from the study are interesting; the media were expected to wait until the speaker arrived." Incorrect are "The data is interesting" and "the media was expected."

A summary of the recommendations for the use of pronunciation, articulation, and grammar is presented in the checklist in Table 12.4.

Table 12.4

Checklist for Using Pronunciation, Articulation, and Grammar

By speaking correctly, you ensure that the listeners understand what you say. Errors distract from your message and reflect negatively on your credibility.

1. Pronounce words correctly.

- Avoid regionalisms and dialect.
- Look up words that you can't pronounce ahead of time.

2. Articulate speech sounds correctly.

- Avoid the errors of omission, substitution, and addition.
- Avoid slurring.

3. Use correct grammar.

- Avoid the incorrect use of the verb *to be.*
- Use the pronouns *self, me,* and *I* correctly.
- Use the correct subject/verb agreement for problem words such as *data* and *media.*

Using Nonverbal Cues

Understanding and using nonverbal cues to support and enhance the spoken message is crucial to public speaking competence. In Chapter 5 you learned that nonverbal cues have a large impact on how people react to messages. The nonverbal cues important to public speaking are appearance, posture and body movement, gestures, facial expression, and eye contact.

Appearance

Recall or consult the discussion of first impressions in Chapter 5 and modify your **appearance** accordingly—your clothing, shoes, jewelry, hairstyle, and even hair adornments. All these nonverbal cues influence what the audience thinks of you before you even begin to speak.

In a study conducted in a public speaking classroom, students like you rated other student public speakers more favorably as a result of the greater formality of their attire (Sellnow & Treinen, 2004). That said, although you want to present yourself in the best possible light, don't manipulate your appearance in any way that would seem artificial to the audience or make you uncomfortable. In general, avoid trying out a new hairstyle or outfit when you give your speech. Instead, a relaxed but professional and attractive appearance is best with any audience.

Posture and Body Movement

You're dressed to impress and there you sit, waiting to present your first speech. When it's your turn, stand up straight, hold your head up, shoulders back, and walk with confidence to the front of the room. A confident walk conveys a sense of self-assurance that will move the audience to respect you. Further, by acting assured, you will actually begin to feel more confident.

After arriving at the lectern, stand relaxed but maintain an alert body posture, with your shoulders held up and in line with your hips and knees. This posture will communicate that you're in control and ready to speak. **Posture** is defined as a position or attitude of body parts, and that is just what it communicates, your attitude. For instance, if you slouch and lean on the lectern, your posture communicates a lack of confidence and enthusiasm.

During your speech, move about voluntarily and purposefully within the speaking area. By moving with purpose, you can emphasize a transition or focus the audience's attention on an important point you want to make. If you're about to tell a story, move closer to the audience to draw them in, and then back to your notes as you conclude it and move on. Moving toward the audience or from one side of the lectern to the other communicates a sense of immediacy and involvement that increases credibility (Thweatt & McCroskey, 1998).

Pacing, however, or letting your body rock unconsciously from one foot to the other distracts listeners and communicates public speaking anxiety. So use body movement only intentionally, and try to become aware of any unconscious movements that may take attention away from your message.

Gestures

Whether standing or moving, competent speakers keep their hands and arms free and relaxed, so they are ready to incorporate natural movements or gestures into their presentations. **Gestures** reinforce what you say, emphasize important points, and make presentations more interesting to watch as well as more natural and relaxed.

Gestures also communicate openness to the audience and a sense of involvement, a small gesture less and a larger gesture more. The important thing is to gesture in a way that's natural for you and matches the content of what you're saying. Here are a few suggestions.

- When you aren't gesturing, let both arms relax and drop to your sides.
- If you feel unsure about what to do with your hands, rest them lightly on the lectern during your speech. This helps you appear much more in control of what you're saying.
- Vary your gestures from one hand to the other and sometimes gesture with both hands at the same time. Many speakers use their dominant hand more, leaving the other arm hanging like a limp dishrag (note the use of simile!).
- Try to hold your gestures longer when speaking publicly than in normal conversation, and avoid quick or jerky movements.
- Don't clasp your hands for too long in front or in back of you, which will keep you from gesturing.
- Finally, avoid gesturing in a way that appears artificial to the audience. If you feel your gestures are contrived, they will certainly appear that way to the audience.

Two more nonverbal cues you can use to your advantage as a public speaker are facial expression and eye contact. In one study of U.S. college students, a relaxed facial expression rather than a nervous facial expression and direct eye contact rather than indirect eye contact resulted in higher credibility ratings of the students as speakers (Aguinis, Simonsen, & Pierce, 1998).

Facial Expression

Facial expression is the vehicle you use to communicate how you feel about what you're saying to the audience. If you don't believe in your claim, your facial expression will reveal your doubt. If you're nervous, your facial expression may be too strained and you won't appear enthusiastic about the topic. Instead, try for a facial expression to match and reflect the content of your speech. If it's on a lighthearted topic, your facial expression should reflect this. If your topic is serious, look serious. Moreover, try to avoid either a deadpan expression—no feeling at all—or a smile pasted on your face like some newscasters.

As we mention in Chapter 5, research indicates that men and women use facial expressions differently when speaking (Wood, 1994). Women express more emotion on their faces and smile more, even if they're unhappy or the message is not worth smiling about. If a woman is presenting a speech on a serious topic and smiles too much, it is confusing and distracting to the listeners. By contrast, men tend to limit the amount of emotion they display on their faces, so listeners in the audience might not be able to tell how they feel about what they're presenting. The way to get around these gender differences is simply to match your facial expression to the content of your speech. Whether you are a man or a woman, use facial expressions that are appropriate to your topic and communicate your true feelings about it.

Eye Contact

Eye contact is a tool you can use to promote a sense of involvement with audience members. In North America, eye contact communicates honesty, openness, and respect for others—all crucial aspects of credibility for a public speaker. If you avoid making eye contact with listeners in an audience of North Americans, they may perceive you as nervous at best or deceitful at worst.

learning link

How can a public speaker figure out what nonverbal behaviors are appropriate and thus achieve a truly competent delivery?

• • •

To get better at using eye contact as a public speaker, mentally divide your audience into four quadrants, like a window with four panes. Look directly at and speak to at least one person in each quadrant at some point during the speech. Don't just gaze in their direction, but actually stop and make eye contact with a specific member of the audience seated in each quadrant. Not only will this communicate interest and involvement to the entire audience but you also will learn how your listeners are reacting to your speech. If they're losing interest, you can speed up or talk a little louder to regain their attention. If it's appropriate to do so, you can invite audience participation by asking questions about their opinion of what you're saying.

By now you may need some kind of guideline for making decisions about using all the presentation skills just described in this chapter. The *Frank & Ernest* cartoon provides one suggestion—just "wag your tail now and then." On a more serious note, Frank Dance, an expert on public speaking, offers a useful recommendation for deciding how to use the presentation skills outlined in this chapter most competently (Dance, 1999). Dance coined the phrase **transparent delivery,** which means presenting a speech in such a way that the audience doesn't focus on the elements of the delivery but instead pays full attention to the message—thus the delivery itself is transparent.

To achieve a transparent delivery, watch yourself present a speech on videotape. Examine the way you use all the various presentation skills and decide what your strengths are and what skills you should use the most. Then practice your speech and record it on videotape several more times, just as Sergio and Wen Shu did as they prepared for the

Nonverbal cues made easy . . . just wag your tail now and then!

statewide tour promoting their campus. Rehearsing your speech several times is critical to achieving a competent presentation.

Table 12.5 provides a checklist of all the nonverbal cues you can use to help present your speech most competently. Review that summary, and next we will discuss how presentational aids can enhance the delivery of your speech.

Using Presentational Aids

Presentational aids are any materials you show to or share with the audience that assist in illustrating or supporting the content of your speech and add interest and excitement to it. They are useful when you need to clarify a difficult concept, present a complex idea, or demonstrate a process the audience would have difficulty understanding.

Incorporating a presentational aid of any kind in your speech can be challenging. If poorly used, it detracts from your speech; but effectively used, it decidedly enhances it. Scholars who study persuasive communication agree. They have confirmed that people may forget texts and lists, but they recall visual images (Messaris, 1997).

Types of Aids

Your choice of a presentational aid is limited only by your imagination and creativity and by the amount of time you are willing to spend preparing it. Types of presentational aids include objects and models, diagrams and drawings, pictures, photographs, maps, charts and graphs, and tables and lists.

Objects and Models

Objects are useful presentational aids when you want to show your listeners what something looks like or how it works. A set of gardening tools would be helpful if you're explaining aspects of horticulture. If you use an object of any kind, be sure it's large enough for all audience members to see, but small enough so you can conceal it until the point in your speech when it becomes relevant. To avoid distracting the audience from what you're saying, show the object only when you're actually talking about it and try not to pass it around during the speech. If the object is too large and cumbersome to bring in or too

Would noodles for brains be a good presentational aid for a speech?

Table 12.5

Checklist for Using Nonverbal Cues in Public Speaking

Make use of a variety of nonverbal cues to support and enhance your verbal message.

1. Appearance

- Modify your appearance to make a good first impression.
- Don't modify your appearance in a way that looks artificial or makes you uncomfortable.

2. Posture and body movement

- Walk confidently.
- At the lectern, relax but maintain an alert body posture.
- Move about in the speaking area voluntarily and purposefully.
- Avoid pacing, body rocking, or fiddling with objects.

3. Gestures

- Make use of both hands and gesture naturally.
- Relax and drop arms to your sides when not gesturing.
- Rest hands lightly on the lectern.
- Hold gestures longer.
- Don't clasp hands in front or in back of you.

4. Facial expressions

- Use your face to communicate how you feel about your speech.
- Let your facial expression reflect the mood and tone of the speech.
- Avoid a deadpan expression.
- Match your facial expression to what you're saying.

5. Eye contact

- Use eye contact to communicate interest and involvement to the audience.
- Use eye contact to gauge how the listeners are reacting to your speech.

One diagram and some impressive words do not result in a competently presented speech.

small for the listeners to see clearly, you can show your audience a model rather than the object itself. If you want to talk about the solar system and how planets relate to one another, a scaled-down model using plastic balls would make a good presentational aid.

Diagrams and Drawings

If you prefer not to create a model, you can use a diagram or a drawing to explain how something looks or operates. These types of aids are particularly useful for explaining steps in a process or for simplifying and clarifying relationships, but they must be clear and accurate. For example, if you want to explain how a car engine works, a diagram will help the listeners follow your explanation.

Pictures, Photographs, and Maps

If your speech would benefit from a realistic depiction of a person, a place, or an object, a picture or photo can bring it to life more effectively than a diagram or drawing. For example, a photograph of the face of a young child would humanize a request to contribute to a charity for children in developing countries. A picture or photograph needs to be large enough to be seen by everyone, and it should be cropped or framed to eliminate any distracting details.

When you want to pinpoint a location or highlight a geographical area, you can use a map as a presentational aid. If your speech is about a historical period, a map of what the world or area looked like at that time makes an intriguing presentational aid.

Charts and Graphs

When you're planning to present statistics or a series of numbers to support a point in your speech, you need a presentational aid that will help your listeners grasp the meaning of the figures. Charts and graphs clarify the relationships among the numbers and reveal any trends or patterns. Among the most frequently used are line graphs, bar graphs, pie charts, and flow charts (Figure 12.3).

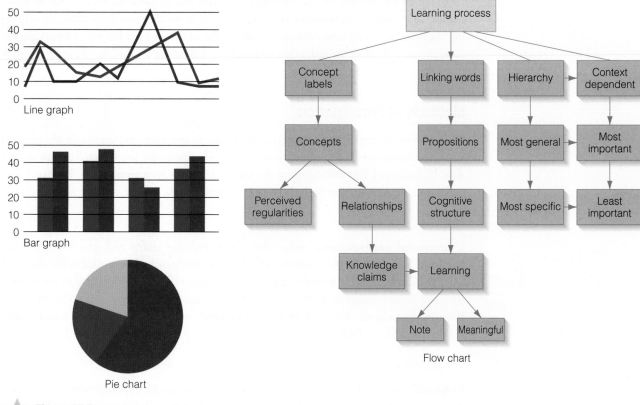

Figure 12.3

Types of Charts and Graphs

Using charts and graphs as visual aids helps clarify relationships among numbers and explain trends or patterns that you mention in your speech.

A line graph shows changes over time or the relationship between two or more sets of numbers. They are simple to read and can show the patterns of change in more than one series of numbers without confusing the audience. A bar graph portrays numbers as rectangular, vertical bars, making a series of numbers or trends over time even easier to understand. When you want to portray numbers as parts of a whole, use a pie chart. Most of the time, it's best to put the largest slice of the pie at 12 o'clock and arrange the other slices clockwise in descending order of size. A flowchart is effective for illustrating a sequence of steps. A symbol or a geometric shape represents each step on the chart, so the listeners can trace a path through the sequence.

Tables and Lists

When you want to organize, summarize, and present detailed information, use a table, an all-text presentational aid in which numbers or words are arranged in a grid of columns and rows. Articles in academic journals often present the results of research studies in table form. By using short phrases for headings and minimizing text entries, you can include a lot of data in a small space. In a speech, you can use color in a table to focus your audience's attention on specific information. But avoid confusing the audience by using too much color or too much information and detail.

Like tables, lists are all-text presentational aids that can communicate a lot of information in a simple way, showing at a glance which items are most important, by arranging them in ascending or descending order. If the items on your list are of equal importance, arrange them in the order that you prefer to talk about them. Lists are most effective if you keep them short and to the point.

Methods of Presentation

Once you've chosen the type of presentational aid to use, then you decide on the method you'll use to present it. You can choose between two methods: unprojected and projected aids. Unprojected aids don't require the use of electricity to present them. Projected aids make use of electricity and include computer-assisted aids.

Unprojected Aids

Unprojected presentational aids—the chalkboard, flip charts and poster boards, and handouts—are among the easiest to use. They are inexpensive, unbreakable for the most part, and can be used in lighted rooms for ease of note taking. Their disadvantages are that they can be cumbersome, hard for large groups to see, and may require you to turn your back on the audience. For suggestions on using each of the unprojected aids competently, see the checklist in Table 12.6.

Projected Aids

Projected presentational aids—including slides, overhead transparencies, videotapes, audio tapes, and computer-generated images—can be more trouble to prepare but often are more impressive than unprojected aids. They are more dramatic and colorful, easier for members of large groups to see, and can create a desired mood or effect for your speech. Their disadvantages are their higher cost and limited availability in some situations, the possibility of breakdowns because they require technology, the potential to be noisy, and difficulty of use in a lighted room. A checklist for the competent use of projected aids is presented in Table 12.7.

Table 12.6
Checklist for Using Unprojected Presentational Aids

Flip Charts and Posters

1. Decide where you'll position and display the flip chart or poster ahead of time.
2. Don't block the audience's view of the chart or poster, and don't face it while you're speaking.
3. Conceal material, then reveal it as you discuss it.

Handouts

1. Use handouts to help the listeners follow or recall your main points, but don't let them take over your presentation.
2. Wait to distribute your handouts until the end of your speech, so audience members don't read them while you're speaking.
3. If the handouts are essential to understanding your speech, distribute them before you start but not during the speech itself, which is time consuming.
4. If you use a computerized presentation and have printed handouts of the computer images, distribute those ahead of time. Then the audience members can listen to you rather than write everything down off each computer image.

Computerized Aids

Computerized presentations are increasingly popular projected aids (Ringle & Thompson, 1998). If you have an Internet browser and a connection to the Internet during your presentation, you can move easily from a computerized presentation to the Internet.

To put together a computerized presentation, you need access to a specialized software program such as PowerPoint, a computer on which to develop the presentation, and a suitable projector for presenting it. If you haven't used a presentation software program before, an easy way to get started is with the tutorial assistant built into most programs. For example, PowerPoint contains a tutorial called AutoWizard. Computer centers on college campuses often provide free training as well.

Despite their popularity, computerized presentational aids have their detractors (Brandt, 1998; Zuckerman, 1999). Some critics say such programs take the life and vitality out of public speaking. To support their claim, they ask us to imagine what Martin Luther King Jr.'s "I Have a Dream" speech or Ronald Reagan's "Challenger" speech would have been like if either of those great speakers had presented with PowerPoint. Of course, those special occasion speeches were persuasive and commemorative and did not lend themselves well to computerized presentational aids.

King Features, 2004, Bizarro.com.

PowerPoint is considered a magic trick by some presenters.

Table 12.7

Checklist for Using Projected Presentational Aids

Slides

1. Put the slides in order and set up the projector ahead of time.
2. Load and test slides and focus the projector before the speech.
3. Practice using the remote control.

Overhead Transparencies

1. Don't cram too much information and detail onto one overhead.
2. Test transparencies for size, focus, and visibility ahead of time.
3. Conceal information on the transparency, until it's time to talk about it.
4. Practice standing next to the projector or the projected image, whichever you prefer.
5. Use a pointer or pen to point to the screen or projector.
6. Shut off the projector when it's not in use.

Audiotape and Videotape

1. Cue up tapes or images to the correct start point ahead of time.
2. Check picture quality and volume ahead of time.
3. Practice using the remote control.

Table 12.8

Checklist for Using Computerized Presentational Aids

1. Be sure each slide focuses on only one main concept and information to support that topic.

2. Use a font size for the text that can be read easily by all audience members no matter where they are sitting. Use 36-point type for major headings, 24 points for subheads, and at least 18 points for text.

3. Use a typeface that is visually pleasing but simple, such as Times New Roman, Courier, Arial, or Helvetica.

4. Use uppercase and lowercase type because reading text printed in all capital letters is difficult.

5. Enliven your slides by using the clip art that comes with programs like PowerPoint. Just clip and paste it onto the slide wherever you want it.

6. Use a color scheme that is pleasing to the eye but not so bold it's distracting. PowerPoint allows you to choose among preselected blends of colors for slides.

7. Keep visual transitions between slides fairly simple. If you're using a computer program, use a consistent transitional device or dissolve to move from one visual to the next. Don't have lines of text flying in from all different directions throughout the presentation.

8. Finally, if you make use of anyone else's work as part of your computerized presentation, get permission and give credit when necessary.

Despite this criticism, computerized presentations have become standard in business settings. Provided you don't allow the aid to upstage you as a speaker, being able to use a computer program such as PowerPoint is essential to public speaking competence. Prepare relatively simple visual graphics, so you can speak to the audience when presenting rather than read off the slide. Control the quantity of information in each slide and the amount of action in each graphic display. Table 12.8 contains a checklist for the effective use of computerized presentational aids, several of which apply to traditional overheads as well.

If you plan to use any type of presentational aid, whether it's a flip chart or a computerized presentation, see whether it passes the NICE test:

N   Necessary to the speech and to prove your thesis, not just an add-on.

I   Impact on the audience is what you intend.

C   Clear and simple.

E   Easily seen or heard by all audience members.

learning link

Can presentational aids be used to best advantage with informative speeches or with persuasive speeches?

• • •

How-Tos for Presenting with Aids

If you decide to use a presentational aid as part of your speech, include it in at least one practice session before you actually present with it. If you're using a projected image of some kind, experiment with standing next to the projector or next to the projected image and decide which feels most comfortable to you. Also experiment with pointing to each item on the aid as you talk about it, or just letting the listeners read for themselves what is displayed. Practice with a pointer if you're going to use one, and plan what you'll do with it when it's not in use. Here's a summary of suggestions for using presentational aids most effectively:

- Speak to the audience, not to the presentational aid. If you face the aid, the audience won't hear what you're saying and your eye contact with listeners will be limited.

- Use a pointer, pencil, or laser pointer if you want to focus audience attention on the part of the aid you're talking about.

- If possible, cover up the sections of the aid you have yet to discuss. Reveal each section just as you begin to talk about it.

- Don't read the text of the aid verbatim to the audience, unless you want to emphasize a definition or description of something contained in it.

- Don't shuffle through handouts or transparencies while you're presenting. Instead, have them in the right order ahead of time and plan how you'll pick them up and where you'll put them after presenting with them.

By now, you know how to prepare and present a speech with competence. The only remaining challenge to making a successful presentation is feeling confident and self-assured about giving that speech. If you cannot manage public anxiety effectively, then all the planning and preparing in the world won't save the day. Let's now consider this challenge to public speaking competence and some specific strategies for overcoming it.

The Challenge of Public Speaking Anxiety

Public speaking anxiety, popularly referred to as stage fright, refers to a person's fear or anxiety associated with a real or anticipated public speaking event. Generally, the more formal and unfamiliar the occasion, the larger the audience, and the more important the goals, the more nervous people become about giving a speech.

Researchers have studied students' patterns of anxiety about giving speeches and learned quite a bit (Behnke & Sawyer, 1999, 2004). Students, and most people for that matter, demonstrate anticipatory anxiety for 2 weeks preceding the actual presentation. The highest level of anxiety occurs right at the beginning of a speech, during the first minute of the presentation. Suddenly, hands shake, legs quiver, and voices quake. Speakers are frequently surprised by these physiological reactions, particularly if they aren't aware of feeling very anxious before the speech. The second highest level of anxiety occurs at the time the assignment is announced and explained. The lowest level is during the time students are preparing their speeches. In a related study, the researchers discovered some gender-based differences with female speakers reporting higher anticipatory anxiety before their speeches (Behnke & Sawyer, 2000).

In addition to understanding patterns of anxiety, it is helpful to know why people have public speaking anxiety in the first place. One cause of anxiety is the psychological threat to your self-esteem, which sometimes results from remembering previous negative experiences when you spoke in public (Sawyer & Behnke, 1997). Perhaps someone laughed or failed to take you and your comments seriously. Or perhaps you forgot the most important points you wanted to make. In either case, you learned a negative lesson: when I speak publicly, I feel foolish or stupid.

A second cause of anxiety is identifying with the wrong public speakers as your role models. You watch people speak in public who appear nervous and made mistakes. You identify personally with them, rather than with someone who speaks with confidence and competence. You say to yourself, "Now that's the kind of speaker I am." The lesson is learned: when I speak in public, I make mistakes, embarrass myself, and appear inept.

A third cause of public speaking anxiety is the tendency to hold unrealistic attitudes and expectations about public speaking as a process and about yourself as a speaker. You may expect some disaster or catastrophic failure to occur when you speak, such as

learning link

Is it helpful to talk about public speaking anxiety and how to control it, or is it better not to discuss it too much?

• • •

Despite research that says public speaking anxiety is the number one fear of many people, approaching the gallows may be more frightening.

blanking out and forgetting everything you want to say. Or you may have an unrealistic desire to be accepted by everyone, to please everybody, and to have all of the listeners like you. You may think your speech has to be flawless in content and delivery. Finally, you may want to feel totally confident and completely calm and in control when you present your speech. All these attitudes and expectations are unrealistic.

Table 14.3 summarizes the three causes of public speaking anxiety and suggests some ways to handle each. See which causes you relate to most and note the suggestions for handling those.

You can learn to give speeches quite effectively and to manage any anxiety. In one study, students in an introductory public speaking course were tested right before and right after presenting a speech (MacIntyre & MacDonald, 1998). The majority of the students, even those with the highest level of anxiety at the beginning of the speech, showed significant improvement in their perceptions of their own communication competence and they also perceived the audience as more pleasant and supportive by the end of the speech. In another study, students demonstrated significant decreases in anxiety from the beginning to the end of the semester of an introductory public speaking course (Morreale, Hackman, & Neer, 1995).

Overcoming Public Speaking Anxiety

Now that you understand public speaking anxiety and why it happens, we can discuss strategies to overcome this challenge. Communication researchers and classroom instructors have tested and experimented with different kinds of treatments and discovered that this anxiety can be reduced successfully in a variety of ways (Robinson, 1997).

Public speaking students who engaged in small group activities to address anxiety every week throughout an entire semester decreased their level of communication apprehension significantly (Crump & Dudley, 1996). Regular participation in workshops on reducing anxiety made a difference for another group of students (Hopf, 1995). Viewing videotapes designed to reduce public speaking anxiety helped still other students. Students who viewed videotapes of themselves giving speeches reported a decrease in apprehension and an increase in perceptions of their own communication competence, in work and social settings, but with the largest improvements for the classroom setting (Ayres, Ayres, Baker, & Colby, 1993; Hinton & Kramer, 1998).

You can choose among three approaches to reducing anxiety: systematic desensitization, cognitive modification, and goal setting (Watson, 1990). You may find that you prefer one of these methods over another, or you may benefit from using more than one technique at the same time.

Systematic Desensitization

Systematic desensitization is a process that desensitizes a person's feelings and emotional reactions to public speaking by using positive visualization and encouraging the person to relax when contemplating a particular speaking event. With this approach, the anxious speaker learns to relax while vividly visualizing giving a speech (Ayres & Hopf, 1999). Here is how systematic desensitization works.

An instructor or a trainer teaches you general methods of relaxation and then asks you to envision a series of situations that lead up to a feared public speaking event. First, you think about a comfortable, nonthreatening situation such as the day you registered for the public speaking class along with several other courses. Then you visualize increasingly threatening and anxiety-producing situations. You get the course syllabus, you read about the speaking assignments, you choose a topic for your first speech. As you learn to relax in each situation, the trainer helps you use more advanced visualization techniques, such as recalling the situation and trying to see, hear, and feel what it actually would be like. Eventually, you should be able to relax, without feeling an overwhelming amount of anxiety, while thinking about the fear-producing event of presenting a speech.

Systematic desensitization works because you cannot be relaxed and fearful at the same time. By repeatedly visualizing a feared communication event but relaxing at the same time, you gain control of the fear.

Cognitive Modification

Cognitive modification is a process that changes or modifies unrealistic beliefs about public speaking. This approach enables a public speaker to confront his or her beliefs and fears and question their validity and value. It works as follows.

Start by identifying any unrealistic beliefs and expectations you hold about yourself as a public speaker. Write down any unrealistic or negative thoughts and expectations that come to mind when you think about an upcoming public speaking event, such as "I'm certain something terrible will happen while I'm giving my speech, and there's nothing I can do about it." Then rewrite each thought in a more reasonable and positive way, for example, "It's unlikely anything will go wrong, and by planning and practice I can help avert any problems." Throughout the preperformance period, jot down any negative thoughts and rewrite them positively. Periodically review the positive thoughts. Some speakers even post their new statements by their computers or the work area where they prepare their speeches. It is important to note that the unrealistic statements are extreme, misleading, and produce high anxiety. In contrast, the revised statements are less extreme, more realistic, and result in a more moderate reaction to anxiety.

Cognitive modification works because it provides you with a different way of looking at yourself. It derails your negative thinking and replaces it with positive statements about yourself as a public speaker.

Goal Setting

Goal setting is a process for alleviating anxiety that makes use of a structured plan for changing a person's public speaking behaviors. You begin by identifying a general area of improvement for your goals, such as reducing your overall level of communication apprehension. For that general area, you formulate specific goal statements in behavioral terms, such as contribute more frequently and confidently to class discussions, contribute more frequently in small groups, and discuss ideas (for speeches) more comfortably with your professor. Next, you write down behaviors and criteria for success for each statement, so you have benchmarks for accomplishing each goal. The success criteria might be to make a minimum of one contribution per day to class discussions, offer two comments in each group meeting in which you participate, and discuss your ideas with your professor once a week.

Goal setting works because it provides a tangible framework for accomplishing behavioral change. If you follow the steps to accomplish your goals, change is inevitable; and when you start behaving confidently, you begin to feel more confident.

In addition to these three basic approaches to reducing anxiety, this final suggestion may be helpful to you. Several leading researchers on anxiety discovered that 38.2% of student worries about giving a speech can be predicted by their concerns about receiving evaluative feedback after their performance (Kopecky, Sawyer, & Behnke, 2004). Instead of worrying about the feedback you may receive, concentrate all your energy on preparing and delivering your speech effectively—not on what others will say to you afterward.

At this point, you should be quite ready to give a speech in a highly competent manner. The next two chapters focus on preparing and presenting the two most common forms of speeches—informative and persuasive.

 ## Chapter Summary

Research studies show that training in public speaking is the best way to improve public speaking skills. The competent use of language and words, vocal variety, pronunciation, articulation, grammar, nonverbal cues, and presentational aids are all essential to presenting a speech successfully.

Competent language enhances the listeners' understanding and enthusiasm for a speech by the use of words that are clear, vivid, and appropriate. Vividness and style are achieved through the use of imagery, figures of speech (simile, metaphor, and analogy), and techniques such as the rhetorical question, alliteration, and repetition. In addition to language, vocal variety is used to heighten and maintain audience attention and interest in a speech, by varying the rate (fast versus slow), pitch (high versus low), and volume (loud versus soft) of the voice. A competent speaker also pronounces words correctly, articulates sounds and words clearly, and uses correct grammar. Beyond words and how they are spoken, a competent speaker uses the following nonverbal cues to support and enhance the spoken message: appearance, posture and body movement, gestures, facial expression, and eye contact. These cues are incorporated into a transparent delivery, which means that the audience doesn't focus on the delivery but instead pays full attention to the speaker's message. Finally, a competent speaker uses presentational aids, unprojected, projected, or computerized, to enhance the delivery of the speech.

To make best use of these presentation skills, it is critical to address the challenge of public speaking anxiety, which often is caused by concern about psychological threats to self-esteem, identifying with the wrong public speakers, or holding unrealistic attitudes and expectations about giving a speech. Public speaking anxiety can be reduced by using any one of three approaches: systematic desensitization, cognitive modification, or goal setting.

Study and Review

The premium companion website for *Human Communication* offers a broad range of resources that will help you better understand the material in this chapter, complete assignments, and succeed on tests. The website resources include

- Interactive self-assessments, competency grids, and other tools
- Web links, practice activities, self-quizzes, and a sample final exam

For more information about this text's electronic learning resources, including Speech Builder Express, consult the *Guide to Online Resources for Human Communication* or visit **http://communication.wadsworth.com/morreale2.**

Key Terms

The key terms below are defined in the chapter on the pages indicated. They are also presented alphabetically with definitions in the Glossary, which begins on page 467. The book's website includes flashcards and crossword puzzles to help you learn these terms and the concepts they represent.

Building Knowledge

The following questions are among the practice activities on the book's website.

1. In what creative ways can a novice speaker, not well known to her or his audience, improve initial credibility with those listeners?
2. Competent language calls for using words that are clear, vivid, and appropriate. However, words that are clear may not be vivid and words that are vivid may not be appropriate for the particular audience or speaking situation. How can a speaker balance the use of all three types of words?
3. As speakers strive for variety in rate, pitch, and volume, how can they retain the genuineness of their own voices?
4. Is it always appropriate for a speaker to use correct pronunciation, articulation, and grammar? When is it not, and why?
5. Of all the nonverbal cues a speaker can use, which is the most important and why—appearance, posture, body movement, gestures, facial expression, or eye contact?
6. What aspects of a speech help decide the type of presentational aid to use?
7. Of the three basic approaches to reducing public speaking anxiety, which would work best for you, and why?

 ## Building Skills

The exercises below are among the practice activities on the book's website.

Individual Exercises

1. Make a videotape of your next speech during one of your practice sessions. Watch yourself and evaluate your presentation skills, based on the content of this chapter. Identify your key strengths and weaknesses and make a list of what you will try to improve when you present the speech to an audience.
2. Attend a live lecture or speech. Evaluate the speaker's presentation skills using the content of this chapter.

3. If you are using InfoTrac College Edition, enter *public speaking* as a subject search. Select several articles that appear to offer helpful hints on presenting a speech. Read the articles and synthesize a list of hints that you could use as the topic of an in-class speech.
4. Go the website of the Public Address Division of the National Communication Association (**http://www.ncapublicaddress.org/PublicAddressArchives.htm**), which links to many other sites that contain speeches, including, for example, the Top 100 Speeches of the 20th Century. Find a speech that appeals to you and, using its text, examine the speaker's use of language. Is it clear, vivid, and appropriate? Does the speaker use correct grammar and effective figures of speech?
5. On the Internet, access the White House website (**http://www.whitehouse.gov**) and find the web page that provides manuscripts of the president's recent major speeches. Select a speech that interests you and present an analysis of it in a speech to your class.
6. Try employing systematic desensitization to change how you feel about giving a speech. Put yourself in a relaxing environment, perhaps at home listening to

soothing music. Lie down or sit in a comfortable chair and close your eyes. Envision yourself in a series of situations that coincide with the steps you will take to prepare your next speech. Completely relax while thinking about each step in the speech preparation process. First relax your toes, then your feet, then your ankles, and so on, moving up through your body to the top of your head. Relax as you envision each step, and then see if you can envision yourself feeling relaxed when presenting a speech.

7. Try using cognitive modification to change your unrealistic beliefs about public speaking. Think ahead to your next assigned speech and write down any beliefs and expectations you can think of about either the speaking event or yourself as a public speaker. Number each belief and then rewrite each as a more positive and reasonable expectation. Type up the new beliefs and print them out using fairly large letters. Make several copies and post them in conspicuous places for several days to help change your thinking. Crumple up and throw away the piece of paper with your old thoughts after you have revised them into new beliefs.

8. Use goal setting to handle your anxiety by developing your skills. Choose an aspect of public speaking that is problematic for you and write it at the top of a pad of paper. For that general area, list several specific behavioral goal statements, which if achieved, would change how you behave.

Group Activities

1. Get another student to be your rehearsal and practice partner. Ask your partner to watch carefully how you present your speech. Then have that person critique your posture, body movement, gestures, facial expression, and eye contact. Reverse roles, watch, and then critique your partner's nonverbal cues.

2. Ask your practice partner to provide you feedback during your in-class presentation on two factors: volume and speaking rate. Your partner should sit toward the rear of the room and communicate with you using four hand signals. A flat hand, facing up and lifted toward the ceiling means "Increase your volume, you're talking too softly." A single finger pointed up and held at the mouth means "Softer, you're too loud." A circular motion with the hand means "Speed it up, you're too slow." A stretching motion with both hands means "Slow it down, you're talking too fast."

3. In small groups, practice your ability to walk to, stand in, and move around in the speaking area. Have each student take a turn walking to the speaking platform, standing at the lectern, and moving deliberately away from the lectern to another part of the speaking area. Group members should provide feedback to each student.

4. In small groups, practice presenting your speech using your presentational aid. Again, the group should provide feedback to each student.

5. If there are bilingual or trilingual students in the class, get in groups and discuss those students' personal experiences with code switching.

 ## References

Aguinis, H., Simonsen, M., & Pierce, C. (1998). Effects of nonverbal behavior on perceptions of power bases. *Journal of Social Psychology, 138*(4), 455–470.

Auer, P. (Ed.). (1998). *Code-switching in conversation: Language, interaction, and identity.* London: Routledge.

Ausmus, W. A. (1998). Pragmatic uses of metaphor: Models and metaphor in the nuclear winter scenario. *Communication Monographs, 65,* 67–82.

Ayres, J., Ayres, F., Baker, A., & Colby, N. (1993). Two empirical tests of a videotape designed to reduce public speaking anxiety. *Journal of Applied Communication Research, 21,* 132–147.

Ayres, J., & Hopf, T. (1999). Vividness and control: Factors in the effectiveness of performance visualization? *Communication Education, 48*(4), 287–294.

Behnke, R., & Sawyer, C. (1999). Milestones of anticipatory public speaking anxiety. *Communication Education, 48*(2), 165–173.

Behnke, R., & Sawyer, C. (2000). Anticipatory anxiety patterns for male and female public speakers. *Communication Education, 49*(2), 187–195.

Behnke, R., & Sawyer, C. (2004). Public speaking anxiety as a function of sensitization and habituation process. *Communication Education, 53*(2), 164–174.

Brandt, D. S. (1998). Digital presentations: Make your delivery effective. *Computers in Libraries, 18*(5), 35–38.

Clair, R. P. (1998). *Organizing silence: A world of possibilities.* Albany: SUNY Press.

Crump, C. A., & Dudley, J. A. (1996). Methods for dealing with communication apprehension in higher education: Speech instruction via use of small group modalities. (ERIC Document Reproductive Service No. ED 390 100.)

Dance, F. E. X. (1999, July). Successful presenters master the art of being transparent. *Presentations,* p. 80.

Dance, F. E. X. (2002). Speech and thought: A renewal. *Communication Education, 51*(4), 355–359.

Detz, J. (1992). *How to write and give a speech.* (pp. 60–61). New York: St. Martin's Press.

Ellis, K. (1995). Apprehension, self-perceived competency, and teacher immediacy in the laboratory-supported public speaking course: Trends and relationships. *Communication Education, 44,* 64–78.

Fatt, P. T. (1999, June–July). It's not the way you say, it's how you say it. *Communication World, 16*(6), 37–41.

Haleta, L. L. (1996). Student perceptions of teachers' use of language: The effects of powerful and powerless language on impression formation and uncertainty. *Communication Education, 45,* 16–28.

Harris, R. M. (1994). Practically perfect presentations. *Training & Development, 48*(7), 55–58.

Hayakawa, S. I. (1964). *Language in thought and action.* New York: Harcourt Brace.

Hinton, J. S., & Kramer, M. W. (1998). The impact of self-directed videotape feedback on students' self-reported levels of communication competence and apprehension. *Communication Education, 47,* 151–161.

Hopf, T. (1995). Does self-help material work? Testing a manual designed to help trainers construct public speaking apprehension reduction workshops. *Communication Research Reports, 21,* 34–38.

Huspek, M. (2000). Oppositional codes: The case of the penitentiary of New Mexico riot. *Journal of Applied Communication Research, 28*(2), 144–164.

Kopecky, C. C., Sawyer, C. R., & Behnke, R. R. (2004). Brief reports. *Communication Education, 53*(3), 281–286.

Logue, C. M. (1997). *Representative American speeches, 1937–1997.* New York: Wilson.

MacIntyre, P. S., & MacDonald, J. R. (1998). Public speaking anxiety: Perceived competence and audience congeniality. *Communication Education, 47,* 359–365.

Martin, J. N., Hecht, M. L., & Larkey, L. K. (1994). Conversational improvement strategies for interethnic communication: African American and European American perspectives. *Communication Monographs, 61,* 236–255.

May, J. M. (1988). *Trials of character: The eloquence of Ciceronian ethos.* Chapel Hill: University of North Carolina Press.

Messaris, P. (1997). *Visual persuasion: The role of images in advertising.* New Delhi: Sage.

Morreale, S. P., Hackman, M. Z., & Neer, M. (1995). Predictors of behavioral competence and self-esteem: A study assessing impact in a basic public speaking course. *Basic Communication Course Annual, 7,* 125–141.

Robinson, T. E. (1997). Communication apprehension and the basic public speaking course: A national survey of in-class treatment techniques. *Communication Education, 46,* 188–197.

Samovar, L., & Porter, R. (2004). *Communication between cultures* (5th ed.). Belmont, CA: Thomson/Wadsworth, Inc.

Sawyer, C. R., & Behnke, R. R. (1997). Communication apprehension and implicit memories of public speaking state anxiety. *Communication Education, 45,* 211–222.

Seibold, D., Kudsi, S., & Rude, M. (1993). Does communication training make a difference? Evidence for the effectiveness of a presentation skills program. *Journal of Applied Communication Research, 21,* 111–131.

Sellnow, D. D., & Treinen, K. P. (2004). The role of gender in perceived speaker competence: An analysis of student peer critiques. *Communication Education, 53*(3), 286–297.

Sparks, J. R., Areni, C. S., & Cox, K. C. (1998). An investigation of the effects of language style and communication modality on persuasion. *Communication Education, 65,* 108–125.

Thweatt, K. S., & McCroskey, J. C. (1998). The impact of teacher immediacy and misbehaviors on teacher credibility. *Communication Education, 47,* 348–358.

Watson, A. K. (1990). Helping developmental students overcome communication apprehension. *Journal of Developmental Education, 14,* 10–17.

Wolff, M. (1998). Perfect pitch. *Success, 45*(8), 18.

Wood, J. T. (1994). *Gendered lives: Communication, gender, and culture.* Belmont, CA: Wadsworth.

Zuckerman, L. (1999, April 17). Words go right to the brain, but can they stir the heart? *New York Times,* pp. A17–A19.

Chapter 13

LEARNING OBJECTIVES | After studying this chapter, you should be able to

1. Describe what informative speaking is and why it is crucial in your professional and community life.

2. Explain the three types of informative speeches on the basis of their objective.

3. Prepare an outline and present an informative speech using the most appropriate of the five informative organizational patterns.

4. Demonstrate the competent use of support materials in your informative speech, choosing among definitions, descriptions, examples, stories, testimonies and quotations, and facts and statistics.

5. Describe the critical role of ethics in informative public speaking and apply appropriate ethical standards to your own informative speeches.

Speaking to Inform

By the time Nicholas started to prepare his informative speech, he had already learned a lot about speaking with competence. Now it was time to apply his newly learned preparation and presenting skills to the informative assignment in his public speaking class. He chose a topic he knew something about—the popularity of coffee shops and coffee drinking in American society. Because of his job as a manager at the Starbucks near school, Nicholas had observed how much business had grown over the last few years. Plus, he thought the topic would appeal to his classmates, most of whom dropped by frequently for a cup of java. Nicholas located some impressive statistics in the library demonstrating a year-by-year increase in coffee consumption, so he decided to describe how much coffee drinking had increased in the United States during the past decade and why that happened. To support his speech, he interviewed students who explained why they liked coming to Starbucks.

When he presented the speech, "The Joy of Java," in class, Nicholas expected the other students to be fascinated, but that wasn't what happened. Some of them appeared a little bored as Nicholas told them about the increase in coffee drinking. His grade improved over the last speech, as he had hoped, but he wondered why his classmates weren't more attentive. After class, he was anxious to review the professor's feedback form to find out what he did well and what he could have done better. He was sure his topic was a good one for the audience. But had he provided too much or too little information—and was it the right information? Was the speech organized in a way that was easy to follow? Why weren't his listeners motivated to learn more about the dramatic increase in coffee drinking?

The instructor said that his presentation style was fine, and he definitely had chosen a topic the other students could relate to. He had organized the speech well and it was easy to follow as he talked about his two main points—how much coffee consumption had increased and why that had happened. But to gain and maintain the attention of the other students, the instructor said Nicholas needed to be more creative in his use of support materials such as presentational aids and examples to liven up the facts and statistics. Although his testimonies were effective, he could have used a better attention getter, perhaps a story to open his speech. His support materials could have included some information and quotations from high credibility sources in the coffee industry. Nicholas had done a good job, but he still had something to learn about giving an informative speech.

This chapter covers key ideas about speaking to inform that will help you prepare and present an informative speech most competently. We begin by clarifying what an informative speech is and why it's an important form of public speaking competence. Then we describe three types of informative speeches, discuss five patterns for organizing and outlining them, and offer ideas for using support materials effectively. The chapter concludes with a description of ethical informative speaking and some final suggestions for making your informative speech the best it can be. ■

Understanding the Informative Speech

An informative speech may range from a description of the intangible, such as understanding the law of gravity, to a set of tangible instructions, such as how to change a flat tire or prepare for final exams. Whether the speech describes, explains, or instructs the audience about something, it's considered informative.

What Is an Informative Speech?

An informative speech about an object could be about a national or local memorial. The newest national memorial in Washington D.C. commemorating World War II has garnered national attention for its unique design.

As we stated in Chapter 11, the general purpose of an informative speech is to communicate new information or a new perspective on a topic to an audience and bring the listeners to greater understanding or insight. Given that general purpose, an informative speech may be about an object, process, event, person, issue, or concept.

If you choose to present a **speech about an object,** it is usually about something tangible that can be seen, touched, or otherwise experienced through the physical senses, such as a car, a computer, a place, or even a monument of some kind, such as the Lincoln Memorial or the new World War II Memorial, both of which are in Washington, D.C. If you decide to describe a system or sequence of steps that lead to a result or change taking place, such as the steps in applying for a loan or shopping for a new car or computer, that is an informative **speech about a process.** An **event speech** describes something that has occurred, such as a historical event—the dawning of the new millennium—or a noteworthy event that has happened in your community—such as the results of an election or reactions to a local catastrophe. A **speech about a person** describes an individual in much the same way that an object speech describes an object.

"Senator, the American people, whom you often mention in your speeches, would like a word with you."

A speech about a person or people may result in those people wanting a word with you after the speech.

A **concept speech** is about abstract ideas—theories, principles, or values—such as the theory of relativity or the principles of freedom of the press or human rights underlying democracy. If you choose to present an **issue speech,** it would examine a debatable topic from various points of view, such as the right to die, environmental concerns, or the banning of certain music and books. To better understand these six possibilities for your informative speech, Table 13.1 suggests topics for each.

An informative speech about an issue brings up an important concept that any competent public speaker must understand—that there is a fine line between informative speaking and persuasive speaking, which is the topic of Chapter 14. Some public speaking experts say that all public speeches—including speeches to inform—are partly persuasive. According to this perspective, whenever you present information, you're attempting to persuade the audience that the information is true and right. Because you believe you are telling the truth about the information, and because you are trying to convince the audience of that truth, perhaps any informative speech could be considered mildly persuasive.

To understand this viewpoint better, take a look at Figure 13.1, where speeches are positioned on a continuum. At one end of the continuum, the speeches are more objective and less opinionated—mostly informative. At the other end of the continuum, the speeches are more subjective and more opinionated—therefore more persuasive.

The sample student speech at the end of this chapter fits on the continuum in the figure. Kelly Bender's speech, "The Race for a Cure: Rethinking the Course of AIDS Research," is an issue speech that presents new information about AIDS research (2004). It took second place at the 132nd annual Interstate Oratorical Association Contest in 2004. We include it with this chapter as an example of well-organized and effective informative speaking. But read the speech and think about where you would position it on the informative versus persuasive continuum.

Table 13.1

Possible Topics for Informative Speeches

Here's a list of possible topics for your speech based on the nature of its content. You may find a topic for your informative speech by examining these suggestions.

Content of Speech	Possible Topics for Each Type of Speech
An object speech	Things you collect—books, stamps, antiques; an extraordinary place you've visited or know about—a town, city, state, or country; a new gadget—a palm computer, CD recorder, or household item.
A process speech	Things you do or know how to do—snowshoeing, skiing, hiking, traveling, refinishing furniture, cooking, saving money, spending, getting along with others, living in another country, planning your life.
An event speech	A local or national current event, a noteworthy event from history, an event that marked a turning point in history, an event that occurred in the life of a noteworthy person, a special event that occurred in your life.
A people speech	A contemporary or historical person of significance to the audience, someone you know or have known of particular interest.
An issue speech	Nuclear disarmament, affirmative action, recycling, conservation laws and practices, violence in the media, grading systems, substance abuse and regulation, health care and policies, political and governmental policies or programs, abortion laws and practices, unions and strike policies, lifestyles.
A concept speech	Nuclear power, multiculturalism/diversity, the world ecosystem, media literacy, the information age, ethical communication, theory of evolution, principles of communication, democracy, friendship, love.

Figure 13.1

A Continuum for Informative and Persuasive Public Speaking

Public speeches may be considered to be on a continuum from highly informative to highly persuasive. Informative speeches at one end are more objective and less opinionated. At the other end are persuasive speeches that are more subjective and more opinionated.

Why Do You Need Informative Speaking Skills?

The ability to present an informative speech may be one of the most valuable public speaking competencies you'll learn, because you'll use these skills so frequently. In the information age in which we live, the majority of us earn our living by handling information in some way and conveying it to one another. Therefore, informative speaking of all sorts is a crucial aspect of most people's professional and community lives.

A professor's lecture obviously is an informative speech, but businesspeople often are called on to present information. In the corporate world, informative speaking can take the form of a briefing that summarizes large amounts of information, a report of progress on projects and activities, or a training session that provides instructions about how to carry out a task or assignment. In our communities, most of us belong to various groups and

learning link

Why is informative speaking so crucial in contemporary society?

• • •

organizations. At parent-teacher meetings and at civic or political gatherings, we often have to stand up and present our ideas informatively.

In giving any of these informative speeches, our goal is to promote understanding of the information, as well as to encourage the audience to retain a significant amount of the message. Retention of information is a very real problem. According to one listening expert, after as little as 10 minutes of a lecture or informative speech, some listeners experience "micro-sleep," during which they only partially attend to what is said (Roberts, 1998). As a result, one day after hearing an informative speech, they recall only about half of it. Two weeks later, they're fortunate if they recall even 25% of what was presented. Given these realities, improving your informative speaking competence is a must, and that begins with an understanding of the three different types of informative speeches.

Types of Informative Speeches

We can categorize informative speeches by their objectives. Three possible objectives for an informative speech are to describe, to explain, and to instruct. These are general objectives, similar to the general purpose for a speech discussed in Chapter 11, but they are tailored to informative speaking. They emphasize audience understanding or abilities—what the audience should know or be able to do by the end of the speech.

Speaking to Describe

Descriptions are used when the listeners are unfamiliar with the topic of the speech and need new information to understand it. If you want the audience to become aware of and remember something new, your objective is to describe it, or provide a verbal picture. If your speech is about a vacation to an exotic or unfamiliar place, you will need to describe what it's like there, perhaps by contrast to a more familiar place. If you want to introduce a new product line to your sales force, it's necessary to describe the new items and their advantages over older products. This informative objective could be stated as follows. Take note in this example of how concrete the speaker's expectation of the audience is.

The sales force members will understand and be able to describe four advantages of the new product line, compared with last year's products.

Speaking to Explain

Explanations are necessary to explain how something works or to clarify something that is already known but not well understood. If you want listeners to understand why something exists or has occurred, or how it operates, your objective is to explain it. If your speech is about public speaking anxiety, for example, the other students are probably familiar with what it is, but they would appreciate an explanation of why they have it and what can be done about it. If your speech is about an increase in recreational drug usage, you could explain why the problem exists and what measures are being taken to address the situation. An informative objective for this speech would be this:

The audience will be able to explain the underlying causes of the increase in recreational drug use, as well as two strategies now in use to combat this problem.

To further clarify the distinction between an informative and a persuasive speech, if you were to move beyond explaining the problem of increased drug usage and take a position on how to decrease it, your speech would become persuasive.

learning link

Which objective—to describe, to explain, or to instruct—would be most useful in most jobs in our contemporary society?

• • •

Speaking to Instruct

Instructions are useful when the objective is to teach the audience something or tell them how to use something. If you want the listeners to be able to apply what is presented, you provide instructions. For example, if you want the other students to be able to use a particular method for reducing public speaking anxiety, such as changing how they think and feel about giving speeches, then you need to provide instructions for applying that method. If a new product available through your company needs to be demonstrated to customers by a salesperson, directions for its use should be provided in an instructional speech. Here's an informative objective statement for that speech:

> Each salesperson will understand how to use the new product and be able to perform the six steps essential to its use.

Why do we need to clarify the objective of an informative speech? Think about Nicholas's speech at the beginning of this chapter. After choosing the topic of coffee consumption, Nicholas decided, perhaps unintentionally, that his speech was to be both descriptive and explanatory. His objectives were to describe the surprising changes in coffee drinking patterns in the United States and to explain why those changes had occurred. Given that he had two objectives, Nicholas needed to provide sufficient information to accomplish both effectively. He provided statistics to support his claim of an increase in coffee drinking, but he had testimonial evidence from only students who frequent Starbucks to explain why the increase had occurred. That oversight might have accounted in part for his speech not being quite as effective as he would have liked. If he decided to stay with both objectives, he should have researched the second objective more, perhaps contacting marketing experts at coffee companies for additional explanations of the increase in coffee consumption.

The sample student speech at the end of this chapter effectively illustrates the importance of understanding the relationship between the objective of a speech and what is included in its content. Like Nicholas's speech, it has two objectives—to describe and to explain—but Bender's speech contains substantial information to accomplish both these objectives.

Organizing and Outlining an Informative Speech _____

The principles of speech organization and outlining discussed in Chapter 11, although important for all speeches, are especially helpful for a competent speaker who wants to achieve the objective of an informative speech. Because the goal is often to communicate an abundance of new information, good organization is essential for the audience to understand what is presented and not be overwhelmed by it. Furthermore, informative speeches are frequently about complex or complicated topics that can be hard to understand.

A communication researcher summarized why it's difficult to organize and present complex ideas and topics in informative speeches (Rowan, 2003). The information in the speech may be confusing because it includes difficult concepts or language, structures or processes that are hard to envision, or ideas that are hard to believe. In all of these cases, Rowan suggests first analyzing the informative topic to discover what aspects of it will be most difficult for your listeners to understand and then organizing and outlining your speech accordingly. Developing a working outline for your speech (see Chapter 11) will help you with this task. You will be able to determine what complex information must be

Figure 13.2

Organizing the Informative Speech

The body of an informative speech is structured using any one of five different organizational patterns. The introduction and conclusion remain the same as we discussed in Chapter 11.

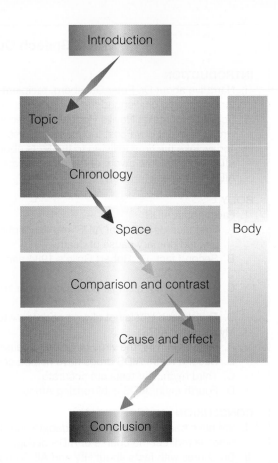

included, the best location for it in your speech, and what form of support or presentational aid is essential to understanding it.

Five possible ways to organize the body of an informative speech are by topic, chronology, space, comparison and contrast, and cause and effect (Figure 13.2). Several of these patterns clearly could be used for a persuasive speech. Cause and effect, for example, is frequently recommended for both informative and persuasive speeches.

As we look in more detail at these five patterns for the body of the speech, recall that an informative speech also has an introduction and conclusion as described in Chapter 11.

Topic

Topical organization divides information about a subject and topic into subtopics or subcategories that will constitute the main points of the body of the speech. This structure is advantageous when your topic naturally clusters into subtopics or lists of items you want the listeners to understand or know how to use. Various aspects of an object or a person, steps in a process, or dimensions of a concept are subcategories that you can effectively organize by topic. The body of the AIDS speech at the end of this chapter is organized by topic and covers two subtopics, or main points—facts about AIDS research and myths about it. Figure 13.3 contains an outline for that speech to illustrate how the subtopics make up the two main points of the body of the speech.

One problem with topical organization is that the main points may sound unrelated if you fail to provide clear transitions as you move from one point to the next. Also, you

learning link

Of the five organizational patterns described here for informative speeches, which would also be useful for persuasive speeches and why?

• • •

Figure 13.3

This informative speech at
the end of this chapter is
organized topically with
two well-developed main
points making up the body
of the speech.

AIDS Speech Outline

INTRODUCTION

I. Narrative about Dr. Peter Duesberg, recipient of an NIH Outstanding Investiga-tor Grant, who challenged the HIV/AIDS theory (attention getter)

II. Scientific journalist Neville Hodgkinson who stated that if the HIV theory is wrong, it might have cost thousands of lives (thesis/statement of significance)

III. Today, take the time to listen to the facts about AIDS, some of the myths about AIDS, and become aware of the AIDS debate so we can start spreading true AIDS awareness (preview)

BODY

I. Facts about AIDS

   A. First fact: definition of AIDS and description indicating that it is the second-ary, not primary cause of death

   B. Second fact: Dr. Robert Gallo's 1984 announcement that HIV was probable cause of AIDS

   C. Third fact: not a single published paper supports HIV as probable cause of AIDS

   D. Fourth fact: HIV is not always necessary for AIDS to exist

II. Myths about AIDS

   A. First myth: HIV, the virus believed to cause AIDS, is infectious

   B. Second myth: AIDS drugs have helped control AIDS

   C. Third myth: HIV tests are accurate

   D. Fourth myth: AIDS is terrorizing Africa

CONCLUSION

I. We have been misled about the debate surrounding the cause of AIDS, and it's time we redirect the course of AIDS dialogue (restatement of thesis)

II. Brochures with facts about HIV and AIDS and list of support groups and chari-ties (review and summary)

III. Robert Gallo, who announced the HIV-AIDS connection, was found guilty of fal-sifying and stealing scientific data related to HIV and AIDS; Dr. Luc Montegnier admitted that his isolation of HIV as the cause of AIDS might have been a labo-ratory contamination (closing device)

---

risk boring the audience and sounding like you're droning on and on, from one topic of discussion to another. To avoid this problem, structure an introduction that builds a strong case for the importance of your topic, use transitions between main points, and use a pre-sentational aid to help your listeners stay focused and interested.

Chronology

Chronological organization is used to describe changes or developments in any situation or circumstance. It can be historical—linked to actual dates—or sequential—related to a sequence of steps that occur or are performed over time.

A *historical structure* would work well if you're describing an event such as a war, the founding and development of your college or company, or the development and decline of the labor movement in the United States. In a speech about the labor movement, you could use a historical timeline to structure the main points in this way:

   I. 1792 to 1929: labor unions grew to be a powerful economic force in the United States.

II. 1930 to 1950: union membership grew in the 1930s and 1940s and began to decline in the 1950s.

III. 1960 to present: membership has continued to decline; labor unions are searching for a new foothold in the information age economy.

Two problems can occur if you organize a speech historically. First, the audience may not think something that happened in the past is relevant to them. If that's the case, demonstrate early in the speech the relevance of the speech topic to their lives. Second, you'll bore the audience if your speech is little more than a recounting of dates and times. To avoid that problem, include precise dates only to provide a context for appreciating the significance of the event. Also, try to make the particular time in history memorable using lively and colorful examples of life back then.

A *sequential time structure* is effective in describing the series of steps in a process. You could use this pattern to describe how the stock market ebbs and flows or how weather systems form and move around the globe. You might present a topic such as the steps a college graduate takes to find a new job with the following sequential pattern:

I. Gather information about job possibilities that align with your qualifications.

II. Develop or revise your résumé, highlighting your strengths that match the job of your dreams.

III. Circulate your résumé to employment agencies.

IV. Apply to your top three choices and await acceptance notification.

Space

Spatial organization presents information on the basis of the positioning of objects in physical space or the relationships between locations. This structure works well when you want listeners to visualize the arrangement of objects, locations, or distances. For example, if you're describing what your home is like, or the architectural design of a building or a mall, you would structure your speech spatially around the layout of the building, beginning with the front hall, say, or the ground floor. Spatial organization would also work well to describe the shifting battle lines held by the North and South during the Civil War; the best places to visit in a major city such as London or New York; or even the various regions of the human brain and their functions, which could be organized in the following way:

I. Cerebellum

II. Cerebral cortex

III. Pituitary

IV. Thalamus

V. Spinal cord

The main problem with spatial organization is making certain that the listeners follow along and can visualize the spaces you are describing. Providing a map, layout, or diagram of the spaces, like the one of the human brain in Figure 13.4, will solve that problem.

Comparison and Contrast

Organization by comparison and contrast helps describe or explain how a subject is similar to, or different from, something else. *Comparison* means pointing out the similarities; *contrast* means pointing out the differences. This structure works particularly well if the

Figure 13.4

Presentational Aid for
Organizing by Space

A speech about the func-
tions of the different parts
of the brain could use a
diagram of the various
areas.

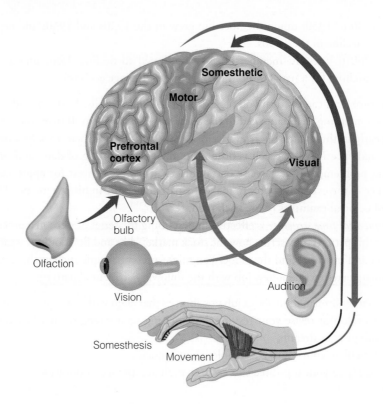

subject of the speech is unfamiliar but can be easily related to something the audience already knows about.

For example, comparison and contrast would be useful for describing a visit to another country. You could first describe how the country is similar to one the listeners are
familiar with, and then talk about how the country and its customs are dissimilar. A speech
on health care reform could compare and contrast programs in the United States to those
in other countries with two main points as the body of the speech:

I. How the U.S. health care program is like (compares to) that in Canada and
England.
II. How the U.S. health care program is unlike (contrasts to) programs in other
countries.

One challenge is structuring the speech so listeners know when you're talking about a
similarity and when you're describing a difference. You could present all the comparisons
first, followed by all the contrasts; then your speech's structure would be like that of the
health care speech. Another approach would be to select important aspects of the subject
and talk about the similarities or the differences of each aspect. Then the body of the
speech would have as many main points as aspects that you choose to talk about. Here's
the health care example again, organized on the basis of aspects of the issue:

I. Historical background to the two health care systems
II. Benefits and costs of both systems for patients
III. Advantages and disadvantages of each system for health care providers
IV. Advantages and disadvantages of each system for health care facilities

Cause and Effect

Organization by cause and effect examines why something happens—the causes—and what happens as a result—the effects. This structure is good for understanding an event or an action of an individual, an organization, or an institution. It is also useful for describing a controversial issue, because it can illustrate connections between the issue and its consequences. You could use a cause-and-effect speech to describe a significant historical event, such as the development of nuclear power in so-called rogue states, or the emergence of a domestic social problem, such as an increase in smoking by young people.

Be aware that you may want to reverse the order and describe the effects or results first and then their cause. This reverse approach is recommended when the audience is already interested in the topic and knows something about it. By first calling attention to the significant impact of the effects, you heighten interest in the causes before you discuss them. That's what Nicholas did in his speech about coffee drinking. He first described the effects—how much coffee consumption had increased in the United States—and then the cause—why people are drinking more coffee. In a speech about smoking, you could first describe the effects—the devastation of lung cancer—before you proceed to the cause—marketing cigarettes to young people. Here's how the body of that speech could be structured:

I. Statistics on the increase in lung cancer and early deaths (effect)
II. Story about a young person who died of lung cancer (effect)
III. Amount of money tobacco companies spend annually to reach a young market (cause)
IV. Ads designed to appeal to young smokers (cause)

Two cautions are in order when using cause-and-effect organization. First, be sure you are clear about whether you are speaking to inform or to persuade, because this organizational pattern lends itself to both types of speeches. For instance, the informative speech about smoking would become persuasive if you urged the audience to take some action about the situation. Second, be certain you have a true cause-and-effect relationship and that the situation (cause) you're describing is really what is causing the result (effect). To be both competent and ethical, you must be sure it's not just a series of coincidences.

To decide which of the five organizational patterns will work best for organizing and outlining the body of your informative speech, think about the actual content of the speech. Depending on whether the speech is about an object, process, event, person, issue, or concept, one or more of the organizational patterns just described will be most effective. Table 13.2 summarizes suggestions for organizing the body of your informative speech according to what the speech is about.

Using Support Materials to Inform

Deciding how to organize your informative speech is a vital step. But to make your speech as effective as possible, you also need to be inventive and creative in using support materials. In Chapter 11 you learned about the sources of information from which to gather support materials, such as the Internet, the library, and your own experiences and those of other people. From these sources you will have access to definitions and descriptions, examples, stories, testimonies and quotations, and facts and statistics. These forms of support are essential to informative speaking, and they are equally effective for use in persuasive speeches. Let's see how you can best use them.

Table 13.2	
Organizing Informative Speeches	
Depending on the content of the informative speech, certain organizational patterns will work better than others.	
If the Speech Is About . . .	**Then Organize it This Way:**
An object	*By topic:* Use if aspects of the object you're describing naturally cluster into categories. *By chronology:* Use if aspects of the object can easily be visualized in a spatial relationship to one another.
A process	*By chronology:* Use if the process you're describing occurs sequentially over time or as a sequence of steps. *By space:* Use if the steps in the process can be easily visualized as connected to each other.
An event	*By chronology:* Use when an event or a series of events can be described as they occurred over time. *By cause and effect:* Use when the event can be understood by describing why it happened and what resulted.
A person	*By topic:* Use when you want to describe various aspects, characteristics, achievements, or actions of a person. *By comparison and contrast:* Use to understand a person based on how she or he is either like or unlike someone else. *By cause and effect:* Use to understand the cause and effects of the person's actions or decisions.
An issue	*By cause and effect:* Use to promote understanding of an issue by presenting why the issue exists and what is happening as a result. *By comparison and contrast:* Use to provide insights into an issue, based on how it is like or unlike another issue. *By topic:* Use to describe the main ideas that comprise the issue.
A concept	*By topic:* Use to describe main ideas that comprise the concept. *By comparison and contrast:* Use to provide insights into an unfamiliar concept by describing how it is like or unlike something else.

learning link

How would definitions and descriptions be most effective in a speech to describe?

• • •

Definitions and Descriptions

We achieve clarity and understanding in an informative speech in part by providing definitions and descriptions. In Chapter 2, you learned that clarity is essential to communicating competently, whether with one other person or with a large audience. To achieve clarity, first realize that uncommon terms that are new or unfamiliar to the listeners must be explained. You can accomplish this by defining the new word or term and providing a description of it early in your speech.

Second, members of the audience may interpret common or familiar words differently from what you mean. So if a familiar word or phrase is a key term in your speech, provide a simple and concise definition of it to let your listeners know exactly how you're using it. As we saw in the discussion on language in Chapter 4, words mean different things to different people. So words that may be somewhat controversial, such as abortion, affirmative action, or welfare, need to be defined. Use a dictionary to determine the most acceptable definition for the key term.

In her speech about AIDS, Kelly Bender provided both a definition and a description of the topic early in her speech:

AIDS stands for Acquired Immune Deficiency Syndrome and it's just that: a syndrome in which the afflicted person's immune system does not work. Consequently,

AIDS is always a secondary cause of death; the primary cause is the disease that killed tissues in the body. Examples are Kaposi's sarcoma and pneumonia. AIDS is the condition that allows these diseases to exist. According to the CDC's webpage, last updated September 23, 2003, there are over 30 AIDS related diseases.

By providing this information to her listeners, Bender ensured that they were *on the same page* and clearly understood the meaning of the topic of her speech.

Examples

Another simple but effective form of support is the example. An **example** is a specific item, person, or event that helps explain or illustrate an idea, clarify a difficult concept, or make anything you say more interesting or real to the audience. You can choose real examples or hypothetical ones. A **hypothetical example** is something that hasn't actually happened but could, which can be just as effective as a real example. In using a hypothetical example, you ask your listeners to imagine a situation related to the speech topic. It is important that a hypothetical example be plausible. For instance, in Nicholas's speech about drinking coffee at Starbucks, he could have said, "Imagine how nice it will be to relax this weekend with a few friends sipping cups of cappuccino together!"

A competent speaker carefully plans the use of powerful examples, realizing that one strong example is more effective than several inadequate ones. In an award-winning student speech about the dangers of eating infected produce imported into the United States, Nicolle Carpenter used this example (2004):

> Tainted produce is a growing plague that is threatening Americans. This problem is leading to sickness and even death. On October 25, 2003 NBCnews.com reported that 40 people in the Southern California area contracted E-coli from impure lettuce, including children [who] ate the lettuce as part of their school lunch program.

Even though an example such as this is effective, it would not be ethical to use an example to prove a point if you know it's only an isolated incident that is not true on a larger scale. A good informative speech must also contain statistics or other information that demonstrates the widespread nature or prevalence of the problem.

learning link

How could examples and stories be used to enhance a speech to explain?

• • •

© CNN

Stories

When you tell a **story,** which is actually just a long example, it serves the same purpose—to illustrate an idea, clarify a concept, or make a point more interesting or real. The ability to tell a good story is one of the most valuable skills a public speaker can have—it fuels a speech with energy and inspires and influences the audience through their involvement in the tale (Simmons, 2002). It is also an ideal tool for eliciting an emotional response from the audience and for setting the tone or mood for a speech as part of the introduction (Wylie, 1998). Nicolle Carpenter opened her speech about infected, imported produce with the following powerful story (2004):

A person who can tell a good story is sometimes referred to as a *raconteur*. Here's a raconteur telling a tale that is entrancing the listeners.

On October 5, 2003 Jack Spratt went out to dinner with his 17-year-old daughter. On October 11, Jack missed the annual Pittsburgh/Notre Dame football game with his brother, John. At this point, his brother John knew something was seriously wrong [with Jack]. On November 3, 2003 Jack was admitted to the hospital for severe dehydration and abdominal pain, and his family soon learned that he had contracted Hepatitis A, a potentially devastating liver disease. *Fox News* noted that doctors thought that Jack would recover quickly, but after just one day in the hospital, Jack went into liver failure. He spent the next ten days incoherent due to the extreme medications being used to try to save his life. However, on November 4, 2003 Jack Spratt died at the age of 46, having never been able to say goodbye to his wife Robin and daughters, Jacqueline, 17, and Kristen, 12. The cause of the infection was traced back to green onions he had eaten just over a month earlier.

A story like this would certainly grab the audience's attention. However, a story that is either poorly told or not relevant to the content of your speech can have a negative impact. To avoid this situation, choose your story carefully, be sure it's relevant to your topic, and don't include it just to fill up time or amuse the audience. Keep the story short and concise, and if possible, describe real people and events. Create a mental picture of the action that takes place in the story by describing what actually happened or what someone actually did.

Testimonies and Quotations

Two more valuable forms of support make use of someone else's words to support the ideas in your speech. **Testimony** uses the opinion of an expert or the account of an event by a witness. A **quotation** makes use of a person's exact words. Either or both of these techniques can be used to provide authoritative evidence for your speech when your own credibility with the listeners isn't as impressive as you would like. In Nicholas's speech about drinking coffee, he did provide testimony from visitors to Starbucks, but his professor said he should have also used some direct quotations from coffee manufacturers.

For a testimony or quotation to be effective, it must come from the right source. Find experts or people who hold respected positions in the subject area you are speaking about, preferably someone your listeners know about. You can use a person who is not highly expert if she or he has experience relevant to your speech topic. You can use a person who is not well known if you tell the audience why the individual's opinion is important. In the speech about tainted produce, Carpenter made effective use of a short but emphatic quotation from a credible source (2004):

> In a November 23, 2003, *Seattle Times News* article, Dr. Glen Morris, chairman of the department of epidemiology and preventive medicine at the University of Maryland said, "Produce is emerging as an important cause of food-borne illness in this country."

Facts and Statistics

A final way to provide support for an informative speech, as we already highlighted in Chapter 11, is to present facts and statistics. A **fact** is an individual piece of information that listeners could verify for themselves if they wanted to. **Statistics** are numerical summaries of facts, figures, and research findings that provide pictures of data about people, ideas, or patterns of behavior. To be effective, a fact or statistic should be highly relevant

learning link

Would testimonies and quotations be helpful in a speech to instruct? How could they be used?

• • •

learning link

Would facts and statistics be most effective in a speech to describe, to explain, or to instruct? Why?

• • •

98% not inspected

2% inspected

▲ Figure 13.5

Presentational Aids Clarify and Simplify an Informative Speech

As we recommend in Chapter 12, a presentational aid in an informative speech can dramatize a statistic, such as the small percentage of imported fruits and vegetables that are inspected for viral and bacterial infection.

to the speech topic, and it should contain enough evidence so that it can stand on its own as a solid piece of information. Here is an example of the effective use of statistics in Carpenter's exemplary speech on tainted imported produce (2004):

> The Centers for Disease Control's website, updated July 23, 2003, reports that food-borne contamination is "estimated to cause 76 million illnesses, 325,000 hospitalizations, and 5,200 deaths in the United States each year."

If you use statistics, select your figures carefully and don't overwhelm the audience with numbers. More is not necessarily better—in fact, too many numbers can be confusing. If you need to present a lot of numbers, provide a simple interpretation of the statistics, such as these two examples from the Carpenter speech (2004):

> According to tests conducted and published by the FDA (Food and Drug Administration) in 2001, imported fruits and vegetables are three times more likely to contain dangerous contamination as [those] grown in the United States.
>
> Worse still, according to the FDA's own website, only 2% of imported fruits and vegetables are inspected for viral and bacterial infection. This is a huge lack of control that is allowing 98% of produce to be imported and distributed to Americans without any quality control.

Another way to simplify the presentation of a statistic is to use a presentational aid. Chapter 12 discussed the use of various types of charts and graphs to present statistics more clearly. Figure 13.5 uses a pie chart to illustrate the statistic on inspection of imported produce. You can also consider strengthening your statistical evidence by combining it with a strong example. An example makes a situation or event real and personal, and statistics indicate that the example is widespread.

Close-Up on Ethics

Ethics and Informative Speaking

An important part of public speaking competence is being able to make ethical decisions as an informative speaker. In public life, examples of ethically questionable informative speaking abound. When his personal conduct was under scrutiny in early 1999 because of his relationship with a White House intern, then president Bill Clinton gave a televised informative speech to the American public. His remarks were considered unethical by some critics who said Clinton used misleading language to misrepresent the nature of his relationship with Monica Lewinsky. More recently, in corporate America, chief executive officers (CEOs) have presented information unethically to their employees. For instance, some officers of Enron informed all the company's employees at a public meeting that the company would survive and their stock and retirement holdings invested in Enron were safe. Days later, the company folded and some employees lost their life savings.

These are extreme examples of unethical informative speaking, but they clearly suggest that you must respect the prevailing cultural rules of conduct, referred to in Chapter 3, while trying to achieve the objectives of your informative speech. That means you present information and support materials to accomplish your objective but with an awareness of the inherent links between communication and culture and a respect for cultural rules for communicating ethically (Miller, 2004).

A credo for ethical communication, referred to in Chapter 2 and developed by members of the National Communication Association, provides insight into the cultural rules for communicating ethically in U.S. society (1999). The prologue to the credo states that "Ethical communication enhances human worth and dignity by fostering truthfulness, fairness, responsibility, personal integrity, and respect for self and others. Truthfulness, accuracy, honesty, and reason are essential to integrity in communication."

This credo challenges a competent speaker to strive for an optimal balance of appropriateness and effectiveness. It's acceptable to attempt to achieve the objective of your speech (effectiveness) but not at the price of violating any prevailing cultural rules for ethical communication (appropriateness), such as distorting the truth or presenting information inaccurately. According to this cultural rule, as an ethical informative speaker you must provide sufficient information to the listeners so they can make informed choices and decisions about any matter of importance to them that you mention in your speech.

Ethics and Informative Speaking

Just as ethics is indispensable to speech preparation in general, it plays a critical role when preparing an informative speech. As you plan your informative speech and choose support materials and evidence, you will face ethical challenges and decisions. Should you use statistics or other support materials that would accomplish your informative objective but perhaps misrepresent the truth or lead your listeners to faulty conclusions? If you discover some evidence that could be manipulated ever so slightly to make your informative speech more interesting, is manipulating it really unethical? The Close-Up on Ethics box discusses the ethics of deciding what support materials to use and how to present your informative speech most ethically.

Final Suggestions for Informative Speaking

No matter how carefully you prepare your informative speech, it may not be as effective as you would like if your listeners aren't motivated to listen to it. Remember that Nicholas's informative speech was effective in some ways, but he didn't fully motivate his audience to want to learn about coffee drinking patterns and their causes.

One way to motivate listeners to learn is to involve them in caring about the topic early in the speech. Figure out an aspect of the topic that will be most intriguing to the audience, and incorporate it into your introduction. Come up with an attention-getting device, a story, or a startling statistic related to that aspect of your topic.

Once you've motivated the audience to want to learn more, assure them that you will provide good and reliable information on the topic. Even if they decide they're interested in what you're going to say, that interest will fade if you appear not to know what you're talking about. A solid preview will assure them that you have gathered good information and organized it effectively for them.

Finally, as you proceed through your informative speech, keep your listeners actively involved in what you are saying. Educators and teachers are well aware that listeners learn more if they become active participants in their own learning process (Rubin & Hebert, 1998; Wulff & Wulff, 2004). One way you can encourage your listeners to get involved and relate to your speech topic is to ask them questions. Nicholas could have asked his audience, "How many of you really like a good cup of coffee to start the day? Raise your hands." The speech about tainted produce could have included a couple of questions, such as "How many of you have already had a fresh fruit or vegetable today? Do you have any idea whether that apple or carrot was grown in the United States or imported?" You can develop questions such as these for practically any informative speech. Or if time allows, you could hand out a short questionnaire with a few questions related to your topic. You could collect the answers and respond immediately or tell the audience you will review their answers after your speech.

Another way to promote involvement in an informative speech is to make use of volunteers from the audience. Even if you use only one or two volunteers, other members of the audience will feel more involved in your speech as a result. You could have volunteers demonstrate a dance step, an exercise, or even point to areas on a map as you talk about them. Finally, at the end of your speech, a simple way to encourage audience participation is to conclude with a short question-and-answer period.

The steps to giving an informative speech outlined in this chapter would have helped Nicholas present his "Joy of Java" speech with a bit more competence. They will help you as well, as you determine the type of informative speech to present, how to organize it, and how to use support materials most effectively. The next and final chapter on public speaking will introduce you to similar concepts but apply them to persuasive speaking.

THE NEIGHBORHOOD

First, get your audience's attention.

© Creators Syndicate, Inc.

There are limits on what a competent speaker should use as an attention-getting device in an informative speech.

learning link

How can the concept of appropriate communication introduced in Chapter 2 help you make decisions about ethical informative speaking?

• • •

 ## Chapter Summary

The purpose of speaking to inform is to communicate new information or a new perspective to an audience about an object, process, event, person, concept, or issue. We categorize informative speeches on the basis of their objective, including speeches to describe, explain, or instruct. Descriptions serve when the listeners are unfamiliar with the topic of the speech and need new information to understand it. Explanations clarify something that is already known but not well understood, or they explain how something works. Instructions are useful when the objective is to teach the audience something or tell them how to use it.

There are five ways to organize the body of an informative speech. Organization by topic divides information about a subject and topic into subtopics or subcategories. Organization by time is used to describe changes or developments in any situation or circumstance, which can be historical or sequential. Organization by space organizes information on the basis of the positioning of objects in physical space or relationships between locations. Organization by comparison and contrast is used to describe or explain how a subject is similar to or different from something else. Organization by cause and effect examines why something happens (the causes) and what happens as a result (the effects).

To present an informative speech most effectively, a competent speaker should be inventive and creative in the use of these support materials: definitions and descriptions, examples, stories, testimonies and quotations, and facts and statistics. When preparing and presenting an informative speech, a competent speaker is mindful of ethical concerns and of the need to motivate listeners to learn by encouraging involvement and participation.

Study and Review

The premium companion website for *Human Communication* offers a broad range of resources that will help you better understand the material in this chapter, complete assignments, and succeed on tests. The website resources include

- Interactive self-assessments, competency grids, and other tools
- Web links, practice activities, self-quizzes, and a sample final exam

For more information about this text's electronic learning resources, consult the *Guide to Online Resources for Human Communication* or visit **http://communication .wadsworth.com/morreale2.**

Key Terms

The key terms below are defined in the chapter on the pages indicated. They are also presented alphabetically with definitions in the Glossary, which begins on page 467. The book's website includes flashcards and crossword puzzles to help you learn these terms and the concepts they represent.

Building Knowledge

The following questions are among the practice activities on the book's website.

1. What are some of the key benefits of acquiring effective informative speaking skills?
2. Could one informative speech have all three objectives: to describe, explain, and instruct? If yes, provide an example. If no, explain why not.
3. Of the five ways to organize an informative speech—by topic, chronology, space, comparison and contrast, and cause and effect—is any one easier or harder to use than the others? Explain your answer.
4. In your opinion, which of the various types of support materials are most essential for giving an effective informative speech? Explain your reasoning.
5. How can a public speaker know when he or she has crossed the line and is presenting an informative speech in an unethical manner?
6. Analyze the speech about AIDS research at the end of this chapter using what you have learned about informative speaking. Is there anything the speaker could have said or done that would have made this speech even more effective? What aspects of the speech make it more informative than persuasive?

 ## Building Skills

The exercises below are among the practice activities on the book's website.

Individual Exercises

1. Make three columns on a piece of paper. Label your columns Types of Informative Speeches, Speech Topic, and Organizational Pattern, from left to right. In column 1, list the three types of informative speeches on the basis of objective. In column 2, come up with one speech topic that appeals to you for each type of speech. In column 3, decide which organizational pattern would work best for each topic you listed.
2. Attend an informative public speech or lecture. Identify the type of speech and how it's organized, and evaluate the support materials used. Write up a summary of your evaluative comments.
3. If you are using InfoTrac College Edition, choose a topic for an informative speech and enter that topic as a keyword search. Locate three to four pieces of information that could be used as support material (definition, example, testimony, fact, statistic) for that topic.
4. Visit the Quotations Home Page at **http://www.theotherpages.org/quote.html**. This site contains links to 30 collections of quotations and more than 24,000 quotes. Find a quotation that could be used for the topic you chose in the previous exercise.

Group Activities

1. Form a small group of four to five students and choose any one of the topics presented in Table 13.1. Each student in the group should write the topic on a piece of paper and decide on an objective and organizational pattern for that topic. Compare and discuss each student's ideas.

2. Attend an informative speech in a small group with several other students (a lecture will do). Each student should analyze the speech with respect to the speaker's use of an organizational pattern and support materials. After you leave the presentation, compare your evaluations.

3. Form groups of four students and choose one of the topics listed in Table 13.1 as issue speeches. Form pairs and assign to the first pair the development of an informative objective and an outline using the comparison and contrast organizational method. The second pair should use cause-and-effect organization to develop an objective and outline for the topic. Compare the two outlines to see which organizational pattern works best and discuss why. Then stay in the group of four students and discuss what types of support materials would help achieve the objective of each outline.

4. In a small group of four to five students, practice telling a personal story to the group. First, have each group member choose one of these topics for his or her story: (1) your most memorable communication experience; (2) an event that influenced the course of your life; or (3) a meeting with a person who contributed something memorable to your life. Take 5 minutes to organize and make notes about your story. Then have each person tell his or her story and the rest of the group provide feedback to the storytellers.

 ## References

Bender, K. (2004). The race for a cure: Rethinking the course of AIDS research. In L. Schnoor (Ed.), *Winning Orations of the 132nd Annual Contest of the Interstate Oratorical Association* (pp. 97–98). Mankato, MN: Interstate Oratorical Association.

Carpenter, N. (2004). What you don't know. In L. Schnoor (Ed.), *Winning Orations of the 132nd Annual Contest of the Interstate Oratorical Association* (pp. 5–6). Mankato, MN: Interstate Oratorical Association.

Miller, V. R. (2004). A cultural twist to the informative speech. *Communication Teacher, 18*(1), 17–21.

National Communication Association. (1999). A credo for ethical communication. Washington, DC: Author.

Roberts, C. (1998, March). Developing willing listeners: A host of problems and a plethora of solutions. Paper presented at the annual meeting of the International Listening Association, Kansas City, KS.

Rowan, K. E. (2003). Informing and explaining skills: Theory and research on informative communication. In J. O. Greene & B. R. Burleson (Eds.), *Handbook of communication and social interaction skills* (pp. 403–438). Mahwah, NJ: Erlbaum.

Rubin, L., & Hebert, C. (1998). Model for active learning: Collaborative peer teaching. *College Teaching, 46*(1), 26–31.

Simmons, A. (2002). *The story factor: Inspiration, influence and persuasion through the art of storytelling*. Philadelphia: Perseus Books Group.

Wulff, W. S., & Wulff, D. H. (2004). "Of course I'm communicating: I lecture every day": Enhancing teaching and learning in introductory statistics. *Communication Education, 53*(1), 92–103.

Wylie, A. (1998, February-March). Story telling: A powerful form of communication. *Communication World, 11*(3), 30–33.

Exemplary Informative Speech

The following informative speech was presented by Kelly Bender at the 132nd Annual Contest of the Interstate Oratorical Association in April 2004 and took second place in the competition. This issue speech both describes and explains the current situation surrounding AIDS research. The speech is organized topically into two main points—facts and myths about AIDS research.

The Race for a Cure: Rethinking the Course of AIDS Research

Kelly Bender
University of Wisconsin, Eau Claire
Coached by Karen Morris and Kelly Jo Wright

(1)   When the National Institutes of Health awarded Dr. Peter Duesberg their 7-year Outstanding Investigator Grant in 1986, they expected him to pick apart and criticize scientific research. After all, that is the entire purpose of the grant. What the NIH did not expect, was the research Duesberg would choose to investigate would be AIDS. In fact, you probably have heard Duesberg's name before—described with the negatively-connotated term AIDS dissident. You may have heard of other AIDS dissidents, such as the San Francisco chapter of ACT UP that has loudly vocalized their disbelief in the HIV/AIDS theory. And while mainstream media and science portrays these dissidents as extreme and uneducated, I want you to take ten minutes today and ask yourself this question:

(2)   What if they're right?

(3)   Scientific journalist Neville Hodgkinson answers this question in his 1996 book, stating, "If the HIV theory is wrong, it may have cost thousands of lives. The neglect of other ways of thinking or lines of research means thousands had been denied information or treatment that might have saved them." While my accounting major puts me a far cry from a scientific expert,

(4)   I have spent the past four years reading and researching this debate, and let me present you with a stark, undisputed reality: 20 years ago, HIV was announced as the cause of AIDS, and since then nearly all AIDS research has been based on that hypothesis.

(5)   However, after 20 years of research we are no closer to finding a cure or even understanding the disease. This lack of progress demands that we question our own perceptions of HIV and AIDS, and at the very least listen to alternative AIDS theories.

(6)   So today, take the time to listen to the facts about AIDS, then listen as I unveil some of the myths about AIDS, and become aware of the AIDS debate so we can start spreading true AIDS awareness.

(7)   Before I begin, I know that it is hard for us to leave the forensics norm of 2003–2004 sources, but I would like to stress that all of the sources used are journal articles and books written by scientists. They are used because of their historical context, scientific credibility, and because all of them are unrefuted. Information on where more recent sources can be found will be provided at the end of the speech.

(8)   The first diagnosed case of AIDS was in 1981, and ever since then, the facts surrounding the disease have been hard to determine. But here's the first fact: AIDS stands for Acquired Immune Deficiency Syndrome and it's just that: a syndrome in which the afflicted person's immune system does not work. Consequently, AIDS is always a secondary cause of death; the primary cause is the disease that killed tissues in the body.

(1) *Introduction:* The speaker begins with a credible story of an "AIDS dissident" and indicates respect for the listeners by saying they might have heard of this person and of groups of dissidents.

(2) Here the speaker uses a rhetorical question—what if they're right?—to encourage the audience to think about the dissidents' opinion of the HIV/AIDS theory.

(3) Immediately, a credible source, a scientific journalist, is used to answer the rhetorical question.

(4) The speaker emphasizes her credibility regarding the topic—4 years of research.

(5) The thesis statement is presented here, calling into question 20 years of research that has not found a cure; therefore we must question our perceptions and listen to alternative theories about AIDS research.

(6) Now that the speaker has told the listeners that the topic is important, this preview clearly states that the speech will be organized into two subtopics—facts and myths about AIDS. The statement about spreading true awareness of AIDS tends to make this speech somewhat persuasive rather than informative. However, the speech has informative objectives—to describe and to explain AIDS research; and the topical

organizational pattern of the body of the speech is informative.

(7) This statement about the speaker's sources serves as a transition to the body of the speech.

(8) *Body of the Speech:* The speaker begins the first main point—facts about AIDS— with a definition and description. The four facts about AIDS are clear and easy to follow because the speaker numbers them. The quantity of support materials could be overwhelming without the speaker's use of this technique.

(9) The second and third facts combine to question the credibility of the researcher who posited the HIV/AIDS theory.

(10) The theory is further challenged in the fourth fact.

(11) Here the speaker provides a transition from the first main point of the speech to the second main point— four myths about AIDS. The first myth, that AIDS is infectious, is challenged by evidence from an article in a well respected journal. Note how clearly the speaker explains what was probably a very complex article.

(12) The second myth, that AIDS drugs have helped control AIDS, uses evidence from two articles to challenge the effectiveness of current treatments. One of the sources is the highly respected and well known *New England Journal of Medicine.*

(13) The third myth, that HIV tests are accurate, is challenged using the results from a summary of 64 published scientific papers.

(14) And the final myth, that AIDS is terrorizing Africa, is dispelled using a report from an advisory panel in South Africa and quotations from two medical doctors whose credibility comes from years of working in Africa. Note that the second doctor

Examples are Kaposi's sarcoma and pneumonia. AIDS is the condition that allows these diseases to exist. According to the CDC's webpage, last updated September 23, 2003, there are over 30 AIDS related diseases.

(9)   Second fact: In 1984 Dr. Robert Gallo announced HIV was the probable cause of AIDS. As John Crewdson details in his 2002 book, Dr. Gallo made this announcement at a press conference before he had even submitted a paper to a scientific journal for peer review. Which leads to the third fact: currently, there is not a single published scientific paper that supports the hypothesis that HIV is the probable cause of AIDS. Noble Laureate Kary Mullis expresses his anger in his 1998 [writing] asserting that the lack of such a paper is unacceptable.

(10)   The fourth fact: HIV positive does not equal AIDS. Being HIV positive simply indicates that HIV, the virus believed to cause AIDS, is present. And the fifth fact: HIV is not always necessary for AIDS to exist. The *Journal of the American Medical Association* reported in December of 1988 that 8–11% of AIDS' victims have tested negative for HIV. Dr. Robert Root-Bernstein explains in his 1993 book that even a handful of HIV negative AIDS patients should be alarming because it means that HIV may not be the sole cause of AIDS.

(11)   Now that we have defined the AIDS facts, it is time to unveil the myths; and there are four major myths surrounding AIDS dogma today. First myth: HIV, the virus believed to cause AIDS, is infectious. In 1997 the *American Journal of Epidemiology* reported that in order to contract HIV heterosexually, one needed an average of 1,000 sexual contacts, which is much higher than any other sexually transmitted disease. But most importantly, as Peter Duesberg explains in his 1996 book, HIV doesn't meet a single one of the scientific criteria for an infectious disease. These criteria are known as Koch's postulates. Currently, every single infectious disease in the world meets every single postulate—except one—HIV. Details on these postulates will be available in a handout at the end of my speech.

(12)   The second myth is that AIDS drugs have helped control AIDS. First, it must be known that AZT, a common drug prescribed to HIV-positive patients was originally researched as a cancer drug, but was banned because AZT was found to be too toxic for human consumption. Furthermore, the *Lancet* of 1994 reported that AIDS drugs, including AZT, were so potent that their side effects were nearly identical to the side effects of AIDS. But the most damning evidence against AIDS drugs was reported by the *New England Journal of Medicine* in 1995: patients that had lived as HIV-positive for twelve years or longer all shared one common thread: they were not on any AIDS drugs.

(13)   Third myth: HIV tests are accurate. In 1999, the Women's Health Interaction published *Uncommon Questions,* a report that found there are over 50 factors known to cause false positive HIV tests. These factors were taken from 64 published scientific papers. Some of the factors include the flu, tetanus vaccination, and blood transfusions.

(14)   The final myth is that AIDS is terrorizing Africa. The AIDS Advisory Panel Report for South Africa reported in March 2001 that reliable statistics on AIDS in Africa do not exist. The reason is that in order to be diagnosed with AIDS in Africa, you don't need to take a test; all you need is a persistent cough, fever and diarrhea. These are the exact same symptoms found in malnourished people with parasitic disease. As Dr. Okot-Nwang explained in a 2000 broadcast of *Meditel,* "I cannot distinguish between AIDS and other diseases." Dr. Harvey Bialy, who has been in Africa since 1975, further explains that he has seen an increase in malaria, TB and diarrheal disease due to a decline in economy and health care. He has not seen any evidence of a new disease such as AIDS, forcing him to remark, "AIDS in Africa is based on so little evidence. It is a tragic myth."

(15)   These facts and myths surrounding AIDS are a lot to digest in ten minutes. But back to the question at hand: What if AIDS dissidents are right? Because in terms of time, money, research, and most importantly lives, we literally cannot afford to be wrong. After four years of personal research, I don't know the cause or cure for AIDS. But what I do know is this: we have been misled by the media and the public about the debate surrounding the cause of AIDS, and it is time we re-direct the course of AIDS dialogue to include the public, because AIDS is a public health issue. To help spread the message about the AIDS debate, I have composed these brochures that contain facts about HIV and AIDS as well as a list of alternative AIDS support groups and charities with contact information. In addition, you will also find an insert that contains a complete biography of all the sources used for this speech and the brochure. If you are questioning the facts of any of my sources or simply would like more information, I urge you to take the time and check them yourself.

Finally, if you have any questions about HIV, AIDS or anything stated in my speech, I ask you not to talk about it on the way home, but to come up to me at any point this weekend and ask me. If I do not know the answer to your question, I will gladly research it for you and send you a response.

(16)   Then, do talk about this speech in the van—because all I'm asking you to do is question AIDS research and spread awareness that the AIDS debate exists.

(17)   Truthfully, we should have begun questioning AIDS research in 1992. Because in 1992, Dr. Robert Gallo, the scientist who announced the HIV-AIDS connection, was found guilty by the Federal Office of Research Integrity for falsifying and stealing scientific data related to HIV and AIDS. Dr. Luc Montegnier, the French researcher from whom the data was stolen, also came forward in 1992 admitting that his isolation of HIV may have been a laboratory contamination, and that he cannot find any solid evidence of an HIV-AIDS connection. These events were largely uncovered [and ignored] by the American media, which I find to be the most shocking fact of the AIDS debate. I assure you, I didn't write this speech to challenge the traditional format of persuasion or some forensics norm on current sources. I wrote this speech because I believe we have been misled, and that by failing to question AIDS research, we only allow this deception to continue.

(18)   Because if there is one fact, one fact that you remember about HIV and AIDS today, let it be this: if we don't question AIDS research, we will lose the war against AIDS—because we were too afraid to fight.

actually refers to "a tragic myth."

(15) *Conclusion:* The speaker begins the conclusion with an expansive restatement of the thesis and central claim of the speech. To support the claim, she gives out additional literature that is intended to help the listeners spread the word about the AIDS debate.

(16) This request for action, to some extent, moves this speech in the direction of a persuasive speech.

(17) The speech concludes with an effective and surprising attention-getter in which the listeners learn that the scientist who announced the HIV-AIDS connection is guilty of a federal crime— falsifying and stealing data about HIV and AIDS. Moreover, another key researcher admitted that his isolation of the HIV virus might have been a laboratory contamination.

(18) The speaker ends the speech by sharing one simple fact that she wants the audience to remember about AIDS.

© David Young-Wolff/PhotoEdit

LEARNING OBJECTIVES | After studying this chapter, you should be able to

1. Describe what persuasive speaking is and its crucial function in a democratic society.

2. Explain the three types of persuasive speeches and guidelines for using each type.

3. Demonstrate the use of logical, emotional, and credibility appeals to persuade.

4. Outline and present a persuasive speech using the most

   appropriate of the four persuasive organizational patterns.

5. Reason logically by avoiding logical fallacies in your persuasive speech.

6. Describe the critical role of ethics in persuasive public speaking and apply appropriate ethical standards to your own persuasive speeches.

Speaking to Persuade

Spencer was about to finish his first semester at Southeast University. He had taken a public speaking class because he knew it would help him give better presentations at work and in other classes. The final assignment in the class was to prepare and present a persuasive speech. The instructor recommended that students choose a significant topic or an issue they felt strongly about, but also one that would appeal to the student audience. Spencer reviewed the list of suggested topics but didn't see anything on the list that excited him.

Two weeks before the assignment was due, Spencer ran into Zola, a classmate who was quite involved in campus politics. As she had done before, Zola tried to persuade Spencer to help her fight for the interests and needs of students on campus. She described a few of the current problems she was working on with a student activist organization, such as insufficient parking and the latest tuition increase. She said that if Spencer and other students didn't organize to fight for their rights, campus administrators would assume they didn't care what was happening and tuition would continue to go up.

Zola's persuasive argument impressed Spencer so much that he attended a meeting of the student activist group with her that afternoon. Later that evening, Spencer thought about how Zola had persuaded him, a relatively nonpolitical type of person, to get involved in campus life. He felt his eyes had been opened to the administration's shifting priorities and indifference to students' needs. He had even signed a petition to protest tuition hikes and to protect other important student rights. But how had Zola motivated him to overcome his ambivalence and finally attend the student meeting?

Zola had effectively persuaded Spencer by changing what he believed to be true and moving him to action. She had presented a logical argument and appealed to him emotionally by explaining how hard it was for some students at Southeast to absorb the repeated tuition hikes. A committed and credible role model herself, Zola appeared to care genuinely about the welfare of others. She stressed the importance of every contribution to one united voice for all students. It wouldn't take much of Spencer's time to participate and add to that collective voice.

Not only was Spencer pleased to be working with Zola and the other students, he realized there was another immediate benefit—he had found a topic for his persuasive speech. He would try to persuade his classmates in the public speaking class to join him in protesting the tuition hike and signing the petition. This was a topic Spencer could get excited about and make relevant to his audience.

This chapter covers the key elements and techniques of competent persuasion, similar to what Zola used to influence Spencer to become more of a student activist. We begin by building an understanding of persuasive speaking, including its importance. Then we describe three types of persuasive speeches, strategies for making an argument persuasive, and methods for organizing these speeches. The chapter concludes with a look at the challenge to persuasive speaking of logical fallacies and a description of ethical persuasive speaking. ■

learning link

Does viewing communication as persuasion (as suggested in Chapter 1) reinforce that all public speeches are persuasive?

• • •

Understanding the Persuasive Speech

Communication experts identify four critical components in the persuasive process—the source, appeals, receiver, and setting (Stiff & Mongeau, 2003). Hence, a persuasive speech, as defined in Chapter 11, is a speech presented by a speaker (the source), using the right appeals for the setting, to influence the attitudes, beliefs, values, or actions of the audience (receivers).

As we show in Chapter 13, an informative speaker uses information purely to promote understanding. By contrast, as you will see in this chapter, a persuasive speaker uses information to influence listeners. As a result, persuasive speeches are organized differently from informative ones. Furthermore, although both types of speakers are concerned with the audience's attitudes toward the information presented, knowing the listeners' specific position on the topic is vital to effective persuasive speaking, because the ultimate goal is to influence that position.

Why Do You Need Persuasive Speaking Skills?

Persuasive speaking has been considered an important aspect of social life for centuries. In *The Rhetoric,* his famous book on persuasion, the Greek philosopher Aristotle wrote about how crucial it is for people to discover the available means of persuasion in any situation (Roberts, 1954). Aristotle identified four social values for rhetoric and persuasion.

First, it prevents the triumph of fraud and injustice. It is not enough just to know what is right; people must be able to argue for what is right. Second, rhetoric and persuasion are an effective method of instruction for the public. It is not sufficient just to understand an argument; a speaker must also be able to instruct the audience in a persuasive manner. Third, persuasive rhetoric helps people see and understand both sides of an issue. They determine what they believe to be true by listening to a variety of persuasive arguments. Fourth, rhetoric and persuasion are a viable means of defense. According to Aristotle, just as people need to be able to defend themselves physically, they should also be able to fend off verbal attacks persuasively.

As we discuss in Chapter 1, the effective use of communication, including persuasive speaking skills, continues to be the foundation of our communities in a free and open society. People use persuasion in contemporary society to examine various sides of important issues and then make informed decisions. Whether at the local or national level—in legislatures, schools, businesses, or public meetings—people use persuasive speaking to debate and then set organizational and public agendas for their communities.

In fact, the ability of citizens to express their positions persuasively is so crucial to a free society that teachers in public schools are encouraging even young students to learn to express their ideas clearly and speak persuasively (Lindquist, 1995). In one study of students in an eighth grade class, the ability to speak persuasively was identified as essential to the mastery of other lifelong learning skills (Moebius, 1991). Students who learned to develop and deliver persuasive speeches also learned to understand and respect different points of view, to support their beliefs with evidence, and to present their opinions more effectively. At the college level, students also are learning how to formulate compelling persuasive arguments (Miller, 2004). They are able to think carefully about their arguments before the arguments are made and then show the validity of their position and tell that position to others.

Types of Persuasive Speeches

Like informative speeches, persuasive speeches can be categorized on the basis of the speaker's objective. Zola's objective in talking to Spencer was to change his attitude and encourage him to adopt different future behaviors, which she did successfully. The objective of Spencer's speech to his class was to motivate them to sign a petition opposing tuition hikes. Three types of persuasive speeches, based on their objective, attempt to (1) reinforce the listeners' attitudes, beliefs, and values; (2) change their attitudes, beliefs, and values; or (3) move the listeners to action.

As you'll recall, these audience characteristics—attitudes, beliefs, and values—were discussed in Chapter 11 as crucial to audience analysis. Now you can use what you know about analyzing these characteristics to develop an effective persuasive speech. This entails figuring out your audience's probable reaction to and position on your persuasive topic and developing your speech on the basis of that information. Table 14.1 provides examples of how to analyze potential audience reactions to some typical persuasive topics.

This categorization system for persuasive speeches may be a bit misleading in that it suggests the three types are discrete and unrelated to one another. In reality, the types of speeches sometimes overlap. You may find yourself presenting a speech that has more than one objective. For example, in the opening story, Zola's objective was to change Spencer's attitudes and beliefs but also to move him to action. We now examine these three types of persuasive speeches more closely.

Speaking to Reinforce Attitudes, Beliefs, and Values

A **speech to reinforce** is intended to influence listeners by strengthening their convictions and taking advantage of their tendency to seek out and attend to messages with which they already agree. Most listeners are more likely to pay attention to and remember information that supports or resembles their own attitudes and opinions (Furnham & Procter,

Table 14.1

Attitudes, Beliefs, Values, & Behaviors

When preparing a persuasive speech topic, you must determine the audience's attitudes, beliefs, values, and possible behaviors. That information will help you develop a speech that's more likely to achieve your persuasive objective.

Topic/issue	Attitude	Belief	Value	Behavior
Prayer In Public Schools	Favorable toward nondenominational prayer	It's the responsibility of the public school system to encourage moral values	Morality and religious values	Petition the school board to rule in favor of prayer in schools
Capital Punishment	Favorable toward life sentences for those committing murder or other violent crimes	It's wrong to take another person's life	Sacredness of all human life	Vote against putting people to death by use of the electric chair or lethal injection
First Amendment Rights	Favorable toward no control or interference by the government on the Internet	People have a right to express their opinions in any way they prefer	Individual liberty	Vote for a hands-off policy relative to web pages and pornography on the Internet
Euthanasia	Favorable toward assisted suicide	People have a right to control their own destiny	Freedom of choice	Encourage the use of living wills that allow people to die as they choose

1989–1990). So by reinforcing your listeners' attitudes, beliefs, or values, without compromising your own position, you can increase the likelihood that they'll pay attention and remember what you say.

Speaking to reinforce works well if there is a need to raise your listeners' consciousness about an issue or concern. Your audience may already agree with your position but have no sense of urgency about the topic. In this case, you want to encourage them to care more about it. For example, if your audience believes governmental aid to education is (or is not) a good idea, your job would be to reinforce their current beliefs and influence them to pay more attention to the messages of political candidates who agree with your position.

To reinforce listeners' attitudes and beliefs, provide them with additional information that supports their existing attitudes and what they already believe to be true. Reinforce their values by indicating your respect for what they hold to be right or important (Johannesen, 2002). You shouldn't say you agree with them if you do not. But merely by respecting their values, you build rapport and goodwill, which enhances your credibility as a persuasive speaker and helps accomplish the objective of speaking to reinforce.

learning link

How can nonverbal cues be used most competently when presenting each of these types of persuasive speeches?

• • •

Speaking to Change Attitudes, Beliefs, and Values

A **speech to change** is intended to convince the audience to change what they like or dislike, what they hold to be true or untrue, or what they consider important or unimportant.

To change listeners' attitudes—what they like or dislike—you have to first provide them with information that motivates them to listen to you and then try to modify or change their attitudes. You could accomplish this by reinforcing an attitude they already hold to get their attention and establish mutual understanding, and then make your own point. For example, if you're presenting a speech against government regulation of the Internet to listeners who are politically conservative, you would want to reinforce their existing attitudes that are probably favorable toward minimizing government regulations. If the audience is more liberal, you would reinforce their concerns about the loss of freedom of speech that might occur through governmental regulation. Then you would provide your argument against regulation.

The best way to change listeners' beliefs—what they hold to be true or untrue—is to present them with solid facts and evidence from highly credible sources. Because beliefs are based on what people know, if you want to change beliefs, you need compelling evidence to counteract their previous experiences and knowledge. Information from credible sources and your own credibility as a speaker are essential to convince the audience that their current beliefs are not necessarily true and they should change them.

To change your listeners' values—what they consider important or unimportant—is to make a fundamental change in something very basic to each individual (Johannesen, 2002). Because they are embedded in a person's self-concept, values are much harder to change than attitudes or beliefs. Therefore success in changing listeners' values is rare, but appealing to values is an effective technique for influencing attitudes and beliefs.

"I'll tell you what this election is about. It's about homework, and pitiful allowances, and having to clean your room. It's also about candy, and ice cream, and staying up late."

Speaking to Move Listeners to Action

A **speech to move to action** is intended to influence listeners to either engage in a new and desirable behavior or discontinue an undesirable behavior. If you give a speech and ask your listeners to vote for your candidate, buy a product, or start recycling their trash, you are asking them to adopt a new behavior. If your speech asks them to stop smoking or littering, the action you're recommending is one of discontinuance.

To change people's behaviors, remember that attitudes, beliefs, and values shape and direct behaviors. For example, you may hold a favorable attitude toward climbing the corporate ladder, believe that education is the best way to get a good job, and value professional success. As a result of these attitudes, beliefs, and values, you'll engage in behaviors such as trying hard to succeed at work, going directly from high school to college, or returning to college after several years in the work force.

Consequently, if you want to change people's behaviors—which is hard to do—you must demonstrate that their current behaviors aren't consistent with their attitudes, beliefs, or values. Most people prefer to think that they are acting according to what they believe and value. If you can demonstrate to your listeners that another set of behaviors is more consistent with their attitudes, beliefs, and values, your speech is more likely to result in at least some behavioral change.

To better understand the three types of persuasive speeches we've just discussed, take a look at the student speech at the end of this chapter, "Core Stories," which won first place at the Interstate Oratorical Association's Winning Orations Competition in 2004 (Moorehead, 2004). The speech is about the need for people to record oral histories of their own and others' life experiences. The speaker, Antonio Moorehead, believes that history is being written by scholars, not by lay people, and it isn't as rich and reflective of historical

Try reinforcing listeners' attitudes, beliefs, and values—even if it's about candy, ice cream, and staying up late.

learning link

How does a listener's sense of personal identity influence your attempt to change that individual's attitudes, beliefs, values, and actions?

• • •

events as it should be. The speech has two objectives: to change existing beliefs about how history should be recorded and to move the audience to the action of getting involved in recording oral histories.

Making Your Arguments Persuasive

As you now know, each of the three types of persuasive speeches uses different strategies to persuade. But whether you're trying to influence attitudes, beliefs, values, or actions, you can make your argument much more persuasive by using one or more of three types of persuasive appeals. An **appeal** is the subtle technique speakers use to get the audience to accept their persuasive argument.

Current thinking on this topic is derived from the classical tradition of rhetoric, begun in the 4th century BC when Greek rhetoricians recommended that persuasive speakers make use of **logos**—a form of logical appeals—**pathos**—emotional appeals—and **ethos**—or credibility appeals (Kennedy, 1963, 1994). Although there is some debate about which of these appeals is most effective—logic, emotion, or credibility—persuasion experts agree that all three techniques can be effective depending on the particular situation, the audience, and the persuasive goal (Stiff & Mongeau, 2003).

Logical Appeals

A **logical appeal** is based on knowledge and reasoning, which describes how people think. It consists of presenting evidence and encouraging the listeners to draw a conclusion from that information. Logical arguments are particularly effective for audiences made up of people from Western or North American cultures, who prefer to make decisions by examining evidence and information. At the beginning of this chapter, Zola persuaded Spencer to become a student activist partly by using a logical argument. She provided solid evidence about how and why unfair tuition increases were affecting students negatively on their campus.

Logical arguments can be made in two ways—using deductive or inductive reasoning. **Deduction** is a process of reasoning in which a specific conclusion follows from a general principle that is often made up of a major and a minor premise. If the audience accepts the two premises as true, then they must also accept that the specific conclusion is true. Here's a classic example that teachers of rhetoric use to illustrate deductive reasoning:

Major premise: All of humanity is mortal.

Minor premise: Socrates is human.

Specific conclusion: Socrates is mortal.

Here's how a college professor might use deductive reasoning to arrive at a conclusion:

Major premise: College students avoid public speaking whenever they can.

Minor premise: Students in my class are typical college students.

Specific conclusion: My students will avoid taking a speaking part in the group presentation project, so I must require them to participate as speakers.

Induction is a process of reasoning in which a general conclusion follows from considering a series of specific instances or examples. If the listeners accept the specific

"Edwardson, this address brings the art of obfuscation to a new high."

Despite what this speaker thinks, obfuscating (blurring) the message is not the best way to present a logical appeal.

instances and examples as true, then they must also accept the general conclusion as true. The more credible the specific examples and illustrations, the more logical the conclusion will seem to the listeners. Using the topic of students presenting a group project, the professor could use an inductive argument to come to a general conclusion in this manner:

Instance: John did not take a speaking role in his group's presentation this semester.

Instance: Arisa declined a speaking role last semester.

Instance: Two other professors told me students in their classes have chosen not to speak during group presentations.

General conclusion: All college students will avoid speaking during group presentations if they possibly can.

In the student speech about oral histories, the speaker uses an inductive logical argument to describe a problem and change the listeners' beliefs about how history should be preserved (Moorehead, 2004). The following evidence is presented to encourage the listeners to draw the desired conclusion:

- The social importance of stories is undeniable. Andrew Buckser argues in the *Anthropological Quarterly* of January 1999 that to tell the story of one's past or one's group is to ground one's own identity.
- The late Justice Harry Blackmun (of the Supreme Court), who wrote the Court's decision on *Roe v. Wade,* in the March 5, 2004, Washington Post shared his stories about how *Roe v. Wade* was very nearly overturned in 1992.

learning link

How can a competent speaker decide which type of appeal—logic, emotion, or credibility— is most appropriate for a given speech?

• • •

- The *Christian Science Monitor* of September 10, 2003, says mass media are ignoring these stories in favor of the Official Truth.
- Studs Terkel—the most renowned oral historian in America—told the *Washington Journalism Review* in October 1989 that the Official Truth is the story that goes into newspapers and history books; it's not so much true as convenient for the establishment.
- The *Oral History Review* of spring 2002 calls this result America's collective amnesia.

The speaker then states the following desired conclusion:

If we forget our stories, we will forget our struggles, and without those, we're just consumers; made homogeneous by the media, and accepting of the Official Truth.

Emotional Appeals

An **emotional appeal** is based on psychology and passion, which describe how people feel. Despite what most people would like to think, they are not always logical. If your argument appeals to your listeners' emotions, it will get their attention and hold it. By reaching them emotionally and convincing them that they should care about your topic, you will more likely achieve your persuasive goal.

To use emotional appeals effectively, you can appeal to any of a variety of your listeners' emotions, such as love, hate, sympathy, guilt, or even fear. A **fear appeal** is based on changing listeners' attitudes or behaviors through the use of an anxiety-arousing message. This type of appeal is useful in situations where you need to motivate the audience to pay attention and get more involved in your topic (Roser & Thompson, 1995).

A fear appeal is not inherently ethical or unethical persuasion. For example, campaigns promoting antismoking or breast self-exams often use fear appeals appropriately to convince people of the danger of ignoring the given health issue. However, fear appeals should be used cautiously, realizing that too strong a fear appeal may backfire. In fact, some studies indicate that good or more positive forms of persuasion may be more effective in gaining compliance than the use of threats or fear appeals (Fink, Cai, Kaplowitz, Sungeun, Van Dyke, & Jeong-Nam, 2003).

For a fear appeal to be effective, it must include information that poses a real threat or danger to the listeners, and it must prescribe an effective action for handling the threat (Witte, 1994). Moreover, the listeners must believe the threat is real and could actually happen, and the speaker and his or her information must be perceived as highly credible. In a study of the use of fear appeals, parents were effectively persuaded to immunize their preschool children against disease after they were given highly credible information stating that getting immunizations is realistic, affordable, safe, and effective (Smith, 1997).

Emotional and logical appeals can be used together to accomplish the objective of a persuasive speech effectively. Listeners typically respond to the emotional content of a speech first and then examine the logical evidence. So combining emotion and logic can be particularly effective. In the opening story, Zola might have started out by emotionally describing the plight of several unfortunate students who could no longer take a full load of courses because of the latest tuition hike. Then she might have provided concrete evidence of the pattern of increases in tuition over recent years.

Credibility Appeals

A **credibility appeal** relates to the way listeners perceive the reputation, prestige, and authority of the speaker. If you establish the credibility of your sources of information and of yourself as a speaker, you are more likely to be believable and therefore persuasive. By contrast, if the audience disrespects or distrusts you, you'll have a harder time persuading them, regardless of any logical or emotional appeals you use. Furthermore, if you lack credibility, they may not even have an interest in what you have to say (Taylor, 1996).

Because their reputations precede them, some speakers are automatically perceived as more credible. But how can a novice speaker establish credibility with an audience? Three factors influence whether you will impress your audience as credible: expertise, trustworthiness, and charisma.

"But, seriously..."

Some speakers' credibility precedes them; others have a harder time appearing expert and trustworthy.

Expertise

You need to be perceived by the listeners as someone who is competent and an expert on the subject of your speech. This kind of competence requires you to know the topic well, be prepared to talk about it, and bring your own experience to the discussion. If you prepare your speech according to the guidelines in Chapter 11 and include credible sources of information, the audience will respect you as more expert on the topic. Or if you have any personal experience relevant to the topic, they'll more likely listen to your advice. For example, if your speech is on smoking cessation and you have successfully stopped smoking, your expertise on the topic will be respected.

Trustworthiness

You need to be perceived as a person of high character, so listeners feel they can trust and believe what you say. Character implies honesty and objectivity. Being an honest person who tells the truth enhances your credibility, because sincerity and openness can quickly build the trust that is crucial to audience respect. In addition, you can demonstrate character by speaking objectively about your speech topic. For instance, acknowledging opposing viewpoints and quoting sources that challenge your position will communicate to the audience that you are a person of integrity.

Charisma

Finally, you need to be perceived as a speaker with charisma, which means the audience finds you engaging. All the nonverbal cues for competent public speaking outlined in Chapter 12 will help you become more charismatic and therefore a more credible speaker. Such a speaker is dynamic, energetic, and enthusiastic and therefore able to gain and hold the audience's attention. There have been many charismatic speakers in the world of politics—Tony Blair, Bill Clinton, Ronald Reagan—and even dictators, such as Saddam Hussein was, have charisma. Whether you agree with the politics of these leaders, their ability to impress audiences is due in part to their personal charisma.

Having thought about the various appeals, next you need to consider how you will organize your persuasive speech.

Organizing and Outlining a Persuasive Speech

The general principles of speech organization discussed in Chapter 11 apply to the persuasive speech as well. An effective persuasive speech is carefully organized and structured to accomplish its objective. Although there are a variety of ways to organize a persuasive speech, four patterns are best known and most accessible for beginning speakers. The problem-solution pattern and the motivated sequence are arguably the most popular. Refuting the opponent and comparing alternatives are useful when it's necessary to take opposing arguments into account.

Problem-Solution Organization

Problem-solution organization first identifies a problem and then proposes a workable solution to it. You can choose this organizational pattern to plan the body of the speech, using the basic structure introduced in Chapter 11. Draft an introduction, body, and conclusion but cover only two main points in the body of the speech. Your first main point describes the problem and persuades the audience that the problem must be overcome. The second main point proposes a solution to overcome the problem. For an outline of problem-solution organization, see Figure 14.1.

Zola might have attempted to get Spencer involved in campus life by using problem-solution organization. She might have described what she saw as a crucial problem on campus and then offered a constructive solution to it.

Problem: Campus administrators make decisions with too little concern for the students' welfare.

Solution: Get involved in campus life and contribute to policy-making decisions.

Despite being perceived by many voters as charismatic and expert on some topics, President George W. Bush's credibility suffered somewhat in his second term due to the war in Iraq and the government's response to Hurricane Katrina.

learning link

Of the four organizational patterns, which would prove most valuable to a speaker who is attempting to facilitate a controversial decision among community members?

• • •

▶ **Figure 14.1**

The Problem-Solution Pattern

This organizational pattern for a persuasive speech is structured similarly to the standard outline format described in Chapter 11. The body of the speech is organized as a problem and a solution.

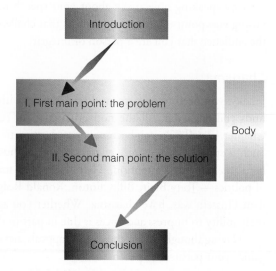

Introduction

I. First main point: the problem

II. Second main point: the solution

Body

Conclusion

Motivated Sequence

An enhanced version of problem-solution organization has dominated the persuasion literature for years since it was first introduced in 1935 by Alan Monroe, a professor at Purdue University (Monroe, 1935). The **motivated sequence** organizational pattern is an effective model for persuasive speaking that moves through a sequence of five steps, designed to motivate and persuade listeners psychologically (McDermott, 2004). This pattern is effective because it makes use of a natural sequential pattern of human thought: gaining the listeners' attention, convincing them of a need or problem, offering a solution to satisfy the need or solve the problem, and then helping them visualize the solution and take action relative to it.

Returning to the basic speech structure you learned from Chapter 11, you present the attention step in your introduction, the need and satisfaction steps in the body of the speech, and the visualization and action steps in your conclusion. These five steps are outlined in Figure 14.2. To help you understand how to use each step, here we provide a short

---

Motivated Sequence Organizational Pattern

Speech Title	Indicate the issue of persuasion (pique curiosity).
General Purpose	Type of speech—to persuade.
Specific Purpose	State whether the speech has the objective to influence the audience's beliefs, attitudes, values, or behaviors about a need or problem.

Five Sequential Steps

INTRODUCTION

I. ATTENTION (STEP 1)	Grab the audience's attention and forecast the theme of the speech.

BODY

II. NEED/PROBLEM (STEP 2)	Describe the problem or need, provide evidence of its importance, and relate it to the audience's desires and/or needs.
III. SATISFACTION/ SOLUTION (STEP 3)	Present a plan of action to address the problem or need.

CONCLUSION

IV. VISUALIZATION (STEP 4)	Describe the results of the proposed plan or consequences of the audience's failure to change or to act.
V. ACTION (STEP 5)	Summarize main ideas and call for the audience to change their beliefs or to act or react in the desired manner.

Figure 14.2

Outline of Motivated Sequence Organizational Pattern

As with any speech, your outline for this organizational pattern should state the title and general and specific purposes of the speech. Then the motivated sequence goes on to include the five sequential steps: attention, need, satisfaction, visualization, and action.

Figure 14.3

Sample Working Outline Using the Motivated Sequence Organizational Pattern

The speech about oral histories illustrates the effective use of this organizational pattern. Each step in the motivated sequence is identified with a Roman numeral, and the alphanumeric system for outlining is used to indicate subordination of points and subpoints. When you prepare a formal outline using this approach, be sure to apply the guidelines for outlining presented in Chapter 11.

Speech Title:	Core Stories
General Purpose:	To persuade
Specific Purpose:	To change the listeners' beliefs about how history should be recorded and move them to the action of collecting oral histories

INTRODUCTION

I. ATTENTION (Step 1)
  A. Narrative about StoryCorps in Grand Central Station
  B. Importance of history from one person's viewpoint—history from the bottom up—as a vital part of the human experience

Preview: We must first outline the growing need to foster history from the bottom up. Having done this, we can construct solution criteria that will keep it alive. Finally, we may illustrate the benefits in our future once we act to save our past.

BODY

II. NEED/PROBLEM (Step 2)
  A. Social importance of stories
    1. To tell the story of one's past or one's groups is to ground one's own identity (*Anthropological Quarterly,* January 1999)
    2. Rondo Oral History project and 100-year-old Mary Hamilton's story about her neighbor (*Minneapolis Star Tribune,* March 1, 2004)
    3. Justice Harry Blackmun shares his stories about *Roe v. Wade* (*Washington Post*, March 5, 2004)
  B. Mass media's role in preserving stories
    1. Mass media ignoring these stories in favor of the Official Truth (*Christian Science Monitor,* September 10, 2003)
    2. Studs Terkel—oral historian—the Official Truth is the story that goes into newspapers and history books (*Washington Journalism Review,* October 1989)
    3. Result is America's collective amnesia (*Oral History Review,* spring 2002)

Transition: The solution to this problem must be multifaceted, but on the whole, it will represent increased participation in creating and maintaining historical records.

III. SATISFACTION/SOLUTION (Step 3)
  A. Take part in history by doing oral histories (Women in Journalism Oral History Project, interview with Ethel Payne, 1987)
  B. Oral history as opposed to a diary or web page (*Atlanta Journal-Constitution,* interview with Sue Davis, February 7, 2004)

Transition: Staying connected to history and keeping it alive requires only a pair of ears and an open mind.

CONCLUSION

IV. VISUALIZATION/BENEFITS (Step 4)
  A. Personal view of history won't make the world different, but we would know much more about it
    1. Individual point of view versus a political one more accurately illustrates historical events (*Columbia Chronicle,* May 7, 2001)
    2. Former slaves' oral accounts required history of slavery to be rewritten (Alessandro Portelli, *The Death of Luigi Trastulli,* 1991)

(Cont'd)

    B. Today, oral history is being used to find the truth
       1. Interviews with soldiers, activists, civilians, and leaders on ground in Iraq as opposed to White House press conferences (Bill Katovsky, *Embedded: The Media @ War in Iraq,* 2003, and *Rocky Mountain News,* February 26, 2004)
    C. In the future, oral histories are necessary if history is to be representative
       1. Fifty years from now, we need to have various views of September 11: the victimized American, the person who felt we had it coming, and the Middle Eastern American who suffered the effects of prejudice in the aftermath
V. ACTION (Step 5)
    A. People are honored that somebody wants to hear their story (*New York Daily News,* February 22, 2004)
    B. Interview of mother and daughter encouraged 4 hours of talking and questioning (*Hartford Courant,* December 18, 2003)

Summary and Call to Action: Having outlined the needs, some features, and the implications of oral history, I ask you now . . . to consider "the voices [you] have heard, and the ones [you] haven't, and the ones [you] wished [you] had recorded to listen to again and again." Whether their stories were remarkable or simply unique, their legacy and wisdom are what history was meant to be (*Baltimore Sun,* November 12, 2003).

description of each and an excerpt to illustrate it from the speech about oral histories. The speaker's outline for the oral histories speech, which uses the motivated sequence, is presented in Figure 14.3.

Step 1: Get the audience's attention. In this first step, create interest in the topic of your speech and a desire on the part of your listeners to hear what you have to say. Also provide a statement of the purpose of your speech and forecast the importance of the need or problem that will be the general theme of your speech. Here's how Moorehead began his persuasive speech and used a narrative to draw the audience's attention to the value of oral histories (Torronen, 2000; see I. A. in the speech outline):

> New York's Grand Central Station is one of the world's prime locations for people-watching, and sometimes it gets scary. You have street punks, hookers, local politicians. The trained eye can even pick out minor celebrities like what's-his-face. But if you happen to notice a booth of bright, translucent honeycomb plastic, you will see that Grand Central Station is now America's prime location for people-listening. This rather curious booth is called the StoryCorps booth, the brainchild of documentarian David Isay. NPR's *Morning Edition,* October 23, 2000 explains that a StoryCorps booth is designed for people like us to interview people close to us, and come away with a broadcast-quality oral history CD.

Step 2: Establish that a need or problem exists. In this step, describe and develop the need or problem by providing evidence of its existence and importance. Use examples, testimony, statistics, and other forms of support to emphasize the seriousness of the situation. Explain why the problem exists and relate it to the listeners by pointing out how it affects them. Motivate them to feel that a decision needs to be made or some action taken. Moorehead's speech follows this recommendation, as the outline in Figure 14.3 shows. First, he describes the social importance of stories (II. A. in the outline):

> The StoryCorps project literally began as the idea of one person. And even though our participation may not garner as much attention, we must take the same initiative to start recording history for ourselves. This history is both socially valuable and increasingly ignored. The social importance of stories is undeniable. Andrew Buckser argues in the *Anthropological Quarterly* of January 1999 that to tell the story of one's past or one's group is to ground one's own identity.

Next, Moorehead explains why a problem exists, which is that the mass media are ignoring these stories (II. B.):

> But more and more, says the *Christian Science Monitor* of September 10, 2003, mass media are ignoring these stories in favor of The Official Truth. As Studs Terkel—the most renowned oral historian in America—told the *Washington Journalism Review* in October 1989, the Official Truth is the story that goes into newspapers and history books; it's not so much true as convenient for the establishment. The *Oral History Review* of Spring 2002 calls the result America's collective amnesia.

Step 3: Propose a satisfying solution. This step presents a plan of action to meet the need or solve the problem you established in the previous step. Explain to the listeners specifically how your plan addresses the need or problem. To do this, you may have to demonstrate how your plan is superior to any other solution. The speaker in the oral histories speech first presents an action step that is necessary to solve the problem and also says what solutions won't work (III. B.):

> The solution to this problem must be multifaceted, but on the whole, it will represent increased participation in creating and maintaining historical records.
>
> The most popular way to take part in history is to start doing oral histories. Just get somebody with interesting experiences to tell you a story, and record it.
>
> I urge oral history as opposed to a diary or webpage because of the words of Sue Davis, an everyday person interviewed by the *Atlanta Journal-Constitution* February 7, 2004. It means so much, she says, to have a videotaped interview with her father.

Step 4: Help the audience visualize the solution. This step helps the audience to imagine the benefits of the solution you propose or the negative consequences of not adopting your solution. You ask your listeners to picture the proposed plan being implemented or what the world will look like if they fail to act. Here's the effective visualization step from Moorehead's speech:

> A more personal view of history wouldn't make the world a different place, we would just know much more about it. History from the bottom up is valuable because as the *Columbia Chronicle* stated on May 7, 2001, an individual's point of view versus a political one more accurately illustrates historical events. Even today, oral history is being used to find the truth. When we make history our own, we make history representative [of everyone].

Step 5: Motivate the audience to take action. Finally, ask the audience to act on the solution that you proposed to solve the problem. Summarize your main ideas as you would in any conclusion. Then clearly identify the specific action that is called for. If your objective is to change attitudes or beliefs, try to motivate the audience to reconsider their past positions and believe what you propose instead. If you want the listeners to change their behaviors, urge them to take the specific actions you recommend to solve the problem. In the following action step, the oral histories speaker summarizes and then asks the audience members to take action:

> Having outlined the needs, some features, and the implications of oral history, I ask you now, as the *Baltimore Sun* of November 12, 2003 does, to consider "the voices [you] have heard, and the ones [you] haven't, and the ones [you] wished [you] had recorded to listen to again and again." Whether their stories were remarkable or simply unique, their legacy and wisdom are what history was meant to be.

learning link

Can a public speaker use refuting the opponent as an organizational pattern and still persuade ethically?

• • •

Refuting the Opponent

Refuting the opponent organization dismantles your opponent's argument to persuade the audience that your argument is superior. In this organizational pattern, your goal is to convince the audience that the opposition's ideas are false, misinformed, or in some way harmful.

There are two basic approaches to refuting the opponent. The first is to convince the audience that the other argument is flawed—that something is wrong with your opponent's line of reasoning. You examine his or her argument for any inconsistencies or errors in the way evidence is presented or interpreted. The second approach is to convince the listeners that the actions recommended by your opponent will lead to undesirable results or consequences. You refute your opponent's argument by stressing its negative results for your audience.

A word of caution if you decide to use the refuting the opponent organization. Avoid engaging in personal attacks and stay strictly with the issues involved. Use solid evidence to criticize only your opponent's argument, because attacking the person instead can backfire and damage your own credibility. Moreover, mudslinging and personal attacks are unethical approaches to persuasion and therefore not competent.

Comparing Alternatives

Comparing alternatives organization first asks listeners to examine two or more alternatives, and then it makes a strong appeal for the preferred choice. This organizational pattern is designed to convince the audience that, among all the possible ways to solve a problem, there is but one choice with significant advantages over the others.

To use this organizational pattern, you present a series of alternatives and provide reasons to reject each alternative and then present the alternative you prefer last. Just as with refuting the opponent, you can use the comparing alternatives organization to structure the body of your speech. You would then have several main points, each containing a different alternative, and end with the presentation of your preferred choice.

The comparing alternatives organization is useful if the listeners will be exposed to other arguments from other speakers. When a politician or policy maker presents a new program, there are usually other opinions or alternative ways to handle the issue. As a result, the speaker often reviews the other alternatives and then presents his or her proposal as the logical choice.

Regardless of how you organize your persuasive speech, you need to be aware of some challenges to persuasive speaking, sometimes referred to as logical fallacies.

Reasoning Logically _____

Logical fallacies are errors in reasoning and logic that lead the listeners to false conclusions. The speakers are so intent on achieving their persuasive goals that they present evidence or information that is in error, is unreasonable, or misrepresents the truth in some way. Whether intentional or unintentional, if fallacies in reasoning are detected, they reflect negatively on your credibility as an ethical speaker and call into question your integrity. Researchers have identified literally hundreds of logical fallacies to avoid, but the following examples show some of the dangers inherent in faulty reasoning.

- Ad hominem. The **ad hominem** fallacy occurs when a speaker attacks another person as opposed to attacking the argument the person is making. (*Ad hominem* is Latin for "to the person.") Candidates in political campaigns commit this error in reasoning by attacking their opponents personally and failing to stick to the issues. For example, labeling the opponent a left-wing liberal or a right-wing conservative would focus the audience's attention on the other person and not on her or his argument. Unfortunately, some candidates for public office have discovered that this approach to negative campaigning has a benefit—it often works.

- Non sequitur. Although a claim may be correct and true, if it does not necessarily follow from the evidence presented, a **non sequitur** (literally, "it does not follow") occurs. For example, a speaker who is discussing health care could discuss the benefits of nationalized health insurance but would commit a non sequitur by concluding with a claim about the benefits to the defense industry.

- Red herring. A **red herring** diverts the audience's attention from the real issue by presenting irrelevant arguments or issues. The expression "red herring" derives its meaning from the practice of dragging a smelly fish across a trail to divert the attention of hunting dogs. This technique might be used in a budget debate on a college campus about financial aid policies. A speaker could divert attention from financial aid issues by bringing up the red herring of insufficient funds for additional parking lots.

- Slippery slope. A speaker who suggests one event automatically leads to a series of other undesirable events is using **slippery slope** reasoning. The speaker implies that if the listeners take one action, they are setting themselves up to slide down a slope from which there is no return. This implication that a situation results from a single cause, when in fact it likely has multiple causes, is another way of misleading an audience. If you know there are additional causes, you have an obligation to describe them to the audience. For example, to suggest that teenage pregnancy is the result only of coming from a broken home is erroneous. There are many other contributing factors such as poor school attendance and lack of education, lack of parental support or access to contraceptives, and peer influence.

- Straw man argument. The speaker who attacks an entire argument by selecting a weak example or aspect of it is making a **straw man argument,** knocking the weak example over and thus discrediting the entire argument. In a business or corporation, the personnel manager could say that the company should not be subject to affirmative action policies because women are

learning link

How can a public speaker become more aware of any tendency to use a logical fallacy to accomplish the objective of a persuasive speech?

• • •

learning link

How can a persuasive speaker ethically combine emotional and logical appeals to accomplish the objective of a persuasive speech on a highly controversial topic?

• • •

CloseUp *on Ethics*

Ethics and Speaking to Persuade

PUBLIC SPEAKERS FACE PARTICULARLY CHALLENGing ethical dilemmas when they are speaking to persuade. An ethic based on objectivity says public speakers should share only the truth with their audience. But a persuasion ethic suggests persuaders may want to present their argument in its most favorable light. Advocates such as lawyers believe the persuasion ethic is appropriate to use in a participatory democracy. In a free and democratic society, when all sides of an issue are argued openly, ultimately the truth is revealed. Furthermore, the presentation of varying perceptions of the truth is justified by the democratic ideal that everyone has a right to express the truth as he or she sees it. A question for a competent speaker is "Do I present the whole truth, or just the truth as I see it?"

Given this ethical dilemma, here are some pitfalls to avoid when making decisions about ethical persuasive speaking:

- Don't allow the end to justify the means. Your end in a persuasive speech is to accomplish your persuasive goal. But if you withhold information to accomplish that goal, you're assuming the audience isn't capable of weighing all the evidence and making a good decision. If you suppress or distort information or deliberately lie to adapt your speech to the audience, that is unethical. As a public speaker, you are ethically responsible to present all viewpoints—openly and fairly—so your listeners will be in a position to form their own opinions.

- Don't use numbers or statistics to mislead the audience. Most people think statistical studies are precise and reliable, so they're easily persuaded by the use of numbers to support an argument. However, researchers who generate statistics, and public speakers who make use of them, can interpret and slant what numbers mean. Using the persuasive ability of statistics to misrepresent the truth is not ethical. If you discover statistics that contradict your position, you have an ethical responsibility to report that evidence to your listeners.

- Don't misrepresent your position on the topic to the listeners. If the listeners strongly disagree with your position, it may be tempting to distort or misrepresent your claim or position. To say what you do not mean, to fabricate enthusiasm for a topic, or to endorse a policy with which you disagree is unethical.

- Don't use emotion to distract the listeners from the truth. Emotional evidence can sometimes be more effective than a logical argument. Therefore you may be tempted to use an extremely emotional story or example to persuade the audience of the rightness or importance of your claim. That is acceptable only if you have carefully considered the impact of that evidence on the audience. Moreover, to use emotion as a substitute for sound reasoning is unethical.

SOURCES: Barney & Black, 1994; Murray, 2004.

already sufficiently represented in the work force. The issue of affirmative action is more complex than simply female representation, so this would be the use of a "straw woman" argument.

- Sweeping or hasty generalization. A **sweeping generalization** that clusters ideas, people, or objects into one group and implies that all the items in the group are the same, obscures vital and relevant differences. For example, a sweeping generalization would be to say that "AIDS is the penalty people pay for having casual sex" or "All Americans eat too much." A **hasty generalization** results from moving to a conclusion too quickly and basing it on too few specific cases or examples. If a speaker describes one basketball or soccer player who is a notoriously bad student and quickly generalizes that trait to all players, he or she is making a hasty generalization.

These logical fallacies suggest that it is critical for a competent public speaker to develop an understanding of what it means to engage in ethical persuasion.

Ethics and Persuasive Public Speaking

Over many years, scholars have studied the topics of ethics, communication, and persuasion (Johannesen, 2002). Some say that persuasive speaking can easily be misunderstood and confused with coercion or manipulation, which are not ethical ways of influencing others. **Coercion** is a negative form of influence that occurs when a speaker persuades others to act in a particular way out of fear, or by using force, or by giving them no choice but to cooperate. In Nazi Germany, some people were coerced by Hitler's speeches to betray their friends and family members who were providing safe havens for Jews.

Manipulation is also a negative and unethical form of influence that is used to control people's actions or reactions but in a devious or deceitful way. Political campaign speeches sometimes border on manipulation when they deliberately distort or misrepresent an opponent's programs or positions on an issue.

By contrast to these unethical approaches, **ethical persuasion** leaves the decision about what to think or do up to the person or the audience members. The speaker presents information, without coercing or manipulating the listeners, and allows them to make up their own minds. Building on the information about ethics introduced in Chapter 1, the Close-Up on Ethics box highlights some ethical challenges that professionals and public speakers often face.

The advice provided in this chapter helped Zola get Spencer involved in student activism. And it helped Spencer present an effective speech on tuition hikes. No doubt most of the students in the class signed his petition opposing the hike. Like Zola and Spencer, if you follow the guidelines provided here for preparing and presenting persuasive speeches competently, you too will influence listeners and reinforce, modify, and change their attitudes, beliefs, values, and behaviors.

 ## Chapter Summary

A persuasive speaker uses appeals appropriate for the setting to influence the audience, or receivers', attitudes, beliefs, values, or actions. Because of its goal to influence, a persuasive speech is organized differently from an informative speech and is more concerned with the listeners' specific position on the speech topic. Aristotle emphasized the importance of persuasive speaking skills in society, which continues to be crucial today.

The three types of persuasive speeches, based on the speaker's objective, attempt to (1) reinforce the listeners' attitudes, beliefs, and values; (2) change attitudes, beliefs, and values; or (3) move the listeners to action. Whether the speech is intended to influence attitudes, beliefs, values, or actions, a competent speaker uses one or more of three types of appeals. A logical appeal is based on knowledge and reasoning, what people know, and makes use of deductive or inductive reasoning to influence listeners. An emotional appeal is based on psychology and passion, how people feel, and calls on emotions such as love, hate, sympathy, guilt, or even fear to influence the audience. A third type of appeal, credibility, is based on the listeners' perceptions of the reputation, prestige, and authority of the speaker. The speaker's perceived expertise, trustworthiness, and charisma affect perceptions of credibility.

A persuasive speech can be organized in any one of four ways. Problem-solution organization first identifies a problem and then proposes a solution. The motivated sequence consists of five steps: attention, need, satisfaction, visualization, and action. Refuting the opponent organization dismantles the opposing argument. The comparing alternatives organization examines two or more alternatives and makes an appeal for the preferred choice. An ethical persuasive speaker does not use coercion or manipulation to influence the audience.

Study and Review

The premium companion website for *Human Communication* offers a broad range of resources that will help you better understand the material in this chapter, complete assignments, and succeed on tests. The website resources include

- Interactive self-assessments, competency grids, and other tools
- Web links, practice activities, self-quizzes, and a sample final exam

For more information about this text's electronic learning resources, consult the *Guide to Online Resources for Human Communication* or visit **http://communication .wadsworth.com/morreale2.**

Key Terms

The key terms below are defined in the chapter on the pages indicated. They are also presented alphabetically with definitions in the Glossary, which begins on page 467. The book's website includes flashcards and crossword puzzles to help you learn these terms and the concepts they represent.

speech to reinforce 373
speech to change 374
speech to move to action 375
appeal 376
logos 376
pathos 376
ethos 376
logical appeal 376
deduction 376
induction 376
emotional appeal 378
fear appeal 378
credibility appeal 379
problem-solution organization 380

motivated sequence 381
refuting the opponent 385
comparing alternatives 385
logical fallacies 386
ad hominem 386
non sequitur 386
red herring 386
slippery slope 386
straw man argument 386
sweeping generalization 387
hasty generalization 387
coercion 388
manipulation 388
ethical persuasion 388

Building Knowledge

The following questions are among the practice activities on the book's website.

1. Of the three types of persuasive speeches—to reinforce, change, or move to action—which poses the greatest challenge for a public speaker and why?
2. When you are considering the use of appeals in a persuasive speech—logical, emotional, or credibility appeals—what aspects of the speech or the speaking situation will help you decide what appeals will work best?
3. Is any one of the persuasive organizational patterns better to use or more effective than the others? Explain your answer.
4. Which of the logical fallacies do you see used most frequently in contemporary organizations? In contemporary political life? Provide examples.
5. If there is a fine line between persuasion and manipulation or coercion, what might you as a persuasive speaker say or do to avoid becoming manipulative or coercive?
6. Analyze the speech about oral histories at the end of this chapter in light of what you have learned about persuasion. Is there anything the speaker could have said that would have made this prize-winning speech even more effective?

Building Skills

The exercises below are among the practice activities on the book's website.

Individual Exercises

1. Identify several topics for a persuasive speech. Label five columns on a piece of paper as follows: topics, attitudes, beliefs, values, and actions. List your speech topics in the left-hand column and then answer these questions for each topic in the remaining four columns. What would the other students in the class believe about the topic? What attitude would they hold toward it? What values might be related to the topic? What actions or behaviors might they demonstrate regarding the topic?
2. On the Internet, visit a site that contains links to historical or contemporary speeches, such as the National Gallery of the Spoken Word at **http://www.ngsw.org**. Go to one of those links and find a persuasive speech that interests you. Read the speech and identify what type of persuasive speech it is, what types of appeals are used, and its organizational pattern. On the basis of your analysis, decide how effective you think the speech is.
3. Make a list of the occasions you can remember during the last year or so when you changed your mind or your behavior in some way. What persuaded you to change?
4. Make a list of the occasions you can remember when someone or something (for example, an advertisement) tried to influence or persuade you but failed. Why did that persuasive act fail, and what could have improved its effectiveness?

Group Activities

1. Form groups of four students and choose a topic for a persuasive speech that appeals to all of you—something you know or care about and the other students in your class would find interesting. As a group, decide on a position on the topic and

state that position as a specific purpose statement for a persuasive speech. Decide what type of persuasive speech to develop for the topic and what types of appeals will work best. Choose the best way to organize the speech.

2. Form dyads and develop a case for your credibility as public speakers. Each person should choose a topic for a persuasive speech and determine how to build his or her credibility when presenting that speech. Compare how each student would build a case for his or her expertise, trustworthiness, and charisma.

3. Attend a persuasive speech either on or off campus with a small group of students. Evaluate the effectiveness of the speech using what you learned from this chapter. After you leave the presentation, compare your analyses.

 ## References

Barney, R., & Black, J. (1994). Ethics and professional persuasive communications. *Public Relations Review, 20,* 233–248.

Fink, E. L., Cai, D. A., Kaplowitz, S. A., Sungeun, C., Van Dyke, M. A., & Jeong-Nam, M. A. (2003). The semantics of social influence: Threats vs. persuasion. *Communication Monographs, 70*(4), 295–317.

Furnham, A., & Procter, E. (1989–1990). Memory for information about nuclear power: A test of the selective recall hypothesis. *Current Psychology Research and Reviews, 8,* 287–297.

Johannesen, R. L. (2002). *Ethics in human communication* (5th ed.). Long Grove, IL: Waveland Press.

Kennedy, G. (1963). *The art of persuasion in ancient Greece.* Princeton: Princeton University Press.

Kennedy, G. (1994). *A new history of classical rhetoric.* Princeton: Princeton University Press.

Lindquist, T. (1995). Talking the talk: How to teach kids the gentle art of persuasion. *Instructor, 105*(4), 26–28.

McDermott, V. M. (2004). Using motivated sequence in persuasive speaking: The speech for charity. *Communication Teacher, 18*(1), 13–14.

Miller, V. R. (2004). "Show and tell" persuasion. *Communication Teacher, 18*(1), 28–30.

Moebius, M. (1991). What do you believe? Persuasive speeches in eighth grade. *English Journal, 80,* 38–42.

Monroe, A. H. (1935). *Principles and types of speech.* Glenview, IL: Scott, Foresman.

Moorehead, A. J. (2004). Core stories. In L. Schnoor (Ed.), *Winning Orations* (pp. 3–4). Mankato, MN: Interstate Oratorical Association.

Murray, J. W. (2004). The face in dialogue, Part II: Invitational rhetoric, direct moral suasion, and the asymmetry of dialogue. *Southern Communication Journal, 69,* 333–347.

Roberts, W. R. (Trans.). (1954). *The rhetoric,* by Aristotle. New York: Modern Library.

Roser, C., & Thompson, M. (1995). Fear appeals and the formation of active publics. *Journal of Communication, 45,* 103–121.

Smith, S. L. (1997). The effective use of fear appeals in persuasive immunization: An analysis of national immunization intervention messages. *Journal of Applied Communication Research, 25,* 264–292.

Stiff, J. B., & Mongeau, P. A. (2003). *Persuasive communication* (2nd ed.). New York: Guilford.

Taylor, L. (1996). How did "a great deal of interest" for my talk dwindle to "unexpected lack of demand"? *New Statesman, 128,* 63–64.

Torronen, J. (2000). The passionate text: The pending narrative as a macrostructure of persuasion. *Social Semiotics, 10*(1), 81–98.

Witte, K. (1994). Fear control and danger control: A test of the extended parallel process model. *Communication Monographs, 61,* 113–134.

Exemplary Persuasive Speech

The following persuasive speech, about the need for oral histories, was presented by Antonio Moorehead at the 132nd Annual Contest of the Interstate Oratorical Association in April 2004 and took first place in the competition. The objectives of the speech are to change existing beliefs about how history should be recorded and move the audience to get involved in the recording of oral histories. The speech follows the five steps of the motivated sequence organizational pattern and makes effective use of logical and emotional appeals and credible sources of information.

Core Stories
Antonio Jean Moorehead
Arizona State University
Coached by Kelly McDonald and Marianne Palmisanno

(1)   New York's Grand Central Station is one of the world's prime locations for people-watching, and sometimes it gets scary. You have street punks, hookers, local politicians. The trained eye can even pick out minor celebrities like what's-his-face. But if you happen to notice a booth of bright, translucent honeycomb plastic, you will see that Grand Central Station is now America's prime location for people-listening.

(2)   This rather curious booth is called the StoryCorps booth, the brainchild of documentarian David Isay. NPR's *Morning Edition,* October 23, 2000 explains that a Story Corps booth is designed for people like us to interview people close to us, and come away with a broadcast-quality oral history CD. One copy is yours to keep, and with permission, one copy is sent to the American Folklife Center at the Library of Congress to help build an oral history of America. StoryCorps is not valuable solely because of what it is doing, but because it reminds us of what we should be doing.

(3)   Since the project has garnered several big name sponsors and, in the words of the *Hartford Courant* of December 18, 2003, "everyone who does this is a convert,"

(4)   History from one person's viewpoint—history from the bottom up—may well be a vital part of the human experience. So where is it? History as most of us know it is in books, not CDs; written by scholars, not recorded by laypeople, but it should be. People who don't happen to study history should also be seeking out interviews and bottom-up history.

(5)   To understand why, we must first outline the growing need to foster history from the bottom up. Having done this, we can construct solution criteria which will keep it alive. Finally, we may illustrate the benefits in our future once we act to save our past.

(6)   The StoryCorps project literally began as the idea of one person. And even though our participation may not garner as much attention, we must take the same initiative to start recording history for ourselves. This history is both socially valuable and increasingly ignored. The social importance of stories is undeniable. Andrew Buckser argues in the *Anthropological Quarterly* of January 1999 that to tell the story of one's past or one's group is to ground one's own identity.

(7)   This is the idea behind the Rondo Oral History project, described in the *Minneapolis Star Tribune* of March 1, 2004. Rondo was a very close-knit black neighborhood in Minnesota that was all but destroyed when I-94 was built through it in the 1950s. One-hundred-year-old Mary Hamilton remembers her neighbor in Rondo who built a ballroom in his house for black people who had no place to dance back then.

(1) *Attention step:* The speaker first calls the audience's attention to a successful national oral history project—StoryCorps.

(2) Next the speaker describes the StoryCorps project and references its notable developer.

(3) A respected publication is used to tell the listeners that StoryCorps (and therefore recording oral histories) is a good idea.

(4) In this thesis statement, the speaker uses language effectively and coins a memorable phrase—history from the bottom up—saying that it's a vital part of the human experience.

(5) In this preview, the speaker forecasts the exact content of the speech.

(6) *Need or problem step:* The speaker presents his first main point—the social importance of stories to the identity of both individuals and groups.

(7) Here an example of a local, neighborhood-based oral history project is provided.

(8) A different kind of oral history exists relating to the late Justice Harry Blackmun, the man who wrote the Court's decision on *Roe v. Wade*. Justice Blackmun took this initiative for himself, and the March 5, 2004 *Washington Post* shares his stories. He tells how *Roe v. Wade* was very nearly overturned in 1992, and how whenever the court viewed films to determine if they were pornographic, the nearly blind Justice John Harlan would always ask "What are they doing now? You don't say!" From tiny neighborhoods to the Supreme Court, our identities depend on details and exchanges like these.

(9) But more and more, says the *Christian Science Monitor* of September 10, 2003, mass media are ignoring these stories in favor of The Official Truth. As Studs Terkel—the most renowned oral historian in America—told the *Washington Journalism Review* in October 1989, the Official Truth is the story that goes into newspapers and history books; it's not so much true as convenient for the establishment.

(10) The *Oral History Review* of Spring 2002 calls the result America's collective amnesia. We are forgetting, the article says, what it was like to not have an 8 hour work day, what it was like to not be able to vote, what it was like to have your entire country be poor. If we forget our stories, we will forget our struggles, and without those, we're just consumers; made homogeneous by the media, and accepting of the Official Truth.

(11) By definition, our history and identity will only move away from us unless we actively keep them near. The solution to this problem must be multifaceted, but on the whole, it will represent increased participation in creating and maintaining historical records.

(12) The most popular way to take part in history is to start doing oral histories. Just get somebody with interesting experiences to tell you a story, and record it.

(13) Consider the experience of the Women in Journalism Oral History Project, when they interviewed Ethel Payne in 1987. As one of only two black women credentialed to cover the White House from 1953 to 1973, Ms. Payne represented exactly the kind of unique perspective that oral history was made for. She passed away four years after her interview, underscoring the urgency of the oral historian's task; it's likely that her story would have been lost if not for the oral history project.

(14) I urge oral history as opposed to a diary or webpage because of the words of Sue Davis, an everyday person interviewed by the *Atlanta Journal-Constitution* February 7, 2004. It means so much, she says, to have a videotaped interview with her father. "We can hear his voice and see his facial expressions when he talks about growing up, his love for my mother, and his career as a doctor." When you write history on paper, you preserve it; but if you use a video or audio tape, you keep it alive. Finally, remember that oral histories are no good unless you consume them! Read transcripts of Studs Terkel's interviews in *My American Century* and *Working;* listen to StoryCorps excerpts at www.storycorps.com and www.npr.org.

(15) Staying connected to history and keeping it alive requires only a pair of ears and an open mind.

(16) A more personal view of history wouldn't make the world a different place, we would just know much more about it. The increase in bottom-up history would serve to make the discipline more accessible and accurate, with similar changes in one's personal life. History from the bottom up is valuable because as the *Columbia Chronicle* stated on May 7, 2001, an individual's point of view versus a political one more accurately illustrates historical events.

(17) Alessandro Portelli makes this clear in his 1991 book *The Death of Luigi Trastulli.* He writes that when former slaves were interviewed in the 1930s by the federal government, their oral accounts required the entire history of slavery to be rewritten.

(18)   Even today, oral history is being used to find the truth. In his 2003 book *Embedded: The Media @ War in Iraq,* Bill Katovsky, by interviewing soldiers, activists, civilians and leaders on the ground in Iraq, tries to avoid a repeat of the 2001 Afghanistan Conflict, which was essentially closed to the media. As he told the *Rocky Mountain News* of February 26, 2004, the mass media have signed off on Iraq, agreeing to White House Press Conferences with only pre-written questions, and going along with the Pentagon's avoidance of a civilian casualty count. Oral history is often the only way to find what really happened or is happening.

(19)   When we make history our own, we make history representative. 50 years from now there will be many views of September 11th: the victimized American, the person who felt we had it coming and the Middle-Eastern American who suffered prejudice in the aftermath. To say that the latter two will be the predominant views is a bit naive. But to claim that the less mainstream views aren't important is more than a bit ignorant. You don't have to be famous for your life to be history.

(20)   History is about soldiers who are now grandpas and hippies who are now Mom and Dad. David Isay has seen people break down and cry before interviews, because they're so honored that somebody wants to hear their story. As he told the *New York Daily News* of February 22, 2004, when a person sees their story on a CD or in a book, they get this amazing feeling: I exist. The previously cited *Hartford Courant* mentions that four hours after Karin Miller-Lewis interviewed her mother, they were still talking and questioning. That's when the real stories came out. Everyone has the right to say "I exist, I will be remembered," especially if you say they're close to you.

(21)   Having outlined the needs, some features, and the implications of oral history, I ask you now, as *The Baltimore Sun* of November 12, 2003 does, to consider "the voices [you] have heard, and the ones [you] haven't, and the ones [you] wished [you] had recorded to listen to again and again". Whether their stories were remarkable or simply unique, their legacy and wisdom are what history was meant to be.

(18)   The speaker next suggests that today oral histories are used to find the truth, for example, interviews on the ground in Iraq.

(19)   Looking to the future, the speaker says that 50 years from now, we need oral histories of the September 11 experience if we want to make history representative of all people.

(20)   *Action step:* The speaker points out that people are honored that somebody wants to hear their story; and through the story-telling interview, people talk to one another more.

(21)   The speaker concludes by reviewing what has been said about the implications of oral history and then the listeners are asked to consider the voices and stories they could have recorded and then listened to again and again.

Public Speaking Presentation Competence Skills Grid

To help you understand how to use this grid, the skills displayed by Sergio and Wen Shu in the opening vignette of Chapter 12 have been analyzed below. Examine that analysis and then think about a recent speech and what you could have done more competently. On the next page, first describe the context of the speech in the spaces provided. Next, analyze your presentation skills based on the four presentational skills explained in this chapter. In the first column, briefly describe and give examples of how your skills were less than competent.

Using these less competent skills as a point of comparison to fill in the second column, describe the skills you think would have been perceived as more competent in the particular context. With practice, you will find you can use this grid to help you plan how to present future speeches more competently and avoid behaviors that could be perceived as less competent.

ANALYZING WEN SHU AND SERGIO'S PRESENTATION SKILLS

Context

CULTURE: A Chinese and a Mexican American student on a statewide speaking tour

TIME: Daytime and evening

RELATIONSHIP: Older students-younger students; student-faculty

PLACE: Rural high schools

FUNCTION: To promote the university and encourage students to attend it

PRESENTATION SKILLS	LESS COMPETENT	MORE COMPETENT
WORDS AND LANGUAGE	Sergio used fancy words, jargon, and unfamiliar terms.	Sergio needs to speak clearly, vividly, and appropriately for the particular audience. Wen Shu chose her words carefully and spoke at the right level.
VOCAL VARIETY	Wen Shu spoke too quietly.	Wen Shu needs to vary her vocal variety and increase her volume. Sergio projected his voice effectively.
PRONUNCIATION, ARTICULATION, AND GRAMMAR	Sergio committed errors in pronunciation and articulation and used filled pauses.	Sergio needs to pronounce words and articulate sounds correctly and pause silently. Wen Shu pronounced clearly and used grammar correctly.
NONVERBAL CLUES	Wen Shu rocked from one foot to the other, kept looking down, doodled nervously, and had an expressionless face.	Wen Shu needs to use posture, gestures, body movement, facial expressions, and eye contact to enhance her verbal message.

ANALYZING YOUR PRESENTATION SKILLS

Context

CULTURE:

TIME:

RELATIONSHIP:

PLACE:

FUNCTION:

PRESENTATION SKILLS	LESS COMPETENT	MORE COMPETENT
WORDS AND LANGUAGE		
VOCAL VARIETY		
PRONUNCIATION, ARTICULATION, AND GRAMMAR		
NONVERBAL CLUES		

Chapter 15

© Javier Pierini/age Fotostock

LEARNING OBJECTIVES | After studying this chapter, you should be able to

1. Compare and contrast the nature of computer-mediated communication to face-to-face communication.

2. Identify advantages and disadvantages of different media with which to communicate, on the basis of whether a message needs richness or openness.

3. Diagnose your own level of technophobia and identify steps to manage it.

4. Identify the ways changes in communication technology are changing society and the role of the individual in society.

5. Translate and adapt face-to-face communication skills into mediated communication skills (attentiveness, composure, co-ordination, expressiveness).

6. Apply your motivation, knowledge, and skills in different contexts to select the most competent media for communicating messages.

Computer-Mediated Communication

Sloane had heard about how much fun chat rooms could be. Given her interest in the television show *The Apprentice,* a chat room seemed a natural way of keeping up with the current buzz of the show. However, Sloane had also heard that women tended to be in the minority in such chat rooms, and as a result, got hit on by geeks and lonely guys who could not meet people any other way. She decided to enter the chat room under an assumed male identity, Ted, and went by the nickname "Bad Hair Decade."

Sloane immediately found the daily chats to be fun and gossipy, dishing on the show's contestants and arguing about whether the show was pitting one racial group against another. She even found someone, Chad, nicknamed "Magnate Magnet," whose conversation she particularly enjoyed. They began leaving the chat room and moving to e-mailing directly to each other, disclosing more and more personal information about their past, their beliefs, their values, and their career aspirations. Sloane and Chad rarely let a message go more than a few hours without some type of response. They started developing their own code names for the ideas they came up with during discussion of *The Apprentice.* They found they had much in common and that they wanted to attend the same season debut party in New York City soon. In a matter of weeks, Sloane felt herself strongly attracted to Chad, but as she found herself wanting to start an honest and trusting relationship with him, she faced the problem of having deceived him all this time about her actual identity. What advice would you give Bad Hair Decade? ∎

In this chapter, we will examine how the model of communication competence applies to the emerging contexts of computer-mediated communication. In Sloane's case, the model accounts for the role of motivation, both in her initial interest in a mass communication show, *The Apprentice,* and in her later motivation to pursue a relationship. The model also reveals the importance of her knowledge, in that her careful following of *The Apprentice* gave her credibility in the chat room and an ability to impress the others in the digital space of the interaction. Finally, the model illustrates the importance of her computer-based communication skills. She was expressive with her disclosure, coordinated with her responsiveness, composed with her expertise, and attentive with her display of interest in what Magnate Magnet had to say. But the model needs further development to make complete sense of this particular environment. Media introduce a variety of unique characteristics into the communication process. This chapter applies the model of communication competence to both the mass communication and computer-mediated communication (CMC) context.

What Is Computer-Mediated Communication Competence?

Today, most of us think of mediated communication as "computer-based" communication. **Computer-mediated communication,** generally referred to as **CMC,** is any human symbolic interaction that takes place through digitally based technologies. Digital simply means that the information contained in sounds, images, and procedures is converted into combinations of the digits one and zero. Unlike *analogic* information (see Chapter 4), which is continuous and typically nonverbal, digital communication generally has precise meanings and precise beginnings and endings.

The word "mediated" comes from the Latin *media,* meaning "middle." It has come to mean anything that comes between one person's message and an audience. Computers in one way or another are the channels or intermediaries through which CMC messages travel from one person to other persons.

Computers are technological media, which we can contrast with natural media. **Natural media** are those that send and translate symbols using only our bodies and minds, such as spoken words, gestures, posture, and all the other verbal, nonverbal, and listening processes examined in the previous chapters. **Technological media** are those devices that translate, amplify, or otherwise alter the information in these natural media and typically include telephones, instant messaging, teleconferencing, videophones, videoconferencing, e-mail, and other computer-assisted interactions such as telemarketing, group-decision support systems, computer chat-lines, blogging, multiuser domains (MUDs), and some virtual reality systems.

This chapter focuses mainly on CMC. The most commonly used forms of CMC are e-mail, the World Wide Web (WWW), chat rooms, blogging, and videophone communication via the computer, including instant messaging (IM). We'll also look at telephone communication, still the preferred mode of everyday conversation (Rideout, Roberts, & Foehr, 2005). Finally, there are also other forms of computer interaction, such as video games, that can be clearly communicative in the sense that they involve multiparty interactions as part of the games.

Sometimes computer-mediated communication helps some forms of communication and limits others.

Characteristics of Computer-Mediated Communication

The nature of computers makes certain characteristics of communication more important to competence than others. Two such basic characteristics of CMC are richness and openness.

Richness

When you talk with people face to face, you see them, hear them, and perhaps even touch and smell them. Such natural media are very rich in sensory information. Media **richness** is the extent to which a medium represents all the information available in the original message. It is also called "presence" (Witmer & Singer, 1998), which is the extent a medium allows communicators to feel like they are in the physical space of another. Richer media permit more feedback; greater immediacy; more types of verbal, visual, and audio cues or information; more tailoring of messages to particular individuals; and more use of informal language (Trevino, Daft, & Lengel, 1990). For example, a videophone offers you more sense of presence than a telephone, and a telephone offers more interactivity than sending letters through the mail. The concept of richness is the foundation of most current theories of mediated interpersonal communication.

Interactivity and completeness determine the richness of a medium. "Poor" or "lean" media lack these characteristics. **Interactivity** is the extent to which parties can communicate simultaneously in response to each other's messages (Sohn & Lee, 2005). Standard e-mail and IM are not very interactive because a writer must complete an entire message, send it, and wait for transmission systems to receive, transfer, and deposit the message to the recipient's system. Many chat rooms, in contrast, are more interactive because they allow a recipient to see the words of the other person as they are being typed and permit interruptions in midsentence almost like a face-to-face conversation. The more interactive the medium, the richer it is.

Completeness is the extent to which a medium represents the nonverbal and emotional content of messages. The telephone reflects a wider range of *vocalic* information about speaker intent and emotion than letters and e-mail, but all these media are less complete

learning link

What is the nature of media richness and media openness, and how do they differ?

• • •

Figure 15.1

Media Richness Continuum

Media vary in their ability to represent both verbal and nonverbal information in communication.

Source: Adapted from Trevino et al. (1990).

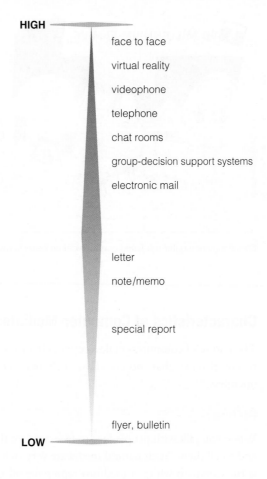

than video-telephony. Yet even video-telephony presents only a fairly flat, two-dimensional picture of a person. The more complete the medium, the richer it is. Figure 15.1 displays a traditional way of organizing media in terms of their richness.

We all adapt our messages to the medium and to the context, such as our goal or the type of relationship we have with the receiver. For example, in one survey, almost three-quarters of teens say they prefer the telephone for a "serious conversation," but for "quick conversations with friends" about 60% prefer the phone and 26% routinely use IM (Lenhart, Madden, & Hitlin, 2005). Competence in CMC is a combination of media richness, context, and message. For example, if you are in a hurry to inform a large number of people of something simple such as a deadline for homework, a brief e-mail, though relatively poor in terms of richness, is quick, efficient, and perfectly acceptable. In such cases, a leaner rather than richer medium seems most competent.

Openness

Openness is the extent to which messages sent through the medium are publicly accessible. Erving Goffman (1973), a sociologist, argued that people have two areas of action, front stage and back stage. **Front-stage** behavior is public and accessible to all who are present. That makes it high in openness. When you give a speech to a class of students, it is front stage. However, when you change your seating to get a better look at the person you intend to ask out on a date, it is more back stage than front stage.

Table 15.1		
CMC in Society		
Computers are integrated into most of our society, and their role is becoming increasingly important to everyday life in a wide variety of ways and contexts.		
The Prevalence of Technology		

- Worldwide number of telephone lines: 1.2 billion
- Worldwide number of cellular telephone subscribers: 1.3 billion
- Worldwide number of personal computers: 650 million
- Worldwide Internet users: 665 million
- Percentage of U.S. youth who use a computer daily: 54%
- Percentage of U.S. youth who go online daily: 47%
- Percentage of U.S. youth who play a video game daily: 41%
- U.S. Internet users visiting blog sites in early 2005: 50 million
- Percentage of U.S. population with main telephone line, cellular phone, and personal Internet access: 62%, 55%, 63%
- Percentage of Chinese population with main telephone line, cellular phone, and personal Internet access: 21%, 22%, 6%
- Percentage of Congolese population with main telephone line, cellular phone, and personal Internet access: 1%, 2%, 1%
- Percentage of worldwide population with no access or prior use of the Internet: 85%

The Personal Dimension of Technology

- The average number of CD or tape players, TVs, and radios in a U.S. youth's home: 3.6, 3.5, 3.3
- The average number of VCR or DVD players and video game consoles in a U.S. youth's home: 2.9, 2.1
- The average number of personal computers in a U.S. youth's home: 1.5
- The average number of hours a day a U.S. youth spends with media: 6½

SOURCES: ComScore (2005); Hudson (1997); Internet World Stats (2005); Rideout et al. (2005); U.S. Department of Commerce (1998).

Computers permit a wide range of front-stage and backstage action. In one survey, more than half of teen IM users (more than one-third of all U.S. teens) reported that "they have created an IM profile and have posted it so that others can see it" (Lenhart et al., 2005, p. 20). By contrast to such intentional front-stage behavior, "21% of online teens report that a private email, instant message or text message that they sent in confidence had been forwarded on to someone else" (Lenhart et al., 2005, p. 32).

To some extent, computer-based media have begun to blur the lines between private and public communication. Virtually everything sent by e-mail is recorded somewhere. Unlike letters that can be burned, voice mail that can be erased, and telephone and face-to-face conversations that are rarely recorded, computer-based messages are commonly copied, manipulated, forwarded, and reproduced for many eyes to see. The fact that messages often take on a life of their own on computer-based networks is one of the many features any communicator needs to consider when choosing to send a message.

The Importance of Computer-Mediated Communication

The invention of the printing press made the transfer and accumulation of generalized knowledge far more accessible than ever before. The Industrial Revolution gave way to the service economy. Most contemporary observers believe that the microchip and computer have ushered in the next revolution.

How many CMC technologies is this meeting depending on?

The Extent of Mediated Communication

Take a moment and read the estimates of CMC in society in Table 15.1. While you are doing so, ask yourself how you are reflected in the profile and how someone from a less developed country in a village that has only two or three telephones might view the trends.

The sheer pace of change is often difficult for people today to fully comprehend. According to researchers Mike Bloxham, Robert Papper, Mark Popovich, and Michael Holmes (Ball State University Newscenter, 2005), people in America now spend more time per day engaged in media activities (30%) and in media while engaged in some other activity (39%) than in work (21%). Indeed, almost one-third (30%) of all time using media use involves using more than one medium at a time. People still spend more time with the television (241 minutes a day), but the computer appears to be catching up (120 minutes a day).

The first programmable computer, named ENIAC (for electronic numerical integrator and computer), was unveiled in 1946. It was 10 feet tall and 150 feet wide. ENIAC cost millions of dollars and executed about 5,000 operations per second. Today's personal computers execute millions of operations per second using microchips the size of thumbnails. However, all this computing power is potentially useless if a person has no access, no motivation, no knowledge, and no skills to use it.

Information Haves and Have-Nots

The information **haves,** those who have computer resources and the skills to use them, will have enormous advantages over the **have-nots.** For example, "13% of American teenagers—or about 3 million people—still do not use the internet" (Lenhart et al., 2005). About three-fourths of the U.S. population does not know the meaning of the terms "phishing" (sending unsolicited e-mails to acquire personal or sensitive information) or "podcasting" (uploading downloadable audio files for play on MP3 and iPod players; Raimie & Madden, 2005). The problem of have-nots is far worse in developing countries and cultures in the world.

The result of such media illiteracy and lack of access can be devastating. Those with no access to media and no competencies with it will become increasingly powerless and dependent on others, which will result in lower status and lower economic potential (Ronfeldt, 1992). However, some trends suggest the gap between the haves and the have-nots is narrowing. Computer power grows cheaper and more user friendly every year. Many countries are bypassing expensive cable and telephone lines and moving straight to cellular and wireless infrastructure, which is likely to be far more affordable for the governments and for their publics. However, having access and knowledge do not necessarily imply CMC competence in using these technologies.

If you now feel like you've got it made because you have media access and some level of competence, don't be fooled. There is a dark side to this brave new world in the possibility some see of a **dystopia,** a world of constant surveillance, technological dependence, and manipulation. Even the popular image of the information highway is sug-

ALTHOUGH NOT NECESSARILY COMMON, THESE TRUE stories or issues of abuses of CMC have shown up in the news and they illustrate some of the potential problems that can arise with technological advances in our communication abilities.

- A married couple separates. Before moving out, the husband sets up the daughter's new computer. In the coming weeks, the mother realizes the husband knows details of the daughter's home life that he should not have been able to know. Suspicious, the mother finds that the husband had set up the computer to be an audio and text monitoring system with which he could listen to whatever was said nearby or download whatever was typed into it.

- In 2005 a police sting operation led to the arrest of a person who came to Colorado intending to meet a 13-year-old girl and instead met the police who had been phishing for such predators. The surprise? The person was almost immediately freed on diplomatic immunity.
- People in surveys continue to report frequent experiences of "flaming," episodes in which Internet correspondents engage in outrageous and seemingly unedited insult and criticism.
- Research is accumulating that video games, especially first-person violent games, increase the likelihood of engaging in aggressive behavior, aggressive thoughts, and physiological arousal associated with aggression (Anderson, 2004; Sherry, 2001).

gestive of a problem: either get on with everyone else or get left behind or run over (Berdayes & Berdayes, 1998). The Close-Up on Technology box reveals just a few of the problems the new communication technologies are introducing to our social and work environments.

CMC competence in the future will increasingly consist of being able to recognize people's deceptions, scams, and exploitations and being more selective in choosing the media that are appropriate for specific messages. The communication competence model can serve as a framework for better understanding this computer-mediated environment.

The Computer-Mediated Communication Competence Model

Recall that communication is more likely to be perceived as competent to the extent that a person is motivated, knowledgeable, and skilled in a given context. These same components apply to CMC situations.

The model in Figure 15.2 shows how the basic model of communication competence applies to the CMC environment. The middle components of the model represent the context in which the media are used and the characteristics of the media and messages. You'll recall from Chapter 2 that context defines functions and situations of communication. In this CMC model, the same types of context apply. However, because CMC uses specific media, we've added more components to the message aspects of the model. The final component of the model represents the outcomes that help define a mediated interaction as competent.

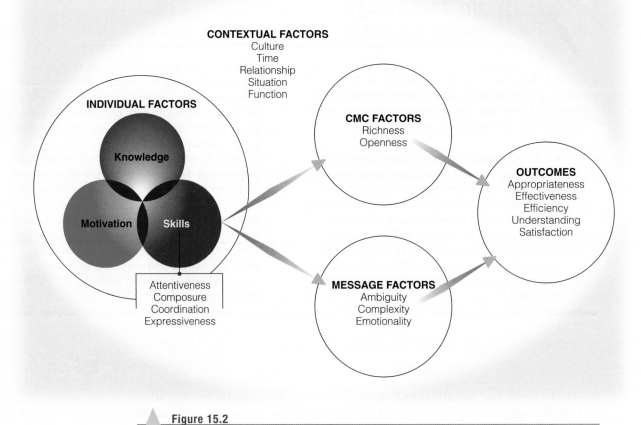

CONTEXTUAL FACTORS
Culture
Time
Relationship
Situation
Function

INDIVIDUAL FACTORS

Knowledge

Motivation   Skills

Attentiveness
Composure
Coordination
Expressiveness

CMC FACTORS
Richness
Openness

MESSAGE FACTORS
Ambiguity
Complexity
Emotionality

OUTCOMES
Appropriateness
Effectiveness
Efficiency
Understanding
Satisfaction

▲   **Figure 15.2**
_____

The Model of Communication Competence Adapted to the Computer Mediated Context

The more motivated, knowledgeable, and skilled a communicator is in selecting and using CMC for a given type of message in a given medium, the more likely the communicator is to achieve competent outcomes.

learning link

How does a technological dystopia relate to the postmodern self discussed in Chapter 3?

● ● ●

Motivation

Motivation in the mediated world has two sides: positive and negative. *Positive motivation* in mediated communication is the feeling or belief that a given medium can enhance our preferred outcomes. If you believe a PowerPoint presentation will be more likely to land a big contract or motivate your sales force than a chalkboard or flip charts, you are positively motivated to use that software in a computer-based medium.

Negative motivation is the feeling or belief that you are incapable of using a given medium competently. The fear of incompetence in sending or receiving CMC is **technophobia.** (Wheeless, Eddleman-Spears, Magness, & Preiss, 2005). In societies such as the United States, in which technology is common, but relatively new, the average eighth grader may well know more about computers than his or her parents. Such familiarity makes the younger generation more comfortable and less afraid to use and experiment with the technology.

Knowledge

One of the reasons people are afraid of technology is that they don't know how to use it, and few people ever learned how by reading user manuals for computer hardware or software. Videos, menu-driven programs, on-screen instructions, in-store demonstrations, and workshops are now being designed to make adopting media easier. These are more formal means of knowing. Informal ways include tinkering and social resource means.

Tinkering is experimenting and trial and error (Turkle, 1995), pushing buttons, exploring drop-down menus, and trying options until you find something that does what you need to do or gets you one step closer. From the perspective of the competence grid introduced in Chapter 2, many tinkerers are engaging in a sufficing approach, doing only what is necessary to get by. Others enjoy the process of learning, and hunt and peck their way into the bells and whistles.

Using **social resources** means learning one on one, perhaps with a help-desk or help-line source or by having a knowledgeable friend or acquaintance show you how to use the medium. Many people are more comfortable with informal learning, but they may skip important areas of knowledge that don't seem important at the time. Most people don't know what to do when they inadvertently delete a file or an LCD projector does not project in the middle of a presentation, because they learned how to use the technology only in the best possible situation when everything was working the way it should.

Interpersonal means of learning about the computer are often the most relaxed and comfortable.

Skills

Skills, as explained in Chapter 2, are the repeatable goal-oriented behaviors a person uses to communicate. In the mediated context, and specifically in the computer-mediated context, skills are displayed in four ways: attentiveness, composure, coordination, and expressiveness.

Attentiveness

People need to feel that their presence and ideas matter. *Attentiveness* is the ability to show interest in, concern for, and attention to others when communicating. Many qualities of CMC, generally a much colder and more impersonal medium than face-to-face or telephone communication, make attentiveness difficult. More often than not, you cannot see the other person directly, message replies are delayed, and messages are often sent to groups of people rather than just to one person. Even so, there are many ways of being attentive even when communicating by computer.

Attentiveness on the computer consists of adding a personal touch to the message. For example, in a traditional business letter you can still direct questions to the particular recipient, display awareness of past correspondence and revisions, and so on. To show interest, you might begin a business e-mail memo with a question or pleasantry about the recipient's recent business trip. As with natural media, responding rapidly and relevantly to someone's message shows attention. The medium alters the way attentiveness is shown but not its importance.

Communication media often have unintended consequences in affecting how others view our competence.

Composure

Composure is the ability to display comfort with, control of, and confidence in communication. In the mediated environment, composure reflects knowledge of and mastery of both the medium and your communication behavior with that medium.

A person who knows more about a medium and has overcome technophobia is generally going to come across as more composed, as is a person who accepts and meets the challenges of new programs, new techniques, and new technologies and displays confidence. Some people go out of their way to learn how to scan images and digitize sound waves and set up their own web pages. Others may only enter online environments, "lurking" rather than contributing.

Composure is also reflected in a person's language choices. Consider two opening statements for an e-mail memo:

1. "I'm not sure if you will get this or not, but if so, please respond to the following message."
2. "Please respond to the following message."

The two writers might feel equally unsure of the technology, but the latter displays greater composure. The very fact that the first opening statement does not make much sense detracts from its competence.

Coordination

Coordination in the computer-mediated environment is the management of time and relevance. Senders who are managing their time send and respond to messages when they should and send messages that are neither too long nor too dense to process. Managing relevance means that messages are about what they are supposed to be about.

If you have ever sent an urgent message by e-mail requesting an answer to a question, only to get a response a few days later that does not respond to the original question, you have experienced the sender's poor coordination in two senses. First, the message was not topically connected with the message to which it was supposed to respond. Second, it was not sent immediately in response to a message titled "urgent."

Coordination requires that you respond to messages in a timely fashion. Timeliness obviously varies from message to message and from relationship to relationship. Some studies suggest that people become hyperpersonal in CMC contexts, disclosing too much

Six Chix by Rina Piccolo

Even the best efforts at "warming up" a cold medium may not always work.

Table 15.2

Acronyms, Jargon, and Emoticons

Acronym (meaning)	Emoticon	Meaning
BTW (by the way)	:-)	smile
F2F (face to face)	:- (	frown
FAQ (frequently asked question)	:'	cry
FWIW (for what it's worth)	;-)	wink
IIRC (if I recall correctly)	:D	laughter
IMO (in my opinion)	:P	sticking out tongue
IOW (in other words)	:-0	yell
IRL (in real life)	:-	anger
LOL (laughing out loud)	:X	my lips are sealed
MEGO (my eyes glaze over)	:Q	smoking
OTOH (on the other hand)	:*	a kiss
TMOT (trust me on this)	%-)	confusion

SOURCES: Adapted from: http://www.computeruser.com/resources/dictionary/emoticons.html, http://www.computeruser.com/resources/dictionary/chat.html, and Higgins, B. (1996, November). How email changed everything, *San Francisco Focus* (pp. 59–67). A list of thousands of dictionary style definitions of computer emoticons and symbols can be found at http://www.netlingo.com/smiley.cfm.

learning link

What is technophobia and what causes it?

● ● ●

too fast (Walther, 1996). If such rapid escalation of intimacy seems inappropriate to one of the communicators, it suggests a lack of sensitivity to issues of coordination on the part of the other.

Expressiveness

Expressiveness in the computer-mediated environment is the vividness of the message. Vividness describes how alive and how animated a message is. When, for example, e-mail first became popular for day-to-day communication, people realized the limited extent to which it could convey emotions. They began to invent **emoticons,** or icons that framed the emotion underlying a verbal statement, and acronyms and abbreviations to make messages more efficient, as well as help frame the meaning. Look at Table 15.2 for some popular acronyms, new terms, and emoticons to enhance the expressiveness of a cold medium.

Context Factors

Recall from Chapter 2 that context has the levels of culture, relationship, situation, and function. Mediated communication primarily affects the situational level, but the other levels also play a role.

As Table 15.1 makes clear, *cultural* factors influence media use. It is easy for people in the United States to take CMC for granted. So it is often a surprise to learn that much of the world's population has never made a telephone call. In addition, some cultures may value ambiguity or politeness more than others, and this may discourage people from flaming (O'Sullivan & Flanagin, 2003). Other cultures, such as the Japanese, may value the slow development of trust in business relationships, a preference that the impersonal feel of e-mail does not support.

The *relational* level of context is extremely important to the choice and use of media (Walther, 1995). In a study of teen uses of CMC, "Teens . . . said that they view email as something you use to talk to 'old people,' institutions, or to send complex instructions to large groups. When it comes to casual written conversation, particularly when talking with friends, online instant messaging is . . . clearly the mode of choice for today's online teens" (Lenhart et al., 2005, p. ii). A 2001 survey found that 17% of respondents had asked someone out using IM, and amazingly, 13% had broken up with someone using IM (Pew, 2001)!

learning link

What are the four mediated communication skills? Give some examples of each.

● ● ●

E-mail encourages rapid development of relationships, at least in terms of disclosure of personal information. In much the same way that flaming is thought to occur because we feel less emotionally involved and empathic with the receiver in e-mail, people may disclose more because they cannot see the recipient's reaction to their disclosures. However, it is not yet known whether such disclosure and relational development through computer media promotes relationships as normal and healthy compared with face-to-face paths of development (Walther, 1996).

In contrast to the culture and relationship, the *situational* level of CMC is obviously different from face-to-face communication by virtue of the physical medium itself. Consider **media access,** which is the extent to which CMC technologies are available to your intended audience. In attempting to coordinate a family reunion, it makes little sense to operate strictly through e-mail if only a fraction of the extended family uses or has access to e-mail. The second important aspect of the situation is distance. Teens appear to use IM more with people they are likely to see frequently, whereas they are more likely to use e-mail with people who do not live nearby (Lenhart et al., 2005).

The *functional* level of the context refers to the purpose of the communication and to pressures such as time (Sitkin, Sutcliffe, & Barrios-Choplin, 1992). When a message has to get out to people immediately, a communicator often uses multiple media—sending e-mail and leaving voice mail at the same time, for example. Even though overnight mail takes only a day to reach the recipient, more and more people are choosing to attach files to an e-mail message instead because it is even faster.

Like the frame of a painting, the context of CMC shows us what is and what is not part of the picture, but it is not the picture itself. The message is the picture. Competence in CMC requires attention to the message as much as the context. Let's look at the message next.

Message Factors

One of the most influential writers on media in the last century, Marshall McLuhan, claimed that the medium *is* the message. That is, the medium influences a message so much that the meaning itself changes. To some extent, seeing video of a tsunami crushing whole villages on TV creates a very different experience of the disaster than if it had been reported only by radio or newspaper. The medium made the tsunami emotionally "hot," real, and intense.

The medium is certainly part of the message, but the message itself is at least as important. Aspects of messages that influence the competence of mediated communication are ambiguity, complexity, and emotionality.

Message ambiguity is the extent to which a message has either unknown or multiple meanings. Most people assume that ambiguous messages are incompetent. But this is not true. Every day of our lives we get through conversations, group decisions, and public presentations by relying on ambiguity (Spitzberg, 1993, 1994). Most people are more likely to vote for political candidates who speak about vague concepts such as freedom and democracy than for candidates who speak only in concrete terms about issues like the cost of this program and the amendments on that policy. When your friend asks what you think of his new haircut and you say, "It's . . . interesting," you are using ambiguity.

CMC generally increases the possibility of ambiguity because it is a poorer medium. When nonverbal information cannot be included in a message, the receiver has more ways to interpret it. Although this may sound useful, it can backfire in unintended ways. Sarcasm and humor, for example, may not translate well in e-mail precisely because the intended meaning is lost without accompanying nonverbal information.

Message complexity refers to the amount of detail, density, and integration of information in a message (Sitkin et al., 1992). More meaning can be derived from messages that have a large amount of information. For example, many e-mail messages now routinely include visual, video, or sound files as well as the sender's introductory text. Highly complex messages are generally difficult to communicate in face-to-face interaction. They may benefit from media that permit both careful production of the entire message and then careful opportunity for review and contemplation by the recipient.

Message emotionality is the extent to which a message attempts to communicate feelings. Some messages have almost no emotional content, whereas others are highly emotional. Feelings can be part of the message, such as when you say, "I love you," or they can be nonverbal, as in messages that imply "I've been thinking about you."

Messages that have a strong affective component are likely to require different media than messages that are emotionally "lean." Despite the convenience of breaking off a relationship by letter, e-mail, IM, or over the phone, most receivers would probably consider such media incompetent for such an emotionally serious message. As McLuhan would suggest, there are times when the medium actually becomes part of the emotional message. In general, the more emotionally based the meaning of a message is, the more competent a richer medium will be to send it.

Media Factors Revisited

When research first examined CMC in the 1980s, media were viewed as essentially richer or poorer. This view, however, did not take the unpredictable and creative human element into account. When faced with relatively poor media, people invented emoticons and used more humor to add an emotional and expressive touch to a relatively lean medium. When

New communication technologies alter traditional ideas of how we interact with one another.

"Big date tonight, Dad. Can I borrow the compter?"

faced with overly difficult DOS-based computer systems, people invented user-friendly icon-based programs. We continue to make mediated forms of communication more like face-to-face forms of communication. Progress in virtual reality systems reflects this ongoing trend.

Indeed, research indicates that computer-mediated relationships may be quite similar to nonmedia-based relationships in many ways (Parks & Floyd, 1996). People who use one medium to communicate with another person tend to use multiple media to communicate with this person (Baym, Zhang, & Lin, 2004). We don't select a single medium for a given receiver; instead we use multiple media to communicate what we need to communicate to a given receiver. And as media in general become richer, the lines between face-to-face and mediated communication will continue to blur. Telephones, for example, preserve the richness of voice and increasingly, imagery. Yet new-generation telephones are becoming interlinked and even merged with computers to serve many of the same functions. People can now be linked to information, and to each other, as never before. For better or worse, telephone conversations are now routine on buses, in restaurants, and even in movie theaters.

Outcomes

Competence cannot be achieved in a vacuum. We've seen that messages, behaviors, and media are not competent or incompetent by their nature. Instead, communication is competent in a given context based on the outcomes of the communication.

The appropriateness and effectiveness of outcomes determine the competence of the communication and medium. Recall from Chapter 2 that a message is *effective* if it accomplishes preferred goals and *appropriate* if it is acceptable to the participants in the context. These outcomes are not really different in the mediated context. They may, however, depend on somewhat different factors. Instead of evaluating only the appropriateness of the message as in a face-to-face encounter, the recipient in a CMC encounter is also likely to evaluate the competence of the choice and use of the medium. If you send an emotionally rich message with important consequences through a poor medium, you risk incompetence. Firing an employee via e-mail is likely to be seen as quite different in its competence than doing so face to face.

Efficiency is an outcome that is particularly important in businesses. **Efficiency** is the relationship between the amount of resources used, such as people, time, and money, relative to the benefits, such as profits or public awareness. When time is money, computers are cheap and very fast for distributing information. Efficiency is also valued in everyday conversations when the context is very simple or task oriented (Bertacco & Deponte, 2005). However, appropriateness and effectiveness should still serve as the key touchstones of competence. It may be efficient to fire an employee through an e-mail message, but it is hardly appropriate for the long-term interests of the organization.

As we discuss in Chapter 2, *understanding* is another common standard for evaluating competence. If you want to meet someone for dinner or a movie at a particular place or time, the most important aspect of the message is that the other person understands clearly the place and time. Again, however, understanding can be achieved in more and less appropriate and effective ways. Telling someone not to be late or you'll go on without them is hardly the most appropriate way of achieving understanding.

Finally, sometimes the most important purpose a message serves is to make people feel good about it. You send many messages because you are part of a relationship or you want to make the other person smile. In short, we often seek satisfaction for ourselves as well as for others through communication (Spitzberg & Hecht, 1984). *Satisfaction* is a feeling that desired outcomes have been achieved. Many people routinely send jokes, greeting cards, humorous video clips, and other feel-good messages to their address list of friends. Sloane and Chad in the chapter's opener conducted much of their e-mail correspondence for the sole purpose of feeling good, of feeling as though there was someone else who saw the world the same way.

Overcoming Challenges to Mediated Communication

Given that much of the economy, and therefore your own livelihood, will depend significantly on how competently people use evolving media, it is vital to have some road map to help navigate the technological jungle. The model of CMC competence shows some directions for better communication in this mediated world. The most significant challenges to competence are access and mastery.

Access is the extent to which different types of media and many types of options in these media are available. **Mastery** is the extent to which a user understands how to use the media. Clearly it is difficult to have mastery without access. However, access alone is not enough to achieve mastery.

Access

Most of the world does not have access to high-technology communication media. Access represents more of a challenge than merely being able to physically touch a keyboard; it has both depth and breadth dimensions. **Breadth** means how many different types of communication media a person has access to. You can own a pager, cellular telephone, and computer but not be able to afford access to an Internet service provider. You may have a computer and dial-up Internet service, but only one telephone line, so you can access only one mode of communication at a time. **Depth,** in contrast, refers to your access to the various options available within a medium. You may have an Internet service provider but a dial-up connection too slow to allow full access to the content available on the network. You may have a computer but not the appropriate imagery software to edit the images from your digital camera.

Both the depth and breadth of access may sound like merely economic issues. Make more money and buy better upgrades. However, upgrades depend not only on money but also on mastery.

Mastery

Your level of mastery in CMC depends on three factors: the pace of change, information overload, and technophobia. The sheer pace of change has been one cause of technophobia, affecting many people's perception of their ability to master communication media. Imagine how intimidating it seems to someone who has never gotten online to consider buying a computer, much less becoming expert at it. Many people feel left behind in the information revolution.

Information overload is the feeling of having more media content and access to and from people than we can process meaningfully. About a quarter (26%) of 8–18-year-olds use more than one medium at a time. Although most youth seem to adapt well to such multitasking, those who are least contented spend more time using media than their most contented peers (Rideout et al., 2005). Such multitasking may permit more to get done, but at the cost of the quality of the average interaction. A person goes on a weekend vacation and returns to 40 to 50 e-mail messages, 20 or 30 voice mail messages, a stack of snail-mail, and several pages and cellphone calls. Such overload makes it challenging to devote attention to all messages equally. People have less time to compose their thoughts, much less their mediated response to messages.

The media through which we communicate are changing more rapidly than at any time in history. The effects on society, and on the relationships we have within that society, are changing rapidly as well. It is not clear yet whether CMC media are making our relationships better or worse—the truth is probably that they make some of our relationships better and some of them worse. Regardless, being prepared to navigate the increasingly complex waters of this mediated environment is more important than ever.

With new CMC technologies comes the convenience, and the potential overload, of information and access.

Chapter Summary

The competence potential of CMC depends significantly on media richness and openness. The extent to which these factors affect our competence depends on motivation, knowledge, skills with communication media, the context in which the communication occurs, and the nature of the message itself.

Communication, whether face to face or mediated, is intended to produce an outcome, even if it is only satisfaction as opposed to understanding or efficiency. The extent to which mediated communication is efficient, understood, and satisfying significantly influences the competence of the message, although even these outcomes are competent only to the extent they are appropriate and effective.

Two significant challenges to achieving CMC competence are access and mastery. Becoming more selective regarding which media are used for what purposes and with which audiences is an essential ingredient of competence in overcoming the challenges to mastery and access.

Study and Review

The premium companion website for *Human Communication* offers a broad range of resources that will help you better understand the material in this chapter, complete assignments, and succeed on tests. The website resources include

- Interactive self-assessments, competency grids, and other tools
- Web links, practice activities, self-quizzes, and a sample final exam

For more information about this text's electronic learning resources, consult the *Guide to Online Resources for Human Communication* or visit **http://communication .wadsworth.com/morreale2.**

Key Terms

The key terms below are defined in the chapter on the pages indicated. They are also presented alphabetically with definitions in the Glossary, which begins on page 467. The book's website includes flashcards and crossword puzzles to help you learn these terms and the concepts they represent.

computer-mediated communication 400
natural media 400
technological media 400
richness 401
interactivity 401
completeness 401
openness 402

front stage 402
haves 404
have-nots 404
dystopia 404
technophobia 406
tinkering 407
social resource 407

Building Motivation

This self-assessment begins on page 422. An interactive version of it is also available on the book's website.

 ## Building Knowledge

The following questions are among the practice activities on the book's website.

1. How have communication media and computers changed your everyday interactions and relationships? List the changes in a first column, and then in two columns next to each change indicate whether there are any positive or negative consequences to the change. Do you think these changes are common to everyone, or are they unique to you? Why?

2. Some people think that media are changing the fundamental way we relate to one another. Others say that we are simply transforming our media into something more like face-to-face interaction, and thus no big changes are likely to occur. Do you think the changes are fundamental or only superficial? Why?

3. Where do you feel most comfortable relating to people, online or in person? Why? Does it depend on the type of situation, and if so, in what ways?

4. Think about where communication technology seems to be going in our society. What changes do you think media will bring to the way we relate to one another 10 years from now, if any? If you see changes occurring, will these be mainly positive or negative?

5. How competent do you think you are in relating to people in various communication media (telephone, letter, e-mail, MUDs)? How competent do you think other people think you are when you communicate using these media?

 ## Building Skills

The exercises below are among the practice activities on the book's website.

Individual Exercises

1. Choose a topic, perhaps a topic you will be doing speeches or papers on in this course, and enter the same search terms into three different search engines. Note the differences in what sites are located and the order in which they are listed. Which engine did a better job? In what sense was it better? That is, did it present the information in more usable form, or did it simply list the most relevant sites before the less relevant sites?

2. Find out more about CMC via the World Wide Web. Enter "computer-mediated communication" into a search engine. Among other things, you should find an entire journal devoted to the study of this phenomenon: *Journal of Computer-Mediated Communication*. Now, search for particular topics of interest. For example, is it true that CMC is dominated by men more than women? If so, why?

3. Not too long ago, it was said that the average person was only six degrees of separation from anyone else in the world. For example, you probably don't know Gwyneth Paltrow or Chris Martin, but you probably know someone (first degree), who knows someone else (second degree), who knows someone else (third degree), and so on to a sixth someone who actually knows Chris or Gwyneth. Technology may have reduced the number of degrees you are from contacting someone. Search for information about *yourself* using all the search tools available to you. How accessible are you to others because of technology? How much privacy do you have, and do you need more, or less? A recent study found that the more time people spent on the Internet, the fewer people they had in their social network, and the more depressed and lonely they became (Kraut et al., 1998). Over the span of a week, at the end of each day note in the following log every medium you used directly and indirectly. By *direct* use is meant a technology that you used to send or receive a message. By *indirect* use is meant that you send or receive or are influenced by a message through someone else who used a medium. For example, you have someone send a fax or you are out with friends when one of them receives a page. By week's end, tabulate the number of different media you were affected by and whether direct or indirect influences were more significant. How media competent are you on the basis of just the number of different media you use? How dependent upon media are you and how comfortable are you with this level of media dependence? Do you feel highly connected or disconnected to communication media? Are your friends and acquaintances more or less media connected than you? Why?

	F2f = Face to face	Fax = Fax
	Ph = Telephone	Ltr = Letter
	CF = Cell phone	CMC = Computer

	Direct						Indirect					
	F2f	Ph	CF	Fax	Ltr	CMC	F2f	Ph	CF	Fax	Ltr	CMC
Monday												
Tuesday												
Wednesday												
Thursday												
Friday												
Saturday												
Sunday												

4. Assess your own media sensitivity:

Measuring Your Media Sensitivity

NSTRUCTIONS: RATE THE APPROPRIATENESS (APP) and effectiveness (EFF) of using each medium in each situation, using a rating scale from 1 (inappropriate, ineffective) to 5 (appropriate, effective). There are no right or wrong answers. For each medium, rate the appropriateness and the effectiveness for each context. For appropriateness, consider how the message fits the situation described. Will it offend others or, instead, be perfectly legitimate? For effectiveness, consider whether the medium will best permit you to achieve what you want to achieve.

Situation	Face to Face		Telephone		Letter/Memo		E-mail	
	APP	EFF	APP	EFF	APP	EFF	APP	EFF
You need to fire a friend								
You want to ask someone out on a date								
You need to inform a large number of people of an upcoming concert								
You want to chat with a friend who lives in another state about how their week went								
You need to get student group members together for an immediate meeting								

Interpretation: Media sensitivity implies making choices about when one medium will be more competent to use relative to another. Thus the greater the difference between your ratings across media and contexts, the more sensitive you are. In contrast, if you rated one medium as best for all contexts, you probably need to reevaluate the competence of that medium across those contexts.

Group Activities

1. In a group of classmates, decide which of the following types of encounters would be best for which media.

Encounter/Message
- Informing people of an upcoming party
- Asking someone out on a date
- Criticizing someone for something careless she or he said to you
- Lifting the spirits of a friend who is feeling depressed
- Introducing yourself to other employees in your organization but who do not work in your department

Medium
- Face to face, one to one
- Face to face, in a group, or in a public context
- Letter (that is, snail mail)
- E-mail, one to one
- E-mail, chat room, or group virtual environment
- Announcement on bulletin board
- Allow gossip or rumor to work its way to someone else

2. Compare group assignments accomplished by computer to those accomplished face to face and by telephone. At some point in the semester, you are likely to have one or more group assignments. See to what extent you can arrange to conduct one entirely over some medium, and then compare it to group projects accomplished more through face-to-face interaction. Analyze what differences there were, if any, in the way you related to others and how you felt about the experience.

3. The instructor creates pairs of groups that will debate utopia and dystopia. A *utopia* is a world in which everything meets some ideal sense of what is best. A *dystopia* is a world in which everything is disastrous or dysfunctional. Scholars have been debating the world that communication technology is likely to create. Form teams in your class. Each team will either be arguing for a utopian vision or for a dystopian vision of communication technology. Each team will have an amount of time to research the topics and then as teams present 15 minutes of arguments for their side and 10 minutes each of rebuttal. Which vision seems more probable, and why?

4. As individuals first, complete the items below. Then, form groups of three to five persons, and identify the group's typical preferences by tallying how many people in the group chose each answer.

   For the following situations, check the *best* answer for each statement or hypothetical situation. For each situation, assume that all the listed media are available to all the parties and that all concerned know how to use them. To what extent did your answers differ? Why or why not?

Situation	Face to Face	Rumor	Letter or Memo	E-mail	Phone or Voice Mail
1. If you needed to talk to a friend about how you are feeling depressed lately, you would most likely use:					
2. If you needed to inform a department's employees of an upcoming retirement party, you would most likely primarily use:					
3. If you wanted to start flirting with an employee in another department, you would most likely primarily use:					
4. If you had a complicated conflict with a boss you needed to work out over a project you were working on, you would most likely primarily use:					
5. If you had a complicated conflict with a subordinate you needed to work out over a project you were working on, you would most likely primarily use:					
6. If you had a small task team organized to make recommendations for ways of improving workplace safety, you would most likely primarily use:					

References

Anderson, C. A. (2004). An update on the effects of playing violent video games. *Journal of Adolescence, 27,* 113–122.

Ball State University Newscenter. (2005, September 23). Average person spends more time using media than anything else. Retrieved October 18, 2005, from http://www.bsu.edu/news/article/0,1370,7273-850-36658,00.html.

Baym, N. K., Zhang, Y. B., & Lin, M-C. (2004). Social interactions across media. *New Media & Society, 6,* 299–318.

Berdayes, L. C., & Berdayes, V. (1998). The information highway in contemporary narrative. *Journal of Communication, 48,* 109–124.

Bertacco, M., & Deponte, A. (2005). Email as a speed-facilitating device: A contribution to the reduced-cues perspective on communication. *Journal of Computer-Mediated Communication, 10,* article 2.

ComScore. (2005, August). Behaviors of the blogosphere: Understanding the scale, composition and activities of weblog audiences. Reston, VA: Author. Retrieved August 10, 2005, from http://www.comscore.com/blogreport/comScoreBlogReport.pdf.

Goffman, E. (1973). *The presentation of self in everyday life.* Woodstock, NY: Overlook Press.

Hudson, H. E. (1997). *Global connections: International telecommunication infrastructure and policy.* New York: Van Nostrand Reinhold.

International Telecommunication Union. (2005). Key global telecom indicators for the world telecommunication service sector. Retrieved July 26, 2005, from http://www.itu.int/ITU-D/ict/statistics/at_glance/KeyTelecom99.html.

Internet World Stats. (2005, July). Internet usage statistics—The big picture. Retrieved July 25, 2005, from http://www.internetworldstats.com/stats.htm.

Kraut, R., Patterson, M., Lundmark, V., Kiesler, S., Mukophadhyay, T., & Scherlis, W. (1998). Internet paradox: A social technology that reduces social involvement and psychological well-being? *American Psychology, 53,* 1017–1031.

Lenhart, A., Madden, M., & Hitlin, P. (2005, July). *Teens and technology: Youth are leading the transition to a fully wired and mobile nation.* Washington DC: Pew Internet and American Life Project.

O'Sullivan, P. B., & Flanagin, A. J. (2003). Reconceptualizing "flaming" and other problematic messages. *New Media & Society, 5,* 69–95.

Parks, M. R., & Floyd, K. (1996). Making friends in cyberspace. *Journal of Communication, 46,* 80–97.

Pew Internet and American Life Project. (2001, June 20). *Teenage life online: The rise of the instant-message generation and the internet's impact on friendships and family relationships.* Washington DC: Author.

Raimie, L., & Madden, M. (2005, July). Data memo. Retrieved August 5, 2005, from http://www.pewinternet.org/pdfs/PIP_podcasting.pdf.

Rideout, V., Roberts, D. F., & Foehr, U. G. (2005, March). *Generation M: Media in the lives of 8–18-year-olds.* Washington DC: Kaiser Family Foundation.

Ronfeldt, D. (1992). Cyberocracy is coming. *The Information Society, 8,* 243–296.

Sherry, J. L. (2001). The effects of violent video games on aggression: A meta-analysis. *Human Communication Research, 27,* 409–431.

Sitkin, S. B., Sutcliffe, K. M., & Barrios-Choplin, J. R. (1992). A dual-capacity model of communication media choice in organizations. *Human Communication Research, 18,* 563–598.

Sohn, D., & Lee, B-K. (2005). Dimensions of interactivity: Differential effects of social and psychological factors. *Journal of Computer-Mediated Communication, 10,* article 6.

Spitzberg, B. H. (1993). The dialectics of (in)competence. *Journal of Social and Personal Relationships, 10,* 137–158.

Spitzberg, B. H. (1994). The dark side of (in)competence. In W. R. Cupach & B. H. Spitzberg (Eds.), *The dark side of interpersonal communication* (pp. 25–49). Hillsdale, NJ: Erlbaum.

Spitzberg, B. H., & Hecht, M. L. (1984). A component model of relational competence. *Human Communication Research, 10,* 575–599.

Trevino, L. K., Daft, R. L., & Lengel, R. H. (1990). Understanding managers' media choices: A symbolic interactionist perspective. In J. Folk & C. Steinfield (Eds.), *Organizations and communication technology* (pp. 71–94). Newbury Park, CA: Sage.

U.S. Department of Commerce. (1998). *The emerging digital economy.* Washington, DC: Author. http://www.ecommerce.gov./digital.htm.

Walther, J. B. (1995). Relational aspects of computer-mediated communication: Experimental observations over time. *Organization Science, 6,* 186–203.

Walther, J. B. (1996). Computer-mediated communication: Impersonal, interpersonal, and hyperpersonal interaction. *Communication Research, 23,* 3–43.

Wheeless, L. R., Eddleman-Spears, L., Magness, L. D., & Preiss, R. W. (2005). Informational reception apprehension and information from technology aversion: Development and test of a new construct. *Communication Quarterly, 53,* 143–158.

Witmer, B. G., & Singer, M. J. (1998). Measuring presence in virtual environments: A presence questionnaire. *Presence, 7,* 225–240.

Building Motivation

Self-Assessment: CMC includes all forms of e-mail and formal or informal computer-based networks (for example, the World Wide Web, chat rooms, electronic bulletin boards, MUDs, terminal-based video-telephony, and so on) for sending and receiving written messages. In the following you'll see 27 statements about your activities and your impressions of various communication media. Using the following scale, indicate the degree to which you agree or disagree with each statement.

1 = STRONGLY DISAGREE   3 = NEITHER AGREE NOR   4 = MILDLY AGREE
2 = MILDLY DISAGREE   DISAGREE; UNDECIDED   5 = STRONGLY AGREE

Skills

Coordination (3–15, midpoint = 9)
1 2 3 4 5   (1)   When I receive a message from someone, I generally reply within a day.
1 2 3 4 5   (2)   I always reply to all the aspects of someone's message.

Expressiveness (3–15, midpoint = 9)
1 2 3 4 5   (3)   I use a lot of the expressive symbols (emoticons) in my CMC messages.
1 2 3 4 5   (4)   I try to use a lot of humor in my CMC messages.

Attentiveness (3–15, midpoint = 9)
1 2 3 4 5   (5)   I adapt my words and writing style to the person I'm corresponding with.
1 2 3 4 5   (6)   I ask a lot of questions of the other person in my CMC.

Composure (3–15, midpoint = 9)
1 2 3 4 5   (7)   I have no trouble expressing my opinions forcefully on CMC.
1 2 3 4 5   (8)   I use the first-person pronoun ("I") frequently in my CMC messages.

Motivation (3–15, midpoint = 9)
1 2 3 4 5   (9)   I enjoy communicating via computer media.
1 2 3 4 5   (10)   I never get nervous using CMC.

Knowledge (3–15, midpoint = 9)
1 2 3 4 5   (11)   I am very knowledgeable about computer-based communication techniques.
1 2 3 4 5   (12)   I am familiar with e-mail and communication networks.

Contextual Factors

Culture (1–5, midpoint = 3)
1 2 3 4 5   (13)   I consider the culture of people when I write messages on CMC.

Relational Context (1–5, midpoint = 3)
1 2 3 4 5   (14)   CMC messages are opportunities to work on relationships as well as tasks.

Distance (1–5, midpoint = 3)
1 2 3 4 5   (15)   I tend not to use CMC messages for people I could talk to face to face.

Media Access (1–5, midpoint = 3)
1 2 3 4 5   (16)   I have access to a variety of media for communicating with people.

Time Pressure (1–5, midpoint = 3)
1 2 3 4 5   (17)   Computers give me time to prepare drafts of my messages.

Message Factors

Message Ambiguity (1–5, midpoint = 3)
1 2 3 4 5   (18)   I try to be as specific as possible in all my task-related CMC messages.

Message Complexity (1–5, midpoint = 3)
1 2 3 4 5   (19)   The more technical a message, the more selective I am in who I send it to.

Message Emotionality (1–5, midpoint = 3)
1 2 3 4 5   (20)   The more emotional a message, the less likely I am to use a computer to send it.

Media Factors

Richness (1–5, midpoint = 3)
1 2 3 4 5   (21)   I choose media (that is, CMC, mail, phone, or face to face) based on how lively the interaction and feedback need to be.

Access (1–5, midpoint = 3)
1 2 3 4 5   (22)   I choose media (that is, CMC, mail, phone, or face to face) based on how much access others have to each medium.

Outcomes

Understanding (1–5, midpoint = 3)
1 2 3 4 5   (23)   I get my ideas across clearly when I use CMC.

Efficiency (1–5, midpoint = 3)
1 2 3 4 5   (24)   I am more efficient using CMC than other forms of communication.

Satisfaction (1–5, midpoint = 3)
1 2 3 4 5   (25)   My CMC conversations are often more pleasant than my face-to-face interactions.

Appropriateness (1–5, midpoint = 3)
1 2 3 4 5   (26)   I avoid saying things I shouldn't on CMC.

Effectiveness (1–5, midpoint = 3)
1 2 3 4 5   (27)   I generally get what I want out of my CMC interactions.

Interpretation: Each heading represents a component of the CMC competence model. For each component, add your responses to the items (for single items, your score is whatever rating you replied with) and then compare the result with the range and midpoint specified in parentheses. Generally speaking, scores below the midpoint suggest you need to work on your competence, and scores above the midpoint suggest that you consider yourself fairly competent in that component.

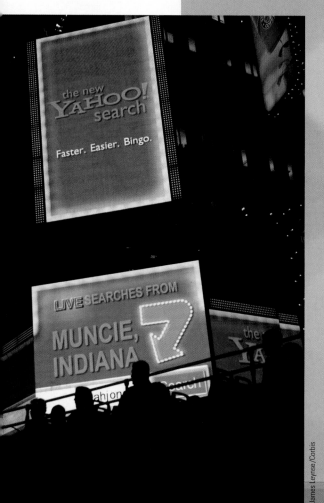

© James Leynse./Corbis

LEARNING OBJECTIVES | After studying this chapter, you should be able to

1. Define mass communication and mass media.

2. Recognize the effects that historical trends in mass communication development have on your everyday communication.

3. Explain the effect of mass communication according to different models of media effects.

4. Distinguish the roles and functions of mass communication professions, such as marketing, advertising, public relations, and journalism.

5. Demonstrate media literacy by engaging in critical thinking, skepticism, and counterarguing to control media biases and stereotypes.

Mass Communication

om is the director of emergency preparedness for a five-county area. He had recently returned from a national conference that made him aware of the need to rework his communication plan for a particular population during an emergency. He convened a team to discuss media strategies to accomplish this goal most effectively.

"What I'd like to do is get a feel for the issues and problems involved in getting information to shut-ins during an emergency," said Tom.

Pat said, "Well, I think one issue is how to let shut-ins know ahead of time where to look for information during a crisis. One way to do this is to put flyers in people's water bills so everyone would have access to the information. Or we could create a series of PSAs (public service announcements) for radio or TV. If we have the money, we could place ads in magazines that shut-ins are likely to read."

"So there are a lot of options we can use to educate the shut-in population," Rashid said. "We just have to make a decision whether we want to use the media to disseminate the information broadly, like ads in water bills, or target the shut-in population specifically by placing ads in magazines. Another issue we need to think about is what media we want to use to communicate information *during* an emergency."

"Well, if they're shut-ins," said Nicole, "the media they probably use are TV and radio."

"True," said Kiera, "but we need to determine what kinds of TV programs and radio stations. Do we need to get the information out on talk radio, Top 40, Christian radio, or what? We need to determine what kind of media they use."

Sith chimed in: "Would it be more effective to use something simple like a recorded message on a crisis hotline?"

The meeting continued for another 30 minutes. At the end, Tom said, "Before our next meeting, there are two issues we need to think about. First, what kind of media do we think the shut-in population uses? Second, if we go with media like magazines, radio, or TV, do we need to select those outlets that specifically cater to shut-ins? Pat and Kiera, would you please tackle the first issue, and Sith and Nicole, could you take on the second issue? If both teams could propose a strategy for media use at our next meeting for your issue, that would be great." Tom left the meeting feeling optimistic that the two teams could develop an effective media plan for reaching the shut-ins during an emergency. ■

Tom faced the same problem that governments, managers and decision makers, organizations, advertisers, public relations and public information officers, community groups, and even individuals who have lost a cat or are holding a garage sale all face: how to communicate to a larger audience than can congregate at a single physical location. In this chapter we examine many of the forces at work influencing how media are produced, as well as various theories that have been developed to explain these forces. In a mass mediated world, it becomes increasingly important to be a critical consumer of media content and form, so a model of media competence is introduced that extends the motivation, knowledge, and skills model to the media environment.

Mass Communication and Media Competence

In 2003 Yahoo! announced a $10,000 prize for the nation's best yodeler to celebrate Yahoo's trademark sound. Yodeling developed to extend the ability to communicate to people over distances. It seems quaint by today's standards of mass communication, but it probably represents the earliest human efforts at mass communication. **Mass communication** is the process of managing messages for the purpose of creating meaning in a large audience. What makes the communication mass is the large audience, one that typically will not be operating as a collective group. That is, mass audiences tend to consist of people who may have common reasons to be in a given audience for a message, but otherwise they usually have relatively little opportunity to interact with the other members. This is one of the features that distinguishes such an audience from a group and mass communication from group communication.

As technologies have evolved to improve human ability to send messages to large audiences, mass communication has evolved parallel to mediated communication (Chapter 15). The term **mass media** commonly represents the various media—television, radio, advertising, public relations, newspapers, book and magazine publishing, music publishing, movies, as well as Internet and World Wide Web publishing and advertising, as well as the organizations that own, produce, and distribute mass communication.

Trends in Mass Communication

Humans have a short history of communicating ideas to larger audiences. The first newspapers date to the early 1700s, the telegraph to the mid-1800s, photoengraving and the telephone to the late 1800s, and Marconi demonstrated wireless transfer of information only in 1901. From these beginnings, mass communication technology has experienced exponential growth, making the last century the information age and producing an information society (Webster, 1995).

Let's consider some of the trends that describe how mass mediated communication has changed over the past century.

From Broadcasting to Narrowcasting

First, mass communication is increasingly moving from broadcasting to narrowcasting. **Broadcasting** is sending messages out indiscriminately to large audiences, whereas **narrowcasting** is sending messages out to large audiences, but adapted to individuals or groups within that audience for whom the message has special relevance. For example, *Reason* magazine recently linked earth satellite imaging software with its subscriber list and sent 40,000 subscribers magazines with *their own home and neighborhood* on the cover (Carr, 2004)! This is a clear example of a mass publication narrowly adapted to individuals within that group. Marketing companies and advertisers are increasingly seeking ways of adapting their messages to individuals and groups within larger audiences.

The Downfall of Distance

A second trend in mass communication is greater flexibility in sending and receiving. In the 1700s, messages had to travel by foot, horse, and ship over great distances. In the 1800s, news would often take months to travel across oceans, languages, and national borders. Even in the days of the telegraph, people on the west coast of the United States might discover events on the east coast weeks or months after their occurrence. But the advent of radio; satellite communications; and digital transfer of visual, textual, and auditory information has collapsed time and space to make information available in real time almost anywhere. Communication is less and less dependent on proximity, even though it is simultaneously finding its way into personal spaces. This has made our everyday environment saturated with exposure to the media of mass communication, as well as the contents of those media.

We may instant message people in the same room or building, but we generally use communication technologies to span distances (Baym, Zhang, & Lin, 2004). Try to think of a place you can go to without being exposed to advertising on the way. Mass communication is becoming ubiquitous. "The typical 8- to 18-year-old lives in a home with an average of 3.6 CD or tape players, 3.5 TVs, 3.3 radios, 2.9 VCRs/DVD players, 2.1 video game consoles, and 1.5 computers. . . . And when they leave home, many young people carry their media with them: almost two-thirds have a portable CD, tape, or MP3 player (65%) and half (55%) have a handheld video game player" (Rideout, Roberts, & Foehr, 2005, p. 9). The Internet, bulging with pop-up ads, corporate sponsors, and spam, was accessed by 80% of the population 12 and older in 2003 (ResearchandMarkets, 2004). All told, surveys indicate that young people spend an average of 6.5 hours a day using media, and about a quarter of that time they are using more than one medium at a time (Rideout et al., 2005).

From Divergence to Convergence

A third trend in mass communication is **convergence,** the integration of media technologies. Your cell phone is increasingly likely to have a camera and video, instant messaging, and e-mail capability; downloading and wireless Internet capability; and calendar and personal data assistant (PDA) capabilities. It will not be long before these phones have two-way interactive video capabilities so that you will be able to see the person you are

learning link

How are the contexts of computer-mediated communication and mass communication converging, and what influences are these having on your everyday life?

• • •

talking with. Convergence is creating a truly multimedia environment by vastly increasing the convenience of access to these various media. Some of the effect of this convergence is greater convenience for the user, but consider the role of pop-up advertising, the extent to which tuning in to TV and movie and music spots in these convergent media include exposure to corporate and sponsor messages. Increasingly, convergence means that the average media consumer finds no place in which their media is not saturated with corporate messaging and branding messages.

How Mass Communication Works

At the root of most explanations of mass media effects is social learning theory, as described in Chapter 7 (Bandura, 1977). We learn some things through trial and error, by trying something and remembering what worked and what did not work. However, we learn much of what we know about our social world by observing others, both real and fictional, seeing what they do that works and does not work in certain situations, and recalling and attempting successful behaviors when we experience a similar situation. We are unlikely to observe all possible social situations in our immediate interpersonal network of acquaintances, so one of the primary sources of social learning is what we experience in the mass media. Have a problem dating someone who is a former dating partner of your friend? How did Chandler and Ross handle it on *Friends*? How does Seth deal with problems with his dad on *The OC*? If these examples seem unrealistic, at the more general level the research clearly shows, for example, that there are still a number of stereotypes of women that continue to occur on TV and that "as the amount of television watched increases, so does the acceptance of stereotypical images of women" (Herrett-Skjellum & Allen, 1996, p. 176). The contents of media seep into our minds in subtle and complex ways.

Obviously, however, we are not blank slates upon which the mass media write their

messages. We select some messages and not others, and some messages have more impact than others, and in more complex ways. A number of models have been put forward to help explain how this process of message influence in mass communication operates (McQuail & Windahl, 1993).

Strong Effects Models

Given the rapid pace of change and societal adoption of mass communication and media in the early part of the 20th century, it is not surprising that early theorists anticipated that mass communication and media would have **strong effects**. This is the prediction that media operate with direct causal force on audience attitudes, beliefs, and behaviors. It seemed bolstered by the rise to power through propaganda by people such as Hitler and the enormous consumerism that followed World War II in concert with a vast increase in television ownership and advertising (Samuel, 2001). To some extent, strong effects models viewed mass communication messages as a hypodermic needle or magic bullet that inserted the desired messages into the passive minds of the audience. These models propose a type of one-step flow of mass communication messages (Figure 16.1).

The media have stronger effects on some people than on others.

Mass media

Information

Figure 16.1

The One-Step Flow of Mass Communication

The one-step flow model represents a strong effects model of influence.

Moderated Effects Models

Such models did not last long, because it became obvious that audiences played an active role in processing information and images from mass communication. **Moderated effects** models viewed both the mass communication and the audience as having influence on the impact of messages. Some of the earliest research suggested, for example, that a large part of the influence of mass communication was based on opinion leaders. **Opinion leaders** are people who receive mass communication messages, form an opinion on the basis of those messages, and then influence others who might or might not have received the messages. Opinion leaders' influence is based more on credibility and interpersonal persuasion.

The notion that opinion leaders serve as a filter of media influence led theorists to think about how society processes media content. The media industries control what we are exposed to, but we then gather around the watercooler or over coffee and talk about what's in the news. Consider news cycles in which for weeks or even months certain topics seem to dominate the popular and news media: Monica Lewinsky, the capture of Saddam Hussein, the Terry Schiavo case, the Michael Jackson case, and so forth. Despite exposure to an onslaught of opinions, audiences are exposed to some diversity of opinion in the media and are generally able to reach their own opinion on the basis of these messages and their own personal values. However, there is little doubt that large segments of the population think about and talk about these topics.

Agenda setting theory claims that the mass media do not determine *what* we think, but they do have significant influence over what we think *about* (Kiousis & McCombs, 2004; Figure 16.2). Thus the degree to which we consider topics important is predicted to correspond to how much coverage those topics receive in the media. If all the political ads are about Kerry's heroism or lack of heroism in Vietnam, then the public will consider this an important issue in the campaign, regardless of what their personal opinion is about Kerry's actions during that time.

Some agenda-setting effects are short-lived. As soon as it was concluded, Michael Jackson's trial disappeared from the news. However, the media can have subtle, long-term effects as well. Research shows, for example, that the more people watch television, which tends to publicize violence and crime both real and fictional, the more they significantly overestimate their risk of becoming the victim of a violent crime (Romer, Jamieson, & Hall, 2003). Watching more television also appears to promote unrealistically idealized beliefs about marriage (Segrin & Nabi, 2002). Such results are referred to as **cultivation effects** (Signorielli & Morgan, 1996). Over time, audience perceptions of reality grow closer to what it is portrayed in the media (Figure 16.3).

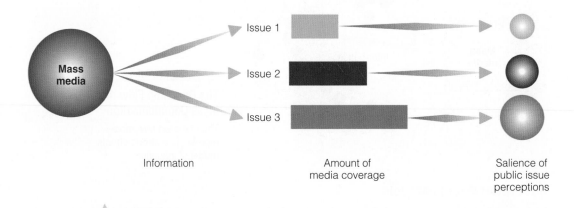

▲ **Figure 16.2**

Agenda Setting Theory

Agenda setting theory says that media don't tell us what to think, but they do tell us what to think about.

Audience-Centered Models

Audience-centered models reverse the early views of mass media by viewing the process of persuasion as residing primarily in the minds of the audience rather than primarily in the messages or media. Most early views of mass communication tended to view the media and their contents as a dominant influence, even if the audience played a role in buffering or filtering those messages. Now, however, the audience is increasingly recognized as playing a primary role in selecting and choosing to use media. Different individuals seek different uses and gratifications from the media they consume (Rubin & Rubin, 2001).

Uses and gratifications are the needs or goals being served by media consumption (Ruggiero, 2000). **Gratifications sought** are the needs or goals we use media to fulfill. **Gratifications obtained** are the needs or goals that media effectively satisfy. For example, people who have been lonely for a short while may be more inclined to seek entertainment sources of media such as prime-time soaps and comedies to compensate for their lack of a social life, whereas chronically lonely people may have given up on using media, finding the relationships displayed a frustrating image of what they lack (Canary & Spitzberg, 1993). Consumers of media are satisfied or dissatisfied with media to the extent that the gratifications they seek from media are obtained from those media (Figure 16.4).

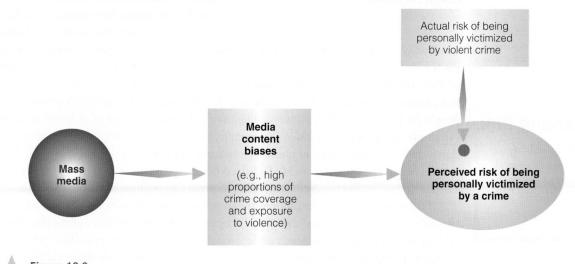

Figure 16.3

Cultivation Theory

Cultivation theory represents how our views of the world come to reflect the world depicted in the media.

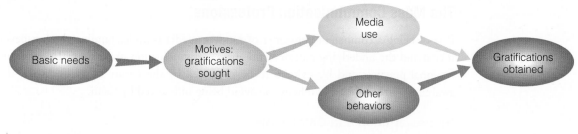

Figure 16.4

Uses and Gratifications Theory

Uses and gratifications theory examines how individuals use different media to satisfy different needs.

"Honey, I'm home."

Our media are increasingly becoming our companions.

People may seek media to be entertained, to find out what is going on around them, to escape the stresses of everyday life, to develop self-concept or identity, or to develop parasocial relationships with those portrayed in the media. **Parasocial relationships** are perceived attachments to characters, real or fictional, portrayed in the media. For example, people who follow certain shows experience feelings not unlike those in a relationship breakup when they know that a character will be leaving the show or breaking up with someone on the show (Cohen, 2003, 2004). The nationwide phenomenon of people gathering in groups to watch the final episodes of *Sex and the City* or *Friends* demonstrates that audiences develop personal relationships with characters, reflecting their own personal needs and desires.

Audience-centered models of mass communication all predict that as exposure to mass mediated messages increases the more effects these messages are likely to have on consumers of those media and messages. For example, after five decades of research on media effects, little doubt remains that exposure to violence in television has damaging effects on young people (Wilson et al., 1997). However, identifying the precise nature of such effects can be extraordinarily difficult. Consider, for example, the influence of the commercial music industry and the various forms of music it distributes and plays. Can listening to music have strong effects? The Close-Up on Media Effects box examines the impact that some rap music may have on its listeners and fans, which illustrates all the models discussed above.

If the messages of mass communication can have such wide-ranging, subtle, and complex effects on individuals and society, it becomes vital to know who is pulling the strings of those media. If there is an agenda underlying the mass media, if there are vast right-wing conspiracies or a monolithic liberal bias to the media, then the models discussed here have far-ranging implications for society. The makers of media, the mass communication organizations of society, are extremely diverse. Some of the most important of these industries and the functions they serve are examined next.

learning link

What kinds of uses and gratifications do parasocial relationships fulfill?

• • •

The Mass Communication Professions

Part of being a competent consumer of modern media is understanding the business of media and the underlying nature of the mass communication profession. If certain professional practices and biases tend to be produced by the nature of the industry, then awareness of these biases can help you avoid being influenced by them.

Representation and Gatekeeping

As the cartoon suggests, distinguishing between news and entertainment is increasingly challenging. When Michael Jackson moonwalks on a car in front of the media covering his trial for child molestation and when *The Daily Show* host Jon Stewart is criticized by

CloseUp on *Media Effects*

What's the Rap on Rap?

MUSICAL GENRES SUCH AS RAP MIGHT HAVE begun as countercultural forms of expression (Martinez, 1997), but the mass communication marketplace recognizes there is profit to be made in such music. The genre of rap has evolved into various subgenres, such as hip hop, trip hop, crunk, and east coast and west coast gangsta/hardcore, so it is difficult to generalize about the entire genre. Nevertheless, as countercultural strands evolved in much of rap music, some of the specific themes of sex and violence drew increasing attention from social critics who feared the lyrics would have damaging cultivation and social learning effects on listeners.

The issue of media effects is particularly difficult to sort out. If an association is found between those who listen to rap music and violence, misogynistic attitudes, or risky sexual activities, is it there because these people listened to rap and the music reinforced the legitimacy of such activities or because people who engage in such activities tend to be drawn to this type of music? Although the research is still in its infancy, so far studies indicate that rap does have some undesirable effects on listeners, although the effects depend in part on the particular genre (Miranda & Claes, 2004) and perhaps on the gender of the listener (Lynxwiler & Gay, 2000). For example, a 12-month study of 522 teenagers (14–18-year-olds) found that more exposure to rap music over this period was associated with a 3-fold increase in the likelihood of hitting a teacher, a 2.5-fold increase in likelihood of being arrested, a 2-fold increase in likelihood of having multiple sexual partners, and a 1.5-fold increase in

likelihood of having contracted a sexually transmitted disease (Wingood et al., 2003).

Experimental research has shown that exposure to violent and misogynistic rap music, compared with popular music, led to more unconscious mental associations with prejudicial stereotypes (Rudman & Lee, 2002). In other words, rap may reinforce gender and racial stereotypes well below the typical listener's level of awareness.

Fans tend to view rap in quite a different way, perceiving it for the most part as a life-affirming experience (Sullivan, 2003). Some rap artists are consciously attempting to move the mainstream into less gender-stereotypical and less violent directions. In addition, more and more women are entering the genre and with them may evolve more gender-egalitarian depictions of men's and women's relationships.

When an association between something in the media, such as violence, is found with something in society, such as violence, media consumers often go into denial: "Well, I watch a lot of violent TV, and I'm not a murderer, so those studies can't be true." Such simplistic denials represent media illiteracy. Such studies are not suggesting that *everyone* who watches violent TV becomes violent. They propose that, out of an entire population of millions, some viewers who may already be prone to violence will be moved just over the threshold to enact violence. Therefore the net effect of such media violence is that across society it is likely to contribute to the amount of aggression. Part of being a competent media consumer is recognizing the possibility of such effects and to be more selective as a result.

Crossfire "news" journalists for not giving a serious interview of his guests, it is clear that the lines between news and entertainment are rapidly dissolving. Newscasters increasingly make cameo appearances in fictional movies, make product endorsements and voice-overs, and are themselves celebrities. Reporters covering hurricanes are sent to report while standing in the wind and rain, which may not add anything beyond reporting wind speed and conditions but is more visually entertaining. This blurring of the distinctions between the nature of news and entertainment has led to the term *infotainment*. **Infotainment** is the inclusion of content, format, and style in news intended to enhance the attention and retention of media consumers on emotional and aesthetic grounds.

Not all journalism seeks to blur the lines. There are many serious print and electronic media for news analysis and presentation. But even when entertainment is not a primary motive of news production, true objectivity is still clouded by other biases and influences.

One of these is gatekeeping. **Gatekeeping** is the decision making that determines what gets investigated, reported, aired, or printed and how this information is edited, formatted,

"What'll it be—entertainment news or entertainment?"

The dividing line between news and entertainment appears to be dissolving in contemporary media.

and styled. For example, in a news organization, editors assign reporters or journalists to certain stories. Some of these stories will be clearly forms of news, such as a State of the Union address, or the capture of a local murder suspect, or the outbreak of war. Other stories will be far less obvious as news, such as the opening of a new art exhibit or the results of an annual report on agricultural subsidies. Some journalists influence their editors by finding out about things they believe ought to be a story. In short, there are various "gates" through which media content must pass, and each gate can add, delete, or modify that content.

Gatekeeping can ensure that only solid, ethical, informative, balanced, and comprehensive journalism gets reported (Benoit, Hansen, & Stein, 2004). Conversely, when practiced incompetently, gatekeeping can simply open the information floodgates and let anything and everything become news (Williams & Carpini, 2000) or permit any number of personal, organizational, and cultural biases to skew the news.

The story the journalist wants to tell can be altered at numerous levels in its course through the news organization. Advertisers pressure the media for optimal placement of their ads, which compete for time and space with the news stories. So the editor has to consider the time or inches of space available. Furthermore, news organizations are generally owned or controlled by corporate interests. Stories get subtly slanted in directions that may slightly favor one political orientation or the other, depending on the political affiliations of the editorial staff and ownership. Research suggests that such biases tend to be relatively minor, at least in terms of presidential campaigns (D'Alessio & Allen, 2000), but biases other than political ones can arise.

One gatekeeping influence, which illustrates the blurring of the line between entertainment and news, is represented by the maxim "If it bleeds, it leads." Violence, accidents, disasters, crises, disgrace, and the fallout from such events tend to garner greater exposure in the media (Chermak, 1995). When extreme, such coverage can lead to charges of sensationalism in the media, but journalists often defend such coverage as informing the public of the threats it faces.

"Those are the headlines, and we'll be back in a moment to blow them out of proportion."

News is never completely unfiltered—it is always an extension of an organization's efforts to reach a given audience.

Even sensational coverage can be biased. For example, Meyers (1997) analyzed coverage of domestic and sexual violence against women. She argues that by reporting such incidents as individual crimes, the media imply that the perpetrators are isolated examples of deviant or disturbed individuals rather than part of a patriarchal society in which women are systematically victimized by large numbers of men. Gatekeeping decisions to report crimes of violence against women under the crime beat mask the larger gendered pattern of the crime.

Gatekeeping also occurs in the entertainment industry. In their competition for ratings and market share, both news and entertainment media seek to do better than their competitors, and that means doing things differently enough to provide a unique relative advantage for consumers and yet similarly enough to compete for the same viewers. Scheduling *The Simpsons* opposite a news program on another network is clearly intended to capture a different viewer market for each show, but when four or five channels offer a news program at the same time, each viewer gained by one network is a viewer lost by another. Management in the entertainment industry strategically determines which audiences they can take from their competition, and they decide that certain shows and media content or format are more likely to compete against their competition than others.

As an example of how subtly organizational factors can affect gatekeeping and thereby the communication of culture, studies by Lauzen and Dozier (2002; Lauzen, Dozier, & Hicks, 2001) have found that the television networks with more males in the management of the organization have fewer women in lead roles in their programming and the women who do have roles tend to employ language that is less powerful in style. The prominence of a male-oriented view of the world thereby gets filtered throughout the culture of the network, from writers to programmers, and that subsequently becomes the image that dominates the airwaves.

Advertising and Public Relations

The tendency to think in terms of market share is a primary task of any media organization. The **marketing** function performs the management processes by which an organization seeks to identify, anticipate, expand, and satisfy its current and potential market. Marketing

learning link

How might the gatekeeping functions of media relate to media consumption as envisioned by cultivation and uses and gratifications theories?

● ● ●

is typically thought of as a tool of for-profit industries, but government agencies, nonprofit organizations, and even celebrities often seek to improve their market strategies.

Advertising and public relations are among the primary tools through which organizations engage in marketing communications. **Advertising** is any nonpersonal form of communication intended to persuade or influence people favorably with respect to the sponsor of the communication. Advertising is nonpersonal in the sense that it is accomplished through things (such as TV commercials) rather than through personal selling or persuasion. A candidate giving a speech to encourage voting for him or her is engaged in personal persuasion; a candidate's commercial or billboard or flyer is an advertisement. Advertisements seek to influence people's behavior, typically by influencing their attitudes, values, or beliefs.

Advertising is most often associated with getting people to buy a product, but it has many other functions. Companies may want to increase the confidence of their stockholders and investors or reinforce their identity in the eyes of the marketplace. For example, one business-to-business (B2B) TV ad for BASF claims that "We don't make a lot of the products you buy. We make a lot of the products you buy better." This company is relatively invisible to the average consumer, so its ad is directed more toward investors and other companies that sell to the consumer. Oil companies may advertise about their environmental efforts, partly to promote sales, but also to diminish public frustration at price increases or to lower public resistance to legislation their lobbyists may be seeking in Congress. PSAs advertise to change public behavior with regard to certain sponsor objectives, such as stopping smoking, wearing seat belts, practicing safe sex, or preventing forest fires.

Advertising generally operates by the processes of attention and relative advantage. Despite the popular interest in subliminal advertising, most advertisers believe that the audience needs to be aware of the product being advertised, and that means gaining attention (Wilmshurst, 2005). There are numerous techniques to get attention. Among the most important are novelty, repetition, pathos, curiosity, and appeal to interests.

learning link

What are the differences and interrelations among marketing, advertising, and public relations?

• • •

Ads that are **novel** represent a new sound, a new look, a variation on an old theme, or any radical departure from what has gone before. An ad for Citroën shows a car reassembling itself into a robot that then dances like a rock star. The rock star dance is familiar, the car may be familiar, and the image of a robot may be familiar, but the three of them together are quite novel. **Repetition** is well known by anyone who consumes media—some commercials or ads are everywhere and seem to be repeated constantly. But as a result, you tend to become aware of the product or service. **Pathos** refers to the ability of an ad to appeal to the emotions. Ads that show babies or cute animals are seeking to endear their product to the audience, whereas a political attack ad that shows the number of criminals an incumbent has released from prison is intended to elicit anger.

Curiosity is sometimes used by multipart ads that give the audience something to anticipate and then later deliver what is anticipated. Some Super Bowl advertisers tease their audience with partial ads weeks before the Super Bowl to prime the audience to watch. Finally, many ads **appeal to interests** that represent needs or values a person is already aware of. Many medicines are advertised with the knowledge that only those people with a particular ailment are likely to be interested in the ad, but that audience is likely very willing to listen.

Once the ad has the audience's attention, it must demonstrate some degree of relative advantage (Brierley, 2002). Having a relative advantage means that the sponsor or product or service being advertised is, or is viewed as, somehow different from, and better than, its competitors. Products are advertised as "new," "improved," "bigger," "faster," "longer lasting," "a brand you can trust," or "better than all the rest." Sometimes relative advantage is created almost out of thin air. DeBeers is famous for creating a cultural shift simply by getting people to associate love and marriage with diamonds, which was far from a widely accepted association before the company began to advertise.

Advertising itself has become an integral part of culture (Alperstein, 2003; Berger, 2000). Pop-up ads and web banners became so commonplace (Adams, 2003) that software packages were designed to reduce them, and telemarketing became so bothersome that, according to a Harris Poll, 57% of Americans claim to have registered with the national Do Not Call Registry (Taylor, 2004). Advertisements now precede movies, sports teams have ads emblazoned on their clothing and equipment and stadiums, product placements occur routinely in movies, corporations make exclusive deals for vending machine rights in schools and universities, and corporate logos are probably prominently displayed on the clothing of half or more of your classmates on any given day (Bhatnagar, Aksoy, & Malkoc, 2004; Galician, 2004). As competition for attention and relative advantage continues to grow, advertisers will continue to find new ways of getting their message out.

Public relations is one of the other ways organizations fulfill their marketing objectives. **Public relations** is the management of communication relationships between an organization and its publics, or audiences (Broom, Casey, & Ritchie, 1997; Grunig, Dozier, Ehling, Grunig, Repper, & White, 1992). Public relations professionals tend to strategize less about a particular product or service and focus instead on how the entire organization is perceived by its employees, stockholders, regulators, suppliers and subcontractors, donors, and of course, consumers. These groups can represent conflicting interests. A company may lay off employees to cut costs, which hurts its image with its remaining employees but improves its image with stockholders.

The earliest conceptions of public relations tended to view communication in the one-step flow model discussed earlier (see Figure 16.1)—as an asymmetric flow of information from the organization to the public. Later views saw public relations as a symmetric relationship in which the publics participate in negotiation of the organization's identity. For example, many organizations today invest significantly in their local communities as a way of developing ongoing relationships with the public. This **asymmetric–symmetric** dimension is one dimension of the evolution of public relations.

The second dimension is the contrast between practicing propaganda and practicing journalism. Early conceptions of public relations assumed that organizations could sell anything to the public and viewed it as similar to propaganda. In contrast, later approaches treated it more like the professional craft of **journalism**.

If these two dimensions are crossed, they provide a model of distinct approaches to public relations (Figure 16.5). The first model is the **press agentry model,** in which the stereotypical press agent distributes messages reflecting just what the organization wants the public to know and think. The **public information model** is more oriented to telling the public what the public needs to know—keeping the public informed about what the organization is doing. The **two-way asymmetric** model reflects that organizations research their publics to develop better understandings of how to communicate and manipulate the public on the basis of those understandings. Finally, **two-way symmetric** public relations represents the most competent model (Grunig, Grunig, & Dozier, 2002), in which the publics are viewed as coequal partners in the process of developing an ongoing and thriving relationship.

Although the approach public relations take toward their audiences varies across these models, all public relations serve similar functions. Public relations must be prepared to

Figure 16.5

Public Relations
Models

Public relations can be
understood in relation to
how the public is
viewed—whether as a re-
ceiver or a coparticipant.

	Asymmetrical	*Press agenty model*	*Public information model*
DIRECTIONALITY			
	Symmetrical	*Two-way asymmetrical model*	*Two-way symmetrical model*
		Propaganda	Journalism

NATURE OF THE CRAFT

serve preparatory, maintenance, and crisis response functions. **Preparatory** functions represent a strategic anticipation or setting of the stage for anticipated changes in an organization or its publics. For years U.S. automakers rode high on the sales of SUVs, but as gasoline prices began to escalate, both public relations and advertising had to start framing their organizations as more concerned with economy and the environment. **Maintenance** functions serve the everyday image of the organization and include newsletters to employees, pamphlets for the public, branding practices that associate the organization and its philosophy with appropriate values, and even such practices as giving tours of the organization.

Crisis response (also called *crisis management*) functions help the organization recover from damage done to its image by a crisis associated with it. NASA faced a series of significant crises that shook public confidence. An organization of literally rocket scientists crashed two spacecraft on Mars and sent *Columbia* astronauts to their deaths, all because of problems that could have been avoided. When crises occur, it is the job of the public relations professionals to craft message strategies for the organization to manage its relationship with the public. NASA invested almost 2 years in rethinking, redesigning, and retesting to attempt to reassure the public that its investments, both economic and human, would be safe in space once more.

Mass communication is a highly complex, multilayered set of processes. The First Amendment and other statutes have guaranteed mass communication a fundamental role in maintaining the democracy and individual liberties and protections. With a set of processes this complex, however, it is challenging to competently navigate the waters of mass communication.

Overcoming Challenges to Media Literacy and Competence

If indeed we are in the midst of an information age, and to whatever extent Marshall McLuhan (1964) was correct in claiming that "the medium is the message," one thing is clear: the media of mass communication have significantly elevated the importance of literacy. Mass communication reaches humanity not in the thousands or millions, but in the billions. As far back as Aristotle, it was understood that the best protection from being manipulated and exploited by communication was understanding how communication does

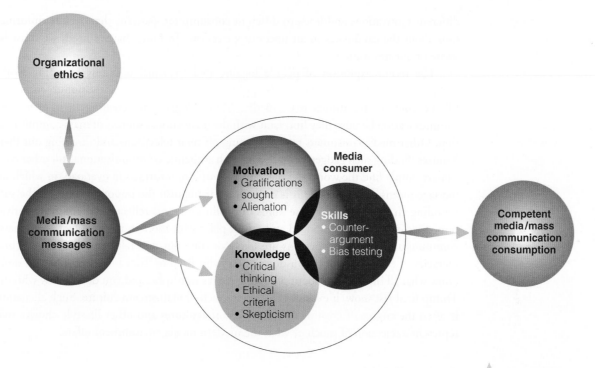

▲ Figure 16.6

Media Competence

Competence in a mass
mediated world involves
both the ethical produc-
tion of messages as well
as motivated, knowledge-
able, and skilled audience
consumption of the
messages produced.

what it does—it is now possible to begin understanding how the *media* of mass communication do what they do. Such an understanding is commonly referred to as media literacy, what in our view is media competence.

Media competence is the critical consumption of mass communication. The term
critical here means more than criticizing the messages of the mass media. It refers to critical thinking, which requires motivation, knowledge, and skills. These components are displayed in Figure 16.6.

We've already discussed many of the factors in producing and distributing mass
communication messages. Obviously the more highly ethical the organization, the more
competent it will be in producing and distributing mass communication (Sanders, 2003).
A large part of producing ethical messages consists of balancing their effectiveness and their
appropriateness (which means balancing the interests of the sender and the audience). Different mass media industries translate that balance into different codes of conduct. For example, the Society of Professional Journalists lists no fewer than 37 codes of conduct organized under four basic ethical standards: (1) seek truth and report it, (2) minimize harm,
(3) act independently, and (4) be accountable (see www.spj.org/ethics_code.asp). In part
because the commercial television stations in this country license the electronic spectrum,
which is owned by the public and regulated by the federal government, the stations have
to abide by standards of decency. It is in this context, for example, that Janet Jackson's in-
famous wardrobe malfunction resulted in a fine levied on CBS and its subsidiary Viacom
of more than half a million dollars. CBS claims the fine was unjust because "one cannot
pander by accident." In other words, there was no unethical intent. Yet the FCC found the
organization in ethical contempt of the standards of law and society.

Once messages have been communicated through mass media, competent media
consumption is up to the individual. Seeking companionship through the media, by using online dating services or developing parasocial relationships with characters, relies on

different motivations and leads to different consumption patterns than seeking information about the candidates in an upcoming election. To find what we need, we must be aware of our motivation.

The recent explosion of people logging their personal opinions regarding world and personal events on the web, or **blogging,** illustrates people's motivation to correct or fill the voids in traditional mass media. Many bloggers are creating their own mass communication because they find fault with the institutional sources of mass communication. Other media consumers take to turning off their televisions and throwing out their X-boxes, finding such gadgetry interfering with authentic communication. Still other consumers simply find the world too mediated, a world of information overload, in which no message means much because it is difficult to distinguish the important ones in the surrounding chaos of voices. These kinds of disillusionments reflect an **alienation** motivation, a feeling of being distanced and out of place with modern media. Over time, mass-communication-alienated persons are likely to tune out and fall behind in the cultural literacies of everyday life. If you don't know who Brad or Tom is dating, and you don't know what all the flap was about regarding Janet's wardrobe, and you don't know who the Trump fired last show, it excludes you from much of mainstream culture. Such alienation is often the engine of creating conscious countercultures and other lifestyle choices that represent a rejection of much of what the modern media environment offers.

Critical Thinking

There are three components of media literacy knowledge: critical thinking, ethical criteria, and skepticism. **Critical thinking** is the ability to analyze, hypothesize, synthesize, and criticize. **Analyzing** a mass communication message means being able to break it down into its surface text or meanings and its underlying subtexts. The text is simply the content of a message, including where relevant the verbal, oral, and visual structure of a message. The verbal text has both relatively standard *denotative* and *connotative* meanings (see Chapter 4). But the subtexts of media messages represent implicit claims or evidence.

For example, if a political candidate criticizes an incumbent for previously voting in favor of taxes, there are several implicit claims: (1) the incumbent may do so in the future if reelected, (2) the candidate promises not to do so, and (3) avoiding raising taxes is a good thing for you the voter, in particular, and for society in general. The message may also have as an unspoken subtext that (4) the incumbent is a liberal.

learning link

In what senses is blogging interpersonal, and in what senses is it mass communication?

• • •

One of the most important analytical distinctions to make in critical thinking about media messages is between facts and inferences. **Facts** are informational claims that are verifiable and are likely to achieve relatively widespread consensus on their validity. **Inferences,** in contrast, are general conclusions intended to represent some set of specific examples, facts, observations, or experiences. Inferences are typically about the implications of facts, but they often are presented as if they were also facts. In the example of the political ad, the criticism is offered *as if* raising taxes is a bad thing when this is not a fact; it is an inference drawn from the possible or probable implications of a history of facts. Inference is where most political debate occurs, because it is relatively easy for different people to reach different inferences from any particular set of facts. Understanding the subjectivity of such inferences will make it easier for you to use critical thinking to form your own independent judgments of media messages (Forsberg, 1993).

Hypothesizing is the ability to draw messages out to their implications and engage in what-if scenarios. For example, using the political example above, what are the societal implications of not raising taxes—what happens to government services, to economic investment, and to new policy initiatives? What is the relationship between taxes and poverty, the stock market, government debt, and the politician's likelihood of reelection?

Synthesizing is the ability to reassemble mass communication messages into a coherent whole after they have been analyzed. For example, given all the implications of an incumbent's having raised taxes, how might you have better designed the challenger's communication campaign?

Criticizing is the ability to apply standards of evaluation to a message to determine its value. But criticism can be issue specific as well. A consumer may ask which is more important: letting the government determine how society's resources should be invested or letting each individual decide. Once more, the balance between self-interests and the interests of others helps us evaluate the competence of the message.

Criticism tends to be more competent if it applies well-thought-out standards, such as the ethical standards we discussed above. For example, determining whether the government should be permitted to wage war based on secret information and sequester enemy combatants without due process requires a complex balance between the public's right to know and the government's right to protect its citizenry. Criticism necessarily implies that underlying the criticism is some ethical standard of judgment regarding what is good or bad. As a competent consumer of media, you need to formulate ethical standards for evaluating mass communication messages.

The final knowledge component is skepticism. You probably accept at face value some messages you receive from the media. When a tsunami hits Southeast Asia, and you see the images and hear the reports, you assume them to be true. But when the reports differ on the number of casualties, the estimated size of the precipitating earthquake, and the likelihood of the United States experiencing a similar type of tsunami, do you accept these statements on their face value or do you wait to form an opinion until after consuming more media or conducting some independent research of your own? **Skepticism** is not simple rejection of all messages, but a healthy tendency to delay forming an opinion until you can complete a more thorough processing of the message.

Counterarguing

Counterarguing is the ability to identify and construct persuasive discourse against the text and subtexts of media messages—that is, to argue against what the message is arguing for. A useful approach to developing counterarguments is to come up with the data, warrant, and claim you want to make in response to the message. **Data** are facts, evidence, examples, or experiences that support conclusions about what is or what isn't, what should be or what shouldn't be. **Warrants** are reasons or justifications. A warrant answers the question why and can generally be introduced with a because. Finally, a **claim** is a conclusion you make to contradict the media message. In the previous example, upon hearing a candidate criticize an incumbent for raising taxes, you could construct a counterargument something like that shown in Figure 16.7.

This model, developed by Stephen Toulmin (1958), reflects the way people construct arguments in their everyday discourse. Using it also improves media literacy skills by making it more apparent when a mass communication message is lacking one or more of these components. For example, if a candidate simply accuses the incumbent of "not being honest with the public," it leaves open the question what the data and warrant of such a claim is.

learning link

What is the difference between facts and inferences, and what are some example statements of each?

● ● ●

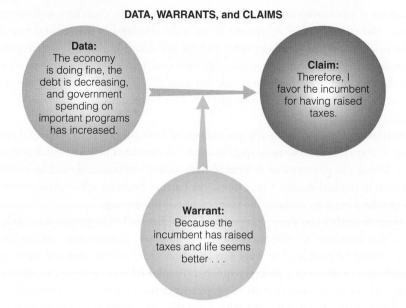

▶ **Figure 16.7**

Example Toulmin
Counterargument

Learning to counterargue
claims made in the mass
media helps avoid the
passive reception of
information.

Bias Testing

Finally, competent mass communication relies on bias testing. **Bias testing** is identifying distortion in the way a message depicts or describes something. Television companies with more men in their management portray more men in leading roles and women in less powerful language. This leads to questions of bias in the ways in which gender is represented in the media. Some of these biases, you may conclude, represent reality, but remember, some of what you perceive as real may reflect media portrayals and not reality.

The invention of the computer changed everything, including the media through which we communicate. As communication media have been changing, so have the competencies required to communicate in everyday life.

 Chapter Summary

Mass communication, the process of managing messages for the purpose of creating meaning in a large audience, has experienced exponential growth over the last three centuries. The term *mass media* is used to represent all the various types of media, such as television, radio, advertising, public relations, newspapers, book and magazine publishing, music publishing, movies, the Internet, advertising, and the organizations that own, produce, and distribute mass communication. Various theories and models of strong and moderated effects, as well as audience-centered models, help explain how and why mass communication works the way it does. These models in turn inform those who work in the professions associated with mass communication: marketing, advertising, public relations, and journalism. Media competence is the critical consumption of mass communication. Among the competencies required to be media competent and to achieve media literacy are critical thinking, counterarguing, and bias testing.

Study and Review

The premium companion website for *Human Communication* offers a broad range of resources that will help you better understand the material in this chapter, complete assignments, and succeed on tests. The website resources include

- Interactive self-assessments, competency grids, and other tools
- Web links, practice activities, self-quizzes, and a sample final exam

For more information about this text's electronic learning resources, consult the *Guide to Online Resources for Human Communication* or visit **http://communication.wadsworth.com/morreale2.**

 Key Terms _____

The key terms below are defined in the chapter on the pages indicated. They are also presented alphabetically with definitions in the Glossary, which begins on page 467. The book's website includes flashcards and crossword puzzles to help you learn these terms and the concepts they represent.

mass communication 426
mass media 426
broadcasting 427
narrowcasting 427
convergence 427
strong effects 428
moderated effects 429
opinion leaders 430
agenda setting 430
cultivation effects 430
uses and gratifications 431
gratifications sought 431
gratifications obtained 431
parasocial relationships 432
infotainment 433
gatekeeping 433
marketing 435
advertising 436
novel 436
repetition 436
pathos 436
curiosity 436
appeal to interests 436
public relations 437
asymmetric–symmetric 437

journalism 437
press agentry model 437
public information model 437
two-way asymmetric 437
two-way symmetric 437
preparatory 438
maintenance 438
crisis response 438
media competence 439
blogging 440
alienation 440
critical thinking 440
analyzing 440
fact 440
inference 440
hypothesizing 440
synthesizing 441
criticizing 441
skepticism 441
counterarguing 441
data 441
warrant 441
claim 441
bias testing 442

Building Motivation

The following questions are among the activities on the book's website.

1. Take a look at the current movie or television listings, or go to a stand with a big selection of magazines, or go to a music store. Select something you would never ordinarily be interested in. Before seeing the movie or reading the magazine or listening to the CD, identify why you have no interest in it. Then, after seeing the movie, television show, reading the magazine, or listening to the CD, consider if there was any change in your opinion and why.

2. List the various media that you regularly choose to be exposed to. Speculate on how your preference for some media over others affects your life—what do you miss, and what do you gain?

3. Go to the book's website to complete an interactive self-assessment similar to the other Building Motivation Self-Assessments in the text. The online Media Self-Assessment asks you to consider a range of statements that describe different ways of interacting with media and rate to what degree each statement represents your own behavior.

 ## Building Knowledge

The following questions are among the practice activities on the book's website.

1. Tape a 30-minute segment of at least two local evening newscasts or two national evening newscasts. Watch each news show and answer the following in columns on a page:
   - What was the topic of the first news story presented?
   - How much time was devoted to that story?
   - Was an expert or someone involved interviewed? What were the person's credentials for being interviewed?
   - Were scholarly or expert studies cited? Was enough detail provided?
   - Was a "person on the street" interviewed? Did his or her comments affect the story?
   - Were graphics used, and if so, how?
   - Did the announcer or reporter offer inferences or opinions? If so, were they positive or negative?
   - What types of gatekeeping decisions could you identify? Were there any biases evident, and if so, what?

2. Choose and tape one story from a local evening newscast and one from a national evening newscast. Use the model of media competence to criticize the claims presented in each story.

 ## Building Skills

The exercises below are among the practice activities on the book's website.

Individual Exercises

1. Locate a newsstand (or library) with an extensive selection of newspapers from U.S. cities and other countries. Select at least four different papers all dated the same

day. Find a front-page story all the papers cover, and compare their coverage of the articles. Summarize the main differences you see across these stories, and think about the reasons for the differences.

2. Get a popular culture magazine from a newsstand or from your library's current periodicals. List all the advertisements in that issue according to the following categories: Who is the advertiser? What do they want you to do (or buy)? What is their warrant? Who is their primary audience? Then, describe how the advertisers adapted their campaigns to the audience they are seeking to influence.

3. How can knowledge and an appreciation of advertising techniques help you become a more competent consumer of media?

Group Activities

1. In a small group of four to five students, identify the significant ways that your lives have changed as a result of the trends and growth of mass media. Consider in the discussion the concepts of movement from broadcasting to narrowcasting, the downfall of distance, and divergence to convergence. What are the positive and the negative effects of the changes you identified?

2. In a small group of four to five students, select a media presentation of some kind to analyze together. This could be a television advertisement, a newspaper or magazine story, or an advertisement. Examine the presentation in terms of media biases and stereotypes by applying critical thinking, skepticism, and counterargument.

 ## References

Adams, R. (2003). *www.advertising*. New York: Watson-Guptill Publications.

Alperstein, N. M. (2003). *Advertising in everyday life*. Cresskill, NJ: Hampton Press.

Bandura, A. (1977). *Social learning theory*. Englewood Cliffs, NJ: Prentice-Hall.

Baym, N. K., Zhang, Y. B., & Lin, M-C. (2004). Social interactions across media. *New Media & Society, 6,* 299–318.

Benoit, W. L., Hansen, G. J., & Stein, K. A. (2004). Newspaper coverage of presidential primary debates. *Argumentation & Advocacy, 40,* 246–258.

Berger, A. A. (2000). *Ads, fads, and consumer culture: Advertising's impact on American character and society*. Lanham, MD: Rowman & Littlefield.

Bhatnagar, N., Aksoy, L., & Malkoc, S. A. (2004). Embedding brands within media content: The impact of message, media, and consumer characteristics on placement efficacy. In L. J. Shrum (Ed.), *The psychology of entertainment media: Blurring the lines between entertainment and persuasion*. Mahwah, NJ: Erlbaum.

Brierley, S. (2002). *The advertising handbook* (2nd ed.). New York: Routledge.

Broom, G. M., Casey, S., & Ritchie, J. (1997). Toward a concept and theory of organization-public relationships. *Journal of Public Relations Research, 9,* 83–98.

Canary, D. J., & Spitzberg, B. H. (1993). Loneliness and media gratifications. *Communication Research, 20,* 800–821.

Carr, D. (2004, April 5). Putting 40,000 readers, one by one, on a cover. *NYTimes.com*. Retrieved July 24, 2005, from http://reason.com/putting.

Chermak, S. M. (1995). *Victims in the news: Crime and the American news media*. Boulder, CO: Westview Press.

Cohen, J. (2003). Parasocial breakups: Measuring individual differences in responses to the dissolution of parasocial relationships. *Mass Communication & Society, 6,* 191–202.

Cohen, J. (2004). Parasocial break-up from favorite television characters: The role of attachment styles and relationship intensity. *Journal of Social & Personal Relationships, 21,* 187–202.

D'Alessio, D., & Allen, M. (2000). Media bias in presidential elections: A meta-analysis. *Journal of Communication, 4,* 133–156.

Forsberg, G. E. (1993). *Critical thinking in an image world: Alfred Korzybski's theoretical principles extended to critical television evaluation.* Lanham, MD: University Press of America.

Galician, M-L. (2004). Product placements in the mass media: Unholy marketing marriages or realistic story-telling portrayals, unethical advertising messages or useful communication practices? *Handbook of product placement in the mass media: New strategies in marketing theory, practice, trends, and ethics.* New York: Haworth Press.

Grunig, L. A., Grunig, J. A., & Dozier, D. M. (2002). *Excellent public relations and effective organizations: A study of communication management in three countries.* Mahwah, NJ: Erlbaum.

Grunig, J. E., Dozier, D. M., Ehling, W. P., Grunig, L. A., Repper, F. C., & White, J. (1992). *Excellence in public relations and communication management.* Hillsdale, NJ: Erlbaum.

Herrett-Skjellum, J., & Allen, M. (1996). Television programming and sex stereotyping: A meta-analysis. In B. R. Burleson (Ed.), *Communication yearbook 19* (pp. 157–186). Thousand Oaks, CA: Sage.

Kiousis, S., & McCombs, M. (2004). Agenda-setting effects and attitude strength: Political figures during the 1996 presidential election. *Communication Research, 31,* 36–57.

Lauzen, M. M., & Dozier, D. M. (2002). Equal time in prime time? *Journal of Broadcasting and Electronic Media, 46,* 137–153.

Lauzen, M. M., Dozier, D. M., & Hicks, M. V. (2001). Prime-time players and powerful prose: The role of women in the 1997–1998 television season. *Mass Communication and Society, 4,* 39–59.

Lynxwiler, J., & Gay, D. (2000). Moral boundaries and deviant music: Public attitudes toward heavy metal and rap. *Deviant Behavior, 21,* 63–85.

Martinez, T. A. (1997). Popular culture as oppositional culture: Rap as resistance. *Sociological Perspectives, 40,* 265–286.

McLuhan, M. L. (1964). *Understanding media: The extensions of man.* New York: McGraw-Hill.

McQuail, D., & Windahl, S. (1993). *Communication models for the study of mass communication* (2nd ed.). New York: Longman.

Meyers, M. (1997). *News coverage of violence against women: Engendering blame.* Thousand Oaks, CA: Sage.

Miranda, D., & Claes, M. (2004). Rap music genres and deviant behaviors in French-Canadian adolescents. *Journal of Youth and Adolescence, 33,* 113–122.

ResearchandMarkets. (2004, June). US online, 2004. Retrieved July 19, 2004, from http://www.researchandmarkets.com/reports/225196.

Rideout, V., Roberts, D. F., & Foehr, U. G. (2005, March). *Generation M: Media in the lives of 8–18-year-olds.* Washington DC: Kaiser Family Foundation.

Romer, D., Jamieson, K., & Hall, A. S. (2003). Television news and the cultivation of fear of crime. *Journal of Communication, 5,* 88–104.

Rubin, A. M., & Rubin, R. B. (2001). Interface of personal and mediated communication: Fifteen years later. *Electronic Journal of Communication, 11* (1). Retrieved

July 23, 2005, from http://p7979-shadow.cios.org.libproxy.sdsu.edu/journals/EJC/011/1/01114.html.

Rudman, L. A., & Lee, M. R. (2002). Implicit and explicit consequences of exposure to violent and misogynous rap music. *Group Processes and Intergroup Relations, 5,* 133–150.

Ruggiero, T. E. (2000). Uses and gratifications theory in the 21st century. *Mass Communication and Society, 3,* 3–37.

Samuel, L. R. (2001). *Brought to you by: Postwar television advertising and the American dream.* Austin, TX: University of Texas Press.

Sanders, K. (2003). *Ethics and journalism.* Thousand Oaks, CA: Sage.

Segrin, C., & Nabi, R. L. (2002). Does television viewing cultivate unrealistic expectations about marriage? *Journal of Communication, 52,* 247–263.

Signorielli, N., & Morgan, M. (1996). Cultivation analysis: Research and practice. In M. B. Salwen & D. W. Stacks (Eds.), *An integrated approach to communication theory and research* (pp. 111–126). Mahwah, NJ: Erlbaum.

Sullivan, R. E. (2003). Rap and race: It's got a nice beat, but what about the message? *Journal of Black Studies, 33,* 605–622.

Taylor, H. (2004, February 13). Do not call registry is working well. *The Harris Poll, 10,* retrieved July 22, 2005, from http://www.harrisinteractive.com/harris_poll/index.asp?PID=439.

Toulmin, S. E. (1958). *The uses of argument.* Cambridge, UK: Cambridge University Press.

Webster, F. (1995). *Theories of the information society.* New York: Routledge.

Williams, B. A., & Carpini, M. X. D. (2000). Unchained reaction: The collapse of media gatekeeping in the Clinton-Lewinsky scandal. *Journalism, 1,* 61–85.

Wilmshurst, J. (2005). How advertising works. In A. R. Mackay (Ed.), *The practice of advertising* (pp. 23–43). Boston: Elsevier.

Wilson, B. J., Kunkel, D., Linz, D., Potter, J., Donnerstein, E., Smith, S. L., Blumenthal, E., & Gray, T. (1997). *National television violence study* (Vol. 1). Thousand Oaks, CA: Sage.

Wingood, G. M., DiClemente, R. J., Bernhardt, J. M., Harrington, K., Davies, S. L., Robillard, A., & Hook, E. W., III. (2003). A prospective study of exposure to rap music videos and African American female adolescents' health. *American Journal of Public Health, 93,* 437–439.

Media Competence Skills Grid _____

Listed in the following chart are some skills grouped together by skill area examined in this chapter. Select one skill in each skill area, describe the skill you have chosen, and define five levels of competence for each skill. Two knowledge areas have been completed as examples.

SKILL AREA	LESS COMPETENT	MORE COMPETENT
KNOWLEDGE—CRITICAL THINKING: ANALYSIS The ability to explain a complex message in the media in terms of its separate parts and subparts of fact, inference, and claims. 1. Generally listen to and watch media rather passively, without much paying much attention or giving much consideration to the particular messages being communicated. 2. Occasionally "tune into" what the media messages are and how they are functioning. 3. Occasionally recognize particular facts, inferences, claims, arguments, language choices, images, and stereotypes being used in media messages. 4. Frequently recognize particular facts, inferences, claims, arguments, language choices, images, and stereotypes being used in media messages. 5. Almost always recognize particular facts, inferences, claims, arguments, language choices, images, and stereotypes being used in media messages.		
KNOWLEDGE—CRITICAL THINKING: HYPOTHESIZING The ability to understand the causal implications of claims made in the media (e.g., if the message is that X leads to Y, and Y leads to Z, hypothesizing means understanding that X leads to Z, and wondering what Z relates to next). 1. Generally listen to and watch media rather passively, without paying much attention to or giving much consideration to the particular cause-effect reasoning being used in the media. 2. Occasionally "tune into" the cause-effect implications of media opinions and messages. 3. Frequently recognize the cause-effect reasoning and implications of specific arguments and claims made in media opinions and messages. 4. Almost always recognize the cause-effect reasoning and implications of specific arguments and claims made in media opinions and messages.		

5. Analyze the specific claims and/or arguments made in various media messages in terms of each claim/argument's cause-effect implications, and whether or not there are any unstated cause-effect implications.		
KNOWLEDGE—CRITICAL THINKING: SYNTHESIZING		
KNOWLEDGE—CRITICAL THINKING: CRITICISM		
KNOWLEDGE—CRITICAL THINKING: SKEPTICISM		
KNOWLEDGE—ETHICS		
SKILLS—COUNTERARGUING		
SKILLS—BIAS TESTING		

Appendix: Communication Competence in Interviews

Marie looked forward to getting a job in human resources in a local firm. She had heard the campus job center had a good library for researching the job market, so she spent several days there looking up contact information for local companies and hours poring over the want ads in the local papers. She sent out dozens of letters with résumés and was disappointed when after 2 months she had received only one call for an interview.

To prepare for the interview, Marie used what she knew from her communication courses, such as dressing professionally, practicing responses to some questions she assumed would be asked, looking at the company website, and asking people what they knew about the company. On the day of the interview, she arrived early to have some time to relax, and before entering the personnel office, she took several deep breaths, stretched, and focused on her introductory manner and approach. She felt good and ready.

She soon found herself sitting in a cold office staring at a secretary, who informed Marie that the interviewer was backed up and the interview wouldn't begin for another 30 minutes. After about 20 minutes of sitting in an uncomfortable chair, Marie saw a person exit the interviewer's office looking visibly shaken and distressed. After another few minutes, a stern-looking man introduced himself as Arthur Short and escorted her into his office.

Arthur explained that the job was demanding, would involve a fair amount of overtime, and required travel at least 20 weeks a year to the various locations of the company, such as Cincinnati, Detroit, Lincoln, Houston, and Phoenix. In addition, the job required using both PowerPoint presentation software and PeopleSoft human resources accounting software. Marie recognized almost immediately that she probably couldn't compete for the job. After answering a few standard questions about her background and interests, Marie was completely surprised by the following request: "In this job, you constantly get surprised by employee questions during your presentations. Let's see how you handle yourself on your feet. Stand up, and tell me an interesting story that has a moral you could apply to an issue of sexual harassment in the workplace." ■

Few of us would be composed and creative enough to handle such a situation well. Despite using what communication knowledge and skills she learned in school, Marie quickly realized that she was not prepared for the situation. She found her own skills limited by the extent to which the interviewer controlled the encounter and directed her comments. In short, Marie found communication competence rather elusive in this interview.

Basics of the Interview Context _____

Though she probably won't get the job, Marie has at least realized something very important about the interview context. Every single action has the potential to communicate something about the candidate's competence. Behavior in interviews is constantly evaluated in terms of its appropriateness and its implications for the interviewee's fit with the job and for the larger organization (Chuang & Sackett, 2005).

Most of the interviewing process can be viewed from the perspective of interpersonal communication competence. Although some interviews call upon public, group, and on-line presentations skills, most are still face-to-face interviews, which most companies view as more fair and effective (Chapman, Uggersley, & Webster, 2003). The model of interpersonal communication competence elaborated in the text provides a way to understand competence in the various types of communication involved in interviewing.

An **interview** is an encounter oriented toward the possibility of mutual gain through the exchange of information, a process consisting largely of question-and-answer sequences. Let's look at the features of this definition in more detail.

It is the possibility of mutual gain, always implicit in interviews, that leads people to engage in interviews even when many do not lead to the outcomes the participants hoped to achieve. The interviewee is seeking something, whether it's help with a personal problem, recognition for expertise in a given topic area, or a job. The interviewer is seeking to help, to complete an assignment, or to fulfill his or her duties for an organization.

Many people assume that the interviewer receives information and the interviewee gives information. This stereotype is incorrect on at least two counts. First, communication is transactional, which means that information is being indirectly exchanged whenever people are communicating. You are interpreting the other person's nonverbal messages and attributing meaning to his or her comments and questions, even when the person is doing little more than asking questions.

Second, interviews almost always include the direct exchange of information. That is, both parties ask questions, provide answers, and attempt to reach conclusions about each other. For example, if you are interviewing for a job, you are likely to ask about the organization's benefits, whom you will report to, and so forth. In campus screening interviews, interviewers spend much more time providing information about their organization than they do asking questions (DeBell, Montgomery, McCarthy, & Lanthier, 1998).

Interviews consist of much more than questions and answers. But questions and answers are one of the most identifiable features of almost any interview (Ramsay, Gallois, & Callan, 1997).

People engage in interviews for important reasons, and understanding these reasons can enhance your motivation in interview contexts.

Why? Motivation in the Interview _____

Few encounters carry as much life-changing potential as interviews. In job interviews, careers are gained and lost on the basis of minutes of interaction. In counseling, interviews provide the keys to insight and healing. In journalism, interviews hold the potential to persuade masses, to bring down governments, to expose corruption, or to bring entertaining or useful information to light. Interviews are thus short-term goals that serve as a bridge to long-term goals.

Anxiety in interview contexts is often a major impediment to competent performance. For example, job interviewees can experience anxiety about their communication, their appearance, their social comfort with the interviewer, their overall performance, and their ability to control their physical actions, such as keeping their hands or their heart rate steady. The levels of these kinds of anxiety alone may account for as much as a tenth of your competence as perceived by the interviewer (McCarthy & Goffin, 2004). Unlike public speaking anxiety, which tends to decrease once a person begins speaking, interview anxiety appears to remain relatively level throughout most of an interview (Young, Behnke, & Mann, 2004). Clearly, identifying the positive motivations and managing the negative ones are essential requirements for achieving competence in this context.

Interview Contexts

Three interview contexts—organizational, investigative, and therapeutic—help illustrate the importance of interviews. The **organizational interview** is a transaction between institutional representatives and a prospective employee for the purpose of ascertaining the appropriateness and terms of contracting the services of the interviewee. It is most often associated with hiring decisions and generally implies salary or remuneration. As little as $5,000 less in your starting year's base salary, multiplied out to retirement over 40 to 45 years, can make a difference of hundreds of thousands of dollars. Thus if a positive impression during an organizational interview means the difference between a higher and a lower base salary, you can see its importance. Organizational interviews can also occur if you want to volunteer for a nonprofit campaign or adopt a pet.

Success in the organizational (job) interview is about more than money. Not getting the job you want and having to take a less desirable one, perhaps in a different industry, can be a serious career setback. By the same token, the organization is investing a lot in the interview as well. The estimated average cost of attracting a high-quality manager or professional is $2,000 (DeBell et al., 1998), and this investment is compounded significantly if the wrong person is hired for the job. Given that the candidate's decision to accept a job is based in part on the interviewer's or recruiter's communication skills (Turban, Forret, & Hendrickson, 1998), all parties have a significant interest in the competence of the interview process (Kikoski, 1998).

The **investigative** (or informational) **interview** is a transaction between parties in which the interviewer is seeking information from the interviewee for the purpose of enhancing decision making and understanding in a specified issue or situation. It typically is associated with journalistic interviews but may include situations as varied as a police interrogation or a sexual harassment investigation. Heads of state and company presidents have kept or lost their jobs because of an ill-placed phrase or a poorly chosen word in an interview with a journalist. Virtually everything we know through the media is generated, illustrated, or reinforced through the interview process. Imagine a news story with no expert testimony or statements, or a biography of a celebrity with no questions asked of the star or the star's acquaintances. Indeed, the interview may become even more important in a world of instant access to information and information overload. People need experts more than ever to help distinguish between valid and invalid information. The investigative interview is a powerful force for knowledge, discovery, and the pursuit of truth.

The **therapeutic interview** is a transaction in which interviewees, typically clients or patients, seek information from a service provider to enhance their health or performance. Generally, people think of the therapeutic interview as the doctor-patient exchange in which a patient tells a physician about symptoms, but it includes other situations such as psychological and marital counseling. Even many instructional conversations between instructor and student could be considered therapeutic, in the sense that the objective is to assist in improving the interviewee's performance in the academic context. An incorrect diagnosis, whether physical, mental, or emotional, can lead to incorrect therapies (pharmaceutical or psychological) that can do more harm than good. Thus it is vital in the therapeutic interview that the interviewer obtain valid and relevant information.

Interview Goals

Interacting competently in interviews is typically a short-term goal in the service of a longer term goal. Understanding the longer term goals can help focus the short-term goals and lead to more competent interview experiences.

Do you want a job or a career? A job is a commitment that pays you a salary. A career is making a living from a profession you want or need to do or for which you feel your talents are particularly well suited. Assessing your goals plays a significant role in guiding your actions in the interview itself. Goals also determine your motivation to a large extent. The more important the goal, the more preparation you will need and the more openness, the more honesty, and the more your performance is likely to matter to the outcome.

What? Knowledge in the Interview _____

Assuming you have analyzed the goals of an interview and concluded they are important, next you must obtain the knowledge you need to perform competently. You have learned much about communication through this and other courses, and you interact with people every day of your life. Yet, although interviews operate by many of the same kinds of processes that fuel other communication contexts with which you are familiar, they are also quite different from most everyday encounters. They have rules few everyday encounters have.

Let's look at the different types of interviews and the rules they follow.

Understanding Types of Interviews

When someone mentions that he or she just participated in an interview, you are likely to picture a situation like the one Marie experienced. However, not only are there different contexts for interviews such as organizational, investigative, and therapeutic, within each context there are many different types of interviews. Consider, for example, the list of interview types in Table A.1. This list is not exhaustive, but it does illustrate why you are likely to encounter some form of interview almost every day.

Each type of interview is likely to have its own rules, roles, and expectations. **Bilateral interviews** are those in which both parties have relatively equal power and roles. Such interviews are likely to be characterized by extensive reciprocity and interchange of roles. Both relational partners are likely to inquire about the other's day or the other's feelings. In contrast, **unilateral interviews** are typified by considerable division of power and roles.

Table A.1

Typical Types of Interviews

Organizational Interviews

    Institutional Interviews

Selection	To determine who is chosen for employment
Appraisal	To assess a person's performance adequacy in a position
Grievance	To investigate the merits of an employee's complaint or accusation of an infraction
Disciplinary	To investigate an infraction or inform an employee of organizational decisions regarding the infraction
Feedback	To obtain information relevant to organizational functioning (for example, exit interviews of departing employees, product or customer satisfaction surveys)
Information Seeking	To understand more about a given person or organization, with the intent to make better future decisions
Negotiation or persuasion	To ascertain information relevant to the prospects for a mutually beneficial exchange or contract among parties (for example, interviewing parties to a conflict, a salesperson interviewing a potential client)

Investigative Interviews

    Media Interviews

Journalistic	To obtain information and commentary relevant to an investigative report intended for publication or display
Conference	To obtain remarks and elaboration of remarks of a person for broadcast (for example, press conference, scientific conference)

    Research Interviews

Survey	To obtain information for a particular study project or set of questions, with prepared questions, via telephone, computer, or face to face
Focus Group	To obtain rich, open-ended information to discover reactions or opinions of people who have an experience in common (for example, interviewing people who have just seen an advertisement or movie)
Ethnographic	To obtain rich, open-ended information to discover individuals' perceptions of a given culture of experience (for example, interviewing homeless people or undocumented immigrants about their experiences)
Relational Interviews	To obtain information relevant to relationship maintenance or resolution of relational problem (for example, inquiring how a spouse's day went, a first-date interchange of information to determine whether a second date is likely)
Interrogation Interviews	To seek information relevant to a mystery, crime, or potentially problematic event (for example, police interrogation of prisoner or witness, FBI interview with prospective employee regarding potential security risks)

Therapeutic Interviews

Physical	To obtain information relevant to treating physical illness or enhancing physical wellness (for example, a doctor or chiropractor diagnosing illness, or a physical therapist preparing you for a massage)
Mental or Emotional	To obtain information relevant to enhancing emotional well-being (for example, a rabbi counseling a couple about to be married, a psychiatrist counseling a student witness after a shooting at school)

For example, in an interrogation, typically the interviewer has almost total control over the questions, the environment, the procedure, and so forth (Sear & Stephenson, 1997).

During your lifetime, you may participate in many, if not most, of these types of interviews. However, some are both more typical and more problematic than others. We have chosen to focus primarily on three interview contexts—organizational, investigative or journalistic, and therapeutic or helping interviews—and specific types of interviews that occur within each.

Identifying You

Now that you have an idea of the types of interviews, it is important to understand which you may face and how you should present yourself in those interviews. As we discuss in Chapter 7, many social situations are guided by rules and scripts. Interviews are guided more than most situations. The interviewers probably will have conducted dozens, perhaps hundreds, of the type of interview you are encountering. This familiarity with the type of communication and the specific topic means the interviewer has a fairly well-established agenda to pursue. Each person may be unique, but a doctor will have interviewed thousands of patients and diagnosed many similar types of ailments. Over time, the doctor will get a sense of what information is needed to diagnose illness. Similarly, a personnel interviewer might have interviewed hundreds of prospective employees for a certain type of position, and a journalist, hundreds of subjects.

You probably behave at least somewhat differently around your best friend than you do around your parents or grandparents. Yet you are also yourself in both situations. People adapt their behavior to the situation to be appropriate and effective. Interviews are no different. You adapt your behavior to fit the interview situation, and yet you generally want the other person to see the real (or at least, the best) you in the interview. To be competent, therefore, know who you are and how you want to be seen in the interview.

"Know thyself" is a far more difficult prescription than it seems. In investigative interviews, stories won't get uncovered if you don't appear sincere and objective, even if at some level you are suspicious and biased. In short, it is important to analyze any potential interview encounter and determine what is expected of you and to what extent you can balance your true self with what is expected. Recall from Chapter 2 that competence carries with it ethical implications. Sometimes you can be effective in the short term through deception, but such deception tends to be more threatening to long-term effectiveness because if it is found out, it is likely to be viewed as inappropriate by others. A journalist who lies to interviewees about keeping sources secret is not likely to get many other interviews with sensitive sources. Similarly, employees who severely exaggerate their abilities in selection interviews may find themselves unable to perform their job duties.

To know yourself and know how you want to appear, engage in **self-analysis,** the systematic examination of your own values, career objectives, and likes and dislikes regarding work and service. How important to you are material possessions, a particular lifestyle, and intangible rewards? Numerous career, aptitude and vocational surveys, and books are available to assist you in determining your core values and interests. When you have a better sense of self, it will be easier for you to determine how to construct the impression you want to convey in an interview.

Identifying the Organization

Marie miscalculated her interview in several ways, but one of the most correctable was in the background research she did on the organization. Virtually every campus, library, and employment agency has a collection of resources for investigating the nature of companies and organizations, from their charters to their size to their public or private status to their benefits. Many organizations have a web presence. If you locate a particular organization's website, look for About Us or Company Profile web pages to learn more about the organization. People can be investigated through newspaper indexes, through regulating professional associations, and by interviewing the organization to which they belong.

Identifying *Your* Fit

Interviews are not supposed to be simple one-way flows of information. The word interview begins with the prefix *inter,* which means *between* and implies something is going on between two or more persons. At the same time someone is interviewing you, you should be obtaining information that will help you determine your course of action.

In a selection interview, as the interviewee you need to obtain information that will allow you to decide whether you want to accept the job should it be offered. This means finding out both whether you understand the expectations for the job and how well you fit into the larger organization (Chuang & Sackett, 2005). If interviewed by a physician or nurse, you want to determine whether that person is sufficiently caring and skilled to help you. In short, a competent interview requires that both (or all) parties to the encounter fulfill their roles and obtain the information relevant to their respective decisions.

How? Skills in Interviews

Interviews are now often multistage events, in which preliminary interviews occur via computer screening of electronically submitted résumés. Subsequent interviews may occur in a group context in which a panel of interviewers from various locations ask questions in a teleconference or videoconference. Negotiations for higher level positions might include discussion of health insurance, child care, housing allowances, and stock options. In this brave new world of interviewing, remember that at its core the interview is still a communication event whichever role you play. Thus the same skills that tend to lead to success in interpersonal encounters are those that tend to lead to competence in interviewing contexts: attentiveness, composure, coordination, and expressiveness.

Attentiveness

Attentiveness in the interview context consists primarily of listening and empathy skills, best illustrated in therapeutic interviews. Research shows that patients evaluate the competence of physicians in large part based on the physician's attentiveness to their concerns (Cegala, McNeilis, McGee, & Jonas, 1995; Tamburrino, Lynch, Nagel, & Mangen, 1993). The ability to pay attention, appear focused on the other person, orient body posture toward the other person, reveal involvement in the other person's statements and concerns, and demonstrate understanding of the other person's agenda and statements all reveal attentiveness.

However, personnel interviewers list eye contact, listening, and feedback response as among the most deficient skills among interviewees (Peterson, 1997). The interview can be a very distracting encounter, and the extent to which you let your thoughts become self-focused detracts from your ability to pay attention to the other person in the encounter.

Composure

Interviews make people nervous because they tend to have more well-defined roles, the stakes are high, and the level of interpersonal evaluation is fairly explicit. Despite such pressures, or perhaps because of them, one of the characteristics being evaluated in many interview situations is the interviewee's ability to maintain self-control and composure (the state of being relaxed and confident). Many personnel interviewers, for example, mention the importance of "self-confidence," "fluency control," "pressure situations," and "preparation" as important skills interviewees need to display (Peterson, 1997). Indeed, appearing self-confident, using positive language, and demonstrating preparation are among the most important rules to follow in job interviews (Ramsay et al., 1997).

Displaying composure in an interview, whether you are the interviewee or interviewer, means displaying vocal confidence and assertiveness, keeping control of posture and movement, and avoiding nervous tapping, fidgeting, and verbal slips or incoherent rambling. Composed persons appear to know what they are doing and are confident in doing it.

Coordination

Coordination is the ability to manage turn taking, transitions, topic flow, and beginnings and endings of interaction. In the interview context, much of the direction and movement is determined by the interviewer but both participants play a significant role in how smoothly and competently such action takes place.

For example, one of the most obvious aspects of coordination in interviews is how well questions are answered. A good answer directly relates to the question, addresses all the implications of the question, and comes promptly without unnecessary digression or inefficiency of response. Indeed, in a survey of personnel interviewers, "topic relevance," "response organization," and "response clarity" were among the most commonly mentioned skill inadequacies noted among interviewees (Peterson, 1997). Displaying verbal fluency and providing focused answers are among the most important skills (Ramsay et al., 1997).

Part of the coordination on the interview's part is asking questions that get at the information relevant to the goal of the interview. **Primary questions** introduce a particular topic, and **secondary questions** are follow-up, or probing, questions that elaborate on the material that surfaces through primary questions. Interviewers should determine before the interview what information they need to collect and select primary and secondary questions that meet their purpose. For example, during an employment interview, an interviewer may want to know more about a job applicant's work history. The interview may then use the following primary and secondary questions to inquire into this area:

- Primary question: could you tell me a little about the jobs that you have held?
- Secondary question: what has been your favorite job? Least favorite? Why?
- Secondary question: what skills have you learned as a result of your work experience?
- Secondary question: what was the biggest challenge you faced on the job?

The wording of a question often influences its effectiveness in eliciting the desired information. Three types of questions are particularly useful.

Open-ended questions permit any range of response. Questions such as "Why did you decide to live here?" and "What motivated you to become a communication major?" are open-ended. **Close-ended questions** typically suggest and are satisfied by simple answers. "So you grew up in Texas?" requires only a yes or no answer, with the possibility of brief elaboration ("Yes, well, mostly, but my parents were in the military, so we moved around a lot").

Second, interviewers may want to select hypothetical or behavioral questions. **Hypothetical questions** ask the interviewee to respond to what-if situations. For example, in a job interview, an interviewer may ask hypothetical questions dealing with specific topics:

- Difficult employees: "What would you do if a co-worker continually came to work late and you needed to motivate that co-worker to come to work on time?"
- Conflict: "Imagine that a co-worker has just made an incredibly inappropriate remark to you. What would you do?"
- Leadership: "Suppose you were promoted to supervisor. What kind of leadership style would you use?"

Hypothetical questions are particularly useful if you want to assess skills and abilities that an individual may not yet have had an opportunity to develop as well as how this individual may act in future situations.

Some interviewers who feel that past experience best predicts future behavior may prefer **behavioral questions,** which solicit detailed and specific responses grounded in interviewees' past experience (Barclay, 2001). These are examples of behavioral questions:

- Difficult employees: "Think of a time when you had to work with a difficult co-worker. How did you manage that situation?"
- Conflict: "Tell me about a situation where you had to manage a conflict between yourself and another co-worker."
- Leadership: "Describe an instance where you acted as a leader. What did you do?"

When asking behavioral questions interviewers typically give an interviewee a specific situation that may be problematic or challenging and invite the interviewee to specifically describe the action they performed to manage the situation and describe the results.

Finally, interviewers need to determine whether they should ask objective or interpretive questions. **Objective questions** are fact based and ask the interviewer for impartial descriptions of events and situations. For example, during a therapeutic interview, a therapist may ask a series of objective questions to acquire the client's personal history ("You got married when?" "How many children do you have?"). Although objective questions may be useful for obtaining relatively straightforward information that is not open to dispute, interviewers may also want to ask questions that provide glimpses into the way people think, their attitudes, and their beliefs. **Interpretive questions** solicit a person's subjective opinions and perspectives. For example, during a therapeutic interview, a therapist may ask interpretive questions such as "How do you make sense of the situation?" or "What do you think would happen if . . . ?" to gain an understanding of the client's opinions and perspectives on the situation.

Competence in interviewing requires not only the skillful use of these kinds of questions by the interviewer but the skillful recognition of them by the interviewee. Brainstorm possible questions you may be asked in an interview and anticipate how to respond. A number of books and articles list typical questions asked during employment interviews (see Stewart & Cash, 2003).

Expressiveness

Expressiveness is the ability to appear animated, involved, and energized in communication. Messages have both verbal and nonverbal aspects, and both are important to making a memorable and vivid impression on another person in interview contexts (Goldberg & Cohen, 2004; Tsai, Chen, & Chiu, 2005). In the interview context, expressiveness consists of facial and vocalic expressiveness, gesturing, and articulateness of pronunciation and opinion expression. Interviewers, for example, note that many applicants are deficient in "vocabulary," "descriptive language," "gesturing," "voice projection," "volume control," and "facial expressiveness" (Peterson, 1997). The vast majority of job interviewers point to articulateness as an element of the interviewee's desirability as a prospective employee (Wright & Multon, 1995), and "ability to express ideas" has been shown to be a significant determinant of interviewer impressions of candidates (Wade & Kinicki, 1997). Expressiveness can distinguish a merely capable interviewee from a memorable one (Bobevski, Holgate, & McLennan, 1997). For example, in a study of interviewees with physical disabilities, those with good nonverbal communication skills were rated as significantly more employable than those with poor nonverbal communication skills (Wright & Multon, 1995). That is, regardless of a person's technical competence for a job, his or her communication competence, in particular, expressiveness, can significantly determine whether this person will be hired (Bretz, Rynes, & Gerhart, 1993).

Overcoming Challenges to Competence in the Interview

Given the importance of communication skills to everyday organizational activity (McPherson, 1998), it is no surprise that demonstrating communication competence in the interview is widely taken to be an important indicator of an interviewee's ability to function in the organization (Ramsay et al., 1997). In addition, the competence of the interviewer is often taken to be an indicator of the competence of the interviewer's organization itself (Turban et al., 1998).

A survey was sent to 500 personnel interviewers in a midwestern city (Peterson, 1997). Almost 70% of the interviewers strongly agreed with this statement: "Oral and nonverbal communication skills significantly impact hiring decisions." Almost exactly as many strongly agreed that "higher level positions require more effective communication skills." In all, half the respondents strongly agreed that jobs in the 21st century require "increased communication skills." However, only about 5% strongly agreed that "job applicants display adequate communication skills." Clearly, there seems to be significant room for improvement of communication competence in the interview context. Why are interviews so difficult to manage competently? Next we consider two important and interrelated challenges to competence in interview contexts: anxiety and impression management.

Anxiety Management

Many aspects of communication situations can make people nervous, and most interview contexts seem to combine a host of them. In the employment interview context, a job or possibly even a career is at stake. The situation is generally formal, unfamiliar, and with little time and opportunity for you to get to know one another. In medical or therapeutic interviews, wellness may be at stake. The prospect of disclosing very private, perhaps very negative, information about one's self looms in almost all such interviews. In journalistic interviews, the interviewee must consider that every word may reflect on his or her competence and each word may show up in print or be broadcast on television or the Internet. High stakes and intense focus may be factors as well. It is not surprising that people are anxious in such encounters.

Most of these factors can, however, be managed if you increase your experience and familiarity with interviews. One of the best ways to prepare yourself for an interview is to conduct an information-seeking interview with a person who is knowledgeable about the area and the kind of interview you will be undertaking (Stewart & Cash, 2003).

In **information-seeking interviews,** a person seeks to understand more about a given person or organization, with the intent to make better future decisions. People sometimes engage in information-seeking interviews with prospective physicians, therapists, or health-care organizations to decide which one ultimately to select. In the most common type of information-seeking interview, candidates interview various organizations primarily to find out more about a given job market, employer, or set of career options.

Information-seeking interviews often are relatively straightforward. A person calls the personnel or human resources department of an organization and asks for an information-seeking interview. If the organization engages in such interviews, a time is set up and the person goes in with a set of questions to ask the organizational representative about various career opportunities in the field that the organization represents. A competent information seeker will have done what homework is possible in researching the organization and have a prepared set of questions to ask. A competent information seeker will also be prepared, should the interview take such a turn, to talk about himself or herself as a prospective employee and what he or she aspires to in a career.

Impression Management

Anxiety is a common problem in interview contexts because of the potential for evaluation. But to some extent, we are always being evaluated in communication. So what makes interview situations so different? One key difference is that the competence of a person's impression is explicitly at stake in interviews. Not only that, but a person's worth (at least in the eyes of the interviewer) is at stake as well. Is a patient's illness "worth" the physician's valuable time? Is the expert's expertise worth quoting in the story? Is the candidate worth hiring?

Impression management is a factor that's more of an issue in interviews than in other communication, because the rules of job interviews are so much more defined than in most other situations (Ramsay et al., 1997). In many situations you can afford to take risks with rules or work your way out of rule violations, assuming the rule is either not very important or not very well defined. But what rules in a job interview could be said to be unimportant or unclear? A good example of the rule-bound nature of job interviews is reflected in the area of illegal questions. The Equal Employment Opportunity Commission (EEOC) and the federal government have created guidelines about the kinds of questions that can be asked during job interviews, primarily to prevent discrimination in hiring decisions. Several questions should never be asked because of the risk of significant legal action but also because they may generate a negative impression of the interviewer.

1. Don't ask applicants whether they currently have children or are planning to have children. This has the potential to lead to gender discrimination.
2. Don't ask for an applicant's age. Questions about age have the possibility of leading to age discrimination.
3. Refrain from asking whether the applicant has physical or mental disabilities that may interfere with job performance. Disabilities can be explored once a job offer has been made, conditional on completion of physical, medical, or job-skills tests.

4. Don't ask questions that try to identify physical characteristics such as height or weight. Obesity can be considered a disability.

5. Don't ask female candidates for their maiden, or family, name. Such questions establish marital status, and consideration of candidates' qualifications cannot include their marital status.

6. Don't ask about citizenship because you may be setting yourself up for a national-origin lawsuit. You may ask for documentation that indicates the employee has a legal right to work in the United States.

7. Don't ask questions about arrest records; such records are not proof of anything. Employers are entitled to inquire into convictions of crimes (adapted from Pouliot, 1992).

What is a job applicant to do if asked an illegal question? On the one hand, you can stand your ground and refuse to answer. However, you may not be offered the job if you directly confront or embarrass the interviewer. On the other hand, you could answer the question and create a favorable impression, but you might feel you have compromised your personal standards. Or you could politely ask whether the job or job offer is dependent on your answering the question. In the first response, your refusal may result in the interviewer's forming a negative impression of you. In the second, the interviewer may view you positively, but you have violated your own personal standards. In the last response, even though it is tactful and reflects your own personal standards, you still run the risk of having the interviewer form a negative impression because you challenged his or her authority.

Even though the preceding example is somewhat extreme, the struggle between self-expression and rule conformity remains one of the most significant challenges of interview situations. Making a better impression in interview contexts is more likely if you know both the general rules of more competent interaction and the specific rules of a particular interview context. Research the specifics by investigating the organization, the topic areas likely to be covered, and any standard rules such as the EEOC standards.

At the more general level, interview contexts typically follow rules similar to everyday conversation, but perhaps with greater expectation of these rules being followed. Many of these rules were summarized by Grice (1975) in terms of conversational maxims. The **maxim of quantity** says a response should be informative but provide only the information required by the previous statement or question. The **maxim of quality** requires that responses be honest. The **maxim of relevance** suggests responses be topically related to prior statements. Finally, the **maxim of manner** says that responses should be orderly and clear. These maxims represent a reasonably solid foundation for competence in an interview.

 ## Summary

Among communication situations the interview is unique in the significance of the goals at stake, the relative formality of the rules, and the difference between the participants in status and role. Interviewing is similar to other communication contexts, especially interpersonal contexts, in that the competence model of motivation, knowledge, and skills applies equally to both contexts. Competent interviewing requires being motivated to be competent, knowledgeable in the types and expectations of interviews, and skilled in selecting appropriate questions. Needed skills, as in interpersonal communication in general, include attentiveness, composure, coordination, and expressiveness.

The challenges to competent interviewing include the level of anxiety candidates tend to experience, brought on largely by the formality and significance of the context. The other major challenge is the intensity with which a person's face, which conveys much of the impression a person makes, is onstage in an interview context. Competent management of these challenges means achieving experience and familiarity through information-seeking interviews and understanding the rule-based nature of interview contexts.

 ## Key Terms

The key terms below are defined in the chapter on the pages indicated. They are also presented alphabetically with definitions in the Glossary, which begins on page 467. The book's website includes flashcards and crossword puzzles to help you learn these terms and the concepts they represent.

interview 452	hypothetical questions 458
organizational interview 453	behavioral questions 459
investigative interview 453	objective questions 459
therapeutic interview 454	interpretive questions 459
bilateral interview 454	expressiveness 459
unilateral interview 454	information-seeking interviews 461
self-analysis 456	maxim of quantity 462
primary questions 458	maxim of quality 462
secondary questions 458	maxim of relevance 462
open-ended questions 458	maxim of manner 462
closed-ended questions 458	

 ## Building Skills

The following activities are among the practice activities on the book's website.

Individual Exercises

1. Develop a draft of a résumé, including a heading that summarizes your career objectives and values. Then show your résumé to a family member, a professional, and a fellow student to receive feedback not only on formatting but also on content. What did you learn about yourself during this process? How well can you summarize who you are in the form of a résumé?

2. Engage in three information-seeking interviews. If you are interested in conducting organizational interviews, select professionals in an industry that represents your current career objective. If you are interested in journalism, select three professional journalists or managers of journalistic enterprises. If you are interested in one of the helping professions, select administrators or helping professionals. Take careful notes at each interview, and at the end, summarize what you learned from the interviews in terms of what changes you would, or intend to, make to your education. How were the interviews different from what you expected?

3. Videotape or audiotape 5 minutes of an interview by an expert (such as Larry King or Charlie Rose) and transcribe it. Then critique the interview. What would you have done differently, asked differently, followed up on differently? Where, if

anywhere, did the interviewer not manage the interview well? What is one question that should have been asked and wasn't?

Group Activities

1. Choose a fellow student in your class and exchange the résumés you developed for individual activity 1. Given a week with each other's résumé, (1) do some research in classified ads and write a job description that would be relevant to the other person's résumé, (2) develop a set of 20 questions you would want to ask the other person if you were an interviewer for an organization that would advertise such a job, and (3) interview each other, one student taking the role of interviewer and the other of interviewee for 15 minutes and then reversing roles for another 15 minutes. How competent were you as an interviewee? As an interviewer? Complete a conversational skills rating form on your own behavior as an interviewee and on the other person as an interviewee. Give each other your ratings of the other person as an interviewee and compare with your own self-evaluations. How do they compare?

2. After the activity has been completed, exchange lists of questions with each other. Provide written feedback to each other by rewriting questions and developing at least one closed-ended question and one open-ended question for each topic area covered. Furthermore, add questions not asked that you wish had been.

 # References

Barclay, J. M. (2001). Improving selection interviews with structure: Organisations' use of "behavioral" interviews. *Personnel Review, 30,* 81–92.

Bobevski, I., Holgate, A. M., & McLennan, J. (1997). Characteristics of effective telephone counselling skills. *British Journal of Guidance and Counselling, 25,* 239–249.

Bretz, R. D., Rynes, S. L., & Gerhart, B. (1993). Recruiter perceptions of applicant fit: Implications for individual career preparation and job search behavior. *Journal of Vocational Behavior, 43,* 310–327.

Cegala, D. J., McNeilis, K. S., McGee, D. S., & Jonas, A. P. (1995). A study of doctors' and patients' perceptions of information processing and communication competence during the medical interview. *Health Communication, 7,* 179–203.

Chapman, D. S., Uggersley, K. L., & Webster, J. (2003). Applicant reactions to face-to-face and technology-mediated interviews: A field investigation. *Journal of Applied Psychology, 88,* 944–953.

Chuang, A., & Sackett, P. R. (2005). The perceived importance of person-job fit and person-organization fit between and within interview stages. *Social Behavior & Personality, 33,* 209–226.

DeBell, C. S., Montgomery, M. J., McCarthy, P. R., & Lanthier, R. P. (1998). The critical contact: A study of recruiter verbal behavior during campus interviews. *Journal of Business Communication, 35,* 202–223.

Goldberg, C., & Cohen, D. J. (2004). Walking the walk and talking the talk: Gender differences in the impact of interviewing skills on applicant assessments. *Group & Organization Management, 29,* 369–384.

Grice, H. P. (1975). Logic and conversation. In P. Cole & J. L. Morgan (Eds.), *Syntax and semantics* (Vol. 3, pp. 41–58). New York: Academic Press.

Kikoski, J. F. (1998). Effective communication in the performance appraisal interview: Face-to-face communication for public managers in the culturally diverse workplace. *Public Personnel Management, 27,* 491–513.

McCarthy, J., & Goffin, R. (2004). Measuring job interview anxiety: Beyond weak knees and sweaty palms. *Personnel Psychology, 57,* 607–637.

McPherson, B. (1998). Student perceptions about business communication in their careers. *Business Communication Quarterly, 61,* 68–79.

Peterson, M. S. (1997). Personnel interviewers' perceptions of the importance and adequacy of applicants' communication skills. *Communication Education, 46,* 287–291.

Pouliot, J. S. (1992, July). Topics to avoid with applicants. *Nation's Business, 20,* 57–58.
Pulakos, E. D., Schmitt, N., Whitney, D., & Smith, M. (1996). Individual differences in interviewer ratings: The impact of standardization, consensus discussion, and sampling error on the validity of a structured interview. *Personnel Psychology, 49,* 85–102.

Ramsay, S., Gallois, C., & Callan, V. J. (1997). Social rules and attributions in the personnel selection interview. *Journal of Occupational and Organizational Psychology, 70,* 189–203.

Sear, L., & Stephenson, G. M. (1997). Interviewing skills and individual characteristics of police interrogators. *Issues in Criminological and Legal Psychology, 29,* 27–34.

Stewart, C. J., & Cash, W. B. (2003). *Interviewing: Principles and practices* (10th ed.). New York: McGraw-Hill.

Tamburrino, M. B., Lynch, D. J., Nagel, R., & Mangen, M. (1993). Evaluating empathy in interviewing: Comparing self-report with actual behavior. *Teaching and Learning in Medicine, 5,* 217–220.

Tsai, W-C., Chen, C-C., & Chiu, S-F. (2005). Exploring boundaries of the effects of applicant impression management tactics in job interviews. *Journal of Management, 31,* 108–125.

Turban, D. B., Forret, M. L., & Hendrickson, C. L. (1998). Applicant attraction to firms: Influences of organization reputation, job and organizational attributes, and recruiter behaviors. *Journal of Vocational Behavior, 52,* 24–44.

Wade, K. J., & Kinicki, A. J. (1997). Subjective applicant qualifications and interpersonal attraction as mediators within a process model of interview selection decisions. *Journal of Vocational Behavior, 50,* 23–40.

Wright, G. E., & Multon, K. D. (1995). Employer's perceptions of nonverbal communication in job interviews for persons with physical disabilities. *Journal of Vocational Behavior, 47,* 214–227.

Young, M. J., Behnke, R. R., & Mann, Y. M. (2004). Anxiety patterns in employment interviews. *Communication Reports, 17,* 49–57.

Glossary

a

abstraction dimension of skills that skills exist at many different levels

access extent that different types of media and options in these media are available

acknowledging communication that helps members indicate that they understand one another

acquaintance stage point of first contact between people

action assembly mental process of putting behaviors together in the pursuit of goals

ad hominem verbal attack on another person rather than the argument the person is making

adaptability ability to alter skills appropriately as contexts and conversations evolve

adaptive work group problems and solutions that are not clearly defined and place the responsibility for change on group members

addition adding extra parts to a word

advertising any nonpersonal form of communication intended to persuade or influence people favorably with respect to the sponsor of the communication

affect blend blending of two or more affect displays into one facial expression

affect displays facial expressions

affective conflict conflict involving the interpersonal relationships formed among group members and the group's emotional climate

affiliation emotional and evaluative dimension of relating

agenda setting the process through which mass media influence what the public thinks about

aggressive communication expression of your rights or views in a way that violates others' rights or views

alienation a feeling of being distanced and out of place with modern media

alliteration repetition of the same consonant sound in a series of words or phrases to draw attention to certain ideas

allness tendency to conclude that what is believed to be true of one part is true of the whole

analogy extended simile or metaphor that suggests that things that seem alike in some respects will be alike in the respect being discussed

analyzing being able to break a media message down into its surface text or meanings and its underlying subtexts

appeal technique speakers use to persuade an audience to accept their argument

appeal to interests explicit or implicit claims in advertisements that represent needs or values a person possesses or is already aware of

appearance presentation of one's physical self

appropriate language language that is respectful, noncondescending, unbiased, and fitting to the context

appropriateness communication that fits a given context

articulation shaping individual speech sounds correctly to produce an understandable word

artifacts objects in an environment that make nonverbal statements about the identity and personality of their owner

assertiveness expression of your rights or views in a way that does not violate others' rights or views

asymmetric–symmetric a dimension of public relations organizations' relationships with their public audiences. Symmetric relationships imply the organization and its publics are co-equal partners and participants in maintaining the organization. Asymmetric relationships imply the organization views its role as sending information to the public, which passively receives it

attentiveness employing good listening and empathy skills

attentiveness skill of showing interest, concern, and attention in an interaction

attitudes psychological reactions to another person, object, or concept that affect people's behaviors

attribution theory framework for determining the motives underlying another's behavior

audience analysis ascertaining relevant information about listeners and a speaking situation that will shape how a speech is prepared and delivered

autocratic leadership leaders having more power than followers and using one-way communication to direct and guide the actions of followers

avoidance skills behaviors that displace, postpone, or shift a conflict

avoidance style conflict management style low in both assertiveness and collaboration

b

behavioral interdependence when an individual's messages affect and are affected by other people's messages

behavioral questions solicit detailed and specific responses grounded in past behavior

beliefs people's basic convictions about what is true or false, based on their own knowledge and experience

467

bias testing identifying distortion in the way a message depicts or describes something

biased language words or phrases that derive their meaning from stereotypes based on gender, race, ethnic group, age, sexual orientation, or disability

bibliography list of source references or related material

bilateral interview both the interviewer and the interviewee have relatively equal power and roles in the interview

blind self aspects of the self known to others but not to the self

blogging process of entering personal information, thoughts, experiences, or opinions in a Web-based log or diary

body of the speech the middle part of a speech that supports the central claim through the presentation of a series of main points

brainstorming group process of generating many uncriticized ideas to improve the chances that high-quality, creative ideas will emerge

brainwriting written method for brainstorming

breadth number of topics we may choose to disclose about ourselves; the number of different communication media to which a person has access

broadcasting sending messages out indiscriminately to large audiences

C

channel medium through which a message is sent

chronemics intentional and unintentional use of time to communicate

chronological speech organization presentation of information in a time sequence

clarifying questions questions that invite another person to elaborate on his or her meaning

clear language word use that is easy to understand and comprehend

closed-ended questions questions that give the respondent limited options in answering

code switching the speaker switches from her or his own way of encoding a message and encodes it the way another person would

coercion negative form of influence that occurs when a speaker persuades others to act in a particular way out of fear of reprisal, or by using force, or giving the listeners no choice but to cooperate

cognitive modification process that changes or modifies a person's unrealistic beliefs

collaboration capability ability of group members to work interdependently in the future

collective behavior joint action that links people together

collectivist culture a culture in which group goals take priority over individual goals

collectivist orientation giving group goals priority over individual goals

communication process of managing messages for the purpose of creating meaning

communication apprehension fear or anxiety of either real or anticipated communication with another person or persons

communication competence use of verbal and/or nonverbal behavior to accomplish preferred outcomes in a way that is appropriate to the context communicator

community group of people who come together in the same physical, mental, or virtual space to interact and/or pursue a common goal

comparing alternatives organizing pattern that examines two or more alternatives and makes an appeal for the preferred choice

comparing questions questions that invite examination of similarities and differences

competence principle plans are selected on the basis of their efficiency in competently achieving a plan's goals

competent language use of words that are clear, vivid, and appropriate

competent listener someone who is motivated, knowledgeable and skillful at listening effectively in a variety of situations

completeness extent that the medium represents the nonverbal and emotional content of messages

composure skill of displaying control and confidence

computerized database collection of information accessed and organized by computer

computer-mediated communication (CMC) any human symbolic interaction through digitally based technologies

concept speech a speech about abstract ideas—theories, principles, or values

conclusion final part of a speech whose main functions are to review and summarize the content and to reinforce the thesis

concurrence seeking trying to achieve a consensus regarding a decision

condescending language language that speaks down to the listener(s)

conflict interaction among interdependent people who perceive others as opposing their goals, aims, or values and having the potential to frustrate them in achieving these goals, aims, or values

conflict management styles distinguishable patterns of behavior that represent different forms of managing disputes

connotative meaning the personal associations people make for a symbol

consistency maintaining similar ways of behaving across contexts and conversations

constitutive rules rules to help sort out the meaning of words or phrases

constructing meaning how listeners attribute and assign meaning to a speaker's message, and mentally clarify their understanding of it

constructing meaning competence motivated, knowledgeable, and skilled assignment of meaning to a speaker's message

content knowledge knowing what topics, words, meanings, and such are required in a situation

context frame within which action occurs

context apprehension fear or anxiety about communicating in a particular context such as interpersonal, small group, or public speaking

context interdependence when a group's environment affects and is affected by a group's actions

context levels number of communicators in a communication and the extent the direction of the communication among them is determined by the nature of the episode

context-oriented code an ethical or moral system based on evaluating the specific circumstances of the situation

context types routine ways we think about and respond to a communication episode

contextual alteration changing something about a situation to see how a person reacts

convergence the integration of media technologies

convergent thinking evaluating and narrowing a wide range of alternatives to select the one most appropriate to the task at hand

conversational narcissism appearance in your communication of caring only about yourself

coordination ability to manage turn taking, transitions, topic flow, and beginnings and endings of interaction

coordination skill of managing the flow of an interaction

cosmopolitan communicators communicators who acknowledge the existence of a number of different, valid meanings for words

counterargument form of inner speech that argues against the persuasive message being presented and for the listener's entrenched point of view

credibility appeal persuasion related to how listeners perceive the reputation, prestige, and authority of the speaker

crisis response (also called *crisis management*) communicative and operational actions that function to help an organization recover from damage done to its image by a crisis associated with the organization

critical thinking process of evaluating evidence, assumptions, and ideas based on sound reasoning and logic

criticizing the ability to apply standards of evaluation to a message to determine its value. But criticism can be issue specific as well

cultivation effects the process by which audience perceptions of reality grow closer to what it is portrayed in the media

cultural characteristics audience characteristics relevant to public speaking that come from the groups they are born into, grow up in, or may choose to belong to

culture enduring patterns of thought, value, and behavior that define a group of people

curiosity audience response to the process of stimulating their interest in a product or service by teasing them with hints or parts of a subsequent revelation of information

d

decision selection among alternative explanations or proposals

decision acceptability degree a decision meets standards of quality, quantity, and timeliness set by the people who will use or be affected by the decision

decision making process of selecting among competing alternatives

deduction process of reasoning in which a specific conclusion follows necessarily from a general principle

deep interruptions interruptions that take over a speaker's turn in the middle of a speaker's statement

delivery presentation of the speech itself, how it is actually delivered to the audience

democratic leadership two-way communication among people with equal power who jointly make decisions

denotative meaning the "dictionary" or objective meaning people give to a symbol

depth the importance and relevance of information to our core sense of self; the various options available within a medium

derived credibility impressions your listeners form as they listen to you speak

description informative speech that gives new information when the listeners are unfamiliar with the topic

devil's advocate procedure process of challenging a group's thinking by introducing contrasting viewpoints and ideas with the assumption that the more minority opinions are included in the final decision, the higher quality the decision

dialectic process of questions and answers used to examine all sides of an issue in search of the truth

dialogue communication process that explores differing perspectives and ideas on problems, issues, or topics; a way of communicating that allows people to stand their own ground while being open to other perspectives

different-cultures thesis men and women are socialized into a masculine or feminine culture given their differential use of language

direct learning the internalization of understanding or behaviors through your individual action and experience in the world

distributive skills ability to divide the outcomes of a conflict so that you win more than the other person

distributive style conflict management style high in assertiveness and low in collaboration

divergent thinking generating multiple ideas and alternatives about issues, problems, and solutions

drivers causes of a particular problem

dystopia vision of a world in which everything has gone wrong

e

effectiveness extent communication accomplishes valued outcomes

efficiency amount of resources such as people, time, and money relative to benefits

emblem nonverbal cue that has meaning for a certain cultural group, substitutes for a word and translates almost directly into a word phrase

emoticons whimsical icons that communicate the emotion underlying a verbal statement

emotional appeal persuasion based on psychology and passion

empathic assertion attempt to recognize and grant legitimacy to others in a situation while simultaneously expressing your own rights or views

empathy ability to experience the feelings similar or related to those of another person

ends-oriented code an ethical or moral system in which evaluation is based on the purpose(s) or outcome(s) of an action

episode sequence of messages that has a clear beginning, an end, and a set of constitutive and regulative rules

equilibrium problem challenge to maintain a constructive tension between getting a group task done and maintaining a positive group environment

ethical persuasion persuasion that leaves the decision about what to think or do up to the person being persuaded or the audience members

ethnocentric communicators communicators who recognize only their own meanings for words as valid and reject alternative meanings as wrong

ethos credibility appeals

evaluation demand the need to assess the information and arguments that emerge in group discussion

event speech a speech that describes something that has occurred, such as a historical event

example specific item, person, or event that helps explain or illustrate an idea, clarify a difficult concept, or make anything you say more interesting or real to the audience

expectation mental picture of what ought to be, or what is likely to occur, in communication situations

explanation informative speech that clarifies something that is already known but not well understood

expressiveness ability to appear animated, involved, and energized in communication

expressiveness skill of animating verbal and nonverbal communication

extemporaneous speech speech carefully planned ahead of time but delivered in a conversational tone using notes for key ideas

eye contact looking directly at a person

f

facial expression nonverbal cues from the face showing emotion and mood

fact individual piece of information that can be verified

fear appeal persuasion based on changing listeners' attitudes or behaviors through the use of an anxiety-arousing message

feedback communication to the speaker that conveys the listener's understanding of and reaction to a message

feng shui Chinese approach to spatial arrangement suggesting that artifacts have unique powers when arranged in a certain way

figures of speech expressions that give color and drama to speech

first impression bias schema formed during the initial meeting of a person that influences how later information about this person is processed

fishbone diagram visual mapping tool to help group members identify and discuss important factors affecting a desired outcome

force field analysis process for analyzing the reasons for a problem and obstacles to its elimination

formal outline final version of a working outline, organized and presented using the standard outline format

front stage behavior that is public and accessible to all who are present

full–thin dimension of voice vocal range from deep and forceful resonance to more rapid and shallow resonance

function what the communication behavior attempts to, or actually, accomplishes

functionalist approach assumption that particular decision-making functions leading to high-quality decision making can be identified

fundamental attribution error common bias of assuming that other people's behavior derives from internal characteristics, while viewing one's own behavior due more to a context or situation

g

gatekeeping the decision making that determines what gets investigated, reported, aired, or printed and how this information is edited, formatted, and styled

gender-as-culture hypothesis men and women are socialized into a masculine or feminine culture given their differential use of language

general purpose speaker's goal to inform or persuade

general-level skills the assembly of specific-level skills to create the performance of general skills such as assertiveness, self-disclosure, social support, conflict management, deception, and wit

generalized others entire social group or community to which one belongs

genuine dissent a disagreement where individuals truly hold differing opinions regarding an issue

gestures large and small movements of the hands and arms that communicate meaning within a society or culture

goal outcome, objective, or purpose sought by communication

goal interdependence when group members share goals

goal setting process for alleviating anxiety that makes use of a structured plan for changing a person's behaviors

grammar rules and structure for putting words together

gratifications obtained the needs or goals that media effectively satisfy

gratifications sought the needs or goals we use media to fulfill

group context interactions among a number of people, typically three to twelve, and usually take place in a more formal, task-oriented context

group phases stages in the group's life span where there are clearly defined purposes and themes for the group activities

group procedure process for performing a function that is central to the group

group role set of prescribed behaviors that individuals are expected to perform

groupthink norm that makes consensus the highest priority and diminishes the vigilant appraisal of possible alternatives to a final decision

h

haptics touch; tactile contact among people

hasty generalization conclusion based on too few specific cases or examples

hate speech speech attacks on other people on the basis of race, ethnicity, gender, religion, or sexual orientation

have-nots those who lack computer resources and the skills to use them

haves those who have computer resources and the skills to use them

hidden self parts of the self known to the self but not to others

household type a description that is based on who is actually living together in the household

hypothesizing the ability to draw messages out to their implications and engage in what-if scenarios

hypothetical example something that hasn't actually happened but could happen

hypothetical questions solicit responses to what-if situations

i

ideational conflict conflict centering on the arguments and issues concerning decision alternatives

illustrator nonverbal cue that complements and accents a verbal message

imagery creation of visual pictures and other sensory experiences through description

I-message statement that labels the speaker's own behavior

implicit personality theory uses one or a few personality traits to draw broad inferences about others

impromptu speech speech delivered with the least amount of preparation

indexing using language that places an issue, event, or person in a specific time or context

indirect learning observation of relevant examples of behavior by others, real or fictional, for the internalization of understanding or behavior

individualistic culture a culture in which personal goals take priority over group or collective goals

individualistic orientation giving individual goals priority over group goals

induction process of reasoning in which a general conclusion follows from the examination of a series of specific instances or examples

inferences general conclusions intended to represent some set of specific examples, facts, observations, or experiences

inflection a change in pitch that reveals the emotional content of the message

information overload feeling of being overwhelmed because of having more media content and access to and from people than can be processed meaningfully

information transfer model linear view of communication in which a message is sent by a source through a channel to a receiver

information-seeking interviews interviews that seek to understand more about a given person or organization, with the intent to make better future decisions

informative speech communication that offers something new to an audience, and attempts to move listeners to greater understanding or insight

infotainment the inclusion of content, format, and style in news intended to enhance the attention and retention of media consumers on emotional and aesthetic grounds

ingratiating communication behavior in interactions that appears to be only interested in seeking favor from the other person

initial credibility impressions listeners have formed of you before hearing you speak

instructions informative speech that teaches something or shows how to use something

integrative skills conflict behaviors that attempt to bring self goals together with another person's goals so both can achieve preferred outcomes

integrative style conflict management style high in assertiveness and high in collaboration

intensity the volume of the speaker's voice

interaction barriers obstacles to listening resulting from verbal battles, inflammatory language, or cultural differences

interactive model model that emphasizes two-way communication, viewing communication as a circular process in which both communicators are senders and receivers of messages

interactivity extent that the parties interacting through a medium can communicate simultaneously

interdependence when two elements are related to and mutually affect one another

interest underlying motivation or reason a person wants to pursue a particular position

interpersonal communication process of exchanging signs or symbols that create meaning in an interactive context of few people

interpersonal context informal interaction among people involved in social and/or personal relationships

interpretive questions solicit a person's subjective opinions and perspectives

interview encounter oriented toward the possibility of mutual gain through the exchange of information, a process consisting largely of question-and-answer sequences

intimacy warmth, closeness, caring, and feeling connected

intimate space space that starts at the skin and extends out 18 inches around a person

introduction beginning part of speech whose purpose is to capture attention, present the main claim, and preview the speech

invention the process of identifying—or inventing—the materials that will make up a speech, including a topic and information to support it

issue framing thoughtful way to define and clarify important questions and choices

issue speech a speech that examines a debatable topic from various points of view

j

Johari Window theory of relational openness based on the dimensions of self and other

journalism the profession and craft of communicating information of public interest or concern to the public

judgmental empathic response a response that provides support but also helps to interpret and evaluate the speaker's situation

k

kinesics body communication that focuses on how people communicate through movement and posture, gestures, and the face and eyes

knowledge in communication, consists of the content of what we say and do, and the procedures by which this content can be performed

knowledge-gaining strategies behaviors a communicator uses to obtain information about others

l

Ladder of Abstraction S. I. Hayakawa's description of language on a continuum from very concrete to the abstract

Ladder of Inference tool to help group members explore the reasoning behind their conclusion by evaluating their assumptions, values, beliefs, data, and procedures

language rule-guided system of symbols that allows us to take messages and utterances in the form of words and translate them into meaning

language community group of people who have developed a common set of constitutive and regulative rules which guide the meaning of words and appropriate reactions to them

leaders individuals within a group who guide and direct the group's activities

leadership communication process that helps groups organize themselves to achieve desirable goals

learning the internalization of a new way of understanding and behaving such that it can be produced on demand. That is, learning translates experiences into information, principles, or ability, any of which we can produce as needed

linguistic determinism language determines what we see in the world and how we think

linguistic tyranny use of a set of words having a certain value or connotation to describe and control the outcome of a situation

listening learned psychological process in which you receive the message, assign meaning to it, and send feedback to the speaker

listening to empathize and understand focusing on the speaker's feelings and attitudes while gaining information

listening to evaluate and critique critically analyzing the meaning and merits of a speaker's message

listening to learn and comprehend listening that involves a search for facts and ideas

logical appeal persuasion based on knowledge and reasoning

logical fallacies errors in reasoning and logic that lead the listeners to false conclusions

logos logical appeals

looking-glass self self as formed by relationships with other people

m

main points key ideas that prove the claim and support the thesis statement of a speech

maintenance function of public relations that serves the everyday image of the organization and includes newsletters to employees, pamphlets for the public, branding practices that associate the organization and its philosophy with appropriate values, and even such practices as giving tours of the organization

managing handling or supervising the process of creating, receiving, and responding to verbal and nonverbal messages and media

manipulation negative and unethical form of influence used to control people's actions or reactions in a devious or deceitful way

manuscript speech speech that is written out ahead of time and read word for word to the audience

marketing the management processes by which an organization seeks to identify, anticipate, expand, and satisfy its current and potential market

mass communication the process of managing messages for the purpose of creating meaning in a large audience

mass media the various media—television, radio, advertising, public relations, newspapers, book and magazine publishing, music publishing, movies, as well as Internet and World Wide Web publishing and advertising, as well as the organizations that own, produce, and distribute mass communication

mastery extent that a user understands how to use the media

maxim of manner responses should be orderly and clear

maxim of quality requires that responses be honest

maxim of quantity a response should be informative, but provide only the information required by the previous statement or question

maxim of relevance responses should be topically related to the prior statements

maximizing communication inappropriately assertive or aggressive, but effective, communication

meaning interpretation people assign to a message

means-oriented code an ethical or moral system that defines what actions are considered moral or immoral, regardless of their outcomes

media any means through which symbols are transmitted and meanings are represented

media access extent that CMC technologies are available to the intended audience

media competence the application of critical thinking to the consumption of mass communication

media richness extent that a medium recreates or represents all of the information available in the original message

mediated context the situation in which the means through which symbols are transmitted and meanings are represented are capable of communication from one to one or one to many

memorized speech speech that is fully written out and memorized ahead of time, then spoken to the audience word for word

message ambiguity extent that a message has either unknown or multiple meanings

message complexity amount of detail, density, and integration of information in a message

message emotionality extent that a message attempts to communicate the sender's feelings

message overload distracting quantity of messages

messages words, sounds, actions, and gestures that people express to one another when they interact

metalogue a set of shared understandings and assumptions

metaphor implied comparison between two dissimilar things without using the words like or as

micromomentary facial flash expression that flashes across the face so quickly it is imperceptible

mindfulness paying close attention to the task at hand

mindlessness engaging in activities without consciously monitoring their operations or processes

minimizing communication inappropriate and ineffective communication that fails to achieve a desired outcome, and may alienate others

mixed message nonverbal cue that contradicts a verbal message

moderated effects model that views both the mass communication and the audience as having influence on the impact of messages

moderation principle as use of communication skills increases, impressions of competence increase, *to a point,* after which the behaviors become excessive and detract from competence

modern self notion that the self is comprised of an "I" and a "Me"

motivated sequence organizational pattern that uses five steps—attention, need, satisfaction, visualization, and action—designed to motivate and persuade listeners

motivation extent a communicator is drawn toward or pushed away from communicating competently in any context

multicodality keeping one's own unique way of using words and language while incorporating some of the unique language patterns of the listener(s)

multiple self concept that we create many different versions of "self" across contexts

n

narrowcasting sending messages out to large audiences, but adapted to individuals or groups within that audience for whom the message has special relevance

natural media face-to-face media such as spoken words, gestures, posture, and all the other verbal, nonverbal, and listening processes using solely body and mind

negative motivation factors that result in fear, anxiety, or avoidance

nested decision making prioritizing questions to ask early in a process that serve as the foundation for subsequent questions and lead to the answer of the major question

noise interference coming from the environment that distracts from the communication

nominal group technique (NGT) generating ideas individually and evaluating them as a group

non sequitor statement that does not follow from anything previously said

nonfluencies frequent use of distracters and interrupters that slip out when you speak

nonjudgmental empathic response a response from a listener that helps both people better understand and probe what is going on

nonverbal communication all behaviors, attributes, and objects of humans—other than words—that communicate messages and have shared social meaning

nonverbal cue any human behavior that communicates a nonverbal message if assigned meaning by a sender, receiver, or social group

nonverbal symbols those sounds, actions, or gestures that people agree have a common meaning

note dependent a public speaker refers to his or her notes too often and loses contact with the audience when giving a speech

novel advertising that represents a new sound, a new look, a variation on an old theme, or any radical departure from what has gone before

O

objective questions fact-based questions asking interviewee for impartial descriptions of events and situations

oculesics using eye contact to communicate

omission leaving out, not saying, part of a word

open self what is known to the self and to others

open-ended questions encourage a wide range of possible responses

openness extent that the messages sent through the medium are public

opinion leaders people who receive mass communication messages, form an opinion on the basis of those messages, and then influence others who might or might not have received the messages

optimizing communication communication that achieves preferred outcomes in a way that preserves the relationship

organization by cause and effect information organized by why something happens (the causes) and what happens as a result (the effects)

organization by comparison and contrast presentation of information organized based on similarities and differences to something else

organizational interview transaction between institutional representative(s) and a prospective employee for the purpose of ascertaining the appropriateness and terms of contracting the services of the interviewee

overlearned the process by which a communication skill is used yet is no longer consciously accessible

p

paralanguage all the nonverbal elements involved in using the voice

paraphrasing summarizing and restating the meaning of a speaker's message in one's own words

parasocial relationships perceived attachments to characters, real or fictional, portrayed in the media

passive communication avoidance of self-expression or the accommodation to others' concerns before your own

pathos emotional appeals

perception active process of making sense of external environment and internal experience

personal characteristics objective demographic information about the audience

personal development decision processes that enhance the personal well-being of group members and facilitate their growth and development

personal space how people distance themselves from one another

perspective taking seeing the world as the other person sees it

persuasion use of communication to reinforce, change, or modify an audience's attitudes, values, beliefs, or actions

persuasive speech speech intended to influence an audience's attitudes, beliefs, values, or behaviors

physical barriers interferences from the physical environment and distracting characteristics or behaviors of the speaker or the listener

pitch highness or lowness of the speaking voice

place environment or physical surroundings where the communication takes place, including lighting, temperature, available space for movement, objects in the space, and media

plan intentional description of the actions involved in achieving a goal

planning the process of anticipating and formulating possible strategies for achieving some goal or goals

plan adjustment use of feedback to change elements of a plan

politically correct (PC) language words and phrases that attempt to remove or compensate for any traces of sexism, racism, ageism, heterocentrism or potentially offensive, derogatory meanings

position stated course of action that a person wants to see pursued

positive motivation result of efforts and desires that drive performance toward excellence

postmodern self self as actually made up of many different selves, not just one stable self

posture position or attitude of the bodily parts

power ability to influence and control another person's thoughts, feelings, or actions

preparatory public relations function that represents a strategic anticipation or setting of the stage for anticipated changes in an organization or its publics

presentational aids any materials a speaker shows to or shares with the audience that assist in illustrating or supporting the content of the speech and add interest and excitement to it

presentational outline key ideas taken from a formal outline with just enough details to remind a speaker what to say

press agentry model the asymmetric approach to public relations in which an organization distributes messages reflecting just what the organization wants the public to know and think

primary questions introduce a particular topic during an interview

principle of consistency we make attributions about people based on the similarity of their characteristics or actions across time and space

principle of controllability we try to determine if the cause of a particular action as internal or external, and the extent to which a person is able to alter or change the outcome

principle of distinctiveness we make attributions about people based on whether particular characteristics and actions are associated with specific outcomes unique to the situation

principle of locus we attempt to determine the extent to which a cause of some outcome is internal or external to a person

prior success principle plans are based on previous plans when previous plans seem effective and appropriate

problem gap between an ideal state and the current state of events

problem solving process in which members assess problems and formulate solutions

problem–solution organization organizational pattern that first identifies a problem and then proposes a workable solution

procedural conflict differences of opinion on what procedures to use during group discussion

procedural knowledge how to assemble, plan, and perform content knowledge in a particular situation

projected presentational aids visual aids that use electricity, including computer-assisted aids

pronunciation accenting of syllables in a word

prototype best example of a particular concept

proxemics study of how people move around in and use space to communicate

psychological barriers mental and emotional distractions to listening

psychological characteristics the audience's needs, motivation, attitudes, beliefs, and values

public information model public relations model oriented to telling the public what the public needs to know—keeping the public informed about what the organization is doing

public relations the management of communication relationships between an organization and its publics, or audiences

public space space that extends outward from 12 feet and beyond the speaker

public speaking communication from one to many

public speaking anxiety fear or anxiety associated with a real or anticipated public speaking event

public speaking context involves one or a small group of people whose task is to speak to a larger number of people, with the general assumption that the audience will have little or no "speaking" role

public voice delivery modified by variety in rate, pitch and volume, to be easily heard and understood by an entire audience

q

questioning explicit or implicit use of verbal or nonverbal behavior to request information from another person

questions of conjecture questions that ask what might happen in the future

questions of fact questions focusing on the accuracy of a particular claim

questions of policy questions that focus on actions that should be taken to solve a problem

questions of value questions that explore issues of intrinsic importance, worth, utility, and desirability of objects, attitudes, and beliefs

quotation a person's exact words

r

rate speed at which a speaker delivers a speech

receiver the ultimate audience for a message

receiving consciously paying attention to verbal and nonverbal aspects of an entire message

receiving competence motivated, knowledgeable, and skilled attention to a speaker's message

reciprocity degree the communicators match each other's levels of disclosure

red herring speech that diverts the audience's attention from the real issue by presenting irrelevant arguments or issues

referent the thing to which a symbol refers

reflecting repeating someone's feelings about what he or she said

reflective thinking model formulation by John Dewey of the series of steps decision makers follow to make high-quality decisions

reframing stating something in a new and constructive way

refuting the opponent persuasive speech organization that dismantles the opposing argument

regulative rules rules that guide a response

regulator nonverbal cue that helps regulate and coordinate communication among people

relational content the implication any message has for a continued connection with another person or a group of people

relational function behaviors that emphasize the importance of building a positive group culture and managing conflict

relationship ongoing, interdependent process of interaction between two or more people

relevance how closely related the information disclosed is to the topic being discussed

repertoire set of all roles a person is capable of playing or enacting and the set of behaviors or actions that comprise the role

repetition use of the same word or phrase several times to emphasize or tie several ideas together

responding process the listener uses to let the speaker know the message has been received and to clarify understanding of it

responding competence motivated, knowledgeable, and skilled communicating to the speaker that the message has been received and understood

restraining forces factors that prevent groups from addressing and solving a problem

rhetoric the art of influencing an audience through words

rhetorical canon basic ideas about rhetoric introduced by the Greeks and Romans that represent five activities all public speakers should engage in when preparing and presenting a speech

rhetorical question question asked for effect rather than to elicit a response

role patterns and style of lines and behaviors a person is able to perform across contexts

role taking imagining the meaning that others attribute to one's own behavior

rules followable prescriptions for behavior in a given context

S

sanction behavior communicating a negative evaluation

Sapir-Whorf hypothesis theory that language determines what we see in the world and how we think

schema concept that organizes information into a coherent and meaningful pattern

script story that needs to occur in a given sequence; expected sequence of events that is coherent to the individual

secondary questions follow-up or probing questions that elaborate on the material that surfaces through primary questions

self-analysis systematic examination of your own values, career objectives, and likes and dislikes regarding work and service

self-disclosure process by which we reveal ourselves to others

self-efficacy the belief that one is able to communicate competently in a given situation

self-fulfilling prophecy behavior or interactions based on unproven assumptions as if those assumptions were true

self-serving bias the tendency to attribute positive outcomes to our selves and negative outcomes to others

self-talk mental or internal conversations with oneself

showing questions questions that invite the respondent to focus on specific actions or activities

shyness tendency to withdraw from social activities

signal monitoring looking for signs that an interaction is not going well because too little or too much of a skill is being performed

significant others important people who shape one's life

significant symbols verbal or nonverbal messages that have shared meaning

signified object or phenomena that is represented by a word or symbol

signifier word or symbol that we associate with an object or phenomenon

simile explicit comparison of two unlike things using the words like or as

simplicity principle communicators are likely to simplify their plans, or make only slight alterations to rather than complicate them

situational analysis analyzing the time and place in which a speech will occur

situational context includes all the physical characteristics that are present—temperature, lighting, amount of space permitted for movement, objects in the space, and the media through which we communicate

skepticism tendency to delay forming an opinion until you can complete a more thorough processing of the message

skills repeatable, goal-directed behaviors

slippery slope the suggestion that one event automatically leads to a series of other undesirable events

slurring running sounds and words together

small group three or more people who perceive themselves to be a group, are interdependent, and communicate with one another

social anxiety real or imagined fear of interacting in an interpersonal encounter

social commitment the values and political positions we hold

social constructionism theory that language creates our perceptions of reality and the mode of our relational interactions

social resource learning one on one through other persons how to use a medium

social self self as emerging from and determined through relationships with other people

social space space that extends from 4 feet to about 12 feet around a speaker

socio-emotional regulator a nonverbal cue that lets others know a person's feelings and communicates roles in a relationship or particular situation

source original producer of a message

spatial arrangement the way spaces are laid out and relate to one another

spatial organization presentation of information based on the positioning of objects in physical space, or relationships between locations

speaker credibility impressions the listeners form of the public speaker in a given public speaking context, at a given time

speaking situation time and place for a speech

specific purpose statement of the desired audience response

specific-level skills the relatively discrete behavioral building blocks of communication, including behaviors such as gestures, eye contact, smiling, vocabulary, articulation, and vocal variety

speech about an object a speech about something tangible that can be seen, touched, or otherwise experienced through the physical senses

speech about a person a speech that describes an individual in much the same way that an object speech describes an object

speech about a process a speech that describes a system or sequence of steps that lead to a result or change taking place

speech to change speech intended to convince the audience to change what they like or dislike, hold to be true or untrue, or consider important or unimportant

speech to move to action speech intended to influence listeners to either engage in a new and desirable behavior or discontinue an undesirable behavior

speech to reinforce speech intended to influence listeners by strengthening their convictions and taking advantage of their tendency to seek out and attend to messages with which they already agree

statistics numerical summaries of facts, figures, and research findings that provide pictures of data about people, ideas, or patterns of behavior

stereotypes characteristics we believe to be true of a category ascribed to a given person or situation

story a long example that is used in a speech to illustrate an idea, clarify a concept, or make a point more interesting or real

straw man argument an attack on an entire argument by selecting a weak example or aspect of it, discrediting that example, and thus defaming the entire argument

strong effects conceptions of mass communication that predict that media operate with direct causal force on audience attitudes, beliefs, and behaviors

style quality of expression

subgoal an objective formulated as part of defining and achieving a larger goal or objective

subject area general area of knowledge

subplans steps that need to be taken to achieve a given stage of a larger plan

substitution replacing part of a word with an incorrect sound

sufficing communication appropriate, but ineffective communication

sweeping generalization clustering ideas, people, or objects into one indiscriminate group and implying that all of the items in the group are the same, obscuring vital and relevant differences

symbol word, sound, action, or gesture that arbitrarily refers to a person, idea, or object

sympathy a desire to offer support for another, generally when that person is in a predicament

synthesizing the ability to reassemble mass communication messages into a coherent whole after they have been analyzed

systematic desensitization process of reducing the intensity of a person's feelings and emotional reactions to a specific situation

t

task function instrumental behavior aimed at goal achievement that clarifies the purpose and scope of the group's task, maintains the group's focus on task, and manages the way the group collects, structures, and uses information in problem solving and decision making

technical work group problems that have clear definitions, solutions, and means of implementation

technological media devices that translate, amplify, or otherwise alter the information from natural media

technophobia fear of incompetence in computer mediated communication

tense–lax dimension of voice vocal range from the harshness of a piercing voice to a continuous more muffled and relaxed voice

terminal credibility long-term impression you leave behind after a speech

territoriality how people stake out space for themselves

testimony opinion of an expert or the account of an event by a witness to it

therapeutic interview transaction between parties in which the parties are seeking information relevant to enhancing the interviewee's mental or physical health from a service provider or provider representative

thesis statement central idea of a speech

time management skill of balancing the relative proportion of time each communicator gets to speak during a conversation

timing consideration of a speaking situation's time allotment and scheduling

tinkering learning approach that involves experimenting and trial and error

topic specific facet or aspect of a subject area

topic development conversational management of a subject under discussion

topic initiation introducing a topic for discussion

topic shift a move of a conversation or interaction away from the preceding subject of discussion to an alternative subject

topical speech organization presentation of information about a subject and topic divided into subtopics or subcategories

transactional model people are senders and receivers of messages simultaneously and communicators bring their own personal fields of meaning to all communication situations

transitions words, phrases, or sentences that demonstrate how main points relate to each other

transparent delivery presenting a speech in such a way that the audience focuses on the message rather than the delivery

trigger words words or phrases that cause emotional reactions, intensify conflicts, and discourage competent listening

two-way asymmetric public relations model in which organizations research their publics to develop better understandings of how to communicate and manipulate them on the basis of those understandings

two-way symmetric public relations model in which publics are viewed as co-equal partners in the process of developing an ongoing and thriving relationship

u

unilateral interview typified by considerable division and inequality of power and roles

unknown self parts of self unknown to both the self and others

unprojected presentational aids visual aids that don't use of electricity

uses and gratifications the needs or goals being served by media consumption

v

valence extent that a message has good or bad implications for the sender

values deeply rooted clusters of attitudes and beliefs that reflect what a person considers very important or unimportant, very worthy or unworthy

verbal communication behavior that exchanges meaning using language as a means; can be written, spoken, or otherwise behaviorally or visually transmitted, as in the case of American Sign Language (ASL)

vigilant interaction commitment to rigorous problem assessment, goal development, and alternatives generation and evaluation

visual aids visual images used to illustrate, support, or enliven the content of a speech

vivid language word use that promotes enthusiasm for a speech by bringing the speaker's message to life and moving the audience emotionally

vocal variety varying vocal rate, pitch, and volume to add interest

vocalics the nonverbal elements of the voice, which includes rate, pitch, and intensity

vocalized pauses meaningless sounds or words a speaker utters during moments of silence

volume intensity, the loudness or softness, of the speaker's voice

w

we-message statement that labels and describes the joint behaviors of two or more people

wide–narrow dimension of voice vocal range from lower frequency tones produced by a relaxed vocal tract to higher frequency tones produced by tense vocal tracts

working outline foundation for organizing materials and ideas into main points during the drafting of a speech

y

you-message statement that labels another person and involves some evaluation of that person's behavior

Photo Credits

Index

Italic page numbers indicate material in tables or figures.

a

Abstract dimension of skills, 188
Abstraction, level of, 94, 97–98, *97*
Access, to computer-mediated communication, 404, 410, 413, 414
Acknowledging skills, 260–261
Acronyms, computer, *409*
Action, move to, persuasive speech, 375–376
Action assembly, 173–175
Action-oriented listeners, 142
Actions
    front-stage and back-stage, 402–403
    skills as, 187
    speeches to move listeners to, 384–385
Activity groups, *217*
Adams, Douglas, 18
Adaptability
    balancing with consistency, 198–199
    of postmodern self, 67
Adaptive work, 252–253
Addition errors, 326
Ad hominem fallacy, 386
Advertising, 428, 434, 435–438
    defined, 436
Affect blend, 116
Affect displays, 116
Affective conflict, 254–256
Affiliation, 40
Age, and audience analysis, 281
Agenda setting theory, 430, *430*
Aggressive communication, 193
Agriculture, U.S. Department of, 222
Aids, visual. *See* Presentational aids
AIDS research speech, 349, *354,* 358–359, 367–369
Alienation motivation, 440
Alliteration, 318–319
Allness, 58–59
AllTheWeb.com, 291
Almanacs, 295
AltaVista, 291
Alternatives
    comparing, organizational pattern, 385
    evaluating, 230–231
    generating, 230
Ambiguous communication, 18

Ambiguous language, 97–98
Ambiguous tasks, 249
American Psychological Association, 94, 95
American Sign Language (ASL), 42
Analogic information, 400
Analogy, 318
Analyzing mass communication messages, 440
Angelou, Maya, 90
Anthony, Susan B., 247
Anxiety
    apprehension, 36
    in interviews, 453, 460–461
    public speaking, 36, 337–340
    social, 36, 191–192
Appeals, 376–379
Appeal to interests, 438
Appearance, physical, 114, 327, *331*
Apprehension, 36
Appropriate communication, 4, 413
Appropriate language, 319
Appropriateness, 29–30, 31–34
    in speech presentation, 319–321, *322,* 324–326, *327*
Argument and debate, 19
Argumentation skills, 187
Arguments, persuasive, 376–379
Aristotle, 32, 276, 372, 438
Arrangement, rhetorical canon, 277
Articulation, 324, 325–326, *327,* 460
Artifacts, 122
Ask Jeeves, 291
Assertiveness, 192, 194–195
Assertiveness skills, 187
Assessment, of decision-making quality, 225–226
Asymmetric–symmetric dimension, 437
Attention
    gaining in advertising, 436
    See also Attentiveness
Attention-getting devices, 301, 303, 318, 383
Attentiveness, 189
    as interpersonal skill, 189–191, *190,* 199, 201
    in interviews, 457
    in mediated context, 407
Attitudes
    of audience, 283, *285*
    and culture, 63–64
    persuasive speeches and, 373–375
    See also Beliefs; Values

Attractiveness, self-concept of, 67
Attribution theory, 60–63, *62*
Audience
    analysis, 280–286, *285,* 373
    attention-getting devices, 301, 303, 318, 383
    diversity, analyzing and adapting to, 284
    motivating to action, 384–385
    See also Listeners
Audience-centered models, 431–432
Audiotape, as presentational aid, *335*
Autocratic leadership, 249
Avoidance conflict management style, 256, 257
Avoidance skills, 194

b

Backstage action, 403
Bar graphs, as presentational aids, 333, *333*
Bartlett's Familiar Quotations, 295
Behavior
    action assembly and, 173–174
    changing with persuasive speech, 375
    roles and, 163–164
Behavioral interdependence, 216
Behavioral questions, 459
Beliefs
    of audience, 283, *285*
    and culture, 63–64
    persuasive speeches and, 373–375
    See also Attitudes; Values
Bender, Kelly, 349, 358–359, 367
Bias
    critical listening and, 140
    first impression, 60
    in language, 95–96
    in mass communication industry, 432–438
    in the news, 434–435
    self-serving, 61, 63
    in speechmaking, 284
    See also Prejudice; Stereotypes
Biased language
    reducing, 95–96
    in speech presentation, 320–321
Bias testing, 442
Bilateral interviews, 454
Biographical reference books, 295
Biography Index, 295
Blair, Tony, 379

Giuliani, Rudy, 247
Goal interdependence, 216
Goal-oriented skills, 187
Goals, 36
    action assembly and, 173–174
    in interviews, 454
    planning and, 171
    transactional nature of, 171
Goal setting, and public speaking anxiety, 339–340
Goffman, Erving, 402
Go Network, 291
Google, 291
Gottman, J., 150
Gouran, Dennis, 224
Government documents, in speech preparation, 296
Grammar, 324, 326, *327*
Graphs, as presentational aids, 332–333, *333*
Gratifications obtained, 431
Gratifications sought, 431
Greek period, rhetorical tradition in, 276
Greetings, 89, *89*
Grice, H. P., 462
Group contexts, 41
Group decision making
    communication and, 222–225
    tasks associated with, 221–222
    when to use, 227–228
Group environment, 259–260
Group phases, 258–259
Group procedure, 233
Group roles, 254, *255*
Groups
    conflict in, 253–256
    creating, 19
    decision making in, 218–226
    knowing how to lead, 247–258
    types, by activity and goal, *217*
    See also Small groups
Groupthink, 231–232, *232*
Group turnover, 258–259

h

Habit, and interpersonal skills, 197–198
Habitat for Humanity, 20
Hall, Edward T., 122, 123
Handouts, as presentational aids, *334*
Haptics, 118, *165*
Hasty generalization fallacy, 387
Hate speech, 93–94
Haves and have-nots, information, 404–405
Hayakawa, S. I., 94
Hidden self, 69
Hierarchical indexes, 294
High five, 119
Hirokawa, Randy, 224

Historical background of messages, 101
Historical structure of speech, 354
Hitchhiker's Guide to the Galaxy, The (Adams), 18
"Hitchhiking rule," 234
Hitler, Adolf, 388, 428
Hofstede, G., 63
Holistic approach to communication, 17–18
Holmes, Michael, 404
Hotbot.com, 291
Household type, and audience analysis, 281
Human needs, 282
Humor, 411
Hussein, Saddam, 379
Hypothesizing, 440
Hypothetical examples, 359
Hypothetical questions, 458–459

i

Idea generators, 287
Ideational conflict, 256
"I Have a Dream" speech, 316, 317, 319, 335
"I" in self, 65, 66
Illegal questions, in interviews, 461–462
Illiteracy, media, 404, 433
Illustrator, 112
Imagery, in speech presentation, 318
I-messages, 102
IM (instant messaging), 400, 401, 403, 427
Immediacy behaviors, 315
Impartial leadership, 232
Implicit personality theory, 60
Impression management, in interviews, 461–462
Impressions, 43
    first, 56, 114
    first impression bias, 60
    interpersonal skills and, 188–189
Impromptu speeches, 278
Incompatibility, 254
Indexes, to newspapers and periodicals, 295–296
Indexing, 101–102
Indians, 57
Indirect learning, 161–162
Individual differences
    in nonverbal communication, 124–126
    See also Diversity
Individualism, 63
Individualistic cultures, 63–64
Induction, 376–378
Inferences, compared to facts, 440
Inflammatory language, 145
Inflection, 323
Information
    haves and have-nots of, 404–405
    See also Knowledge

Informational interviews, 290, 453
Information overload, 414, 440
Information-seeking interviews, 461
Information transfer model, 7–9, *8, 14*
Informative speeches, 278, 346–369
    compared to persuasive speech, 349, *350*
    ethics and, 362
    example of, 367–369
    importance of, 350–351
    organizing, *298,* 352–357, *353, 358*
    outlining, 352–357, *354*
    suggestions for, 362–363
    support materials for, 357–361
    types of, 351–352
    types of content, 348–349, *350*
Infotainment, 433
Ingham, Harry, 69
Ingratiating communication, 201
Initial credibility, 315
Instant messaging (IM), 400, 401, 403, 427
Instructions, informative speech, 352
Insulated groups, 232
Integrative conflict management style, 256, 257
Integrative skills, 195
Intensity, 119
Interaction, group conflict and, 253
Interaction barriers, to listening, 145–146
Interactive model, 9, *10*
Interactivity, 401
Interdependence, in small groups, 216–217, 253–254
Interdependent, 39
Interest, 262
Interests, appeal to, 436
Interior, U.S. Department of, 222
Internet
    evaluating sources, 293
    role in speech preparation, 290–293
    World Wide Web (WWW), 291, 400
Interpersonal communication, ethics and, 33
Interpersonal competence (knowledge), 158–183
    action assembly, 173–175
    challenges to, 175–177
    learning, 161–162
    planning, 168–173
    relationships, 175–177
    repertoires, 163–164, *165*
    scripts, 165–167, *166–167*
    See also Knowledge building
Interpersonal competence (skills), 184–211
    challenges to managing, 197–201
    characteristics of skills, 186–189
    types of skills, 189–197
    See also Skills
Interpersonal context, 41
Interpretation, perception and, 60–63
Interpretations, anticipating, 100–101

McCroskey, J. C., 125
McLuhan, Marshall, 411, 438
Mead, George Herbert, 65–66, 68
Meaning, 6
   constructing, 137
   sharing, 9–11, 14
   of words, curiosity about, 99–100
   of words, in speech presentation, 317
Means-oriented ethical codes, 32, 34
Media, 6, 400
   See also Computer-mediated
     communication (CMC)
Media access, 404, 410, 413, 414
Media competence, 439, *439*
Media consumption, 439–440
Media effects, 433
Media factors, CMC, 411–412
Media illiteracy, 404, 433
Media literacy, 438–442
Media richness, 401
Media sensitivity, 418
Mediated communication, 404
   See also Computer-mediated
     communication (CMC)
Mediated context, 42
Medical interviews. *See* Therapeutic
   interviews
"Me" in self, 65, 66, 68
Memorized speeches, 279
Memory, rhetorical canon, 277
Men. *See* Gender
Mental anxiety. *See* Anxiety
Merrill, Lisa, 142
Message ambiguity, 411
Message complexity, 144, 411
Message emotionality, 411
Message factors, 411
Message interpretation, 100–101
Message overload, 144
Messages, 5–6
   history of sending and receiving, 427
   mixed message, 112
   See also Communication; Nonverbal
     communication
Meta engines, 291–292
Meta-List, 291
Metaphor, 318
Mexico, 64
Meyers, M., 435
Micromomentary facial flash, 116
"Micro-sleep," 351
Mindfulness, 56
Mindlessness, 197–198
Minimizing communication, 31
Minority, meaning of, 85–86
Misrepresentation, in persuasive speeches,
   387
Mixed message, 112
Models, as presentational aids, 330, 332
Models of communication, 7–15

Moderated effects models, 429–430
Moderation principle, 199–200
Modern self, 66
Modification, cognitive, 339
Monroe, Alan, 381
Moorehead, Antonio, 375, 383, 384, 393
Motivated sequence organizational pattern,
   297, *381,* 381–385, *382–383*
Motivation
   in communication competence model,
     35–37
   in interviews, 452–454
   of listeners, in informative speeches, 363
   of listeners, in persuasive speeches,
     375–376, 384–385
   in mediated world, 406
Movable markers, 124
Move to action, persuasive speech, 375–
   376, 384–385
Multicodality, 320
Multiple "me's," managing, 68
Multiple perspectives, 73, 100
Multiple self, 67
Music, rap genre, 433

n

Narrowcasting, 427
NASA crises, 438
National Communication Association
   (NCA), 32
   Credo for Ethical Communication, 34, 362
National Issues Forum, 68
Nationality, 39
National Speakers Association, 296
Native Americans, 57
Natural media, 6, 400
Nature/nurture question, 125
Nazi Germany, 388
Negative motivation, 35, 406
Nested decision making, 222, *223*
New Encyclopedia Britannica, 295
News, and entertainment, 432–433, 435
News organizations, 434–435
Newspapers, in speech preparation, 295–
   296
Newsweek magazine, 296
New York Times Index, 296
"No criticism rule," 234
Noise, 8, 143
Nominal group technique (NGT), 235–236
Nonfluencies, 120
Nonjudgmental empathic response, 141
Nonprofit organizations, and online
   research, 292
Non sequitur fallacy, 386
Nonverbal communication, 43, 108–133
   body communication, 114–118
   challenges to, 124–126
   challenges to, overcoming, 126

defined, 110
functions of, 111–114
gender and, 125
importance of, 110–111, *111*
time and space, 120–124
touch, 118–119
types of, 114–124
voice, 119–120
Nonverbal cues, 110, 111, 115
   in speech presentation, 327–330, 379
Nonverbal symbols, 5–6
Norms, 29
North American cultural context, 39
Note dependent, 301
Noticing
   language and, 91–92
   perception and, 56–58
Novelty, 436

O

Obama, Barack, 90
Objective questions, 459
Objects, as presentational aids, 330, 332
Object speech, 348, *350, 358*
Occupation, and audience analysis, 281
Oculesics, 117, *165*
Office design, 121–122
Ogden, C. K., 87
Oil companies, 436
Omission, errors of, 325–326
Online databases, 294
Open-ended questions, 191, 458
Openness, 69–70, 402–403
Open self, 69
Opinion leaders, 430
Opportunities, language creation of, 92–94
Optimizing communication, 31, 33
Oral histories speech, 375–376, 377,
   382–383, 393–395
Organization
   of informative speeches, 352–357, *353,*
     358
   perception and, 58–59
   of persuasive speeches, 380–385
   role in speech preparation, 296–306
Organizational interviews, 453–454, *455*
Organizational patterns
   of informative speeches, 353–357
   of persuasive speeches, 380–385
   of speeches, 297, *298*
Organizations, identifying for interviews,
   456
Orientation, long-term vs. short-term, 63
Orientation group phase, 258–259
Other-interests, balancing with self-interest,
   200–201
Others, generalized and significant, 65
Outcomes, of communication, 30, 412–413

Thesis statement, 289, *289*, 303
Thinking
    convergent, 235–237
    critically during speech preparation, 296, 297
    divergent, 234–235
Time, 39
    nonverbal messages and, 120–121
    public speaking and, 286
Timeliness, in computer-mediated communication, 408
Time management, 191
Timing, in speechmaking, 286
Tinkering, 407
Tisias, 276, 298
Topical speech organization, 297, 353–354, *358*
Topic development, 191
Topic initiation, 196
Topics
    choosing and narrowing, 287–288
    for informative speeches, 348–349, *350*
Topic shift, 191
Touch, as nonverbal communication, 118–119
Toulmin, Stephen, 441
Transactional model, 10–11, *11*
Transitions, in speeches, 305
Transparent delivery, 329
Trigger words, 145
Trustworthiness, and credibility, 379
Tsunami, 411
Turnover in groups, 258–259
Two-way asymmetric model, 437
Two-way symmetric model, 437

U

Unbiased language, 320, *321*
Uncertainty avoidance, 63
Understanding
    in evaluating competence, 413
    listening and, 141

Unethical behavior, covering for, 33
Unilateral interviews, 454–455
Universities, and online research, 292
Unknown self, 69
Unprojected presentational aids, 334, *334*
USA Today, 316
Uses and gratifications, 431, *431*

V

Valence, of self-disclosure, 70
Value, questions of, 222, *223*
Valued outcomes, 30
Values
    of audience, 283, *285*
    and culture, 63–64
    persuasive speeches and, 373–375
    See also Attitudes; Beliefs
Verbal battles, 145
Verbal communication, 42
Verbal fluency in interviews, 458
Video games, 405
Videophone communication, 400, 401, 402
Videotape, as presentational aid, *335*
Vigilance, 225–226
Vigilant interaction, 226
Violence
    ethics of, 33
    in rap music, 433
    on television, 16, 430, 432
    in video games, 405
    against women, 435
Visual aids. *See* Presentational aids
Vivid language, in speech presentation, 317–319, *322*
Vividness, 409
Vocalic information, 401
Vocalics, 119, *165*
Vocalized pauses, 323
Vocal variety, 321–324

Voice
    expressiveness dimensions of, 196
    nonverbal dimension of, 119–120
    in speech presentation, 321–324
    volume of, 323–324, *325, 460*
Volunteers, in informative speeches, 363

W

Warrants, 441
Weapons of mass destruction (WMD), 57
We-messages, 102
Whorf, Benjamin Lee, 90
Wide–narrow dimension of voice, 196
"Win–lose" approach to conflict, 256
Winslet, Kate, 164, 165
"Win–win" approach to conflict, 256
Women
    stereotypes on television, 428
    in television, 435, 442
    violence against, 435
    See also Gender
Woods, Tiger, 74
Words
    contradictory, 112–113
    curiosity about meanings, 99–100
    in nonverbal communication, 112
    use of, in speech presentation, 316–321
    use of definitions in informative speeches, 358
Work, types of, in small groups, 252–253
Working outlines, 299, *301*
World Wide Web (WWW), 291, 400
    See also Internet
Writing, bias in, 95–96

Y

Yahoo, 291
You-messages, 102